CHAPTER 6   Financing New Ventures

    Case: Stegmart

    Small Business School Video Case: Bridgecreek Development

CHAPTER 7   Writing an Effective Business Plan: Crafting a Roadmap to Success

    Case: Robinson Associates, Inc.

PART | III

Launching the New Venture

CHAPTER 8   The Legal Forms of New Ventures – And the Legal Environment in Which They Operate

    Case: A Question of Incorporation

CHAPTER 9   Marketing in a New Firm

    Case: Scrubadub Auto Wash

    Small Business School Video Case: Rodgers Chevrolet

CHAPTER 10   Strategy: Planning for Competitive Advantage

    Case: The Fantastic Catalogue Company

CHAPTER 11   Intellectual Property: Protecting Your Ideas

    Case: A Patent Matter

    Small Business School Video Case: NoUVIR

PART | IV

Running the Business: Building Lasting Success

CHAPTER 12   Essential Skill for Entrepreneurs: Enhancing Social Competence, Creating Trust, Managing Conflict, Exerting Influence, and Dealing with Stress

    Case: When Everything Isn't Half Enough

    Small Business School Video Case: Gadabout Salon and Spas

CHAPTER 13   Building the New Venture's Human Resources: Recruiting, Motivating, and Retaining High-Performing Employees

    Case: Waterway Industries

    Small Business School Video Case: On Target Supplies

PART | V

Harvesting the Rewards

CHAPTER 14   Exit Strategies for Entrepreneurs: When – And How – To Harvest the Rewards

    Case: The Bonneau Company

    Small Business School Video Case: Selling to a Public Company

entrepreneurship

A PROCESS PERSPECTIVE

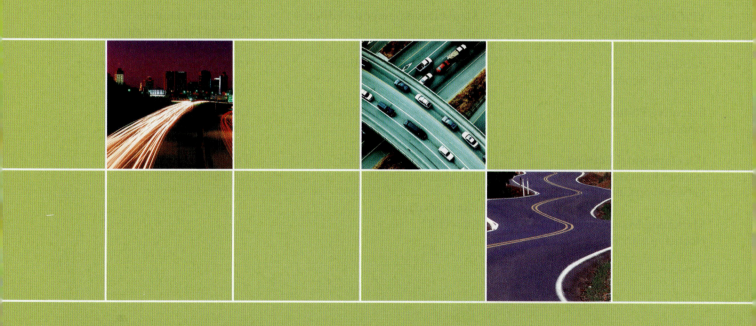

ROBERT A. BARON

Wellington Professor of Management
Lally School of Management & Technology
Rensselaer Polytechnic Institute
Troy, NY

SCOTT A. SHANE

Professor of Economics and Entrepreneurship
Weatherhead School of Management
Case Western Reserve University
Cleveland, OH

THOMSON
SOUTH-WESTERN

Australia · Canada · Mexico · Singapore · Spain · United Kingdom · United States

THOMSON
★
™
SOUTH-WESTERN

Entrepreneurship: A Process Perspective, 1e

Robert A. Baron & Scott A. Shane

VP/Editorial Director:
Jack W. Calhoun

VP/Editor-in-Chief:
Michael P. Roche

Publisher:
Melissa S. Acuña

Executive Editor:
John Szilagyi

Developmental Editors:
Jennifer E. Baker &
Rebecca von Gillern

Marketing Manager:
Jacquelyn Carrillo

Sr. Production Editor:
Elizabeth A. Shipp

Media Developmental Editor:
Kristen Meere

Media Production Editor:
Karen L. Schaffer

Manufacturing Coordinator:
Rhonda Utley

Design Project Manager:
Rik Moore

Photo Manager:
John Hill

Photo Researcher:
Darren Wright

Production House:
Rebecca Gray Design

Internal and Cover Designer:
Liz Harasymczuk

Cover Images:
© PhotoDisc, Inc.

Printer:
CTPS

For permission to use material from
this text or product, contact us by
Tel (800) 730-2214
Fax (800) 730-2215
http://www.thomsonrights.com

For more information
contact South-Western,
5191 Natorp Boulevard,
Mason, Ohio, 45040.
Or you can visit our Internet site at:
http://www.swlearning.com

To Venkat, who opened our hearts and our minds to the challenges—
and joys—of entrepreneurship
(RAB & SAS)

And

To Rebecca, Randy, Paul, Jessica, and Ted—the people who make my
life what, almost always, it is—a journey through warm, golden
sunshine; and to Richard, who, when he was needed, showed the
strength I always knew he had
(RAB)

And

To Lynne for supporting me in writing this book, as well as everything
else I do; and to Hannah for giving my life a central purpose
(SAS)

BRIEF CONTENTS

PART | 1

Entrepreneurship: Who, What, Why? 1

CHAPTER 1   Entrepreneurship: A Field—And An Activity   2

CHAPTER 2   Uncovering Opportunities: Understanding Entrepreneurial Opportunities and Industry Analysis   27

CHAPTER 3   Cognitive Foundations of Entrepreneurship: Creativity and Opportunity Recognition   53

PART | 2

Assembling the Resources 81

CHAPTER 4   Acquiring Essential Information: Why "Look Before You Leap" Is Truly Good Advice for Entrepreneurs   82

CHAPTER 5   Assembling the Team: Acquiring and Utilizing Essential Human Resources   107

CHAPTER 6   Financing New Ventures   133

CHAPTER 7   Writing an Effective Business Plan: Crafting a Road Map to Success   163

PART | 3

Launching the New Venture 185

CHAPTER 8   The Legal Form of New Ventures—And the Legal Environment in Which They Operate   186

CHAPTER 9   Marketing in a New Firm   213

CHAPTER 10   Strategy: Planning for Competitive Advantage   239

CHAPTER 11   Intellectual Property: Protecting Your Ideas   267

PART | 4

Running the Business: Building Lasting Success 291

CHAPTER 12   Essential Skills for Entrepreneurs: Enhancing Social Competence, Creating Trust, Managing Conflict, Exerting Influence, and Dealing with Stress   292

CHAPTER 13   Building the New Venture's Human Resources: Recruiting, Motivating, and Retaining High-Performing Employees   319

PART | 5

Harvesting the Rewards 347

CHAPTER 14   Exit Strategies for Entrepreneurs: When—And How—To Harvest the Rewards   348

CONTENTS

PART | 1

Entrepreneurship: Who, What, Why? 1

CHAPTER 1 Entrepreneurship: A Field—And An Activity 2

The Field of Entrepreneurship: Its Nature and Roots 4

Entrepreneurship: An Engine of Economic Growth 6

Entrepreneurship: Foundations in Other Disciplines 7

Entrepreneurship: A Process Perspective 9

Levels of Analysis: Micro Versus Macro Revisited 12

Entrepreneurship: The Intersection of Valuable Opportunities and Enterprising Individuals 13

Sources of Knowledge About Entrepreneurship: How We Know What We Know 14

Observation, Reflection, and Experimentation: Alternative Routes to Knowledge 15

Theory: Answering the Questions "Why" and "How" 18

A User's Guide to This Text 20

Summary and Review of Key Points 22

CHAPTER 2 Uncovering Opportunities: Understanding Entrepreneurial Opportunities and Industry Analysis 27

Sources of Opportunities: The Origins of New Ventures 29

Technological Change 30

Political and Regulatory Change 31

Social and Demographic Change 31

Forms of Opportunity: Beyond New Products and Services 33

Industries That Favor New Firms: Fertile Grounds for New Ventures 34

Knowledge Conditions 35

Demand Conditions 36

Industry Life Cycles 37

Industry Structure 38

Opportunities and New Firms 40

Why Most Opportunities Favor Established Firms 40

Opportunities That Favor New Firms 42

DANGER! PITFALL AHEAD! Exploiting an Incremental Innovation by Starting a Firm 44

Summary and Review of Key Points 46

CHAPTER 3 Cognitive Foundations of Entrepreneurship: Creativity and Opportunity Recognition 53

The Raw Materials for Creativity and Opportunity Recognition: Mental Structures That Allow Us to Store—And Use—Information 56

Cognitive Systems for Storing—And Using—Information: Memory, Schemas, and Prototypes 56

Limited Capacity to Process Information: Why Total Rationality Is Rarer Than You Think 58

Creativity: Escaping from Mental Ruts 60

DANGER! PITFALL AHEAD! "Too Much Invested to Quit": The Potentially Devastating Effects of Sunk Costs 61

Creativity: Generating the Extraordinary 61

Concepts: Building Blocks of Creativity 62

Creativity and Human Intelligence 64

Encouraging Creativity: The Confluence Approach 65

Opportunity Recognition: A Key Step in the Entrepreneurial Process 67

Access to Information and Its Effective Use: The Core of Opportunity Recognition 68

Opportunity Recognition: Additional Insights from Cognitive Science 69

Practical Techniques for Increasing Opportunity Recognition 72

THE VOICE OF EXPERIENCE Some Thoughts on Avoiding False Alarms 73

Summary and Review of Key Points 75

PART | 2

Assembling the Resources 81

CHAPTER 4 Acquiring Essential Information: Why "Look Before You Leap" Is Truly Good Advice for Entrepreneurs 82

Market Information: Determining What Your Customers Really Want 84

Direct Techniques for Gathering Market Information: Surveys, Perceptual Mapping, and Focus Groups 85

Indirect Techniques for Gathering Market Information: The Entrepreneur as Sherlock Holmes 88

Government Policies and Regulations: How They Affect New Ventures 89

Taxes: An Important Consideration for Entrepreneurs 90

Government Policy: Increasingly Favorable to New Ventures 91

Government Regulations: What Every Entrepreneur Should Know 93

DANGER! PITFALL AHEAD! When Good Ideas Fail: The Costs of Ignoring the Rules 96

Interpreting Information: Potential Pitfalls for Decision-Making Groups 97

Accepting "Early Favorites": Or, Why the Initial Majority Usually Wins 97

v

Group Polarization: Why Groups Often Do Go off the Deep End 98

Groupthink: When Too Much Cohesion Among Group Members Is a Dangerous Thing 98

Ignoring Unshared Information 99

Improving Group Decisions: Techniques for Countering the Pitfalls 100

THE VOICE OF EXPERIENCE Know Your Market—And Your Competitive Edge—Before You Start! 101

Summary and Review of Key Points 102

CHAPTER 5 Assembling The Team: Acquiring and Utilizing Essential Human Resources 107

Similarity Versus Complementarity: "Know Thyself" Revisited 109

Self-Assessment: Knowing What You Have Helps Determine What You Need 110

Choosing Cofounders: Maximizing the New Venture's Human Resources 113

Impression Management: The Fine Art of Looking Good— And How to Recognize It 113

Deception: Beyond Impression Management 115

DANGER! PITFALL AHEAD! The Partner Who Wasn't What He Claimed: When Social Perception Fails 117

Utilizing the New Venture's Human Resources: Building Strong Working Relationships Among the Founding Team 118

Roles: The Clearer the Better 118

Perceived Fairness: An Elusive But Essential Component 119

THE VOICE OF EXPERIENCE Why Your Family Should Be Part of the Team—Or at Least Fully On Board 120

Effective Communication 122

Expanding the New Venture's Human Resources: Beyond the Founding Team 124

Obtaining Excellent Employees: The Key Role of Social Networks 124

Is Bigger Necessarily Better? Number of Employees as a Factor in New Venture Growth 125

Should New Ventures Hire Temporary or Permanent Employees? Commitment Versus Cost 126

Summary and Review of Key Points 127

CHAPTER 6 Financing New Ventures 133

Why Is It so Difficult to Raise Money? The Problems of Uncertainty and Information Asymmetry 135

Information Asymmetry Problems 135

Uncertainty Problems 137

Solutions to Venture Finance Problems 137

Amounts and Sources of Capital: How Much and What Type Do You Need? 140

Amount of Start-Up Capital 140

Estimating Financial Needs: Start-Up Costs, Proforma Financial Statements, Cash Flow Statements, and Breakeven Analysis 141

DANGER! PITFALL AHEAD! The Hazards of Raising Too Little Money 145

Types of Capital: Debt Versus Equity 146

Sources of Capital 147

The Structure of Venture Finance 151

The Equity Financing Process 151

Staging of Investment 152

The Cost of Capital 152

Social Capital and the Behavioral Side of Venture Finance 155

Social Ties and the Process of Raising Money 155

Behaviors and Actions That Encourage Investors 155

Summary and Review of Key Points 157

CHAPTER 7 Writing an Effective Business Plan: Crafting a Road Map to Success 163

Why Write a Business Plan? The Benefits of Clear-Cut Goals 165

Components of a Business Plan: Basic Requirements 167

The Executive Summary 168

Background, Product, and Purpose 170

Market Analysis 171

Development, Production, and Location 172

The Management Team 172

Financial Plans and Projections 173

Critical Risks: Describing What Might Go Wrong 174

Reaping the Rewards: Harvest and Exit 175

Scheduling and Milestones 175

Appendices 176

A Note on the Intangibles 176

DANGER! PITFALL AHEAD! The Seven Deadly Sins for New Venture Business Plans 177

Making an Effective Business Plan Presentation: The Ball Is Definitely in Your Court 178

Summary and Review of Key Points 181

PART | 3

Launching the New Venture 185

CHAPTER 8 The Legal Form of New Ventures—And the Legal Environment in Which They Operate 186

The Legal Forms New Ventures Can Take 187

Sole Proprietorship: One Company, One Owner 188

Partnerships: Different Forms, Different Benefits 189

Corporations: Limited Liability, But at a Cost 192

The S Corporation 193

The Limited Liability Company (LLC) 193

The Joint Venture 194

The Professional Corporation 194

The Legal Environment of New Ventures: Some Basics 195

New Ventures and the Law 195

DANGER! PITFALL AHEAD! What Can Happen When Entrepreneurs Are Ignorant of the Law 197

Business Contracts: Their Essential Components 197

Basic Elements of a Contract 197

Obligations Under Contracts 198

Franchising 199

Types of Franchising 200

The Benefits of Becoming a Franchisee 200

Drawbacks of Becoming a Franchisee 202

Legal Aspects of Franchising 204

The Future Shape of Franchising 205

Summary and Review of Key Points 207

CHAPTER 9 Market in a New Firm 213

Assessing the Market 215

Starting with a Real Need 215

Assessing Customer Preferences and the Market for New Products and Services 217

Conjoint Analysis: Determining Which Dimensions Are Most Important 220

Market Dynamics 222

Knowing Your Market: The Importance of Market Size and Market Growth 222

Timing the Market: The S-Curve Story 222

Achieving Market Acceptance 224

Adoption Patterns: Understanding Which Customers Adopt When 224

Moving from Early Adopters to the Early Majority 226

Focus: Choosing the Right Customers to Target First 227

Dominant Design: Product Convergence and Its Effect on New Ventures 227

Technical Standards: Getting Customers to Adopt Your Design as the Market Standard 228

DANGER! PITFALL AHEAD! *Stymied by the Dominant Design: The Story of Electric Vehicles* 229

The Marketing Process in a New Company 230

Personal Selling: The Central Component of Entrepreneurial Marketing 230

Pricing New Products: The Role of Cost Structure and Supply and Demand 231

Summary and Review of Key Points 233

CHAPTER 10 Strategy: Planning for Competitive Advantages 239

Competitive Advantage: An Essential Ingredient 241

Strategy: Protecting Profits from the Exploitation of Opportunity 242

Secrecy: Keeping Others from Learning About or Understanding How to Exploit the Opportunity 243

DANGER! PITFALL AHEAD! *Arrow's Paradox: The Problem of Disclosure* 245

Establishing Barriers to Imitation 246

THE VOICE OF EXPERIENCE Establishing Competitive Advantage: Recognize Your Strengths 248

Franchising or Licensing? The Choice of Organizational Form 249

Minimizing the Cost of Exploiting the Opportunity 250

Accelerating the Pace to Market 251

Making Use of the Best Capabilities 251

Managing Information Problems in Organizing 252

Managing Information Asymmetry and Uncertainty in the Pursuit of Opportunity 255

Growth from Small Scale 256

Forming Alliances and Partnerships with Established Firms 258

Legitimating the Opportunity and the New Venture 259

Summary and Review of Key Points 261

CHAPTER 11 Intellectual Property: Protecting Your Ideas 267

Capturing the Profits from New Products and Services 269

The Product Development Process 269

New Firm Advantages at Product Development 270

Ease of Imitating Entrepreneurs' Intellectual Property 272

DANGER! PITFALL AHEAD! Nondisclosure and Noncompete Agreements 274

Legal Forms of Intellectual Property Protection 275

Patents 275

Trade Secrets 277

Trademarks 279

Copyrights 280

Nonlegal Forms of Intellectual Property Protection 281

Learning Curves, Lead Time, and the First-Mover Advantage 282

Complementary Assets 284

Summary and Review of Key Points 286

PART | 4

Running the Business: Building Lasting Success 291

CHAPTER 12 Essential Skills for Entrepreneurs: Enhancing Social Competence, Creating Trust, Managing Conflict, Exerting Influence, and Dealing with Stress 292

Getting Along Well with Others: Building Social Competence 294

The Nature of Social Skills 294

The Impact of Social Competence on Entrepreneurs 295

Working Effectively with Others: Building Trust and Managing Conflict 297

THE VOICE OF EXPERIENCE Why People Skills Really Matter 298

Building Cooperation: The Key Role of Trust 298

Managing Conflict: Heading Off Trouble at the Pass 301

DANGER! PITFALL AHEAD! How to Create an Affective Conflict When There Is None 304

Influencing Others: From Persuasion to Vision 305

Tactics of Influence: Which Ones Are Most Common? 305

Other Tactics of Influence: From Ingratiation to the Foot-in-the-Door   306

Managing Stress: How Entrepreneurs Can Survive to Enjoy the Fruits of Their Labor   308

Stress: Its Nature and Causes   308

The Adverse Effects of Stress   310

Personal Techniques for Managing Stress   311

Summary and Review of Key Points   313

CHAPTER 13   Building the New Venture's Human Resources: Recruiting, Motivating, and Retaining High-Performing Employees   319

Recruiting and Selecting High-Performing Employees   321

The Search for High-Performing Employees: Knowing What You Need and Where to Look   321

Selection: Techniques for Choosing the "Cream of the Crop"   322

Motivating Employees: Maximizing the Value of the New Venture's Human Resources   326

Reaching for the Moon—Or at Least, the Next Level Up: The Key Role of Goals—And Vision   326

Tying Rewards to Performance: The Role of Expectancies   328

Fairness: An Essential Ingredient in Motivation   330

DANGER! PITFALL AHEAD!   Employee Theft: Evening the Score with an Unfair Employer   331

Designing Jobs to Make Them Motivating   332

Retaining High-Performing Employees   333

Reward Systems: Linking Pay and Performance   333

Building Employee Commitment   335

Overcoming the "Control Barrier": A Note on the Necessity of "Letting Go"   336

THE VOICE OF EXPERIENCE   The Four Pillars of New Venture Success   337

Summary and Review of Key Points   339

PART | 5

Harvesting the Rewards   347

CHAPTER 14   Exit Strategies for Entrepreneurs: When—And How—To Harvest the Rewards   348

Exit Strategies: The Major Forms   350

Sale or Transfer to Insiders: Succession, Leveraged Buyouts, and Employee Stock Ownership Plans   351

Sale to Outsiders: When Valuation Becomes Crucial   353

Determining the Value of a Business: A Little Art, a Little Science   354

Taking a Company Public: The Lure of IPOs   357

Negotiation: The Universal Process   359

Negotiation: Its Basic Nature   359

THE VOICE OF EXPERIENCE   The Multiple Benefits of an Appropriate Exit Strategy   360

Tactics of Negotiation: Procedures for Reducing an Opponent's Aspirations   360

DANGER! PITFALL AHEAD!   The Costs of Negotiating to Win: Watch Out for the "Ankle-Biters"!   364

Exit Strategies and the Life Span: Different Needs—And Goals—At Different Times of Life   365

Summary and Review of Key Points   368

APPENDIX 1   Case Studies   373

APPENDIX 2   Video Case Library   397

GLOSSARY   415

NAME INDEX   421

SUBJECT INDEX   425

PREFACE

IN SEARCH OF THE IDEAL BALANCE

It almost never fails: at a cocktail party or other social gathering, someone we have just met asks, "What do you do for a living?" When we tell them that we are professors, their next question is usually something like "What do you teach?" When we reply "entrepreneurship," many seem truly fascinated, and they soon make it clear *why* they find this information so intriguing: in their eyes, entrepreneurs are a truly remarkable group—modern-day versions of the mythical character who could spin straw into gold. Instead of starting with straw, though, our new acquaintances assume that entrepreneurs begin with dreams and ideas and spin *these* into gold—new companies that quickly make them fabulously wealthy. In short, many people we meet are convinced that teaching courses about entrepreneurship, and doing research on it, is a very exciting career.

We are certainly not going to argue with *that* conclusion! We both ardently believe that entrepreneurship is a fascinating topic. In fact, it is our personal commitment to the field of entrepreneurship that led us to write this book. More specifically, we believe that in recent years, the field has made rapid progress toward the goal of understanding entrepreneurship as a process, and that this progress, in turn, has yielded important implications for assisting entrepreneurs in their efforts to create new ventures. It was only a small step from these beliefs to asking ourselves the following question: "Could we write a new text that would accurately reflect these changes—a text that would emphasize the growing sophistication and usefulness of our field?" Being optimists by nature (!), we concluded that it was worth a try, and the result is the text you are about to read.

Once we decided to write this book, we immediately realized that we needed a clear strategy for reaching our goals—for preparing a text that would represent the field of entrepreneurship in an accurate, comprehensive, and up-to-date manner. We'll describe this strategy, and the specific steps we took to implement it, here. Before doing so, however, we feel that it is important to comment briefly on several basic principles that have guided our thinking throughout this project.

I. OUR GUIDING PRINCIPLES

Here is an overview of the principles that have guided our efforts in writing this book:

A. Entrepreneurship is a process. We believe that recently, the field has come to view entrepreneurship as an ongoing *process* rather than as a single event (e.g., founding of a company or recognition of an opportunity). We reflect this growing consensus by focusing on the entrepreneurial process as it unfolds through several distinct phases:

- **Generation of an Idea for a New Business and/or Recognition of an Opportunity**
- **Assembly of Resources (Financial, Human, Information) Needed to Develop the Opportunity**
- **Launching the New Venture**
  - **Managing Growth**
  - **Harvesting the Rewards**

While the divisions between these phases are frequently far from distinct, sometimes occur simultaneously, and the cycle often repeats itself even within specific companies, we also believe that entrepreneurs' efforts to start new ventures generally follow this basic process. Thus, this book, too, adopts this sequence and consistently presents a process view of entrepreneurship.

B. At each phase of the process, *individual-level* variables, group or *interpersonal-level* variables, and *societal-level* variables all play a role. Until recently, the field of entrepreneurship was marked by a continuing debate over the following question: In studying the entrepreneurial process, should we focus on the entrepreneur (e.g., this person's skills, abilities, talents, motives, traits, etc.), group-level variables (e.g., information provided by other persons; relations with cofounders, customers, venture capitalists, etc.), or on the societal context in which the entrepreneur operates (e.g., government policies, technology, economic conditions)? We view this question as largely unnecessary because during each phase of the entrepreneurial process, all three types of variables play a role.

For instance, consider the question of opportunity recognition. Certainly, this process occurs in the minds of specific persons and reflects the impact of individual-level variables such as a person's existing knowledge and unique life history. But recognition of opportunities cannot occur unless something that is potentially profitable emerges from ever-changing technological, societal, and economic conditions—societal-level factors. Further, other people with whom the entrepreneur has contact—friends, associates, or even figures in the mass media—are often important sources of information and may play a key role in opportunity recognition (group-level factors). In short, all three levels of analysis (individual, group, societal) are relevant and must be considered in order to fully understand opportunity recognition. **We suggest that the same is true for every other phase of the entrepreneurial process;** in other words, individual-level, group-level, and societal-level factors interact to influence every action and every decision taken by entrepreneurs. Consequently, all three levels of analysis will be represented throughout the book.

C. There is no split or tension between theory and practice; on the contrary, they are two sides of the same coin. The field of entrepreneurship has a dual nature: on the one hand, it seeks greater understanding of the process—how it unfolds and the many factors that shape it and determine entrepreneurs' success. On the other hand, it is concerned with providing entrepreneurs with the practical information and skills they need in order to reach their goals. Is there any "disconnect" between these two goals? In our view, absolutely not! It is a well-established principle that in almost all fields, systematic knowledge and increased understanding are necessary for successful practice. In other words, we must first understand the basic nature of entrepreneurship as a process before we can proceed with the task of providing entrepreneurs with the practical help they seek. For this reason, we have worked hard throughout the text to attain a good balance between theory and research, on the one hand, and practical advice and application on the other. In each chapter, we summarize "state of the art" knowledge about specific aspects of the entrepreneurial process—and then indicate how this information can be applied to solving practical problems faced by entrepreneurs. This is the **ideal balance** mentioned in the title of this preface, and attaining it has been a major goal of the book.

D. Many perspectives can contribute to our understanding of entrepreneurship. The field of entrepreneurship is eclectic by nature: it has important roots in many older and more well-established disciplines, such as economics, psychology, management, and sociology. Each of these fields offers a different perspective, and each can contribute significantly to our understanding of entrepreneurship as a process. Thus, fully representing all of them in this book is yet another guiding principle we have adopted. The fact that together, our training and experience covers virtually all of these fields [psychology, OB/HRM (Baron); management, economics (Shane)], helped assure that we would adopt an eclectic, inclusive approach. But since this is much too important a goal to take for granted, we have also made including these different perspectives one of our guiding principles.

II. SPECIFIC FEATURES DESIGNED TO MAKE THE BOOK MORE USEFUL

Agreeing on guiding principles is one thing; implementing them consistently is quite another. How, then, have we sought to incorporate these principles throughout this book? Here are some specific steps we have taken.

A. Breadth of coverage. First, we have attempted to provide very broad coverage of the field of entrepreneurship. Consistent with this goal, we have included many topics not covered in other texts. Here is a small sample:

- Cognitive bases of creativity and opportunity recognition
- Choosing cofounders wisely
- Indirect techniques for gathering marketing information
- Potential pitfalls faced by decision-making groups
- The legal environment of business (e.g., business contracts)
- The marketing process in a new company
- Complementary assets as a strategy for new firm performance
- Essential people skills for entrepreneurs: creating trust, exerting influence, managing stress
- Recruiting, selecting, and motivating high-performing employees
- The impact of entrepreneurs' personal lives (e.g., their families) on their success
- The role of negotiating skills in exit strategies
- Developing and protecting intellectual property
- How to make an effective business plan presentation

B. Balance between theory and practice. To attain this balance, we have included coverage of the most recent findings and information available in every chapter. The result: The research we draw upon is quite recent, with many citations coming from 2000 or later. To assure that practice is fully represented, we have included two special features:

1. **Danger! Pitfall Ahead!** These sections highlight potential snares and hazards of which entrepreneurs should be aware—ones that can prove fatal to their new ventures, and their dreams! More importantly, these sections provide practical examples of the key concepts outlined in each chapter.

   A few examples:
   - Exploiting an Incremental Innovation by Starting a Firm (Chapter 2)
   - "Too Much Invested to Quit": The Potentially Devastating Effect of Sunk Costs (Chapter 3)
   - What Can Happen When Entrepreneurs Are Ignorant of the Law (Chapter 8)
   - Stymied by the Dominant Design: The Story of Electric Vehicles (Chapter 9)
   - Employee Theft: Evening The Score with an Unfair Employer (Chapter 13)

DANGER! PITFALL AHEAD!

Exploiting an Incremental Innovation by Starting a Firm

You have spent a lot of time thinking about a business idea for your new venture, and you have come up with what you think is a good one—to produce a laptop computer with a built-in MP3 player. You think that this is a really great idea. All of your friends in your dorm think that it would be really cool to have an MP3 player built into their laptops. That way, when they are in the library working on their term papers, they could listen through their headphones to music that they downloaded from the Internet. So why is your entrepreneurship professor telling you that this isn't a very good idea for founding a new firm?

Your business idea is an incremental improvement on a product that existing firms already produce. Sure it is a good idea, and people would buy the laptop if it were made. The problem is that your new company is not the right company to make it.

When existing firms produce a product, like laptop computers, they develop skills and capabilities that make them better at producing and selling a product, the more of the product that they produce and sell. This is the idea behind the learning curve that we described here. The companies, like Dell and Apple, that already make laptops know a whole lot more than you do about how to make and sell those computers. Your idea for putting an MP3 player in a laptop is only a small improvement over their laptops. If Dell and Apple wanted to compete with you, all they would have to do would be to figure out how to put the MP3 player into their existing laptops. On the other hand, to compete with them, you would have to figure out how to make a laptop computer. What you would have to do would be a lot harder to do than what they have to do, and they have more resources (money, knowledge, people) than you to do it. The fact that their innovation is incremental, combined with the experience that they have developed, puts

THE VOICE OF EXPERIENCE

The Four Pillars of New Venture Success

As one of the founders of Axiowave Networks, Mukesh Chatter brings with him more than 18 years' experience in the architecture, design, and development of state-of-the-art networking equipment and supercomputers and also holds several patents in these areas. Prior to founding Axiowave, he was the founder, president, and CEO of Nexabit Networks, Inc., a highly successful terabit switch/router company, which was acquired by Lucent Technologies in July 1999. A noted systems architect, Chatter invented the innovative scalable switching fabric technology that operates at multi-terabits per second. He subsequently served as vice president and general manager of IP products at Lucent. Chatter holds a master's degree in computer and systems engineering from Rensselaer Polytechnic Institute in New York and was its "Entrepreneur of the Year" in 2001.

What factors contribute to an entrepreneur's success? This is certainly a basic question for the field of entrepreneurship and one that can only be answered fully through systematic research. But the insights of highly successful entrepreneurs, too, can be valuable in this respect. This is the topic I discussed with Mukesh Chatter in a recent interview.

Baron: "In your experience, what ingredients are necessary for an entrepreneur to succeed?"

Chatter: "I often think in terms of what I call the 'four pillars'—four things that you absolutely need to succeed. First, you must have a burning need—if you don't have this kind of passion, you really don't have an opportunity. Second, you must have a solution—something that is a lot better than what is out there—a solution that makes you top. Third, you must have money—you can't get anywhere without financial resources. Finally, you need a team that can execute—that can make it all happen. You need all four to really succeed."

Baron: "I'd like to hear more about the team—just what do you mean by 'a team that can execute'? How do you go about building one?"

Chatter: "You do it by building a corporate culture that values fairness and teamwork. Everyone is part of the team, including you. You are not the king—you a member of the team. You must

2. **The Voice of Experience.** Several chapters contain interviews with highly successful entrepreneurs. The entrepreneurs share their views about various aspects of the entrepreneurial process, thus providing concrete examples of how principles covered in a given chapter can be applied. A few examples:

- Some Thoughts on Avoiding False Alarms (Chapter 3)
- Know Your Market—And Your Competitive Edge—Before You Start! (Chapter 4)
- The Multiple Benefits of an Appropriate Exit Strategy (Chapter 14)

III. FEATURES DESIGNED TO MAKE THIS BOOK MORE APPEALING TO READERS

LEARNING OBJECTIVES

After reading this chapter, you should be able to:

1 Explain why cognitive processes provide an important foundation for understanding creativity and opportunity recognition.

2 Describe working memory, long-term memory, and procedural memory, and explain the role they play in creativity and opportunity recognition.

3 Explain why we tend to use heuristics and other mental shortcuts, and how these shortcuts can influence entrepreneurs.

4 Define creativity and explain the role that concepts play in it.

5 Distinguish between analytical, creative, and practical intelligence, and explain how all three are combined in successful intelligence.

6 List several factors that influence creativity, as described by the confluence approach.

7 Explain the role of access to information and utilization of information in opportunity recognition.

8 Describe signal detection theory and distinguish between hits, false alarms, and misses.

9 Explain the difference between a promotion focus and a prevention focus, and describe the effects these contrasting perspectives may have on entrepreneurs' efforts to discover valuable opportunities.

10 List several steps you can take as an individual to increase your skill at recognizing potentially valuable opportunities.

Our own teaching experience (more than 50 years combined), tells us that if students find a textbook difficult or boring to read, its value is sharply reduced. With this thought in mind, we have included several features to make this book more interesting to read, and more convenient to use. First, it is written in what we believe to be a clear and direct style—one that will communicate with readers rather than bore or irritate them. Second, we have included a number of features designed to help students with their studying. All chapters begin with a **Chapter Outline** and **Learning Objectives**. Brief reviews of **Key Points** appear at the end of major sections of the text within chapters. All charts and graphs have been specially prepared for this text, and contain special captions to help readers with correct interpretation (see p. 17 for an example). Each chapter ends with a **Summary and Review of Key Points.**

All **Key Terms** are printed in **boldface** within the body of the text, and are defined in a **Glossary** section at the end of the chapter. End-of-chapter materials for each chapter include **Discussion Questions**, which are designed to stimulate in-class discussion of major points, and several **Getting Down to Business** exercises designed to give readers practice with the principles presented and to help students to write a feasibility study or business plan for their own venture idea. **InfoTrac** exercises are also included at the end of each chapter, and students can find additional InfoTrac exercises on the book support Web site. These exercises are designed to direct readers to relevant articles from established academic journals to illustrate the chapter concepts, as well as to spark further interest in them. Finally, we have included an abundance of case resources. Cases illustrating concepts for each chapter can be found in the **Case Studies Appendix**. Video Cases from the *Small Business School* are available on VHS, and the **Video Case Library Appendix** included in the text provides additional information and discussion questions. Finally, longer, detailed **Comprehensive Cases** can be accessed at http://baron.swlearning.com detailing real businesses whose successes and setbacks illustrate principles covered in the text chapters, as well as each stage of the entrepreneurial process. Teaching notes for all the cases are included in the instructor's manual.

We believe that together, these features will make this a book that students will actually read—and that, of course, is the first, crucial step toward learning.

GETTING DOWN TO BUSINESS

Becoming an Entrepreneur: Is It Right for You?

A key theme of this chapter has been that the entrepreneurial process begins when enterprising individuals identify potentially valuable opportunities. Clearly, this implies that not everyone is suited to becoming an entrepreneur. Just being able to spot potentially profitable opportunities is not, in itself, enough. In addition, entrepreneurs must be willing, ready, and able to "run with the ball"—to take the vigorous and continuing steps necessary to launch a new venture. Are you such a person? Are you capable not only of developing a vision of where you want to get, but also of getting there, because you are willing to learn from your mistakes? If not, you should reconsider, because entrepreneurship definitely lives up to Edison's suggestion that "Success is 2% inspiration and 98% perspiration."

Although there is no single test of "entrepreneurial potential," there is general agreement that becoming a successful entrepreneur requires several key characteristics. Rate yourself on each of these dimensions—and then ask several people who know you well to do the same thing. The results may give you valuable insight into whether you are cut out to be an entrepreneur.

1. **Can You Handle Uncertainty?** Is security (e.g., a regular paycheck) important to you, or are you willing to live with uncertainty—economic and otherwise?

2. **Are You Energetic?** Do you have the vigor and health required to work very long hours for long periods of time in order to reach goals that are important to you?

3. **Do You Believe in Yourself and Your Abilities?** Do you believe that you can accomplish whatever you set out to accomplish, learning what you need along the way?

4. **Can You Handle Reversals and Failures Well?** How do you react to negative outcomes—with discouragement or with renewed commitment to succeeding the next time around and learning from your mistakes?

5. **Are You Passionate About Your Goals or Vision?** Once you establish a goal or a vision of where you want to be, are you willing to sacrifice almost everything else to get there, because you are truly passionate about doing so?

6. **Are You Good with Other People?** Can you persuade them to see the world the way you do? Can you get along with them well (e.g., handle conflicts, build trust)?

7. **Are You Adaptable?** Can you make "mid-course corrections" easily? For instance, can you admit that you made a mistake and reverse course to correct it?

8. **Are You Willing to Take Risks or Leaps of Faith?** Once you establish a goal, are you willing to take reasonable risks to reach it? In other words, are you willing to do what you can to minimize the risks, but then, once you have done so, proceed?

Current evidence suggests that successful entrepreneurs are high on all of these dimensions—higher than other persons. They can handle uncertainty, are energetic, believe in themselves, react well and flexibly to reversals, are passionate about their beliefs, are good with other people, are highly adaptable, and are willing to accept reasonable levels of risk. To the extent you possess these characteristics—or a least most of them—you may be well-suited for the role of entrepreneur. We suspect that if you are reading this book, you fit this description—otherwise, you would not be in this course! If you find that you are relatively low on several of these characteristics, however, you might want to reconsider: perhaps becoming an entrepreneur is not really "your particular cup of tea."

IV. ANCILLARIES

This text is supported by a complement of excellent ancillary materials including an **Instructor's Manual with Test Bank** (ISBN 0-324-28817-4) and **Instructor's Resource CD-ROM** (ISBN 0-324-28972-3), which also includes the Instructor's Manual and Test Bank, as well as **PowerPoint slides** and **ExamView testing software**. A **VHS video** is available with video segments from the Small Business School (ISBN 0-324-28821-2). Last, the book support Web site, http://baron.swlearning.com, is an excellent resource for instructors and students, including additional InfoTrac exercises for students, access to the PowerPoint slides for instructors and students, **case studies**, and full access to instructor ancillaries for registered instructors. Prospective entrepreneurs will also be interested in viewing video **Profiles in Entrepreneurship**, available for download from the Web site.

V. ACKNOWLEDGMENTS

Many of our colleagues graciously offered comments and suggestions during the writing and development of this text. We are grateful for their time and conscientious feedback.

Joseph E. Combs
University of Richmond

Todd A. Finkle
University of Akron

Gerry George
University of Wisconsin

Samuel R. Gray
New Mexico State University

Andrea S. Hershatter
Emory University

Michael Lounsbury
Cornell University

Gary Libecap
University of Arizona

Kenneth Maddux, Jr.
St. Cloud University

Gideon D. Markman
University of Georgia

Peter Marton
Tufts University

Pamela Pommerenke
Michigan State University

George W. Rimler
Virginia Commonwealth University

Harry J. Sapienza
University of Minnesota

Richard L. Smith
Iowa State University

Monica A. Zimmerman
Temple University

VI. SOME CONCLUDING COMMENTS

Looking back, we can honestly say that we have spared no effort to make this book as accurate, comprehensive, up-to-date, and useful to readers as possible. We have also worked hard to meet our goals of representing the field as it exists today, and to obtain the balance between theory, research, and practice that we feel is so crucial. Have we succeeded? Only you, the readers of this book, can decide. So please, share your reactions, suggestions, and comments with us at the e-mail addresses below. We will be genuinely glad to receive your input and, even more important, we will definitely listen carefully to it! Thanks in advance for your help.

Robert A. Baron
baronr@rpi.edu

Scott A. Shane
sas46@cwru.edu

A NOTE TO STUDENTS

This Book: A Useful Tool for Studying...and for Starting Your Own Company

When we think back over our own years in college, both of us can remember using texts that were, to be perfectly honest, *mind-numbing*. Not only were they boring and hard to understand, but they offered absolutely no help when we tried to study from them, often late at night. And because they were so painful to read, it was difficult to remember any useful information they might have contained; we just wanted to forget about them as quickly as possible!

Consequently, when we decided to write this text, we took a personal pledge that this would not be the kind of book we would produce. On the contrary, we would do our best to prepare a text that would be easy to read and useful, both now when you study for exams, and later, when you start your own company. What steps have we taken to reach these ambitious goals? Here is an overview:

- **Chapter Outlines:** Research findings indicate strongly that information that is organized is easier to understand and remember than information that is not. For this reason, we start each chapter with an outline of the major sections. If you take a moment to read through these outlines, they will help you to see how each chapter "flows" and how its various parts fit together; that, in turn, will help you to understand—and remember—the information presented.

- **Review of Key Points at the End of Each Major Section:** Often, it is easy to "lose the forest for the trees"—to get so bogged down in details that the main points are lost from view. To avoid this possibility, each major section of text is followed by a review of the key points made. If you consider these carefully, it will help you to remember the most central points and information, and that, in turn, will make your studying more efficient.

- **Boldface of Key Terms:** Our own students often ask us: "What are the most important points or concepts?" To help you recognize these, they are printed in **bold type** like this.

- **Glossary:** In addition, these key terms are clearly defined at the end of each chapter in a separate Glossary. Having these definitions in one place, as well as in the text, is not only convenient—it will help you remember the meaning of these terms both now, when you study for exams, and later, when you use the information in this book to start your own company.

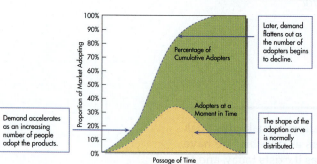

- **Special Labeling of All Charts and Graphs:** Instead of merely copying charts and graphs that appear in other sources, we have specially designed *all* of them so that they are easy to understand. And to help you grasp the main points they illustrate, all charts and graphs contain special labels that call your attention to these points and explain why they are important.

- **End-of-Chapter Summary and Review of Key Points:** All key points are summarized once again at the end of the chapter; this will make it easier for you to review them—and to see how they are related to each other.

- **InfoTrac Exercises:** These are research exercises closely linked to the content of each chapter, designed to illustrate and highlight key points and concepts.

- **End-of-Chapter "Getting Down to Business" Exercises:** These exercises will give you actual practice in using the key principles presented in each chapter. Together, they will help you prepare to write an actual feasibility study or business plan for your new venture.

- **Special Sections Designed to Help You Become a Successful Entrepreneur:** We have included two different kinds of sections that we believe you will find both interesting and useful:
  - *Danger! Pitfall Ahead!* These sections are designed to emphasize potential dangers that lie in wait to trap unwary entrepreneurs. Recognizing them may help you avoid lots of painful experiences in the future!
  - *The Voice of Experience.* Several chapters contain interviews with highly successful entrepreneurs. The entrepreneurs share their views about various aspects of the entrepreneurial process, thus providing concrete examples of how principles covered in a given chapter can actually be applied.

THE VOICE OF EXPERIENCE

The Four Pillars of
New Venture Success

- **Case Studies Appendix (Appendix 1):** The Case Studies Appendix includes case studies for 13 chapters of the text, illustrating with real-world detail the concepts you've learned in each chapter.

- **Video Case Library Appendix (Appendix 2):** The Video Case Library Appendix gives you additional background on the companies in the *Small Business School* Video Cases that your instructor may choose to show. This appendix also includes discussion questions to prompt you to think more about the entrepreneurial issues the video depicts.

- **Online Comprehensive Cases:** You can download case studies from the book's Web site at http://baron.swlearning.com. These cases feature real businesses that have faced the same kinds of opportunities and challenges that you may deal with in your own ventures, illustrating the chapter concepts and the stages of the entrepreneurial process.

We sincerely believe that together, these features make the book more interesting to read, more useful as a tool for studying, and—perhaps most important of all—a good source of practical information you can use when you start your own company. We hope you will agree, and that you will find this book to be one you consult over and over again in the years ahead. Good luck both in your course and in the exciting years ahead when *you* will start the companies that strongly shape the future.

Robert A. Baron   **Scott A. Shane**
baronr@rpi.edu   sas46@cwru.edu

ABOUT THE AUTHORS

Robert A. Baron is Dean R. Wellington Professor of Management and Professor of Psychology; Ph.D., University of Iowa. He recently completed terms of office as Interim Dean and Interim Director of the Severino Center for Technological Entrepreneurship (2001–2002). Professor Baron has held faculty appointments at Purdue University, the University of Minnesota, University of Texas, University of South Carolina, University of Washington, and Princeton University. In 1982 he was a Visiting Fellow at Oxford University. From 1979 to 1981 he served as a Program Director at the National Science Foundation (Washington, D.C.) In 2001 the French Ministry of Research appointed him as a Visiting Senior Research Fellow; he held this post at the Universite des Sciences Sociales, Toulouse. He has been a Fellow of the American Psychological Association since 1978, and is also a Charter Fellow of the American Psychological Society.

Professor Baron has published more than 100 articles in professional journals and 30 chapters in edited volumes. He is the author or co-author of more than 40 books in the fields of management and psychology, including *Behavior in Organizations* (8th ed.) and *Social Psychology* (10th ed.).

Professor Baron served as a member of the board of directors of the Albany Symphony Orchestra (1993–1996). He holds three U.S. patents and was founder, president, and CEO of Innovative Environmental Products, Inc. (1993–2000).

Professor Baron's research and consulting activities focus primarily on the following topics: (1) social and cognitive factors in entrepreneurship, (2) workplace aggression and violence, and (3) impact of the physical environment (e.g., lighting, air quality, temperature) on productivity.

Scott A. Shane is Professor of Economics and Entrepreneurship at the Weatherhead School of Management at the Case Western Reserve University and Academic Director of the Center for Regional Economic Issues; PhD, University of Pennsylvania. Dr. Shane has held faculty appointments at University of Maryland, Massachusetts Institute of Technology, and Georgia Institute of Technology. The author of over 50 scholarly articles on entrepreneurship and innovation management, Dr. Shane's work has appeared in *Management Science, Academy of Management Journal, Academy of Management Review, Strategic Management Journal, Decision Science, Journal of Economic Behavior and Organization, Journal of Management, Journal of Business Venturing, Journal of International Business Studies*, and *Entrepreneurship Theory and Practice*, among other journals. He is currently departmental editor of the R&D, Innovation, Entrepreneurship, and Product Development Division of *Management Science*. His current research examines how entrepreneurs discover and evaluate opportunities, assemble resources, and design organizations. Dr. Shane has consulted to numerous large and small organizations and has taught in executive education programs in Norway, Poland, New Zealand, and the United States. His research has been quoted in *The Wall Street Journal, Inc.,* and *Entrepreneur Magazine*.

PART 1

ENTREPRENEURSHIP: WHO, WHAT, WHY?

CHAPTER 1

Entrepreneurship: A Field—And An Activity

CHAPTER 2

Uncovering Opportunities: Understanding
Entrepreneurial Opportunities and Industry Analysis

CHAPTER 3

Cognitive Foundations of Entrepreneurship:
Creativity and Opportunity Recognition

What precisely is entrepreneurship, both as an activity and a field of study? How does it unfold over time as a process? How can we gather systematic and valid information about it? What are opportunities and how do they emerge? What cognitive factors play a role in creativity and in the generation of ideas for new products or services? Understanding these basic issues is essential for understanding what follows in the remainder of the book—a comprehensive examination of the entire entrepreneurial process—so we focus on them in this initial section of the text.

CHAPTER 1

ENTREPRENEURSHIP:
A FIELD—AND AN ACTIVITY

LEARNING OBJECTIVES

After reading this chapter, you should be able to:

1 Define "entrepreneurship" as a field of business.

2 Explain why the activities of entrepreneurs are so important to the economies of their countries, and why entrepreneurship is an increasingly popular career choice.

3 Describe the process perspective on entrepreneurship, and list the major phases of this process.

4 Explain why entrepreneurship can be viewed as arising out of the intersection of people and opportunities.

5 Explain why certain sources of knowledge about entrepreneurship are more reliable and useful than others.

6 Describe the basic nature of systematic observation, experimentation, and reflection (i.e., the case method and other qualitative methods).

7 Explain the role of theory in the field of entrepreneurship.

The Field of Entrepreneurship: Its Nature and Roots
 Entrepreneurship: An Engine of Economic Growth
 Entrepreneurship: Foundations in Other Disciplines

Entrepreneurship: A Process Perspective
 Levels of Analysis: Micro Versus Macro Revisited
 Entrepreneurship: The Intersection of Valuable Opportunities and Enterprising Individuals

Sources of Knowledge About Entrepreneurship: How We Know What We Know
 Observation, Reflection, and Experimentation: Alternative Routes to Knowledge
 Theory: Answering the Questions "Why" and "How"

A User's Guide to This Text

All photos this page © PhotoDisc, Inc.

"Much of our American progress has been the product of the individual who had an idea; pursued it; fashioned it; tenaciously clung to it against all odds; and then produced it, sold it and profited from it." (Hubert Humphrey, 1966)

In the spring of 1990, I (Robert Baron) had my first chance (but not my last, I suspect) to observe for myself the wisdom of Senator Humphrey's words. The situation went something like this. My daughter was a sophomore at a large state university. She loved her school, but complained incessantly about the dormitory: "It's so noisy that I can't study," she told me, "and the air is terrible—dusty, stale, and it smells bad, too!" Then she said something that, in a sense, changed my life: "Dad, you're an expert on how the physical environment affects people, so can't you come up with an invention that would help?" (She was referring to the fact that for more than 15 years, I had conducted research on the impact of environmental factors such as temperature, air quality, and lighting on human performance.) I had been a consultant to many companies on such matters, but until that point, I had never really thought about "inventing" a product to help deal with such problems as excess noise and stale, dusty air in small spaces like offices or dorm rooms. After my daughter's comment, though, wheels began to turn inside my head: Couldn't I actually design a device that would address the problems she mentioned? If I could, wouldn't it be both useful *and* eminently marketable? I am not an engineer, so I began to search for a partner who could help me convert this idea into an actual product. I soon found one (although, as I'll note later in this chapter, perhaps not the right one!), and together we came up with a working prototype: a device that filtered the air, contained a separate system for reducing noise, and yet another system for releasing pleasant fragrances. Each system could be operated independently by users. At that point, we felt we had something, so we applied for a U.S. patent. We received it, and two others on related products, in the next two years. Now, though, we faced another challenge: how to

bring the product to market. We checked carefully and learned that to produce it ourselves would require several million dollars' worth of equipment, so we decided to seek a corporate partner. That search, too, was successful, and within a year, our product—which we called the PPS (for Personal Privacy System)—was being sold in stores and on TV by our large corporate partner (see Figure 1.1). My own company (IEP, Inc.) handled direct sales through an Internet site and ads in magazines. Our product continued to sell for several years and IEP was modestly—but not wildly—profitable. We ceased operations in 2000, mainly because I had reached a point where I had to choose between my career as a professor and running the company full-time, and also because of my growing realization that I had fallen into several of the major pitfalls that lie in wait for unwary entrepreneurs (e.g., choosing partners unwisely and losing control over the quality of one's products). For seven years, though, I was truly an entrepreneur in every sense of the word; when I feel the "itch" to do it again (which I do with increasing frequency!), I can only conclude that I may be one again in the future.

Figure 1.1 The Author as Entrepreneur

The device shown here—a combination air cleaner, sound-reduction, and fragrance release system—was patented by one of the authors (Baron), manufactured by a corporate partner of the author's company, and sold nationally.

Why do we begin with this bit of personal history? Primarily because it helps us to make several points that will be key themes throughout this text. First, it illustrates the fact that entrepreneurship is a *process*—a chain of events and activities that takes place over time—sometimes, considerable periods of time. It begins with an idea for something new—often, a new product or service. But that is only the start: Unless the process continues so that the idea is converted into reality (actually brought to market through a new business venture, licensing to existing companies, etc.), it is not entrepreneurship. Rather, it is just an exercise in creativity or idea generation.

Second, this brief personal history underscores the fact that both of us have actually "been there"—we have direct, personal experience with being an entrepreneur. As a result, when we write about the processes involved in entrepreneurship—

processes such as recognizing an opportunity and developing the means to exploit it—we understand these events and activities from the *inside*, not simply as observers. As we will note in later discussions, we feel this is very important from the point of view of making this book not only accurate and up-to-date, but also useful to anyone who is now, or wants to become, an entrepreneur.

Having clarified these important points, we will now turn to several tasks that we want to accomplish in this initial chapter. Briefly, these are as follows. First, we will present a definition of entrepreneurship both as an activity and as a field of study. Next, we'll offer a framework for understanding entrepreneurship as a *process*—one that unfolds over time. This process is affected by a multitude of factors, some relating to individuals (i.e., to entrepreneurs), some to their relations with other people (e.g., partners, customers, venture capitalists), and some to society as a whole (e.g., government regulations, market conditions). A major theme of this book will be that all three categories of factors (individual, group, societal) play an important role in every phase of the entrepreneurial process. As part of this discussion, we will emphasize yet another key theme: At the heart of the entrepreneurial process is the intersection of opportunities generated by changing economic, technological, and social conditions and enterprising people capable of distinguishing potentially valuable opportunities from less valuable ones and of actively exploiting them. This theme will be examined in more detail in Chapter 2, which focuses on the emergence of opportunities, and Chapter 3, which focuses on the role of cognition in this process.

Third, we will consider the question of how we know what we currently know about entrepreneurship—in other words, how the information presented in this book was obtained. We think this is important because, in general, it is dangerous to accept *any* information as accurate without knowing something about its source. Finally, we will provide you with an overview of the contents of this book and a description of its special features.

Why do we begin with these preliminary tasks instead of just jumping right into a discussion of various aspects of entrepreneurship? Mainly for this reason: Research findings in the field of cognitive science strongly suggest that people have a much better chance of understanding, remembering, and using new information if they are first provided with a framework for organizing it. We believe that this text contains much new information about entrepreneurship—information you probably have not already encountered. The topics discussed in this introductory chapter will provide you with a framework for making this knowledge your own and for using it in your future life and career. So please read carefully: This will be effort well spent, and it will definitely help you to understand the information presented in later chapters.

THE FIELD OF ENTREPRENEURSHIP: ITS NATURE AND ROOTS

Definitions are always tricky, and for a field as new as entrepreneurship, the task is even more complex. It is not surprising, then, that currently there is no single agreed-upon definition of entrepreneurship either as a field of study in business or as an activity in which people engage. Having said, that, we should note that a definition offered recently by Shane and Venkataraman[1] has received increasing acceptance. Broadly paraphrased, their definition suggests the following: Entrepreneurship, as a field of business, seeks to understand how opportunities to create something *new* (e.g., new products or services, new markets, new production processes or raw materials, new ways of organizing existing technologies) *arise* and are *discovered* or created by *specific persons*, who then use various means to *exploit or develop* them, thus producing a wide range of *effects*. (Italics added by the current authors.) By implication, this definition suggests that entrepreneurship, as an activity carried out by specific persons, involves the key actions we mentioned earlier: identifying an opportunity—one that is potentially valuable in the sense that it can be exploited in practical business terms (i.e., one that can potentially yield sustainable profits)—and identifying the activities involved in actually exploiting or developing this opportunity. In addition, as we will note in a later section of this chapter, the process does not end there, with the launching of a new venture; it also involves being able to run a new business successfully after it has come into existence.

We believe that this definition is a clear and useful one, and does indeed capture the essential nature of entrepreneurship. Although it helps to clarify many important questions, perhaps the most central of these is: "Just what makes someone an entrepreneur?" Obviously, if we can't agree on *that* issue, there is little hope of developing systematic knowledge about what entrepreneurship involves. To see how the definition offered by Shane and Venkataraman helps significantly in this respect, consider the following individuals. For each, ask yourself this question: "Is this person truly an entrepreneur?"

- A woman who enjoys making appetizers for parties in her home, and who is often praised by friends who tell her how delicious these are, starts a company to make and sell them.
- A university scientist engaged in basic research on the biochemistry of life makes important discoveries that advance the frontiers of his field; however, he has no interest in identifying practical uses of his discoveries and does not attempt to do so.
- After being "downsized" from his management-level job, a middle-aged man hits upon the idea of processing old tires in a special way to make edging for gardens (borders that keep different kinds of plants separate).
- A retired army officer develops the idea of purchasing obsolete amphibious vehicles from the government and using them to start a company that specializes in tours of remote wilderness areas.
- A young computer scientist develops new software that is far better than anything now on the market; she seeks capital to start a company to develop and sell this product.

Which of these individuals are entrepreneurs? At first glance, you might be tempted to conclude that only the last two are really entrepreneurs—that only *they* are creating something truly new. We suggest, however, that *all* of these persons with the exception of the university scientist are entrepreneurs. Why? Recall our definition: Entrepreneurship involves recognizing an opportunity to create something new—and that something does not have to be a new product or service. On the contrary, it can involve recognizing an opportunity to develop a new market, to use a new raw material, or to develop a new means of production, to mention just a few possibilities. According to this definition, the appetizer-baking woman is acting as an entrepreneur because she has recognized a new market—one that will pay a premium price for appetizers that taste truly homemade. In fact, this is just what Nancy Mueller did when she started Nancy's Specialty Foods—a company she recently sold for tens of millions of dollars.

Similarly, the downsized executive is using a new "raw material"—old tires—in a new way. This, too, qualifies as entrepreneurship. The retired army officer and the computer scientist are also entrepreneurs: Both have identified opportunities for new products or services, and both have taken active steps to convert these ideas into going business concerns.

In contrast, the university scientist is not an entrepreneur, according to our definition. Although his research does add appreciably to human knowledge, the fact that he makes no effort to apply his discoveries to the development of new products, services, markets, or means of production suggests that he is not an entrepreneur. Certainly, he is playing a valuable role in society, but he is not an entrepreneur.

In essence, then, entrepreneurship requires creating or recognizing a commercial application for something new. The new commercial application can take many different forms, but simply inventing a new technology, product, or service, or generating a new idea is not, in itself, enough. As shown in Figure 1.2 (on page 6), many inventions never result in actual products for the simple reason that they offer no commercial benefits (or, alternatively, no one can think of a marketable use for them), and so they cannot really serve as the basis for a profitable new business. In sum, we agree with Shane and Venkataraman that entrepreneurship emerges out of the intersection of what might be

Figure 1.2 Newness Is Not Enough!

The fact that a product is new is not sufficient to assure that it will be developed and brought to market.

Barry's new Executive Power Stilts™ gave him an air of superiority over co-workers who once intimidated him.

termed "the inspired" and "the mundane," recognizing opportunities for something new that people will want to own or use and taking vigorous steps to convert these opportunities into viable, profitable businesses.

A Note on Intrapreneurship

Before turning to other topics, we should note, briefly, that recognizing opportunities for creating or developing something new can occur within existing organizations as well as outside them. In fact, many successful companies are deeply concerned with encouraging innovations and take active steps to provide an environment in which they can flourish.[2] This involves such steps as developing a corporate culture receptive to new ideas rather than one that routinely rejects them and providing concrete rewards for innovation.[3] For instance, General Electric (GE) offers employees who come up with innovative ideas a share of the profits resulting from them. The result? GE has obtained more U.S. patents during recent decades than any other U.S. company and now holds more than 51,000 in total! Individuals who act like entrepreneurs inside a company are often described as being **intrapreneurs**—persons who create something new, but inside an existing company rather than through the route of founding a new venture. Although our focus will be firmly on entrepreneurs throughout this book, we do want to note that individuals can act entrepreneurially in several different contexts, including large, existing companies.

Entrepreneurship: An Engine of Economic Growth

When one of us (Robert Baron) began his career as a university professor (in 1968), courses such as the one you are now taking simply did not exist. Now, in contrast, they are offered by virtually every school of management or business and have shown a pattern of rapidly growing enrollments in recent years. Why? One reason is that such courses reflect parallel growth in the number of persons choosing to become entrepreneurs—or at least to start their own businesses. Each year, more than 600,000 new businesses are launched in the United States alone, and this number has almost doubled in the past two decades.[4] Although not all of these would meet our definition for involving entrepreneurship, all—to the extent they are successful—contribute to economic growth. Consider the following facts:

- During the 1990s, large corporations in the United States downsized more than 6 million jobs out of existence, yet unemployment fell to record-low levels, mainly as a result of new companies started by entrepreneurs
- In one recent year, more than 900,000 new start-up companies were founded in the United States [U.S. Small Business Administration (SBA), 1999].
- Currently, more than 10 million individuals are self-employed in the United States (U.S. SBA, 1998)—about one in eight adults!
- While the number of new businesses started each year has increased steadily, the number started by women and minorities has risen even more dramatically; for instance, the number of companies owned by minorities increased 168 percent between 1987 and 1997, to a total of 3.25 million businesses, which, together, employ more than 4 million persons and generate $495 billion in revenues (U.S. SBA, 1999).

LEARNING OBJECTIVE

2 Explain why the activities of entrepreneurs are so important to the economies of their countries, and why entrepreneurship is an increasingly popular career choice.

These statistics suggest that the activities of entrepreneurs have a truly major impact on the economies of their societies.

Even a casual glance at history suggests that entrepreneurs have always existed and always "made waves" in their societies: Vast fortunes were certainly amassed by entrepreneurs of the past such as John D. Rockefeller, Andrew Carnegie, and Cornelius Vanderbilt. However, considerable evidence suggests that more people than ever are pursuing, or considering, this role. What factors are responsible for this trend? Many appear to be playing a role. First, the media are filled with glowing accounts of successful entrepreneurs such as Michael Dell, Bill Gates, and Mary Kay Ash (see Figure 1.3). As a result, the role of entrepreneur has taken on a very positive and attractive aura. In an age when political and military heroes are few and far between, entrepreneurs have, in a sense, become the new heroes and heroines, so it is far from surprising that a growing number of persons are choosing to pursue this kind of career.

Second, there has been a fundamental change in what has often been termed "the employment contract"—the implicit understanding between employers and employees.[5] In the past, this implicit agreement suggested that as long as individuals performed their jobs well, they would be retained as employees. Now, in an era of downsizing and "right-sizing," this agreement has been broken, with the result that many individuals feel little loyalty to their current employers. It is just one small step from such feelings to the conclusion, "I'd be better off working for myself!"

A third factor is a change in basic values. In the past, security was a dominant theme for many people: They wanted a secure job with steady increments in salary. Now, surveys indicate that young people, especially, prefer a more independent lifestyle—one that offers choice in place of certainty or predictability.[6] Together, these and many other factors have combined to bolster the allure of becoming an entrepreneur, and as noted earlier, this has translated into the creation of hundreds of thousands of new businesses employing millions of persons. This trend is stronger in the United States than elsewhere, but seems to be picking up steam around the world, as government leaders in many countries recognize that, in fact, entrepreneurs *do* matter—and matter greatly.

Entrepreneurship: Foundations in Other Disciplines

Nothing, it has often been said, emerges out of a vacuum. Where the field of entrepreneurship is concerned, this is certainly true. Entrepreneurship, as a branch of business, has important roots in several older and more established fields—and with good reason. Consider, again, our definition of entrepreneurship—a field of study that seeks to understand how opportunities to create new products or services, new markets, production processes, ways of organizing existing technologies, or raw materials arise and are discovered by specific persons, who then use various means to exploit or develop them. This definition implies that in order to understand entrepreneurship as a process—and as an activity in which entrepreneurs engage—it is essential to consider (1) the economic, technological, and social conditions from which opportunities rise, (2) the people who recognize these opportunities (entrepreneurs), (3) the business techniques and legal structures they use to develop them, and (4) and the economic and social effects produced by such development. All of these elements play a role in entrepreneurship, and all must be taken into account if we are ever to fully understand this complex process. This, in turn, implies that the field of entrepreneurship is closely linked to older and more established disciplines such as economics, behavioral science (psychology, cognitive science), and sociology. The findings and principles of these fields can shed much light on many aspects of entrepreneurship and provide valuable frameworks for understanding key questions addressed by the field—questions such as these: "How do opportunities arise?" (see Chapter 2); "Why do some persons but not others recognize them?" (see

Figure 1.3 The Romance of Entrepreneurship

In a sense, entrepreneurs are the new heroes and heroines: They are often presented in very flattering terms by the media. As a result, the appeal of becoming an entrepreneur has increased greatly in recent years. (Shown here: Michael Dell)

© Reuters NewMedia Inc./CORBIS

Chapter 3); and "What factors influence the success of new ventures after they are launched?" (see Chapters 9, 10, and 13).

Admittedly, all of this is somewhat abstract, so perhaps a concrete example will be helpful. Consider the rapid growth of one successful high-tech company: Expedia.com. Expedia is an online travel service that allows users to book flights, hotel rooms, and rental cars from any computer with access to the Internet. The company's growth has been swift, so it seems clear that its founders recognized an excellent opportunity and have gone on to exploit it well. But consider the following question: Could Expedia.com have been launched 10 years ago? The answer is "Almost certainly no." The reason it could not is straightforward: Technological, economic, and social forces had not yet generated the opportunity that the founders of Expedia.com recognized. From a technological point of view, an online travel service could not exist until many millions of persons had access to the Internet and until software capable of integrating the schedules of dozens of airlines and the rates of thousands of hotels existed. From an economic point of view, such a service could not be viable until a safe and reliable way of making payments over the Internet existed and unless airlines and hotels were willing to pay commissions to an Internet company instead of (or in addition to) traditional travel agents. Finally, from a social perspective, an online travel service could not exist and prosper until large numbers of persons had enough confidence in online information to entrust their travel plans to it and until large numbers of persons became aware of the fact that travelers on the same flights often paid hugely different fares (see Figure 1.4). In sum, the opportunity for founding Expedia.com did not always exist; rather, it emerged—and became available for discovery by specific persons—out of a combination of many factors—economic, technological, and social.

In a similar manner, the disciplines of economics, behavioral science, and sociology can help to provide answers to other basic questions addressed by the field of entrepreneurship, questions such as: "Why do some persons but not others recognize opportunities?" "Why are some entrepreneurs so much more successful than others?" and "Why are some means for developing opportunities more effective than others?" Clearly, then, the field of entrepreneurship does not exist in an intellectual vacuum; rather, its roots rest firmly in several older disciplines that, together, provide it with a firm foundation for understanding one of the most complex—and important—business processes in existence.

One final comment: Are some of these disciplines more useful than others in our efforts to understand entrepreneurship as a process? In other words, should we focus primarily on economic factors, on factors relating to entrepreneurs, or on factors relating

Figure 1.4 An Opportunity in the Making

In recent years, increasing numbers of persons have become aware of the fact that people on the same flights or staying in the same hotels often paid very different rates. This awareness was one factor that created the opportunity Expedia.com and similar companies exploited.

to society as a whole in our efforts to understand the entrepreneurial process? This issue has sometimes been debated in the context of a distinction found in several other branches of management: **macro** versus **micro** approaches.[7] Macro approaches take a "top-down" perspective, seeking to understand how and why new ventures are founded, and why they succeed or fail, by focusing largely on what are often termed "environmental factors"—economic, financial, and political variables. Presumably, these factors, which are largely beyond the direct control of individuals, shape the behavior and decisions of individual entrepreneurs, so understanding their impact is crucial. In contrast, micro approaches take a "bottom-up" perspective, seeking to understand the entrepreneurial process by focusing primarily on the behavior and thoughts of individuals or groups of individuals (e.g., founding partners). Presumably, it is the way in which individuals behave that is the key to understanding the entrepreneurial process. Is either view more accurate or more useful than the other? We strongly doubt it. On the contrary, we believe that full understanding of entrepreneurship can only be gained through careful consideration of both perspectives. In fact, we view them as complementary rather than competing. Thus, both will be represented throughout this book.

KEY POINTS

- Entrepreneurship, as a field of business, seeks to understand how opportunities to create something new (new products or services, new markets, new production processes or raw materials, new ways of organizing existing technologies) arise and are discovered or created by specific persons, who then use various means to exploit or develop them, thus producing a wide range of effects.
- In recent years, the allure of entrepreneurship has increased, with the result that more people than ever are choosing this activity as a career.
- Entrepreneurship, as a branch of business, has important roots in economics, behavioral science, and sociology.
- The field of entrepreneurship recognizes that both the micro perspective (which focuses on the behavior and thoughts of individuals) and the macro perspective (which focuses primarily on environmental factors) are important for obtaining a full understanding of the entrepreneurial process.

ENTREPRENEURSHIP: A PROCESS PERSPECTIVE

Now that we have offered a working definition of entrepreneurship, highlighted its importance, and briefly described its intellectual roots in related disciplines, we will turn to another key task: suggesting a framework for understanding it as a *process*. This will be a guiding theme of the remainder of this book, so it is important that we present it clearly and that you—our readers—understand what it implies.

The view that entrepreneurship is a process rather than a single event is certainly not new or unique to this text. On the contrary, there is a growing consensus in the field that viewing entrepreneurship as a process that unfolds over time and moves through distinct but closely interrelated phases is both useful and accurate.[8] Further, there is general agreement that the key phases in this process are as follows:

LEARNING OBJECTIVE

3 Describe the process perspective on entrepreneurship, and list the major phases of this process.

- *Recognition of an opportunity.* The entrepreneurial process begins when one or more persons recognize an **opportunity**—the potential to create something new (new products or services, new markets, new production processes, new raw materials, new ways of organizing existing technologies, etc.) that has emerged from a complex pattern of changing conditions—changes in knowledge, technology, or economic, political, social, and demographic conditions.[9] Opportunities have the potential to generate economic value (i.e., profit) and are viewed as desirable in the society in which they occur (i.e., development of the opportunity is consistent with existing legal and moral standards and would, therefore, not be blocked or constrained by these standards).

We will examine the emergence of opportunities in Chapter 2 and the cognitive roots of entrepreneurship in Chapter 3, but for the moment, we want to emphasize just one point: In a sense, there really *is* nothing "entirely new under the sun." Ideas do not emerge out of a void; on the contrary, they almost always consist of a novel combination of elements that already exist. What is new is the combination—not the components of which it consists. To take a striking example from history, Alexander Graham Bell did not invent the telephone out of sheer creative genius. Rather, he combined component ideas that already existed and had been generated by other persons (e.g., electric batteries, basic research on the nature of sound, etc.) in a new way—and hence invented a product that revolutionized human communication.

A similar argument holds for recognizing opportunities. The opportunities themselves are generated by economic, technological, and social factors—factors that are in a constant state of change. What is new is the act of noticing a pattern in these changes—somehow "connecting the dots," so to speak, so that the idea for something new emerges in the minds of one or more persons. For instance, consider Nancy Mueller, the founder, in 1977, of Nancy's Specialty Foods. As Mueller describes it, she was a housewife who prepared mini-quiches and other appetizers for a holiday party that she and her husband gave each year. The party had more than 200 guests, so Mueller would prepare the appetizers in advance and freeze them. The appetizers were always a great hit, and many of the guests—especially women—mentioned that they would love to make them too, but had no time. The 1970s was a period of rapidly changing roles for women, and millions were entering the job market for the first time. Taking note of this fact, Mueller began to consider the possibility that there might be a market for frozen appetizers like the ones she prepared. In other words, she began to notice a *convergence* of factors that, together, offered an opportunity for an interesting new venture, one that would prepare and sell frozen appetizers to working women who had little or no time to prepare them (see Figure 1.5). Why did she and not someone else recognize this opportunity? (Like many good opportunities, it seems so obvious in retrospect!) We will consider this question in detail in Chapter 3. Here, we simply want to note that the entrepreneurial process does indeed begin with the recognition of the

Figure 1.5 Opportunities Emerge out of a Confluence of Factors

Opportunities—the potential to create something new (new products or services, new markets, new production processes, new raw materials, new ways of organizing existing technologies, etc.)—emerge from a complex pattern of changing conditions (changes in knowledge, technology, or economic, political, social, and demographic conditions). This was certainly true for Nancy Mueller, who based her highly successful company (Nancy's Specialty Foods) on a convergence of the factors shown here.

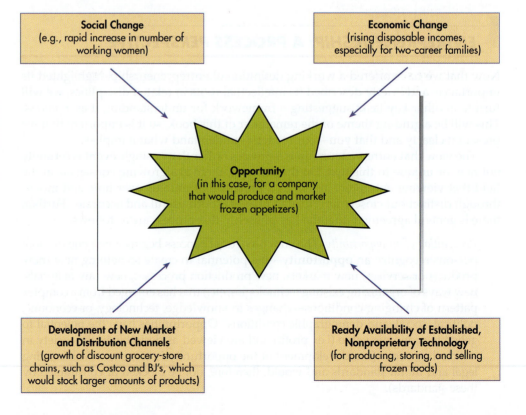

potential for something new in the minds of one or more persons who—if they choose to develop these opportunities—become entrepreneurs.

■ *Deciding to proceed and assembling the essential resources.* Having an idea for a new product or service or recognizing an opportunity is only, of course, the first step in the process. At that point, an initial decision to proceed—to do something *active* about the idea or opportunity—is required. As Shane, Locke, and Collins[10] suggest, the entrepreneurial process occurs because specific persons make this decision and act upon it. In their view, understanding entrepreneurs' motives is crucial to comprehending the entire process. Deciding to start a business is one thing; actually doing so is quite another. Would-be entrepreneurs quickly discover that they must assemble a wide array of required resources: *basic information* (about markets, environmental and legal issues), *human resources* (partners, initial employees), and *financial resources.* Gathering these resources is one of the most crucial phases of the entrepreneurial process, and unless it is completed successfully, opportunities—no matter how attractive—or ideas for new products and services—no matter how good—come to naught. It is at this stage, and especially when seeking financial backing, that entrepreneurs typically prepare a formal **business plan**—a detailed description of how they plan to develop their new venture. (Assembly of required resources will be covered in Chapters 4 through 7).

■ *Launching a new venture.* Once the required resources are assembled, the new venture can actually be launched. Doing so involves a wide range of actions and decisions: choosing the legal form of the new venture, developing the new product or service, establishing the roles of the top management team, etc. Sadly, many new entrepreneurs do not fully grasp the complexities of starting a new venture, and as we will note in later chapters, this can burden them with problems that could, in fact, have been avoided. (The issues involved in actually launching a new venture will be covered in Chapters 8 through 11).

■ *Building success.* Although moving from an idea to an actual, going concern represents major progress, it is just the start of another key phase in the entrepreneurial process: running the new venture and building it into a growing, profitable business. Many entrepreneurs recognize that this requires additional financial resources. However, in our experience, a smaller proportion fully recognizes the importance of human resources in this process. No business can grow without talented, motivated employees, so at this phase of the process, issues such as how to attract such persons, motivate them, and prevent them from leaving (often with vital information that may be shared with competitors!) become crucial. Devising a strong business strategy is yet another aspect of the process during this phase. Finally, we should note that as a new venture grows, entrepreneurs find themselves having to deal with issues such as conflicts within the top management team and negotiating with others outside the company over a wide range of issues. (These aspects of the entrepreneurial process will be covered in Chapters 12 and 13.)

■ *Harvesting the rewards.* In this final phase, founders choose an exit strategy that allows them to harvest the rewards they have earned through their time, effort, and talents. There are many ways of reaping the benefits of successful entrepreneurship (see Chapter 14), and individual entrepreneurs must choose carefully among them so as to maximize the benefits they gain from what, in many cases, is years of sacrifice and commitment.

One additional comment: We do not mean to imply that entrepreneurship can be readily divided into neat and easily distinguishable phases. In fact, the process is far too complex for that to be true. But the activities described here do tend to unfold over time in an orderly sequence, with idea generation or opportunity recognition occurring first; an active decision to proceed, next; and so on. We believe that viewing entrepreneurship in this manner offers several benefits. First, it helps avoid a static view of entrepreneurship—one that sees entrepreneurship as a specific act (launching of a new venture) that occurs and is then complete. Such a view ignores the fact that entrepreneurs face an everchanging array of tasks and challenges, and that they often think and feel differently about them as they change and unfold. Second, viewing entrepreneurship as an ongoing process draws attention to the key activities entrepreneurs must perform as they proceed with their efforts to convert ideas for new products or services into successful businesses. It has long been recognized that how well entrepreneurs perform these activities is often more central to their success than their personal characteristics or background.[11] Attention to entrepreneurs' tasks, in turn, gives us a good handle on identifying the skills, knowledge, and characteristics they need to function effectively in this role. From this angle, too, a process perspective is useful. (An overview of the major phases is shown in Figure 1.6. Please examine it carefully, because it provides a basic framework for understanding much of what follows in later chapters. As we noted earlier, having such mental frameworks is often very useful.)

Levels of Analysis: Micro Versus Macro Revisited

Until recently, the field of entrepreneurship was marked by a controversy over the following question: In studying the entrepreneurial process, should we focus primarily on the entrepreneur (e.g., this person's skills, abilities, talents, motives, and traits) or primarily on the economic, technological, and societal context in which the entrepreneur operates (economic and market conditions, government policy, etc.)? As you can guess from our earlier comments on the macro/micro issue, we view this question as largely irrelevant. On the contrary, we believe that at every stage of the entrepreneurial process, individual-level (i.e., micro) variables, group or interpersonal-level variables, and societal-level (macro) **variables** all play a role (please refer to Figure 1.6).

For instance, consider the question of opportunity recognition. Certainly, this crucial process occurs in the minds of specific persons and must, therefore, reflect the impact of individual-level variables such as the existing knowledge structures and the unique life histories of these persons. But nothing having to do with people—not even basic aspects of cognition—occurs in a social vacuum. On the contrary, the kind of ideas people generate reflect the times in which they live, the current state of technological knowledge, and many other aspects of the societies and times in which they live. Further, other people with whom the entrepreneur has contact—friends, associates, or even figures in the mass media—often suggest the germ of an idea for a new product or service. In short, all three levels of analysis (individual, group, societal) are relevant and must be considered in order to understand idea generation fully.

Here's another example: Why do some persons, but not others, choose to become entrepreneurs? Again, all three categories of variables play a role. With respect to individual factors, some persons have higher energy, are more willing to accept risk, and have greater self-confidence (self-efficacy) than others; those high on these dimensions are probably more likely to choose the entrepreneurial role.[12]

Figure 1.6 Entrepreneurship as a Process: Some Key Phases

The entrepreneurial process unfolds over time and moves through a number of different phases. Events and outcomes during each phase are affected by many individual-level, group-level, and societal-level factors.

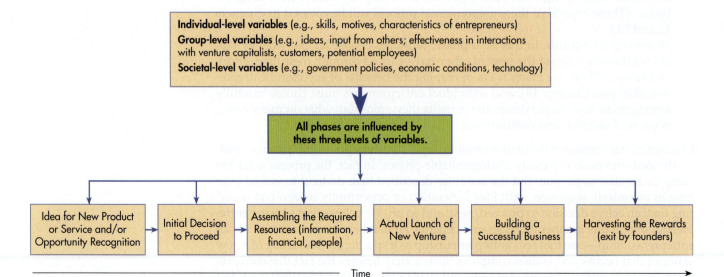

Direct evidence for the role of individual-level factors in choosing to become an entrepreneur is provided by a recent and fascinating study conducted by White, Thornhill, and Hampson.[13] These researchers compared the levels of testosterone shown by male MBA students who had previously started new ventures and those who had not. Results indicated that those who had previously chosen to become entrepreneurs had higher levels of this male hormone! Further evidence suggested that this difference stemmed from a greater tendency toward risk on the part of the entrepreneurs.

Turning to group-level factors, it seems possible that persons who receive encouragement from friends or family members and those who have been exposed to entrepreneurs in their own lives are more likely to proceed than ones who do not receive encouragement and have not been exposed to models of entrepreneurs. For instance, when Enron, a huge energy company based in Houston, imploded as a result of a series of accounting scandals (October 2001), members of the local business community feared that a large number of highly talented people would leave the Houston area. To keep them around, they organized Resource Alliance Group, a company whose sole mission was that of helping former—and highly talented—Enron employees to become entrepreneurs. They succeeded to an amazing degree: Within just three months, they had helped 25 ex-Enron employees to found new ventures. And within a few short years, several of these companies became profitable and added good jobs to the Houston-area economy. Clearly, group-level (i.e., social) factors such as help and encouragement from others can play a key role in the entrepreneurial process.

Societal-level factors, too, are important: Persons who come from certain social and economic backgrounds, or who live in countries where government policies are favorable to starting new ventures, are more likely to choose this role than persons from other backgrounds or who live in other countries. We could continue with other examples, but by now, the main point should be clear: Individual-level, group-level, and societal-level factors influence *every action and every decision taken by entrepreneurs during all phases of the entrepreneurial process.* Taking note of this fact, we will employ all three levels of analysis throughout the text. This will, indeed, add complexity to our discussions of many topics. But it will also, we firmly believe, offer a more complete, accurate, and useful picture of what we know about the process of entrepreneurship today. If that is not the ultimate goal of any text, then we, as authors, researchers, and entrepreneurs, have no idea as to what it should be!

Entrepreneurship: The Intersection of Valuable Opportunities and Enterprising Individuals

About a year ago, one of us (Robert Baron) had the honor of introducing a highly successful entrepreneur, Mukesh Chatter, at a banquet held in his honor. (Chatter was receiving the "Entrepreneur of the Year" award given annually by the university and had just sold his company to Lucent Technologies for almost $1 billion.) During his acceptance speech, Chatter made the following remarks:

> *Success comes from many sources. Yes, you have to recognize an opportunity . . . But to recognize it, it has to be there in the first place—something must have changed so as to generate the opportunity. After that, you have to recognize it and be able to tell that it is a good one—something you can turn into a successful business. Luck definitely plays a role; you have to be in the right place at the right time and know the right people who can help you. But after that, it's largely a matter of hard, mind-bending work; if you are not willing to put in the hours and give up lots of other things in your life, you won't succeed—you won't make it happen.*

We believe these remarks are highly insightful. In just a few sentences, Chatter captured another key theme in entrepreneurship—and this book. Briefly stated, this theme suggests that it is the *intersection of valuable opportunities and enterprising individuals that is the essence of entrepreneurship.* Opportunities, as Chatter pointed out, are generated by changing economic, technological, and social conditions; but nothing happens with respect to these opportunities until one or more energetic, highly motivated persons

LEARNING OBJECTIVE

4 Explain why entrepreneurship can be viewed as arising out of the intersection of people and opportunities.

recognizes them, and the fact that they are worth pursuing. This is an important point: Opportunities vary greatly in their potential value, with the result that only some are worth pursuing. In other words, only for some opportunities is the ratio of risk-to-potential benefits sufficiently favorable to justify efforts to exploit them. As you have probably observed yourself, some business opportunities are superior to others. They occur in industries that are faster growing or more profitable, or ones in which customer needs are easier to identify or satisfy. Further, some opportunities are easier to protect against competition. In Chapter 2, we will carefully examine the specific characteristics that make some opportunities more viable or promising than others. The key point we wish to make here, however, should be obvious: At the very heart of entrepreneurship is a nexus (connection) between opportunities and people. It is this connection or intersection that starts the process—and sometimes changes the world!

KEY POINTS

- Entrepreneurship is a process that unfolds over time and that moves through distinct but closely interrelated phases.
- The entrepreneurial process cannot be divided into neat and easily distinguished stages, but in general, it involves generation of an idea for a new product or service and/or recognition of an opportunity; assembling the resources needed to launch a new venture; launching the venture; running and growing the business; and harvesting the rewards.
- Individual, group, and societal factors influence all phases of the entrepreneurial process. Thus, there is no reason to choose between a micro and a macro approach to entrepreneurship; both perspectives are necessary.
- It is the nexus of valuable opportunities and enterprising individuals that is the essence of entrepreneurship.

SOURCES OF KNOWLEDGE ABOUT ENTREPRENEURSHIP: HOW WE KNOW WHAT WE KNOW

LEARNING OBJECTIVE

5 Explain why certain sources of knowledge about entrepreneurship are more reliable and useful than others.

Throughout this book, we will discuss many aspects of entrepreneurship—how opportunities arise, how some people recognize them, why some means of developing opportunities are better than others (at least in some contexts), why some entrepreneurs are successful while others fail, and so on. As we discuss each of these issues, we will present the most accurate and up-to-date information currently available. This, in turn, raises an important question: How do we know which information fits this description—which information is the most accurate and useful? As any visit to a local bookstore will suggest, many potential sources of information about entrepreneurship exist, and there is no shortage of self-proclaimed experts on this topic. So how have we chosen the information to include in this book? The answer is straightforward: Insofar as possible, we have selected information that has been gathered in accordance with a set of rules or methods for acquiring *reliable* knowledge—methods that have proven extremely helpful in many other fields ranging from the physical sciences, on one hand, through various branches of management on the other. What are these methods, and can they really be applied to the study of entrepreneurship? The methods themselves are quite complex and far beyond the scope of this brief discussion; however, their essential nature was stated concisely by the French philosopher Diderot (1753) more than 250 years ago. Diderot suggested that "There are three principal means of acquiring knowledge: observation, reflection, and experimentation. Observation collects facts; reflection combines them; experimentation verifies the result of that combination . . . ."

That these methods can be used to study entrepreneurship is strongly suggested by the fact that they are currently being employed in a large volume of entrepreneurship research. Because this is the case, and because much of the information presented in this text has been gathered through these methods, it seems useful to describe them briefly here. Our goal is certainly *not* that of turning you into an entrepreneurship researcher; on the contrary, it is simply to provide you with a basic understanding of these methods so that you can become a more informed consumer of knowledge about entrepreneurship, deciding for yourself whether, and to what extent, alleged "facts" about it are really accurate.

Observation, Reflection, and Experimentation: Alternative Routes to Knowledge

Because it is the method most frequently used to study entrepreneurship, we will start with **systematic observation**. The basic idea is straightforward: We observe certain aspects of the world systematically, keeping careful records of what we notice. Then, we use this information as a basis for reaching conclusions about the topics we wish to study—and understand. For example, suppose that a researcher had reason to believe that the number of persons leaving secure jobs to become entrepreneurs is influenced by economic conditions. Further, the researcher reasons as follows: When the economy is strong, and many jobs are available, more people are willing to take the risk of becoming an entrepreneur because they know that if their new ventures fail, they can always find another job. When the economy is weak, in contrast, fewer people are willing to "take the plunge" and become entrepreneurs because they fear that if they give up their jobs, they may not get another one. To study this idea—which would be termed a **hypothesis**—an as yet untested prediction or explanation for a set of facts— the researcher would gather information on economic conditions (e.g., unemployment rate, growth in GDP) and also on the number of persons leaving secure jobs to become entrepreneurs. If the hypothesis were correct, these two variables—aspects of the world that can take different values—would be observed to change together: As economic conditions improve, the number of entrepreneurs increases, and vice versa. In other words, the variables would be correlated—changes in one are accompanied by changes in another. Knowing that two variables are correlated can be very useful because to the extent they are correlated, it is then possible to predict one from the other. (Correlations can range from 0.00 to +1.00 or –1.00. The greater the departure from zero, the stronger the relationship between two or more variables). In this case, for instance, knowing that economic conditions have declined (e.g., that growth in the GDP has declined or that the unemployment rate has increased) would allow us to predict that there would soon be a drop in the number of new ventures started.

So far, so good. But now, imagine that research on this question yielded precisely the opposite finding: As economic conditions decline, the number of persons who start new ventures *increases*, and as economic conditions improve, this number drops—precisely the opposite of the researcher's initial hypothesis. Would this finding still be useful even though it contradicts the researcher's expectations? Absolutely. In fact, if data gathered in systematic observation contradict a hypothesis, this can be extremely informative. In this particular case, the unexpected pattern of results suggests that although economic conditions and entrepreneurship are indeed related, the explanation for this relationship is different from the one initially proposed; in other words, an alternative hypothesis is more accurate. Here is one explanation that has been suggested by economists to explain this finding: When economic conditions are poor and many people are unemployed, the opportunity costs for engaging in entrepreneurship are reduced relative to times when economic conditions are good. An opportunity cost is any cost associated with giving up one activity in order to engage in another. If people are unemployed, their opportunity costs for becoming entrepreneurs are lower than if they were employed; they give up less by choosing to become entrepreneurs.

Although all this may seem a bit confusing, it provides a clear illustration of the value of systematic observation from the point of view of increasing our understanding of entrepreneurship. On the face of it, both explanations seem reasonable, *and it is only through systematic observation* (gathering appropriate data in a careful and systematic manner) *that we can choose between them*. In fact, there is simply no substitute for such research if we really want to understand how the entrepreneurial process unfolds and what factors influence it. All the "educated guesses" offered by self-proclaimed "experts" on entrepreneurship are not, in our view, nearly as informative as the findings of careful research. (By the way, actual research on this issue supports this alternative hypothesis rather than the original one.)[14, 15]

Having made that important point, we should quickly add that although systematic observation and the correlations it yields are invaluable tools, they leave one important point unresolved: causation. We don't know whether changes in one variable cause changes in the other, or vice versa—or whether they are not causally linked at all (i.e., both are affected by some other factor). In the research described earlier, for instance, we don't know whether changes in the economy cause changes in the number of people deciding to become entrepreneurs or whether the number of people becoming entrepreneurs affects the economy. On the face of it, the first interpretation makes more sense; but suppose that it is generally the best people who leave their companies to start new ventures. This might adversely affect the performance of the companies they leave and start the economy on a downward spiral. So, in fact, if large numbers of people decide to become entrepreneurs this could, conceivably, result in negative economic ripples. Again, it seems much more reasonable to suggest that economic conditions make it easier, or harder, for individuals to become entrepreneurs rather than vice versa, but on the basis of a correlation between these variables, we cannot tell for certain.

In order to deal with the issue of causality, researcher in many fields turn to another technique known as **experimentation**. In essence, this involves systematically changing one variable in order to see if such changes affect one or more other variables. Note that this involves active interventions by the researcher; in systematic observation, in contrast, the researcher merely observes the variables of interest and does not attempt to change one. When conducted carefully, experimentation is a very powerful tool. The reasoning behind it is impeccable: If we change one variable while holding everything else constant, and these changes affect another variable, we can conclude that changes in the first do indeed cause changes in the second.

Can this method be used to study entrepreneurship? In many cases, not very readily. Continuing with this example, it would certainly be impossible to change economic conditions in a society in order to determine if more or fewer persons choose to become entrepreneurs! But in some instances—especially research relating to the behavior of individual entrepreneurs—it *is* possible to use experimentation. For example, consider the hypothesis that entrepreneurs' appearance influences their success—the more attractive they are, the more successful they tend to be. (This would not be at all surprising: Research in human resource management and organizational behavior has frequently reported that attractiveness is related to success in many fields.)[16] Systematic observation could be readily used to study this question. For instance, photos of a large number of entrepreneurs could be rated for attractiveness (low to high) by many persons, and then these ratings would be correlated with measures of the entrepreneurs' success (e.g., growth rates of their companies, personal income, etc.). Suppose such research found that the higher the entrepreneurs' attractiveness, the greater their success (e.g., the more rapid the growth of the companies they found, or the greater the companies' profitability). This is interesting, but it does not indicate whether attractiveness *causes* success or whether, alternatively, success boosts attractiveness. For instance, it is possible that successful people have more money to spend on their appearance and so become more attractive.

Experimentation could help to solve this puzzle. One approach would involve obtaining a large number of photos of entrepreneurs and then choosing ones that show entrepreneurs who are either high, moderate, or low in attractiveness. These photos would next be presented to a large number of people (ones holding a wide variety of jobs). Their task would be that of rating the entrepreneurs in the photos on various dimensions—the entrepreneurs' future success, the extent to which they would be able to convince potential customers to use their new products or services, and so on. If the attractive entrepreneurs received higher ratings than the entrepreneurs moderate in attractiveness, who, in turn, received higher ratings than those low in attractiveness, this would provide evidence that entrepreneurs' appearance does influence other people's perceptions of them and so, perhaps, their success (see Figure 1.7).

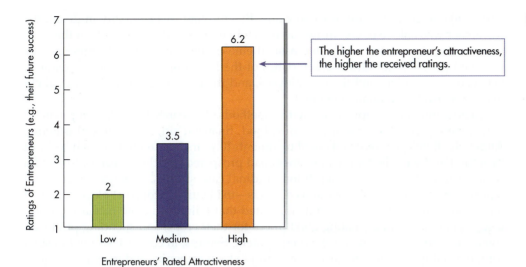

The higher the entrepreneur's attractiveness, the higher the received ratings.

Figure 1.7 Experimentation in Entrepreneurship Research: An Example

In the study illustrated here, photos of entrepreneurs rated as low, medium, and high in attractiveness were shown to a large number of persons working in a wide variety of jobs. These persons rated the entrepreneurs on various dimensions (e.g., likelihood of future success, ability to "sell" their products or services). Results indicate that the more attractive the entrepreneurs, the higher the ratings they received. These findings suggest that entrepreneurs' appearance may play a role in their success.

Going further, the photos could be attached to summaries of ideas for new products or services, and participants in the research would then rate the quality of these ideas on several dimensions (creativity, market appeal, potential to generate profits). The ideas would be identical, but for some persons, the photos accompanying them would show attractive entrepreneurs; for others, the photos would show unattractive entrepreneurs. If the ideas received higher ratings when paired with the attractive photos, this would suggest that entrepreneurs' appearance influences not only ratings of them, but also reactions to their ideas. (In fact, this is just what recent research has found: Ideas linked to attractive entrepreneurs are indeed rated more favorably than ones linked to unattractive entrepreneurs).[17]

Because of practical constraints (e.g., it is difficult to vary the factors of interest systematically), experimentation is not used very often in the study of entrepreneurship. Instead, researchers employ a wide range of statistical techniques to help determine causality on the basis of other methods, such as systematic observation. One way to do this is to determine if one variable or change occurs before another. Something that occurs later in time cannot reasonably be the cause of something that occurred earlier. This concept, called "Granger Causality," can be used to establish the direction of causality in systematic observation. Returning to the previous example, suppose that photos of entrepreneurs appearing in their high school yearbooks were rated for attractiveness by a large number of persons. Because these photos were taken *before* the entrepreneurs started new ventures, differences in their level of attractiveness were there first, before they became entrepreneurs. If these ratings were found to be correlated with their later success as an entrepreneur, this would provide some evidence that attractiveness is a cause of entrepreneurs' success rather than vice versa.

Now, let's turn to the third method of aquiring knowledge mentioned by Diderot—reflection. Does this, too, play a role? Absolutely. Combining facts in a careful and systematic way is central to the **case method** and other qualitative methods of research, methods that are used very frequently in entrepreneurship research.[18] The case method involves gathering large amounts of data about one organization or specific persons and then using this information to reach conclusions about what factors have influenced important outcomes such as economic success. For example, consider a case study of the French information systems and services company Steria, carried out by Pier Abetti.[19] This company was founded on the principle that it would gradually be owned by employees of all ranks. Initially, 51 percent of its shares were owned by the seven founding entrepreneurs and one employee. Thirty years later, 1,000 active or retired employees of the company owned 57 percent of the shares; thus, the plan to gradually transfer ownership to employees had succeeded. But how did this process unfold? Careful study of Steria indicated that it passed through several distinct phases en route to this goal—an initial revolt by dissatisfied employees; managed, gradual growth; a severe drop in profitability; and later, exponential growth coupled

LEARNING OBJECTIVE

6 Describe the basic nature of systematic observation, experimentation, and reflection (i.e., the case method and other qualitative methods).

with a 400 percent increase in share value. By studying this company in detail, the researcher was able to obtain insight into factors that played a major role in the company's ultimate success; and as the basic theme of this book suggests, these factors involved the behavior and characteristics of the founding entrepreneurs, relations between the founders and their employees, and the economic and technological climate in which the company operated.

Here's another example of qualitative methods of research. In 1984, villagers in Sri Lanka were given 2.5 acres of land plus food, financial aid, and technical training. Although all villagers received equal treatment, 10 years later more than half had lost their land and were in debt, while others had prospered greatly. Researchers[20] used a wide variety of sources—in-depth longitudinal case studies, surveys, government reports, commercial documents, and contracts—to identify factors that played a role in these contrasting outcomes. Results indicated that failure was due primarily to villagers' poor skills at negotiating good prices for their crops, and spending profits on consumer goods rather than needed equipment. Success, in contrast, seemed to stem from the ability to negotiate good prices, and to both recognize and manage opportunities over time. The basic idea behind qualitative methods is that they permit us to capture the tremendous complexity of the entrepreneurial process—complexity that can, occasionally, be missed if we attempt to quantify all factors that play a role in it.

In sum, there are several different methods for gathering useful—and accurate—information about various aspects of entrepreneurship. None are perfect, but it is our strong conviction that all three are very useful and are greatly superior to the kind of informal, "shoot from the hip" approaches taken in many popular books on entrepreneurship. Don't misunderstand: We do not mean to imply that the persons writing such books are ill-intentioned or totally lacking in useful insights about the entrepreneurial process. Rather, we only wish to note that the information they communicate is based almost entirely on their own experience and other informal sources. Although these can sometimes provide important insights, they rest on less certain (i.e., reliable) foundations than information gathered through the use of systematic observation, experimentation, or the case method. For that reason, we will emphasize information gathered through those methods throughout this book.

Theory: Answering the Questions "Why" and "How"

LEARNING OBJECTIVE

7 Explain the role of theory in the field of entrepreneurship.

There is one more aspect of the quest for knowledge about entrepreneurship that we should mention briefly before concluding: the role of **theory** in this endeavor. The term "theory" has a special meaning in the realm of science. It refers to efforts to go beyond merely describing various phenomena to the point at which we can explain them—understanding why and how they happen or take place as they do. For instance, with respect to opportunity recognition, we don't want merely to be able to state that some people are better at recognizing opportunities than others or to report the percent of people who are highly skilled at this task. We want to be able to explain *why* this is so and *how* they go about recognizing these opportunities. In other words, we want to know just what it is about certain people that allows them to be so good at recognizing opportunities that other people miss. Theories are frameworks for explaining various events or processes. Given the fact that it has been in existence for only a relatively short period of time, it is not surprising to learn that the field of entrepreneurship has few well-developed theories of its own; in fact, it has sometimes been criticized for lacking such frameworks.[21] Up to this point in time, entrepreneurship has largely borrowed theories from other fields, such as economics, psychology, and cognitive science. For instance, efforts have recently been made to apply prospect theory, a well-developed theory of decision making,[22] to several important issues relating to entrepreneurship (e.g., the question of how entrepreneurs perceive risk)[23] to answer the previous question.

Again, we should emphasize that theories are extremely useful because they help explain why certain events or processes occur as they do. But how are they derived in the first place? Briefly, the process goes something like this:

1. On the basis of existing evidence or observations, a theory reflecting this evidence is proposed.

2. This theory, which consists of basic concepts and statements about how these concepts are related, helps to organize existing information and makes predictions about observable events. For instance, the theory might predict the conditions under which individuals recognize or do not recognize opportunities.

3. These predictions, known as *hypotheses*, are then tested by actual research.

4. If results are consistent with the theory, confidence in its accuracy is increased. If they are not, the theory is modified and further tests are conducted.

5. Ultimately, the theory is either accepted as accurate or rejected as inaccurate. Even if it is accepted as accurate, however, the theory remains open to further refinement as improved methods of research are developed and additional evidence relevant to the theory's predictions is obtained. (Please see Figure 1.8 for a summary of these steps.)

Our discussion so far has been quite abstract, so perhaps a concrete example will help. Suppose that, on the basis of careful observations, an entrepreneurship researcher formulates the following theory: Individuals who choose to become entrepreneurs think differently, in various ways, from people who do not choose this role.[24] Specifically, individuals who choose to become entrepreneurs (1) are more likely than other persons to be susceptible to several kinds of cognitive errors or biases (e.g., they are more likely to be overoptimistic, to suffer from the illusion of control—overestimates of their ability to control the outcomes they experience, etc.) and (2) are more likely than other persons to think about situations in terms of the gains they will give up if they do not launch a new venture; this, in turn, causes them to be more accepting of risk. These predictions are then formulated as specific hypotheses and tested in actual research. For instance, actual or would-be entrepreneurs could be compared with persons who have no interest in starting new ventures in terms of their susceptibility to cognitive errors and their tendency to think about various situations in terms of losses. Measures of all these variables already exist and have been used in previous studies, so designing research to test these hypotheses is quite feasible. If results are consistent with predictions derived from the theory, confidence in it would be increased: There would be increased basis for accepting the theory's premise that entrepreneurs do indeed think differently from other persons.

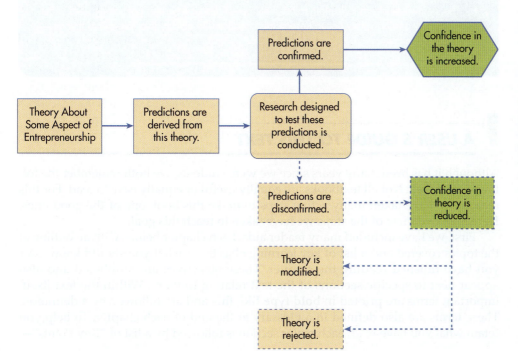

Figure 1.8 The Role of Theory in Entrepreneurship Research

Theories both organize existing knowledge and make predictions about how various events or processes will occur. Once theories are formulated, hypotheses derived logically from them are tested through careful research. If results agree with predictions, confidence in the theory is increased. If results disagree with such predictions, the theory may be modified or—ultimately—rejected as false.

On the other hand, if results were not consistent with predictions derived from the theory, confidence in it would be reduced.

Why should the field of entrepreneurship, which is eminently practical in orientation, be interested in theory? Because, as one social scientist remarked many years ago, "There is nothing as practical as a good theory."[25] By this he meant that having a good theory—a clear understanding of why or how a process occurs as it does—is very useful from the point of view of intervening in beneficial ways. In other words, if we have good and well-verified theories about entrepreneurship, we will understand this process in ways that enhance our ability to assist entrepreneurs in their efforts to start new ventures. That, of course, would be a very positive outcome. In short, developing good theories is more than an exercise in basic science: It is an important step toward attaining valuable, practical results.

Two final points: First, theories are never *proven* in any final, ultimate sense. Rather, they are always open to test and are accepted with more or less confidence depending on the weight of available evidence relating to them. Second, research should *never* be undertaken to prove or verify a theory; it is performed to gather evidence relating to the theory. If a researcher sets out to "prove" her or his pet theory, this is a serious violation of the methods that should be followed to gather accurate information about any topic. Why? Because in this case the researchers may lose objectivity and either subconsciously (or even consciously) design her or his research so that it tips the balance in favor of the theory. Clearly, any results obtained under these conditions are on shaky ground.

KEY POINTS

- Many potential sources of knowledge about entrepreneurship exist, but the most accurate and reliable knowledge is provided by methods found to be useful for this purpose in other fields: systematic observation, experimentation, and reflection.
- Systematic observation involves careful measurement of variables of interest in order to determine if they are related (correlated) in any orderly manner. To the extent they are, one can be predicted from the other.
- Experimentation involves direct interventions: One variable is changed systematically in order to determine if such changes affect one or more additional variables.
- In the case method, large amounts of information are gathered about one organization or specific persons, and this information is then used to reach conclusions about what factors have influenced important outcomes such as economic success.
- Theory involves efforts to explain rather than merely describe various phenomena—to understand why and how they occur. Research is conducted to obtain data relevant to theories—not to prove them.

A USER'S GUIDE TO THIS TEXT

Although it has been many years since we were students, we both remember the following fact well: Not all textbooks are equally useful or equally easy to read. For this reason, we have taken many active steps to make this book one of the good ones. Here is an overview of the steps we have taken to reach this goal.

First, we have included many reader aids. Each chapter beings with an outline of the topics covered and a list of key learning objectives: what you should know after you have finished reading the chapter. These objectives are numbered and also appear next to specific sections of the text relating to them. Within the text itself, important terms are printed in **bold type like this** and are followed by a definition. These terms are also defined in a glossary at the end of each chapter. To help you retain what you have read, each major section is followed by a list of "Key Points"—

a brief summary of major points covered in that section. All figures and tables are clear and simple, and most contain special labels and notes designed to help you understand them (see Figure 1.7 for an example). Finally, each chapter ends with a "Summary and Review of Key Points." Reviewing this section can help you retain more of the information presented and help you to benefit more from this course.

Second, the text contains two special features designed to make it more useful— and interesting. One—labeled "The Voice of Experience"—reports interviews that we have conducted with experienced entrepreneurs. In these interviews, which are presented at the end of various chapters, these entreprneurs give us their perspective on the topics covered in that chapter, discussing factors that contributed to their success— and to their failures. We think you will be amazed by the degree of overlap between what their practical experience has told them and what you find reported on the pages of this book.

The second feature is labeled "Danger! Pitfall Ahead!" These sections, which appear within each chapter rather than at the end, will highlight potential snares and hazards of which entrepreneurs should be aware—ones that can prove fatal to their new ventures, and their dreams. Having been there ourselves, we are only too aware of these pitfalls and think it is crucial that we call them clearly to your attention.

Third, each chapter is followed by experiential exercises labeled "Getting Down to Business." As this title suggests, these exercises are designed to provide you with practice in using the information presented earlier in the chapter. Finally, it is important to note that the chapters follow the time line presented earlier in this chapter (refer to Figure 1.6). Thus, Part 1 (Chapter 1, 2, and 3) examines the field of entrepreneurship and what is perhaps the start of the entire process: emergence and recognition of opportunities. Part 2 (Chapters 4 through 7) focuses on assembly of the resources needed to launch a new venture—information, financial, and people resources. Part 3 (Chapters 8 through 11) examines the actual launch of new ventures, considering such topics as the legal form of such ventures and strategy for success. Part 4 (Chapter 12 and 13) focuses on running the new venture and converting it into a successful, growing business. Finally, Part 5 (Chapter 14) focuses on the logical conclusion to the entrepreneurial process: alternative ways in which entrepreneurs can harvest the rewards of their efforts.

One last word. As authors and teachers, we promise faithfully that we will not lose sight of our major goals in writing this book: providing you with an accurate and up-to-date overview of what we currently know about entrepreneurship as a process. In closing, we wish to add that we agree with Lady Mary Montagu (an English author) who, in writing about personal wealth, once remarked: "'*Tis a sort of duty to be rich, that it may be in one's power to do good . . . .*" We believe that successful entrepreneurs do indeed "do good." True, they add to their own wealth but, in addition, they do much more. The products and services they bring into being improve the lives of countless millions of persons; on top of this, they are often extremely generous in donating substantial portions of their wealth to eminently worthy causes. For instance, a few years ago, one of us visited the beautiful art museum in Los Angeles funded by the John Paul Getty Foundation (see Figure 1.9). What a gift to all humanity! Both of us work in schools of management that are named after the entrepreneurs who made generous donations to support them and the universities in which they are located. If this book helps emerging entrepreneurs to succeed in attaining their dreams—and therefore enhances their ability "to do good" with the wealth they acquire—we will feel that as authors, we too have done our part.

Figure 1.9 Entrepreneurs: Key Contributors to Society

Entrepreneurs do not merely add to their own personal fortunes; in addition, they improve the lives of millions of persons through the new products and services they bring to market. Moreover, they often make generous donations to worthy causes; for instance, the breathtakingly beautiful Getty museum, located outside Los Angeles, was funded by a gift of several billion dollars from the John Paul Getty Foundation.

Summary and Review of Key Points

- Entrepreneurship, as a field of business, seeks to understand how opportunities to create new products or services arise, and are discovered or created by specific persons; these persons then use various means to exploit or develop them, thus producing a wide range of effects.
- In recent years, the allure of entrepreneurship has increased, with the result that more people than ever before are choosing this activity as a career.
- Entrepreneurship, as a branch of business, has important roots in economics, behavioral science, and sociology.
- The field of entrepreneurship recognizes that both the micro perspective (which focuses on the behavior and thoughts of individuals) and the macro perspective (which focuses primarily on environmental factors) are important for obtaining a full understanding of the entrepreneurial process.
- Entrepreneurship is a process that unfolds over time and moves through distinct but closely interrelated phases.
- The entrepreneurial process cannot be divided into neat and easily distinguished phases but, in general, it involves generation of an idea for a new product or service and/or recognition of an opportunity; assembling the resources needed to launch a new venture; launching the venture; running and growing the business; and harvesting the rewards.

- Individual, group, and societal factors influence all phases of the entrepreneurial process. Thus, there is no reason to choose between a micro and a macro approach to entrepreneurship; both perspectives are necessary.
- It is the nexus of valuable opportunities and enterprising individuals that is the essence of entrepreneurship.
- Many potential sources of knowledge about entrepreneurship exist, but the most accurate and reliable knowledge is provided by methods found to be useful for this purpose in other fields: systematic observation, experimentation, and reflection.
- Systematic observation involves careful measurement of variables of interest in order to determine if they are related (correlated) in any orderly manner. To the extent they are, one can be predicted from the other.
- Experimentation involves direct interventions: One variable is changed systematically in order to determine if such changes affect one or more additional variables.
- In the case method, large amounts of information are gathered about one organization or specific persons, and this information is then used to reach conclusions about what factors have influenced important outcomes such as economic success.
- Theory involves efforts to explain rather than merely describe various phenomena—why and how they occur. Research is conducted to obtain data relevant to theories—not to prove them.

Glossary

Business Plan: A detailed description of how entrepreneurs plan to develop their new venture.

Case Method: A research method in which large amounts of data about one organization or specific persons are gathered and then used to reach conclusions about what factors have influenced important outcomes such as economic success.

Experimentation: A research method in which one variable is systematically changed in order to determine whether such changes affect one or more other variables.

Hypothesis: An as yet untested prediction or explanation for a set of facts.

Intrapreneurs: Persons who create something new, but inside an existing company rather than through founding a new venture.

Macro (Perspective): A "top-down" perspective that seeks to understand the entrepreneurial process by focusing largely on environmental factors (i.e.., economic, financial, political factors) that are largely beyond the direct control of an individual.

Micro (Perspective): A "bottom-up" perspective that seeks to understand the entrepreneurial process by focusing on the behavior and thought of individuals or groups of individuals (e.g., founding partners).

Opportunity: The potential to create something new (new products or services, new markets, new production processes, new raw materials, new ways of organizing existing technologies, etc.) that has emerged from a complex pattern of changing conditions—changes in knowledge, technology, or economic, political, social, and demographic conditions.

Systematic Observation: A research method in which certain aspects of the world are observed systematically, keeping careful records of what is detected. This information is then used as a basis for reaching conclusions about the topics under investigation.

Theory: Refers to effort to go beyond merely describing various phenomena and, instead, to explain them.

Variables: Aspects of the world that can take different values.

Discussion Questions

1. Is there any difference between an inventor and an entrepreneur? If so, describe it.

2. Suppose that the government passed a series of laws that made it much more difficult to start a new business. What effect(s) do you think this would have on the economy?

3. One basic question in the field of entrepreneurship is "Why do some persons leave secure jobs and lives to become entrepreneurs?" How would you study this from the micro perspective? From the macro perspective?

4. In this chapter, we suggested that entrepreneurs are the new heroes and heroines in many cultures. Do you think this is really so? If it is, why do so many people see entrepreneurs as being heroic? If you think it is not accurate, why?

5. Suppose you came across an article in a magazine with the following title: "First-Borns Make the Best Entrepreneurs." Reading the article, you discover that it contends that entrepreneurs who are the oldest child in their family are more successful than ones who are the second or third born. What questions should you ask yourself about how this information was obtained in order to decide whether to view it as accurate or valid?

InfoTrac Exercises

1. **Competition Opens the Door for New-Age Entrepreneurs** (includes related article on management expert Peter Drucker's definition of entrepreneurship)
   John E. Gnuschke; Coy A. Jones

   Business Perspectives, July 1997 v10 i1 p2(5)

   Record: A57445160

   Abstract: Entrepreneurs are unquestionably important to economic growth. Statistics indicate that new and small companies have contributed 95 percent of all radical innovations and roughly 50 percent of all innovations since World War I. Entrepreneurs have bridged the gap from science to the consumer market with innumerable, useful products. Even if less than 50 percent of all new businesses survive more than four years, the creation of value and addition of it to the distribution chain have been remarkably critical to economic expansion.

   1. According to the text, more and more people are pursuing the role of entrepreneur. List the reasons cited by the authors for this trend.
   2. According to the article, what role does entrepreneurship play in the economy?
   3. What steps can government take to encourage economic growth via entrepreneurship? Consider the examples in the article; then add your own ideas.

2. **Competition Opens the Door for New-Age Entrepreneurs** (includes related article on management expert Peter Drucker's definition of entrepreneurship)
   John E. Gnuschke; Coy A. Jones

   Business Perspectives, July 1997 v10 i1 p2(5)

   Record: A57445160

   Abstract: Entrepreneurs are unquestionably important to economic growth. Statistics indicate that new and small companies have contributed 95 percent of all radical innovations and roughly 50 percent of all innovations since World War I. Entrepreneurs have bridged the gap from science to the consumer market with innumerable, useful products. Even if less than 50 percent of all new businesses survive more than four years, the creation of value and addition of it to the distribution chain have been remarkably critical to economic expansion.

   1. According to the text, how is entrepreneurship defined?
   2. According to the related article by Peter Drucker, how is entrepreneurship defined?
   3. Compare and contrast these two definitions. Then develop your own definition for entrepreneurship.

GETTING DOWN
TO BUSINESS

Becoming an Entrepreneur: Is It Right for You?

A key theme of this chapter has been that the entrepreneurial process begins when enterprising individuals identify potentially valuable opportunities. Clearly, this implies that not everyone is suited to becoming an entrepreneur. Just being able to spot potentially profitable opportunities is not, in itself, enough. In addition, entrepreneurs must be willing, ready, and able to "run with the ball"—to take the vigorous and continuing steps necessary to launch a new venture. Are *you* such a person? Are you capable not only of developing a vision of where you want to get, but also of getting there? If not, you should reconsider, because entrepreneurship definitely lives up to Edison's suggestion that "Success is 2% inspiration and 98% perspiration."

Although there is no single test of "entrepreneurial potential,"[26] there *is* general agreement that becoming a successful entrepreneur requires several key characteristics. Rate yourself on each of these dimensions—and then ask several people who know you well to do the same thing. The results may give you valuable insight into whether you are cut out to be an entrepreneur.

1. **Can You Handle Uncertainty?** Is security (e.g., a regular paycheck) important to you, or are you willing to live with uncertainty—economic and otherwise?

2. **Are You Energetic?** Do you have the vigor and good health required to work very long hours for long periods of time in order to reach goals that are important to you?

3. **Do You Believe in Yourself and Your Abilities?** Do you believe that you can accomplish whatever you set out to accomplish, learning what you need along the way?

4. **Can You Handle Reversals and Failures Well?** How do you react to negative outcomes—with discouragement or with renewed commitment to succeeding the next time around and learning from your mistakes?

5. **Are You Passionate About Your Goals or Vision?** Once you establish a goal or a vision of where you want to be, are you willing to sacrifice almost everything else to get there, because you are truly passionate about doing so?

6. **Are You Good with Other People?** Can you persuade them to see the world the way you do? Can you get along with them well (e.g., handle conflicts, build trust)?

7. **Are You Adaptable?** Can you make "mid-course corrections" easily? For instance, can you admit that you made a mistake and reverse course to correct it?

8. **Are You Willing to Take Risks or Leaps of Faith?** Once you establish a goal, are you willing to take reasonable risks to reach it? In other words, are you willing to do what you can to minimize the risks, but then, once you have done so, proceed?

Current evidence suggests that successful entrepreneurs are high on all of these dimensions—higher than other persons.[27] They can handle uncertainty, are energetic, believe in themselves, react well and flexibly to reversals, are passionate about their beliefs, are good with other people, are highly adaptable, and are willing to accept reasonable levels of risk. To the extent you possess these characteristics—or a least most of them—you may be well-suited for the role of entrepreneur. We suspect that if you are reading this book, you fit this description—otherwise, you would not be in this course! If you find that you are relatively low on several of these characteristics, however, you might want to reconsider; perhaps becoming an entrepreneur is not really "your particular cup of tea."

Answering Questions About Entrepreneurship: Practice in Thinking Like a Researcher

In this chapter, we discussed various methods for answering questions about entrepreneurship in ways that yield information that is both reliable and accurate. Although we certainly don't expect you to become an expert in using these methods (that takes years of study and practice), we think it is important for you to understand how they work because if you do, you will become an informed consumer of knowledge about entrepreneurship. In other words, you will be able to tell what information is useful to you and what is purely conjecture—or worse!

To gain practice in using these methods, try the following exercise. Consider the following questions and, for each, describe how you might go about answering it through use of (1) systematic observation, (2) experimentation, or (3) qualitative methods, such as the case method. For each, try to specify clearly the variables you would study and the ways in which you would gather information about these variables. Also try to formulate specific hypotheses about how your results will turn out. Finally, consider the implications for entrepreneurs if your findings confirm, or do not confirm, your initial hypothesis.

1. Do companies that are first to market with a new product have a competitive edge over companies that enter the same market later?

2. Do repeat entrepreneurs (people who found one successful company after another) search for opportunities differently than entrepreneurs who found only one company?

3. What factors lead individuals to give up secure and well-paid jobs to become entrepreneurs? Are these factors the same for women and men?

Enhanced Learning

You may select any combination of the case options below to enhance your understanding of the chapter material.

- **Appendix 1: Case Studies** – Thirteen cases provide opportunities to apply chapter concepts to realistic entrepreneurial situations. These brief cases call for careful analysis of real business problems and ask you to think about potential solutions.

- **Appendix 2: Video Case Library** – Nine cases are tied directly to video segments from the popular PBS television series *Small Business School*. These cases and video segments give you unparalleled access to today's entrepreneurs, with expert advice and insights on how to start, run, and grow a business.

- **Comprehensive Cases** – Visit the book support Web site at http://baron.swlearning.com for cases detailing real businesses whose successes and setbacks illustrate each stage of the entrepreneurial process. You will conduct in-depth analysis of entrepreneurial challenges through well-developed case studies.

Notes

1   Shane, S., & Venkataraman, S. 2000. The promise of entrepreneurship as a field of research. *Academy of Management Review* 25: 217–226.

2   Ricchiuto, J. 1997. *Collaborative creativity.* New York: Oakhill.

3   Koen, P.A., & Baron, R.A. 2003. Predictors of resource attainment among corporate entrepreneurs: Executive champion versus team commitment. Paper presented at the Babson-Kauffman Entrepreneurship Research Conference, Babson Park, MA, June, 2003.

4   Dun & Bradstreet, 1999.

5   O'Reilly, B. 1994. The new deal: What companies and employees owe each other. *Fortune* 44–52.

6   Bedeian, A.G., Ferris, G.R., & Kacmar, K.M. 1992. Age, tenure, and job satisfaction: A tale of two perspectives. *Journal of Vocational Behavior* 40: 33–48.

7   Greenberg, J., & Baron, R.A. 2003. *Behavior in organizations.* 8th ed. Upper Saddle River, NJ: Prentice-Hall.

8   Baron, R.A. (in press). OB and entrepreneurship: The reciprocal benefits of closer conceptual links. In B.M. Staw & R. Kramer (eds.). *Research in organizational behavior.* Greenwich, CT: JAI Press.

9   Ardichvili, Al, Cardozo, R., & Ray, S. 2003. A theory of entrepreneurial opportunity identification and development. *Journal of Business Venturing* 18: 105–124.

10 Shane, S., Locke, E.A., & Collins, C.J. (2002) Entrepreneurial motivation. *Human Resource Management Review* 13: 257–280.

11 Gartner, W.B. 1990. What are we talking about when we talk about entrepreneurship. *Journal of Business Venturing* 5: 15–28.

12 Markman, G.D., Balkin, D.B., & Baron R.A. 2002. Inventors and new venture formation: The effects of general self-efficacy and regretful thinking. *Entrepreneurship Theory & Practice* 20: 149–165.

13 White, R.E., Thornhill, S., & Hampson, E. 2003. Entrepreneurs and evolutionary biology: The relationship between testosterone and new venture creation. Paper presented at the Babson-Kauffman Entrepreneurship Research Conference, Babson Park, MA, June, 2003.

14 Evans, D., & Leighton, L. 1989. Some empirical aspects of entrepreneurship. *American Economic Review* 9: 519–535.

15 Alba-Ramirez, A. 1994. Self-employment in the midst of unemployment: The case of Spain and the United States. *Applied Economics* U26: 189–204.

16 Langlois, J.H., Kalakanis, L., Rubenstein, A.J., Larson, A., Hallam, M., & Smoot, M. 2000. Maxims or myths of beauty? A meta-analytic and theoretical review. *Psychological Bulletin* 126: 390–432.

17 Baron, R.A., Markman, G.D., & Bollinger, M. Effects of attractiveness on perceptions of entrepreneurs, entrepreneurs' behavior, and their financial success. Paper submitted for publication.

18 Gartner, W.B., & Birley, S. 2002. Introduction to the special issue on qualitative methods in entrepreneurship research. *Journal of Business Venturing* 17: 387–395.

19 Abetti, P.A. (2003). The entrepreneurial control imperative: A case history of Steria (1969–2000). *Journal of Business Venturing* 18: 125–143.

20 Kodithuwakku, S.S., & Rosa, P. 2002. The entrepreneurial process and economic success in a constrained environment. *Journal of Business Venturing* 17: 431–455.

21 See note 1.

22 Plous, S. 1993. *The psychology of judgment and decision making.* New York: McGraw-Hill.

23 Stewart, W.H., Jr., & Roth, P.L. 2001. Risk propensity differences between entrepreneurs and managers: A meta-analytic review. *Journal of Applied Psychology* 86: 145–153.

24 Krueger, N.F., Jr. 2003. The cognitive psychology of entrepreneurship. In Z. Acs & D.B. Audrestsch (eds.). *Handbook of entrepreneurial research.* London: Kluwer Law International.

25 Lewin, K. 1951. *Field theory in social science.* New York: Harper & Row.

26 Chen, C.C., Green, P.G., & Crick, A. 1998. Does entrepreneurial self-efficacy distinguish entrepreneurs from managers? *Journal of Business Venturing* 13: 295–316.

27 Stewart, W.H., Jr., Watson, W.E., Carland, J.C., & Carland, J.W. 1999. A proclivity for entrepreneurship: A comparison of entrepreneurs, small business owners, and corporate mangers. *Journal of Business Venturing* 14: 189–214.

CHAPTER 2

UNCOVERING OPPORTUNITIES: UNDERSTANDING ENTREPRENEURIAL OPPORTUNITIES AND INDUSTRY ANALYSIS

LEARNING OBJECTIVES

After reading this chapter, you should be able to:

1. Define an entrepreneurial opportunity and explain why such opportunities exist.

2. Describe how technological, political/regulatory, and social/demographic changes generate entrepreneurial opportunities.

3. List the different forms that entrepreneurial opportunities can take, and explain why some forms are better for new firms than others.

4. Explain why new firms are more successful in some industries than in others, and identify the four major types of industry differences that influence the relative success of new firms.

5. Identify the three different dimensions of knowledge conditions, and explain how they influence an industry's supportiveness of new firms.

6. Identify the three different dimensions of demand conditions, and explain how they influence an industry's supportiveness of new firms.

7. Identify the two different dimensions of industry life cycles, and explain how they influence an industry's supportiveness of new firms.

8. Identify the four different dimensions of industry structure, and explain how they influence an industry's supportiveness of new firms.

9. Explain why established firms are usually better than new firms at exploiting entrepreneurial opportunities.

10. Identify the types of opportunities that new firms are better at exploiting, and explain why new firms are advantaged at the exploitation of those opportunities.

Sources of Opportunities: The Origins of New Ventures
    Technological Change
    Political and Regulatory Change
    Social and Demographic Change
Forms of Opportunity: Beyond New Products and Services
Industries That Favor New Firms: Fertile Grounds for New Ventures
    Knowledge Conditions
    Demand Conditions
    Industry Life Cycles
    Industry Structure
Opportunities and New Firms
    Why Most Opportunities Favor Established Firms
    Opportunities That Favor New Firms

"In great affairs we ought to apply ourselves less to creating chances than to profiting from those that offer." (La Rouchefoucauld, *Maxims*, 1665)

In Chapter 1, we explained that entrepreneurs recognize opportunities to create new products or services, to use new means of production, to exploit new ways of organizing, to use new raw materials, and to tap new markets that are made possible by technological, political, regulatory, demographic, or social change. For example, some entrepreneurs have developed new products, like DVD players, that people can use to watch movies. Other entrepreneurs have come up with new ways of organizing, like using retail superstores to make goods less expensive. Others have figured out how to use new materials, like oil, to make gasoline. Still other entrepreneurs have developed new production processes, like computer-aided drug discovery, that allow people to come up with new drugs to cure diseases. One more group worth mentioning has identified new markets for products, like crackers made from seaweed that are popular in Japan.

Not only do entrepreneurial opportunities have different sources and take different forms, but they also differ in value. For example, the potential profits from establishing a new pizza restaurant on the corner of the Case Western Reserve University campus are not as large as the potential profits that one can make from developing a new biotechnology company that has formulated a cure for breast cancer. In fact, research has shown that some industries consistently produce more valuable opportunities for new businesses than others. Jon Eckhardt, a Ph.D. student of mine (Scott Shane), now teaching at the University of Wisconsin, looked at the industries in which the Inc. 500 companies were found. The Inc. 500 is a list put together by *Inc.* magazine that identifies the fastest growing young private companies in the United States. Over an 18-year period (1982–2000), Jon found that some industries had a consistently higher percentage of start-up companies listed on the Inc. 500 than other industries

(see Table 2.1).[1] He also found that many of these same industries had a higher percentage of start-up companies that had gone public. These data show that, if a random entrepreneur started a business in certain industries and not in others, that person would be much more likely to have a very rapidly growing public company. Unless the entrepreneurs that go into certain industries are more talented than the entrepreneurs that go into other industries, Jon's data mean that some industries must have better opportunities for founding new companies than others.

What makes some opportunities better than others for starting new companies? Existing evidence suggests that some industries and opportunities are more favorable to new firms than others—a favorability that helps new firms grow and become profitable.

Table 2.1 Some Industries Produce More High-Growth Companies Than Others

The industries in the top half of the chart are more attractive to entrepreneurs than those at the bottom of the chart because they had a higher ratio of Inc. 500 companies to new firms from 1989–1997.

SIC	INDUSTRY	NUMBER OF Inc. 500 FIRMS	NUMBER OF FIRM STARTS	Inc. 500 FIRMS AS A PERCENT OF STARTS
261	Pulp mills	6	33	0.181818
357	Computer and office equipment	99	2,359	0.041967
376	Guided missiles, space vehicles, parts	2	60	0.033333
335	Nonferrous rolling and drawing	14	581	0.024096
474	Railroad car rental	3	136	0.022059
382	Measuring and controlling devices	49	2,482	0.019742
262	Paper mills	3	152	0.019737
381	Search and navigation equipment	6	310	0.019355
366	Communications equipment	29	1,543	0.018795
283	Drugs	20	1,092	0.018315
384	Medical instruments and supplies	55	3,025	0.018182
316	Luggage	3	172	0.017442
314	Footwear, except rubber	4	271	0.014760
623	Security and commodity exchanges	2	141	0.014184
496	Steam and air-conditioning supply	1	83	0.012048
356	General industrial machinery	26	2,173	0.011965
386	Photographic equipment and supplies	7	646	0.010836
276	Manifold business forms	3	281	0.010676
363	Household appliances	4	390	0.010256
362	Electrical industrial apparatus	11	1,080	0.010185
811	Legal services	10	129,207	0.000077
581	Eating and drinking places	34	494,731	0.000069
175	Carpentry and floor work contractors	4	66,383	0.000060
651	Real estate operators	5	90,042	0.000056
701	Hotels and motels	2	39,177	0.000051
172	Painting and paper hanging contractors	2	43,987	0.000046
546	Retail bakeries	1	22,165	0.000045
541	Grocery stores	5	112,473	0.000045
593	Used-merchandise stores	1	24,442	0.000041
753	Automotive repair shops	5	124,725	0.000040
723	Beauty shops	3	79,081	0.000038
836	Residential care	1	27,710	0.000036
784	Videotape rental	1	27,793	0.000036

Source: Adapted from Eckhardt, J. 2003. *When the weak acquire wealth: An examination of the distribution of high growth startups in the U.S. economy*, Ph.D. Dissertation, University of Maryland.

The remainder of this chapter will expand on the role of opportunities in entrepreneurship. In the first section, we will discuss where new opportunities come from. Three major sources of change—new technology, political and regulatory shifts, and social and demographic changes—make it possible for people to start firms to exploit opportunities to make new products, to develop new production processes, to organize in new ways, to open up new markets, and to use new raw materials.

In the second section, we will explain why opportunities are sometimes exploited through one of these forms and why they are exploited through other forms at other times. For instance, why did the development of the Internet, a new technology, lead to a new way of organizing, e-tailing, but fail to change the types of products sold? In contrast, why did the invention of the internal combustion engine, also a new technology, lead to the development of a new product, the automobile, but not produce changes in the way businesses were organized?

In the third section, we will return to the discussion that we started in the beginning of this chapter about the industry differences that make some industries more attractive than others for the founding of new businesses. We will explain the characteristics of different industries that researchers have shown make some of them more fertile environments than others for founding new firms.

In the final section of the chapter, we will focus on differences across opportunities, and will explain why some opportunities are better for new firms than for established firms. Although established firms are better than new firms at exploiting opportunities most of the time, new firms sometimes have distinct advantages in exploiting entrepreneurial opportunities. We want you to learn how to exploit those advantages.

SOURCES OF OPPORTUNITIES: THE ORIGINS OF NEW VENTURES

As we explained in Chapter 1, an entrepreneurial opportunity is a situation in which changes in technology, or economic, political, social, and demographic conditions generate the potential to create something new.[2] As we mentioned earlier, an entrepreneurial opportunity can be exploited through the creation of a new product or service, the opening of a new market, the development of a new way of organizing, the use of a new material, or the introduction of a new production process. But where do these opportunities come from? Why do they make it possible for people to come up with new business ideas that have the potential to generate a profit?

> **LEARNING OBJECTIVE**
>
> 1 Define an entrepreneurial opportunity and explain why such opportunities exist.

Researchers have provided two explanations for the existence of entrepreneurial opportunities. Israel Kirzner, an economist at New York University, explains that entrepreneurial opportunities exist because people have different information.[3] Some people know about a new technological discovery, while others know about a storefront in a strip mall lying vacant. The different information that people have makes some people better than others at making decisions about a particular business idea. Because people with inferior information make worse decisions, there are always shortages, surpluses, and errors that allow people with better information to make more accurate decisions. For example, you might have better information than a local businessperson about what the people in your dorm would like to do on a Saturday night. As a result, the local businessperson might have put a pizza place on the street just outside the edge of campus. However, you might be able to make a greater profit than the owner of the pizzeria by taking over the spot and putting in a nightclub. Your greater information about what the people in your dorm want to do (go to a club) allows you to take advantage of a prior decision-making error (creating a pizza place) that generates a new business opportunity.

In contrast, Josef Schumpeter, an economist who once taught at Harvard University, argued that truly valuable entrepreneurial opportunities come from an external change that either makes it possible to do things that had not been done before or makes it possible to do something in a more valuable way.[4] For example, the invention of the laser made it possible to develop a new product, the supermarket scanner, that electronically scans the bar codes on food. In the absence of the external change—the invention of the laser—this opportunity would not have existed. Researchers who have followed in the tradition of Josef Schumpeter have identified three major sources of opportunity: technological change, political and regulatory change, and social and demographic change.

These changes really do drive the creation of opportunities for new businesses. Amar Bhide, an entrepreneurship professor at Columbia University, has shown that the founders of half of the Inc. 500 companies started their businesses in response to a specific change in technology, regulation, fashion, or other source of opportunity.[5]

Technological Change

Researchers have shown that technological change is the most important source of valuable entrepreneurial opportunities that make it possible for people to start new businesses.[6] Technological changes are a source of entrepreneurial opportunities because they make it possible for people to do things in new and more productive ways (see Figure 2.1). For example, although people communicated with each other before the invention of e-mail by using faxes, letters, the telephone, and face-to-face meetings, when the Internet was invented, several entrepreneurs discovered that people could use electronic mail to communicate. Although e-mail did not replace these other modes of communication completely (talking to your boyfriend or girlfriend only via e-mail really isn't as much fun as communicating face-to-face!), savvy entrepreneurs realized that e-mail was better than these other modes of communication for certain things. That is, the invention of a new technology made it possible to develop a more productive form of communication, e-mail, and so was a valuable source of opportunity.

Researchers explain that larger technological changes are a greater source of entrepreneurial opportunity than smaller technological changes because larger technological changes make possible bigger changes in productivity from exploiting the new technology. For example, a new material that is 50 percent stronger than steel

Figure 2.1 Technological Change Is an Important Source of Entrepreneurial Opportunities

Technological change makes it possible to do new things or do old things in a more productive way. The possibility of improvement that technology brings makes technological change the greatest source of entrepreneurial opportunity.

GENTLEMEM OUR COUNTRY.

HENRY FORD AND HIS FIRST CAR

© Getty Images/ PhotoDisc; © CORBIS

would be a lesser source of entrepreneurial opportunity than a new material that is 10 times stronger than steel because there would be many more ways that a material that is 10 times stronger than steel could be used. In fact, in a study of the efforts to commercialize inventions belonging to the Massachusetts Institute of Technology, I (Scott Shane) found that the more important the technological advance represented by an invention, the more likely someone was to found a new firm to exploit it.[7]

Political and Regulatory Change

Other important sources of opportunity are political and regulatory changes. These changes make it possible to develop business ideas to use resources in new ways that are either more productive or that redistribute wealth from one person to another. For example, the deregulation of telecommunications, intrastate banking, trucking, and railroads all made it more difficult for established firms to deter the entry of new competitors and allowed entrepreneurs to introduce more productive business ideas into these industries.[8]

However, regulatory or political change does not necessarily enhance productivity. Many times these changes generate entrepreneurial opportunities by simply allowing people who respond appropriately to the change to gain at the expense of others. For example, suppose the town in which you lived passed an ordinance requiring all historic homes to be repainted using the same type of paint that was used 100 years ago. An alert entrepreneur could profit from this regulatory change by obtaining exclusive rights to all paint formulations from 100 years ago. This entrepreneur's profit would have nothing to do with productivity. It would simply come from the higher price that people in the town would have to pay for paint that met the standards of the ordinance instead of the less expensive paint that they would otherwise buy.

Researchers have shown that certain types of regulatory and political change are particularly valuable sources of entrepreneurial opportunities (see Figure 2.2). First, as we mentioned earlier, deregulation is a valuable source of opportunity by making it easier for people to enter industries with their new ideas. Second, regulations that support particular types of business activity encourage entrepreneurs to undertake those activities. For example, researchers have shown that government regulation to certify day-care centers in Toronto, Canada, led to an increase in the formation of new day-care centers.[9] Similarly, pro-cartel policies encouraged the formation of Massachusetts railroads in the nineteenth century, whereas antitrust legislation discouraged the formation of these companies.[10] Third, regulations provide a source of opportunity by providing resources that either increase demand for particular activities or subsidize firms that undertake them. For example, Maryann Feldman, an economist at The University of Toronto, found the U.S. government's procurement policies facilitated demand for information technology and biotechnology, spurring the formation of new companies in these industries.[11]

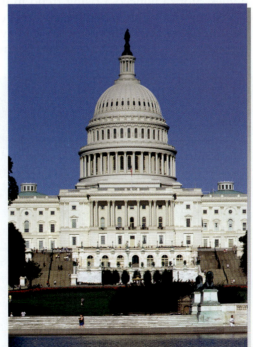

© Getty Images/ PhotoDisc

Figure 2.2 Political and Regulatory Changes Are Sources of Entrepreneurial Opportunities

Many of the regulations passed by the federal and state governments are sources of opportunity for alert entrepreneurs.

Social and Demographic Change

Social and demographic changes are also an important source of entrepreneurial opportunities. Think about the clothes that you wear and the music that you listen to. They are probably different from the clothes and music that your parents favored when they were your age. Changes in people's preferences make it possible for alert entrepreneurs to provide products and services that people demand.

Suppose you knew that next year there was going to be a change in fashion among college students. Instead of jeans, t-shirts, and baseball caps, people were going to start wearing suits to class. You could take advantage of this social change to begin a company to manufacture and sell suits to college students. Does this sound preposterous? Maybe it is. But the reverse shift certainly happened. In the 1950s, college students wore ties and jackets to class, but stopped doing so in the 1960s. The result? Entrepreneurs who started making jeans and t-shirts to sell to college students in the 1960s took advantage of a social trend to exploit an opportunity to sell different clothing to college students than had been sold in the past.

In addition to social trends, demographic changes are also an important source of entrepreneurial opportunities. The demographics of the U.S. population change all the time. Over the past 20 years, the population has become older, generating opportunities for entrepreneurs to make products for the elderly, such as assisted living facilities. The population has become more spread out from major cities, creating opportunities for entrepreneurs to build malls further from the center of cities and to provide products, like books on CD, to entertain people during lengthy commutes. Similarly, as more Spanish-speaking immigrants have entered the country, opportunities for supermarkets with lines of Latin American foods and Spanish language radio stations have grown in many parts of the United States.

Why are social and demographic changes a source of entrepreneurial opportunity? We think there are two reasons. First, social and demographic changes alter demand for products and services. Because entrepreneurs make money by selling products and services that customers want, changes in demand create opportunities to produce different things. Second, social and demographic changes make it possible to generate solutions to customer needs that are more productive than those currently available.[12] For example, the demographic shift of women entering the workforce in large numbers created a need for a more efficient way to prepare food for dinner. This opportunity for more efficient food preparation led to the introduction of frozen dinners, a more efficient solution to food preparation than what had previously existed.

Social and demographic trends certainly created opportunities for Michael Stopka, the founder of Design Toscano, Inc., a company in Illinois that sells historical reproductions. Stopka found that as baby boomers aged and became more affluent, they began to travel more to Europe. Seeing European castles and museums, many of these baby boomers returned home with new ideas about how to decorate their homes. Stopka noticed a rising trend in demand for European reproductions. By increasing the number of reproductions of suits of armor, Italian fountains, and English phone booths his company had available for sale, Stopka was able to turn this social and demographic trend into entrepreneurial profits.[13]

KEY POINTS

- An entrepreneurial opportunity is a situation in which a person can exploit a new business idea that has the potential to generate a profit.
- Entrepreneurial opportunities exist because people differ in their information. This influences the accuracy of their decision making, and creates shortages and surpluses—and the potential for better ways of doing things.
- Entrepreneurial opportunities also exist because of external sources of change, particularly technological change, regulatory and political change, and social and demographic change.
- Technological changes are sources of entrepreneurial opportunity because they make it possible for people to do things in new and more productive ways.
- Political and regulatory changes are sources of opportunity because they make it possible to develop business ideas to use resources in new ways that are either more productive or that redistribute wealth from one person to another.
- Social and demographic changes are sources of opportunity because they alter demand for products and services, as well as make it possible to generate solutions to customer needs that are more productive than those currently available.

FORMS OF OPPORTUNITY: BEYOND NEW PRODUCTS AND SERVICES

Most people tend to think of the sources of opportunities as leading entrepreneurs to develop new products and services. Although this is certainly true, these sources also generate a much wider range of things that entrepreneurs can do. As we explained in Chapter 1, entrepreneurs can develop business ideas to take advantage of five different types of opportunity that result from technological, political/regulatory, and social/demographic change: new products and services, new methods of production, new markets, new ways of organizing, and new raw materials.[14]

New types of accounting software and new surgical devices are examples of business ideas that entrepreneurs use to take advantage of new product opportunities. Amazon.com is an example of a business idea that an entrepreneur, Jeff Bezos, used to take advantage of a new way of organizing—selling books without using physical bookstores. The introduction of seaweed-flavored snack crackers into the U.S. market is an example of an effort to take advantage of a new market because this business idea had existed earlier in Japan, but not in the United States. The production of gasoline from crude oil is an example of an effort to take advantage of an opportunity to use a new raw material. Finally, biotechnology start-ups that come up with new cancer drugs through computer-aided drug discovery are examples of business ideas that come from opportunities to use new modes of production.

Though opportunities exist for all five forms, entrepreneurs who create new businesses focus primarily on the first and second forms. Most of the time, entrepreneurs introduce new products or services or enter new markets, rather than exploit new materials, come up with new ways of organizing, or establish new methods of production.[15] In fact, Jim Utterback, a professor at the Sloan School of Management at MIT, has shown that, in a wide range of industries, entrepreneurs founding new firms are usually the ones to introduce new products and services, and established firms are the ones that introduce new production processes and ways of organizing. Why? Because new production processes and ways of organizing usually demand experience operating in an industry.[16]

However, founding a new business with a form of opportunity that is most commonly used by entrepreneurs might not always be the best approach. As we will describe in more detail in Chapter 10, success at entrepreneurial activity requires the entrepreneur to develop a business idea that he or she can defend against competition. Researchers have shown that entering a new market is a particularly risky form of opportunity exploitation because it is virtually impossible for an entrepreneur to defend this form of exploitation against competition. Moreover, business ideas to exploit new methods of production are often better forms of opportunity exploitation than business ideas to exploit new products, because new methods of production can be kept secret. Because entrepreneurs sell new products to customers, all of the attributes of their new products are available for others to see. Competitors can buy one of the entrepreneur's new products and take it apart to see how it works. Then the competitor can copy the product. In contrast, an entrepreneur does not have to show anyone else the production process that he or she uses. Therefore, it takes much longer, is much more difficult, and costs much more for competitors to imitate business ideas that take the form of new production processes than take the form of new products and services.[17]

Take Seth Hall, the founder of Source One Spares Inc., as an example of an entrepreneur who successfully exploited an opportunity to create something other than a new product. While in school at Southern Methodist University, Hall worked for a company that repaired aircraft parts. That experience showed Hall that there was a need for a company that could provide working aircraft parts in less than the 30 days that his employer took to fix the parts. Hall's business opportunity was to create an aircraft parts exchange. Source One Spares provides spare parts for airlines in return for their damaged part and a fee. The company then repairs the parts and keeps them in inventory for later use. This system of providing spare parts from inventory is

LEARNING OBJECTIVE

3 List the different forms that entrepreneurial opportunities can take, and explain why some forms are better for new firms than others.

profitable because Hall can charge customers an exchange fee for providing them with a spare as well as for repairing parts. Moreover, he gets to use the repaired parts as spares for other customers, keeping his inventory costs down.[18]

To help clarify the relationship between the source of opportunity and the form that the opportunity takes, we show examples of all five different forms of opportunities for a single source of opportunity—technological change—in Table 2.2.

Table 2.2 Examples of Different Forms of Entrepreneurial Opportunities That Result from Technological Change

A single source of opportunity, like technological change, can generate all five forms of opportunity.

FORM OF THE OPPORTUNITY	TECHNOLOGICAL CHANGE	EXAMPLE OF A BUSINESS IDEA IN RESPONSE TO THE OPPORTUNITY	REASONING
New product or service	Internal combustion engine	Automobile	The internal combustion engine is used to power automobiles.
New way of organizing	Internet	Online book sales	The Internet allows people to sell products without retail outlets.
New market	Refrigeration	Refrigerated ship	The refrigerated ship allows ranchers in one country to sell their meat in another country.
New method of production	Computer	Computer-aided design	The computer allows designers to make products without building physical prototypes.
New raw material	Oil	Producing gasoline	Oil is refined into gasoline to power vehicles.

KEY POINTS

- Entrepreneurial opportunities do not only take the form of new products and services. They also take the form of new methods of production, new raw materials, new ways of organizing, and new markets.
- Entrepreneurs' business ideas typically involve the introduction of new products and services or entry into new markets.
- The most common form of opportunity exploitation by entrepreneurs is not necessarily the best. Researchers have shown that new businesses that enter new markets or introduce new products and services tend to perform worse than those that develop new production processes.

INDUSTRIES THAT FAVOR NEW FIRMS: FERTILE GROUNDS FOR NEW VENTURES

One of the most interesting observations that researchers have made about entrepreneurship is that the ability of people to found successful new firms varies dramatically across industries. For instance, if you take two entrepreneurs with exactly the same skills and abilities and you place one in an industry favorable to new firm formation and place another in an industry unfavorable to new firm formation, the probability that the new firm will survive, the likelihood that the new firm will go public, the amount of sales growth it will have, and the level of profits it will earn have been shown to be as much as ten times higher in the favorable industry than in the unfavorable one.[19]

One of the most important things that a budding entrepreneur can learn is to identify industries that are favorable to new firms. After all, if you are going to go through the trouble of starting a new business, you might as well increase your odds that it will be successful. Four different dimensions of industry differences influence the relative success of new firms: knowledge conditions, demand conditions, industry life cycles, and industry structure. In the following sections, we will describe these dimensions of industry differences so that you can learn what industry characteristics to look for as you think about starting your own company.

Knowledge Conditions

"Knowledge conditions" is a term that economists use to refer to the type of information that underlies the production of products and services in an industry. It includes such things as the degree of complexity of the production process, the level of new knowledge creation in the industry, the size of the innovating entities, and the degree of uncertainty. Take, for example, a comparison of the pharmaceutical industry and the retail clothing industry. The production of drugs is much more complex, requires much greater investment to produce new knowledge, requires larger entities to undertake innovation, and is much more uncertain than the production of clothing.

So what does this have to do with starting new firms? You probably guessed it already. Three dimensions of an industry's knowledge conditions are favorable to new firms. First, industries that have greater **R&D intensity** are more favorable to new firms than industries that have lesser R&D intensity.[20] R&D intensity is a measure of how much research and development expense firms incur for every dollar of sales. This measure captures how heavily firms invest in the creation of new knowledge. Researchers have found that R&D intensive industries have more new firms because the invention of new technologies is a source of opportunity for new business ideas. The more R&D there is, the more new technology is invented. The more new technology that is invented, the more opportunities there are for new businesses (see Figure 2.3).

But, you might ask, why don't the companies that invested in the R&D capture these opportunities? Established firms take advantage of many of them. However, they cannot take advantage of all of them because of a concept called **knowledge spillovers**. Knowledge spillovers occur when information about how to develop new technology leaks out to other people.

Fortunately for entrepreneurs, these spillovers occur all of the time. Take, for example, an engineer from Intel who goes out on a date with a man who just graduated from San Jose State University. After a few beers, the young engineer, hoping to impress her date, tells him about her very important work at Intel to develop a new generation computer chip. Unbeknownst to our young Intel engineer, the young man had been thinking of starting a business to produce a new generation of computer chip. However, his undergraduate thesis showed that he was missing a key piece of the puzzle about how to do that. The engineers at Intel had figured out the missing piece. Over a couple of beers, this knowledge spilled over from the Intel engineer to the young man, who then uses it to start a new business.

Another aspect of knowledge conditions that enhance new firm formation is the **locus of innovation**. This term refers to who produces the technology that is a source of opportunity. In some industries, like automobile manufacturing, private sector firms produce most of this knowledge; in other industries, like pharmaceuticals, public organizations—including universities and government research labs—are the source of much knowledge creation. Researchers have shown

"We're looking for a creative, innovative individual to head up our new Research and Development Department."

Figure 2.3 The R&D Intensity of an Industry Influences New Firm Formation

New knowledge is created in every industry, making it possible for people to take advantage of it to found new firms, but some industries are more knowledge intensive than others.

that industries in which public sector organizations produce most of the new technology have more new firm formation.[21] The reason is simple. As you probably suspected, senior management at Intel and other companies are not very big fans of knowledge spillovers. Spillovers allow other firms to exploit opportunities that their companies otherwise would have exploited. As a result, they take great pains to minimize the amount of knowledge that spills over to others through research publications, presentations, and loose-lipped engineers trying to impress their dates. In contrast, universities and research labs have a very different mission. The goal of universities is to put knowledge into the public domain so that society can benefit from it. When electrical engineering professors and students invent new computer chips, they tend to publish their research. This effort of people in the public sector to put knowledge in the public domain makes it easier for people to found new firms using public sector knowledge.

A third dimension of knowledge conditions that makes new firm formation more likely is the nature of the innovation process. In some industries, like automobile manufacturing, innovation and new technology development require a very large scale of operations and lots of capital, leading most of the innovation to be done by large, established companies like General Motors and Ford. In other industries, like computer software, innovation and technology development require flexible and nimble organizations, leading most of the innovation to be undertaken by new and small firms. Because new firms tend to start small, they do better at coming up with new products and services in industries in which small firms are the better innovators. Therefore, industries in which innovation demands smaller organizations tend to have more new firm formation than industries in which innovation demands larger organizations.[22]

Demand Conditions

"Demand conditions" is a term that researchers use to explain the attributes of customer preferences for products and services in an industry. Customers can express light demand or heavy demand for products. That demand can be growing or shrinking; it can be stable or changing; or it can be homogenous or heterogeneous.

Three attributes of demand conditions enhance new firm formation: market size, market growth, and market segmentation. Researchers have shown that new firms perform better in larger markets than in smaller ones because larger markets are more profitable for new firms.[23] Entrepreneurs face a fixed cost to found new firms. This fixed cost can be **amortized**, or spread out, over more sales in a larger market than in a smaller market. As a result, the expected returns to founding a firm are greater in a larger market than in a smaller market.

New firms also perform better in more rapidly growing markets than in less rapidly growing, or shrinking, markets because new firms can enter rapidly growing markets to serve customers that established firms are unable to serve.[24] Not only does this allow new firms to gain customers who are relatively easy to persuade—they have excess demand—but it also allows new firms to avoid trying to take customers away from existing firms as a way to make sales.

Finally, new firm formation is more common in markets that are more heavily segmented. Industries differ in their degree of market segmentation. For example, there are many more types of cars targeted at different types of buyers than there are types of frozen corn targeted at different types of buyers (see Figure 2.4). The reason is that people have more varied preferences for automobiles than they do for frozen corn. Market segmentation enhances new firm formation[25] because niche markets require organizations that can exploit them without producing at a high volume. New firms are better than the average established firm at small scale production. In addition, the exploitation of niches requires quick and agile firms that can take advantage of market segments that other firms have left unsatisfied. New firms tend to be quicker and more agile than other firms. Furthermore, market segmentation allows a new firm to enter a market and obtain a foothold without going after the mainstream

customers of an established firm. As a result, new firms can enter segmented markets without the level of retaliation that they face in entering unsegmented markets where they must attack the customer base of established firms directly.

Industry Life Cycles

Like people, industries are born, mature, and die. Most of you are aware of the birth of electronic commerce as an industry. But you are probably less aware of the death of the Pony Express, unless you watch a lot of late-night Westerns on television. The birth, maturation, and death of industries, what researchers call the "industry life cycle," is important to entrepreneurs because the life cycle has a powerful impact on the ability of entrepreneurs to found successful new firms.

First, researchers have shown that new firms do much better when industries are young than when they are older.[26] As your marketing professor will tell you, the adoption of new products is normally distributed. A small number of people are lead users; a moderately large number of people are early adopters. Most people adopt products in the middle of the curve. A moderately small number of people are late adopters, and a small number of people are laggards. As you may remember from your first course in calculus, a normal distribution of adopters will yield an S-shaped curve of market growth (see Figure 2.5). So if most products are normally distributed, then most markets experience S-shaped growth patterns in which demand will first accelerate and then decelerate. Because we said earlier that it is easier for new firms to enter markets during periods of demand growth, new firms do better in younger markets than in older ones.

Figure 2.4 New Firm Formation Is Easier in More Segmented Markets Than in Less Segmented Ones
The automobile industry is highly segmented because people have very different preferences for the cars that they drive.

LEARNING OBJECTIVE

7 Identify the two different dimensions of industry life cycles, and explain how they influence an industry's supportiveness of new firms.

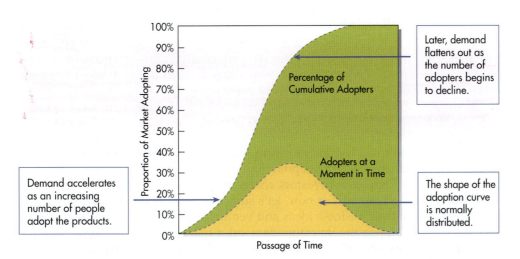

Demand accelerates as an increasing number of people adopt the products.

Percentage of Cumulative Adopters

Later, demand flattens out as the number of adopters begins to decline.

Adopters at a Moment in Time

The shape of the adoption curve is normally distributed.

Figure 2.5 New Firm Formation Is Easier in Younger Industries Than in Older Ones
A normal distribution of adopters generates an S-shaped pattern of market growth.

Source: Adapted from Rogers, E. 1983. *Diffusion of innovations.* New York: Free Press, p. 243.

Moreover, when industries are new, no existing firms are available to meet changes in demand. Without existing firms present to compete with the entrepreneurs to meet demand, new firms do better than when they have to compete with existing firms to serve customers.

Furthermore, firms get better at meeting the needs of customers through experience. Because firms have to operate in an industry to gain experience, new firms are at a disadvantage when compared to established firms. Early in the life of an industry, this disadvantage is very small because even the oldest firms have very little experience. However, when the industry becomes mature, the level of experience that older firms have is much greater than that of new firms, making it very hard for new firms to perform well.

Second, when industries mature, they tend to converge on a **dominant design**. A dominant design is a common approach or standard used to make a product. For example, the internal combustion engine is a dominant design. None of the major auto companies use engines based on steam power anymore. However, this was not always the case. Early in the life of the auto industry, many firms used engines based on steam power rather than the internal combustion engine.

The concept of a dominant design is important to entrepreneurship because new firms tend to do much better before a dominant design emerges in an industry than after it has been established. Before a dominant design is established in an industry, entrepreneurs can adopt any design that they want for the new venture's product or service. However, the establishment of a dominant design limits the approaches that entrepreneurs can take to those designs that fit the standards that established firms are already using. Not only does the new firm have to use a design for its products that the established firms already have greater experience with, but once a dominant design has been established, the basis of competition in an industry changes. Instead of competing to see who has the design that fits the preferences of customers the best, firms compete on who can make a standard design most efficiently. Because established firms are larger and have more experience, they can produce more efficiently and so have distinct advantages once a dominant design has emerged in an industry.

Take VHS tapes for example. Once the video recording industry converged on the VHS standard as the dominant design, it became almost impossible for new companies to introduce other tape formats. The major Japanese companies that produced VHS tapes, like Matsushita, were able to produce the tapes more efficiently than anyone else and were able to out-compete everyone else.

Industry Structure

Industries also differ in their structure, making some of them more hospitable to new firms than others. Researchers have identified four aspects of the structure of an industry that make it easier for a person to found a successful new firm. First, some industries are more **capital intensive** than others. Capital intensity refers to the degree to which the production process in an industry relies on capital rather than on labor. New firms perform relatively poorly in capital-intensive industries.[27] When firms are initially created, entrepreneurs must spend capital to obtain equipment, establish production facilities, set up distribution, and otherwise organize. This expenditure of capital occurs before the new business can sell its products or services and so generate revenue. Because new firms do not generate cash from their existing operations, they must obtain this capital from investors. For reasons we will describe in more detail in Chapter 6, investors charge more for capital than it costs to use internally generated capital. For now, let's suffice it to say that entrepreneurs know much more about their business ideas and venture opportunities than the investors who back them, and so the investors demand a risk premium to compensate for those entrepreneurs who might try to take advantage of their (the investors') relative ignorance. Because existing firms can use capital from their current operations to finance new business ideas, this premium puts new firms at a disadvantage. This disadvantage grows as the capital intensity of the business increases.

Second, new firms perform worse in advertising-intensive industries, like consumer products, than they do in industries that do not rely heavily on advertising, like industrial chemicals. Brand reputations are developed over time through repeated advertising efforts. As a result, it takes considerable time for new firms to develop the same level of brand name recognition as established firms. Moreover, advertising is subject to **economies of scale**. "Economies of scale" is a term that economists use to explain that the cost of each unit of a product goes down as the volume of production increases. Scale economies exist anytime that there is a much larger cost to producing the first unit of something than there is to producing additional units. Because the cost of developing a television or radio advertisement is the same regardless of the number of units of the product that you sell, the cost per unit of advertising is significantly lower as you produce and sell more units of your product. Therefore, the small size of new ventures makes it hard for them to keep their per-unit advertising costs as low as those facing established firms (see Figure 2.6).[28]

Third, new firms perform worse in concentrated industries than they do in fragmented industries.[29] **Concentration** refers to how much market share lies in the hands of the largest firms in the industry. When industries are concentrated, new firms have to challenge the customer base of established firms with the power and resources to drive them out of business. In contrast, when industries are fragmented, new firms can enter by challenging small and weak established firms whose customers are more vulnerable.

Fourth, new firms perform better in industries that are composed of firms of smaller average size.[30] Most new firms are started small because starting small allows entrepreneurs to minimize the cost and risk of establishing their new ventures. Because entrepreneurs are often wrong about their business opportunities, they like to minimize the cost of being wrong, which they accomplish by starting on a small scale and testing whether their business ideas work.

In industries composed mostly of small firms, starting small does not put a new firm at much of a disadvantage relative to established competitors. However, in industries composed mostly of large firms, starting small greatly disadvantages new firms whose established firm competitors can purchase in greater volume, produce at a lower average manufacturing cost, and spread their costs of advertising and distribution over more units. Therefore, new firms do relatively more poorly in industries made up of relatively large firms.

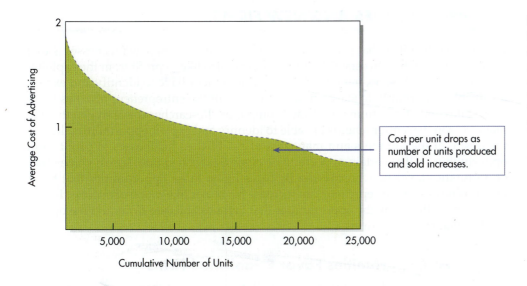

Figure 2.6 New Firm Formation Is More Difficult in Advertising-Intensive Industries

Economies of scale in advertising mean that the per-unit cost to advertise a product or service goes down with the volume of units produced. Because new firms tend to start small, they face significant disadvantages in advertising intensive industries.

Cost per unit drops as number of units produced and sold increases.

KEY POINTS

- New firms perform better in R&D intensive industries because the invention of new technologies is a source of opportunity for new business ideas.
- Industries in which public sector organizations are the locus of innovation have more new firm formation because public sector organizations do not try as hard as private sector firms to minimize knowledge spillovers.
- New firms perform better in industries in which most of the innovation is conducted by small firms because innovation in these industries requires agile and flexible organizations, and new firms are agile and flexible.
- New firms perform better in larger markets than in smaller ones because larger markets allow the fixed cost of firm formation to be amortized over more sales.
- New firms perform better in more rapidly growing markets because new firms can enter rapidly growing markets to serve customers that established firms are unable to serve.
- Market segmentation enhances new firm formation because niche markets require organizations that can exploit opportunities on a smaller scale; because the exploitation of niches requires quick and agile firms; and because market segmentation allows a new firm to enter a market and obtain a foothold without going after the mainstream customers of an established firm.
- Young industries are more supportive of new firms because demand grows more rapidly in young industries than in mature ones; because no existing firms are available to meet demand in young industries; and because firms gain experience operating in industries as they mature.
- Industries are less supportive of new firms after a dominant design has been established because a dominant design means that new firms have to use a design for its products that the established firms already have greater experience with, and because the basis of competition in an industry changes to favor efficiency, which established firms are better at achieving.
- Capital-intensive industries are more hostile to new firms because external capital, on which new firms must rely, is more costly than internally generated capital.
- Advertising-intensive industries are more hostile to new firms because advertising has effects that cumulate over time and because advertising faces strong economies of scale.
- Concentrated industries are more hostile to new firms because concentration means that new firms must try to take customers from large, established firms that have the power to drive them out of business.
- Industries with larger average firm size are more hostile to new firms because new firms, which are established on a small scale so that entrepreneurs can minimize cost and risk, are at a much greater disadvantage in industries with large average firm size than with small average firm size.

OPPORTUNITIES AND NEW FIRMS

One of the difficulties that people face in founding successful new businesses is that the individuals who run established firms would also like to profit from the exploitation of opportunities. So, not only does an entrepreneur have to identify and exploit a valuable opportunity to start a new company, but the entrepreneur also has to do so despite competition from established companies. Researchers have shown that the major reason that entrepreneurs are able to identify and exploit opportunities despite the desire of the founders and managers of established businesses to profit from opportunities is that certain opportunities favor established businesses, while other opportunities favor new businesses. By focusing on those opportunities that favor new businesses, an entrepreneur can increase his or her likelihood of success. In this section, we will review the opportunities that favor established firms and the opportunities that favor new firms.

Why Most Opportunities Favor Established Firms

Most of the time, established companies will do a better job than a new company at exploiting an opportunity. When companies are in business for awhile, they develop sev-

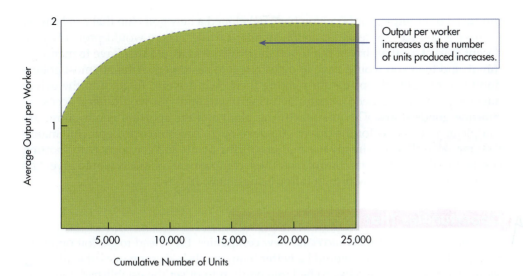

Output per worker increases as the number of units produced increases.

Figure 2.7 The Manufacturing Learning Curve

Because a new company has not manufactured as many products as an established company, it will manufacture those products much less efficiently.

eral advantages over new companies. First, companies face a **learning curve** when they develop any product or service. A learning curve is a graphical depiction of how well someone does at something as a function of the number of times that they have done it (see Figure 2.7). For example, think about how far you rode the first time you rode a bicycle and how much further you went with each additional time you rode. The same is true for companies. Initially, they find it difficult to manufacture products efficiently because they have not worked out the kinks in their production processes. Moreover, they haven't yet figured out the best way to sell products to customers. However, just like you and your bicycle, as companies produce more of something, they get better at doing it. Because new companies have not yet moved down the learning curve, they are worse at manufacturing and marketing products than established companies.

Second, business depends a great deal on reputation. Research has shown that people are much more likely to buy products from suppliers that they know and trust.[31] Experience interacting with a particular supplier gives a customer confidence in the products and services that they supply. Think about going out to dinner. If you've eaten at a restaurant before, you know whether or not you like it. Although you might have a better meal at a new restaurant, you don't know if the meal will be any good. The reputation that the established restaurant has developed with you keeps you coming back and makes it harder for the new restaurant to get you in the door.

Third, if businesses are successful, they develop positive **cash flow**. That is, they bring in more cash than they spend to produce and distribute their products and services. This cash flow is useful for developing new products and services. If an established business has positive cash flow, it can use that cash to invest in producing new products and services that meet the needs of customers. For example, Dell invested the cash it had earned from selling computers into making and selling printers. Because new companies haven't yet sold any products to customers, they do not have positive cash flow and have to borrow money or issue stock to raise money. This costs more than using internal cash and so puts new companies at a disadvantage relative to established companies where producing new products is concerned.

Fourth, many businesses face economies of scale. For example, think about the cost of producing a computer game. To write the software code for the first copy of the game is very expensive. A computer programmer will have to spend several hundred hours writing the code. However, once the game has been written, a person can burn CDs of the game for only pennies. Economies of scale benefit established companies over new companies because the established companies are already producing products and services. If it is buying raw materials or advertising or doing anything else that requires economies of scale, the established company faces lower costs than the new company because it produces more units of the product or service.

Fifth, new companies often find it difficult to compete with established companies because they lack **complementary assets**. Complementary assets are things that are used along with the entrepreneur's new product to produce or distribute that

LEARNING OBJECTIVE

9   Explain why established firms are usually better than new firms at exploiting entrepreneurial opportunities.

product. For example, suppose you have developed a new golf club that can be used to drive a golf ball twice as far as the standard driver. There would probably be a decent market for that driver. But to sell the driver, you would first have to manufacture it, and then you would have to distribute it to customers. After all, most golfers don't want to buy blueprints for making their own drivers. To get into the driver business, you would need a manufacturing plant, and you would need access to sporting goods stores. The manufacturing plant and the sporting goods stores are complementary assets for the driver you developed. An established golf club manufacturer, say Callaway, already has manufacturing plants and contracts with sporting goods stores. Therefore, its control over these complementary assets would give it an advantage over your new firm in introducing a new driver.

Opportunities That Favor New Firms

For entrepreneurs to found *successful* new companies, they need to exploit opportunities that new companies would be better than established companies at exploiting. Moreover, this advantage has to be large enough to offset the established company advantages that we just described. What kinds of advantages do new companies have in exploiting opportunities?

One major advantage that new companies have is that they are better at exploiting **competence-destroying** change. Earlier in the chapter, we explained that one of the major sources of opportunity is technological change. Technological change makes it possible to introduce a new product or service, open up a new market, use a new raw material, develop a new way of organizing, or introduce a new production process. Researchers have explained that technological change can be competence enhancing or competence destroying. Competence-enhancing technological change is a change that makes people better at what they are already doing; competence-destroying technological change is a change that makes people worse at what they are doing.[32]

LEARNING OBJECTIVE

10 Identify the types of opportunities that new firms are better at exploiting, and explain why new firms are advantaged at the exploitation of those opportunities.

Most change is competence enhancing. For instance, companies that have been exploiting a technology for awhile are better at doing things that make use of further advances of the technology because of the learning curve that we described earlier. As long as the effort to produce a new product, develop a new production process, exploit a new product, use a new raw material, or organize in a new way takes advantage of something that had been learned before, the established firm, which has moved further up the learning curve, has an advantage. But sometimes, change is competence destroying. In those cases, having done something in the past doesn't make you any better at exploiting a business idea than someone who hasn't done that thing—in fact, it makes you worse. Why? Because, as we explained earlier, people get locked into old ways of thinking and doing things, and they find it harder to do new things than people with no experience at all.

For example, when the Internet first came into existence, experience with bricks-and-mortar retailing didn't help established clothing companies very much as e-tailers. In fact, it made the established companies worse. Their managers kept trying to use the experience that they gathered from their retail stores in their online sites without realizing that people cannot try on or touch clothes online the way that they can in a retail store. The managers' experience got in the way of approaching the online sales of clothing in a new way—a way that new companies with no experience in retailing were able to figure out because the Internet was a competence-destroying technological change.

Not only does a competence-destroying technological change, like the Internet, undermine the learning curve advantages of established companies, but established companies face several other disadvantages in exploiting competence-destroying changes. To invest in a competence-destroying technological change, an existing company has to **cannibalize** its existing business. Cannibalization occurs whenever a company launches a new product or service that replaces its existing products or services. For example, unlike Amazon.com, Internet book sales cannibalize Barnes & Noble's existing business. By introducing Barnesandnoble.com, Barnes & Noble ended up serving many customers that would have bought books in its stores, but at an additional cost—the cost of setting up the online business. New companies have an advantage over existing companies when a technological change requires the existing company to make investments that cannibalize its existing products and services because established companies do not like to make these types of investments (see Figure 2.8).[33]

Moreover, companies develop routines for doing business efficiently. These routines allow the company to do things without having to evaluate whether those activities are worthwhile everytime they do them. For example, companies might have procedures for manufacturing a CD player that focus the company on using a certain technology to make the player. Although these routines are useful for manufacturing the CD player efficiently, they hinder efforts to explore new technologies, like the technology behind MP3 players. New companies often have an advantage in doing things that are new, like investigating the MP3 technology, because they are not constrained by existing routines for doing something else.

Established companies also seek to satisfy their existing customers. As your marketing professor will tell you, satisfying customers is important if a company is going to sell its products. But keeping your customers happy has a downside. When companies develop new products, they often ask their customers what they think of those products. Much of the time, customers reject new products either because those products aren't useful to them, because they simply cannot envision changing to something new, or because changing requires effort. Because established companies run the risk of losing their existing customers by pursuing products that these people do not want, they often avoid pursuing those products.[34] For example, when IBM developed the laser, its lawyers weren't sure that the company should patent it because IBM's customers couldn't find any use for the technology. But as we know, there is a huge market for lasers in everything from supermarket scanners to making CDs. The lesson here is that new companies are often better than established companies at developing new products or services because established companies are constrained by their existing customers. If their existing customers tell them that they don't like a new product, the company risks losing customers by pursuing it. A new company, in contrast, has no customers to lose by pursuing new products.

New companies are also more successful when they develop products and services that are **discrete**. An example of a discrete product is a new drug. Any company that produces a drug can sell that drug without embedding it in other devices. In contrast, a windshield wiper is not discrete, but is part of a system. Disconnected from the rest of a car, bus, or other vehicle, a windshield wiper is pretty much useless. The reason that discrete products are better for new companies is that they can be developed without the cost and difficulty of trying to replicate existing companies' systems.[35] Think about how difficult it would be to produce an entire car if all you wanted to do was sell windshield wipers. As hard as it might be to develop a new drug, at least the drug can be used independently.

New companies are also more successful when their business ideas are embedded in **human capital**. Human capital is value invested in people, and it is different from physical capital like machines and equipment. New businesses do better with business ideas that are embedded in human capital rather than physical capital

Figure 2.8 Established Companies Do Not Like to Make Investments That Cannibalize Their Existing Assets

Because Barnes & Noble had spent a large amount of money to build a network of bookstores, it resisted efforts to sell books over the Internet, fearing that its customers would stop going to its stores and make all of their purchases electronically.

© James Leynse/CORBIS SABA

because human beings can move relatively easily from an existing organization to pursue an entrepreneurial opportunity; physical assets are much less mobile. For example, if you developed an idea for how to better fit customers to snowboards while working at a ski shop, you could quit and start your own shop. If you are right about how to fit the customers to the snowboards, you could attract a lot of customers away from your old employer and do pretty well. But suppose, instead, that your employer had a great machine for fitting customers to snowboards. If you left and took that machine with you to start your own ski shop, you would be stealing. The ability to fit customers is better than a machine to fit customers for starting a company because the first lies in human capital and is mobile, but the second lies in physical capital, and is not.

This is only a small sample of the many differences in the types of opportunities that favor new and established firms that have been uncovered in careful research. Some others are summarized in Table 2.3. The main point of the current discussion is simply this: Because new firms are different from established firms, new firms are better at pursuing some opportunities, while established firms are better at pursuing others. Differentiating between these different types of opportunities is crucial for entrepreneurs, so we focus on it in our discussion of opportunities. (For a discussion of one type of opportunity that can be problematic for entrepreneurs founding new firms, please see the **"Danger! Pitfall Ahead!"** section.)

DANGER! PITFALL AHEAD!

Exploiting an Incremental Innovation by Starting a Firm

You have spent a lot of time thinking about a business idea for your new venture, and you have come up with what you think is a good one—to produce a laptop computer with a built-in MP3 player. You think that this is a really great idea. All of your friends in your dorm think that it would be really cool to have an MP3 player built into their laptops. That way, when they are in the library working on their term papers, they could listen through their headphones to music that they downloaded from the Internet. So why is your entrepreneurship professor telling you that this isn't a very good idea for founding a new firm?

Your business idea is an incremental improvement on a product that existing firms already produce. Sure it is a good idea, and people would buy the laptop if it were made. The problem is that your new company is not the right company to make it. When existing firms produce a product, like laptop computers, they develop skills and capabilities that make them better at producing and selling a product, the more of the product that they produce and sell. This is the idea behind the learning curve that we described here. The companies, like Dell and Apple, that already make laptops know a whole lot more than you do about how to make and sell those computers. Your idea for putting an MP3 player in a laptop is only a small improvement

over their laptops. If Dell and Apple wanted to compete with you, all they would have to do would be to figure out how to put the MP3 player into their existing laptops. On the other hand, to compete with them, you would have to figure out how to make a laptop computer. What you would have to do would be a lot harder to do than what they have to do, and they have more resources (money, knowledge, people) than you to do it. The fact that their innovation is incremental, combined with the experience that they have developed, puts you at a disadvantage.

But, what if your business idea was to put a device under a person's skin so that they could download music from the Internet and then listen to it wherever they went? Okay, this might be a little too science fiction for today, but suppose you could do it. Because no one else has figured out how to do this yet, the new technology would not just be an incremental improvement on an existing product or service. It would be a radical change. No one in the business of making devices for downloading and listening to music, or making computers, has any experience with the type of device that you are thinking of making. So they are not ahead of you on a learning curve. As a result, you would stand a chance of creating a valuable company to exploit this type of business idea.

The moral of the story: Don't waste your time trying to develop incremental innovations—there is too much against you.

DIMENSION OF THE OPPPORTUNITY	WHO IT FAVORS	REASONS WHY	EXAMPLE
Relies heavily on reputation	Established firm	People are more likely to buy from those whom they know and trust.	Jewelry store
Has a strong learning curve	Established firm	Established firms can move up the learning curve to get better at producing and distributing products.	Automobile manufacturer
Takes a lot of capital	Established firm	Established firms have existing cash flow that they can use to produce a new product or service.	Jet aircraft manufacturer
Demands economies of scale	Established firm	The average cost of producing a product or service goes down with the volume produced when economies of scale exist.	Steel plant
Requires complementary assets in marketing and distribution	Established firm	The ability to meet customer needs often requires access to retail distribution.	Maker of running shoes
Relies on an incremental product improvement	Established firm	The established firm can add the incremental improvement to its products more easily and cheaply than the new firm can imitate their product or service.	Manufacturer of DVD players
Employs a competence-destroying innovation	New firm	Established firm experience, assets, and routines are undermined.	Biologically-based computer maker
Does not satisfy the needs of existing firms' mainstream customers	New firm	Established firms focus on serving their mainstream customers and will not pursue products or services that do not meet the needs of those customers.	Computer disk drive manufacturer
Is based on a discrete innovation	New firm	New firms can exploit discrete innovations without replicating the entire system belonging to established firms.	Drug maker
Lies in human capital	New firm	Whoever has the knowledge can produce a product or service that meets customer needs.	Personal chef

Table 2.3 Some Opportunities Are Better for New Firms Than Others

Some opportunities favor new firms, while others favor established firms.

KEY POINTS

- The managers of established companies would like to exploit many of the same opportunities as entrepreneurs.
- Established firms are better than new firms at exploiting most opportunities.
- Established firms have the advantage of the learning curve, which improves their ability to introduce a new product or service, tap a new market, use a new material, take advantage of a new production process, or organize in a new way.
- Established firms have reputations, which encourage customers and suppliers to do business with them.
- Established firms have cash flow from existing operations, which they can invest in the exploitation of new opportunities at a lower cost than new firms can tap external capital.
- Established firms have access to complementary assets in manufacturing, marketing, and distribution, which are necessary to exploit opportunities.
- To found *successful* new firms, entrepreneurs must exploit opportunities that favor new firms.
- Competence-destroying technology favors new firms because competence-destroying change undermines the capabilities of existing firms and forces established firms to cannibalize their existing assets.
- Opportunities that an established firm's mainstream customers reject are good for new firms because established firms focus on activities to serve those mainstream customers.
- Opportunities that are discrete are good for new firms because entrepreneurs can exploit them without having to replicate established firms' entire system of assets.
- Opportunities that are embedded in human capital are better for new firms because entrepreneurs can leave their employers to found firms that exploit the knowledge in their heads, but they cannot take their employer's physical assets with them.

Summary and Review of Key Points

- An entrepreneurial opportunity is a situation in which a person can exploit a new business idea that has the potential to generate a profit.
- Entrepreneurial opportunities exist because people differ in their information. This influences the accuracy of their decision making, and creates shortages and surpluses, and the potential for better ways of doing things.
- Entrepreneurial opportunities also exist because of external sources of change, particularly technological change, regulatory and political change, and social and demographic change.
- Technological changes are sources of entrepreneurial opportunity because they make it possible for people to do things in new and more productive ways.
- Political and regulatory changes are sources of opportunity because they make it possible to develop business ideas to use resources in new ways that are either more productive or that redistribute wealth from one person to another.
- Social and demographic changes are sources of opportunity because they alter demand for products and services, as well as make it possible to generate solutions to customer needs that are more productive than those currently available.
- Entrepreneurial opportunities do not only take the form of new products and services. They also take the form of new methods of production, new raw materials, new ways of organizing, and new markets.
- Entrepreneurs' business ideas typically involve the introduction of new products and services or entry into new markets.
- The most common form of opportunity exploitation by entrepreneurs is not necessarily the best. Researchers have shown that new businesses that enter new markets and introduce new products and services tend to perform worse than those that develop new production processes.
- The likelihood of founding a successful new firm varies dramatically across industries, making it important for entrepreneurs to assess how supportive an industry is to new firms.
- Researchers have identified four different dimensions of industry differences that influence the relative success of new firms: knowledge conditions, demand conditions, industry life cycles, and industry structure.
- Three different dimensions of knowledge conditions influence the industry's supportiveness of new firms: R&D intensity, the locus of innovation, and the nature of innovation.
- New firms perform better in R&D intensive industries because the invention of new technologies is a source of opportunity for new business ideas.

- Industries in which public sector organizations are the locus of innovation have more new firm formation because public sector organizations do not try as hard as private sector firms to minimize knowledge spillovers.
- New firms perform better in industries in which most of the innovation is conducted by small firms because innovation in these industries requires agile and flexible organizations, and new firms are agile and flexible.
- Three different dimensions of demand conditions influence the industry's supportiveness of new firms: large markets, growing markets, and segmented markets.
- New firms perform better in larger markets than in smaller ones because larger markets allow the fixed cost of firm formation to be amortized over more sales.
- New firms perform better in more rapidly growing markets because new firms can enter rapidly growing markets to serve customers that established firms are unable to serve.
- Market segmentation enhances new firm formation because niche markets require organizations that can exploit opportunities on a small scale; because the exploitation of niches requires quick and agile firms; and because market segmentation allows a new firm to enter a market and obtain a foothold without going after the mainstream customers of an established firm.
- Two aspects of industry life cycles influence the benevolence of an industry toward new firms: industry age and the presence of a dominant design.
- Young industries are more supportive of new firms because demand grows more rapidly in young industries than in mature ones; because no existing firms are available to meet demand in young industries; and because firms gain experience operating in industries as they mature.
- Industries are less supportive of new firms after a dominant design has been established because a dominant design means that new firms have to use a design for their products that the established firms already have greater experience with, and because the basis of competition in an industry changes to favor efficiency, which established firms are better at achieving.
- Four aspects of industry structure make industries more supportive of new firms: capital intensity, advertising intensity, concentration, and average firm size.
- Capital-intensive industries are more hostile to new firms because external capital, on which new firms must rely, is more costly than internally generated capital.
- Advertising-intensive industries are more hostile to new firms because advertising has effects that cumu-

late over time, and because advertising faces strong economies of scale.

- Concentrated industries are more hostile to new firms because concentration means that new firms must try to take customers from large, established firms that have the power to drive them out of business.
- Industries with larger average firm size are more hostile to new firms because new firms, which are established on a small scale so that entrepreneurs can minimize cost and risk, are at a much greater disadvantage in industries with large average firm size than with small average firm size.
- The managers of established companies would like to exploit many of the same opportunities as entrepreneurs.
- Established firms are better than new firms at exploiting most opportunities.
- Established firms have the advantage of the learning curve, which improves their ability to introduce a new product or service, tap a new market, use a new material, take advantage of a new production process, or organize in a new way.
- Established firms have reputations, which encourage customers and suppliers to do business with them.
- Established firms have cash flow from existing operations, which they can invest in the exploitation of new

opportunities at a lower cost than new firms can tap external capital.

- Established firms have access to complementary assets in manufacturing, marketing, and distribution, which are necessary to exploit opportunities.
- To found *successful* new firms, entrepreneurs must exploit opportunities that favor new firms.
- Competence-destroying change favors new firms because competence-destroying change undermines the capabilities of existing firms and forces established firms to cannibalize their existing assets.
- Opportunities that an established firm's mainstream customers reject are good for new firms because established firms focus on activities to serve those mainstream customers.
- Opportunities that are discrete are good for new firms because an entrepreneur can exploit them without having to replicate the established firm's entire system of assets.
- Opportunities that are embedded in human capital are better for new firms because entrepreneurs can leave their employers to found firms that exploit the knowledge in their heads, but they cannot take their employer's physical assets with them.

Glossary

Amortized: A method of distributing the cost of an investment over the number of units produced or sold.

Cannibalize: An effort to produce and sell a product or service that replaces a product or service that one already produces and sells.

Capital Intensive: The degree to which the production process in a firm or industry relies on capital rather than on labor.

Cash Flow: The internally generated funds available to a firm after costs and depreciation are subtracted from revenues.

Competence-Destroying: A form of change that undermines the skills and capabilities of people who are already doing something. It is contrasted with competence-enhancing change, which enhances the skills and capabilities of people who are already doing something.

Complementary Assets: Assets that must be used along with an innovation to provide a new product or service to customers, typically including manufacturing equipment, and marketing and distribution facilities.

Concentration: The proportion of market share that lies in the hands of the largest firms in an industry. This concept is commonly measured by the four-firm concentration ratio, a government measure of the market share that lies in the hands of the four largest firms in an industry.

Discrete: A characteristic of a new product or service that makes it independent of a system of other assets necessary to use the product or service.

Dominant Design: A common approach or standard to making a product on which firms in an industry have converged.

Economies of Scale: A reduction in the cost of each unit produced as the volume of production increases.

Human Capital: Investment or value in human resources rather than physical assets.

Knowledge Spillovers: The accidental transfer of information about how to create new products, production processes, ways of marketing, or ways of organizing, from one firm to another.

Learning Curve: A relationship that measures the per-unit performance at production as a function of the cumulative number of units produced.

Locus of Innovation: The location, both within the value chain and between the public and private sector, in which efforts to apply new knowledge to the creation of new products, production processes, and ways of organizing occurs.

R&D Intensity: The proportion of a firm's sales that are devoted to creating new scientific knowledge and applying that knowledge to the creation of new products and production processes.

Discussion Questions

1. Say you discovered a cure for lung cancer. Is that an entrepreneurial opportunity? What about if you invented a perpetual motion machine?

2. What do you think are the major sources of entrepreneurial opportunities over the next five years? Why are these things sources of opportunity?

3. Think of five entrepreneurial opportunities. What forms do these entrepreneurial opportunities take? Are some of these forms of opportunities better for entrepreneurs founding new firms? Why or why not?

4. Pick three industries you know well. What dimensions of these industries make them favorable or unfavorable to new firm formation? Why or why not?

5. Go back to the five entrepreneurial opportunities that you thought of in response to question 3. Would established firms have an advantage over new firms in exploiting those opportunities? Why or why not?

InfoTrac Exercises

1. **Fall River, MA, Technology Entrepreneur Works Overtime to Lure Investors**

   Knight Ridder/Tribune Business News, August 21, 2002 pITEM02233052

   Record: CJ90610001

   Full Text: COPYRIGHT 2002 *Knight Ridder/Tribune Business News,* by Andrea L. Stape, *Providence Journal,* RI *Knight Ridder/Tribune Business News*

   1. What type of external change made it possible for Tracey Dodenhoff to start a new business?
   2. What is the locus of innovation for Dodenhoff's new business venture? How is this an advantage to her?
   3. How would you assess Dodenhoff's new business opportunity in light of your reading in Chapter 2? Are conditions favorable for her success? Why or why not?

2. **Tomorrow's Entrepreneur** (brief article)

   Inc., May 29, 2001 p86

   Record: A75318268

   Full Text: COPYRIGHT 2001 Goldhirsh Group, Inc. Graying Boomers, Booming Teens

   1. According to the text, how is demographic change related to entrepreneurial opportunities?
   2. According to the article, what changes in demographics are creating new entrepreneurial opportunities?
   3. Research new ventures in senior or teen markets. Pick one new company and analyze how it is leveraging demographic change to develop and sell a new product or service.

Enter

GETTING DOWN
TO BUSINESS

The Hunt for Opportunities: Building Your Skills

We defined an "opportunity" as the potential to create something new and desirable (new products or services, new markets, new production processes, new raw materials, new ways of organizing existing technologies, etc.) that has emerged from a complex pattern of changing conditions. You will need to identify an entrepreneurial opportunity to start your business. We believe that you can use some of the things that we discussed in this chapter to identify an entrepreneurial opportunity. To do so, please follow these steps:

Step 1: Construct a list of recent changes in (1) technology, (2) demographics (changes in the makeup of the population), (3) lifestyle and other social changes, (4) markets, and (5) government policies.

Changes You Observe

Technology:
1.
2.
3.

Demographics (changes in the makeup of the population):
1.
2.
3.

Lifestyle and other social changes:
1.
2.
3.

Markets:
1.
2.
3.

Government policies:
1.
2.
3.

Step 2: Once you have constructed this list, try to identify the following: (1) new products or services that these changes make possible, (2) new markets that they open up, (3) new production processes that they allow firms to use, (4) new raw materials that they make possible, and (5) new ways of organizing that these changes would lead to. Remember to identify the source of the opportunity that you identified along with the new products or services, new markets, new production processes, new raw materials, and new ways of organizing that result from these changes.

Example: The invention of the Internet (technological change) creates an opportunity to sell books without having a free-standing bookstore (new way of organizing).
1.
2.
3.
4.
5.

If you succeed, congratulations! You have accomplished the first, crucial stage in the entrepreneurial process: identifying a bona fide entrepreneurial opportunity.

Industry Analysis

We discussed the importance of analyzing the industry that your new business will enter to make sure that it is a good one for new firms. We believe that you can use some of the things that we discussed in this chapter to analyze the industry that your new business will enter. To do so, please follow these steps:

Step 1: For each of the five business opportunities that you listed in exercise 1, identify the industry where that opportunity would be found. Define the industry in which the business will operate. Then match that business description to the U.S. government's list of national industrial codes at http://www.census.gov/epcd/naics02/naicod02.htm.

Step 2: Once you have a definition of the industry in which your five business opportunities will operate and the national industrial codes that correspond to the industry, evaluate the favorability of the those industries to new firm formation across the three main dimensions we described earlier in the chapter: knowledge conditions, industry life cycles, and industry structure. Consider all of the aspects of each of these dimensions of industry. For each of your five opportunities, provide evidence for why the industry is favorable or not favorable for a new firm.

1.
2.
3.
4.
5.

Should a New Firm Pursue the Opportunity? Comparing the Opportunity Fit with Established Firms

We discussed the advantages that established firms have in exploiting entrepreneurial opportunities. Consider the possibility that a large, established firm has also identified each of the five business opportunities you identified on page 49. Explain why that company would be better or worse than your new venture at exploiting each of the opportunities. Consider all of the advantages that large, established firms have in pursuing opportunities that we discussed in this chapter: learning curves, reputation, positive cash flow, economies of scale, complementary assets, greater ease in managing systemic innovations, and advantages in exploiting incremental change.

Enhanced Learning

You may select any combination of the case options below to enhance your understanding of the chapter material.

- **Appendix 1: Case Studies** – Thirteen cases provide opportunities to apply chapter concepts to realistic entrepreneurial situations. These brief cases call for careful analysis of real business problems and ask you to think about potential solutions.

- **Appendix 2: Video Case Library** – Nine cases are tied directly to video segments from the popular PBS television series *Small Business School*. These cases and video segments give you unparalleled access to today's entrepreneurs, with expert advice and insights on how to start, run, and grow a business.

- **Comprehensive Cases** – Visit the book support Web site at http://baron.swlearning.com for cases detailing real businesses whose successes and setbacks illustrate each stage of the entrepreneurial process. You will conduct in-depth analysis of entrepreneurial challenges through well-developed case studies.

Notes

1   Eckhardt, J. 2003. *When the weak acquire wealth: An examination of the distribution of high growth startups in the U.S. economy*, Ph.D. dissertation, University of Maryland.

2   Ardichvili, Al, Cardozo, R., & Ray, S. 2003. A theory of entrepreneurial opportunity identification and development. *Journal of Business Venturing* 18: 105–124.

3   Kirzner, I. 1997. Entrepreneurial discovery and the competitive market process: An Austrian approach. *The Journal of Economic Literature* 35: 60–85.

4   Schumpeter, J.A. 1934. *The theory of economic development: An inquiry into profits, capital credit, interest, and the business cycle.* Cambridge, MA: Harvard University Press.

5 Bhide, A. 2000. *The origin and evolution of new businesses.* New York: Oxford University Press.

6 Shane, S. 1996. Explaining variation in rates of entrepreneurship in the United States: 1899–1988. *Journal of Management* 22(5): 747–781.

7 Shane, S. 2001. Technology opportunities and new firm creation. *Management Science* 47(2): 205–220.

8 Holmes, T., & Schmitz, J. 2001. A gain from trade: From unproductive to productive entrepreneurship. *Journal of Monetary Economics* 47: 417–446.

9 Baum, J., & Oliver, C. 1992. Institutional embeddedness and the dynamics of organizational populations. *American Sociological Review* 57: 540–559.

10 Dobbin, F., & Dowd, T. 1997. How policy shapes competition: Early railroad foundings in Massachusetts. *Administrative Science Quarterly* 42: 501–529.

11 Feldman, M. 2001. The entrepreneurial event revisited: Firm formation in a regional context. *Industrial and Corporate Change* 10(4): 861–891.

12 Eckhardt, J., & Shane, S. (forthcoming). The individual-opportunity nexus: A new perspective on entrepreneurship. In Z. Acs (ed.) *Handbook of entrepreneurship.*

13 *Future shift: Illinois matures.* http://www. entrepreneur. com/mag/article/0,1539,230606-6,00.html.

14 Schumpeter, J.A. 1934. *The theory of economic development: An inquiry into profits, capital credit, interest, and the business cycle.* Cambridge, MA: Harvard University Press.

15 Ruef, M. 2002. Strong ties, weak ties, and islands: Structural and cultural predictors of organizational innovation. *Industrial and Corporate Change* 11(3): 427–450.

16 Utterback, J. 1994. *Mastering the dynamics of innovation.* Boston, MA: Harvard Business School Press.

17 Mansfield, E. 1985. How rapidly does technology leak out? *Journal of Industrial Economics* 34(2): 217–223.

18 Smith, P. *Burn, baby, burn: Fixing aircraft parts.* http://www. entrepreneur.com/Your_Business/YB_SegArticle/0,4621,2751 55-4,00.html.

19 Shane, S. (forthcoming). *A general theory of entrepreneurship: The individual–opportunity nexus.* London: Edward Elgar.

20 Dean, T., Brown, R., & Bamford, C. 1998. Differences in large and small firm responses to environmental context: Strategic implications from a comparative analysis of business formations. *Strategic Management Journal* 19: 709–728.

21 Audretsch, D., & Acs, Z. 1994. New firm startups, technology, and macroeconomic fluctuations. *Small Business Economics* 6: 439–449.

22 Acs, Z., & Audretsch, D. 1989. Small firm entry in U.S. manufacturing. *Economica* 255–266.

23 Eisenhardt, K., & Schoonhoven, K. 1990. Organizational growth: Linking founding team, strategy, environment, and growth among U.S. semiconductor ventures, 1978–1988. *Administrative Science Quarterly* 35: 504–529.

24 Mata, J., & Portugal, P. 1994. Life duration of new firms. *The Journal of Industrial Economics,* 42(3): 227–243.

25 Shane, S. 2001. Technology regimes and new firm formation. *Management Science* 47(9): 1173–1181.

26 Barnett, W. 1997. The dynamics of competitive intensity. *Administrative Science Quarterly* 42: 128–160.

27 Audretsch, D. 1991. New firm survival and the technological regime. *Review of Economics and Statistics* 441–450.

28 Shane, S. (forthcoming). *A general theory of entrepreneurship: The individual–opportunity nexus.* London: Edward Elgar.

29 Eisenhardt, K., & Schoonhoven, K. 1990. Organizational growth: Linking founding team, strategy, environment, and growth among U.S. semiconductor ventures, 1978–1988. *Administrative Science Quarterly* 35: 504–529.

30 Audretsch, D., & Mahmood, T. 1991. The hazard rate of new establishments. *Economic Letters* 36: 409–412.

31 Aldrich, H. 1999. *Organizations evolving.* London: Sage.

32 Tushman, M. & Anderson, P. 1986. Technological discontinuities and organizational environments. *Administrative Science Quarterly* 31: 439–465.

33 Arrow, K. 1962. Economic welfare and the allocation of resources for inventions. In R. Nelson (ed.). *The rate and direction of inventive activity.* Princeton, NJ: Princeton University Press.

34 Christensen, C., & Bower, J. 1996. Customer power, strategic investment, and the failure of leading firms. *Strategic Management Journal* 17: 197–218.

35 Winter, S. 1984. Schumpeterian competition in alternative technological regimes. *Journal of Economic Behavior and Organization* 5(3–4): 287–320.

COGNITIVE FOUNDATIONS OF ENTREPRENEURSHIP: CREATIVITY AND OPPORTUNITY RECOGNITION

LEARNING OBJECTIVES

After reading this chapter, you should be able to:

1 Explain why cognitive processes provide an important foundation for understanding creativity and opportunity recognition.

2 Describe working memory, long-term memory, and procedural memory, and explain the role they play in creativity and opportunity recognition.

3 Explain why we tend to use heuristics and other mental shortcuts, and how these shortcuts can influence entrepreneurs.

4 Define creativity and explain the role that concepts play in it.

5 Distinguish between analytical, creative, and practical intelligence, and explain how all three are combined in successful intelligence.

6 List several factors that influence creativity, as described by the confluence approach.

7 Explain the role of access to information and utilization of information in opportunity recognition.

8 Describe signal detection theory and distinguish between hits, false alarms, and misses.

9 Explain the difference between a promotion focus and a prevention focus, and describe the effects these contrasting perspectives may have on entrepreneurs' efforts to discover valuable opportunities.

10 List several steps you can take as an individual to increase your skill at recognizing potentially valuable opportunities.

The Raw Materials for Creativity and Opportunity Recognition: Mental Structures That Allow Us to Store—and Use—Information
  Cognitive Systems for Storing—and Using—Information: Memory, Schemas, and Prototypes
  Limited Capacity to Process Information: Why Total Rationality Is Rarer Than You Think

Creativity: Escaping from Mental Ruts
  Creativity: Generating the Extraordinary
  Concepts: Building Blocks of Creativity
  Creativity and Human Intelligence
  Encouraging Creativity: The Confluence Approach

Opportunity Recognition: A Key Step in the Entrepreneurial Process
  Access to Information and Its Effective Use: The Core of Opportunity Recognition
  Opportunity Recognition: Additional Insights from Cognitive Science
  Practical Techniques for Enhancing Opportunity Recognition

In Chapter 1, we suggested that the entrepreneurial process begins when one or more persons either formulate an idea for something new (a new product or service, a new means of production, a new raw material, etc.) or recognize an opportunity that has emerged out of economic, technological, and social factors. To the extent this is true, an intriguing question arises: Why do some persons, but not others, create new ideas for products, services, or markets or recognize emerging opportunities that can be developed into successful new ventures? The answer is certainly complex, but as we have already noted in Chapters 1 and 2, we believe that in essence, it involves a convergence between opportunities and specific individuals. In other words, some people, but not others, come up with useful ideas or recognize promising opportunities because they are, in a sense, the right *person*, at the right *place*, at the right *time*. What makes specific persons "right" in these respects? Existing evidence suggests that the answer involves two key factors: (1) such persons have better access to crucial information—information helpful in recognizing opportunities or formulating new ideas and (2) they are better able to utilize—to combine it or interpret in ways that reveal the opportunities other persons overlook.[1]

This was certainly true for Lissa D'Aquanni, who created a gourmet chocolate business—The Chocolate Gecko—in 1998. Like many entrepreneurs, D'Aquanni started her new venture in her basement. But her experience as a former executive for several nonprofit organizations had equipped her with a wealth of experience in rallying community support. When a nearby abandoned building suitable for her business became available, she used these skills to solicit financial support from the local community for revitalizing the building. This support was forthcoming: Within a few weeks, she had raised the $25,000 needed for a down payment. She then worked with a local development group to secure low-cost financing that enabled her to move forward with the purchase. Volunteers contributed free labor for essential repairs and improvements, and a local community development financial institution tapped a state program to fund major upgrades, such as new windows, lighting fixtures, furnaces, and siding. The result? D'Aquanni was able to move her growing business into desirable new quarters at a tiny fraction of the normal costs. As she puts it: "There were lots of different pieces of the puzzle to identify and figure out how to access." Clearly, her previous experience and current access to useful information made her the right person to recognize this particular opportunity and to move forward with it.

The remainder of this chapter will expand upon these basic ideas about access to, and utilization of, information. It focuses on three key, and closely related, processes in entrepreneurship: **idea generation**—the production of ideas for something new, **creativity**—the generation of ideas that are both new and potentially useful, and **opportunity recognition**—the process through which individuals conclude that they have identified the potential to create something new that has the capacity to generate economic value (i.e., potential future profits).[2] In a sense, these processes fall along a continuum of increasing relevance to the process of founding new ventures—a dimension that moves from sheer production of new ideas (idea generation), to ideas that are also potentially useful (creativity), and finally to ideas that can also potentially serve as the basis for a profitable new venture—*bona fide* opportunities (see Figure 3.1).

Although many approaches to understanding these processes exist, we believe that among them, a cognitive perspective is especially helpful. Because new ideas and the recognition of emerging opportunities must, ultimately, occur inside the skulls of particular persons, important insights into these processes can be gained by focusing on basic aspects of **human cognition**—the mental processes through which we acquire information, enter it into storage, transform it, and use it to accomplish a

Figure 3.1 Idea Generation, Creativity, and Opportunity Recognition

These three processes—which all play a role in entrepreneurship—can be viewed as falling along a dimension moving from origination of ideas that may or may not be useful (idea generation), to ideas that are not only new but also potentially useful (creativity), and finally to ideas that are not only new and useful but also have the potential to generate economic value (opportunity recognition).

Idea Generation	Creativity	Opportunity Recognition
Production of ideas for something new.	Production of ideas for something new that is also potentially *useful*.	Recognition that ideas are not only new and potentially useful, but also have the potential to generate economic value.

— Increasing Relevance to Founding New Ventures ———→

wide range of tasks (e.g., making decisions, solving problems).[3] Indeed, we believe that trying to understand idea generation, creativity, and opportunity recognition without careful attention to their cognitive origins is like to trying to solve complex mathematical problems without a basic knowledge of algebra and calculus: In both cases, essential tools are lacking. In the discussion that follows, therefore, we will focus on the cognitive foundations of these crucial, initial steps in the entrepreneurial process.

Ideas, including those for new products or services, do not emerge from nowhere; on the contrary, they occur when individuals use existing knowledge they have gained (and retained) from their experience to generate something new—thoughts they did not have before. Often, this process is stimulated by some external event or occurrence, for instance, a new experience, information provided by other people, or simply by observing changes in the world around us. But no matter how or why the process begins, it depends heavily on the "raw materials" individuals already possess—their unique store of knowledge. For this reason, we will begin with a brief overview of the cognitive systems and structures that allow us to store knowledge and transform it in various ways—including changing it into something new. Following this discussion, we will turn to creativity—the act of coming up with something that is both novel and useful. As shown in Figure 3.2, just being new is not enough; in order to be viewed as creative, ideas must also have the potential to be useful. If they are not, then they are better viewed as mere "flights of fantasy" than as the potential basis for new venture. As part of this discussion, we will consider ways in which you can enhance your own creativity. Finally, we will turn to opportunity recognition. Here, we will focus on the basic nature of this process and the question of why some persons are better than others at identifying opportunities that have emerged from changes in technology, markets, economic conditions, government policies, demographics, and other factors. Several theories of human cognition are relevant to this issue, so we will briefly examine them here. Finally, we will conclude with a discussion of steps that you—as nascent entrepreneurs—can take to enhance your own ability to recognize valuable opportunities.

© Getty Images/
PhotoDisc

© CORBIS

© CORBIS

Figure 3.2 Creativity: Ideas for What's New—*and* Useful

New products that survive and gain widespread use are not only novel, they are also useful to large numbers of people.

THE RAW MATERIALS FOR CREATIVITY AND OPPORTUNITY RECOGNITION: MENTAL STRUCTURES THAT ALLOW US TO STORE—AND USE—INFORMATION

In an ultimate sense, everything we think, say, or do is influenced by, and reflects, cognitive processes occurring inside our brains. Are you reading and understanding these words? Can you conjure an image of what you ate for dinner last night, the house where you grew up, the face of the person you love most dearly? Can you play a musical instrument? Ride a bicycle? Speak more than one language? Do you have plans for the future? Memories of events that occurred many years ago? Goals? Intentions? All these activities, and countless others, reflect complex neurochemical events occurring within your brain. Indeed, recent advances in neuroscience now permit us to observe these activities that occur within our brains as we think, reason, and make decisions.[4]

It is clear that cognitive processes are the basis for generating new ideas, for creativity, and for opportunity recognition. But why do some persons generate ideas for new products or services or identify opportunities for profitable new ventures overlooked by others? To take one concrete example, why did Jack Kelly and Bob Ohly, founders of Caffe Ladro, a rapidly growing chain of coffeehouses, come up with the idea of selling only coffee certified by independent sources to have been purchased at fair prices from growers (many of whom are poor peasants)? That this was a good idea is indicated by the fact that Caffe Ladro competes successfully against Starbuck's in its own hometown of Seattle. The answer, we suggest, involves the fact that Kelly and Ohly had just the right combination of past experience—and just the right store of information at their disposal—to permit them to formulate and execute this excellent business strategy. To repeat: We are suggesting that the raw materials for new ideas and for recognizing opportunities are present in the cognitive systems of specific persons as a result of their life experience. Because everyone's experience is unique, the information they have at their disposal, too, is unique, and this is a key reason why specific ideas occur to some persons but not others.

To the extent that this reasoning is correct, two basic questions arise: (1) What are these cognitive systems for retaining and processing information like? (2) Can they be stretched or augmented in ways that enhance creativity and the ability to recognize viable opportunities? We will consider the second question in detail as part of our discussion of opportunity recognition. Here, though, we think it is important to pave the way for our later discussions of creativity and opportunity recognition by briefly describing the nature of our cognitive systems for storing and processing information.

Cognitive Systems for Storing—And Using—Information: Memory, Schemas, and Prototypes

A basic finding in entrepreneurship research is that the more experience people have in a given field, the more likely they are to identify opportunities in it.[5] Similarly, the more experience venture capitalists have—at least to a point—the better *they* are at spotting good opportunities.[6] Why should this be so? In part, because such experience provides a wealth of useful information people can store and later use in various ways to create or recognize something new. The most basic cognitive system for storing information is known as **memory**, and life without it would be unthinkable. Without memory, we would be unable to recall the past, retain new information, solve problems, or plan for the future. So clearly, memory is a very central aspect of our cognitive systems.

Actually, memory consists of several closely related systems. One, known as *working memory*, holds a limited amount of information for brief periods of time—perhaps up to a few seconds. If you look up a phone number and then try to remember it just long enough to dial it, you are using working memory. Another is known as *long-term memory*. This system allows us to retain truly vast amounts of information for long periods of time. In fact, research findings indicate that there may be no limits to how much long-term memory can hold or how long it can retain information stored in it. So, you can, indeed, go on learning throughout life: There is no apparent limit to the amount of information you can retain or the number of skills you can acquire.

As you already know from your own experience, memory can hold several different kinds of information. Some involve *factual information* that you can readily put into words (e.g., How far is it from New York to Los Angeles? Who was the first President of the United States?). Some involve more personal knowledge about events we have experienced as individuals (e.g., memories of a trip to the dentist, your first love, the first time you had an idea for a new venture).

Still other information we retain in memory is much harder to put into words than the preceding two types. For instance, skilled athletes can't readily explain to other persons why they perform so well. Similarly, musicians can't state how they remember a long piece of music—they just do. In fact, trying to express this kind of information in words can interfere with these activities (see Figure 3.3). Such information is stored in *procedural memory*.

What does procedural memory have to do with entrepreneurship? More than you might guess. For instance, suppose you asked highly successful venture capitalists to explain how they go about choosing new ventures in which to invest. Could they do so? Research findings provide the following answer: not very well. Yes, the venture capitalists can offer explanations about how they reach their decisions. But, in fact, these explanations are not closely aligned with what they actually do—how they really seem to make their decisions, as assessed by data relating to their choices.[7] In short, successful venture capitalists have indeed learned how to recognize good opportunities and have stored information and strategies useful in making such decisions in memory. But after years of practice, this information has become mainly automatic (i.e., it is now a part of procedural memory) so they can't readily describe it in words. The same is true for entrepreneurs: If asked how they go about recognizing opportunities, most can provide some sort of answer. But, in fact, this process seems to involve a large component of information that cannot be readily put into words, so it, too, is related to procedural memory.

Using and Transforming Information: Schemas and Prototypes.

Retaining information we acquire from experience is important, but it is only part of the total picture. In addition, we must also be able to interpret new information as we encounter it and to integrate it with the information already present in memory. This is essential for creativity and for recognizing opportunities, because these activities involve generating or recognizing something *new*—something that is not already present in memory.

Research in the field of cognitive science suggests that we accomplish these tasks by creating mental frameworks—mental "scaffolds" that help us to understand new information and to integrate it (often in original ways)—with information we already possess. Several kinds exist, but among the most important are **schemas**—

Figure 3.3 Procedural Memory in Action

Information stored in procedural memory allows us to perform skilled actions such as the one shown here. Such information, while present in memory, cannot readily be described verbally. In fact, trying to do so can have negative effects. If the person shown here tried to think about what she was doing while doing it, her performance might well suffer. Research findings indicate that venture capitalists cannot explain clearly how they choose the new ventures they wish to support; this is another example of procedural memory in action.

© Getty Images/PhotoDisc

cognitive frameworks representing our knowledge and assumptions about specific aspects of the world. Here is one example: You undoubtedly have a well-developed schema for eating in a restaurant. A host seats you, a waiter asks for your drink order and later returns for your food order, and so on. (Schemas of this type that provide us with an outline for a series of events are known as *scripts*.) Another important kind of mental framework we possess are **prototypes**—abstract, idealized mental representations that capture the essence of a category of objects (e.g., a prototype of a gym: a room filled with exercise equipment, sweating people, a locker room, and so on).

As we will note in our later discussion of creativity and opportunity recognition, schemas and prototypes are important because they can facilitate or hinder both processes. For instance, continuing with our restaurant example, what's your idea of a menu? Probably, a list of set dishes: Customers choose the one they like from what is offered. Does it have to be this way? Your schema for eating in a restaurant would lead you to expect that it does; it would, in a sense, restrict your creativity. But think again: Brian Winders, proud owner of several Genghis Grills, had a different idea. Why not let customers build their own dishes from a list of ingredients? In other words, they could have any meats, sauces, vegetables, and spices they wished, in any combination they preferred. The result? A new concept in dining, and one that is quickly gaining popularity. On the other hand, schemas can facilitate creativity and opportunity recognition because they help us to relate new information to what we already know—and perhaps come up with an entirely new combination.

Prototypes, too, can facilitate or hinder creativity and opportunity recognition. For instance, consider a new product I (Robert Baron) recently purchased—a rotary grater for parmesan cheese known as the "Microplane." Over the years, I have purchased many cheese graters and none has worked well: All tend to jam up and to compress the cheese instead of grating it. This one, though, works like a dream (see Figure 3.4). Why? Because the cutting edges are modeled on high-quality woodworking tools. Why didn't someone think of this sooner? Perhaps because the prototype for "cheese grater" did not include this type of blade. In this case, an existing prototype interfered with creativity—and the development of an excellent new product. In other cases, prototypes can facilitate creativity by providing a framework for interpreting new information (e.g., by relating it to existing prototypes).

Limited Capacity to Process Information: Why Total Rationality Is Rarer Than You Think

Now that we have outlined what is, in a sense, the "production facilities" for creativity and opportunity recognition, we should call your attention to one other basic aspect of human cognition—the fact that it has limited capacity to process (i.e., deal with, interpret) information at any given time. So although our ability to add to the knowledge stored in memory and other mental systems seems unlimited, there appear to be fairly firm limits on how much information we can handle at once. This results from the fact that *working memory*—the short-term system we described earlier—can hold only a limited amount of information at once. Because this system seems to be the contact point between what we are thinking about right now and information stored in memory, this creates a bottleneck in our efforts to make sense of our ongoing experience—and to create something new.

As a result of this limited capacity to process information, we often adopt mental shortcuts—tactics for stretching our limited capacity as far as possible. These are helpful from the point of

Figure 3.4 Prototypes and Creativity

The cheese grater shown here is far superior to others currently on the market because the cutting blades are based on tools used in fine woodworking. These tools have existed for centuries, so why didn't anyone incorporate them into cheese graters before now? Perhaps because the prototype for such graters did not include this kind of blade and that prevented people from seeing that it could be used in this kind of product.

Photo courtesy of R.A. Baron

view of conserving precious mental capacity, but they can also lead us into serious errors. Further, our tendency to rely on such shortcuts is strongest at times when our cognitive systems are strained to the limit—when we are required to process large amounts of information in a short period of time (e.g., make important decisions quickly or on the basis of incomplete information). If this sounds like the situation faced by many entrepreneurs much of the time, it is! For this reason, it has been suggested that entrepreneurs may be more susceptible to these cognitive biases and errors than people in many other fields or occupations.[8] We will refer to the potential role of these errors in various aspects of entrepreneurship in later chapters, so it is useful to briefly describe some of them here.

Although many of these exist, among the most useful are **heuristics**—simple rules for making complex decisions or drawing inferences in a rapid and seemingly effortless manner. Perhaps the most important of these is the *availability heuristic.* This mental rule suggests that the easier it is to bring information to mind, the more important or accurate we perceive it to be, and hence the greater its impact on our subsequent judgments or decisions. Further, the more information we can bring to mind, the greater the importance we assign to it.[9] Although this heuristic seems reasonable, it can lead to important errors, primarily because dramatic or unusual information is easier to recall than more mundane information. Thus, it may influence our thinking and our decisions to a greater extent than is justified. For instance, imagine an entrepreneur who is trying to choose a key employee. There are several applicants, one of whom is much more expressive and outgoing than the others. Later, when trying to remember the interviews, the entrepreneur finds it easier to recall what this person said, and that may tip the decision in his favor, even though other applicants are actually better qualified.

In addition to heuristics, there are many other "tilts" or potential errors in our thinking that result from the same general tendency to conserve our limited processing capacity. Among these, three are especially common and dangerous: the *optimistic bias*, the *confirmation bias*, and the *illusion of control.*[10] In its most basic form, the optimistic bias refers to the tendency to expect things to turn out well even when there is no rational basis for such expectations. Susceptibility to the optimistic bias may be one reason why some persons choose to become entrepreneurs: They expect to attain success even though the odds are strongly against them.[11] One common form of this bias is known as the *planning fallacy*—the tendency to believe that we can complete more in a given period of time than we actually can. Do you ever observe this tendency in your own thinking? Unless you are very unusual, you probably do. This, and other aspects of the tendency to be overoptimistic, has been observed among both entrepreneurs[12] and venture capitalists.[13]

The *confirmation bias* is even more insidious in its impact. This refers to the tendency to notice, process, and remember information that confirms our current beliefs (or, at least is consistent with them) much more readily than information that disconfirms our current beliefs. This means that all too often, we live in a self-constructed "echo chamber"—the only information that gets through is information that strengthens our current views. Clearly, this is a very dangerous tendency for entrepreneurs who cannot afford to ignore information contrary to their current beliefs—for instance, market information or information about actual or potential competitors.

The *illusion of control* refers to the tendency to assume that our fate is under our control to a greater extent than is actually the case—to believe that we have more control over what happens to us than rational considerations suggest. Research findings indicate that this belief may be another important factor in many persons' decisions to become entrepreneurs; they believe that the fate of the new ventures they start is largely under their control and so underestimate the potential impact of economic conditions, competitors, and many other factors that are, in fact, largely outside their influence.[14]

This is only a small sample of the many potential sources of error in human cognition that have been uncovered in careful research. Others are summarized in Table 3.1 on page 60. The main point of the present discussion is simply this: Because we must deal with a basic dilemma—restricted capacity to process information in the face of

LEARNING OBJECTIVE

3 Explain why we tend to use heuristics and other mental shortcuts, and how these shortcuts can influence entrepreneurs.

SOURCE OF POTENTIAL ERROR	DESCRIPTION OF ERROR	EXAMPLE
Representative heuristic	A mental rule-of-thumb suggesting that the more closely an event or object resembles typical examples of some concept or category, the more likely it is to belong to that concept or category	An individual is assumed to belong to some occupation or group because she or he resembles the stereotype for that group or occupation.
Availability heuristic	A mental rule-of-thumb in which the importance or probability of various events is judged on the basis of how readily information concerning them can be brought to mind, or how much information can be readily recalled	People assume that the chances of dying in a fire or airplane crash are greater than those of dying in an automobile accident because the media report fatal fires and airplane crashes more dramatically than automobile accidents, thus making them easier to remember.
Anchoring-and-adjustment heuristic	A cognitive rule-of-thumb in which existing information is accepted as a reference point but then adjusted to take account of various factors	Negotiators accept their opponent's opening offer as a framework for further bargaining.
Confirmation bias	The tendency to notice and remember information that confirms our views	An entrepreneur becomes increasingly convinced that an idea for an new product is viable because he notices and remembers only information that supports this view.
Optimistic bias	The tendency to assume that things will turn out well even though there is no rational basis for this prediction	Entrepreneurs believe that the odds they will succeed are much higher than they actually are.
Planning fallacy	The tendency to assume that we can accomplish more in a given period of time than is true (or to underestimate the amount of time it will take to complete a project)	An entrepreneur assumes that each stage in starting a new venture will take less time to complete than is actually true.
Escalation of commitment (sunk costs)	The tendency to stick with decisions that yield negative results even as the negative results continue to mount	An entrepreneur continues efforts to market her product in a specific way even though these efforts produce a mounting string of failures.
Affect infusion	Emotions have powerful effects on thinking (e.g., when in a good mood we notice and remember positive information while when in a bad mood, we notice and remember negative information)	An entrepreneur who is in a bad mood when she interviews a job applicant recalls mainly negative information about this person; in contrast, she recalls mainly positive information about an applicant she interviews while in a good mood.

Table 3.1 Potential Sources of Error in Human Cognition

Because we possess limited capacity to process information, we often adopt "mental shortcuts" to stretch this capacity and to reduce our effort. As shown here, this tendency underlies many different potential errors in our thinking.

large amounts of information—many aspects of our cognition are far from entirely rational. On the contrary, they are subject to a wide range of tilts and biases that do indeed save effort, but also increase the odds of serious errors. Successfully navigating through these dangerous waters is crucial for entrepreneurs, so we will have reason to refer to this basic theme at many points in this book. (For discussion of one potential cognitive error that can be especially dangerous for entrepreneurs, see the **"Danger! Pitfall Ahead!"** section.)

KEY POINTS

- Cognitive processes provide the foundation for creativity and opportunity recognition.
- Memory involves cognitive systems for storing information. Working memory can retain limited amounts of information for short periods of time. Active processing of information occurs in working memory, so it is the system in which consciousness exists.
- Long-term memory holds vast (perhaps unlimited) amounts of information for long periods of time. Such information can be factual or procedural in nature.
- Because our capacity to process information is limited, we often adopt shortcuts to reduce mental effort. These include heuristics and various "tilts" in our thinking (e.g., the confirmation bias). These shortcuts *do* save effort, but they can lead to serious errors.
- Among these shortcuts, one of the most dangerous for entrepreneurs is sunk costs (escalation of commitment)—a tendency to stick with decisions that yield increasingly negative results.

CREATIVITY: ESCAPING FROM MENTAL RUTS

Now that we have provided you with the necessary "toolkit" concerning human cognition, we can turn to one of the two central topics of this chapter: creativity (the gener-

DANGER! PITFALL AHEAD!

"Too Much Invested to Quit": The Potentially Devastating Effects of Sunk Costs

Have you ever heard the phrase "Throwing good money after bad"? It refers to the fact that in many situations, people who have made a bad decision—one that is yielding negative outcomes—tend to stick to it even as the evidence for its failure mounts. They may even commit additional time, effort, and resources to a failing course of action in the hope of somehow turning it around. This tendency to become trapped in bad decisions is known as **sunk costs** or *escalation of commitment* and is very common; it happens to investors who continue to hold on to what are clearly bad stocks and to people in troubled relationships, who often remain in them when all their friends urge them to withdraw.[15] Escalation of commitment also happens in decision-making groups. They, too, find it difficult to admit that they made a mistake and so cling to bad decisions that generate increasingly negative results. Research findings indicate that such effects—sometimes described as *collective entrapment* (a group becomes trapped in a bad decision)—are especially likely to occur in cases where groups have exerted a lot of effort to make the initial decision and so feel strongly committed to it.

Why do such effects occur? For several reasons. First, sticking with a decision is, initially, quite rational. Giving up too quickly can be a mistake, and if the decision was made carefully to start with, it makes sense to continue with it, at least for awhile. As losses mount, though, other processes that are *not* so rational come into play. People are unwilling to admit that they made a mistake because doing so will cause them to lose face and look foolish. Similarly, those who made the initial decision want to justify their actions, and the best way to do so is to continue on the current course and somehow make it turn out well.

Whatever the precise basis for escalation of commitment, it poses a very real danger to entrepreneurs. New ventures generally have limited resources, so there is little capacity to absorb mounting losses. Further, in any decision made by several persons, some will feel more responsible for this choice than others, with the result that dissension may occur among members of the founding team. Those who "back away" from the decision, claiming that they were against it all along, may come into conflict with those who feel more strongly committed to it. Overall, the results may be devastating for the new venture, so clearly, escalation of commitment is one cognitive error entrepreneurs should try to avoid.

What steps can entrepreneurs take to minimize the risk of this kind of error? Several have been found to be useful. One involves deciding, in advance, that if losses reach certain limits, or negative results continue for a specific period of time, no further resources will be invested and the decision will be changed. This is hard to do, but it is similar to "stop loss" orders in the stock market: It does tend to limit the losses that will be sustained. Another strategy involves charging persons other than the ones who made the original decision with the task of deciding whether to continue. Because they did not make the original commitment, they are often less committed to it. A third approach involves creating a culture in which people do not feel that they will lose face if they reverse earlier decisions now found to be poor ones. Rationally, this approach makes a lot of sense, but as you can guess, it can be difficult to implement.

Overall, it is clear that escalation of commitment and collective entrapment in bad decisions represent serious threats to the success of new ventures. For this reason, entrepreneurs should be fully aware of these potential pitfalls and take active steps to avoid them. Doing so can be a challenging task, but one well worth the effort: The companies they save will be their own!

ation of ideas that are both new *and* useful). A cognitive perspective offers important new insights into the nature of this crucial process and how, precisely, it occurs.

Creativity: Generating the Extraordinary

Suppose you were asked to name people high in creativity: Who would be on your list? When faced with this question, many persons come up with names such as Albert Einstein, Leonardo DaVinci, Thomas Edison, and Sigmund Freud. They worked in very different domains, so what do they all have in common? Essentially, this: All created something almost everyone agreed was *new*—theories, inventions, and other contributions that did not already exist. As we noted earlier, however, newness is not enough. Most researchers who have studied *creativity* define it as involving two key

LEARNING OBJECTIVE

4 Define creativity and explain the role that concepts play in it.

aspects: the items or ideas produced are both novel (original, unexpected) and appropriate or useful—they meet relevant constraints.[16] By this definition, the action shown in Figure 3.5 does not illustrate true creativity. Although the idea it involves is original, it really isn't practical. The U.S. Patent Office applies the same criteria to patent applications: Not only must an idea be new, but it must be practical, too.

Creativity is important for several reasons: It provides new knowledge, products, and other advances that can improve the quality of human life. It is somewhat surprising to learn, therefore, that until recently, it was *not* the subject of systematic research. Why not? Primarily because our understanding of human cognition was not sufficiently advanced to offer a solid framework for interpreting creativity in terms of basic cognitive processes. During the past two decades, this situation has changed greatly, and at present, there is general agreement that creativity in all domains—science, medicine, the arts, and day-to-day living—emerges from a relatively small set of basic cognitive processes. What are these processes? Most research suggests that two are central. One involves the stretching or expanding of internal mental structures we construct to organize information. The second involves the operation of various facets of human intelligence.

Concepts: Building Blocks of Creativity

The amount of information in long-term memory is vast, so in order to make it easier to retrieve and use this information, we organize it in various ways by creating internal mental structures to hold it. These structures take many different forms, but among them, **concepts**—categories for objects or events that are somehow similar to each other in certain respects—are especially important. Consider, for instance, the words "bicycle," "airplane," "automobile," and "elevator"; all are included in the concept "vehicle." Similarly, the words "shoes," "shirts," "jeans," and "jackets" are all included in the concept "clothing." As you can see, the objects within each of these concepts differ greatly, but are also similar to each other in certain underlying respects (e.g., all vehicles are used to move people from one point to another). In a sense, then, concepts act as a kind of "filing system" in memory, and once established, can help us to store new information. For instance, if you observed an entirely new kind of clothing you had never seen before, you would probably have no difficulty including it in the concept "clothing."

Concepts exist in memory in hierarchical networks that reflect the relationships between them. For instance, the concept "animals" includes "birds," "fish," and "insects." Animals, in other words, is higher in our hierarchy of concepts than birds, fish, and insects. "Birds," in turn, includes "penguins" and "canaries." Similarly, "fish" includes "sharks" and "salmon." "Insects" includes "butterflies" and "mosquitoes." The same is true for many other concepts; they, too, are organized into a hierarchical structure.

The fact that we store information in memory in an organized manner has two major implications for creativity—one positive and the other negative. On the "plus" side of the ledger, such internal structure enhances our ability to retrieve the vast amount of knowledge included in long-term memory, and this gives us better access to the raw materials from which new ideas can emerge. On the downside, however, the fact that knowledge is organized in memory often constrains our thinking, assuring that, in general, it stays pretty much within what have sometimes been

Figure 3.5 Creative Ideas Are Both Novel *and* Useful

The idea illustrated here is certainly new, but it is not useful or practical. Therefore, it does not meet the basic criteria for being described as creative.

At the National E-Mail Addiction Rehabilitation Center.

described as mental ruts. In other words, the internal structures we have created for ourselves are so strong that we find it very difficult to escape from, or think outside, them. Here's a striking example. In the mid 1970s, engineers and scientists at SONY Corporation were charged with the task of developing music CDs. They made great progress but ultimately gave up for the following reason: The CDs they produced stored fully 18 hours of music, and that was viewed as being too large to be marketable. Why did the CDs hold so much? *Because the engineers made them the same size and shape as existing LP records!* Although they were brilliant scientists and engineers, they simply could not escape from the "mental ruts" created by their past experience to realize that the new CDs could be any size they wished!

Here's yet another and perhaps even more amazing example of how cognitive organization can interfere with creativity. The Inca of South America had a very advanced civilization—one whose achievements astounded the Spaniards who first encountered them. But one invention they did not possess was wheeled vehicles; items to be transported were loaded on animals or dragged on poles—no carts or wagons existed. Yet—and here's the really surprising fact—Inca children played with models of wheeled carts! So the Inca had the *idea* of putting wheels on vehicles, but for some reason, they viewed this design as suitable only for toys! It is hard to imagine a more dramatic illustration of the power of mental ruts to constrain human thought.

If the impact of mental ruts can be this strong, you may be wondering, how do people ever escape from them? How, in short, does creativity ever occur? The answer seems to involve the fact that concepts can sometimes be expanded, thus paving the way for creativity. In other words, creativity emerges when basic mental processes allow for the expansion or transformation of concepts so that something new appears. This did not occur among the Inca, who seemed unable to expand the concept of "wheeled toy" into "wheeled full-scale wagons," but it does occur and can be encouraged. Specifically, concepts can be stretched or expanded in several different ways.

First, they can be *combined*, with the result that something very new is generated. For instance, consider the concept of the "Luxury SUV." The concept of "all-wheel drive, off-road vehicle" has been combined with the concept of "luxury vehicle" to produce something that never existed before—and is currently very popular. When concepts that appear to be initially opposite are combined, the result can be novel indeed—at least, when they are first introduced (e.g., nonalcoholic beer).

Concepts can also be *expanded*. In fact, this is often what happens with new products—even ones that represent a major breakthrough. For instance, the first railroad cars looked very much like the horse-drawn carriages they replaced. The concept of "carriage" had been expanded to include a vehicle for moving people, but what resulted was very similar to the original concept in appearance, if not means of propulsion. Similarly, early television sets were often placed in beautiful wooden cabinets because they were a form of home entertainment like radios and phonographs, and that's how *those* items had been presented to consumers.

A third way in which concepts can be changed or expanded is through *analogy*. Analogies involve perceiving similarities between objects or events that are otherwise dissimilar. For instance, statements such as "Knowledge is like a light in the dark" or "My love is like a red, red rose" involve analogies. Knowledge is not really like a light, and lovers are not like red roses—except in special ways. By making such comparisons, however, it is sometimes possible to break out of the mental ruts described earlier. The history of science, technology, and the arts is filled with examples of creative advances based, in part, on analogy. For instance, Rutherford's view of the hydrogen atom as similar to a planetary system in some respects (a large nucleus in the center with electrons revolving around it) and de Mestral's invention of Velcro after examining how burrs clung to his clothing with minute hooks are examples of reasoning by analogy that led to important advances. When concepts are stretched through analogy, in short, creativity is encouraged and important advances can result (see Figure 3.6 on page 64).[17]

Does the creativity shown by entrepreneurs emerge from the same processes? There seems little doubt that it does; after all, why should entrepreneurs present an exception to a pattern shown over and over in science, medicine, and the arts? In

Figure 3.6 Expanding Concepts Through Analogies: An Important Source of Creative Theory

When Swiss scientist Georges de Mestral looked at the burrs that stuck to his clothes after walking through fields, he noticed that the burrs had tiny hooks that became attached to the threads of the fabric. Through analogy, he reasoned that he could create a useful means of attaching things to each other with a similar system of tiny plastic hooks—and Velcro was born!

short, we agree with Robert Bresson, a French film director, who once noted: "An old thing becomes new if you detach it from what usually surrounds it." When concepts are separated from the hierarchical mental structures of which they are a part by combining them with other concepts, by expanding them, or through analogy, they may indeed become new—or at least, point the way toward acts of creativity that, in the hands of energetic and motivated entrepreneurs, generate something truly new.

Creativity and Human Intelligence

Another important factor in creativity (and in opportunity recognition, too) is human intelligence. Here's a vivid illustration of this point:

Two individuals, a university professor and an entrepreneur, are walking in the woods when they spot a ferocious grizzly bear charging in their direction. The professor, whose field is physics, estimates the speed of the bear and the speed at which they can run away from it. He then states: "Stop running. There's no way we'll ever be able to escape from that bear. He will catch us in 15 seconds." The entrepreneur, however, keeps on running. When the professor asks why, the entrepreneur shouts back over his shoulder: "You're right—I can never outrun the bear. But I don't have to outrun it; all I have to do is outrun you!"

This apocryphal tale has an important moral: Intelligence is indeed an important ingredient in success, but it is not necessarily the kind of intelligence measured by standard IQ tests. Instead, it is intelligence useful in meeting the many challenges of life—challenges posed by an everchanging world. This fact is widely recognized by psychologists, who currently define **intelligence** as individuals' abilities to understand complex ideas, to adapt effectively to the world around them, to learn from experience, to engage in various forms of reasoning, and to overcome a wide range of obstacles. As you can see, this definition suggests that intelligence has several different facets: It is not a unitary phenomenon. In fact, it is now widely recognized that human intelligence can be divided into several different kinds:[18] *analytic* intelligence, which involves the abilities to think critically and analytically (this is the kind measured by traditional IQ tests); *creative* intelligence, which involves the ability to formulate new ideas and gain insights into a wide range of problems (this is the kind shown by scientific geniuses and inventors such as Einstein, Newton, and Edison); and **practical intelligence**, which involves being intelligent in a practical sense (persons high in such intelligence are adept at solving the problems of everyday life and have "street smarts"). Another component in this mixture may be what is sometimes described as *social intelligence*, which involves the ability to understand others and get along well with them.

A growing body of evidence suggests that in order to be creative—and successful—entrepreneurs need a balanced mixture of all three components, something one expert

LEARNING OBJECTIVE

5 Distinguish between analytical, creative, and practical intelligence, and explain how all three are combined in successful intelligence.

in human intelligence, Robert Sternberg, terms **successful intelligence**.[19] Specifically, entrepreneurs need *creative* intelligence to come up with new ideas, *practical* intelligence to identify ways to develop these ideas, and *analytic* intelligence to evaluate the ideas and determine whether they are worth pursuing (see Figure 3.7).[20]

Although Sternberg does not specifically mention social intelligence—the skills required to get along effectively with others—there is little doubt that it, too, plays a role. We will consider this topic in more detail in Chapter 12. Here, we will simply note that growing evidence suggests that social intelligence, too, is a key ingredient in entrepreneurs' success. Without it, entrepreneurs can experience major problems in obtaining the financial and human resources they need to convert their dreams into reality.[21] So this aspect of intelligence, too, is important.

In sum, human intelligence does indeed play a role in creativity and in entrepreneurship, but in a more complex way than was once assumed. The intelligence required by entrepreneurs to be creative and to found successful new ventures is much richer and more multifaceted than the kind measured by standard IQ tests. In this respect, informal observation about entrepreneurs (and other creative persons) is correct: Such individuals do not necessarily "shine" in settings that require mainly analytical intelligence (e.g., in school); rather, their intellectual assets are more apparent in practical settings such as the modern world of business.

Encouraging Creativity: The Confluence Approach

Now that we have considered the role of practical and successful intelligence in creativity, it seems appropriate to consider another important question: "What can be done to enhance it?" Perhaps the best way of answering this question is by considering the factors that contribute to its occurrence; to the extent these factors are maximized, then creativity, too, should be encouraged. So, what factors have been found to contribute to creativity? As we have already noted, the field of cognitive science suggests that basic cognitive processes underlie creative thought. Creativity emerges from the operation of several kinds of memory, the expansion or merging of concepts, and related processes.[22]

Although the cognitive approach to creativity provides important insights into the factors that contribute to it, a somewhat broader view that includes additional factors has gained increased acceptance in recent years. This is known as **confluence approach**, and as its name suggests, it proposes that creativity emerges out of the confluence (i.e., convergence) of several basic resources:[23]

- *Intellectual abilities*—the ability to see problems in new ways, the ability to recognize which ideas are worth pursuing coupled with persuasive skills—being able to convince others of the value of these new ideas (a combination of successful and social intelligence)
- *A broad and rich knowledge base*—a large store of relevant information in memory; without such knowledge, the cognitive foundations for creative thought are lacking

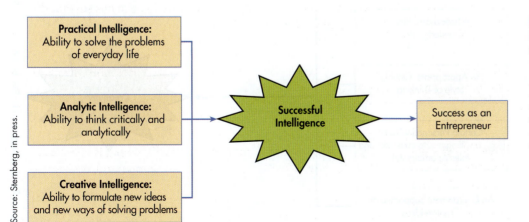

Source: Sternberg, in press.

Figure 3.7 Successful Intelligence: A Basic Requirement for Entrepreneurs

One expert on human intelligence, Robert Sternberg, has recently suggested that in order to succeed, entrepreneurs need a high level of successful intelligence—a good blend of practical, analytic, and creative intelligence.

- *An appropriate style of thinking*—a preference for thinking in novel ways, and an ability to "see the big picture"—to think globally as well as locally; in essence, a propensity for escaping from mental ruts
- *Personality attributes*—such traits as willingness to take risks and to tolerate ambiguity; these traits help individuals to consider ideas and solutions others overlook
- *Intrinsic, task-focused motivation*—creative people usually love what they are doing and find intrinsic rewards in their work
- *An environment that is supportive of creative ideas*—one that does not impose uniformity of thought and one that encourages change

The confluence approach suggests that to the extent these factors are present, creative thought can emerge (see Figure 3.8). A large body of evidence offers support for this view, so it appears to be quite useful.[24] This, in turn, suggests several techniques you can use to increase your own creativity, and so enhance the likelihood that you will generate ideas that can be the basis for successful new ventures.

First, and most important, it is clear that new ideas do *not* emerge out of a vacuum. Rather, they derive from combining, stretching, or viewing existing information in a new way. This means that in order to be creative, it is essential to have lots of information at your disposal. There are many ways of gaining a broad and rich knowledge base, but research findings indicate that among the most useful from the point of view of becoming an entrepreneur are (1) having varied work experience (e.g., the more jobs people have held, the more likely they are to become self-employed[25]), (2) having lived in many different places,[26] and (3) having a broad social network—many friends and acquaintances who can share their knowledge with you.[27] All of these factors increase the amount of information individuals have at their disposal and make them more creative. So, if you want to enhance your own creativity, you might consider structuring your life so as to broaden your own knowledge base—the foundation from which creative ideas spring.

Second, as the confluence approach suggests, you should cultivate a style of thinking that helps you break out of mental ruts. This is more difficult than it sounds because it is always easier to think in routine ways than to question our own beliefs. One way of doing so is to make sure that the people with whom you spend time are *not* all highly similar to yourself. To the extent they are, you will tend to agree with one another about most issues and will not challenge each others' beliefs. If, instead, you count among your friends people from different backgrounds and occupations, and who have contrasting views on a wide range of issues, this can help you develop flexible, open modes of thoughts—and these, in turn, can enhance your creativity.

Third, you should try to work in environments that encourage rather than discourage creativity. One reason many people choose to become entrepreneurs is that they feel stifled by the corporate world, which often leaves little room for imagination or origi-

Figure 3.8 Creativity: The Confluence Approach

The confluence approach suggests that creativity stems from the convergence of several factors. The most important of these include a broad and rich knowledge base, an appropriate style of thinking, certain personality attributes, and high intrinsic motivation.

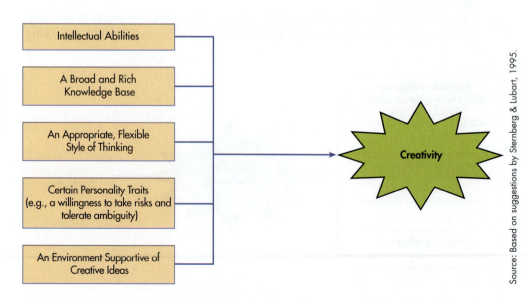

Intellectual Abilities

A Broad and Rich Knowledge Base

An Appropriate, Flexible Style of Thinking

Certain Personality Traits (e.g., a willingness to take risks and tolerate ambiguity)

An Environment Supportive of Creative Ideas

Creativity

Source: Based on suggestions by Sternberg & Lubart, 1995.

nality. The very best organizations, in contrast, tolerate or even encourage innovation among their employees. They also often tend to be more open about distributing information to employees. Many studies suggest that working in such jobs can broaden your knowledge base while simultaneously encouraging you to think creativity.[28]

In sum, there are a number of steps you can take to increase your own tendency to think creatively. To the extent you make these part of your daily life, you will become more creative and increase your ability to come up with ideas that can lead to successful ventures. Creativity *is* impressive, and in the hands of the right persons, it can literally change the world. But we now know that it stems from factors that are far from mysterious, and that are, to an important degree, under our own control.

KEY POINTS

- Creativity involves producing ideas that are both novel and appropriate.
- Existing evidence suggests that creative thought emerges from the combination and expansion of concepts, and from reasoning by analogy.
- To be creative and succeed, entrepreneurs need successful intelligence—a good balance of analytic, practical, and creative intelligence. They also need a high degree of social intelligence—the ability to get along well with others.
- The confluence approach to creativity suggests that it emerges out of a convergence of several factors (intellectual abilities, a broad and rich knowledge base, appropriate style of thinking, etc.).
- This approach, and others, suggests concrete steps you can take to increase your own creativity and, hence, your capacity for formulating new ideas that can lead to successful business ventures.

OPPORTUNITY RECOGNITION: A KEY STEP IN THE ENTREPRENEURIAL PROCESS

As we noted in Chapter 1, identification of a potentially valuable opportunity is a key initial step in the entrepreneurial process. Entrepreneurs' decisions to found new ventures often stem from their belief that they have identified an opportunity no one else has yet recognized, and so can benefit from being first to enter the marketplace.[29] Because it is the start of the entrepreneurial process, it is not at all surprising that opportunity recognition has long been a central concept in the field of entrepreneurship. Until recently, however, little effort has been made to examine it as a *process*. Rather, opportunities have been defined largely in economic terms: Any idea for a new product, service, raw material, market, or production process that can be successfully exploited so as to generate economic benefits for stakeholders has been viewed as constituting an opportunity.[30] Although this certainly makes sense, defining opportunities entirely from an economic perspective overlooks several key questions.

First, it largely ignores the question of *how* this process occurs; in other words, how do specific persons go about identifying opportunities that have been generated by shifting economic, technological, and social conditions (described in Chapter 2)? Clearly, this is an active process involving human perceptions and cognition, so understanding how it occurs might well suggest ways of enhancing its occurrence— techniques for helping would-be entrepreneurs identify opportunities that will benefit not only them, but millions of persons who ultimately use the new products or services they develop.

Second, and closely related, why are some persons better at this process—at identifying opportunities—than others? The opportunities generated by economic and technological conditions are there for anyone to notice; yet, only some individuals do so. What is it about these persons that allows them, and not others, to perform this task? Third, all opportunities are certainly not equal in potential value; some are blind alleys leading to economic disaster, while others have real potential for generating personal and societal wealth. Why, then, are some individuals so much better than others at separating the "wheat from the chaff"—at discerning which opportunities provide real potential for economic gains? In this section, we will review existing evidence concerning these issues. As we will soon see, this evidence suggests that two factors—having better access than others to certain kinds of information and being able to use this information effectively—play a crucial role.[31] For this reason, we will consider these factors first. In addition, however, cognitive processes, too, influence opportunity recognition.[32] When entrepreneurs conclude that they have noticed an opportunity, this implies that they believe they have recognized something "out there" that exists and is worth developing, but that other persons have not yet detected. Theories and concepts in cognitive science that focus on perception and related processes offer intriguing insights into the nature of opportunity recognition, so we will consider these, too. Finally, we will comment on ways in which you, as budding entrepreneurs, can enhance your own ability to spot opportunities worth pursuing.

One more point before proceeding: Recently, there has been a debate in the field of entrepreneurship over the question of whether opportunities exist in the external world or are created by human minds.[33] We believe that there is in fact no basis for controversy over this issue. As we noted in Chapter 2, opportunities, as a *potential* (i.e., a pattern that could be observed) come into existence in the external world as a result of changes in knowledge, technology, markets, political, and social conditions. However, they remain merely a potential until they emerge within specific human minds as the result of active cognitive processes. So in a sense, opportunities both exist "out there" and are the creation of human thought. Choosing between these two ideas is not necessary, because both are valid. Now, back to our discussion of opportunity recognition as a process.

Access to Information and Its Effective Use: The Core of Opportunity Recognition

The question of why some people and not others discover opportunities is both an intriguing and a practical one: If we can understand why certain people recognize opportunities that others don't yet notice, this can provide important insights into how this process can be enhanced. In other words, it may offer valuable clues as to how individuals can increase their ability to recognize opportunities.

Research on this question offers fairly clear answers, all revolving around the central role of information. Specifically, it appears that some people are more likely than others to recognize opportunities because (1) they have better access to certain kinds of information, and (2) they are able to utilize this information once they have it.

Greater Access to Information

With respect to the first of these points (greater access to information), it appears that specific persons gain increased access to information useful for identifying opportunities in several ways. For example, they may have jobs that provide them with information "on the cutting edge" that is not widely available to others. Jobs in research and development or marketing appear to be especially valuable in this respect.[34] Another way in which individuals gain superior access to information is through varied work and life experience—factors that, because they contribute to individuals' knowledge base, also increase their creativity.[35] Yet another way in which specific persons gain enhanced access to information is through a large social network.[36] As you may know from your own experience, other people are a valuable source of information, and often the information they provide cannot be acquired easily in any other way. Finally—and not surprisingly—persons who discover opportunities are often ones who actively search for them. They do not just wait for opportunities to "drop into their laps"; rather, they go out and look for them—often in places others overlook. In this respect, Gaglio and Katz[37] have recently suggested that entrepreneurs—and especially successful ones—possess a *schema* (mental framework) that assists them in being alert to, and therefore recognizing, opportunities. As we noted earlier, schemas are a kind of "mental scaffold" built up through experience that help us to process information efficiently. They do so because they provide a framework into which new information can be readily placed. In other words, schemas assist us in linking new information to information already stored in memory. This, in turn, makes it easier to retain the new information and to use it in various ways.

Applying this concept to opportunity recognition, Gaglio and Katz suggest that some persons possess a schema of *entrepreneurial alertness*—an internal mental framework that helps them search for and notice changes that might yield valuable opportunities, changes in markets, technology, competition, and so on. The result? They are more likely to recognize opportunities than other persons. In sum, many factors give specific persons "an edge" where access to useful kinds of information is concerned, and this, in turn, increases the likelihood that they will recognize potentially valuable opportunities.

Superior Utilization of Information

Greater access to valuable information is not the entire story, however. Entrepreneurs who recognize opportunities not only have greater access to information than other persons, they are also better at using such information. First, because of their greater access to information, they often have richer and better-integrated stores of knowledge than other persons—for instance, more information (in memory) about markets and how to serve them.[38] This, in turn, enhances their ability to interpret and use new information because not only do they have more information at their disposal, but it is also better organized. As we noted earlier, large quantities of well-organized information play a key role in creativity. After all, it is hard to stretch information or combine it in new ways if it is not present or if it is not well-organized. Persons who identify opportunities have been found to possess richer and better organized stores of information, so it is not surprising that they are better able to perceive opportunities others often miss. In addition, individuals who recognize opportunities may also be better at the process of improvisation—at formulating plans and strategies "on the fly," as they go along.[39] In other words, they don't necessarily engage in a systematic or detailed search for opportunities; rather, recognition of these emerges out of their continuing efforts to adapt to, and deal with, everchanging conditions around them.

Other cognitive processes, too, play a role. For instance, persons who found new ventures are higher in intelligence than persons who do not (e.g., managers). Moreover, entrepreneurs have been found to be higher in intelligence even when this was measured many years in the past—when they were, on average, 12 years old![40] Additional evidence suggests that entrepreneurs are especially likely to be higher than other persons in practical intelligence—the ability to solve the varied problems of everyday life.[41] Finally, and again, far from surprising, entrepreneurs are higher in creativity than other persons.[42] In other words, they are more adept at combining the information at their disposal into something new.

In sum, it seems clear that a key component in opportunity recognition is information—greater access to it and better cognitive tools for putting it to good use (see Figure 3.9 on page 70 for a summary of these points). In this sense, the answer to the question "Why some people and not others?" with respect to opportunity recognition is far from mysterious: It stems from basic cognitive processes and well-practiced skills with which we are all very familiar.

Opportunity Recognition: Additional Insights from Cognitive Science

In earlier chapters, we noted that opportunities emerge from a complex pattern of changing conditions—changes in knowledge, technology, economic, political, social, and demographic conditions. In other words, they come into existence at a given point in time because of a combination of conditions that did not exist previously, but is now present. They are only a potential, however, until one or more persons "connects the

Figure 3.9 Opportunity Recognition: The Central Role of Information

Opportunity recognition stems, to an important degree, from greater access to information and greater capacity to utilize it.

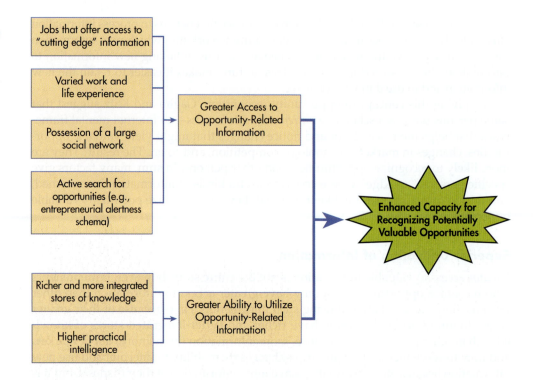

dots" between diverse and seemingly unrelated changes or events to form the perception of a pattern that links them together—until one or more persons perceives the existence of the opportunity.[43] If this is indeed true, then two important theories relating to human cognition can help us understand the process through which specific persons identify opportunities.

One is known as **signal detection theory**,[44] and it is concerned with a very basic question: "How do we decide whether there really *is* anything out there to notice?" This is an important question because opportunities don't always leap out at entrepreneurs—or anyone else. On the contrary, they are often hard to discern against a background of noise. So a key task faced by would-be entrepreneurs is deciding whether an opportunity is or is not actually present. Signal detection theory suggests that in situations like this—ones in which individuals attempt to determine whether a stimulus is present or absent—four possibilities exist: (1) The stimulus does indeed exist and the perceiver concludes (correctly) that it is present (this is known as a *hit* or *correct identification*); (2) the stimulus does exist but the perceiver fails to recognize it (this is known as a *miss*); (3) the stimulus does not exist and the perceiver concludes, erroneously, that it is present (this is a *false alarm*); (4) the stimulus does not exist and the perceiver correctly concludes that it is not present (a *correct rejection*—another kind of hit). (See Figure 3.10 for a summary of these possibilities.)

The theory further notes that many factors determine the rate at which individuals experience hits, misses, and false alarms in any given situation. Some of these are physical and relate to the properties of the stimuli (e.g., the brighter a light or louder a sound, the easier it is to be certain that it is present). Other factors, however, reflect the current state of the person making this judgment (e.g., is this person fatigued? highly or weakly motivated to make correct judgments?). Still other factors involve the subjective criteria such persons apply to the task—whether they are more concerned about attaining "hits" or more concerned about avoiding false alarms, for instance. Perhaps at this point, a concrete example will be helpful.

Consider a security officer at a busy airport. A routine electronic scan of a busy terminal provides data suggesting that a bomb may be present, but the data are far from conclusive. What does she do next? One alternative is to keep the airport open while conducting a careful search. That will prevent delays for many travelers, but it runs the risk of tragic consequences if a bomb does in fact exist: Hundreds of people may be killed in an explosion. Another alternative is to close the airport and conduct

Actual Presence of Opportunity

		Yes	No
Judgment About Presence	**Yes**	**Hit** Opportunity is present and is recognized.	**False Alarm** Opportunity is not present but is judged to be present.
	No	**Miss** Opportunity is present but is not judged to be present.	**Correct Rejection** Opportunity is not present and is judged to be absent.

Figure 3.10 Signal Detection Theory and Opportunity Recognition

Signal detection theory is concerned with the basic question, "How do we decide whether a stimulus is or is not present?" It suggests that there are four possibilities, which, in the context of opportunity recognition, are as follows: An opportunity is present and we recognize it (a hit); an opportunity is present and we overlook it (a miss); there is no opportunity present and we realize that none exists (a correct rejection); or there is no opportunity but we conclude that one exists (a false alarm).

an even more thorough search. But what if this is done, and the search turns up nothing? Thousands of travelers will have been inconvenienced, and if the airport is a major one, closing it may disrupt the entire air travel system—all for nothing.

What will the security officer do? Because public annoyance is strongly preferable to being responsible for the deaths of hundreds of travelers if a bomb actually explodes, she would probably set her subjective criterion for concluding that there is a serious danger quite low. In other words, she would accept even weak data suggesting that a bomb may be present as sufficient grounds for closing the airport. The security officer, in brief, would much rather experience false alarms (closing the airport when there is no reason to do so) than misses (not closing it when there really is a bomb present).

In other situations, the opposite might be true: Misses are preferable to false alarms. For instance, consider the case of a radiologist examining medical scans in order to determine whether a cancerous tumor is or is not present in a 90-year-old patient. The radiologist does not want to overlook tumors that exist and could, potentially, kill the patient if not removed (that would constitute a miss), but the costs of false alarms are even higher: This type of exploratory surgery is extremely dangerous for someone 90 years old and, if the cancer is a relatively slow-growing type, the patient might well die of other causes before the cancer becomes fatal. Under these circumstances, the radiologist might well set a relatively high criterion for concluding that a stimulus is present (i.e., he would require very clear evidence that a tumor is present before recommending exploratory surgery).

Now that we have described the basic concepts of signal detection theory, we can explain why it is directly relevant to opportunity recognition. Entrepreneurs are strongly motivated to obtain hits—to recognize opportunities that actually exist. But they also wish to avoid false alarms—perceiving opportunities that do not in fact exist and that, if pursued, will waste their time, effort, and resources. Further, they also desire to avoid misses—overlooking opportunities that actually exist. So in a sense, signal detection theory provides a very useful framework for understanding how opportunity recognition actually occurs.

But where do entrepreneurs set their personal criteria for deciding whether opportunities are, or are not, present? In other words, what factors determine whether they are primarily motivated to attain hits, avoid false alarms, or avoid misses? Another cognitive theory, known as **regulatory focus theory**,[45] offers an answer. Briefly, this latter theory suggests that in regulating their own behavior to achieve desired ends (something entrepreneurs do all the time!), individuals adopt one of two contrasting perspectives:[46] a *promotion focus*, in which their primary goal is attaining positive outcomes, or a *prevention focus*, in which their primary goal is avoiding negative outcomes. Many studies[47] indicate that individuals differ in their personal preferences for a promotion or prevention focus. In addition, people can be induced to adopt one or the other of these two foci by situational factors (e.g., instructions to focus either on achieving gains or avoiding losses[48]).

When regulatory focus theory is combined with signal detection theory, it generates intriguing insights into the process of opportunity recognition. Specifically, it suggests that entrepreneurs who adopt a promotion focus (an emphasis on accomplishment) will be more concerned with attaining hits (recognizing opportunities

LEARNING OBJECTIVE

9 Explain the difference between a promotion focus and a prevention focus, and describe the effects these contrasting perspectives may have on entrepreneurs' efforts to discover valuable opportunities.

that actually exist) and with avoiding misses (failing to recognize an opportunity that exists), while entrepreneurs who adopt a prevention focus will concentrate mainly on avoiding errors—on avoiding false alarms (pursuing opportunities that don't really exist) and on correct rejections (correctly recognizing when opportunities do not exist).

Is either of these patterns better from the point of attaining success? Not really; both offer advantages and disadvantages.[49] However, it seems possible that overall, entrepreneurs who are successful at identifying valuable opportunities adopt a mixture of these two perspectives: They are eager to identify real opportunities (hits), but they are also motivated to avoid false alarms, which implies that they have better cognitive systems or structures not only for recognizing opportunities, but for evaluating them, too—for estimating their potential economic value.[50] In contrast, entrepreneurs who are less successful at identifying valuable opportunities may adopt a pure promotion focus: They focus on attaining hits (recognizing real opportunities) and are less concerned about the dangers of false alarms. These and related predictions are summarized in Table 3.2.

Together, signal detection theory and regulatory focus theory shed intriguing light on the question of why some entrepreneurs are more adept than others at recognizing viable opportunities. Successful ones, in essence, have a more realistic view of the risks involved and their chances of obtaining success. They are strongly motivated to maximize hits—to correctly identify real opportunities. At the same time, though, they are also strongly motivated to avoid the false alarms and the dangers of wasting their time, effort, and resources pursuing opportunities that don't really exist. That conclusion brings us back to the quote presented at the start of this chapter: "When written in Chinese the word *crisis* is composed of two characters. One represents danger and the other represents opportunity." These words, spoken by John F. Kennedy, propose that *danger* and *opportunity* are two sides of the same coin. The findings of cognitive science agree with this view, suggesting that in entrepreneurship, as in many other spheres of life, victory does not necessarily go to the strongest or the swiftest, but rather to those whose judgment is most closely aligned with reality. (How do successful entrepreneurs avoid false alarms? Some important insights are offered by Chester J. Opalka, a cofounder of Albany Molecular Research, Inc. See **"The Voice of Experience"** section.)

Practical Techniques for Increasing Opportunity Recognition

We will now conclude on a very practical note: How can you increase your own ability to recognize potentially valuable opportunities? Though we still have a lot to learn about opportunity recognition as a process, existing evidence points to several steps that should prove very helpful in this respect. Here are the most important:

- *Build a broad and rich knowledge base.* The capacity to recognize opportunities, like creativity, depends in large measure on how much information you have at your disposal. The more you possess, the more likely you are to recognize the connections and patterns that constitute opportunities—before others do so. Learn everything you can, whenever you can; the result will be an enhanced capacity to recognize opportunities.

Table 3.2 Predicted Motivation to Identify Hits, Misses, False Alarms, and Correct Rejections Among Successful and Unsuccessful Entrepreneurs

A key difference between successful and unsuccessful entrepreneurs may relate to their adoption of one of two styles of regulatory focus, and to the effects this has on their motivation to obtain hits, correct rejections, avoid misses, and avoid false alarms.

SUCCESSFUL ENTREPRENEURS (Mixed Promotion and Prevention Focus)		UNSUCCESSFUL ENTREPRENEURS (Pure Promotion Focus)	
High motivation to attain:	Hits Correct identification of false alarms	High motivation to attain:	Hits Avoidance of misses
Moderate motivation to attain:	Correct rejections	Low motivation to attain:	Correct identification of false alarms
Low motivation to attain:	Avoidance of misses		Correct rejections

THE VOICE OF EXPERIENCE

Some Thoughts on Avoiding False Alarms

Chet Opalka is a cofounder of Albany Molecular Research, Inc. (AMRI), a drug discover and development company focused on applications for the pharmaceutical, biotechnology, and life sciences industries. The company, which is based in Albany, NY, employs more than 800 people. Opalka, who worked at Sterling Drug, Inc., prior to founding AMRI, is the inventor or co-inventor in nearly 30 patents. He has coauthored several scientific publications relating to his accomplishments in the field of pharmaceutical chemistry. Opalka received his BS in chemistry from Niagara University. Since his retirement in 2002, he has become very active in the local business and philanthropic community and currently serves on the nonprofit boards of the Sage Colleges and Northeast Health.

If there is one thing no entrepreneur can afford, it is wasting precious time, resources, and energy pursuing false alarms—opportunities that don't really exist, or—if they do—are impossible to develop. In a recent interview, I asked Chet Opalka, cofounder of AMRI and currently president of Opalka Family Investment Partners, Inc., how he and his partner, Tom D'Ambra, avoided such traps.

Baron: "A potential problem for all entrepreneurs is that of wasting their time, effort, and money on a 'false alarm'—an idea for a new product or service that looks good, but is actually not feasible. How do *you*, personally, go about distinguishing between ideas that are truly good ones and ideas that are likely to be false alarms?"

Opalka: "That really *is* a big issue for entrepreneurs, because no one can afford to make huge mistakes. First, you have to develop a network of people whose experience base and knowledge base you can trust—people you can draw on as consultants. You have to bounce your ideas off these people. They can be on your board of directors or board of advisors, but what's important is soliciting their input and perspective. People will tend to put on blinders, so they tend to see what they want or expect to see. You have to pull off the blinders and avoid being stubborn or assuming that you are smarter than everyone else; believing that you know it all can be really deadly. You have to begin by realizing that you *don't* know it all. Then, you have to get good advice; that can save you from committing to false alarms."

Baron: "Anything else?"

Opalka: "Belonging to an angel network or some other type of investment forum whose members are individuals with some experience in entrepreneurship. The composition of these groups varies from region to region but the value of having them as a resource has incredible value to new entrepreneurs. They can provide investment, but what I sometimes consider of higher value to the young CEO is the wealth of knowledge that can only be obtained by having 'been there and done that.' They are the mentors that every 'newbie' needs to help avoid some of the pitfalls that start-ups face. In some cases, experienced people will leave the angel groups because they have invested all they personally can invest, but it's important to keep them engaged and around the table somehow. They all have different perspectives, offer advice, and ask questions other people might not think of asking. For instance, one might be a chemist, another a biologist, and another might be experienced in finance. Because of these different backgrounds, they look at problems from different angles, and they can be a tremendous help in making decisions about where to go next—what to do and what to avoid."

Baron: "So your advice to budding entrepreneurs about avoiding false alarms centers mainly around getting help from other people—especially ones with different backgrounds and knowledge from each other, and perhaps from you, too."

Opalka: "That's right. No one knows everything, and the more good brains you have sitting around the table when you make decisions, the better off you will be—and the less likely you are to go off the deep end and get into serious trouble. That's how we always operated, and it worked well for us."

Commentary: We agree with Mr. Opalka's advice. One important way to avoid false alarms is to get smart people with different backgrounds to examine potential opportunities you are considering. Although you have to have confidence in your own judgment and recognize that in the final analysis, the decision is yours, moving ahead *without* good input and advice from people whose opinions, experience, and common sense you trust can truly be suicidal. So do follow Opalka's suggestions and do two things: (1) Surround yourself with intelligent, experienced people and (2) listen to their advice!

■ *Organize your knowledge.* Knowledge that is organized is much more useful than knowledge that is not. This means that as you acquire new information, you should actively seek to relate it to what you know so that connections between existing and new information come clearly into focus. Information that is connected and organized in this manner is easier to remember—and to use—than information that it is not.

■ *Increase your access to information.* The more information that is potentially related to opportunities you receive on a regular basis, the more likely you are to recognize opportunities that have just emerged. You can do this by holding jobs that put you on "the cutting edge" (e.g., jobs in research and development or marketing), by building a large social network, and by having rich and diverse job—and life—experiences.

■ *Create connections between the knowledge you have.* Research findings indicate that the more richly interconnected knowledge structures are, the more readily the information in them can be combined into new patterns. This suggests that establishing such connections between information stored in memory and other cognitive systems can be a useful strategy. One way in which such connections can be formed involves what is known as *deep processing*—actively thinking about information and connections between it. This is something you can readily do, and the result may be an increased ability to recognize emerging opportunities.

■ *Build your practical intelligence.* Entrepreneurs are sometimes accused of being "dreamers"—people who think so large that they lose touch with reality. In fact, this is far from the truth. They are usually people high in practical intelligence—the ability to solve the highly varied problems of everyday life. Practical intelligence is definitely not set in stone—it can be cultivated. The best way to increase it is to avoid accepting the solutions to problems suggested by "mental ruts." Try, instead, to think of new and better ways to handle various problems. The result may be an increase in your own practical intelligence—and hence your ability to recognize opportunities.

■ *Temper eagerness for hits with wariness of false alarms.* It has long been assumed that entrepreneurs are optimists—that they suffer from the optimistic bias to a greater extent than other persons (i.e., they expect positive results even when there are no rational grounds for such predictions). In fact, there is a healthy grain of truth in this idea. This implies that it is important for entrepreneurs to focus not only on the potential gains offered by hits—by recognizing opportunities that really do exist—but also on the potentially devastating costs of pursuing false alarms (opportunities that aren't really there). In other words, if you want to be successful as an entrepreneur, and at identifying genuine opportunities, fight against your own tendencies to be optimistic and consider the downside, too. Doing so may go against your personal inclinations, but the result may be that you avoid one of the most dangerous pitfalls lying in wait for unsuspecting entrepreneurs: the quicksand of illusory opportunities.

KEY POINTS

- In the past, opportunities have been viewed primarily in economic terms. This is reasonable, but largely ignores such questions as how the process of opportunity recognition actually occurs, and why some persons are better at it than others.
- A cognitive perspective addresses these and other questions. It suggests, for instance, that information—access to it and the capacity to utilize it—plays a crucial role in opportunity recognition.
- Two cognitive theories—signal detection theory and regulatory focus theory—offer further insights into the cognitive foundations of opportunity recognition. Signal detection theory addresses the basic question: "Is an opportunity really present?" and suggests that entrepreneurs seek to maximize hits (recognizing opportunities that exist) while avoiding false alarms.
- Regulatory focus theory suggests that successful entrepreneurs may be more adept than unsuccessful ones at combining two contrasting perspectives (promotion and prevention focus) in their search for opportunities.
- As a nascent entrepreneur, there are several steps you can take to increase your ability to recognize valuable opportunities. These include building a broad, rich, and organized knowledge base, increasing your access to information, actively searching for opportunities, increasing your practical intelligence, and tempering eagerness for "hits" with a healthy fear of false alarms.

Summary and Review of Key Points

- Cognitive processes provide the foundation for creativity and opportunity recognition.
- Memory involves cognitive systems for storing information. Working memory can retain limited amounts of information for short periods of time. Active processing of information occurs in working memory, so it is the system in which consciousness exists.
- Long-term memory holds vast (perhaps unlimited) amounts of information for long periods of time. Such information can be factual or procedural in nature.
- Because our capacity to process information is limited, we often adopt shortcuts to reduce mental effort. These include heuristics and various "tilts" in our thinking (e.g., the confirmation bias). These shortcuts *do* save effort, but they can lead to serious errors.
- Among these shortcuts, one of the most dangerous for entrepreneurs is escalation of commitment—a tendency to stick with decisions that yield increasingly negative results.
- Creativity involves producing ideas that are both novel and appropriate.
- Existing evidence suggests that creative thought emerges from the combination and expansion of concepts, and from reasoning by analogy.
- To be creative and succeed, entrepreneurs need successful intelligence—a good balance of analytic, practical, and creative intelligence. They also need a high degree of social intelligence—the ability to get along well with others.
- The confluence approach to creativity suggests that it emerges out a convergence of several factors (intellectual abilities, a broad and rich knowledge base, appropriate style of thinking, etc.).

- This approach and others suggest concrete steps you can take to increase your own creativity—and hence your capacity for formulating new ideas that can lead to successful business ventures.
- In the past, opportunities have been viewed primarily in economic terms. This is reasonable, but it largely ignores such questions as how the process of opportunity recognition actually occurs and why some persons are better at it than others.
- A cognitive perspective addresses these and other questions. It suggests, for instance, that information—access to it and the capacity to utilize it—plays a crucial role in opportunity recognition.
- Two cognitive theories—signal detection theory and regulatory focus theory—offer further insights into the cognitive foundations of opportunity recognition. Signal detection theory addresses the basic question: "Is an opportunity present?" and suggests that entrepreneurs seek to maximize hits (recognizing opportunities that exist) while avoiding false alarms.
- Regulatory focus theory suggests that successful entrepreneurs may be more adept than unsuccessful ones at combining two contrasting perspectives (promotion and prevention focus) in their search for opportunities.
- As a nascent entrepreneur, there are several steps you can take to increase your ability to recognize valuable opportunities. These include building a broad, rich, and organized knowledge base, actively searching for opportunities, increasing your practical intelligence, and tempering eagerness for "hits" with a healthy fear of false alarms.

Glossary

Concepts: Categories for objects or events that are somehow similar to each other in certain respects.

Confluence Approach: A view suggesting that creativity emerges out of the confluence (i.e., convergence) of several basic resources.

Creativity: The generation of ideas that are both novel (original, unexpected) and appropriate or useful; they meet relevant constraints.

Heuristics: Simple rules for making complex decisions or drawing inferences in a rapid and seemingly effortless manner.

Human Cognition: The mental processes through which we acquire information, enter it into storage, transform it, and use it to accomplish a wide range of tasks.

Idea Generation: The production of ideas for something new; very close in meaning to *creativity*.

Intelligence: Individuals' abilities to understand complex ideas, to adapt effectively to the world around them, to learn from experience, to engage in various forms of reasoning, and to overcome a wide range of obstacles.

Memory: Our cognitive systems for storing and retrieving information.

Opportunity Recognition: The process through which individuals conclude that they have identified the potential to create something new that has the capacity to generate economic value (i.e., potential future profits).

Practical Intelligence: Being intelligent in a practical sense; persons high in such intelligence are adept at solving the problems of everyday life and have "street smarts."

Prototypes: Mental representations of categories of events or objects.

Regulatory Focus Theory: A theory that suggests that in regulating their own behavior to achieve desired ends, individuals adopt one of two contrasting perspectives: a promotion focus (main goal is accomplishment) or a prevention focus (main goal is prevention of losses).

Schemas: Cognitive frameworks representing our knowledge and assumptions about specific aspects of the world.

Signal Detection Theory: A theory suggesting that in situations where individuals attempt to determine whether a stimulus is present or absent, four possibilities exist: The stimulus exists and the perceiver concludes that it is present; the stimulus exists but the perceiver fails to recognize it; the stimulus does not exist and the perceiver concludes, erroneously, that it is present; the stimulus does not exist and the perceiver correctly concludes that it is not present.

Successful Intelligence: A balanced blend of analytic, creative, and practical intelligence. Successful intelligence is the kind of intelligence needed by entrepreneurs.

Sunk Costs or Escalation of Commitment: The tendency to become trapped in bad decisions and stick to them even though they yield increasingly negative results.

Discussion Questions

1. People are not very good at describing information stored in procedural memory (the kind of memory that allows you to perform skilled tasks such as playing a musical instrument). Why do you think this is so?

2. Many people who are afraid of flying in airplanes are not afraid to drive their own cars. When asked, they often answer: "Because there is greater danger of being killed in airplanes." This is not true—there is actually a greater chance of being killed in an automobile. Do you think the availability heuristic might play a role in this error?

3. Repeat entrepreneurs—people who start one successful venture after another—seem to have a knack for recognizing good opportunities. Do you think they may have better prototypes for opportunities than other people? If so, how did they acquire them?

4. Can you think of people you have known who were high in analytic intelligence (the kind measured by IQ tests) but low in practical intelligence? What about the opposite pattern—have you known people high in practical intelligence but low in analytic intelligence? Which would make better entrepreneurs? Why?

5. In your opinion, do opportunities exist "out there" in the external world? Or are they purely a construction of human thought? Why?

6. Have you ever been trapped in mental ruts—forced by your own experience and training to view a situation or problem in a way that blocked your creativity? If so, what should you have done to escape from this kind of cognitive trap?

InfoTrac Exercises

1. **"The Rusty Ribbon": John Herbert Orr and the Making of the Magnetic Recording Industry, 1945–1960.**
   David L. Morton
   Business History Review, Winter 1993 v67 n4 p589(34)
   Record: A15638145

   Abstract: Orradio Industries Inc. was founded in 1949 by the late John Herbert Orr, an Alabama entrepreneur and former U.S. Army intelligence official. Orradio was a pioneer in the manufacture of magnetic recording tape, a technology invented by the Germans in the 1930s. Orradio's sales expanded rapidly in the late 1950s as magnetic tape became the standard medium for magnetic recorders. The history of Orradio is presented to show the organizational, technological, and locational challenges encountered by a small firm starting a new industry.

   1. According to the text, what is successful intelligence?

2. How do you see the concept of successful intelligence reflected in the entrepreneurial ventures of John Orr?

3. Would you say that Orr's business life also reflected social intelligence? Why or why not?

2. **Opportunity Recognition: An Exploratory Investigation of a Component of the Entrepreneurial Process in the Context of the Health Care Industry**
   Richard L. McCline; Subodh Bhat; Pam Baj

   Entrepreneurship: Theory and Practice, Winter 2000 v25 i2 p81

Record: A74524634

Full Text: COPYRIGHT 2000 Baylor University

1. According to the text, how can you increase your ability to recognize opportunities?

2. Robinson et al. (1991) suggested a 3-part measure of "entrepreneurial-attitude orientation" after the tradition established in social psychology. In this line of research, an attitude is believed to have what three components?

3. What two new exploratory scales were developed for the health care study?

GETTING DOWN
TO BUSINESS

What Is Your Prototype for an "Opportunity"?

In our discussion of opportunity recognition, we suggested that individuals may possess prototypes for opportunities. In other words, we have mental representations that capture the essence of what we believe "opportunities" to be. To the extent this is true, then one reason why some people may be better at recognizing opportunities is that they possess clearer or better-developed prototypes with which to compare potential opportunities.

What is *your* prototype of an opportunity like? To find out, follow these steps:

1. List the features you think are required for something to qualify as an opportunity. (*Hint:* These might include newness, feasibility, etc.)

   a. Feature:
   b. Feature:
   c. Feature:
   d. Feature:
   e. Feature:

(Continue with others if necessary.)

2. Now, rate how central you think each of these features are—in other words, how important is each feature you listed for recognizing an opportunity? Do this by assigning a number from 1 to 5 to each feature, where 5 = highly central and 1 = not very central.

3. Next, ask several of your friends to carry out the same steps. To what extent did you list the same or similar features? To what extent did you rate these the same in terms of their centrality to the idea of "opportunity"?

4. If you can, find an actual entrepreneur and ask her or him to do the same thing. Then, compare this person's list of features to yours and to those produced by your friends.

5. Do you think the list of features you have compiled can be helpful to you in identifying opportunities for new ventures in the future?

Are You Promotion-Focused or Prevention-Focused?
Testing Your Own Regulatory Focus

Research findings indicate that people have preferences for a promotion focus or a prevention focus. Those who show a preference for a promotion focus tend to concentrate on achievement—on attaining goals they find desirable. Those who show a preference for a prevention focus tend to concentrate on avoiding negative outcomes and on minimizing risks. Neither is better, but they do have important implications for becoming an entrepreneur. Early on, a promotion focus may be better because it can facilitate the search for opportunities. Later, a prevention focus may be useful because it helps entrepreneurs avoid false alarms. To find out where you stand on this dimension, follow these instructions:

Event Reaction Questionnaire

This set of questions asks you about specific events in your life. Please indicate your answer to each question by circling the appropriate number below it.

1. Compared to most people, are you typically unable to get what you want out of life?

1	2	3	4	5
never or seldom		sometimes		very often

2. Growing up, would you ever "cross the line" by doing things that your parents would not tolerate?

1	2	3	4	5
never or seldom		sometimes		very often

3. How often have you accomplished things that got you "psyched" to work even harder?

1	2	3	4	5
never or seldom		a few times		many times

4. Did you get on your parents' nerves often when you were growing up?

1	2	3	4	5
never or seldom		sometimes		very often

5. How often did you obey rules and regulations that were established by your parents?

1	2	3	4	5
never or seldom		sometimes		always

6. Growing up, did you ever act in ways that your parents thought were objectionable?

1	2	3	4	5
never or seldom		sometimes		very often

7. Do you often do well at different things that you try?

1	2	3	4	5
never or seldom		sometimes		very often

8. Not being careful enough has gotten me into trouble at times.

1	2	3	4	5
never or seldom		sometimes		very often

9. When it comes to achieving things that are important to me, I find that I don't perform as well as I ideally would like to do.

1	2	3	4	5
never true		sometimes true		very often true

10. I feel like I have made progress toward being successful in my life.

1	2	3	4	5
certainly false				certainly true

11. I have found very few hobbies or activities in my life that capture my interest or motivate me to put effort into them.

1	2	3	4	5
certainly false				certainly true

Scoring: Here's how to score your answers: Add your scores for items 1, 3, 7, 9, 10, and 11 and take an average: This is your Promotion Focus Score. Now add the scores for items 2, 4, 5, 6, and 8 and average these: This is your Prevention Focus Score. Which is higher? If the Promotion Focus Score is higher, that is your preferred regulatory focus. If the Prevention Focus Scores is higher, then that is your preferred regulatory focus. Remember: Neither is better, but both are relevant to becoming an entrepreneur—and to being successful in this role.

Enhanced Learning

You may select any combination of the case options below to enhance your understanding of the chapter material.

- **Appendix 1: Case Studies –** Thirteen cases provide opportunities to apply chapter concepts to realistic entrepreneurial situations. These brief cases call for careful analysis of real business problems and ask you to think about potential solutions.

- **Appendix 2: Video Case Library –** Nine cases are tied directly to video segments from the popular PBS television series *Small Business School*. These cases and video segments give you unparalleled access to today's entrepreneurs, with expert advice and insights on how to start, run, and grow a business.

- **Comprehensive Cases –** Visit the book support Web site at http://baron.swlearning.com for cases detailing real businesses whose successes and setbacks illustrate each stage of the entrepreneurial process. You will conduct in-depth analysis of entrepreneurial challenges through well-developed case studies.

Notes

1. Shane, S. (in preparation). *The individual-opportunity nexus: Perspectives on entrepreneurship.* Aldershot, United Kingdom: Eward Elgar.
2. Herron, L., & Sapienza, H.J. 1992. The entrepreneur and the initiation of new venture launch activities. *Entrepreneurship Theory and Practice* 16: 49–55.
3. Matlin, M.W. 2002. *Cognition.* 5th ed. Fort Worth, TX: Harcourt College Publishers.
4. Haxby, J.V., Horwitz, B., Ungerleider, L.G, Maisog, J.M., Pietrini, P., & Grady, C.L. 1994. The functional organization of human extrastriate cortex: APET-CBV. *Journal of Neuroscience* 1:, 6336–6353.
5. Shepherd, D.A., & DeTienne, D.R. 2001. Discovery of opportunities: Anomalies, accumulation and alertness. In W.D. Bygrave et al. (eds.). *Frontiers of Entrepreneurship Research* (pp.138–148). Babson Park, MA: Center for Entrepreneurial Studies.
6. Shepherd, D.A., Zacharakis, A., & Baron, R.A. 2003. VC's decision processes: Evidence suggesting more experience may not always be better. *Journal of Business Venturing* 18: 381–401.
7. Zacharakis, A.L., & Shepherd, D.A. 2001. The nature of information and overconfidence on venture capitalist's decision making. *Journal of Business Venturing* 16: 311–322.
8. Baron, R.A. 1998. Cognitive mechanisms in entrepreneurship: Why and when entrepreneurs think differently than other people. *Journal of Business Venturing* 13: 275–294.
9. Rothman, A.J., & Hardin, C.D. 1997. Differential use of the availability heuristic in social judgment. *Personality and Social Psychology Bulletin* 23: 123–138.
10. Kunda, Z. 1999. *Social cognition: Making sense of people.* Cambridge, MA: MIT Press.
11. Busenitz, L.W. & Barney, J.B. 1997. Differences between entrepreneurs and managers in large organizations: Biases and heuristics in strategic decision-making. *Journal of Business Venturing* 12: 9–30.
12. Krueger, N.F., Jr. 2003. The cognitive psychology of entrepreneurship. In Z. Acs & D.B. Audrestsch (eds.). *Handbook of entrepreneurial research.* London: Kluwer Law International.
13. See Note 7.
14. Simon, M., Houghton, S.M., & Aquino, K. 2000. Cognitive biases, risk perception, and venture formation: How individual decide to start companies. *Journal of Business Venturing* 15: 113–134.
15. Ross, J., & Staw, B.M. 1993. Organizational escalation and exit: Lessons form the Shoreham nuclear power plant. *Academy of Management Journal* 36: 701–732.

16 Lubart, T.T., & Sternberg, R.J. 1995. An investment approach to creativity: Theory and data. In S.M. Smith, T.B. Ward, & R.A. Finke (eds.). *The creative copgnition approach* (pp. 269–302). Cambridge, MA: MIT Press.

17 Ward, T.B. (in press). Cognition, creativity, and entrepreneurship. *Journal of Business Venturing.*

18 Sternberg, R.J., & Grigorenko, E.L. 2000. *Practical intelligence in everyday life.* New York: Cambridge University Press.

19 Sternberg, R.J. 1999. (ed.). T*he nature of cognition.* Cambridge, MA: MIT Press.

20 Sternberg, R.J. (in press). Successful intelligence as a basis for entrepreneurship. *Journal of Business Venturing.*

21 Baron, R.A., & Markman, G.D. 2000. Beyond social capital: The role of social skills in entrepreneurs' success. *Academy of Management Executive* 14: 106–116.

22 See note 14.

23 Sternberg, R.J., & Lubart, T.I. 1995. *Defying the crowd: Cultivating creavity in a culture of conformity.* New York: Free Press.

24 Sternberg, R.J., & Lubart, T.I. 1995. *Defying the crowd: Cultivating creativity in a culture of conformity.* New York: Free Press.

25 See note 20.

26 Lerner, M., & Hendeles, Y. 1993. New entrepreneurs and entrepreneurial aspirations among immigrants from the former USSR in Israel. In N. Churchill, S. Birley, W. Bygrave, J. Coutriaux, E. Gatewood, F. Hoy, & W. Wetzel (eds.). *Frontiers of entrepreneurship research.* Babson Park: Babson College.

27 Johansson, E. 2000. Self-employment and liquidity constraints: Evidence from Finland. *Scandianivian Journal of Economics* 102: 123–124.

28 Klepper, S. & Sleeper, S. 2000. Entry by spinoffs. *Working Paper*, Carnegie Mellon University.

29 Durand, R., & Coeurderoy, R. 2001. Age, order of entry, strategic orientation, and organizational performance. *Journal of Business Venturing* 16: 471–494.

30 Dollinger, M.J. 2003. *Entrepreneurship.* 3rd ed. Upper Saddle River, NJ: Prentice-Hall.

31 Shane, S. 2000. Prior knowledge and the discovery of entrepreneurial opportunities. *Organizational Science* 11(4): 448–469.

32 Sarasvathy, D., Simon, H., & Lave, L. 1998. Perceiving and managing business risks: Differences between entrepreneurs and bankers. *Journal of Economic Behavior and Organization* 33: 207–225.

33 See note 12.

34 See note 25.

35 Blanchflower, D., & Oswald, A. 1998. What makes an entrepreneur? *Journal of Labor Economics* 16: 26–60.

36 Aldrich, H. 1999. *Organizations evolving.* London: Sage.

37 Gaglio, C., & Katz, J. 2001. The psychological basis of opportunity identification: Entrepreneurial alertness. *Small Business Economics* 16: 95–111.

38 See note 28.

39 Hmieleski, K.M., & Corbett, A.C. 2003. Improvisation as a framework for investigating entrepreneurial action. Paper presented at the Meetings of the Academy of Management, August, 2003, Seattle, WA.

40 Van Praag, C., & Cramer, J. 2001. The roots of entrepreneurship and labour demand: Individual ability and low risk aversion. *Economica*, February, 45–62.

41 Sternberg, see note 17.

42 Hyrsky, K., & Kangasharju, A. 1998. Adapters and innovators in non-urban environment. In P. Reynolds, W. Bygrave, N. Carter, S. Manigart, C. Mason, G. Meyer, & K. Shaver (eds.). *Frontiers of entrepreneurship research.* Babson Park: Babson College.

43 Baron, R.A. (under review). *Opportunity recognition: A cognitive perspective.*

44 Swets, J.A. 1992. The science of choosing the right decision threshold in high-stakes diagnostics. *American Psychologist* 47: 522–532.

45 Brockner, J., Higgins, E.T., & Low, M.B. (in press). Regulatory focus theory and the entrepreneurial process. *Journal of Business Venturing.*

46 Higgins, E.T., 1998. Promotion and prevention: Regulatory focus as a motivational principle. In M.P. Zanna (ed.). *Advances in experimental social psychology* (Vol. 30, pp. 1–46). New York: Academic Press.

47 Higgins, E.T., & Silberman, I. 1998. Development of regulatory focus: Promotion and prevention as ways of living. In J. Heckhausen & C.S. Dweck (eds.). *Motivation and self-regulation across the life span* (pp. 798–113). New York: Cambridge University Press.

48 Liberman, N., Idson, L.C., Camacho, C.J., & Higgins, E.T. 1999. Promotion and prevention choices between stability and change. *Journal of Personality and Social Psychology* 77: 1135–1145.

49 Brockner, J., Higgins, E.T., & Low, M.B. (in press). Regulatory focus theory and the entrepreneurial process. *Journal of Business Venturing.*

50 Fiet, J.O., Gupta, M., & Zurada, J. 2003. Evaluating the wealth creating potential of venture ideas. Paper presented at the Babson-Kaufman Entrepreneurship Research Conference, June 2003, Babson Park, MA.

PART 2

ASSEMBLING THE RESOURCES

CHAPTER 4

Acquiring Essential Information: Why "Look Before You Leap" Is Truly Good Advice for Entrepreneurs

CHAPTER 5

Assembling the Team: Acquiring and Utilizing Essential Human Resources

CHAPTER 6

Financing New Ventures

CHAPTER 7

Writing an Effective Business Plan: Crafting a Road Map to Success

It is one thing to have an idea for a new product or service, but quite another to turn it into an actual new venture. In this section, we describe the resources needed to actually launch a new company. These include information about markets, environmental and legal issues, human resources—the people whose skills, knowledge, motivation, and energy will provide the forward momentum of the new venture, and financial resources—the capital needed to launch the business. An overview of these resources and how they will be used to create a viable company is provided by a formal business plan, which many entrepreneurs prepare for two reasons: to assist them in obtaining financial support from investors and to help them formulate specific goals and appropriate strategies for reaching them.

ACQUIRING ESSENTIAL INFORMATION: WHY "LOOK BEFORE YOU LEAP" IS TRULY GOOD ADVICE FOR ENTREPRENEURS

LEARNING OBJECTIVES

After reading this chapter, you should be able to:

1. Explain why entrepreneurs need to gather several kinds of information before launching their new venture and describe the nature of that information.

2. Explain why entrepreneurs need marketing information before beginning, and ways of gathering this information.

3. Define perceptual mapping and explain how its results can assist entrepreneurs in designing their products.

4. List and describe various ways in which taxation can affect new ventures.

5. List and describe government regulations and laws concerning the health, safety, and well-being of employees with which entrepreneurs should be familiar.

6. Describe sources of error in the interpretation of information by decision-making groups. Be sure to include early favorites, group polarization, and groupthink.

7. Describe various techniques for countering the effects of these sources of error.

Market Information: Determining What Your Customers Really Want
  Direct Techniques for Gathering Market Information: Surveys, Perceptual Mapping, and Focus Groups
  Indirect Techniques for Gathering Market Information: The Entrepreneur as Sherlock Holmes

Government Policies and Regulations: How They Affect New Ventures
  Taxes: An Important Consideration for Entrepreneurs
  Government Policy: Increasingly Favorable to New Ventures

Government Regulations: What Every Entrepreneur Should Know

Interpreting Information: Potential Pitfalls for Decision-Making Groups
  Accepting "Early Favorites": Or, Why the Initial Majority Usually Wins
  Group Polarization: Why Groups Often *Do* Go off the Deep End
  Groupthink: When Too Much Cohesion Among Group Members Is a Dangerous Thing
  Ignoring Unshared Information
  Improving Group Decisions: Techniques for Countering the Pitfalls

> "The facts: nothing matters but the facts:
> worship of the facts leads to everything,
> to happiness first of all, and then to wealth."
> (Edmond De Goncourt, 1888)

Like many men, I (Robert Baron) like tools and gadgets. In fact, I often buy them at flea markets, antique shows, and estate sales. I have a complete array of modern tools in my woodworking shop, so what I tend to collect, mainly, is unusual tools and gadgets—ones I have never seen before. For instance, in my desk drawer I have a "Stapleless Stapler," a device that connects pieces of paper without staples; in my kitchen is an all-purpose tool known as "The Open All" for opening every kind of bottle, jar, and can—and for cracking nuts, too! As you can see from Figure 4.1, these are beautiful tools, made of high-quality stainless steel. But I'm also willing to bet you have never seen one. Why? Because these tools, and many others I have collected over the years, were *not* commercial successes. In fact, they have generally disappeared without a trace and without generating a large volume of sales. The companies that produced them, too, have vanished, and this suggests that many of these tools were invented by entrepreneurs who founded companies to bring them to market. (In fact, I know that this is true for the two items shown in Figure 4.1, because I traced them through the U.S. Patent and Trademark Office's Web site.)

So far, none of this is surprising: As we noted in Chapter 1, most new ventures founded by entrepreneurs fail within a few years. What's surprising about these products, though, is the fact that they got as far as they did: That they were actually manufactured and sold, despite the fact that they do not work very well. In fact, when I ask friends who try them out whether they would buy one, they uniformly reply "No way!" So how did these products ever come to exist? Why did entre-preneurs invest their time, energy, and perhaps life savings in bringing these essentially useless products to market? The answer, I believe, centers around the fact that the entrepreneurs in question simply did not do their homework: they did not attempt to find out whether there was a potential market for their products—whether people would actually want to buy and use them—and whether other, competing (and perhaps superior) products already existed. Instead, they "fell in love" with their inventions and managed to convince other persons that these products had a real future. In fact, though, these inventions were probably doomed from the start. For instance, the Stapleless Stapler appeared in the mid-1950s, just when small staplers that could fit in a pocket or purse were introduced. These were so convenient, and so inexpensive, that the Stapleless Stapler never had a chance!

Figure 4.1 Products That Quickly Vanished Without a Trace

Have you ever seen these products? Probably not. They were introduced and then quickly vanished from the marketplace. One reason they suffered this sad fate is that the entrepreneurs who invented them and launched new ventures to manufacture and promote them did not do their homework. They did not gather essential information on such issues as the reactions of potential customers, competing products, and so on. The result? Economic disaster!

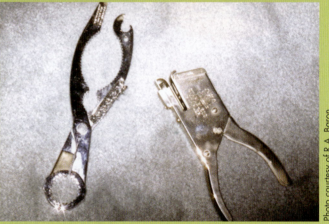

Photo courtesy of R.A. Baron.

Clearly, there is an important moral for entrepreneurs in this and many other tales of failed new products: Before launching a new company, it is *crucial* for entrepreneurs to gather several kinds of basic information—information that will tell them whether their new venture is really feasible, what specific form their new products and services should take, and how these products and services can be effectively marketed. In other words, as the quote suggests, entrepreneurs should pay careful attention to the *facts*—to gathering and interpreting them; failure to do so can lead to truly disastrous outcomes.

What kinds of information do entrepreneurs need before launching their new ventures? As noted in Chapter 2, many aspects of an industry strongly determine the likelihood that new ventures in it will succeed. For instance, it is easier for new ventures to succeed in industries that are experiencing rapid growth, in which most innovations come from small companies, that are *not* advertising intensive, and in industries that are early in their life cycle. So certainly, entrepreneurs should begin by carefully considering such information.

In addition, however, entrepreneurs need to gather other kinds of information before getting started. Doing so can help them avoid many problems and pitfalls that can destroy their young companies—and their hopes. Many different kinds of information can prove useful in this regard. However, several are especially crucial: (1) marketing information—information about the markets entrepreneurs hope to enter, including the preferences and needs of potential customers, (2) information regarding government regulations and policies, including taxation, and (3) information regarding various laws that strongly affect all businesses, including new ventures. We will return to all of these topics in later chapters of this book, when we address the growth and development of new ventures, but it is important to begin consideration of them here because information about them is definitely part of the total package of resources entrepreneurs should acquire before launching new ventures.

In the first sections of this chapter, we will focus on each of these topics: marketing information, information about taxation, government regulations and policies, and laws. Then, in a final section, we will examine the next step in the process: interpretation of facts and information about these issues. As we'll soon see, performing this task is neither simple nor straightforward because there are many factors that influence—and sometimes strongly distort—the accurate interpretation of information, and the decisions based on such interpretation. We will examine several of the most important of these factors and will also suggest ways of minimizing the dangers they pose.

KEY POINTS

- Many new products that are brought to market disappear without attaining widespread use.
- One major reason why this is so is that the entrepreneurs who found new ventures to develop these products or services do not do their homework: They fail to acquire essential information before beginning.
- Among the most important kinds of information entrepreneurs need are (1) marketing information, (2) information about government regulations and policies, including taxation, and (3) information about relevant laws.
- Information on these issues should be gathered prior to the launch of new ventures, because it can help entrepreneurs avoid many problems and pitfalls.
- Even if entrepreneurs gather information on these topics, they face the task of interpreting it accurately; this, too, can pose hazards for new ventures.

MARKET INFORMATION: DETERMINING WHAT YOUR CUSTOMERS REALLY WANT

Daniel J. Borstein, a well-known historian, once remarked (1961): "We read advertisements . . . to discover and enlarge our desires. We are always ready . . . to discover, from the announcement of a new product, what we have all along wanted without really knowing it." Borstein was a historian but, in a sense, he was a good psychologist, too, because the findings of modern cognitive science confirm his words: Often, we are *not* very good at describing our needs or, to put it slightly differently, at identifying the factors that affect our behavior. For instance, we know that we like (or dislike) something— a new product, a prospective employee, a new idea—but we aren't clear as to *why* we have these reactions; like the character in Figure 4.2, we know that we want to do something—but we aren't sure why.

This raises a perplexing question for entrepreneurs. On the one hand, they need marketing information before launching their companies—information on how potential customers will react to and evaluate the products or services they provide, and who these potential customers really are. (As we will note later, there can be some interesting surprises in this respect, because new products or services are often adopted by different customers than entrepreneurs initially anticipate.) Marketing information, and a detailed marketing plan explaining how the new product or service will be promoted, are usually included in business plans, and venture capitalists and other potential investors often read this information carefully. Further, existing evidence suggests that new ventures that draw a careful bead on specific markets or specific geographic areas are more successful than ones that do not focus their efforts and products in this way.[1] In Chapter 9, we will discuss marketing in new ventures and examine some of these topics in greater detail. But, even before the company gets to the stage of marketing a new product, it needs to gather information from customers. This raises an important question that entrepreneurs should begin considering before they launch a new venture: How can such information be gathered? The overall answer is:

Figure 4.2 Often, We Don't Know the Causes of Our Own Preferences or Behavior

Like the character in this cartoon, we often do not fully understand the reasons why we behave in various ways.

Through several different techniques. None are perfect, but together, they can give entrepreneurs a useful "handle" on how potential customers will react to their product, and why they will—or will not—be willing to buy it.

Direct Techniques for Gathering Market Information: Surveys, Perceptual Mapping, and Focus Groups

The most obvious approach to finding out how people will react to a new product or service is simply to ask them. This is true for most products except those that are really novel and create new markets. Marketing such products requires different techniques, which we will discuss in Chapter 9. However, just asking customers how they feel about a new product also creates some problems even when the product isn't totally new because it can yield jumbled information that is difficult to interpret. Even worse, it is a basic principle in the field of marketing, and in the study of human behavior generally, that the answers you get from people depend strongly on the questions you ask. For instance, consider the "Stapleless Stapler" once again. Perhaps the entrepreneur who invented it did try to gather marketing information before launching a new venture. But consider what she or he would have learned if they posed questions such as these to prospective customers: "Isn't it a nuisance when a stapler runs out of staples?" "Do you ever cut yourself or break a nail trying to pull staples out of documents?" The answers might well suggest that people are greatly dissatisfied with existing staplers; in fact, though, these are petty annoyances that are more than offset by the convenience of this product. Yet, the entrepreneur might not realize this because she or he has asked "loaded" questions almost certain to put the new product in a favorable light. Although this may sound absurd—who would fall prey to such obvious traps?—it is not: Cognitive science indicates that we are all subject to a strong *confirmation bias*—a powerful tendency to notice and collect information that confirms our beliefs and preferences. So, never underestimate the power of commitment to an idea (or product): The dangers of falling in love with one's own invention are all too real to overlook.

In order to obtain useful marketing information about their new products or services, therefore, entrepreneurs need to approach this task in a more systematic manner and assure that they do indeed ask appropriate questions that do not load the dice in favor of the conclusions they want to reach (e.g., that their new product is one consumers badly want and will rush out to buy). There are several techniques for obtaining such information, but because we will return to marketing again later in this text, here we will just touch on a few.

Customer Surveys

One useful way to obtain marketing information is to have persons in the target group (the people you expect to be future customers) compare your product with existing ones. This can be done by showing them each product and asking them to rate each one on a number of different dimensions (e.g., low to high in terms of quality, usefulness, value, etc.). In such surveys, it is often common practice to use 5-point scales: Each product is rated as Very Low, Low, Moderate, High, or Very High on each dimension being considered. If the questions on such surveys are chosen carefully and the people who evaluate the products and respond to the questions are truly representative of potential customers, valuable information can be obtained.

Please note, though, that such surveys rest on an assumption that is sometimes very shaky: We already know the dimensions along which potential customers perceive and evaluate products. Sometimes this is obvious. For instance, a travel alarm that fails to keep accurate time or fails to go off at the time set is useless, so *accuracy* and *reliability* are almost certainly key dimensions for such a product. Size, too, probably matters—although it is difficult to tell in advance whether customers weight this as heavily as accuracy and reliability. Perhaps they are willing to trade off size for a loud alarm, for instance. With respect to other products—especially very new ones, however—it is often difficult to tell, in advance, what features will be most important to customers. To get at this very basic question, another technique is often useful—one known as *perceptual mapping*.

Perceptual Mapping: Identifying Key Product Dimensions

Have you ever left your keys, eyeglasses, or checkbook somewhere in your home or apartment and then couldn't find it? If so, welcome to the club. Almost everyone has experiences like this, and some of us have them every day! This suggests an interesting possibility for a new product: a small device that can be attached to "disappearing" items like keys or eyeglasses, one that can then be triggered to emit an audible (or visible) signal by a handheld control device. Sound interesting? In fact, the idea is not new: Several products that accomplish this feat already exist, but none has been very successful to date. This raises an intriguing question: Why not? What is it about these existing products that fails to satisfy the needs of potential customers, so that they are not rushing out to buy these products? More importantly, how would an entrepreneur who wants to fill this need find out just what's lacking in existing products so that she or he can design a better one?

This is where **perceptual mapping** enters the picture.[2] Perceptual mapping refers to a kind of diagram of potential customer's perceptions—a map that reveals the key dimensions along which they perceive products and evaluate them. The central idea is this: When people choose among existing, competing products, they are obviously comparing them on various dimensions and then selecting the product that they perceive most favorably on some, or all, of these dimensions. But what, exactly, *are* these dimensions? Some are obvious, such as price, perceived quality, and various aspects of a product's appearance. But others are not so easy to discern. For instance, consider the lost object locating devices mentioned earlier. On what dimensions are potential customers evaluating them? Several possibilities come to mind: size, loudness (or brightness) of the signal they emit, ease with which they can be attached to various objects, and so on. But these are just guesses: Until we conduct careful market research, we really don't know whether potential customers are actually comparing and evaluating the products on these dimensions or on others we haven't been able to guess. To find, out we use perceptual mapping.

Focus Groups: One Technique for Understanding How Consumers Perceive and Evaluate Products

Although this can be a complex process and can be carried out in several ways, one popular means of conducting it involves **focus groups**—groups of about 8 to 12 people who are similar to potential customers and who meet for one to two hours to describe their perceptions of and reactions to relevant products. Focus groups are conducted by a moderator, whose task it is to elicit a broad range of opinions from participants. The moderator does this by creating a relaxed, friendly atmosphere for the discussion and by assuring that all participants get a chance to express their views. The moderator also probes for the meaning of statements people make—the thoughts, ideas, and reactions behind the words. The basic goal is to identify the key dimensions along which focus group members perceive and evaluate various products. In order to reach this objective, a procedure known as the *repertory grid* is often used. Each product being considered is listed on a separate index card. The deck is then shuffled and three cards are chosen, often by a participant in the focus group. The moderator then asks members of the focus group to describe ways in which any two of the products are similar and the third is different. This leads to initial identification of a dimension along which people perceive the product. For instance, for item-locator devices, size might emerge as one dimension and weight as another. The process is repeated with new sets of three cards until no new dimensions appear. Then, after the key dimensions have been identified, participants rate the products along each of these dimensions and discuss these ratings until consensus is reached.

The overall result is identification of the dimensions along which products of the type being considered are actually perceived and evaluated by potential customers, plus relative rankings of the products in question along these dimensions. Results are then often presented in the form of a chart, such as the one in Figure 4.3. Each item is rated on each dimension, and comparisons between them can then be made. As you can see, none of the products is an obvious "winner"—products that score high on one dimension often score low on others, and vice versa. This suggests why none of the products considered in this focus group have reaped large sales: None does a good overall job of meeting customer needs. A product that scored high on several of the key dimensions, in contrast, might well be more successful—and this, in turn, can constitute a major opportunity for astute entrepreneurs. Please note: Such charts are definitely *not* a "magic formula" for understanding customer preferences—far from it. Interpreting human judgments is *always* a complex matter, and market research is often more art than science; at best, it provides a general guide to consumers' views and reactions—not precise measurements of these in the sense that physical measurements can be precise. So please do interpret charts such as the one shown in Figure 4.3 with a healthy degree of caution. Still, the entrepreneur that launches a new venture without attempting to determine, in advance, how potential customers will react to a new product or service is on very shaky ground indeed. For this reason, market information is an essential, not a luxury, and should definitely be part of entrepreneurs' pre-launch agenda.

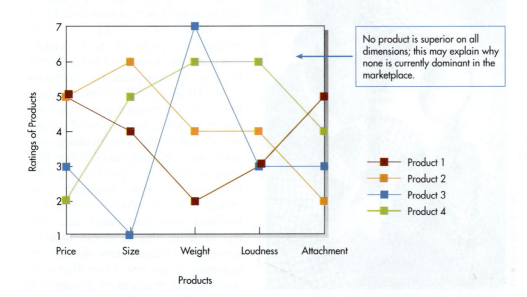

Figure 4.3 Perceptual Maps for Object Locaters: No Clear Winner

Products for locating lost objects vary along several key dimensions (price, size, weight, loudness of signal), but no single product is high on all these dimensions. The fact that there is no clear "winner" may explain why none of these products has yet generated large sales. (Please note: Such charts should be interpreted with a healthy degree of caution; they provide rough estimates of customers' preferences—not precise measurements of them.)

No product is superior on all dimensions; this may explain why none is currently dominant in the marketplace.

Indirect Techniques for Gathering Market Information: The Entrepreneur as Sherlock Holmes

In one famous story involving Sherlock Holmes, Sir Arthur Conan Doyle's famous detective, Holmes amazes Dr. Watson by stating—correctly, it turns out—that one physician's practice is in decline while that of another physician, whose office is next door, is on the rise. When Watson asks Holmes how he knew this, Holmes points to the steps leading into the two offices: One shows much more recent wear than the other. "Elementary, my dear Watson," Holmes remarks (see Figure 4.4).

In this case, Holmes has used an *indirect method* for measuring the preferences of patients—who can be viewed as the physician's customers. Similarly, if they are perceptive, entrepreneurs, too, can profit from indirect methods for gathering such information. In other words, they can use what is often known as *secondary data*—data they do not collect themselves, but which can still be very useful. For instance, they can examine the sales of competing products to see if any trends emerge—some rising in popularity, others declining. This may suggest that certain features or combinations of features are gaining or losing appeal to potential customers. Similarly, they can examine demographic data (e.g., the *Statistical Abstract of the United States* or the *Sourcebook of Zip Code Demographics*) to see how populations are changing: growing or declining in a given area, changing in terms of age makeup, ethnic background, and so on.

Such sources of data can help entrepreneurs identify the best markets for their products before they launch a new venture. In some cases, they can even suggest the basis for a successful company. For instance, consider Brian Scudamore, CEO of 1-800-Got Junk? This Canadian company, which is now located in more than two dozen U.S. cities, helps people get rid of . . . their junk! Because most of us are incredibly weak when it comes to deciding to get rid of things we have had for years but no longer use, you might wonder how Scudamore came up with this idea. Mainly on the basis of indirect marketing information. He noticed, for instance, that storage facilities were experiencing a sharp drop in business. This suggested to him that more people were getting rid of their unneeded possessions at a higher rate than in the past. Why? Perhaps tough economic conditions play a key role: An increasing number of persons were concluding that they could no longer afford to pay to store items they did not use or want. By carefully observing these trends (forms of indirect market information), Scudamore was able to come up with the idea for his new company, and to cash in handsomely on the new "Get rid of it!" ethic that seems to be emerging.

Figure 4.4 Indirect Marketing Information: Often Useful

Sherlock Holmes often used indirect methods to solve mysteries. In one of his many adventures, he correctly determined that one physician was much more popular than another, whose office was next door. How did he do it? By noticing that the steps leading to the popular doctor's office showed greater recent wear than those leading to his neighbor's office. In a similar manner, entrepreneurs can use indirect methods (secondary data) for gathering information about potential markets for their new products or services.

Index Stock Imagery, Inc.

Before concluding, we should emphasize one additional point: Marketing information—even if excellent in every respect—is no guarantee of success. To the extent a product or service is truly new, it may be difficult for consumers to compare it with existing products. We will consider this point in more detail in Chapter 9, but here are a few examples of what we mean. History is filled with products that were designed for one use and one market but, in fact, found success in a different one. For instance, consider personal computers. When IBM launched this new product in 1981, the company was absolutely convinced that it would be used only in business contexts: After all, who would want this business tool for home use? Within a few short years, however, it became clear that consumers were much more inventive at developing uses for a personal computer than IBM's engineers—or their marketing division!—ever dreamed.

Here's another one: Silly Putty was developed, quite by accident during World War II, when chemists were searching for a silicone-based rubber substitute. It was unsuitable for that use, but soon—and unexpectedly—became a popular children's toy. Recently, however, it has found another market: as an aid to stress-reduction among harried adults.[3] Busy executives seem to find bouncing and stretching this elastic substance quite relaxing. But small amounts (the package for children contains 0.5 ounces) are not enough to satisfy these adult appetites, so they buy it by the pound. In fact, groups of Silly Putty fans join together to order the manufacturer's minimum amount of pounds. This gives each person 10 pounds or more of the bouncing wonder. Certainly, this is a dramatic example of a product that has found a new market niche—one its makers probably never dreamed would emerge. So yes, market information is often very helpful to entrepreneurs, but it is just one of several kinds of information they need in order to achieve the success they hope to achieve.

KEY POINTS

- Before launching a new venture, entrepreneurs need reliable marketing information—information on how potential customers will react to and evaluate the products or services they provide.
- Because people are not very successful at identifying the factors that influence their behavior, simply asking them why they like or dislike various products is not an effective approach.
- Perceptual mapping, one technique for identifying the dimensions along which customers evaluate various products, is often a useful initial step.
- One useful procedure for gathering such information is focus groups—groups of about 8 to 12 people who are similar to potential customers and who meet for one to two hours to describe their perceptions of and reactions to relevant products.
- In addition to gathering their own marketing information, entrepreneurs can also often use indirect or secondary data, information gathered by others.
- Although marketing data are often useful to entrepreneurs, they are no guarantee of success, especially with respect to new products or services because consumers may find comparing these to existing products a difficult task, and because unexpected uses for such products may quickly emerge.

GOVERNMENT POLICIES AND REGULATIONS: HOW THEY AFFECT NEW VENTURES

Opinions concerning the proper relationship of government to business—including new ventures—differ greatly. There is little doubt, however, that the policies and regulations governments adopt strongly affect the fortunes of new ventures: These policies and regulations make it harder or easier to start a new venture, harder or easier to run one, and harder or easier to attain success. I (Robert Baron) had firsthand experience with this fact recently, when I lived in France. While there, I asked my colleagues in the school of management to describe how one would go about starting a new company in France. Their replies were quite discouraging. The French government is deeply involved in the entire economy, and starting a business would require dealing with a vast array of regulations and "red tape."

In the United States, in contrast, I was able to start a new company within a matter of days, and with a minimum of government-erected barriers. In other words, the economy is more centralized in France than in the United States, where centralization refers to the degree to which one political actor (in this case, the government) coordinates the economic, political, and social activity in a society. So to start a business in France, one needs many more permits from the central government than it takes to start the same business in the United States. Clearly, then, from "day one," the policies adopted by specific governments play a role in the entrepreneurial process.

For this reason, it is crucial that entrepreneurs contemplating a new venture gather relevant information on the government policies and regulations that will, potentially, affect their business. What kind of information should they seek? This depends, to an important degree, on the kind of business in question. For instance, companies that engage in manufacturing or handle potentially dangerous or toxic substances may be subject to more numerous and stronger regulations than ones that provide services. In this discussion, therefore, we will focus on regulations and policies that are likely to have an impact on a very wide range of new ventures.

Taxes: An Important Consideration for Entrepreneurs

No one likes taxes, but like it or not, we all have to pay them—and new ventures are no exception to this general rule. For this reason, it is important for entrepreneurs to gather information on taxation before launching a new venture. Tax codes are immense documents (the one for the federal government in the United States is more than 1,600 pages long!), so here we can only touch briefly on some of the key issues for entrepreneurs.

Overall Tax Rate

The marginal tax rate is the highest rate at which individuals or corporations are taxed, and not surprisingly, there is considerable evidence suggesting that as these rates rise, the level of entrepreneurial activity in a taxing unit (state, country) falls. For instance, the higher the marginal tax rate in the United States, the lower the rate of self-employment.[4] Similarly, the higher the marginal tax rates in several European countries, the lower the self-employment rates.[5] Perhaps most revealing of all is a study comparing tax rates and firm formation in the United States and Sweden.[6] Results indicated that firm foundation rates are higher in the United States, which has a lower tax rate, while at the same time, new technology is actually produced at a higher rate per capita in Sweden. This suggests that government taxation policies influence the decisions of individual entrepreneurs to found new ventures, but do not in and of themselves inhibit technological progress. Of course, if tax rates rise to very high levels, entrepreneurs may seek ways of reducing them, for instance, converting profits to capital gains insofar as this is feasible. In that case, increases in marginal tax rates may not reduce entrepreneurial activity. In general, though, high marginal tax rates do seem to have a negative impact on the formation of new ventures.

Overall, it appears that if governments wish to encourage the formation of new ventures, they should reduce marginal tax rates. When these rates are high, the potential gains to entrepreneurs, who can keep only a small fraction of the profits they earn, are too small to offset the risks involved in starting new ventures. The result? Economic growth of the entire society may be slowed.

Legal Forms of New Ventures and Tax Rates

We will consider the legal forms new ventures can take in detail in Chapter 8. Here, therefore, we will simply call attention to the fact that the legal form of a new venture can affect the taxes it, and its founders, must pay. One of the first decisions entrepreneurs have to make is whether their company should be a regular C corporation or a Subchapter S corporation. The difference? In a regular corporation, profits and losses remain in the company, and the corporation pays taxes on any declared profits. In a Subchapter S corporation, in contrast, profits and losses flow through to the shareholders, and they pay any taxes due as individuals, according to their own tax bracket. Many new ventures opt for the latter choice, but then, if they grow and prosper, switch to regular status. In any case, taxation is an important issue and entrepreneurs should gather information about it before beginning. When a company is new and profits seem a distant goal, it is easy to focus attention elsewhere. But unless appropriate decisions are made early on, total tax burden can be increased, and it may be too late to take steps to reduce it. So as is true with respect to all tax planning, "early" and "in advance" are far better than "late" or "after the fact."

Tax Incentives

So far, this discussion has been somewhat discouraging: We have emphasized the adverse effects of taxation on entrepreneurial activities. Before concluding this brief consideration of tax-related issues, therefore, we should note that some government policies are designed specifically to help new ventures. One issue entrepreneurs should consider carefully, for example, is whether their new ventures are eligible for special tax incentives. For instance, manufacturing companies—or companies that purchase equipment—can benefit from *depreciation*, an aspect of the tax code that allows businesses to deduct from earnings a portion of the cost of the equipment on a yearly basis for a set period of time. Similarly, the interest on bank loans may be deductible to a corporation, while other forms of financing, such as equity-financed loans, receive less favorable treatment.

Here's yet another example: Both federal and state governments often offer tax incentives to companies that locate in certain geographic regions, or that choose to renovate and improve older buildings that have been designated as having historical significance. For instance, I (Robert Baron) recently visited an antique mall located within an old factory. The developers of this mall received substantial tax breaks for bringing this historic structure back to life (see Figure 4.5). A new venture seeking to hold its taxes to a minimum might well consider such options to the extent they are feasible.

Another form of tax relief offered to new ventures is a *tax credit* for research and development activities. Companies that engage in such activities can deduct the costs dollar-for-dollar from their tax bills. To qualify, though, they must demonstrate that their efforts are directed toward discovering information that is "technological in nature," a so-called *discovery test*. But what is the precise definition of information that is "technological in nature"? One small company, Tax and Accounting Software Corp. of Tulsa, Oklahoma, tested the existing Internal Revenue Service definition when it claimed that its new software offered features not available in existing accounting software; on this basis, it claimed a tax credit for expenses associated with developing this product. The IRS challenged this claim and although it lost the first round, won on appeal. However, even while rejecting TAASC's claim for a tax credit, the court broadened the definition of "technological in nature," and so opened the door to this credit for many new ventures. Moreover, the IRS, seeking to avoid a further appeal by TAASC, is now working on a revised—and broadened—definition. So stay tuned: The outcome is almost certain to be beneficial for new ventures.

One final point: It is important to note that in the United States (and in many other countries, too), there are several layers of government: federal, state or provincial, and local (county, city, etc.). All of these must be considered carefully because the taxes they impose can be far from trivial. So once again, entrepreneurs should gather pertinent information on these matters before launching a new venture.

Figure 4.5 Tax Incentives for Specific Locations: A Potential Break for New Ventures

The antique mall shown here is in a former factory building that has been designated by the state where it is located as a historic site. As a result, the entrepreneurs who developed this business received substantial tax incentives for doing so.

Government Policy: Increasingly Favorable to New Ventures

We should also briefly mention the fact that the relationship between entrepreneurs and government is a two-way street. Government tax policies and regulations affect new ventures in many ways. But entrepreneurs, in turn, have acquired a growing voice in shaping government policy, especially during the past two decades and especially in the United States, where their contribution to the strength of the economy has been increasingly recognized. Legislation specifically designed to reduce

Photo courtesy of R.A. Baron.

the financial burdens of government regulations on new businesses has been enacted and has helped lessen these burdens to a degree. For instance, the Small Business Regulatory Enforcement Fairness Act (1996) requires agencies issuing regulations to assist small-business operators in understanding and complying with the rules. Further, these agencies were empowered to reduce or waive penalties for violations of regulatory requirements for small businesses. Similarly, the Unfunded Mandates Reform Act (1995) requires agencies to consider the cost of new federal mandates and to assure that these do not pose an unfair burden on small businesses.

Government Support of Innovation

In the United States and many other countries, governments have become increasingly aware of the importance, for economic health, of encouraging innovation. In the United States, this awareness was translated into concrete action in 1982, with the passage of the Small Business Innovation Development Act (further strengthened and expanded by the Small Business Research and Development Enhancement Act of 1992). These acts created the **Small Business Innovation Research (SBIR)** program, which requires participating federal agencies to set aside 2 percent of their budgets for funding contracts, grants, or cooperative agreements through the SBIR. The agencies identify research and development needs, and these are published in a master list by the SBA (Small Business Administration). The amounts involved are truly large: In recent years, they have exceeded $4 billion per year.

Start-up ventures (or any small business) can submit proposals for research projects directly to the appropriate agencies. Awards are made on a competitive basis and generally involve three distinct phases. During Phase 1, which lasts about six months, funds (up to $100,000) are used to evaluate the technical merit and feasibility of an idea. During Phase 2, which can last for up to two years, promising projects are continued and evidence of progress toward commercialization is required. New ventures can receive up to $750,000 during this phase. In Phase 3, it is expected that private sector support will be attained, and that the new product or service will be brought to the point at which it can enter the marketplace. During this phase, the agency or agencies involved may offer production contracts and other financial incentives. The overall goal is that of helping bring innovative ideas to the point at which they become new products or services. The program is widely regarded as highly successful, and each year, thousands of new ventures participate.

Minority Entrepreneurs

In addition to the SBA, the federal government in the United States has also established a series of programs designed to help minority entrepreneurs. One of these is the *8(a) Business Development Program*. This program is designed to help minority-owned businesses enter the economic mainstream. It seeks to accomplish this goal by encouraging federal agencies to award a certain percentage of their contracts to what are known as Small Disadvantaged Businesses—businesses that are at least 50 percent owned by a socially and economically disadvantaged individual or group of individuals. Persons included in this category are African-Americans, Hispanic Americans, Asian-Pacific Americans, Subcontinent-Asian Americans, and Native Americans. Women, too, may qualify under certain conditions. Not only do minority-owned businesses receive preference with respect to contracts (a percent is "held-back" or reserved for such companies) but they also receive mentoring in the form of technical and management assistance, as well as financial assistance in the form of equity investments and/or loans. In short, the federal government in the United States has taken a number of steps to assist new ventures started by minority entrepreneurs.

That such programs have been successful is indicated by the fact that although the number of new businesses started each year has increased steadily, the number started by women and minorities has risen even more dramatically. For instance, the number of companies owned by minorities increased 168 percent between 1987 and 1997, to a total of 3.25 million businesses, which, together, employ more than 4 million persons and generate $495 billion in revenues.[7]

Yet another effort to assist minority entrepreneurs is the HubZone Empowerment Contracting Program. This program is designed to stimulate economic development in specific geographic areas by providing preferences in contracting to small businesses that are located in a HubZone or that hire employees who live in one. To be eligible for the program, the small business must meet three criteria: (1) It must be located in a historically underutilized business zone, (2) be wholly owned and controlled by U.S. citizens, and (3) draw at least 35 percent of its employees from a HubZone. HubZones are generally areas in which median household income is less than 80 percent of that for the state in which it is located, unemployment is 140 percent or more of the statewide average, or are located within federally recognized Indian reservations. The goal, of course, is to pump new life into economically disadvantaged areas by assisting new companies established in these areas (see Figure 4.6).

Overall, then, the current picture concerning the impact of government on new ventures is complex, but improving. Taxation can impose a heavy burden on new ventures, but special incentives can greatly lessen this load. Moreover, government programs designed to encourage innovation, such as the SBIR and the 8(a) Business Development Program, and to assist minority entrepreneurs can be very helpful. Entrepreneurs should acquire familiarity with these programs because in many instances, they can provide valuable resources—financial and otherwise—that can greatly assist new ventures.

Figure 4.6 HubZones: New Life for Old—and Poor—Communities

Under the HubZone Empowerment Contracting Program, new businesses started in economically disadvantaged areas receive preference in government contracting. This encourages new ventures to locate in such areas.

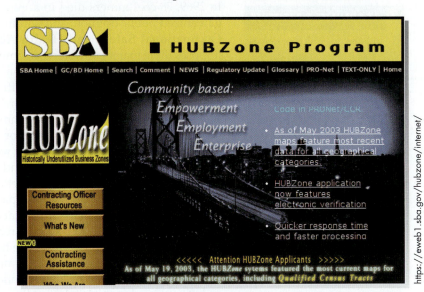

https://eweb1.sba.gov/hubzone/internet/

KEY POINTS

- Government policies concerning new ventures vary greatly from country to country, but no matter where they reside, entrepreneurs should pay careful attention to these issues.
- Taxation strongly affects the profitability of all businesses, so entrepreneurs should consider federal, state, and local tax codes carefully in planning their new ventures.
- Government policies concerning new ventures have become more favorable in many countries in recent years, and special programs designed to encourage innovation, such as the SBIR and programs designed to assist minority entrepreneurs, have been instituted.
- Entrepreneurs should be familiar with these programs because they can provide valuable resources for new ventures.

GOVERNMENT REGULATIONS: WHAT EVERY ENTREPRENEUR SHOULD KNOW

Taxation and government policies are only part of the total picture where the impact of governments on new ventures is concerned. In addition, new ventures—like all businesses—must comply with a wide array of government regulations. How many regulations exist? This should give you some idea: In the United States, the Code of Federal Regulations contains more than 65,000 pages of new and modified regulations, and these regulations are administered by 52 separate agencies employing more than 120,000 persons![8] Clearly, it is impossible for entrepreneurs to be aware of all the regulations that may impinge on their new businesses, but it is crucial that they be familiar with some of the most important ones. Failure to comply with these regulations can result in fines—or worse! So please read the following sections carefully: They outline some key regulations concerning the health, safety, and well-being of employees (important focal points of government regulations). In addition, many regulations exist for specific industries; these are so varied that it would be impossible to mention all of them here. Suffice it to say that it is truly *crucial* for entrepreneurs to be familiar with major government regulations when starting a new venture because this is definitely a case where preventing trouble is far preferable to dealing with it after it arises.

Regulations Concerning the Health and Safety of Employees: OSHA

In 1969, 78 coal miners died in a mine explosion in the United States. This tragedy galvanized public opinion, and within a year, the federal government had passed the **Occupational Safety and Health Act of 1970** (also known as **OSHA**). This act imposes three major provisions on employers: (1) to provide a safe and healthy work environment—a workplace free from recognized hazards likely to cause harm to employees; (2) to comply with specific occupational safety and health standards—rules dealing with various occupations and industries; (3) to keep records of occupational injuries and illnesses. Being small is no excuse for ignoring these provisions; in fact, businesses with 10 employees or more must keep records of any occupational injury or illness resulting in death, lost work time, or medical treatment, and retain these records for five years. These injuries and illnesses must be recorded on OSHA forms and posted annually on an employee bulletin board. This law has important "teeth" behind it: The government set up the Occupational Safety and Health Administration and charged it with the task of assuring that all companies comply with OSHA. The agency sets occupational standards, keeps a record of violations of these standards, and conducts workplace inspections to assure that the provisions of the law are being met (see Figure 4.7). Employers who fail to meet OSHA standards can receive stiff fines. Executives of firms who recklessly endanger employees may be charged with crimes and, if convicted, go to jail. In fact, in some famous cases, senior executives have been charged with murder!

It is certainly *not* our intention to frighten you: Hundreds of thousands of new ventures are started in the United States each year, and only a tiny fraction run into serious problems with respect to OSHA or other government regulations. But as an entrepreneur, you absolutely *must* become familiar with these regulations and make certain that you keep them in mind as you move from the idea stage to the functioning company stage. Failure to do so can be very costly in a many different ways.

Figure 4.7 OSHA in Action: On-Site Inspections

In the United States, OSHA conducts on-site inspections to assure that all provisions of the law it enforces are being met. New ventures are no exception to this law and must be careful to protect the health and safety of their employees.

Equal Employment Opportunity Laws: Protecting Employees Against Discrimination

Suppose that you have launched a new venture and are interviewing people for jobs in it. You ask one applicant the following question: "Are you married or single?" You ask another, "How would you describe your general physical health?" followed up by "Do you have any medical conditions that might interfere with your doing this job?" You ask a third, "Do you have any religious beliefs that would keep you from working on weekends?" Although these may seem like innocent questions, *watch out*! Asking them could get you in serious trouble. Each of these questions would be in violation of government regulations and laws protecting employees from discrimination. Perhaps a brief description of major laws and regulations designed to prevent workplace discrimination will help you see why.

The most important law protecting employees from discrimination is **Title VII of the Civil Rights Act of 1964**. This law prohibits employers from basing employment decisions on a person's race, color, religion, sex, or national origin. Although the law applies to everyone, it is focused primarily on people belonging to what is known as a **protected class**—a group that suffered discrimination in the past. In the United States, this includes African-Americans, people of Hispanic descent, Native Americans, and women. Discrimination against these groups has been defined by the courts as involving either of two major forms: *disparate treatment*—people belonging to the protected groups are treated differently simply because they belong to these groups (e.g., they are excluded from employment because they are women, African-American, and so on), and *adverse impact*—the same standard is applied to all employees, but that standard affects members of a protected class more negatively. Here's an example of adverse impact: In the past, many police departments had minimum height requirements. These have now been dropped because they produced adverse impact on women and on men of Hispanic or Asian descent, who were excluded from employment by the height requirement. Please note: Height regulations would be illegal under the law even if no intention of excluding specific groups existed.

How serious are charges of discrimination brought by an employee or a prospective employee? This should give you an idea: If someone lodges a complaint against a company with the Equal Employment Opportunity Commission (the government agency charged with enforcing this and other antidiscrimination laws), *the burden of proof falls largely on the employer*, who must then prove that company policies are not in violation of the law. Clearly, then, entrepreneurs starting new ventures should take careful note of this law, and others related to it (e.g., laws designed to prevent discrimination based on age or gender). Failure to do so can result in serious consequences. By the way, Title VII and many related laws apply to all private employers, state and local governments, and educational institutions that employ 15 or more individuals. So they are certainly relevant to new ventures once they reach this relatively small size.

Another important law of which entrepreneurs should be aware is the **Americans with Disabilities Act** of 1990 (**ADA**). This law prohibits discrimination against persons with disabilities who, despite these disabilities, are able to perform the essential functions of the job. Further, and perhaps even more important, it requires employers to provide reasonable accommodation for such persons—actions that accommodate the known disabilities of applicants or employees. Here's an actual example: A truck driver who weighed 360 pounds applied for a job as a driver and was rejected by a company because he could not fit through the doors of the company's trucks. He filed a lawsuit on the grounds that the company could have widened the doors, thus providing reasonable accommodation—and he won! Reasonable accommodation is required under the law if the person in question has all the qualifications required by the job, and if the cost will not be prohibitive to the employer. "Prohibitive" is still being defined by the courts, and would be a lower figure for a new start-up venture than for a multibillion-dollar corporation. However, our advice to entrepreneurs is straightforward: Be fully aware of this law because failure to comply with it can lead to serious consequences. Again, ADA applies to small businesses as well as large ones; once a business employs 15 or more persons, it is fully subject to this law.

We could go on to list other laws and regulations—ones relating to environmental hazards (pollution, toxic substances) are especially important and should be considered carefully. Similarly, local restrictions and regulations concerning the geographic locations of businesses can be crucial. Although it might be permissible to start a software company in a basement or garage (this has certainly been done successfully in the past!), it would almost certainly be a violation of local codes and laws to start a manufacturing operation in such locations. In such cases, what seems to be a great idea for a new venture may not seem nearly as appealing when it is considered in the light of relevant government regulations.

Overall, then, the main point we wish to make should be clear: Government regulations and laws are an important consideration for each entrepreneur preparing to launch a new venture, so knowledge of them should absolutely be on the entrepreneur's "must have" list, along with marketing information and knowledge of tax codes. What can happen to a new venture when entrepreneurs do *not* pay careful attention to these considerations? Please see the following **"Danger! Pitfall Ahead!"** section for an example that one of us experienced personally.

DANGER! PITFALL AHEAD!

When Good Ideas Fail: The Costs of Ignoring the Rules

I (Robert Baron) have spent most of my career at universities having a strong technological leaning, so over the years, I have encountered many ideas for new ventures. Most are interesting but so far away from becoming actual profit-generating businesses that I have little interest in investing in them. But one that was brought to my attention about eight years ago literally knocked me over. Basically, it was this: Huge numbers of used tires are pilling up in dumps all over the United States. Why not use these as a source of valuable raw materials? The people who came up with the idea also believed that they knew how to extract valuable resources (rubber, nylon, steel) from the tires. When tires are cooled to extremely low temperatures, they become very brittle. They can then be pulverized, thus allowing easier separation of various recyclable components.

Here, I thought, was a wonderful idea! On the one hand it solved a serious environmental problem: When tire dumps catch fire, which they often do, huge amounts of toxic smoke are released; such fires are very difficult to put out. On the other, it permitted recycling of valuable raw materials. Further, businesses actually pay tire storage facilities to take their used tires off their hands. In essence, then, the new venture would not have to pay anything for its raw materials; on the contrary, other businesses would pay it to accept them!

I was sold, and I made a personal investment in the company, Cycletech Inc. For a while, things went well. Then, lightning struck: The state Environmental Protection Agency came to our facility and closed it down. Why? Because the founders of the company (scientists and engineers) had not done their homework—they did not know about, and had neglected to meet, various state-established standards that applied to tire-holding or tire-recycling facilities. Moreover, the company was also in violation of federal regulations regarding use of the gases that froze the tires.

The result was a disaster for the new venture: Because it could no longer receive tires, it was in violation of its agreements with suppliers who promptly sued for damages. To make matters worse, the founder of the company was an abrasive person who reacted to the situation with anger and public attacks on top officials at the state environmental agency. They retaliated by finding additional violations, so that operations remained closed. Ultimately, the company became one of the "living dead"—it continues to exist but, in reality, I and everyone else who put money into it lost their investments.

This sad story is repeated over and over again: New ventures fail because their founders do not gather essential information before proceeding. Truly, in such cases, haste does make for waste—waste of capital, effort, and potentially good ideas.

KEY POINTS

- Governments have established many regulations and laws designed to protect the health and safety of employees and to regulate various industries (e.g., ones that handle dangerous or toxic substances).
- Entrepreneurs should be familiar with these because they can have major effects on new ventures.
- In the United States, the Occupational Safety and Health Act requires all employers—even very small ones—to take active measures to safeguard the health and safety of employees.
- Additional regulations and laws are designed to protect employees from discrimination (e.g., the Americans with Disabilities Act).
- Entrepreneurs must be familiar with these laws and regulations to assure that their new ventures comply with them. Failure to do so can produce truly disastrous results.

INTERPRETING INFORMATION: POTENTIAL PITFALLS FOR DECISION-MAKING GROUPS

We hope that the first section of this chapter suggests why we chose the chapter subtitle that we did: Entrepreneurs should definitely "look before they leap"—gather information on a number of important topics before actually launching a new venture. In a sense, though, this is only one side of the coin. Once information is obtained, it must be *interpreted*—in other words, it must be understood so that it can be used a basis for making good decisions and mapping future strategy. This, unfortunately, is where things become truly complicated. We noted in Chapter 3 that as human beings we are definitely *not* perfect information-processing machines. On the contrary, our thinking, reasoning, and decision making are often influenced by errors and biases that prevent these processes from being completely rational[9] (see Figure 4.8.). Thus, once information is gathered, entrepreneurs must work hard to hold these errors to a minimum. If they do not, they stand the real risk of misinterpreting the information they have gathered, and so reaching false conclusions or decisions. In Chapter 3, we described several of these potential errors and biases—ones that affect the thinking of individuals. Here, we will focus instead on processes that can strongly affect decision making by groups. Because most new ventures are founded by teams of entrepreneurs (see Chapter 5), this context is very relevant to the success of new ventures. Among the factors that can badly distort the interpretation of information, four stand out as most important: the tendency to accept "early favorites," group polarization, groupthink, and a tendency to ignore unshared information.

Accepting "Early Favorites": Or, Why the Initial Majority Usually Wins

Most people believe—often implicitly—that decisions made by groups are safer and more accurate than decisions made by individuals. After all, group members can help keep each other from going off the deep end, and one member's misinterpretation of available information can be readily corrected by one or more other members whose interpretation is more accurate. Unfortunately, research findings concerning decisions by groups suggest that these potential benefits often fail to materialize. On the contrary, what often happens in groups is that the final decision reached is the one favored by the initial majority—a choice sometimes known as the **implicit favorite**.[10] In other words, there is a tendency for groups (and individuals, too) to begin with a bias toward one interpretation or decision and then to move toward accepting it. In fact, as the process unfolds, other interpretations or options, known as **confirmation candidates**, are suggested and rejected. These are alternatives that are not really considered seriously; rather, they are raised mainly for the purpose of helping groups convince themselves that the initial favorite is indeed correct. The moral for entrepreneurs is clear: When trying to interpret information and use it as a basis for decisions, be very wary of a drift toward the implicit favorite. True, it may ultimately prove to be the right one. But it is *crucial* to consider alternative interpretations

Figure 4.8 Total Rationality: An Impossible Dream!

Mr. Dithers' reaction to an important business outcome is strongly influenced by his current mood. This is indicative of many other situations in which our thinking is influenced by numerous forms of cognitive bias or error. The upshot? Our thought is often far from totally rational.

or decisions carefully to avoid jumping to conclusions by prematurely closing the decision-making process.

Group Polarization: Why Groups Often *Do* Go off the Deep End

Earlier, we noted that many people assume that groups are less likely to make extreme decisions than individuals. In fact, however, precisely the opposite seems to be true. When several persons discuss information in order to reach a group decision about it, they show a strong tendency to shift toward views more extreme than the ones with which they began. This is known as **group polarization**, and it seems to occur in many different contexts.[11] There appear to be two major reasons why this is so. First, during group discussion of information, most arguments presented are ones favoring the group's initial preference or leaning. As a result of hearing such arguments, members literally persuade one another that the view favored initially is correct, and so they shift toward this position with increasing strength. One old saying captures this effect very neatly: "We all say it's so, we all say it's so, we all say it's so, so it *must* be so!" This is precisely what happens in many decision-making groups, as members convince each other that their interpretation of available information is correct.

A second reason why group polarization occurs involves the desire, shared by virtually everyone, to be better than average. That means that they want the views they hold to be better than those held by other groups members. What does "better" mean in this context? This depends on the specific group, but in general, it means holding the view favored by the majority even more strongly than the other members do. Again, this tendency causes group members—and the decision-making group itself—to shift further and further toward extremity.

Group polarization effects appear to be strong ones, and they are hard to resist. For this reason, entrepreneurs should be on guard against their occurrence; once they take hold, they can lead to truly disastrous decisions. For instance, there is some indication that group polarization played a role in Apple Computer's decision *not* to license its software to other manufacturers—a decision that ultimately cost it most of the personal computer market when Microsoft chose the opposite route, thus permitting many companies to produce computers using their operating system. We will consider ways of minimizing group polarization as part of a general discussion of techniques for improving the entire process of interpreting information and making decisions.

Groupthink: When Too Much Cohesion Among Group Members Is a Dangerous Thing

In Chapter 5, we will emphasize the importance of good relationships between members of a new venture's founding team.[12] In general, we will suggest, effective relationships among founding entrepreneurs is an essential ingredient in a new venture's success. But like anything else, a high level of cohesion among group members can cut both ways and pose a serious threat to effective decision making. When cohesion (unity) among group members is very high, they run the real risk of falling prey to **groupthink**—a strong tendency for decision-making groups to close ranks, cognitively, around a decision, assuming that the group *can't* be wrong, that all members must support the decision strongly, and that any information contrary to the decision should be rejected.[13] Once this collective state of mind develops, groups become unwilling—perhaps even unable—to change their decisions, even if external events suggest that these decisions are very poor ones.

For instance, consider the decision by General Electric Corporation (GE) to release PCBs (dangerous, cancer-producing chemicals) into the Hudson River in New York state. Although corporate records are generally closed to outsiders, government investigations of this issue suggest that top executives at GE decided over and over again to proceed with releasing these dangerous chemicals. They did so even though they realized that this action was a violation of various laws and regulations designed to protect the environment. Why did this happen? Perhaps because they convinced themselves—falsely—that could get away with this action indefinitely. The result: The company must now pay for costly dredging to remove these chemicals from the Hudson River—operations estimated to cost more than $1 billion.

Corporations are not the only organizations subject to groupthink, however. Consider what is, in a sense, the other side of the coin where GE is concerned: when it was sinned against rather than being the culprit itself. GE was located in the upstate New York city of Schenectady for many decades, and at one time, employed more than 40,000 persons in this area. Over the years, city and county officials repeatedly raised taxes on GE, ignoring strong protests from the company and statements suggesting that if this process were not altered, it would move to other locations. Despite these warnings, however, local governments continued to raise GE's taxes, even as the company began building new plants in other states. The result? GE reduced its payroll in the Schenectady area to fewer than 4,000 and destroyed unused buildings to remove them from the tax rolls (see Figure 4.9). How could local officials continue on this disastrous course of action? Records of their decision-making sessions suggest that groupthink played a role: Somehow, they convinced themselves over and over again that GE would never move away.

Ignoring Unshared Information

One major advantage of groups is that members can pool their information and experience. In other words, each has something unique to contribute, and combining members' unique knowledge increases the pool of information available to the group. Presumably, the richer this pool, the better the decisions the group can make. This makes eminent good sense, but in fact, it turns out that groups do *not* automatically share information held by individual members. On the contrary, when groups discuss an issue and try to reach a decision about it, they tend to consider information shared by most if not all members and generally tend to ignore information that is known to only one or a few members. Why is this so? Partly because information known to most members has a high probability of being reported by one or more members: Because most people know it, it is very likely that one or more will state it. In addition, people tend to prefer information that confirms their existing knowledge, and group members encourage this process by agreeing with such statements. The result is that groups never become aware of unique information held by individual members, and so cannot use it in their decisions.[14] Ultimately, this can lead to misinterpretation of information and very poor decisions.

Surprisingly, this tendency for groups to ignore information held by one or a few members occurs even in contexts involving life-and-death decisions. For instance, teams of interns and medical students tend to discuss more shared than unshared information, and juries, too, discuss information known to most members while ignoring information known to one or a few members.[15] Because entrepreneurs need to employ all the information at their disposal—some of which they have gathered through great effort—this tendency, too, can be a costly one with devastating results for new ventures. For instance, if the founding team of a new venture simply discusses information already known to all members, the decisions reached about a wide range of issues, ranging from new product developments through financing, may be adversely affected, with harmful consequences for the new venture.

Figure 4.9 The Results of Groupthink?

Despite strong protests from the company, local governments in upstate New York raised taxes on General Electric Corporation repeatedly over several decades, despite warnings from GE that it would move away if this process continued. The result? GE largely abandoned its Schenectady operations, which had employed more than 40,000 people in the 1950s, and knocked down unwanted buildings to remove them from the tax rolls (grassy areas shown in photo). It cut its workforce to fewer than 4,000.

Photo courtesy of R.A. Baron.

Improving Group Decisions: Techniques for Countering the Pitfalls

If our discussion of potential pitfalls in group decision making sounds discouraging, this is by design: We feel it is very important for you, as nascent entrepreneurs, to be aware of these dangers; ignoring them can be costly—or even fatal—to new ventures. Being optimists by nature, though, we want to end on a positive note by reporting that there are effective techniques for countering all of these traps—techniques you can use to protect your own decisions from their impact.

One that is especially useful is the **devil's advocate technique**.[16] In this procedure, one founding team member is assigned the task of disagreeing with and criticizing whatever plan or decision is the initial favorite. This tactic is very helpful, because it induces members to think carefully about the information available and the decisions toward which they are leaning; this can slow the shift toward initial favorites. It is also effective in countering groupthink, because it suggests very clearly that the group has *not* attained consensus and focuses discussion on the fact that it is indeed possible to hold alternative views.

Another useful technique for improving the interpretation of information and group decision making involves asking group members to list all pertinent information known to them before beginning the discussion. This reduces the tendency to ignore unshared information and limit the amount of time spent discussing views shared by most members, thus reducing the likelihood of reciprocal persuasion and the development of group polarization effects.

A third technique that new ventures can adopt—one that is often very helpful to them—is to appoint individuals with technical or business experience to a board of advisers. The advice and guidance provided by these individuals can help founding teams improve the decisions they make—provided the founders are wise enough to listen! The advice of an outside board of advisers can be extremely valuable because not only do these people have expertise that may not be present among members of the founding team, but they are also on the outside looking in. This means that they are less subject to the effects of group polarization, groupthink, and other factors that can affect decisions by groups. For all these reasons, they can be a big plus for new ventures. (For the thoughts of a highly experienced entrepreneur on decision making by groups and on what entrepreneurs need to know before launching their new ventures, please see **"The Voice of Experience"** section.)

KEY POINTS

- Once information is obtained, it must be interpreted—understood so that it can be used as a basis for making good decisions and mapping future strategy.
- Unfortunately, many sources of bias and error can affect the interpretation of information, thus leading to bad decisions. Entrepreneurs must make strenuous efforts to avoid these errors.
- One common source of error is the tendency of decision-making groups to drift toward acceptance of the group's initial preference—the implicit favorite.
- A second source of error in the interpretation of information by groups is group polarization— a strong tendency to shift toward views more extreme than the ones with which they began.
- Another potential source of error in decision-making groups is groupthink—a strong tendency for decision-making groups to close ranks, cognitively, around a decision, assuming that the group can't be wrong, that all members must support the decision strongly, and that any information contrary to the decision should be rejected.
- Although a key advantage of groups is that they can pool information held by individual members, this does not always occur. In fact, groups often fail to share information known to only one or a few members. Instead, they tend to discuss information already known to most members; this, too, can lead to poor decisions.
- Several procedures for reducing these potential errors exist, including the devil's advocate technique. Another involves appointing a board of advisers who, as outsiders, are less subject to forces that can distort group decisions.

THE VOICE OF EXPERIENCE

Know Your Market—and Your Competitive Edge—*Before* You Start!

Paul Severino received an electrical engineering degree in 1969 from Rensselaer Polytechnic Institute, Troy, New York. He serves as a trustee at Rensselaer and The Dana Farber Cancer Institute, Boston, Massachusetts. In 1981, Severino was a founder of Interlan, Inc, and served as president, chief executive officer, and director until 1985, when Micom Systems acquired Interlan. Interlan was the first company to provide Ethernet adapter products and became the leading supplier of Ethernet connectivity products for mini- and microcomputer systems. In 1986, Severino was a founder of Wellfleet Communications, Inc., and served as president, chief executive officer, and director until 1994. Wellfleet Communications was the leading supplier of high-performance, fault resilient internetworking systems and services for Enterprise network environments. Wellfleet was named "The Fastest Growing Company" in the United States by Fortune *magazine for two consecutive years, 1992 and 1993.*

Prior to his current activities as an investor in and adviser to emerging technology companies and venture funds, Severino was a cofounder and chairman of Bay Networks, Inc. He served as chairman of Bay Networks until November 1996. Nortel Networks acquired Bay in 1998. Severino is currently a director of Media 100, MCK Communications, Sonus Networks, NASDAQ (SONS), and a number of private companies. He also serves on industry and government business groups. He is chairman of the Massachusetts Technology Development Corp. (MTDC), was a cofounder of the Massachusetts Telecommunications Council, and served as chairman in 1997.

Before starting a new venture, it is important for entrepreneurs to gather several kinds of information—facts and data that will tell them whether their new venture is really feasible, what specific form their new products and services should take, and how these can be effectively marketed. I spoke recently to Paul Severino, founder of Wellfleet Communications, about this issue.

Baron: "Let's start with marketing. How did you go about determining what kind of markets existed for the products and services your new company would provide?"

Severino: "What I did was to focus on the networking side of computers. In 1980, when we began, there really were no standardized computer networks. I realized that there was a real need for a standard high-speed network for computers. We considered the number of computers and projected how many there would be in the future. That made us think that this was a really big opportunity. At the time, there were a few network standards around that I thought might work—for instance, the Ethernet—so we decided to focus on that. I started Wellfleet in 1986, and by that time, there was already a large number of local area networks, so we decided to focus on these. But again, we wanted to project how big the whole concept would get. The bottom line is this: If by the time you are in a market opportunity for a start-up

and you are reading about details of the market in magazines or newspapers, it is probably too late. You have to have a vision, a sense of the future, and to take some risk. But you do this with a clear idea of what the market size will be."

Baron: "Let's turn to another type of information—information about government policies and regulations. What do you think entrepreneurs need to know before getting started?"

Severino: "That depends on the business you are in. If government policies affect you, you have to know as much about them as you can. That was not a big issue for me, because I worked in industries that were essentially unregulated at the time. But now, I'm working with people in the medical field, and there, you have all kinds of issues—government policies, insurance companies payment policies. Any entrepreneur starting a company in an industry that is regulated should know about the regulations. If these are really complex, you might want to ask yourself 'Is this the right place to start a company?' These change all the time, and they could put you out of business before you know it. Biotech companies are a good example. There has been lots of entrepreneurial activity in that field, and they have to deal with a large number of government regulations and policies."

Baron: "Anything else?"

Severino: "Government regulations and policies have another effect: They can be the basis for start-up companies that provide information about them and help companies formulate policies to meet them. For instance, recent legislation about corporate governance has created real opportunities for new companies that are telling boards of directors what policies and rules they must put in place to meet these regulations."

Baron: "Let's turn to another issue. There's a general belief that groups make better decisions than individuals—at least, are less likely to off the deep end than individuals. Does this fit with your experience? Or do you feel that decision-making groups are subject to errors and potential pitfalls?"

Severino: "I think that the key thing in such groups is the founder's vision. Many entrepreneurs start their companies and then realize that they need a marketing person, a finance person, a production person. The founder hires these people, and then the collaboration begins—working with these people to make key decisions. But in this process, the founder's vision and leadership are always crucial. If the founder doesn't keep things focused, they can get out of hand. For instance, in my company, Wellfleet Communications, we reached a point where we had to decide whether to take our present platform and continue adding features to it or build the next generation platform. We had a debate about this—even the board of directors was involved. But finally, I had to go to the group, as founder, and say: 'I feel strongly that

continued

if we don't keep our differentiated platform, we will be less competitive.' So I made the decision to build the next generation platform, and that turned out very well. In the end, because we had lots of mutual respect, everyone pulled together and we had a big success."

Baron: "Anything else you'd like to add?"

Severino: "Yes. There's another very important piece of the puzzle: Entrepreneurs really have to understand a competitive environment before they enter it. As a start-up, you must have a compelling reason why a customer should buy from you. That's why I like a marketplace without big players—competition is more my size. Ultimately, you want to be #1 or #2, and to do that, you have to understand the competitive environment and how you fit it into, and how you can win. So, opportunities are best when you can enter a market where the competitors are relatively small. The key is to be certain you bring something to the table that is so compelling that customers will say 'I want this.'"

Commentary: We think that Mr. Severino's points are very well taken. Because entrepreneurs are entering emerging markets, they cannot expect to have complete information about these markets; but they should certainly gather as much information as possible in order to estimate the potential size and value of the opportunity they are pursuing. Information about government regulations and policies is also important, and as Severino notes, in some industries they can make or break a new company. Severino's comments about decision-making groups are also right on target: Although several heads are often better than one, this is only true under certain conditions—when founders exert leadership and keep the groups focused. Finally, and perhaps most important of all, we agree with Severino's view that entrepreneurs should try to understand the competitive environments they plan to enter *before* getting started. Jumping in without this knowledge is like setting off on a cross-country hike without a map or compass: You might get there, but the most likely outcome is disaster!

Summary and Review of Key Points

- Many new products that are brought to market disappear without attaining widespread use.
- One major reason why this is so is that the entrepreneurs who found new ventures to develop these products or services do not do their homework: They fail to acquire basic and essential information before beginning.
- Among the most important kinds of information entrepreneurs need are (1) marketing information, (2) information about taxation, (3) information about government regulations and policies, and (4) information about relevant laws.
- Information on these issues should be gathered prior to the launch of new ventures, because it can help entrepreneurs avoid many problems and pitfalls.
- Even if entrepreneurs gather information on these topics, they face the task of interpreting it accurately; this, too, can pose hazards for new ventures.
- Before launching a new venture, entrepreneurs need reliable marketing information—information on how potential customers will react to and evaluate the products or services they provide.
- Because people are not very successful at identifying the factors that influence their behavior, simply asking them why they like or dislike various products is not an effective approach.
- Perceptual mapping, one technique for identifying the dimensions along which customers evaluate various products, is often a useful initial step.
- One useful procedure for gathering such information is focus groups—groups of about eight to twelve people who are similar to potential customers and who meet for one to two hours to describe their perceptions of and reactions to relevant products.
- In addition to gathering their own marketing information, entrepreneurs can also often use indirect or secondary data, information gathered by others.
- Although marketing data is often useful to entrepreneurs, it is no guarantee of success, especially with respect to new products or services because consumers may find comparing these to existing products a difficult task, and because unexpected uses for such products may quickly emerge.
- Government policies concerning new ventures vary greatly from country to country, but no matter where they reside, entrepreneurs should pay careful attention to these issues.
- Taxation strongly affects the profitability of all businesses, so entrepreneurs should consider federal, state, and local tax codes carefully in planning their new ventures.
- Government policies concerning new ventures have become more favorable in many countries in recent years, and special programs designed to encourage innovation, such as the SBIR and programs designed to assist minority entrepreneurs, have been instituted.
- Entrepreneurs should be familiar with these programs because they can provide valuable resources for new ventures.
- Governments have established many regulations and laws designed to protect the health and safety of employees and to regulate various industries (e.g., ones that handle dangerous or toxic substances).

- Entrepreneurs should be familiar with these because they can have major effects on new ventures.
- In the United States, the Occupational Safety and Health Act requires all employers—even very small ones—to take active measures to safeguard the health and safety of employees.
- Additional regulations and laws are designed to protect employees from discrimination (e.g., the Americans with Disabilities Act).
- Entrepreneurs must be familiar with these laws and regulations to assure that their new ventures comply with them. Failure to do so can produce truly disastrous results.
- Once information is obtained, it must be interpreted—understood so that it can be used as a basis for making good decisions and mapping future strategy.
- Unfortunately, many sources of bias and error can affect the interpretation of information, thus leading to bad decisions. Entrepreneurs must make strenuous efforts to avoid these errors.
- One common source of error is the tendency of decision-making groups to drift toward acceptance of the group's initial preference—the implicit favorite.

- A second source of error in the interpretation of information by groups is group polarization—a strong tendency to shift toward views more extreme than the ones with which they began.
- Another potential source of error in decision-making groups is groupthink—a strong tendency for decision-making groups to close ranks, cognitively, around a decision, assuming that the group can't be wrong, that all members must support the decision strongly, and that any information contrary to the decision should be rejected.
- Although a key advantage of groups is that they can pool information held by individual members, this does not always occur. In fact, groups often fail to share information known to only one or a few members. Instead, they tend to discuss information already known to most members; this, too, can lead to poor decisions.
- Several procedures for reducing these potential errors exist, including the devil's advocate technique. Another involves appointing a board of advisers who, as outsiders, are less subject to forces that can distort group decisions.

Glossary

Americans with Disabilities Act (ADA): This law prohibits discrimination against persons with disabilities who, despite these disabilities, are able to perform the essential functions of the job. The law also requires employers to provide reasonable accommodation for such persons—actions that accommodate the known disabilities of job applicants or employees.

Confirmation Candidates: Alternatives that are not really considered seriously; rather, they are raised mainly for the purpose of helping groups convince themselves that initial favorite is indeed correct.

Devil's Advocate Technique: A procedure for improving group decision making in which one group member is assigned the task of disagreeing with and criticizing whatever plan or decision is the initial favorite.

Focus Groups: Groups of from 8 to 12 people who are similar to potential customers and who meet for one to two hours to describe their perceptions of and reactions to relevant products.

Group Polarization: The tendency for members of decision-making groups to shift toward views more extreme than the ones with which they began.

Groupthink: A strong tendency for decision-making groups to close ranks, cognitively, around a decision, assuming that the group can't be wrong, that all members must support the decision strongly, and that any information contrary to the decision should be rejected.

Implicit Favorite: The decisions initially favored by a majority of members of a decision-making group. Often, this is the decision made by the group.

Occupational Safety and Health Act of 1970 (OSHA): An act designed to protect the health and safety of employees in the United States. The act requires employers to (1) provide a safe and healthy work environment—a workplace free from recognized hazards likely to cause harm to employees; (2) comply with specific occupational safety and health standards—rules dealing with various occupations and industries; (3) keep records of occupational injuries and illnesses.

Perceptual Mapping: A technique for identifying the key dimensions along which potential customers evaluate products.

Protected Class: A group that suffered discrimination in the past.

Small Business Innovation Research (SBIR): A government program designed to encourage innovation in the United States by requiring participating federal agencies to set aside 2 percent of their budgets for funding contracts, grants, or cooperative agreements through the SBIR.

Title VII of the Civil Rights Act of 1964: A law designed to prevent dicrimination in workplaces. The law prohibits employers from basing employment decisions on a person's race, color, religion, sex, or national origin.

Discussion Questions

1. The most straightforward way to obtain information on how potential customers will react to a new product is simply to ask them. Why is this method sometimes misleading?

2. Suppose that you have an idea for a new service—one that will help future brides plan their wedding. How could you use perceptual mapping to decide which kind of information and help would be most attractive to potential customers?

3. In this chapter, we noted that marketing information, even if it is excellent in every respect, is no guarantee of success. Why is this so? Is there any kind of information that *could* guarantee success for new ventures?

4. What government programs might be helpful to your new venture? How would you go about obtaining help from these programs?

5. Suppose you were interviewing prospective employees for your new venture. What kinds of questions could you ask them? What kinds of questions would be violations of government regulations designed to protect employees from discrimination?

6. Imagine that an individual with a serious physical disability applied for a job in your new venture. Could you deny her employment because of her disability? If your answer is "no," what would you have to do, if you employed her, to meet the requirements of laws concerning persons with disabilities?

7. It is widely believed that groups are less likely to "go off the deep end" than individuals when making decisions. Do you think this is true? If not, what processes, working together, could push groups toward extreme (and poor) decisions?

InfoTrac Exercises

1. **Forget Focus Groups: Just Watch Users, Innovator Says** (news)
   Tom Kelley, product innovator, IDEO Product Development Inc.)
   Machine Design, March 20, 2003 v75 i6 p28(1)
   Record: A99378451
   Full Text: COPYRIGHT 2003 Penton Media, Inc.
   1. According to the text, what role do focus groups play in innovation?
   2. According to Tom Kelly, what is the value of focus groups in product innovation?
   3. What approach does Kelly take to innovation?

2. **Help Needed? Does Uncle Sam Owe Entrepreneurs a Helping Hand, or Should the Government Just Get Out of Small Business's Way? Two Experts Face Off** (interview)
   Joshua Kurlantzick
   Entrepreneur, April 2003 v31 i4 p72(2)
   Record: A99388282
   Full Text: COPYRIGHT 2003 Entrepreneur Media, Inc.
   1. According to the text, how does government support innovation?
   2. Summarize the positions of Chris Edwards and Nydia Velazquez.
   3. What is your position on government support for small business? Do you tend to agree with Velazquez or Edwards? Why?

GETTING DOWN
TO BUSINESS

When Entrepreneurs Play Detective: Using Indirect Methods for Acquiring Marketing Information

Suppose that you are considering the possibility of starting a new venture. You are trying to decide what specific products to offer, what potential markets to develop, and which specific marketing techniques to use. You have very limited funds, so you can't afford to do full-scale marketing studies. As a result, you decide to focus on indirect methods for gathering market information—methods that are virtually free. To gain experience in performing this kind of task, please do the following:

1. **Identify the specific kinds of information you need.** What do you want to know about competing products, who uses them, and what they like and dislike about them? Formulate a list of specific kinds of information you believe to be important. For each item you list, explain why it is important to have this kind of information.

   a.

   b.

   c.

   d.

   e.

2. **Identify ways in which you can obtain this information.** What sources can you use that are available to you free—or practically free? List these, and explain how would you go about obtaining them.

   a.

   b.

   c.

   d.

   e.

3. **Decide how you would use this information to plan your marketing strategy.** Now, describe what you would do with this information—how would you use it to develop your product, match it to its potential market, and develop specific techniques you will use to build sales.

Improving Group Decisions

Poor decisions are costly to all organizations, but they are especially deadly to new ventures: Such businesses simply can't afford major errors because their resources are often so limited. Most new ventures are formed by two or more entrepreneurs, so decision making often involves face-to-face meetings between the cofounders, who discuss current problems and consider various options. Although this process can be effective, it also faces serious obstacles—processes that tend to distort decision made in groups and push them toward extreme (and often poor) choices. How can you protect your own decision-making process from these risks? By applying the following steps to decisions *you* must make in running your own new venture.

1. **Resist groupthink.** Groupthink develops when members of a group convince themselves that they *must* be right; after all, they all agree. Several steps are useful in countering this tendency, but one of the best is to appoint a board of expert advisers—and listen to their advice! If you choose these people carefully, they will point out potential pitfalls and tell you—frankly!—when you are about to make poor decision. The key is to (1) choose them wisely and (2) listen carefully to their advice. If you do this, you will gain considerable protection against groupthink—and other causes of poor decisions.

2. **Be certain to share information.** A major problem for decision-making groups is that they generally talk mainly about information everyone already has. This is not surprising; such information is known to everyone, so it is likely to come up during discussions. You can counter this problem by assigning each member of the group to address different topics or issues. For instance, one person can focus on finance-related issues, another on marketing tasks and problems, and still another on production-related issues. By structuring meetings so that each participant specializes with respect to topics, the likelihood that unshared information will be presented can be increased.

3. **Appoint a devil's advocate.** Groups often move rapidly toward agreement; often, their final position is more extreme than the initial views of all the members (i.e.,

group polarization occurs). One good way of slowing down this rush toward extremity is by appointing a devil's advocate. This person has the role of asking "Why?" over and over again. In other words, he or she prods other group members to explain their assumptions, to clarify the reasons why they are recommending specific views or actions, and, in general, urges them to consider other alternatives. Obviously, this can't go on forever—decisions have to be made in a timely manner. But by forcing the group to hold all options up to close scrutiny, the person playing this role can be very helpful in terms of avoiding poor decisions. Try appointing one persons to play this role in your own new venture; you may be pleasantly surprised by the results.

Enhanced Learning

You may select any combination of the case options below to enhance your understanding of the chapter material.

- **Appendix 1: Case Studies –** Thirteen cases provide opportunities to apply chapter concepts to realistic entrepreneurial situations. These brief cases call for careful analysis of real business problems and ask you to think about potential solutions.

- **Appendix 2: Video Case Library –** Nine cases are tied directly to video segments from the popular PBS television series *Small Business School*. These cases and video segments give you unparalleled access to today's entrepreneurs, with expert advice and insights on how to start, run, and grow a business.

- **Comprehensive Cases –** Visit the book support Web site at http://baron.swlearning.com for cases detailing real businesses whose successes and setbacks illustrate each stage of the entrepreneurial process. You will conduct in-depth analysis of entrepreneurial challenges through well-developed case studies.

Notes

1 Wesson, T., & DeFigueiredo, J.N . 2001. The importance of focus to market entrants: A study of microbrewery performance. *Journal of Business Venturing* 16: 377–403.

2 Knott, A.M. 2002. *Venture design.* Philadelphia: Entity Press.

3 Warren, S. 2002. When grown-ups go for silly putty they do it in a big way. *The Wall Street Journal*, September 11, pp. A1, 9.

4 Gentry, W., & Hubbard, R. 2000. Tax policy and entrepreneurial entry. *American Economic Review Papers and Proceedings* 90(2): 283–292.

5 Robson, M., & Warren, C. 1999. Marginal and average tax rates and the incentive for self-employment. *Southern Economic Journal* 65: 757–773.

6 Goldfarb & Henrekson (in press).

7 Heilman, M.E., & Chen, J.J. (in press). Entrepreneurship as a solution: The allure of self-employment for women and minorities. *Human Resource Management Review.*

8 Murray, L., 1986. *Business, government, and the public.* 4th ed. Englewood Cliffs, NJ: Prentice-Hall.

9 Kunda, Z. 1999. *Social cognition: Making sense out of people.* Cambridge, MA: MIT Press.

10 Nemeth, C., Connell, J.B., Rogers, J.D., & Brown, K.S. 2001. Improving decision making by means of dissent. *Journal of Applied Social Psychology* 31: 45–58.

11 Burnstein, E. 1983. Persuasion as argument processing. In M. Brandstatter, J.H. Davis, & G. Stocker-Kriechgauer (eds.). *Group decision processes.* London: Academic Press.

12 Ensley, M.D., Pearson, A.W., & Amason, A.C. 2002. Understanding the dynamics of new venture top management teams: Cohesion, conflict, and new venture performance. *Journal of Business Venturing* 17: 365–386.

13 Janis, I.L. 1982. *Victims of groupthink.* 2nd ed. Boston: Houthgon Mifflin.

14 Gigone, D., & Hastie, R. 1993. The common knowledge effect: Information sharing and group judgment. *Journal of Personality and Social Psychology* 65: 959–974.

15 Larson, J.R., Jr., Foster-Fishman, P.G., & Franz, T.M. 1998. Leadership style and the discussion of shared and unshared information in decision-making groups. *Personality and Social Psychology Bulletin* 75: 93–108.

16 Hirt, E.R., & Markman, K.D. 1995. Multiple explanations: A consider-an-alternative strategy for debiasing judgments. *Personality and Social Psychology Bulletin* 69: 1069–1086.

CHAPTER 5

ASSEMBLING THE TEAM: ACQUIRING AND UTILIZING ESSENTIAL HUMAN RESOURCES

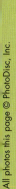
LEARNING OBJECTIVES

After reading this chapter, you should be able to:

1 Explain the difference between similarity and complementarity and the relevance of these concepts to the task of choosing cofounders in a new venture.

2 Explain why entrepreneurs should conduct a careful self-assessment as part of the process of choosing potential cofounders.

3 Define "impression management" and describe various tactics used by individuals for this purpose.

4 Explain how entrepreneurs can use nonverbal cues to determine when others are engaging in deception.

5 Define "self-serving bias" and explain how it plays an important role in perceived fairness.

6 Explain the difference between constructive and destructive criticism.

7 Describe the role of social networks in new ventures' efforts to hire additional employees.

8 Describe the relationship of number of employees to new venture success.

9 List the relative advantages and disadvantages of temporary and permanent employees

Similarity Versus Complementarity: "Know Thyself" Revisited
  Self-Assessment: Knowing What You Have Helps Determine What You Need

Choosing Cofounders: Maximizing the New Venture's Human Resources
  Impression Management: The Fine Art of Looking Good—and How to Recognize It
  Deception: Beyond Impression Management

Utilizing the New Venture's Human Resources: Building Strong Working Relationships Among the Founding Team
  Roles: The Clearer the Better
  Perceived Fairness: An Elusive But Essential Component
  Effective Communication

Expanding the New Venture's Human Resources: Beyond the Founding Team
  Obtaining Excellent Employees: The Key Role of Social Networks
  Is Bigger Necessarily Better? Number of Employees as a Factor in New Venture Growth
  Should New Ventures Hire Temporary or Permanent Employees? Commitment Versus Cost
  Some Concluding Thoughts

"Union may be strength, but it is mere blind brute strength unless wisely directed."
(Samuel Butler, 1882)

Although the popular view of entrepreneurs suggests that they are "loners"—energetic and creative people who prefer to do things in their own, unique way—most new ventures (more than two-thirds) are actually started by teams of entrepreneurs working closely together.[1] This is not surprising: Cooperation and teamwork often allow individuals to accomplish tasks they could never accomplish alone. The fact that many entrepreneurs choose to work with cofounders, however, raises an intriguing question: Is the whole greater than the sum of its parts in this context, as it is in many others? In other words, are new ventures started by teams of entrepreneurs more successful than ones started by individuals? Although no definite answer to this question currently exists, we agree with the quotation, which suggests that teams are indeed a "plus," but only when the persons involved work together wisely—and well. This, in turn, implies that two tasks are crucial for entrepreneurs who decide to work with others (cofounders) to convert their ideas into reality. First, they must choose these persons carefully, selecting ones who will help them to reach their goals. Second, they must work effectively with these people so that the potential benefits of teamwork can actually be obtained.

Clearly, it is much easier to state these goals than to attain them. Choosing excellent cofounders and developing good working relationships with them are complex tasks requiring considerable effort. In our view, though, this is effort well spent because the success of any new venture depends, to an important degree, on the human resources it assembles—the knowledge, skills, talents, abilities, reputations, and social networks of its cofounders, plus those brought to it by initial, early employees. Research findings indicate that these and related factors play an important role in the launch and success of new ventures.[2] How, then, can these important tasks be performed effectively? How can entrepreneurs assemble the human resources needed to launch a successful new venture? This is the central focus of this chapter. In order to answer this question in a useful way, we will consider four closely related topics.

First, we will examine the issue of complementarity versus similarity: Should entrepreneurs choose cofounders who are similar to themselves in various respects or ones who are different in complementary ways, providing what they themselves lack in terms of knowledge, skills, or abilities? As we will note later in this discussion, both similarity and complementarity offer advantages, but we believe that emphasizing complementarity may, in many instances, be a somewhat better strategy because it provides new ventures with a strong and diverse base of human resources. In any case, the process of choosing appropriate cofounders should certainly start with a careful self-assessment by prospective entrepreneurs. The reason for this requirement can be stated simply: In a very real sense, it is impossible for entrepreneurs to know what they need from cofounders unless they (the entrepreneurs) know what they already have. After considering why and how entrepreneurs should engage in careful self-assessment, we will turn to the task of actually choosing cofounders. This requires skill at assessing others accurately and is far trickier than you might at first imagine. Most people are quite adept at managing their "image" and appearing to be what they are not, so being able to cut through such tactics is a skill worth developing. (In fact, this is a theme that we will be concerned about throughout this book. We will return to this problem in Chapter 10, where we explain why entrepreneurs often franchise their businesses to avoid having problems with employees who misrepresent their abilities.) Third, we will turn to the issue of establishing effective working relationships with cofounders and new employees. This requires such preliminary steps as a clear division of roles and obligations, plus careful attention to basic principles of fairness and effective communication. Finally, we will close with a brief consideration of human resources beyond the founding team—how new ventures recruit the talented people they need and whether these persons should be temporary or permanent employees. If these four tasks are performed successfully, a new venture can begin life with the pool of human resources it needs to grow and prosper; if, instead, they are *not* carried out effectively, a new venture may begin with serious handicaps—ones from which it may never be able to recover.

SIMILARITY VERSUS COMPLEMENTARITY: "KNOW THYSELF" REVISITED

It is a basic fact of life that people feel most comfortable with, and tend to like, others who are similar to themselves in various ways. In fact, a very large body of research evidence points to two intriguing conclusions regarding the appeal of similarity: (1) almost any kind of similarity will do—similarity with respect to attitudes and values; demographic factors such as age, gender, occupation, or ethnic background; shared interests—almost anything; and (2) such effects are both general and strong. For instance, similarity has been found to influence the outcome of employment interviews and performance ratings: In general, the more similar job applicants are to the persons who interview them, the more likely they are to be hired. Correspondingly, the more similar employees are to their managers, the higher the ratings they receive from them.[3] You can probably guess why similarity is so appealing: When people are alike on various dimensions, they are more comfortable in each other's presence, feel that they know each other better, and are more confident that they will be able to predict each others' future reactions and behavior. In short, everything else being equal, we tend to associate with, choose as friends or cofounders, and even marry people who are similar to ourselves in many respects.

Entrepreneurs are definitely no exception to this similarity-leads-to-liking rule. In fact, most tend to select people whose background, training, and experience is highly similar to their own. This is far from surprising: People from similar backgrounds "speak the same language"—they can converse more readily and smoothly than persons from very different backgrounds. Often, they already know one another because they have attended the same schools or worked for the same companies. The overall result is that many new ventures are started by teams of entrepreneurs from the same fields or occupations: Engineers tend to work with engineers; entrepreneurs with a marketing or sales background tend to work with others from these fields; scientists tend to work with other scientists, and so on (see Figure 5.1).

In one sense, this is an important "plus": As we will note in a later section, effective communication is a key ingredient in good working relations, so the fact that "birds of a feather tend to flock together" in starting new ventures offers obvious advantages. On the debit side of the ledger, however, the tendency for entrepreneurs to choose cofounders whose background and training is highly similar to their own has several serious drawbacks. The most important of these centers around redundancy: The more similar people are, the greater the degree to which their knowledge, training, skills, and aptitudes overlap. For instance, consider a group of engineers who start a company to develop a new product. All have technical expertise, and this is extremely useful in terms of designing a product that actually works. But because they are all engineers, they have little knowledge about marketing, legal matters, or regulations concerning employees' health and safety. Further, they may know very little about writing an effective business plan, which, as we will see in Chapter 7, is often crucial for obtaining

LEARNING OBJECTIVE

1 Explain the difference between similarity and complementarity and the relevance of these concepts to the task of choosing cofounders in a new venture.

Figure 5.1 Similarity in Founding Teams of Entrepreneurs
Because people find it more pleasant and comfortable to work with others who are similar to themselves, teams of entrepreneurs often consist of persons with similar background, training, and experience. This can be detrimental to the success of the new ventures they found.

© Getty Images/PhotoDisc

required financial resources and determining how to operate a company effectively. Moreover, although all of them have excellent quantitative skills, they are not proficient at preparing written documents or in "selling" their ideas; as is often the case with persons from a technical or scientific background, they are better with numbers than words. Further, because all were trained in the same field (and may even have studied at the same school), they have overlapping social networks: They tend to know the same people and, hence, have a limited range of contacts from whom they can obtain needed resources—information, financial support, and so on.

By now the main point should be clear: What this particular team of entrepreneurs—or any other—needs for success is a very wide range of information, skills, aptitudes, and abilities. This is less likely to be present when all members of the founding team are highly similar to one another in important ways. Ideally, what one team member lacks one or more others can provide so that, as the quote offered at the start of this chapter suggests, the whole is indeed greater than the sum of its parts because the team can pool its knowledge and expertise. Rule number one for entrepreneurs in assembling their founding teams, then, is this: *Don't yield to the temptation to work solely with people whose background, training, and experience is highly similar to your own. Doing so will be easy and pleasant in many ways. but it will* not *provide the rich foundation of human resources the new venture needs.*

KEY POINTS

- In general, people tend to like, and feel more comfortable around, persons who are similar to themselves in various ways.
- This leads entrepreneurs to select cofounders whose background, training, and experience closely matches their own.
- Because a wide range of knowledge, skills, and experience among the founding team is advantageous to new ventures, selecting cofounders on the basis of complementarity rather than similarity is often a more useful strategy.

Self-Assessment: Knowing What You Have Helps Determine What You Need

Now that we have clarified the dangers associated with the potential downside of choosing to work exclusively with cofounders similar to oneself, we will take a step back and briefly examine a related issue: the importance in this process of an accurate self-assessment. As we noted earlier, it is difficult, if not impossible, to know what you need from prospective cofounders without first understanding what you, yourself, bring to the table. For this reason, a crucial initial step for all entrepreneurs—one they should perform *before* beginning the task of assembling required human resources (cofounders or additional employees)—is a careful **self-assessment**, an inventory of the knowledge, experience, training, motives, and characteristics they themselves possess and can contribute to the new venture.

This is far from a simple task: The dictum "Know thyself" sounds straightforward, but in reality, it is exceedingly difficult to put into actual practice. There are two major reasons why this is so. First, we are often unaware of at least some of the factors that affect our behavior. As we noted in Chapter 4, we know what we did but are less certain about *why* we did it. The powerful effect of similarity is a prime example of this fact. Often, people like others, including prospective cofounders, because of subtle similarities—they are alike in various ways but are not fully aware of these similarities. In short, they know that they like each other and find it pleasant to work together, but don't really know why. To the extent we are unaware of the factors that influence our behavior and reactions, the task of knowing ourselves becomes complex.

Second, and perhaps even more important, we do not gain knowledge of our major traits, abilities, or even attitudes directly, through self-reflection. Rather, we gradually gain insight into these important aspects of ourselves through our relations

LEARNING OBJECTIVE

2 Explain why entrepreneurs should conduct a careful self-assessment as part of the process of choosing potential cofounders.

with other persons. Only they—and their reactions to us—can tell us how intelligent, energetic, charming, or well-informed about various topics we are. There are no direct physical measures of these and many other attributes, so we have to gather them, gradually, from what other people tell us, directly or indirectly (see Figure 5.2).

Although the task of acquiring clear self-knowledge is a complex one, we can perform it quite well—if we take the trouble to do so. There are concrete steps you, as a prospective entrepreneur, can take to develop an accurate view of your own human capital—the resources you bring to any new venture you choose to launch. You can complete several key portions of this personal inventory yourself, but for others, you will need the help of people who know you well—and hence, can provide insights you can't readily acquire alone. Remember: The reason for engaging in this activity is to understand what you already have—your own human capital—so that you can determine what you need from other persons, including potential cofounders.

- *Knowledge base.* This is a good place to begin, because it is something you can do alone. Ask yourself the following questions: "What do I know?" "What information and knowledge do I bring to the new venture?" Here, your education and experience are directly relevant and can suggest what you know and what you don't know, and therefore need to acquire from others, including potential cofounders.

- *Specific skills.* Quite apart from your knowledge base are specific skills—proficiencies that enable you to perform certain tasks well. Are you very good with numbers? Adept at making oral presentations? Good with people? Everyone has a unique set of skills, and you should try to understand—and inventory—yours as a preliminary step in developing your new venture.

- *Motives.* This is more difficult, but also quite important. Why do you want to start a new venture? Because you like a challenge? Because you fervently believe in your new product? To earn a huge fortune? To escape from corporate life and become self-employed? You can hold all of these motives at the same time, but it is useful to ponder their relative importance to you because if your personal motives do not match those of potential cofounders, you may be laying the foundation for serious future problems.

- *Commitment.* This is related to motivation, but not identical to it. Commitment refers to the desire to seeing things through—to continue even in the face of adversity—and to reach your personal goals relating to the new venture (e.g., the ones listed under motives). Recent findings indicate that this is an important factor in new venture success.[4]

- *Personal attributes.* Here is where you will need help from other persons because only they can tell you where you stand on a number of key dimensions. Human beings differ along a tremendous number of dimensions, but in recent years, it has become increasingly clear that five of these are the most central, and most relevant in business contexts. These are known as the **"Big Five Dimensions" of personality**,[5] and growing evidence suggests two important facts about them: They are indeed central—in fact, they are so basic that where individuals stand on these dimensions is usually apparent even after knowing them for only a few minutes; and they are indeed strongly related to many aspects of behavior in business settings, including job performance.[6] What are these dimensions? Briefly, they can be described as follows:

Conscientiousness. The extent to which individuals are hardworking, organized, dependable, and persevering versus sluggish, disorganized, and unreliable.

Extraversion-introversion. The degree to which individuals are gregarious, assertive, and sociable versus being reserved, timid, and quiet.

Agreeableness. The extent to which individuals are cooperative, courteous, trusting, and agreeable versus uncooperative, disagreeable, and belligerent.

Figure 5.2 Self-Reflection Does Not Always Equal Self-Knowledge

We cannot determine many of our most important abilities or traits directly, through self-reflection. Rather, we can only gain such information from other persons, whose reactions provide us with valuable insights into our relative standing on many important dimensions (e.g., intelligence, energy, charm, talent, etc.).

Emotional stability. The degree to which individuals are insecure, anxious, depressed, and emotional versus calm, self-confident, and secure.

Openness to experience. The extent to which individuals are creative, curious, and have wide-ranging interests versus practical and with narrow interests.

As we noted earlier, these dimensions are important. For instance, they have been found to be linked to work performance across a large number of occupations.[7] In general, conscientiousness shows the strongest association with task performance: The higher individuals are on this dimension, the higher their performance. Recent findings indicate that the higher entrepreneurs are in conscientiousness, the more likely are their new ventures to survive.[8] Emotional stability, too, is related to task performance, although not as strongly or consistently; again, the more emotionally stable individuals are, the better their performance.

Other dimensions of the big five are also linked to task performance, but in more specific ways. For instance, agreeableness and extraversion are both positively related to the interpersonal aspects of work (e.g., getting along well with others). Especially relevant to entrepreneurs is the fact that individuals' standing on several of the big five dimensions of personality is related to performance of the teams to which they belong.[9] Specifically, it has been found that the higher the average scores of team members on conscientiousness, agreeableness, extraversion, and emotional stability, the higher was teams' performance (as rated by managers). Finally, we should note that two of these dimensions—openness to experience and conscientiousness—are related to creativity and innovation.[10] Openness to experience seems to facilitate such behavior while conscientiousness can reduce it.

How can you assess your own standing on these dimensions? Performing the "Getting Down to Business" exercise on page 129 is a good start. By following the instructions in that, you will gain helpful insights into where you stand on each of the big five dimensions. Knowing that, in turn, can help you draw a bead on what you need in prospective cofounders. In general, conscientiousness and emotional stability are important pluses in almost any context. Further, people high in agreeableness are easier to get along with than people low on this dimension. Keeping these points in mind, you will probably want to choose cofounders who are high on these characteristics. But for other dimensions, complementarity may be worth considering. For instance, if you are high in extraversion and have good "people skills," it is less crucial that your cofounders be high on this dimension, too; one good spokesperson may be all you need most of the time.

Similarity or Complementarity: A Final Word

So which should you seek in prospective team members, similarity or complementarity? The answer depends largely on the dimensions you are considering. Complementarity is very important with respect to knowledge, skills, and experience. In order to succeed, new ventures must acquire a rich and useful inventory of human resources. Choosing cofounders whose knowledge and experience complement your own can be very useful in attaining this important goal. On the other hand, similarity, too, offers benefits: It enhances ease of communication and facilitates good personal relationships. Similarity with respect to motives is very important: If the cofounders of a new venture have sharply contrasting motives or goals, conflict between them is almost certain to develop.

Over all then, we suggest a balanced approach: Focus primarily on complementarity with respect to knowledge, skills, and experience, but bring similarity into the picture with respect to personal characteristics and motives.[11] Doing so will provide good symmetry between acquiring the broad range of human resources new ventures require and establishing a good working environment in which all members of the founding team can work hard to convert their vision into reality.

Good luck with your personal inventory—and with the task of choosing excellent cofounders. As you proceed, keep the words of Lao-Tzu, a philosopher of ancient China, firmly in mind: "He who knows others is clever; He who knows himself has discernment."

- In order to choose cofounders who bring knowledge, skills, and attributes complementary their own, entrepreneurs must first conduct a careful self-assessment of their own human capital.
- This is a difficult task because often we are unaware of the causes of our own behavior and also because in many instances, we can acquire understanding of our own characteristics only from others' reactions to us.
- Entrepreneurs' self-assessment should carefully consider their knowledge base, specific skills, motives, and personal attributes (e.g., where they stand on each of the "Big Five" Dimensions of personality).
- In choosing cofounders, it is often useful to focus on complementarity with respect to knowledge, skills, and experience, but on similarity with respect to personal characteristics and motives.

CHOOSING COFOUNDERS: MAXIMIZING THE NEW VENTURE'S HUMAN RESOURCES

As we noted in the preceding section, it is considerably harder to "know thyself" than you might at first assume. With a little hard work, however, it *is* possible to formulate an accurate inventory of your own human capital—what you bring to the new venture in terms of knowledge, skills, experience, and personal characteristics. This, in turn, can help you determine what you need from other persons (e.g., cofounders, employees) in terms of these basic dimensions. Once you have drawn a bead on this issue, though, things do not necessarily get simpler, because knowing what you need is no guarantee that you will find it—or that you will recognize it when you do. Superb cofounders do not appear, conveniently, just when you need them. On the contrary, identifying such persons usually requires considerable work. Accomplishing this task is very worthwhile, because choosing badly can have disastrous consequences. (Please see the **"Danger! Pitfall Ahead!"** section on page 117 for further discussion of this issue.) These points raise an important, practical question: How should entrepreneurs go about selecting potential cofounders—what guidelines should they use in assembling the human resources required for their new ventures? Answering this question involves many activities, but perhaps most central among these is developing skill at what is known as **social perception**—the process through which we come to know and understand other persons.[12]

This is a key task because unless we form accurate perceptions of others, it is impossible to determine whether, and to what extent, they offer the knowledge, skills, and characteristics we seek. For this reason, developing skill at this task is very useful for entrepreneurs. In fact, recent evidence indicates that entrepreneurs who are adept at social perception (ones who are good at perceiving others accurately) attain greater financial success than ones who are less proficient.[13] Unfortunately, perceiving others accurately is more difficult than it sounds because other people do not always portray themselves accurately. On the contrary, they often seek to disguise their true feelings or motives and frequently seek to present themselves in a favorable light. If we accept these external masks at face value, we can be seriously misled. In order to perceive others accurately, therefore, we must learn to be adept at distinguishing reality from image where other people are concerned. In this respect, developing skill at dealing with two related issues—**impression management** and **deception**—is extremely useful.

Impression Management: The Fine Art of Looking Good— And How to Recognize It

At one time or another, virtually everyone engages in efforts to make a good first impression on others—to present themselves in a favorable light.[14] To accomplish this goal, individuals use a wide range of tactics. Most of these, however, fall into two major categories: *self-enhancement*—efforts to increase their appeal to others, and *other-enhancement*—efforts to make the target person feel good in various ways.

Specific strategies of self-enhancement include efforts to boost one's physical appearance through style of dress, personal grooming, and the use of various "props" (e.g., eyeglasses, which have been found to encourage impressions of intelligence; see Figure 5.3).[15] Additional tactics of self-enhancement involve efforts to appear highly skilled, or describing oneself in positive terms, explaining, for instance, how they (the person engaging in impression management) overcame daunting obstacles.

Turning to other-enhancement, individuals use many different tactics to induce positive moods and reactions in others. A large body of research findings suggests that such reactions, in turn, play an important role in generating liking for the person responsible for them.[16] The most commonly used tactic of other-enhancement is flattery—making statements that praise the target person, his or her traits, or accomplishments, or the organization with which the target person is associated.[17] Such tactics are often highly successful, provided they are not overdone. Additional tactics of other-enhancement involve expressing agreement with the target person's views, showing a high degree of interest in this person, doing small favors for them, asking for their advice and feedback in some manner, or expressing liking for them nonverbally (e.g., through high levels of eye-contact, nodding in agreement, and smiling).[18]

These are not the only strategies people use; for instance, individuals sometimes employ intimidation—pretending to be dangerous or angry in order to wring concessions from others. This tactic does not generate positive reactions to the people using it, but it does often produce the results they desire. Have you ever known anyone who relies on this approach? Such persons are far from rare, and they often enter meetings with an approach suggesting: "I'm mad as hell and am not going take any more!" If this tactic is recognized for what it is, its impact is reduced; but it does work well in many situations, at least for some persons.[19]

Do other tactics of impression management, too, actually succeed? The answer provided by a growing body of literature is clear: *yes*, provided they are used with skill and care. For example, one large-scale study involving more than 1,400 employees found that social skills (including impression management) were the single best predictor of job performance ratings and assessments of potential for promotion for employees in a wide range of jobs.[20] Overall, then, it appears that impression management tactics often do enhance the appeal of persons who use them effectively. We should hasten to add, however, that the use of these tactics involves potential pitfalls: If they are overused, or used ineffectively, they can backfire and produce negative rather than positive reactions from others. For instance, people often form very negative impressions of others who play up to their superiors, but treat subordinates with disdain and contempt—sometimes known as the *slime effect*.[21] The moral of these findings is clear: Although tactics of impression management often succeed, this is not always the case, and sometimes they can boomerang, adversely affecting reactions to the persons who use them.

By now, it should be obvious that being able to "cut through" these various tactics of impression management is very important for prospective entrepreneurs engaged in the task of choosing prospective cofounders and initial employees. Accepting others' statements about their skills, experience, and past accomplishments without *due diligence* (carefully checking on the accuracy of such information) can lead entrepreneurs to form inflated views of the persons using such tactics.

Figure 5.3 Impression Management in Action

At one time or other, almost everyone engages in impression management—efforts to present themselves in a favorable light. To accomplish this goal, people use many different tactics. Careful grooming—which is often effective—is just one of these tactics.

© Getty Images/PhotoDisc

Similarly, failing to recognize flattery, exaggerated agreement or similarity, and related tactics can lead entrepreneurs to "go with their hearts instead of their heads" in assembling the initial team for their new venture. Developing the ability to recognize such tactics when they are used requires considerable practice, but simply calling them to your attention is useful, because some research findings indicate that where impression management is concerned, "to be forewarned is to be forearmed." Certainly, we are not suggesting that you adopt a cynical approach to other persons—that, too, can be harmful. But accepting the information or outward façade presented by strangers without due diligence is not only naïve, but it can also be very costly to the fortunes of a new venture. As Peter Dunley, a humorist of the early twentieth century put it: *Trust everybody, but cut the cards.*

Deception: Beyond Impression Management

If the only thing we had to worry about in terms of perceiving others accurately was impression management, our task would be complex but far from unmanageable. In fact, though, efforts by others to put themselves in a favorable light is only part of the problem. In addition we often confront outright deception—efforts by others to actively mislead us, either by withholding vital information or providing false information (see Figure 5.4). The use of deception raises serious ethical issues, and there is general agreement that engaging in it, especially to promote one's selfish interests at a high costs to others, is inappropriate and reprehensible. Unfortunately, however, deception is far from rare, so once again, it is important for prospective entrepreneurs to be able to recognize it when it occurs during the process of assembling required human resources.

How can they accomplish this important task? Existing evidence suggests that part of the answer involves judicious use of **nonverbal cues**. When people lie, subtle changes often occur in their facial expressions, body posture or movements, and certain nonverbal aspects of speech (aspects that are not related to the meaning of the words they speak—for instance, the tone of their voices). These changes, in turn, can provide valuable clues to the occurrence of deception. Here is a brief summary of the changes that are most useful in this respect:

- *Microexpressions.* These are fleeting facial expressions lasting only a few tenths of a second. Such reactions appear on the face very quickly after an emotion-provoking event and are difficult to suppress. As result, they can be very revealing about others' true feelings or emotions. For instance, if you ask other persons whether they like something (e.g., an idea you have expressed, a new product), watch their faces closely as they respond. If you see one expression (e.g., a frown), which is followed very quickly by another (e.g., a smile), this can be a useful sign that they are lying— they are stating one opinion or reaction when in fact, they really have another.
- *Interchannel discrepancies.* A second nonverbal cue revealing of deception is known as interchannel discrepancies. (The term "channel" refers to type of nonverbal cues; for instance, facial expressions are one channel, body movements are another.) These are inconsistencies between nonverbal cues from different basic channels. These result from the fact that persons who are lying often find it difficult to control all these channels at once. For instance, they may manage their facial expressions well, but they may have difficulty looking you in the eye as they tell their lie.

Figure 5.4 Deception: An All-Too-Frequent Occurrence in the World of Business

Entrepreneurs, like everyone else, often confront deception on the part of others. Being able to recognize such dishonesty is a valuable skill.

- *Nonverbal aspects of speech.* A third cue to deception involves nonverbal aspects of speech. When people lie, the pitch of their voices often rises, and they tend to speak in a more hesitating manner and to make more errors. If you detect these kinds of changes in another person's voice, this too, can be a sign that he or she is lying.
- *Eye contact.* Efforts at deception are often frequently revealed by certain aspects of eye contact. Persons who are lying blink more often and show pupils that are more dilated than persons who are telling the truth. They may also show an unusually low level of eye contact or—surprisingly—an unusually high one, as they attempt to fake being honest by looking others right in the eye.
- *Exaggerated facial expressions.* Finally, persons who are lying sometimes show exaggerated facial expressions. They may smile more—or more broadly—than usual or may show greater sorrow than is typical in a given situation. A prime example: Someone says no to a request you've made and then shows exaggerated regret. This is a good sign that the reasons the person has supplied for saying "no" may not be true.

Through careful attention to these nonverbal cues, we can often tell when others are lying—or merely trying to hide their own feelings from us. Success in detecting deception is far from certain; some persons are very skillful liars. But if you pay careful attention to the cues described here, which are summarized in Figure 5.5, you will make their task of "pulling the wool over your eyes" much more difficult. (What happens if entrepreneurs do *not* pay careful attention to the task of social perception and form inaccurate views of others? For a discussion of this important issue, please see the **"Danger! Pitfall Ahead!"** section.)

What about the use of deception by entrepreneurs? Is this ever justified? Ethically, the answer is clear: *No!* Intentionally misleading others by withholding information or providing false information is contrary to widely accepted standards of business ethics.[22] But it is clear that some unscrupulous persons, representing themselves as entrepreneurs, do engage in deceptive practices. Recently, in fact, business fraud has become a serious problem for *e-tailers*—companies that sell their products or services on the Internet. These entrepreneurs are currently being hit with a double "whammy"— not only is the economy weak, but there is also growing concern among consumers about deception on the Internet. Newspapers and TV news shows have recently carried many reports of cases in which online shoppers' credit card numbers have been hijacked, or in which unsuspecting shoppers have been the victims of "bait and switch": They order and pay for one item, but receive another of much lower quality. Clearly, the persons who engage in such practices are *not* entrepreneurs: They are criminals. But there is a danger that their unscrupulous actions will reflect negatively on legitimate e-tailers. So far, there has been no large-scale defection from e-commerce sites, but since fraud is even harder to detect on computers than in person, only time will tell whether

Figure 5.5 Recognizing Deception

By paying careful attention to the cues summarized here, it is often possible to tell when others are engaging in deception.

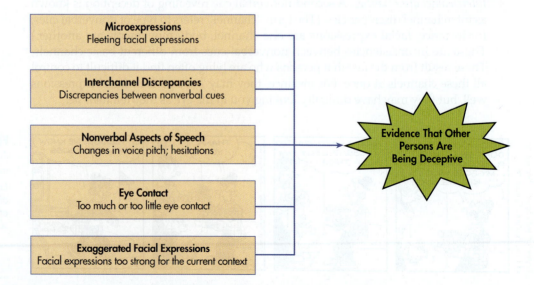

DANGER! PITFALL AHEAD!

The Partner Who Wasn't What He Claimed: When Social Perception Fails

In 1991, I (Robert Baron) became an entrepreneur. I had an idea for a new product (the special kind of air cleaner I described in Chapter 1) and believed that it might well have a substantial market. I realized that I did not have the knowledge and experience I needed to develop this opportunity alone, so I immediately launched efforts to identify one or more appropriate cofounders. Friends urged me to talk to the director of my university's technology park because he might be a good source of contacts for me. He directed me to a group of entrepreneurs running a small company that manufactured air cleaners. All of them claimed to have a lot of expertise with respect to design, manufacturing, and intellectual property rights—just what my self-assessment told me I needed most. So soon, I entered into an agreement with one of them to start a new company and begin the process of seeking a patent for my invention. Why did I choose this particular person? Mainly because I liked his candor—he seemed very down-to-earth—and because I thought that he could provide just what I needed most. Not only did he claim to have had lots experience in product design and manufacturing, but he had also run his own marketing company. That seemed just about perfect, so we moved ahead with our plans to found a new venture.

We agreed that in this venture, I would put up the needed funds to get the patent, so he would be a junior partner, holding about 20 percent of the shares. Because he had already helped me to design the new product, we applied for the patent jointly, as co-inventors. We received it, and that's when my major surprises began. It soon became clear that my new partner knew much less about manufacturing than he originally claimed. In fact, he did not really have a clue as to the costs involved in manufacturing our product. When these turned out to be more than $2 million, we decided to license our technology to a large company rather than try to make the product ourselves. We divided our duties in the new venture very clearly: I would deal with our corporate partner and focus on building markets for our product, while my cofounder would run day-to-day operations. But all too soon it became obvious that he either would not, or could not, handle these tasks. Our phones went unanswered (we were doing considerable business in direct sales to consumers), our financial records were a mess, and shipments of our product were painfully slow—if they happened at all. Gradually, I had to take over all these activities. The final result was that I ended up running the entire show—but sharing the profits with my partner, who often complained about the "pitiful return" he was getting for his valuable time!

Truly, I learned some painful lessons from these events, and when our agreement with the manufacturer expired, I told my partner that I could not continue and wanted to dissolve the company. He agreed, and that was the end of our working relationship. Looking back, I can see that although I did a fairly good self-assessment and understood what I needed from a cofounder, I then proceeded to make every mistake in the book. I did *not* do appropriate due diligence, did *not* try to separate verbal claims from reality, and did *not* try to determine when I was receiving the truth and when I was not. Don't misunderstand: I don't think my former partner harbored evil intentions toward me; on the contrary, I think that he was basically honest, but was lacking in self-knowledge and was seriously confused about what he could supply to our new venture. Still, I would have saved myself a lot of personal grief if I had followed the advice presented in earlier sections of this chapter. Will I do better the next time? Absolutely! After all, I don't see how I could do much worse!

this problem will have a long-term chilling effect on new ventures that do the bulk of their business on the Web.

Putting such instances of outright fraud aside, it is important to note that in order to assemble the resources they need (financial and otherwise), entrepreneurs—even ones who are 100 percent legitimate—sometimes do stretch the truth to a degree. Often, this takes the form of expressing greater optimism about their new ventures than current facts merit. Convincing others to "get on board" in one way or another is a challenging task and sometimes requires emphasizing the upside while minimizing the downside. In a sense, then, entrepreneurs must often walk a fine line between enthusiasm and optimism on the one hand, and intentional misrepresentations on the other. This is a difficult task, but one the founders of new ventures should approach with care; as one venture capitalist put it recently: "I try to balance sincerity against trust. If entrepreneurs are being super-optimistic, I don't mind, as long as I think, they are also sincere. If I think they are trying to mislead me, though, trust flies out the window and the game is over as far as I'm concerned."

KEY POINTS

- In order to choose excellent cofounders, entrepreneurs must perform the task of social perception well—they must form accurate perceptions of other persons.
- This is often a difficult task, because others do not always portray themselves accurately. They often engage in impression management—various tactics designed to place them in a favorable light. Entrepreneurs should take careful note of these tactics when choosing cofounders and should carefully check claims and information provided to them by these persons.
- Entrepreneurs often confront deception—efforts by others to actively mislead them. Important clues to the occurrence of deception are provided by nonverbal cues relating to facial expressions, eye contact, and nonverbal aspects of speech.
- Although they are sometimes tempted to do so, entrepreneurs should avoid engaging in deception themselves. This is unethical and will ultimately undermine trust in the entrepreneurs and their new ventures.
- If entrepreneurs do not choose cofounders carefully, they can experience disastrous results—as one of the authors did in connection with his own start-up company.

UTILIZING THE NEW VENTURE'S HUMAN RESOURCES: BUILDING STRONG WORKING RELATIONSHIPS AMONG THE FOUNDING TEAM

Assembling the resources needed to perform a task is an essential first step; indeed, there is no sense in starting unless the required resources are available or easily obtained "on the fly." But it is only the beginning; the task itself must then be performed. The same principle holds true for new ventures: Assembling the necessary human resources—an appropriate pool of knowledge, experience, skills, and abilities—is only the beginning. The people who constitute the founding team must then work together in an effective manner if the new venture is to succeed. Unfortunately, this key point is often overlooked, or at least given very little attention, by new entrepreneurs. They are so focused on the opportunity they have identified and wish to develop that they pay scant attention to building strong working relationships with one another—working relationships that will permit the new venture to utilize its human resources to the fullest. Growing evidence suggests that such relationships are an essential ingredient in new ventures' success.[23] For instance, in one recent study of 70 new ventures, higher levels of cohesion among the founding team (positive feelings toward one another) were strongly associated with superior financial performance by these new ventures.[24] In view of such evidence, a key question arises: How can strong working relationships between founding team members be encouraged? Although there is no simple answer to this question, three factors that appear to play a crucial role are these: a clear initial assignment of roles (responsibilities and authority) for all team members; careful attention to the basic issue of perceived fairness; and developing effective patterns and styles of communication (especially with respect to feedback) among team members.

Roles: The Clearer the Better

A major source of conflict in many organizations is uncertainty concerning two issues: responsibility and jurisdiction. Disagreements—often harsh and angry ones—often develop over the question of who is supposed to be accountable for what (responsibility), and over the question of who has the authority to make decisions and choose among alternative courses of action (jurisdiction).[25] One effective way of avoiding such problems is through the clear definition of **roles**—the set of behaviors that individuals occupying specific positions within a group are expected to perform, and the authority or jurisdiction they will wield. Once established, clear roles can be very useful. For instance, consider a new biotechnology venture with two cofounders. One holds an M.D. and is a practicing physician with a specialty in cardiology; the other holds an

MBA. To maximize their effectiveness as a team, these individuals should negotiate clearly defined roles at the outset. One possibility: the M.D. runs the laboratory, because it is conducting medical research and he is intimately familiar with the rules and regulations governing such activities; in addition, he is also responsible for interfacing with other M.D.s and for choosing the drugs on which to focus—after all, he is an expert on the symptoms and causes of various medical conditions. The other founder, in contrast, handles business-related aspects of the company (e.g., purchase and maintenance of equipment, setting up the company's computer systems), and because of his business expertise, oversees hiring of new personnel and financial tasks ranging from securing new capital through maintaining required records. If these roles are specified clearly in advance, the cofounders will truly work in a complementary manner—each will provide unique skills, experience, and knowledge that the other does not possess, or possesses to a lesser degree. The result? The company will operate smoothly and efficiently.

Imagine, however, that the M.D. decides that he should take an active hand with respect to the company's finances. This would not be surprising because bright, talented people often think it will be fun to do something that they haven't done before. Because the M.D. lacks knowledge in this area, he will have to spend considerable time acquiring a working knowledge of financial statements, tax regulations, and so on. This is inefficient. Moreover, his partner, who holds an MBA degree, may find this to be irritating at the least, and downright insulting at worst. The result? Conflict between the cofounders may occur, and the company operates at lower efficiency.

The moral is clear: Once the founding team has come together to form the new venture, its members should stick to the principle of complementarity. This implies dividing responsibilities and authority in accordance with each founder's expertise and knowledge. Anything else may well prove costly and detract from the new venture's success. This sounds very simple, but the sad fact is that many entrepreneurs are highly energetic, capable people, used to "running the show" in their own lives. Unless they can learn to coordinate with their cofounders, though, they may run the risk of seriously weakening their own companies.

A Note on Role Conflict

As we have just noted, it is important for entrepreneurs to establish clear-cut roles for all cofounders; this facilitates coordination between them and also helps to maximize the value of the new venture's human capital. But entrepreneurs, like everyone else, have roles outside their companies as well as within them. For instance, they may be spouses, significant others, or parents; they are certainly sons and daughters to their own parents. It is a classic finding in the field of human resource management that the roles that all of us hold sometimes make incompatible demands upon us; in other words, we experience *role conflict*—contrasting expectations about behavior and responsibilities held by different groups of persons.[26] Spouses and significant others, for example, expect us to be around to fill their emotional needs at least some of the time; similarly, children have legitimate expectations for their parents. So dealing with role conflict can be a very stressful task—and a difficult juggling act—for entrepreneurs, who must devote so much of their time to running their new ventures. Role conflict can be a very serious matter with important consequences; if the significant people in entrepreneurs' lives cannot come to terms with the heavy demands on the entrepreneurs' time and energies, serious interpersonal problems can result. These, in turn, can add to entrepreneurs' stress and reduce their overall performance. Clearly, then, getting one's spouse, significant others, children, and other family members "on board" is a task no entrepreneur can afford to overlook. The importance of this issue is emphasized by one highly successful entrepreneur in **"The Voice of Experience"** section on page 120.

Perceived Fairness: An Elusive But Essential Component

Try this simple exercise: Think back over your past life and remember a specific occasion when you worked with one or more persons on some project. The context is

THE VOICE OF EXPERIENCE

Why Your Family Should Be Part of the Team—Or at Least Fully On Board

David Gibson received a B.S. in economics and a B.S. in mechanical engineering from MIT in 1979; he received an M.S. in management from the Sloan School (MIT) in 1986. In 1990, he founded X-Ray Optical Systems, Inc., a company that focuses on the application of X-ray optics. He currently serves as president of X-Ray Optical Systems, and in this role, he is responsible for corporate strategy, marketing, and resource allocation. Prior to founding his company, Gibson worked at McKinsey & Company as a consultant and engagement manager and at Corning Glass Works, Inc., where he was responsible for sales and marketing for several industrial ceramic product lines and supervised the organization's customer service organization. From 1979 through 1984, he served in the United States Army Berlin Brigade, where he was an expert on urban combat. Gibson holds two U.S. patents and has published more than 10 articles in professional journals.

When entrepreneurs think about the team they must assemble for their new business, they think first of cofounders and then of key employees they must attract. Often, though, they overlook other persons who, although they may not work directly with the entrepreneur in starting the company, also play a crucial role its success: the entrepreneurs' family and close friends. How important are such persons to an entrepreneurs' success? I raised this matter in a recent conversation with David Gibson, founder of XOS, Inc., a company that has developed new technology to focus X-rays—something that was not previously feasible.

Baron: "Many factors enter into entrepreneurs' success—for instance, the quality of their idea; the entrepreneurs' experience, background, and training; the availability of adequate financing; people skills (e.g., persuasiveness, knowing how to make a good first impression). What factors do *you* think are most important in producing success?"

Gibson: "I think you have to have a number of different skills. A varied, eclectic background is valuable. And you have to be able to make decisions; if you can't, you can't run a business, especially a technology-based business. And you must be able to make these decisions under uncertainty, without all the information you'd ideally like to have."

Baron: "Anything else?"

Gibson: "You have to be able to *sell*—that is truly a value-added activity. I spend 70 to 80 percent of my time selling—I have to sell my family on risks, investors and suppliers on why they should give us 90 days to pay our accounts, employees and their families. Selling is really what you do, and you have to be good at it to succeed."

Baron: "I just heard you mention selling families on risks. Can you expand on that?"

Gibson: "Sure. I mean that starting a business is a big risk, and you shouldn't do it unless your spouse and close family are OK with it. They have to understand the downside as well as the upside. If they aren't comfortable with the risks, including the debts you have to take on, you really can't proceed."

Baron: "But what happens if spouses or close family members aren't on board? Can't the entrepreneur deal with that?"

Gibson: "Maybe, but I've seen some real horror stories—happy couples who get divorced after many years together because one couldn't handle the risk, the uncertainty, and the absence of their spouse from home so many hours every week. No one talks about this in entrepreneurship classes, but in my view, it is crucial. In fact, entrepreneurs ought to choose a spouse who can handle risks and uncertainty. If they marry someone for whom that is upsetting life can be very difficult for everyone involved."

Baron: "Well, given that love is often blind, that may be hard to do—but I get what you mean: The more your spouse or significant other shares your willingness to take risks and make big life changes, the better."

Gibson: "Exactly."

Commentary: We think that the points made by Mr. Gibson are both insightful and accurate. Being able to "sell"—to persuade others, to get them to share your enthusiasm for your products or services—is certainly a key skill useful to all entrepreneurs. Among the people entrepreneurs must persuade are the ones closest to them—their spouses, significant others, family, and close friends. Without the strong support of these people, the difficulties they face can be greatly magnified. In a sense, then, the first "selling task" entrepreneurs face is that of overcoming the doubts and concerns—often legitimate—of the people on whose help they will count most heavily. If these people aren't fully on board, entrepreneurs are likely to experience intense role conflict, and this, in turn, can drain their energies, distract them from running their business, and damage those around them. So making sure that family members and close friends are part of the team in the sense that they fully support what the entrepreneur is trying to do is one of the most important steps entrepreneurs can take to enhance their chances of success.

unimportant—it can be any kind of project you wish—but try to recall an incident in which the outcome was positive: The project was a success. Now, divide 100 points between yourself and your partners according to how large a contribution each person made to the project. Next comes the key question: How did you divide the points? If you are like most people, you gave yourself more points than your partners. (For example, if you had one partner, you took more than 50 points; if you had three, you took more than 33.3 points, and so on).

Now, by way of contrast, try to recall another incident—one in which you also worked with partners, but in which the outcome was negative: The project failed. Once again divide 100 points between yourself and your partners, according to how large a contribution each person made to the project and its outcome. In this case, you may well have given them more points than yourself. If you showed this pattern, welcome to the club: You are demonstrating a very powerful human tendency, often known as the **self-serving bias**. This is the tendency to attribute successful outcomes largely to internal causes (our own efforts, talents, or abilities) but unsuccessful ones largely to external causes (e.g., the failings or negligence of others, factors beyond our control).[27] This bias has been found to be a strong one, and it has serious implications for any situation in which people work together to achieve important goals. Specifically, it often leads all the persons involved to conclude that somehow, they have not been treated fairly. Why? Because each participant in the relationship tends to accentuate their own contributions and minimize those of others, they conclude that they are receiving less of the available rewards than is justified. Further, because each person has the same perception, the result is often friction and conflict between the persons involved.

LEARNING OBJECTIVE

5 Define "self-serving bias" and explain how it plays an important role in perceived fairness.

In other words, this tendency raises thorny questions relating to *perceived fairness*—a key issue for entrepreneurs. Because of the self-serving bias (plus other factors, too), we all have a tendency to assume that we are receiving less than we deserve in almost any situation. In other words, we perceive that the balance between what we contribute and what we receive is less favorable than it is for other persons. In specific terms, we perceive that the ratio between what we are receiving and what we are contributing is smaller than that for others. In general, we prefer this ratio to be the same for all, so that the larger any person's contributions, the larger their rewards—a principle known as **distributive justice**. Most people accept this principle as valid, but the self-serving bias leads us to cognitively inflate our own contributions—and hence to conclude that in fact, we are not being treated fairly (see Figure 5.6).

What do people do when they perceive that the distribution of rewards is unfair? Many different things, none of which are beneficial to a new venture. The most obvious tactic is to demand a larger share; because others do not view these demands as legitimate, conflict is the likely outcome. Another approach is to reduce one's contributions—to reduce effort or shirk responsibility. This, too, can be highly detrimental to the success of a new venture. An even more damaging reaction is to withdraw, either physically or psychologically. Disaffected cofounders sometimes pull out of new ventures, taking their experience, knowledge, and skills with them. If they are essential members of the team, this can mark the beginning of the end for the ventures in question.

All this is bad enough, but even worse is the recent finding that although people tend to focus relatively little attention on the issue of fairness when things are going well (e.g., they are getting along well with their cofounders), they devote increasing attention to this issue when things begin to go badly.[28] In short, when a new venture is succeeding and reaching its goals, members of the founding team may show little concern over distributive justice. If things go badly, however, they begin to focus increasing attention on this issue, thus intensifying interpersonal friction.

Given the existence of this cycle, it is truly crucial for the founding teams of new ventures to consider the issue of perceived fairness very carefully. This implies that

Figure 5.6 The Self-Serving Bias and Perceived Unfairness

Because most persons have a strong tendency to perceive their contributions to any relationship as larger than they are, they also tend to perceive that they are receiving a smaller share of available rewards than is appropriate. In other words, they conclude that they are being treated unfairly. This can be a serious problem for founding teams of entrepreneurs.

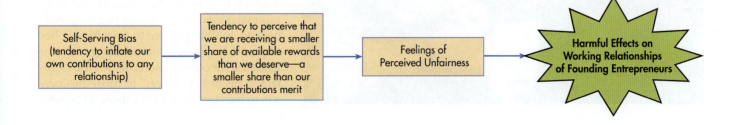

they should discuss this issue regularly to assure that as roles, responsibilities, and contributions to the new venture change (which they will inevitably do over time), adjustments are made with respect to equity, status, and other rewards to reflect these changes. This is a difficult task because all members will tend to accentuate their own contributions (recall the powerful self-serving bias). But because the alternative is the very real risk of tension and conflict between the founding team members, and because conflict is often a major waste of time and energy,[29] it is certainly a task worth performing well—and one that will help the new venture utilize its human resources to the fullest.

One more point: Issues of fairness arise not only between cofounders, but also between companies that form business alliances. As we will note in Chapter 10, such alliances can often be extremely helpful to new ventures, but in order to survive, they must be perceived as fair and mutually beneficial by both sides. Here's one example of an alliance that has been very successful. 8 minute Dating is a young company with an idea that has taken the matchmaking industry by storm. At 8 minute Dating events, single men and women gather at a restaurant, chat in couples for eight minutes, and then move on to the next table, where they meet another person (see Figure 5.7). This allows each person participating in the event to meet many potential partners in one evening instead of just one, as is true in traditional dating. After the event is over, couples who like each other can meet again. Recently, 8 minute Dating has formed an alliance with Tele-Publishing International (TPI)—a company that runs the personal ad pages for 550 newspapers in the United States. How did this occur? The founder of 8 minute Dating, Tom Jafee, learned that Adam Segal, an executive with TPI, was having dinner with his mother at a restaurant where an 8 minute Dating event was being held. Jafee introduced himself and the two entrepreneurs quickly realized that they could form a mutually beneficial alliance: TPI would advertise 8 minute Dating in its personal columns, and 8 minute Dating events would distribute free coupons and sponsor other promotions to encourage its customers to try the personal ads. The alliance has worked like a charm: Both companies have benefited considerably. Both see it as fair, and as helping them to attain their major goals. As Segal puts it: "The beauty of our alliance is that it can expand with 8 minute Dating's growth. Every time they start events in a new city, TPI will already be there with our personal ads in the newspapers. Talk about a match made in heaven." So if you consider forming an alliance with another company, please do devote careful attention to the question of fairness: Alliances that are not perceived as meeting this essential criterion are unlikely to survive.

Figure 5.7 Fairness: A Key Principle in Business Alliances

Business alliances can be highly beneficial to entrepreneurs, but in order to succeed, both sides must perceive them as fair and as yielding real benefits. This is definitely the case for the alliance between 8 minute Dating and TPI, Inc. 8 minute Dating encourages people participating in its dating events to check out the personal columns, and TPI promotes 8 minute Dating events in the personal columns it runs for 550 newspapers.

AP/Wide World Photos/AJ Mast

Effective Communication

Perceived unfairness is not the only cause of costly conflicts between members of a new venture's founding team. Another major factor involves faulty styles of communication. Unfortunately, individuals often communicate with others in a way that angers or annoys the recipients, even when it is not their intention to do so. This happens in many different ways, but one of the most common—and important—involves delivering feedback, especially negative feedback, in an inappropriate manner. In essence, there is only one truly rational reason for delivering negative feedback to another person: to help him or her improve. Yet, people often deliver negative feedback for other reasons: to put the recipient in his or her "place," to cause this person to lose face in front of others, to express anger and hostility, and so on. The result of such negative feedback is that the recipient experiences anger or humiliation in turn, and this can be the basis for smoldering resentment and long-lasting grudges.[30] When negative feedback is delivered in an informal context, rather than formally (e.g., as part of a written performance review), it is known as *criticism*, and research findings suggest that such feedback can take two distinct forms: *constructive criticism*, which is truly designed to help the recipient improve, and *destructive criticism*, which is perceived—rightly so—as a form of hostility or attack.

What makes criticism constructive or destructive in nature? Key differences are outlined in Table 5.1. As you can see from this table, constructive criticism is considerate of the recipient's feelings, does not contain threats, it timely (occurs at an appropriate point in time), does not attribute blame to the recipient, is specific in content, and offers concrete suggestions for improvement. Destructive criticism, in contrast, is harsh, contains threats, is not timely, blames the recipient for negative outcomes, is not specific in content, and offer no concrete ideas for improvement. Table 5.1 also provides examples of each type of criticism.

Research findings indicate that destructive criticism is truly destructive: It generates strong negative reactions in recipients and can initiate a vicious cycle of anger, the desire for revenge, and subsequent conflict. The message for entrepreneurs is clear: Effective communication between cofounders is one essential ingredient in establishing and maintaining effective working relationships. If it is lacking, serious problems may result. For instance, consider a new venture started by partners who have followed the complementarity principle: One is an engineer and the other has a background in marketing. Although the marketing cofounder has selected his partner carefully, he harbors negative feelings about engineers ("They never think about people!"). As a result, he criticizes the engineer's designs for new products harshly. The engineer is offended by this treatment, so he begins to make changes in the company's products without informing his cofounder. Because the marketing entrepreneur doesn't know about these changes, he can't get customer input before they are made. The result? The company's products "bomb" in the marketplace, and soon the new venture is in deep trouble. This is just one example of how faulty communication between members of the founding team can produce disastrous effects. The main point should be clear: Strong efforts to attain good, constructive communication between cofounders are very worthwhile.

One final question: Is all conflict between founding cofounders bad? Absolutely not. Conflict between team members can, if it is focused on specific issues rather than personalities and is held within rational bounds, be very useful. Such "rational" conflict can help to focus attention on important issues, motivate both sides to understand each others' view more clearly, and can, by encouraging both sides to carefully consider all assumptions, lead to better decisions.[31] In sum, conflict between founding

LEARNING OBJECTIVE

6 Explain the difference between constructive and destructive criticism.

Table 5.1 Constructive Versus Destructive Criticism

Constructive criticism is negative feedback that can actually help the recipient improve. Destructive criticism, in contrast, is far less likely to produce such beneficial effects.

CONSTRUCTIVE CRITICISM	DESTRUCTIVE CRITICISM	EXAMPLES
Considerate—protects self-esteem of recipients	Inconsiderate—harsh, sarcastic, biting	Constructive: "I was disappointed in your performance." Destructive: "What a rotten, lousy job!"
Does not contain threats	Contains threats	Constructive: "I think improvement is really important." Destructive: "If you don't improve, you are history!"
Timely—occurs as soon as possible after the poor or inadequate performance	Not timely—occurs after an inappropriate delay	Constructive: "You made several errors in today's report." Destructive: "I've been meaning to tell about the errors you made last year."
Does not attribute poor performance to internal causes	Attributes poor performance to internal causes	Constructive: "I know that a lot of factors probably played a role in your performance." Destructive: "You failed because you just don't give a damn!"
Specific—focuses on aspects of performance that were inadequate	General—a sweeping condemnation of performance	Constructive: "The main problem was that the project was late." Destructive: "You did a really terrible job."
Focuses on performance, not the recipient	Focuses on the recipient	Constructive: "Your performance was not what I expected." Destructive: "You are a rotten performer!"
Offers concrete suggestions for improvement	Does not offer concrete suggestions for improvement	Constructive: "Here's how I think you can do better next time around." Destructive: "You'd better work on doing better!"

team members is not necessarily a bad thing. Rather, it—like all other aspects of the new venture's operations—should be carefully managed so that benefits are maximized and costs held to a minimum. Overall, strong and effective working relationships between founding members are a powerful asset to any new venture, so efforts to foster them should be high on every founding team's "must do" list.

KEY POINTS

- Once an appropriate founding team is assembled, these individuals must work together effectively if their new venture is to succeed.
- One key ingredient in establishing strong working relationships is the development of clearly defined roles, which specify the responsibilities and jurisdiction of each entrepreneur.
- Because of the self-serving bias and other factors, individuals often perceive that they are not being treated fairly by others—that they are not receiving a share of available rewards that is commensurate with the scope of their contributions (i.e., that distributive justice is lacking).
- Reactions to such perceived unfairness range from demanding more or doing less, to actual withdrawal from the relationship. Because all of these reactions are inimical to the success of a new venture, entrepreneurs should take active steps to assure that all members of the founding team feel that they are being treated fairly.
- The same principle holds for business alliances formed by new ventures: In order to be successful, both parties to such alliances must feel that they are fair and mutually beneficial.
- Another ingredient in strong working relationships is effective communication. In particular, entrepreneurs should avoid delivering destructive criticism to one another because such negative feedback often leads to feelings of hostility and intense conflict.

EXPANDING THE NEW VENTURE'S HUMAN RESOURCES: BEYOND THE FOUNDING TEAM

The founding team of any new venture is a key component of its human resources. A first-rate group of founders brings a wealth of knowledge, experience, skills, and commitment to their company.[32] Further, as common sense would suggest, the larger the founding team and the more varied the experience of its members (the principle of complementarity), the greater the likelihood that the new venture will succeed. Specifically, the greater are the new venture's chances of survival[33] and the faster its rate of growth.[34] But no matter how excellent a new venture's founding team is, it cannot possibly supply all required resources or all forms of information. At the very least, new ventures often require the services of experts from outside the company— for instance, lawyers, accountants, or engineers. If the new venture is successful in obtaining financing and in building a customer base, the need for additional human resources in the form of employees beyond the founding team may soon become apparent. This raises several important and related questions: (1) How can new ventures succeed in obtaining the employees they need? (2) How many should they hire? (3) Should these be temporary or permanent employees? Research on these questions provides relatively clear and informative answers.

Obtaining Excellent Employees: The Key Role of Social Networks

LEARNING OBJECTIVE

7 Describe the role of social networks in new ventures' efforts to hire additional employees.

New ventures face serious obstacles with respect to attracting outstanding employees: As new companies, they are relatively unknown to potential employees and cannot offer the legitimacy or security of established firms. Thus, they enter the market for human resources with important disadvantages. How do start-up companies overcome these difficulties? Largely through the use of *social networks*. In other words, they tend to hire people they know either directly, from personal contact, or indirectly, through recommendations from people they do know and trust[35] (see Figure 5.8). This is helpful to new ventures in several ways.

By hiring people they know (often family members, friends, or persons with whom they worked in the past), entrepreneurs are able to acquire human resources quickly, without the necessity for long and costly searches. Second, because they know the people they hire either directly or indirectly, it is easier for entrepreneurs to convince these individuals of the value of the opportunity they are pursuing. Third, new ventures often lack clearly established rules or a well-defined culture; having direct or indirect ties with new employees makes the task of integrating them into this somewhat loose and changing structure somewhat easier.

In sum, new ventures generally hire people known to the founding entrepreneurs either directly or indirectly and in this way are able to expand their base of human resources in a relatively rapid and cost-effective manner.

© Getty Images/PhotoDisc

Figure 5.8 Social Networks: A Major Source of New Employees for New Ventures

Entrepreneurs often rely on social networks as a source of new employees. The persons they hire are ones they know or ones recommended to them by people they trust.

Is Bigger Necessarily Better? Number of Employees as a Factor in New Venture Growth

New ventures face many difficult questions as they grow and develop, but among these, one of the most perplexing concerns the number of employees they should hire. Adding employees—expanding the new venture's human resources—offers obvious advantages. New employees are a source of information, skills, and energy; further, the more employees a new venture has, the greater the number and larger the size of the projects it can undertake. As we noted earlier, there is little doubt that in many contexts, people working together in a coordinated manner can accomplish far more than individuals working alone. But adding employees to a new venture has an obvious downside, too. Employees add to the new venture's fixed expenses and raise many complex issues relating to the health and safety of such persons that must be carefully considered. In a sense, therefore, expanding the company's workforce is a double-edged sword, and the results of expanding the number of employees can truly be mixed in nature.

However, existing evidence suggests that on balance, the benefits of increasing the number of employees outweigh the costs. New ventures that start with more employees have a greater chance of surviving than ones that begin with a smaller number.[36] Similarly, companies with more employees have higher rates of growth than ones with fewer employees.[37] Profitability, too, is positively related to the size of new ventures. For example, the greater the number of employees, the larger the earnings of new ventures, and the greater the income generated by them for their founders.[38]

We should hasten to note that these findings are all correlational in nature: They indicate that number of employees is *related*, in a positive manner, to several measures of new ventures' success. They do not, however, indicate that hiring new employees *causes* such success. In fact, both number of employees and various measures of financial success may stem from other, underlying factors, such as the quality of the opportunity being developed, commitment and talent of the founding team, and even general economic conditions (it is often easier to hire good employees at reasonable cost when the economy is weak than when it is strong). So the relationship between new venture size (number of employees) and new venture success should be approached with a degree of caution. Still, having said this, it is clear that human resources are a key ingredient in the success of start-up companies, so to the extent a new venture can afford to expand its workforce, doing so many be an effective strategy.

Should New Ventures Hire Temporary or Permanent Employees? Commitment Versus Cost

Achieving an appropriate balance between costs and numbers of new employees is not the only issue facing new ventures where expanding their workforce is concerned: In addition, they must determine whether new employees should be hired on a temporary or permanent basis. Again, there are advantages and disadvantages to both strategies. Temporary employees reduce fixed costs and provide for a great deal of flexibility: They can be hired and released as the fortunes of the venture dictate. Further, hiring temporary employees permits the new venture to secure specialized knowledge or skills that may be required for a specific project; when the project is completed, the temporary employees depart, thus reducing costs.

On the other side of the coin, there are several disadvantages associated with temporary employees. First, they may lack the commitment and motivation of permanent employees. After all, they know that they have been hired on a contract basis for a specified period of time (although this can often be extended), so they have little feeling of commitment to the new venture: In a sense, they are visitors, not permanent residents. In addition, there is the real risk that temporary employees will acquire valuable information about the company or its opportunity and then carry this to potential competitors. Certainly, that is a serious danger for any new venture. Permanent employees, in contrast, tend to be more strongly committed and motivated with respect to the new venture and are less likely to leave—especially if, as we will describe in Chapter 13, they gain an equity stake in the company.

Overall, then, the choice between temporary and permanent employees is a difficult one. Which is preferable seems to depend, to a large extent, on specific conditions faced by a new venture, such as the industry in which it operates or the opportunity it is attempting to exploit. In situations where flexibility and speed of acquiring new sets of knowledge and expertise are crucial (e.g., among software start-up companies), temporary employees may be very beneficial.[39] In situations where employee commitment and retention are more important (e.g., employees rapidly acquire skills and knowledge that increase their value to the new venture), then focusing on a permanent workforce may be preferable.[40] In Chapter 12, we will discuss several factors (e.g., the need for speed) that lead entrepreneurs to use contractual modes of business such as hiring temporary workers in place of more hierarchical forms, such as hiring permanent ones.

Some Concluding Thoughts

Many companies—and new ventures are no exception to this generalization—proudly proclaim that "Our people are our most precious resource." In other words, they recognize that the knowledge, skills, talents, and commitment supplied by employees is the single most important ingredient in the company's success—or failure. A vast body of evidence in the field of human resources suggests that this is true: People *are* a crucial factor in determining the success of any business, large existing ones and small start-ups alike.[41] Indeed, they are just as important in this respect as technological, legal, and financial factors. For this reason, it is very important that the founders of new ventures devote careful attention to the issues considered here—hiring excellent employees, carefully determining the optimal size of the company's workforce, and attaining a good balance between temporary and permanent human resources. Lack of attention to these issues can prove as deadly to the new company's fortunes as beginning with a mismatched founding team or allowing working relations between members of this team to deteriorate to the point where they become ineffective. Excellent human resources, in short, are an essential part of the foundation of new ventures, and as we are sure you will agree, only structures built on firm foundations endure.

- As new ventures grow, their requirements for additional human resources, too, increase. Often, these new employees are hired through the founding teams' social network.
- Existing evidence suggests that the greater the number of employees in new ventures, the greater their financial success. However, this does not necessarily imply that increasing the number of employees causes success; rather, both success and number of employees may stem from the same underlying factors (e.g., the quality of the opportunity being exploited).
- The choice between hiring temporary and permanent employees is a complex one; both offer advantages and disadvantages. Ultimately, this decision must depend on the specific situation in which a new venture operates.

Summary and Review of Key Points

- In general, people tend to like, and feel more comfortable around, persons who are similar to themselves in various ways.
- This leads entrepreneurs to select cofounders whose background, training, and experience closely matches their own.
- Because a wide range of knowledge, skills, and experience among the founding team is very advantageous to new ventures, selecting cofounders on the basis of complementarity rather than similarity is often a more useful strategy.
- In order to choose cofounders who bring knowledge, skills, and attributes complementary to their own, entrepreneurs must first conduct a careful self-assessment of their own human capital.
- This is a difficult task because often we are unaware of the causes of our own behavior and, because in many instances, we can acquire understanding of our own characteristics only from others' reactions to us.
- Entrepreneurs' self-assessment should carefully consider their knowledge base, specific skills, motives, and personal attributes (e.g., where they stand on each of the "Big Five" Dimensions of personality).
- In choosing cofounders, it is often useful to focus on complementarity with respect to knowledge, skills, and experience, but on similarity with respect to personal characteristics and motives.
- In order to choose excellent cofounders, entrepreneurs must perform the task of social perception well—they must form accurate perceptions of other persons.
- This is often a difficult task, because others do not always portray themselves accurately. They often engage in impression management—various tactics designed to place them in a favorable light. Entrepreneurs should take careful note of these tactics

when choosing cofounders and should carefully check claims and information provided to them by these persons.
- Entrepreneurs often confront deception—efforts by others to actively mislead them. Important clues to the occurrence of deception are provided by nonverbal cues relating to facial expressions, eye contact, and nonverbal aspects of speech.
- Although they are sometimes tempted to do so, entrepreneurs should avoid engaging in deception themselves. This is unethical and will ultimately undermine trust in the entrepreneurs and their new ventures.
- If entrepreneurs do not choose cofounders carefully, they can experience disastrous results—as one of the authors did in connection with his own start-up company.
- Once an appropriate founding team is assembled, these individuals must work together effectively if their new venture is to succeed.
- One key ingredient in establishing strong working relationships is the development of clearly defined roles, which specify the responsibilities and jurisdiction of each entrepreneur.
- Because of the self-serving bias and other factors, individuals often perceive that they are not being treated fairly by others—that they are not receiving a share of available rewards that is commensurate with the scope of their contributions.
- Reactions to such perceived unfairness range from demanding more or doing less, to actual withdrawal from the relationship. Because all of these reactions are inimical to the success of a new venture, entrepreneurs should take active steps to assure that all members of the founding team feel that they are being treated fairly.

- The same principle holds for business alliances formed by new ventures: In order to be successful, both parties to such alliances must feel that they are fair and mutually beneficial.
- Another ingredient in strong working relationships is effective communication. In particular, entrepreneurs should avoid delivering destructive criticism to one another because such negative feedback often leads to feelings of hostility and intense conflict.
- As new ventures grow, their requirements for additional human resources, too, increase. Often, these new employees are hired through the founding teams' social network.

- Existing evidence suggests that the greater the number of employees in new ventures, the greater their financial success. However, this does not necessarily imply that increasing the number of employees causes success; rather, both success and number of employees may stem from the same underlying factors (e.g., the quality of the opportunity being exploited).
- The choice between hiring temporary and permanent employees is a complex one; both offer advantages and disadvantages. Ultimately, this decision must depend on the specific situation in which a new venture operates.

Glossary

Big Five Dimensions of Personality: Basic dimensions of personality that have been found to strongly affect behavior in a wide range of situations.

Deception: Efforts to mislead others by withholding information or presenting false information.

Distributive Justice: A principle of perceived fairness suggesting that all parties to a relationship should receive a share of the available rewards commensurate with the scope of their contributions.

Impression Management: Tactics used by individuals to make a good first impression on others.

Nonverbal Cues: Cues relating to facial expressions, eye contact, body posture or movements, or nonverbal

aspects of speech. These cues can be very helpful in the detection of deception.

Roles: The set of behaviors that individuals occupying specific positions within a group are expected to perform.

Self-Assessment: An inventory of the knowledge, experience, training, motives, and characteristics they themselves possess and can contribute to the new venture.

Self-Serving Bias: The tendency to attribute successful outcomes largely to internal causes (our own efforts, talents, or abilities) but unsuccessful ones largely to external cause (e.g., the failings or negligence of others).

Social Perception: The process through which we come to know and understand other persons.

Discussion Questions

1. In general, we tend to like people who are similar to ourselves in various ways. Why can this sometimes be counterproductive for entrepreneurs when choosing partners?

2. Do you think that because of their relative standing on the "Big Five" dimensions of personality, some persons are more suited to become entrepreneurs than others? What characteristics would qualify someone to become an entrepreneur? What characteristics might make someone unsuited to becoming an entrepreneur?

3. What tactics of impression management do *you* use? Which are most successful? Why?

4. How good are you at recognizing attempts at deception by other persons? What clues do you use to try

to determine whether others are telling the truth or lying?

5. Everyone wants to be treated fairly. Can you think of factors other than the share of available rewards you receive that could lead you to conclude that you were being treated fairly or unfairly by others? (*Hint:* Do the procedures used to distribute rewards matter?)

6. Do you ever criticize other persons for any reason aside from a desire to help them? When? What effects does this produce?

7. In general, entrepreneurs tend to hire people they know when first increasing the size of their new ventures. Can you think of any potential problems that could result from following this strategy?

InfoTrac Exercises

1. **Resource Complementarity in Business Combinations: Extending the Logic to Organizational Alliances** (technical)

   Jeffrey S. Harrison; Michael A. Hitt; Robert E. Hoskisson; R. Duane Ireland.

   Journal of Management, Nov–Dec 2001 v27 i6 p679(12)

   Record: A81598446

Abstract: Organizations are combining resources through acquisitions and alliances in record numbers. Since publication of our original study in 1991, research has confirmed that resource complementarity creates the potential for greater synergy from acquisitions and alliances, leading to higher long-term firm performance as an end result. The valuable, unique, and inimitable synergy that can be realized by integrating complementary resources provides an opportunity for the firm to create competitive advantages that can be sustained for a period of time. In addition, complementary resources present opportunities for enhanced learning as well as the development of new capabilities. However, we also suggest that the existence of complementary resources is a necessary but insufficient condition to achieve synergy. The resources must be effectively integrated and managed to realize the synergy.

   1. According to the text, which characteristic is more likely to lead to a successful founding team—similarity or complementarity? Why?
   2. What evidence do the authors of the article offer to support their view that complementarity leads to more successful alliances?
   3. According to the article, what benefits result from complementarity?

2. **Offer Constructive Criticism . . . Without Sounding Like a Jerk**

   Info-Tech Advisor Newsletter, Sept 3, 2002 pNA

   Record: A92303209

   Full Text: COPYRIGHT 2002 InfoTech Research Group Sources: (*Business Finance Magazine* article, ITtoolkit.com article, *Software Development Magazine* article)

   1. According to the text, what is the only truly rational reason for delivering negative feedback?
   2. What are the effects of destructive criticism according to the text and the article?
   3. List steps from the text and article that you can use to give feedback more constructively.

GETTING DOWN
TO BUSINESS

Where Do You Stand on the "Big Five" Dimensions of Personality?

A large body of evidence indicates that the "Big Five" dimensions of personality are both basic and important. Where people stand on these factors has a strong impact on their behavior in many situations—and the success they attain. Where do *you* stand on each of these dimensions? To find out, ask several people who know you well to rate you on each of the following items. They should use a 7-point scale for these ratings, where 1 = lowest and 7 = highest. The ratings they provide are a very rough indication of where you stand on each of the "Big Five" dimensions of personality. (*Note*: Because this is an informal exercise, please interpret the findings with a healthy degree of caution.)

DIMENSION	RATING QUESTIONS (TO BE ANSWERED BY PEOPLE WHO KNOW YOU WELL)
Conscientiousness	How reliable is [your name]? How neat and orderly is _____ ? How carefully does _____ complete jobs?
Extraversion	How much excitement does _____ prefer? How readily does _____ make new friends? How cheerful and friendly is _____ ?
Agreeableness	How trusting of others is _____ ? How courteous is _____ toward others? How cooperative is _____ ?
Emotional stability	How much does _____ worry? How often does _____ become emotionally excited? How confident and secure is _____ ?
Openness to experience	How much does _____ like change? How much curiosity does _____ have?

Choosing the Right Partner

Many new ventures are founded by two or more persons, so it is clear that choosing a good partner (or partners) is an important task for entrepreneurs. In order to choose wisely, you need three basic pieces of information: (1) a clear self-assessment (what you bring to the table in terms of skills, abilities, knowledge, etc.), (2) a clear picture of what you need from potential partners, and (3) an ability to assess other people accurately so that you can tell whether they have what you need. This exercise should help you to gather all three kinds of information.

1. **Self-assessment.** Rate yourself on each of the following dimensions. Be as honest and accurate as possible! For each dimension, enter a number from 1 to 5 (1 = very low; 2 = low; 3 = average; 4 = high; 5 = very high).

   a. **Experience related to your new venture** _____ (enter a number from 1 to 5)

   b. **Technical knowledge related to your new venture** _____

   c. **People skills (skills useful in getting along with others, persuading them, etc.)** _____

   d. **Motivation to succeed** _____

   e. **Commitment to the new venture** _____

   f. **Personal attributes that suit you to becoming an entrepreneur** _____

   g. **Personal attributes that do not suit you to becoming an entrepreneur** _____

2. **What you need in a partner.** Taking account of the ratings in part 1, list what you need from your partners. For instance, if you are low in technical knowledge, you would want such knowledge in your partner; if you are low in people skills, you would want a partner high on this dimension, and so on.

   a.

   b.

   c.

   d.

   e.

   f.

3. **How good are you at social perception?** Are you good at assessing other people accurately? To find out, indicate the extent to which each of the following statements is true of you (1 = not true at all; 2 = not true; 3 = neither true nor false; 4 = true; 5 = very true).

   a. I can easily tell when other people are lying.

b.   I can guess others' true feelings, if they want to conceal these from me.

c.   I can recognize others' weak spots.

d.   I'm a good judge of other people.

e.   I can usually recognize others' traits accurately by observing their behavior.

f.   I can tell why people have acted the way they have in most situations.

Add your answers. If you scored 20 or higher, you see yourself as good at social perception. To find out whether this is accurate, ask several people who know you well to rate you on the same items. In other words, change the items to read: " _____ can easily tell when other people are lying" (your name goes in the blank space). If their ratings agree with yours, congratulations—you are good not only at assessing others, but also at assessing yourself!

Enhanced Learning

You may select any combination of the case options below to enhance your understanding of the chapter material.

- **Appendix 1: Case Studies –** Thirteen cases provide opportunities to apply chapter concepts to realistic entrepreneurial situations. These brief cases call for careful analysis of real business problems and ask you to think about potential solutions.

- **Appendix 2: Video Case Library –** Nine cases are tied directly to video segments from the popular PBS television series *Small Business School*. These cases and video segments give you unparalleled access to today's entrepreneurs, with expert advice and insights on how to start, run, and grow a business.

- **Comprehensive Cases –** Visit the book support Web site at http://baron.swlearning.com for cases detailing real businesses whose successes and setbacks illustrate each stage of the entrepreneurial process. You will conduct in-depth analysis of entrepreneurial challenges through well-developed case studies.

Notes

[1] Cooper, A., Woo, C., & Dunkelberg, W. 1989. Entrepreneurship and the initial size of firms. *Journal of Business Venturing* 3: 97–108.

[2] Davidsson, P., & Honig, B. 2003. The role of social and human capital among nascent entrepreneurs. *Journal of Business Venturing* 18: 301–331.

[3] Greenberg, J., & Baron, R.A. 2003. *Behavior in organizations*. 8th ed. Upper Saddle River, NJ: Prentice-Hall.

[4] Erikson, T. 2002. Entrepreneurial capital: The emerging venture's most important asset and competitive advantage. *Journal of Business Venturing* 17: 275–290.

[5] Mount, M.K., & Barrick, M.R. 1995. The big five personality dimensions: Implications for research and practice in human resources management. In K.M. Rowland & G. Ferris (eds.). *Research on personnel and human resources management.* (vol. 13, pp. 153–200). Greenwich, CT: JAI Press.

[6] Hurtz, G.M, & Donovan, J.J. 2000. Personality and job performance: The big five revisited. *Journal of Applied Psychology* 85: 869–879.

[7] Salgado, J.F. 1997. The five-factor model of personality and job performance in the European community. *Journal of Applied Psychology* 82: 30–43.

[8] Ciavarella, M.A., Buchholtz, A.K., Riordan, C.M., Gatewood, R.D., & Stokes, G.S. (in press). The big five and venture survival: Is there a link? *Journal of Business Venturing*.

[9] Barrick, M.R., Stewart, G.L., Neubert, M.J., & Mount, M.K. 1998. Relating member ability and personality to work-team processes and team effectiveness. *Journal of Applied Psychology* 83: 377–391.

[10] George, J.M., & Zhou, J. 2001. When openness to experience and conscientiousness are related to creative behavior: An interactional approach. *Journal of Applied Psychology* 86: 513–524.

11 Keller, R.T. 2000. Cross-functional project groups in research and new product development: Diversity, communications, job stress, and outcomes. *Academy of Management Journal* 44: 547–555.

12 Baron, R.A., & Byrne, D. 2002. *Social psychology*. 10th ed. Boston: Allyn & Bacon.

13 Baron, R.A., & Markman, G. 2003. Beyond social capital: The role of entrepreneurs' social competence in their financial success. *Journal of Business Venturing* 18: 41–60.

14 Ferris, G.R., Witt, L.A., & Hockhwarter, W.Q. 2001. Interaction of social skill and general mental ability on job performance and salary. *Journal of Applied Psychology* 86: 1075–1082.

15 Terry, R.L., & Krantz, J.H. 1993. Dimensions of trait attributions associated with eyeglasses, men's facial hair, and women's hair length. *Journal of Applied Social Psychology* 23: 1757–1769.

16 See note 2.

17 Kilduff, M., & Day, D.V. 1994. Do chameleons get ahead? The effects of self-monitoring on managerial careers. *Academy of Management Journal* 37: 1047–1060.

18 Wayne, S.J., & Ferris, G.R. 1990. Influence tactics and exchange quality in supervisor-subordinate interactions: A laboratory experiment and field study. *Journal of Applied Psychology* 75: 487–499.

19 Olson, J.M., Hafer, C.L., & Taylor, L. 2001. I'm mad as hell and I'm not going to take it any more: Reports of negative emotions as a self-presentation tactic. *Journal of Applied Social Psychology* 31: 981–999.

20 Wayne, S.J., Liden, R.C., Graf, I.K., & Ferris G.R. 1997. The role of upward influence tactics in human resource decisions. *Personnel Psychology* 50: 979–1006.

21 Vonk, R. 1998. The slime effect: Suspicion and dislike of likeable behavior toward superiors. *Journal of Personality and Social Psychology* 74: 849–864.

22 Buchholz, R.A. 1989. *Fundamental concepts and problems in business ethics*. Englewood Cliffs, NJ: Prentice-Hall.

23 Ensley, M.D., Pearson, A.W., & Amason, A.C. 2002. Understanding the dynamics of new venture top management teams: Cohesion, conflict, and new venture performance. *Journal of Business Venturing* 17: 365–386.

24 See note 1.

25 Cropanzano, R.D. 1993. (ed.) *Justice in the workplace*. Hillsdale, NJ: Erlbaum.

26 Greenberg, J., & Baron, R.A. 2003. *Behavior in organizations*. 8th ed. Upper Saddle River, NJ: Prentice-Hall.

27 Brown, J.D., & Rogers, R.J. 1991. Self-serving attribution: The role of physiological arousal. *Personality and Social Psychology Bulletin* 17: 501–506.

28 Grote, N.K., & Clark, M.S. 2001. Perceiving unfairness in the family: Cause of consequences of marital distress? *Journal of Personality and Social Psychology* 80: 281–289.

29 Tjosvold, D. 1993. *Learning to manage conflict: Getting people to work together productively*. New York: Lexington Books.

30 Baron, R.A. 1993. Criticism (informal negative feedback) as a source of perceived unfairness in organizations: Effects, mechanisms, and countermeasures. In R. Cropanzano (ed.). *Justice in the workplace: Approaching fairness in human resource management* (pp. 155–170). Hillsdale, NJ: Erlbaum.

31 Thompson, L. 1998. *The mind and heart of the negotiator*. Upper Saddle River, NJ: Prentice-Hall.

32 Schefcyzk, M., & Gerpott, T.J. 2001. Qualifications and turnover of managers and venture capital-financed firm performance: An empirical study of German venture capital-investments. *Journal of Business Venturing* 16: 145–165.

33 Eisenhardt, K., & Schoonhoven, K. 1995. Failure of entrepreneurial firms: Ecological, upper echelons and strategic explanations in the US semiconductor industry. *Working Paper*. Stanford University.

34 Reynolds, P., & White, S. 1997. *The entrepreneurial process: economic growth, men, women and minorities*. Westport, CT: Quorum Books.

35 Aldrich, H. 1999. *Organizations evolving*. London: Sage.

36 Baum, J. 1996. Organizational ecology. In S. Clegg, C. Hardy, and W. Nord (eds.). *Handbook of organization studies*. (pp. 77–114). London: Sage.

37 Shutjens, V., & Wever, E. 2000. Determinants of new firm success. *Papers in Regional Science* 79: 135–159.

38 Gimeno, J., Folta, T., Cooper, A., & Woo, C. 1997. Survival of the fittest? Entrepreneurial human capital and the persistence of underperforming firms. *Administrative Science Quarterly* 42: 750–783.

39 Matusik, S. 1997. Motives, use patterns and effects of contingent resource use in entrepreneurial firms. In P. Reynolds, W. Bygrave, N. Carter, P. Davidsson, W. Gartner, C. Mason, & P. McDougall. *Frontiers of entrepreneurship research*. (pp. 359–372). Babson Park: Babson College.

40 Aldrich, H., & Langdon, N. 1997. Human resource management and organizational life cycles. In P. Reynolds et al. (eds.). *Frontiers of entrepreneurship research*. Babson Park: Babson College.

41 Gomez-Mejia, L.R., Balkin, D.B., & Cardy, R.L. 2002. *Managing human resources*. 3rd ed. Upper Saddle River, NJ: Prentice-Hall.

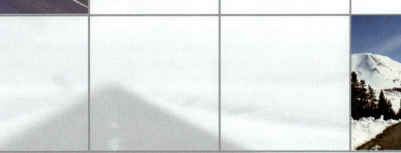
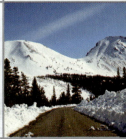

CHAPTER 6

FINANCING NEW VENTURES

LEARNING OBJECTIVES

After reading this chapter, you should be able to:

1 Explain why it is difficult for entrepreneurs to raise money from external investors.

2 Identify specific solutions to venture finance problems created by uncertainty and information asymmetry, and explain why these solutions work.

3 Explain why entrepreneurs typically raise very little start-up capital.

4 Create proforma financial statements and cash flow statements and conduct breakeven analysis.

5 Define debt and equity financing and explain how they differ.

6 Describe the different sources of capital for new ventures.

7 Describe the equity finance process from start to finish.

8 Explain why equity financing in new ventures is typically staged.

9 Describe how venture capitalists calculate the cost of the capital that they provide to new ventures.

10 Explain why direct and indirect social ties are important to raising money from external investors.

11 Identify the behaviors and actions that successful entrepreneurs engage in to encourage investors to back them, and explain why these behaviors and actions are effective.

Why Is It So Difficult to Raise Money? The Problems of Uncertainty and Information Asymmetry
    Information Asymmetry Problems
    Uncertainty Problems
    Solutions to Venture Finance Problems

Amounts and Sources of Capital: How Much and What Type Do You Need?
    Amount of Start-Up Capital
    Estimating Financial Needs: Start-Up Costs, Proforma Financial Statements, Cash Flow Statements, and Breakeven Analysis
    Types of Capital: Debt Versus Equity
    Sources of Capital

The Structure of Venture Finance
    The Equity Financing Process
    Staging of Investment
    The Cost of Capital

Social Capital and the Behavioral Side of Venture Finance
    Social Ties and the Process of Raising Money
    Behaviors and Actions That Encourage Investors

> "Money, it turned out, was exactly like sex; you thought of nothing else if you didn't have it and thought of other things if you did." (James Baldwin, *Nobody Knows My Name*, 1961)

In July 1996, Alex Laats, a technology licensing officer at MIT, and two undergraduate students, Pehr Andersen and Chris Gadda, founded a company named NBX Corporation to make an Internet telephone. Although none of the entrepreneurs had started a previous company, they raised $16.7 million in venture capital, and used the money to build a company that was later sold to 3Com for $80 million. How did three inexperienced entrepreneurs raise millions of dollars of venture capital and build a company?

It happened like this: While he was working at the MIT technology licensing office, Alex Laats met a venture capitalist named Charles Harris. Harris was impressed with Laats and tried to hire him for his venture capital firm, Harris and Harris. Because Laats decided he'd rather be an entrepreneur than a venture capitalist, he turned down the offer. So Harris told Laats to look him up when he had a venture he wanted to start.

In the summer of 1996, Laats called Harris to talk about financing NBX. Harris agreed to provide $500,000.

When Laats left the technology licensing office to start NBX, he agreed to license the Internet phone technology from MIT in return for 5 percent of the company. As a result, Phil Rotner, who worked in the MIT treasurer's office, became responsible for managing MIT's investment in NBX.

One of Rotner's responsibilities was to manage the investments of MIT's endowment in venture capital funds, which put him in contact with a lot of venture capitalists. This proved valuable in the fall of 1996 when NBX Corporation needed to raise additional capital. Harris and Harris couldn't provide all of the additional $3.5 million that NBX Corporation needed, and Laats and Harris began to search for other venture capital firms to provide money.

Harris called Bill Laverack, a partner at J.H. Whitney, a venture capital firm that was very closely tied to Harris and Harris. Because of his relationship with Harris, Laverack supported funding NBX Corporation, figuring if Harris thought it was a good investment, it probably was. In addition, Laverack had close ties to Rotner because MIT was the largest investor in J.H. Whitney's most recent venture capital fund. Based on his relationships with Harris and Rotner, Laverack convinced his partners at J.H. Whitney to finance the second round of NBX.

By October 1997, NBX was running out of capital again. This time it was looking for $12.7 million and needed another investor. Laverack figured that they should try Morganthaler Ventures because of J.H. Whitney's relationship with that firm. Rotner also thought this was a good choice because MIT was a big investor in Morganthaler's fund, and Rotner sat on Morganthaler's advisory board.

The partners at Morganthaler Ventures thought NBX Corporation was a good investment, but there were a lot of good companies in the Internet phone business at that time. They almost didn't invest, but agreed to do so largely on the basis of Morganthaler's relationship with MIT and J.H. Whitney.

The moral of this story is that financing a new venture depends very much on social ties. NBX obtained several stages of venture capital that it otherwise wouldn't have received because of social ties between the founders and investors or between earlier investors and later investors. Given the advantages that venture capital offers new firms (see Table 6.1), one might say NBX's success depended on social relationships.

Table 6.1 Why Entrepreneurs Seek Venture Capital

Venture capital backing offers a wealth of advantages for new firms, from enhanced credibility to operating assistance.

TYPE OF ADVANTAGE	REASONING
Capital	Venture capital is a major source of high-risk capital for new ventures.
Credibility	The prestige of venture capital backing makes it easier for entrepreneurs to persuade customers, employees, and suppliers of the value of their new businesses.
Connections to investment bankers	The high volume of venture capital backed initial public offerings means that venture capitalists have close ties to investment bankers, facilitating going public.
Connections to suppliers and customers	Venture capitalists often link the companies that they finance together as suppliers and customers of each other.
Assistance in recruiting the management team	Venture capitalists have strong ties to executive search firms and can help entrepreneurs attract CEOs and other senior management talent.
Operating assistance	Many venture capitalists were former entrepreneurs and have significant experience building new companies.

We just explained that social ties were very important to the founders of NBX because they helped to raise a large amount of venture capital. But why did it matter that the founders obtained this type of financing? As Table 6.1 indicates, venture capital provides entrepreneurs with a wealth of advantages, from serving as a major source of money for high-risk new businesses to demonstrating the credibility of the new business, to providing connections to important stakeholders, to giving assistance running a new business. We will talk more about venture capital later in the chapter, but for now just remember that venture capital backing provides a lot of value to new firms.

The remainder of this chapter will expand on the new venture financing process. In the first section, we will discuss why it's so difficult for entrepreneurs to raise the money they need for their new ventures. Two broad categories of problems—**information asymmetry**, or the fact that entrepreneurs know more about their opportunities than investors, and **uncertainty**—make raising money difficult, and demand specific arrangements that you will need to understand if you're going to raise external capital for your start-up.

In the second section, we will describe the amount, source, and type of capital that new ventures typically raise. We will explain why entrepreneurs usually raise a small amount of initial capital and then obtain additional financing later. We will teach you important tools for the financial analysis of your new venture, including estimating the amount and use of start-up capital, proforma financial statements, cash flow statements, and breakeven analysis. We will also discuss the difference between *debt* and *equity* financing, and explain why entrepreneurs typically obtain equity financing in the early days of their ventures. Finally, we will outline the variety of sources of financing that entrepreneurs tap.

In the third section, we will describe the structure of venture finance for the high potential ventures that typically receive *business angel* and *venture capital* financing. In particular, we will outline the equity financing process from initial contact with investors to receiving money. We will also explain why equity investors typically stage financing, and how they establish a price for their capital.

In the fourth section, we will return to the discussion that we started in the beginning of this chapter about social capital and the behavioral side of raising money. We'll explain why having direct or indirect social ties to investors is important to raising money, and we'll outline the actions and behaviors that successful entrepreneurs use to encourage venture capitalists or others to back them.

WHY IS IT SO DIFFICULT TO RAISE MONEY? THE PROBLEMS OF UNCERTAINTY AND INFORMATION ASYMMETRY

Most entrepreneurs will tell you that the single most difficult part of starting a company is raising money. In fact, when researchers have asked entrepreneurs what their biggest concerns were in starting their new companies, the most common response is "raising money." When the researchers have asked entrepreneurs what kind of help would have been most valuable in the firm formation process, the most common answer is help with obtaining capital.[1]

But why is raising money for a new venture so difficult? The answer lies in what entrepreneurs are asking investors to do. As we indicated in Chapter 3, entrepreneurs identify uncertain new venture opportunities based on information that other people either do not have or do not recognize. As a result, investors must make decisions about funding new businesses of very uncertain value with less information than the entrepreneur has. This uncertainty and information asymmetry create problems in financing new companies. Because entrepreneurs who want to raise money from external investors need to overcome these problems, it is important that we explain to you what they are.

Information Asymmetry Problems

The fact that entrepreneurs have or recognize information about their business opportunities that investors don't have or can't recognize creates three problems for raising money. First, entrepreneurs are reluctant to disclose information to investors, requiring investors to make decisions on limited information. Entrepreneurs need to keep secret

> **LEARNING OBJECTIVE**
>
> 1 Explain why it is difficult for entrepreneurs to raise money from external investors.

the information that they have about their opportunities and their approaches to exploiting them. If other people learned this information, then they could pursue the same opportunities. Moreover, investors have the money necessary to exploit the opportunities (otherwise the entrepreneurs wouldn't be talking to them about financing). So entrepreneurs don't want to tell investors too much about their opportunities or ways of exploiting them, lest the investors exploit the opportunities without them. As a result, entrepreneurs keep information about their opportunities hidden, and investors have to make decisions about financing ventures with less information than entrepreneurs have.[2]

Second, the information advantage that entrepreneurs have makes it possible for them to take advantage of investors (see Figure 6.1). Entrepreneurs can use their superior information to obtain capital from investors and use it for their own benefit instead of the benefit of the company.[3] For example, suppose an entrepreneur tells his investor that he needs a large expense account to entertain clients. The investor can't really know whether the entrepreneur needs the expense account because clients in that industry will not make purchases unless they are wined and dined or because the entrepreneur likes fine food and wine and will use the expense account as a way to dine out. Why? Because the entrepreneur supplies the information about the need for the expense account, and it might not be true.

Third, the investor's limited information about the entrepreneur and the opportunity creates the potential for a problem called **adverse selection**. Adverse selection occurs when someone is unable to distinguish between two people, one who has a desired quality, and the other who doesn't. Because it's not possible to distinguish between the two people, the one without the desired quality has an incentive to misrepresent her attributes and say that she has the desired quality. For example, some entrepreneurs have what it takes to build a successful new company and some don't. If investors can't tell one from the other, those without the ability to build successful companies will mimic the behavior of the others to get financing. For instance, they will pretend to possess skills, information, or experience that they really don't have. To protect themselves, investors have to charge a premium to pay for the losses incurred from backing the wrong people. Because talented entrepreneurs don't want to pay this premium, they withdraw from the financing market, leaving only the entrepreneurs that investors don't want to back, creating adverse selection.[4]

Figure 6.1 Investors in New Ventures Have to Be Very Careful to Manage Entrepreneurs' Behavior

Entrepreneurs who are unmotivated or who—like the man shown here—misrepresent themselves are a serious problem for investors. To protect themselves against such tactics, investors often adopt mechanisms designed to prevent or control such behaviors by entrepreneurs.

"It's as though everything nice about you had been just some kind of introductory offer."

Uncertainty Problems

Investors also face a variety of problems because new ventures are very uncertain. First, they have to make judgments about the value of opportunities and the ability of entrepreneurs on the basis of very little actual evidence. The factors that determine those ventures that will become valuable investments—things like the demand for the new product, the financial performance of the firm, the ability of the entrepreneur to manage the company, and so on—cannot be known for certain until after entrepreneurs obtain financing and exploit their opportunities because these things cannot occur without the investment of someone's capital.[5] So if the entrepreneur doesn't have a patented technology or a long track record of building successful businesses (which most ventures don't have), then the investor has to make a decision about the venture on the basis of very little hard evidence, making the financing decision very risky.[6]

Second, entrepreneurs and investors often disagree about the value of new ventures. Because new ventures are uncertain, no one really knows for sure how profitable—if at all—a new venture will be. So investors make their financing decisions on the basis of their own perceptions about the profitability and attractiveness of ventures, which are almost always lower than those of the entrepreneur.[7] Why? Remember in Chapter 5, when we indicated that entrepreneurs are overoptimistic about their ventures? To motivate themselves to undertake the hard work of starting a company, entrepreneurs often convince themselves that their ventures' chances are better than they actually are. So when they negotiate with investors, who aren't overoptimistic, they often face difficult bargaining over the value of the venture.

Third, investors want to make sure that entrepreneurs will pay up if their ventures prove not to be valuable, especially if they are lending money to the venture. That way, the investor is risking less. Obviously, the entrepreneur can't tap the venture for funds to pay back the investor if the venture proves to be a failure because a failed venture won't have any money. So investors ask entrepreneurs to provide **collateral**, or something of value that can be sold if the venture fails—such as the entrepreneurs' home! (See Figure 6.2.)[8] The problem with this arrangement is that many entrepreneurs need capital because they don't have anything of value; otherwise, they would finance the new firm themselves.

Why did we tell you about these uncertainty and information asymmetry problems, which might seem like abstract concepts? Because, by telling you about these problems, we can make it easier for you to understand how investors solve them. That way you can learn why venture finance works the way that it does.

Solutions to Venture Finance Problems

Don't worry. The new venture finance business is alive and well. Investors have solved the information asymmetry and uncertainty problems described here. In this section, we will outline the solutions that they've come up with so that you can learn about the things that you will have to do to raise money when you start your new venture.

Self-Financing

When you raise money to finance a new venture, investors will want you to invest your own money in the venture as well. The amount of capital that you put in doesn't really matter. What's important is that you put in an

LEARNING OBJECTIVE

2 Identify specific solutions to venture finance problems created by uncertainty and information asymmetry, and explain why these solutions work.

Figure 6.2 Investors Want Collateral When They Provide Debt Financing

Many entrepreneurs mortgage their homes to provide collateral to obtain the capital that they need to start their businesses.

amount that is a large percentage of your net worth. So if you have $10,000 to your name, investors will want it all invested in the business; but you'll have to kick in closer to a million dollars if that's what you're worth.

Why do you have to put in a lot of your own capital when you are raising money from other people? After all, you probably don't want to risk losing your own money in a failed venture. Actually, that's precisely the point. You know more about the venture opportunity than any investor. So if you don't think a venture is a good enough idea to risk losing your own money, then why should investors risk theirs? Moreover, investors are worried that unscrupulous entrepreneurs will take advantage of them. Suppose that an entrepreneur put none of her own money in a new venture and then used the investor's capital to buy a fancy convertible, which she then used purely for personal pleasure or convenience. The investor really wouldn't have any way to stop this behavior. But the investor could discourage the entrepreneur from doing it in the first place. By making the entrepreneur invest her own money along with theirs, investors give the entrepreneur an incentive to be careful with the venture's capital. If the entrepreneur invests in the venture, it wouldn't just be the investor's money that was wasted on gas for the convertible; it would also be the entrepreneur's.[9]

Although making entrepreneurs self-finance is useful for mitigating venture finance problems, it is not a complete solution, especially not for very large ventures. Most people don't have enough money to self-finance large venture opportunities. For example, when Fred Smith started Federal Express, he needed tens of millions of dollars to assemble trucks, aircraft, and an information management system. He just wasn't rich enough to finance Federal Express out of his own pocket. He needed to raise capital from others. Because entrepreneurial self-finance isn't a complete solution to the problems that investors face, investors use a variety of other mechanisms to manage information and asymmetry problems.

Contract Provisions

To protect themselves against the problems that uncertainty and information asymmetry create, investors include a variety of provisions in their contracts with entrepreneurs. First, they include covenants on entrepreneurs' behavior. **Covenants** are restrictions on someone's actions (see Figure 6.3). Common covenants in new venture finance include precluding the entrepreneur from purchasing or selling assets or shares without investors' permission, as well as **mandatory redemption rights**, which require the entrepreneur to return the investors' capital at any time.[10] Second, investors employ **convertible securities**, or financial instruments that allow investors to convert preferred stock, which gets preferential treatment in the event of a liquidation, into common stock, at the investor's discretion.[11] Third, investors use **forfeiture** and **antidilution provisions**. These provisions require entrepreneurs to lose a portion of the ownership of their ventures if they fail to meet agreed-upon milestones.[12] Fourth, investors give themselves **control rights** to the new ventures that they finance. Control rights are what give someone the discretion to determine how to use a venture's assets. Investors typically take a disproportionate share of control rights—for instance, they own 30 percent of the shares of the company, but take 51 percent of

Figure 6.3 Investors Require Entrepreneurs to Agree to Restrictive Covenants

Investors require entrepreneurs to agree to certain terms and conditions in return for financing.

the seats on the board of directors. Finally, investors make it difficult for entrepreneurs to leave the company without investors' permission, or to retain much ownership of the new venture if they leave. They do this by requiring long **vesting periods**, during which time entrepreneurs cannot cash out of their investments. All of these tools minimize the likelihood that entrepreneurs will act against the interest of the investors, either by restricting the entrepreneur's behavior or reducing the incentive to act that way. These tools also make entrepreneurs bear more of the uncertainty of the new venture, shielding investors against some of the risk of financing new companies.

Specialization

To better choose which new ventures to invest in, and to manage those investments after they're made, investors in new firms tend to specialize in two ways. First, they specialize by industry, with some focusing on, say, the software industry and others on, say, biotechnology. Second, many investors specialize by the stage of development of the venture, with some investors concentrating on making small investments very early in the lives of new firms, and others focusing on making larger, later-stage investments.[13] Specialization helps investors by providing them with contacts among suppliers, customers, and experts who can help evaluate the ventures that they are thinking of backing and ensure that the ventures are on the right track once they have invested in them. Moreover, by specializing, investors can learn the key success factors at a particular stage of a firm's life or in a particular industry—information that makes them better able to assist and monitor new firms. Therefore, specialization helps investors overcome both information asymmetry and uncertainty problems in new venture finance.

Geographically Localized Investing

Unlike investors in the stock market, who often think nothing of buying shares of a foreign company traded on the stock exchange, investors in new ventures almost always make investments in companies located near them. The rule of thumb is typically not to invest in a venture more than a 2-hour drive from one's office.

Why do venture investors limit their investments to local entrepreneurs? First, localized investing makes it easier to for investors to get heavily involved in new companies. This is important because investors want entrepreneurs to give them regular updates about their ventures, and often have to step into the day-to-day operations of new firms if something starts to go wrong.[14] In fact, investors will often replace the entrepreneurial team with new management if they need to, something that requires intense involvement to accomplish.

Second, local investing makes it easier to pick the right companies to back. Investors find it easier to develop a network of sources of information about good start-ups if they focus on a constrained area. Moreover, because investors have to assess the value of information provided by entrepreneurs, they use their contacts to confirm entrepreneurs' claims about their business ideas, their talents, and so on.[15]

Syndication

Many investors in new ventures, particularly venture capitalists and business angels, **syndicate**, or get other investors to join in them in making investments. Syndication allows investors to diversify their risks by putting smaller amounts of money into a variety of companies rather than putting large sums of money into one or two firms. Syndication also helps investors gather information about entrepreneurs and investors. By syndicating, investors can gather information from a greater variety of different people with different experience and knowledge,[16] as well as check their decisions against the decisions of others.[17] Both of these things help investors to make better investment decisions.

KEY POINTS

- The problems of uncertainty and information asymmetry make it difficult for entrepreneurs to raise money from external sources.
- Information asymmetry means that investors must make decisions on less information than the entrepreneur has, that entrepreneurs can take advantage of investors, and that entrepreneurs can engage in adverse selection.
- Uncertainty means that investors have to make decisions about new ventures on very little actual evidence, that entrepreneurs and investors will disagree on the value of new ventures, and that investors will want assurance that the entrepreneur can pay up if the opportunity proves not to be valuable.
- Investors have established several solutions to the financing problems generated by information asymmetry and uncertainty, including self-financing, contract provisions, syndication, specialization, and geographically localized investing.
- Self-financing reduces entrepreneurs' incentive to act against the interests of investors, and provides collateral for new ventures.
- Covenants, mandatory redemption rights, convertible securities, control rights, and forfeiture and antidilution provisions are all contract provisions that help to protect investors against uncertainty and information asymmetry problems in venture finance.
- Investors syndicate their investments to diversify their risks and to gather information that reduces the problems generated by information asymmetry.
- Specialization and geographically localized investing provide investors with information and control that protects them against opportunistic entrepreneurs.

AMOUNTS AND SOURCES OF CAPITAL: HOW MUCH AND WHAT TYPE DO YOU NEED?

Three of the most important questions that an entrepreneur will need to ask herself before starting a venture are: How much money do I need? Where should I get that money? What type of arrangements do I need to make to obtain that capital? Because you are going to need to answer these questions, you need to know some things about the amount and timing of new venture finance; the differences between debt and equity financing; and the sources of new venture finance. In this section, we provide answers to these questions gleaned from academic research and expert entrepreneurs.

Amount of Start-Up Capital

If you read the newspaper regularly, you might be surprised to learn that most new ventures do not require much start-up capital. The financing process for the typical start-up is very different from the one that is described by *The Wall Street Journal* for new ventures that make the pages of that newspaper. According to data provided by the U.S. Census Bureau, 60 percent of all new ventures take less than $5,000 of capital to get started, and only 3 percent take more than $100,000 (see Figure 6.4).[18] Moreover, even really high potential businesses often take very little capital. Amar Bhide, an entrepreneurship professor at Columbia University, reports that the average firm listed in the Inc. 500—the 500 fastest growing private firms in the United States—was capitalized at less than $30,000.[19]

ACM Enterprises in Tucson, Arizona, is a good example of a start-up whose founders figured out how to get a company off the ground without a lot of initial capital. The company produces a metal case to hold credit cards that electronically dispenses the selected card when a button is pushed. The founders of the company, James and Anthony Tiscione, started the company with $50,000 in initial capital even though they had never developed a new product, needed to obtain a patent on the product, and needed to manufacture it. How did they do it? First, James Tiscione went to the U.S. Patent and Trademark Office and searched for patents on inventions similar to his. Only after he had conducted his own search did he approach a patent attorney, cutting his

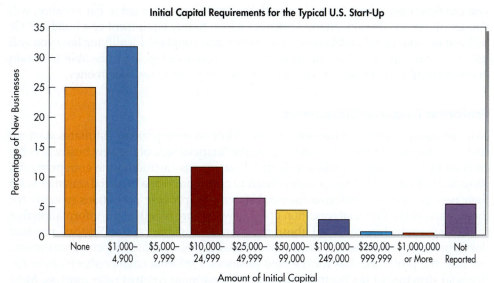

Figure 6.4 Most New Ventures Do Not Require Much Initial Capital

More than half of the new ventures started in the United States require less than $5,000 in initial capital.

Source: Adapted from "Characteristics of Business Owners," U.S. Department of Commerce, Bureau of the Census, Washington, DC: SSGPO, CB087-1, Table 15C, p. 10.

patent costs substantially. Second, the Tisciones partnered with a marketing expert, Steve Pagac, who found all their customers in return for an equity investment in the firm. Third, the founders outsourced their manufacturing to a company in Hong Kong, cutting their manufacturing expenses. Fourth, the Tisciones agreed to distribute their product through SkyMall for free advertising in return for giving SkyMall all the sales from their products until a set sales level had been reached. Through these four decisions, the Tisciones started a company with $50,000 in initial capital that many entrepreneurs would have required hundreds of thousands of dollars to start.[20]

Estimating Financial Needs: Start-Up Costs, Proforma Financial Statements, Cash Flow Statements, and Breakeven Analysis

Okay, so you don't need that much capital to start a business. But how do you figure out how much money you'll need for your new business? Entrepreneurs use four important tools to figure these things out: a list of start-up costs and use of proceeds, proforma financial statements, cash flow statements, and breakeven analysis. Not only will you need to learn to use these tools to start your business, but you'll also have to put these things into your business plan if you want to raise money. Any reputable investor will want to see this information as part of the process of evaluating your business.

List of Start-Up Costs and Use of Proceeds

One of the first things that you will need to do on the financial side of your new business is create a list of start-up costs, or costs that would need to be incurred to get the business off the ground. Examples of start-up costs are the cost of buying the equipment that you'll need to get going—ovens for a bakery, trucks for a delivery service, and so on—as well as inventory or supplies. Because you probably will have to incur costs to produce and sell your product or service, you'll need some working capital to tide you over through the period when cash is flowing out and none is flowing in. Any working capital that your business will need to get off the ground also needs to be included in your start-up costs. Furthermore, if you need to buy any long-term assets for your new business, such as a building in which to operate, that would need to be included as a start-up cost as well.

Once you have estimated your start-up costs, then you can figure out a couple of things that are important to raising money and getting your venture off the ground. First, you can determine the total amount of money that you are going to need to get started. This estimate is crucial to figuring out where to obtain the capital that you need. Second, you can determine what you will do with the capital once you get it. For instance, will you use the proceeds from an investment or a loan to buy equipment or a building? Or will you use the capital to obtain initial inventory and supplies? Identifying how you will use your start-up capital is important because you aren't going to be able to obtain financing until you can show investors how you are going to use their money.

Proforma Financial Statements

Now we can get down to the bottom line. After an entrepreneur estimates start-up costs and the use of funds, the next step on the financial side of the new business is the creation of the venture's projected financial statements (including the entrepreneur's projected bottom line!). Entrepreneurs need to create proforma financial statements for their new businesses. Proforma financial statements provide projections (usually for three years) of the financial condition of the new venture based on the information that the entrepreneur has collected about the market, customers, competitors, product development, operations, and other parts of the business. Proforma income statements estimate the profit and loss for the new business. Proforma balance sheets show the financial structure of the business and allow investors to conduct ratio analysis. Most experts recommend that you calculate the income statement for your business monthly or at least quarterly, and estimate the venture's balance sheet at least quarterly.

When developing their proforma financial statements, most entrepreneurs learn two lessons fairly quickly. First, the estimates of profit or loss shown in income statements depend very much on the quality of the entrepreneur's sales estimates. Therefore, accurate financial statements depend very much on accurate market analysis. In Chapter 9, we will discuss in great detail how to estimate market size and sales in a new venture. This information will be important to you in creating the income statement for your new venture.

Second, the estimates of profit and loss shown in income statements also depend very heavily on accurate estimates of costs. Most entrepreneurs get into trouble here because of people's natural tendency to underestimate costs. Remember that sales are generated through activities like advertising and hiring people, which create costs. So any increases in sales that you project in your financial statements should be accompanied by increases in costs.

In addition, businesses in a particular industry tend to have very similar relationships between costs and sales. Therefore, when you're creating your new business's financial statements, you should carefully compare your financial statements with those of other businesses in your industry. Are your numbers realistic? For example, say you project sales of $1,000,000 per year and plan to hire one saleswoman, but other firms in your industry average sales of $300,000 per year per salesperson. Take another pass at the numbers. Odds are that your venture is not going to be more than three times as good as the average firm in your industry at generating sales. We hope that you are, but potential investors will be skeptical of any claims that you make that are much better than industry averages.

To help you to develop your proforma financial statements (and remind you of what you did in accounting class), we provide an example of a balance sheet and income statement in Table 6.2.

Cash Flow Statements

CIMITYM. Do you know what that stands for? "Cash is more important than your mother." Many venture capitalists provide this abbreviation to the entrepreneurs that they back to make sure they realize how important cash flow management and cash flow statements are to new ventures. Because most venture capitalists believe that cash flow is more important than their portfolio company founders' mothers (okay, probably not really, but it makes a point), we need to spend some time discussing cash flow management.

Cash flow statements are calculations of the amount of cash that your new venture has at a given point in time. You'll need cash flow statements to manage your new

CAMPUS PIES BALANCE SHEET		
	12/31/03	12/31/04
Cash	$ 22,143	$ 26,218
Accounts receivable	$ 14,807	$ 15,801
Inventory	$ 6,284	$ 10,113
Property and equipment	$500,000	$500,000
Less: Accumulated depreciation	($ 47,901)	($ 74,112)
Total Assets	$495,333	$478,020
Accounts payable	$ 7,212	$ 8,216
Notes payable	$412,500	$412,500
Total Liabilities	$419,712	$420,716
Stockholders' equity	$ 75,621	$ 57,304
Total Liabilities and Equity	$495,333	$478,020

CAMPUS PIES INCOME STATEMENT 12/31/04	
Sales	$147,213
Less: Cost of goods sold	$119,612
Gross profit	$ 27,601
Less: Operating expenses	($103,400)
Less: Depreciation	($ 26,211)
Net Loss	($102,010)

Table 6.2 Proforma Financial Statements

This table shows the proforma income statement and balance sheet for Campus Pies, a new venture that sells fruit pies made according to grandma's secret recipe.

business. If a company has negative cash flow, it will be unable pay its bills and will become insolvent.

Managing cash flow is difficult because income statements do not measure the amount of cash in a business. As a result, many a business has become insolvent while remaining profitable. How is this possible? Many expenses in your income statement, such as depreciation, affect profit and loss, but do not involve real cash flows. So your business can have a profit or loss through depreciation of assets that is not reflected in actual cash flows. Moreover, cash inflows and outflows don't always occur at the same time as revenues and expenses are incurred. Sales, in particular, often occur long before customers pay for those sales, as is the case when customers buy on credit or are simply late in paying their bills.

Let's look at an example. Suppose you started a furniture business. In the first month of the life of your business, you sell a couch for $2,000 that cost you $1,000 to obtain. Therefore, you book a profit of $1,000. However, your customer pays you after 30 days, following your 30-days-same-as-cash plan. As a result, your business doesn't have positive cash flow in the first month. If you had to pay $1,000 cash to obtain the couch, you'll have negative $1,000 cash flow in the first month of your business.

This example illustrates that it is important for you to estimate your new business' cash flow as well as its income. To convert information from your income statement to your cash flow statement, do the following, as Table 6.3 on page 144 illustrates:

1. Take your net profit and add back depreciation.
2. Subtract increases in accounts receivable or add decreases in accounts receivable.
3. Subtract increases in inventory or add decreases in inventory.
4. Add increases in accounts payable or subtract decreases in accounts payable.
5. Subtract decreases in notes/loans payable or add increases in notes/loans payable.
6. The resulting figure is your net cash flow.

Suppose your analysis reveals that your venture will have negative cash flow. What can you do to keep your business from becoming insolvent? The short answer is that you can improve your venture's cash flow. How? First, you can minimize your accounts

Table 6.3 Net Cash Flow

This table shows the conversion of information in Campus Pies' income statement to a cash flow statement.

STEP	CALCULATION FOR CAMPUS PIES	RESULT
Take net profit (net loss) from the income statement.	($102,010)	($102,010)
Add depreciation.	($102,010) + $26,211	($ 75,799)
Calculate the increase in accounts receivable between 12/31/03 and 12/31/04.	$ 15,801 – $14,807	$ 994
Subtract the increase in accounts receivable from the result in line 2.	($ 75,799) – $994	($ 76,793)
Calculate the increase in inventory between 12/31/03 and 12/31/04.	$ 10,113 – $6,284	$ 3,829
Subtract the increase in inventory from the result in line 4.	($ 76,793) – $ 3,829	($ 80,622)
Calculate the increase in accounts payable between 12/31/03 and 12/31/04.	$ 8,216 – $ 7,212	$ 1,004
Add the increase in accounts payable to the result in line 6.	($ 80,622) + $ 1,004	($ 79,618)
Calculate the decrease in notes payable between 12/31/03 and 12/31/04.	$412,500 – $ 412,500	$ 0
Subtract the decrease in notes payable from the result in line 8.	($ 79,618) – $ 0	($ 79,618)
Net cash flow for the year ended 12/31/04.		($ 79,618)

receivable by offering customers discounts for paying quickly; limiting the credit that you extent to customers; and selling your receivables to companies that purchase accounts receivable at a discount in return for immediate cash. Second, you can reduce the raw material and finished products inventory that you hold to meet unanticipated customer demand. Third, you can control your spending by avoiding nonessential expenditures, such as nice furniture for your office; by leasing equipment instead of buying it; by recycling and reusing equipment and supplies; and by adding employees slowly. Fourth, you can delay your accounts payable. For instance, you can incur the extra cost of obtaining credit from your suppliers by giving up on early payment discounts. Although it might cost you a little more to approach your business in this way, you might be able to keep the business solvent when cash outflows are larger than inflows.

Breakeven Analysis

Another tool that entrepreneurs need to master is **breakeven analysis**, which allows you to calculate the amount of sales that you need to achieve to cover your costs. Breakeven analysis also lets you figure out the increase in sales volume that you would need to have if you were to increase your business' fixed costs. To calculate your breakeven level of sales, you do the following:

1. Determine the sales price (per unit) of your product or service.
2. Estimate the variable cost (per unit) of your product or service.
3. Subtract the variable cost per unit from the sales price to calculate your contribution margin (per unit).
4. Estimate your business' fixed costs.
5. Divide the fixed costs by the contribution margin percentage to calculate the breakeven sales volume.

Table 6.4 provides an example to illustrate the calculation of the breakeven level of sales. Play around with the numbers shown in the example. You'll soon realize that the higher the proportion of your costs that are fixed, the higher your breakeven level of sales will be. So remember that buying fixed assets is going to increase your fixed costs, your breakeven level of sales, and the risk of your new venture.

STEP	INFORMATION	CALCULATION
Determine the sales price (per unit) of your product or service.	Sales price is $10.00 per pie.	
Estimate the variable cost (per unit) of your product or service.	Variable cost is $3.00 per pie.	
Subtract the variable cost per unit from the sales price to calculate your contribution margin (per unit).	Contribution margin per unit is $7.00 per pie.	$10.00 – $3.00 = $7.00
Estimate your business' fixed costs.	Fixed costs are $500,000.	
Divide the fixed costs by the contribution margin percentage to calculate the breakeven sales volume.	Breakeven level of sales is 71,429 pies.	$500,000 / 7.00 = 71,429
Interpretation	As sales exceed 71,429 pies, Campus Pies earns a profit. Sales of fewer than 71,429 pies result in a loss.	

To summarize: The biggest issue about raising money isn't getting enough money to *start* the business. That's relatively easy. What's more difficult is getting enough money at the right times during the early life of the venture to make sure that the venture doesn't run out of cash. Almost all new ventures experience negative cash flow from operations early in their lives. Negative cash flow means that the operation of the business uses more cash than the business generates. It will kill a new business unless the entrepreneur can obtain additional capital. The key to avoiding negative cash flow is to look for money when you don't need it. In fact, experienced entrepreneurs often say that you should look for money before you need it, and raise more money than you think you need. As the **"Danger! Pitfall Ahead!"** section indicates, it often takes awhile to find money, especially if your business really needs cash.

Table 6.4 Breakeven Analysis

This example shows the calculation of the breakeven level of sales for Campus Pies.

DANGER! PITFALL AHEAD!

The Hazards of Raising Too Little Money

When I (Scott Shane) taught at the DuPree College of Management at Georgia Tech, an MBA student came to my office one day asking for advice on financing his new company, which had just developed a new inventory management software program. The student had just received a phone call from an Atlanta-area venture capital firm that wanted to finance his venture, and he wanted to talk to me about the terms he had been offered.

The venture capital firm proposed providing the new venture with $1 million in financing in return for 30 percent of the company. The plan would be to use the investors' capital to refine the prototype of the software, do a beta test, and launch the product. However, the student wasn't sure he should take the financing offer. He had only asked for $500,000 in seed capital; and he had only wanted to give up 10 percent of the company to get the money. His plan had been to use $500,000 in capital to refine the prototype and then seek more capital when the beta test began. Moreover, he had a business angel willing to take those terms.

I urged the student to take the venture capital financing, arguing that it is more important to raise enough capital than to get the best valuation of the

new company. But the student was stuck on the terms. "Why," he asked, "should I give up 30 percent of the company to get $1 million when I could give up 10 percent of the company to get $500,000. If I do two financing rounds at $500,000, I'd still have 80 percent of the company left. And besides, the venture will be so much further developed by the time of the next round, that I'll get the next round of money for even less equity." I explained that the venture might run into a rough spot along the way, and that he might not be able to raise the money he needed later. "Take the money when you can get it," I said. "You never know when it will be offered to you again."

The student decided to go with the business angel's offer, and put the $500,000 he received toward developing the software. Unfortunately, it proved to be a lot harder to develop the software than the student had originally thought, and he ran through his capital very quickly. When the money started running out, the student went out looking for additional financing. However, because the beta test didn't look good, not very many investors were interested, and the student couldn't find anyone to give him the capital he needed.

The entrepreneur in this story scraped by for six more months by selling equipment and giving employees stock in place of their paychecks. But

continued

continued

DANGER! PITFALL AHEAD!

that wasn't enough. After spending $750,000, he still didn't have a working beta version of his software, and he was out of capital. Although the student probably could have solved the software problems in a few more months, no one would give him the $250,000 that he needed to keep going. So he had to close up shop.

The moral of this story: Always raise more money than your venture needs, and obtain capital when you don't need it. Moreover, make sure that your estimate the **burn rate**, the pace at which you use funds, conservatively. A good rule of thumb: It

will almost always be twice as high as you originally thought! Raising enough money is essential to allowing your venture to survive and grow; to respond to unforeseen circumstances and change directions; to take the best approach to developing the business—hiring the best people, buying the best equipment and so on; and to project an image to external stakeholders of a stable, dependable and legitimate new venture.[21] If you don't raise enough money when money is easy to raise, chances are that you will run out of cash. It's almost impossible to raise money when you really need it.

Types of Capital: Debt Versus Equity

When new ventures are very young, they rarely obtain **debt** financing, and tend to obtain **equity** financing instead. Debt is a financial obligation to return the capital provided plus a scheduled amount of interest; equity is a portion of ownership received in an organization in return for money provided. New ventures tend to be financed by equity for two reasons. First, until ventures have generated positive cash flow, they have no way to make scheduled interest payments. As a result, entrepreneurs need to raise money in a way that doesn't require them to make fixed payments on that capital—that is, obtain equity investments. Second, debt financing at a fixed rate of interest encourages people to take risky actions when investors can't observe entrepreneurs' decisions. Why? If an entrepreneur fails, she can't lose any more money than she put into the venture (although the entrepreneur could lose her house if she put it into the venture by pledging it as collateral on a loan), so her downside loss is the same regardless of how much risk she takes. However, because the entrepreneur pays the same amount of interest on debt regardless of how well her venture does, she keeps all of the returns from success. Thus, with debt, she has an incentive to take high risk–high return actions. In contrast, with equity investments, the entrepreneur would have to share any greater benefit that accrues from success at risky actions and so won't be as inclined to take them.

Figure 6.5 Asset-Based Financing Is an Important Source of Capital for New Ventures

Entrepreneurs finance certain types of equipment, like trucks, through asset-based lending in which the equipment itself provides collateral on the loan.

Occasionally new ventures do obtain debt financing. When new ventures receive this type of financing early in their lives, it tends to be one of three varieties. The first is debt guaranteed by the entrepreneur's personal assets or earning power, as is the case when an entrepreneur uses credit cards or a home equity loan to finance her business. The second is **asset-based financing** (see Figure 6.5). Asset-based financing is debt that is secured by the equipment that it is used to buy. Many products like trucks, computers, and photocopiers can be financed this way. (We will talk more about asset-based lenders later.) The third is supplier credit. In many industries, suppliers offer credit to entrepreneurs to obtain inventory and equipment, as is the case when a restaurant supplier finances a restaurant entrepreneur. The supplier provides the kitchen equipment, and will take it back if the entrepreneur fails to pay interest and principal on the loan to pay for it.

Sources of Capital

Entrepreneurs have a wide variety of sources of capital for their new businesses. Because these sources are very different from one another, and all have advantages and disadvantages, it is important that you know what these sources are, and when they are most useful to entrepreneurs. This section of the chapter describes the different sources of capital for new ventures.

Savings

The single most important source of capital for new ventures is the entrepreneur's own savings. Researchers have shown that approximately 70 percent of all entrepreneurs finance their new businesses with their own capital.[22] Even high potential businesses, like the Inc. 500 companies, are heavily reliant on savings of the founders for initial capital (see Figure 6.6).

Friends and Family

Many entrepreneurs turn to their friends and family members to raise the capital that they need to finance their businesses. Although asking one's father-in-law for the money to buy equipment for a new business is a TV-sitcom standard, it also appears to be true for financing real ventures. In many industries, particularly retail businesses and restaurants, entrepreneurs raise a lot of their capital from family members. Usually these financing arrangements are informal with the entrepreneur promising to pay the money back when she can. However, in some cases, raising money from friends and family members can be systematic, with the entrepreneur signing promissory notes and paying interest, or selling shares of the company to obtain capital.

Business Angels

Business angels are private individuals who invest in new ventures. The typical business angel is a former entrepreneur. Business angels generally invest between $10,000 and $200,000 per venture in businesses that are geographically close to where they live and work, and in industries that they know well. They tend to demand a lower return on their investment than venture capitalists because they are less financially motivated. In addition to having the goal of making money, many business angels invest in new companies to stay involved with the entrepreneurial process.

Venture Capitalists

Venture capitalists are people who work for organizations that raise money from large institutional investors, like university endowments and company pension funds, and invest those funds in new firms. Venture capital firms are generally structured

LEARNING OBJECTIVE

6 Describe the different sources of capital for new ventures.

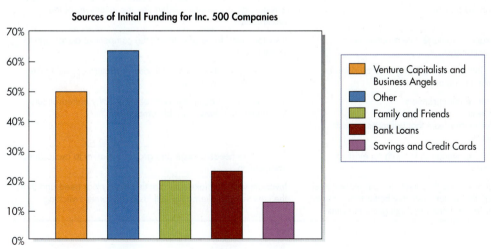

Sources of Initial Funding for Inc. 500 Companies

- Venture Capitalists and Business Angels
- Other
- Family and Friends
- Bank Loans
- Savings and Credit Cards

Source: Adapted from Amar Bhide, *The Origin and Evolution of New Businesses*, New York: Oxford University Press, 2000, p. 38.

Figure 6.6 Where Entrepreneurs Obtain Initial Capital for Their New Businesses: Their Own Savings

Almost two-thirds of even the fastest growing private companies, those listed in the Inc. 500, use the entrepreneur's savings and credit cards as the source of initial capital.

as limited partnerships in which a fund is established for a fixed period of time, typically 10 years. The institutional investors, who provide the capital, are called limited partners because their participation is limited to providing money. The venture capitalists themselves, who make investment decisions in start-ups and manage those investments, are called general partners. At the end of the life of a venture capital fund, the venture capital firm returns the capital invested to the institutional investors plus a percentage of any profits from investing in the start-ups (usually 80 percent). The general partners keep the other 20 percent and also take a management fee (typically 2 percent of the capital in the fund annually) for managing the investments.

In addition to providing money to new firms, venture capitalists provide assistance in operating new businesses; help to identify key employees, customers, and suppliers; and assist with operations and strategy formulation and implementation. Because venture capital backed start-ups are more likely to go public than other start-ups, venture capitalists develop strong relationships with investment bankers who underwrite initial public offerings. As a result, venture capitalists also help new firms to go public.

Although venture capitalists offer a lot to new companies, they are also very demanding investors. Very few businesses meet their criteria for financing. In general, only businesses with a great deal of growth potential are interesting to this class of investors. As Table 6.5 shows, to receive venture capital backing, a new venture typically needs to operate in a high growth industry, have a proprietary competitive advantage, offer a product with a clear market need, and be run by an experienced management team with a plan to go public.

Moreover, venture capitalists impose a large number of restrictions on the behavior of entrepreneurs. Venture capitalists often require entrepreneurs to issue convertible preferred stock, which allows the venture capitalist to have liquidation preference in the event that the venture does not do well, but be able to have common stock ownership in the event that the venture succeeds. Venture capitalists also include a large number of covenants in their agreements with entrepreneurs. For instance, they typically bar entrepreneurs from purchasing assets or issuing or selling shares without their permission

Table 6.5 What Venture Capitalists Want

Venture capitalists have clear preferences in the types of business and entrepreneurs that they finance.

DIMENSION OF THE OPPORTUNITY	VENTURE CAPITALISTS' PREFERENCES	REASONING
Investment size	$3 million to $15 million	Transaction costs are high on small investments, but large investments are risky.
Screening	Invest in less than 1 percent of proposals	Very few ventures meet performance standards that venture capitalists demand.
Industries	High technology	Technology provides the high rate of growth that venture capitalists demand.
Control rights	More control than is proportional to the number of shares owned	Investors want to have the ability to make decisions about the direction of the company.
Ownership	Less than 50 percent	Investors do not want to undermine the incentives of the entrepreneur.
Competitive advantage	Proprietary advantage, like a patent or exclusive contract	Investors need to be able to see the competitive advantage to know it exists.
Exit strategy	Plan for initial public offering or acquisition by established company	Venture capitalists need to cash out and return capital to the investors that provided it.
Management	Experienced entrepreneurs Honest team Complementary team that balances aspects of business	Investors want a complete team of trustworthy entrepreneurs that understand how to build companies.
Market	Large and growing market with no existing competitors	The venture needs a large and growing market to avoid direct competition.
Product	Product or service that meets a clear market need in a way that is demonstrably better than existing alternatives and provides high gross margins	Investors want to make sure that there is a clear need and that the new venture alternative will justify customer switching.

and demand mandatory redemption rights that require entrepreneurs to give them their investment back at any time. Finally, venture capitalists employ forfeiture provisions that cause entrepreneurs to lose ownership if their performance falls below target goals and antidilution provisions that transfer shares from entrepreneurs to their investors if the venture fails to meet performance targets. Given the demands that venture capitalists place on entrepreneurs and venture capitalists' focus on extremely high potential companies, you will need to evaluate very carefully whether venture capital financing is appropriate for your new company.

Corporations

Many companies make strategic investments in new companies. By making these investments, they can obtain access to new companies' products or technology. In return, the established companies provide important marketing and manufacturing support for new ventures, as well as improve the latter's credibility. Another advantage of corporate investors is that they generally offer better valuation than financial investors, like venture capitalists and business angels. However, entrepreneurs need to be careful. Corporations provide favorable financial terms, relative to other investors, because they want to obtain access to the intellectual property and products developed by new companies. Therefore, entrepreneurs have to protect their intellectual property when obtaining financing from large corporations.

Banks

In general, banks are not in the business of lending money to start-up companies. However, commercial banks do provide a variety of types of capital to new businesses under the right circumstances. First, banks occasionally provide new companies with standard **commercial loans**, particularly after those companies have begun to generate positive cash flow and when entrepreneurs can secure those loans with property, equipment, or other assets. A commercial loan is a form of financing in which the borrower pays interest on the money borrowed. Second, banks sometimes provide new companies with **lines of credit**, or agreements to allow entrepreneurs to draw up to a set amount of money at a particular interest rate, whenever they need it. Lines of credit are usually used to finance inventory or accounts receivable. Despite these examples, bank loans are relatively rare for very new businesses; positive cash flow is necessary to pay interest on a loan.

Asset-Based Lenders

Asset-based lenders provide financing by using the assets themselves as collateral for the loan. Take, for example, a new business that needs to purchase some computers and trucks. Both of these assets can be financed by asset-based lenders who offer loans at a certain percentage of the value of the assets (typically around 60 percent). The entrepreneur in our example could purchase ten computers and two trucks by pledging the computers and trucks as collateral against the loan, and borrow about 60 percent of the value of that equipment.

Factors

Factors are specialized organizations that purchase the accounts receivable of businesses at a discount (usually 1 or 2 percent). Because customers in many industries have between 30 and 90 days to pay their bills, new businesses often turn to factors to obtain capital immediately. With factoring, the new venture sells its accounts receivables to the factor for 98 to 99 percent of what they're worth, and receives the cash value of those receivables immediately.

Figure 6.7 The Government Is
an Important Source of Capital
for Entrepreneurs

*Federal, state, and local governments
offer a wide array of programs to
provide capital to entrepreneurs or to
help them to obtain it from the private
sector.*

Government Programs

Federal and state governments offer a variety of programs to finance new businesses. One federal program, which we first mentioned in Chapter 5, is the Small Business Innovation Research Program. Under this program, new businesses can obtain up to $100,000 from government agencies to evaluate a technical idea, and up to $750,000 to commercialize a technology. Another federal program is the 7(A) Loan Guarantee Program of the U.S. Small Business Administration, which guarantees repayment to lenders of any capital that they provide to new businesses, up to a preset limit. The U.S. Small Business Administration also provides the CAPLine Program, a system for guaranteeing loans to new and small businesses to finance inventory or accounts receivable. Small business investment companies (SBICs) are organizations that the U.S. Small Business Administration licenses and to which it lends money. These organizations make minority (less than 50 percent) investments in new companies and often provide debt capital to new companies (see Figure 6.7).

Marlene Cameron is a good example of an entrepreneur who used government funding to get her start-up off the ground. Her company, which makes candy, syrups, and sauces, obtained an $85,000 grant from the Alaska Science and Technology Foundation to purchase birch syrup equipment. Even though her company was not a high technology firm, the foundation provided her with the money she needed to get started because her equipment purchase would help stimulate the creation of a new industry in Alaska. As a result, Cameron was able to start her company without having to give up ownership to a venture capitalist or business angel.[23]

KEY POINTS

- New ventures typically require very little start-up capital, but tend to demand larger amounts of capital later, as they experience negative cash flow from operations.
- To manage the financial side of new businesses, entrepreneurs estimate start-up costs and uses of funds; create proforma financial statements; generate cash flow statements; and undertake breakeven analysis.
- New ventures are generally financed by equity rather than by debt because they lack sufficient cash flow to pay interest, and because debt financing at a fixed rate of interest encourages entrepreneurs to take risky actions with investors' funds.
- Entrepreneurs have a wide variety of capital sources available to them, including their own savings, their friends and family, business angels, venture capitalists, corporations, banks, asset-based lenders, factors, and government programs.

THE STRUCTURE OF VENTURE FINANCE

Because we want you to develop a high potential new venture—one that has the chance to make a lot of money and provide useful products or services to a large number of people—we think that it's important to describe the process by which high potential new ventures get external financing. In this section, we'll describe the typical equity financing process for entrepreneurs who obtain capital from business angels and venture capitalists (because debt financing is fairly uncommon in high potential ventures at the early stages). We focus on how the process works with venture capitalists and business angels because we can't really describe the process for raising money from your friends and family. That would depend a lot on those people, and we don't know your aunts, uncles, and roommates.

In addition to describing the financing process in general, we want to make sure that you understand a key part of the financing process—the staging of capital—so we'll talk about that in detail. We'll also discuss how much equity investors are going to take from you in return for their money, and explain how they calculate the cost of capital.

The Equity Financing Process

In general, the financing process begins with an initial introduction of the entrepreneur to the investor. Although angels and venture capitalists often receive hundreds and even thousands of business plans each year, they ignore most of them. Typically, these investors don't even consider investments unless they are referred to them by someone they know and trust. Investors generally first evaluate business plans by checking to see who referred the venture to them. If they consider the referral to be a good one, then they will take a quick look at the business plan. This means glancing at the executive summary of the business plan to see what the business is, what market it will operate in, what market need it's filling, and what product or service it's offering. Investors will weed out 95 percent of the plans they receive from this type of quick scan.

LEARNING OBJECTIVE

7 Describe the equity finance process from start to finish.

For the remaining 5 percent of plans, the investor undertakes a more formal investigation, looking for characteristics that make a venture a desirable one for external financing. So what are investors looking for? Two things. The first is an excellent venture team. The second is an excellent business opportunity.

On the venture team side of the equation, investors want to see evidence that the entrepreneur is motivated and passionate about the business, as well as being honest and trustworthy. However, this is a relatively limited screen. Not having these characteristics might eliminate an entrepreneur from further consideration. But it doesn't weed out many people; most entrepreneurs are honest, trustworthy, motivated, and passionate about their businesses.

The real screen on the team side of the equation is experience. Investors look for entrepreneurs who they think can build companies. In general this means that they favor people who have started and built companies before, and who have a lot of experience in the industry that they are entering.[24]

On the opportunity side of the equation, investors look for things that demonstrate the value of the venture opportunity and the entrepreneur's ability to capture that value. We'll talk more about these things in Chapters 9, 10, and 11, but, in general, they include such things as a large market, product acceptance, an appropriate strategy, a way to protect the entrepreneur's intellectual property against imitation, a well-designed production plan, a compelling description of a product, and so on.[25] In particular, investors favor new ventures that have an externally observable competitive advantage, like a patent, because such assets are easier to evaluate than intangible things like the entrepreneur's willingness to work hard.[26]

Once the investors are fairly sure that they would like to invest in a new venture, they conduct **due diligence**. Due diligence is a legal term that refers to the effort by investors to verify information about the new venture. It typically includes an investigation of (1) the business—the market, the business model, the intellectual property; (2) the legal entity—the organizational form, board of directors, patents, trademarks; and (3) the financial records—the company's financial statements.

If the new venture passes the due diligence hurdle, then the investor will negotiate the terms of the investment with the entrepreneur. This negotiation usually focuses on the amount of equity that the investor will receive in return for providing capital. We will explain how venture capitalists and angel investors decide on the amount of ownership that they want in return for their investment. But first, we need to explain why the initial investment the entrepreneur receives will be small relative to the total amount of investment that a successful firm will ultimately get, and why the investors make those investments in small pieces over time.

Staging of Investment

LEARNING OBJECTIVE

8 Explain why equity financing in new ventures is typically staged.

New ventures typically raise money from investors in a series of stages, rather than all at once. That is, investors provide a small amount of money to create an **option**—a right, but not an obligation—to make additional investments later. Why? First, investing in new ventures is very risky for investors. To minimize their exposure to this risk, investors put in a small amount of money and see what happens to this initial investment. This way, the most that the investor can lose is the small amount of the initial investment.

The entrepreneur uses the initial investment to reach a **milestone**, or set target that they need to achieve for investors to consider additional financing. Examples of milestones to achieve with initial capital are the development of a prototype for the product or service, obtaining customer feedback through a survey or focus group, organizing the relevant venture team, hiring employees, and so on. If the milestone is achieved, the investor puts more money in. If the milestone isn't met, the investor discontinues investment in the venture.

Second, **staging** helps to protect investors against efforts by entrepreneurs to use their information advantage to gain at the expense of the investor. By putting money into a new venture over time, the investor has the opportunity to gather information about how the venture is doing before putting more money in. If the entrepreneur does anything that the investor doesn't like, such as using the money for private gain (throwing lavish parties, for example) or if the entrepreneur adopts too risky a strategy because it's not his money at risk, the investor can decide not to put more money in.[27] However, if the investor put the entire amount of money that the entrepreneur needed in the venture upfront, then this option would lost.

Last, staging helps investors manage the uncertainty of investing in new ventures. In the very early stages of a new venture—right after the discovery of the opportunity and before a product or service has been developed—new ventures are very difficult for investors to evaluate because so little information about them is available. Over time, however, as a new venture develops, information about the product, the entrepreneur's management style, the firm's strategy, and so on become clearer, making it easier for investors to evaluate the venture. Because uncertainty is reduced as the venture develops, delaying most of the investment until after the venture has reached key milestones allows the investor to manage the uncertainty of investing in new ventures.[28] Table 6.6 summarizes the staging of venture finance.

The Cost of Capital

LEARNING OBJECTIVE

9 Describe how venture capitalists calculate the cost of the capital that they provide to new ventures.

How much will you pay to obtain capital for your new venture? Obviously this is an important question for entrepreneurs, and the answer is a lot! Over the past 40 years or so, equity investors in new ventures have demanded an annual rate of return of between 20 and 100 percent, depending on the venture's stage of development.

Why do investors in new ventures demand—and get—such high rates of return? After all, even Tony Soprano, HBO's popular waste management entrepreneur, doesn't get this kind of return from his investments. There are several reasons: First, new ven-

STAGE	CONDITION OF THE VENTURE	SOURCES OF CAPITAL	USES OF CAPITAL	COST OF CAPITAL
Pre-seed stage	The entrepreneur has an idea, but has not yet formed a company or written a business plan.	Entrepreneur Friends and family Business angels Corporations	Write a business plan. Form a company.	70–100% rate of return
Seed stage	The entrepreneur has formed a legal entity, has a partial venture team, and has written a business plan.	Entrepreneur Friends and family Business angels Venture capitalists Corporations	Develop a prototype of the product. Fill out the venture team. Conduct market research.	60–80% rate of return
First stage	The entrepreneur has organized the company, and the product development and initial market research are compete.	Entrepreneur Friends and family Business angels Venture capitalists Corporations	Make initial sales. Establish production. Buy fixed assets.	40–60% rate of return
Second stage	The entrepreneur has produced and sold initial versions of the product and the organization is "up and running."	Business angels Venture capitalists Asset-based financiers Corporations	Scale up production. Hire additional people for sales and for production.	20–40% rate of return

Table 6.6 Stages of Financing

Investors stage financing to new ventures. Each stage has different sources of financing, different uses of capital, and different expected rates of return.

tures are extremely risky—and returns are inversely related to risk. Very few new ventures are ultimately successful, and investors need a high return to make up for all of the failures that they back. In fact, a rule of thumb used by investors in new ventures is that only one in ten succeeds, requiring the successful venture to pay a high rate of return to make up for the capital lost on the other nine. Second, investors in new ventures can't diversify their risks very well. Most investors in new ventures need to focus on a particular industry and geographic location to develop enough expertise to manage their investments. This means that their investments are dependent on the overall performance of a particular industry—remember the collapse of Internet ventures?—and the vagaries of the local economy. Third, investors demand an **illiquidity premium**, or extra compensation for the fact that they can't sell their investments. (As you probably know, there's no market for shares of start-ups like there is for publicly traded stocks.) Fourth, as we have said earlier, entrepreneurs have information about new ventures that they don't share with investors. Because that information advantage allows some entrepreneurs to take advantage of investors, investors demand a premium for making investments when they have an information disadvantage. Fifth, entrepreneurs are often overoptimistic when they project the future prospects of their new ventures, so investors demand a high rate of return to discount these overoptimistic projections. Sixth, unlike investors in the stock market who are largely passive, investors in new ventures provide several types of assistance to new ventures, including identifying customers, attracting suppliers, and hiring senior management; and investors want compensation for providing this assistance.[29]

The main factor that determines the rate of return that investors receive for financing new ventures is the stage of venture development. As Figure 6.8 on page 154 shows, the rate of return goes down as the venture moves to later stages of development because uncertainty is reduced as ventures develop. However, the maturity of the venture isn't the only factor that influences the cost of capital. Investors also factor in their perception of the capabilities of the venture team and the quality of the business opportunity, including the size and growth rate of the market. Investors weigh the amount of capital required and the risk that is imposed on them. Founders' objectives for how the venture exit will occur and their desire for control, as well as their ability to bargain with investors, also influence the rate of return.

The cost of capital provided to new ventures can be calculated a number of different ways. However, the most common way used by professional investors is called the **venture capital method**. This method, shown in Figure 6.9 on page 154, is as follows: First, the investor looks at the business plan's forecasted earnings and estimates the venture's level of income in the year that the new business is expected to be acquired or go public. Second, the investor calculates the appropriate price-earnings ratio for acquisitions and public offerings in the same industry as the new venture. Third, the investor estimates the **terminal value** of the investment by multiplying the projected income by the price-earnings ratio. Fourth, the investor uses the appropriate **discount rate**, based on the desired rate of return for the investment and calculates the net present value of the terminal value. Fifth, the investor specifies the portion of ownership that they will take by dividing the investment amount by the net present value of the terminal value.

Figure 6.8 Rates of Return and Financing Rounds

The rate of return that investors demand decreases as the venture becomes more developed.

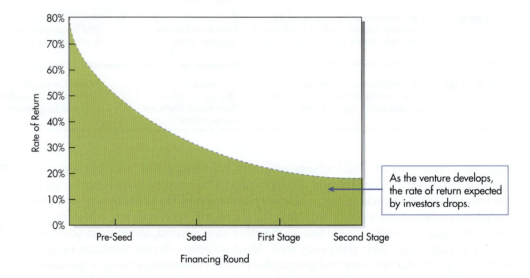

As the venture develops, the rate of return expected by investors drops.

Figure 6.9 The Formula for the Investor's Expected Share of a New Venture

Venture capitalists use the method shown here to calculate how much ownership in a new venture they demand in return for their investment.

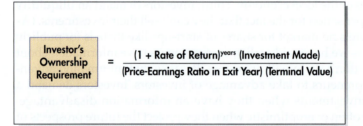

$$\text{Investor's Ownership Requirement} = \frac{(1 + \text{Rate of Return})^{\text{years}} (\text{Investment Made})}{(\text{Price-Earnings Ratio in Exit Year}) (\text{Terminal Value})}$$

KEY POINTS

- Equity financing by business angels and venture capitalists follows a common process that typically begins with a referral, and is followed by an initial screening, a deeper investigation, due diligence, and ends with the negotiation of the terms of the investment.
- Equity investors in new ventures typically stage their investments to minimize risk, to minimize the potential for entrepreneurs to take advantage of the investors' lack of information, and to manage uncertainty.
- Investors in new ventures demand high rates of return to compensate for high risk, limited ability to diversify, illiquidity, information asymmetry, entrepreneurial overoptimism, and a need for investor involvement in the new venture's development.
- Venture capitalists and business angels typically use the venture capital method to calculate how much equity to demand in return for their investment.
- The venture capital method involves taking the business plan's forecasted earnings in the year that the entrepreneur projects the exit, calculating the appropriate price-earnings ratio, multiplying these numbers to estimate the terminal value, calculating the present value of that number on the basis of the investor's discount rate, and dividing the investment amount by the net present value figure.

SOCIAL CAPITAL AND THE BEHAVIORAL SIDE OF VENTURE FINANCE

This chapter began with a story about how three entrepreneurs used their social relationships to obtain capital. Although we have spent most of this chapter discussing the more structural and economic factors involved in venture finance, both research and entrepreneurial experience show that raising money depends heavily on the social and behavioral factors that lie behind the story that introduced this chapter. In this section, we'll turn to a discussion of how and why social relationships, and certain behaviors and actions, help entrepreneurs to raise money from external investors.

Social Ties and the Process of Raising Money

Entrepreneurs typically raise money from people whom they know, tapping their social networks for contacts to sources of capital. Researchers have shown, for example, that investors are much more likely to provide capital to entrepreneurs with whom they have a direct business or social tie—that is, people with whom they have done business before, or their roommates in college—than they are to provide capital to people that they don't have a tie to.[30] Moreover, indirect social ties, or ties to people who can refer an entrepreneur to an investor (for example, a lawyer who does work for a venture capitalist) also increases the likelihood that an entrepreneur will receive financing from an investor.[31]

Why do social ties matter to raising money for new ventures? There are several reasons: First, if the investor knows the entrepreneur, then the entrepreneur will be less likely to try to take advantage of the investor. Social relationships make people act in a less self-interested way by creating a sense of obligation and generosity.[32] Most people know that a good way to kill a friendship is by taking advantage of a friend; this principle influences relationships with investors as well as relationships with roommates.

Second, social ties provide a way to invoke sanctions against people who harm others. Just like a group of friends might rally to your defense or take actions against someone who hurt you, investors use their social networks to keep entrepreneurs in line. Entrepreneurs who break the rules or take advantage of investors are quickly black-balled by the investing community.[33]

Third, social relationships provide an efficient way to gather information about people. Social networks transmit information quickly and cheaply, particularly about hard-to-observe qualities, like a person's competence or honesty.[34] So a referral from a reputable source provides an efficient way of figuring out who the good guys are.[35]

Fourth, social ties—whether direct or indirect—create positive attributions about people. When someone refers you to a third party, that referral elevates you in the eyes of the person who is going to meet you. Why? Because you have been singled out as someone important. This makes people meeting you for the first time be predisposed to thinking that you are better than people who weren't referred to them. Similarly, if you already know someone and are their friend, you'll tend to make positive attributions about their actions in a new setting. So if you are a good doubles partner of a venture capitalist, the positive feelings of the venture capitalist toward your net game will be carried over when you ask him for money.[36]

In short, social ties to investors really do help you to raise money (see Figure 6.10 on page 156). In practical terms, this means that you should go first to those investors you know if you are serious about raising money. You should work your contacts. Getting referrals to investors is a central part of the process of financing a new company.

Behaviors and Actions That Encourage Investors

Entrepreneurs sometimes forget that the investors from whom they are trying to raise money are people. Just like other human beings, investors are influenced by the behaviors

© Getty Images/ PhotoDisc

Figure 6.10 Social Ties Are Important to Facilitating Access to Capital

Entrepreneurs are more likely to receive venture capital or angel financing if they are referred to the investor by someone the investor knows and trusts.

and actions of others. Although you probably don't need us to tell you that it would be hard to persuade investors to give you money if you met them without having washed for a month, or cursed at them when you greet them, you might not be aware of the more subtle behaviors and actions that entrepreneurs can engage in to positively or negatively influence investors.

In Chapter 5, we discussed the importance of impression management to entrepreneurs. Nowhere is that more important than in raising money. To obtain capital, an entrepreneur needs to generate the impression that she is trustworthy and competent, and that her venture is going to be successful. Successful entrepreneurs recognize that no entrepreneur can provide irrefutable evidence that her venture will succeed and that investors, like everyone else in this world, are influenced by appearances as well as actual performance.[37] Successful entrepreneurs are careful to generate a good impression with investors.

They use many of the general impression management strategies that we discussed in Chapter 5. For instance, successful entrepreneurs are careful to create a good story about their ventures in their business plans so that they can persuade investors of the value of their ideas. They use effective verbal and nonverbal communication mechanisms, and avoid inadvertent negative cues, like failing to smile or looking uncomfortable.

But successful entrepreneurs do more than just use these interpersonal techniques. They create a sense of urgency among investors so that they can generate momentum in favor of their business, something we will discuss in more detail in Chapter 12.[38] They also frame their business ideas in ways that make them more appealing to investors. For instance, they describe their businesses in ways that focus attention on their potential value and away from their potential risks, by making associations between their businesses and things that are familiar to investors.[39] An entrepreneur with a space tourism business, for example, might focus attention on the types of exotic vacations, like safaris, that investors are familiar with, rather than on the dangers of space flight.

This is where a good business plan comes in, and why your professor told you that it's important to write a persuasive one if you hope to raise money. We'll return to this theme in Chapter 12 and discuss it in more detail. But for now, we just want to make a couple of points. Your business plan needs to communicate the message of your business—why the need is there, how you are going so solve it, why you are going to make money, and so on—in a clear and compelling way. Remember that investors are people and that a good presentation and cogent argument will often convince people to do something that they might otherwise not do.

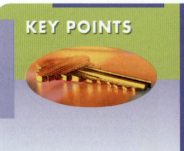

KEY POINTS

- Entrepreneurs typically raise money from people they know because social ties reduce the likelihood that entrepreneurs will take advantage of investors; because social networks provide an effective way for investors to sanction entrepreneurs; because social relationships provide an efficient way to transfer information; and because social ties create positive attributions about people.
- Successful entrepreneurs use impression management strategies to encourage investors to back them. They create good stories about their ventures in their business plans, and use effective verbal and nonverbal communication.
- Framing business ideas in ways that focus attention on potential and away from risks and creating urgency also encourage investors to back entrepreneurs.

Summary and Review of Key Points

- The problems of uncertainty and information asymmetry make it difficult for entrepreneurs to raise money from external sources.

- Information asymmetry means that investors must make decisions on less information than the entrepreneur has, that entrepreneurs can take advantage of investors, and that entrepreneurs can engage in adverse selection.

- Uncertainty means that investors have to make decisions about new ventures on very little actual evidence, that entrepreneurs and investors will disagree on the value of new ventures, and that investors will want assurance that the entrepreneur can pay up if the opportunity proves not to be valuable.

- Investors have established several solutions to the financing problems generated by information asymmetry and uncertainty, including self-financing, contract provisions, syndication, specialization, and geographically localized investing.

- Self-financing reduces entrepreneurs' incentive to act against the interests of investors, and provides collateral for new ventures.

- Covenants, mandatory redemption rights, convertible securities, control rights, and forfeiture and antidilution provisions are all contract provisions that help to protect investors against uncertainty and information asymmetry problems in venture finance.

- Investors syndicate their investments to diversify their risks and to gather information that reduces the problems generated by information asymmetry.

- Specialization and geographically localized investing provide investors with information and control that protects them against opportunistic entrepreneurs.

- New ventures typically require very little start-up capital, but tend to demand larger amounts of capital later, as they experience negative cash flow from operations.

- To manage the financial side of new businesses, entrepreneurs estimate start-up costs and uses of funds; create proforma financial statements; generate cash flow statements, and undertake breakeven analysis.

- New ventures are generally financed by equity rather than by debt because they lack sufficient cash flow to pay interest, and because debt financing at a fixed rate of interest encourages entrepreneurs to take risky actions with investors' funds.

- Entrepreneurs have a wide variety of capital sources available to them, including their own savings, their friends and family, business angels, venture capitalists, corporations, banks, asset-based lenders, factors, and government programs.

- Equity financing by business angels and venture capitalists follows a common process that typically begins with a referral, and is followed by an initial screening, a deeper investigation, due diligence, and ends with the negotiation of the terms of the investment.

- Equity investors in new ventures typically stage their investments to minimize risk, to minimize the potential for entrepreneurs to take advantage of the investors' lack of information, and to manage uncertainty.

- Investors in new ventures demand high rates of return to compensate for high risk, limited ability to diversify, illiquidity, information asymmetry, entrepreneurial overoptimism, and a need for investor involvement in the new venture's development.

- Venture capitalists and business angels typically use the venture capital method to calculate how much equity to demand in return for their investment.

- The venture capital method involves taking the business plan's forecasted earnings in the year that the entrepreneur projects the exit, calculating the appropriate price-earnings ratio, multiplying these numbers to estimate the terminal value, calculating the present value of that number on the basis of the investor's discount rate, and dividing the investment amount by the net present value figure.

- Entrepreneurs typically raise money from people they know because social ties reduce the likelihood that entrepreneurs will take advantage of investors; because social networks provide an effective way for investors to sanction entrepreneurs; because social relationships provide an efficient way to transfer information; and because social ties create positive attributions about people.

- Successful entrepreneurs use impression management strategies to encourage investors to back them. They create good stories about their ventures in their business plans, and use effective verbal and nonverbal communication.

- Framing business ideas in ways that focus attention on potential and away from risks and creating urgency also encourage investors to back entrepreneurs.

Glossary

Adverse Selection: The choice of someone or something without a desired quality because of the inability to distinguish between those who have a desired quality and those who don't.

Antidilution Provisions: Contract provisions that require entrepreneurs to provide investors with additional shares in a new venture so that the investor's percentage of ownership is not reduced in later rounds of financing.

Asset-Based Financing: A type of loan in which the assets being purchased are used as collateral for the loan.

Breakeven Analysis: A calculation that shows the amount of sales that you need to achieve to cover your costs.

Burn Rate: The pace at which a new venture uses capital provided by investors.

Business Angel: A person who invests in new ventures as a private individual.

Cash Flow Statements: Calculations of the amount of cash that your new venture has at a given point in time.

Collateral: Something of value that an entrepreneur pledges to sell to reimburse investors in the event that there are insufficient proceeds from a venture to return the investors' principal.

Commercial Loan: A form of bank financing in which the borrower pays interest on the money borrowed.

Control Rights: The right to decide what to do with a venture's assets.

Convertible Securities: Financial instruments that allow investors to convert preferred stock, which gets preferential treatment in the event of a liquidation, into common stock at the investor's option.

Covenants: Restrictions on the behavior of entrepreneurs contractually agreed upon by investors and entrepreneurs.

Debt: A financial obligation to return money provided plus a scheduled amount of interest.

Discount Rate: The annual percentage rate that an investor reduces the value of an investment to calculate its present value.

Due Diligence: The review of a new venture's management, business opportunity, technology, legal status, and finances prior to investment.

Equity: The ownership of a company, which takes the form of stock. It also equals assets minus liabilities or net worth.

Factor: Specialized organizations that purchase the accounts receivable of businesses at a discount.

Forfeiture Provisions: Contract terms that require an entrepreneur to lose ownership of her venture if she fails to meet agreed-upon milestones.

Illiquidity Premium: Additional return demanded by investors to compensate them for the fact that an investment cannot be sold easily.

Information Asymmetry: The imbalance in knowledge about something between two parties.

Line of Credit: An agreement to allow entrepreneurs to draw up to a set amount of money at a particular interest rate whenever they need it.

Mandatory Redemption Rights: Contract terms that require an entrepreneur to give investors their investment back at any time.

Milestone: A jointly agreed-upon goal between entrepreneurs and investors that the entrepreneur needs to meet to receive another stage of financing.

Option: A right, but not an obligation, to make a future investment.

Staging: The provision of capital in pieces conditional on the achievement of specified milestones.

Syndicate: The sharing of an investment across a group of investors.

Terminal Value: The estimated value of a new venture at the time that the investment is liquidated in an initial public offering or an acquisition.

Uncertainty: A condition in which the future is unknown.

Venture Capitalist: A person who works for an organization that raises money from institutional investors and invests those funds in new firms.

Venture Capital Method: How venture capitalists calculate the amount of equity that they will take in a new venture in return for their investment of capital.

Vesting Periods: A period of time when entrepreneurs cannot cash out of their investments.

Discussion Questions

1. What can entrepreneurs do to "fool" venture capitalists and how can venture capitalists fight back?

2. What is the hardest thing about raising money for a new business? What makes financing a new business so difficult?

3. Why should an entrepreneur agree to give up 40 percent of her company when she used her own blood, sweat, and tears to get it started?

4. How can a new company can be profitable and still fail? What can you do to reduce the chances of this happening?

5. Why will you have more trouble raising debt for your new business than you'll have raising equity?

6. What can you do to make yourself and your new business more attractive to potential investors?

InfoTrac Exercises

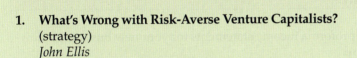

1. **What's Wrong with Risk-Averse Venture Capitalists?** (strategy)
   John Ellis
   Fast Company, July 2003 p54(1)
   Record: A102835146
   Full Text: COPYRIGHT 2003 *Gruner & Jahr USA Publishing.* All rights reserved.

   1. According to the article, why is the venture capital paradigm changing?
   2. What key changes does Daniel L. Burstein predict in the venture capital paradigm?
   3. Do you agree with Burstein? Or with the author of the article? Why?

2. **Don't Count on Venture Capital, Family and Friends More Likely to Help** (*The Orlando Sentinel*)
   Barry Flynn
   Knight Ridder/Tribune News Service, June 24, 2003 pK1986
   Record: CJ104170537
   Full Text: COPYRIGHT 2003 *Knight Ridder/Tribune News Service* Byline: Barry Flynn

   1. According to the article, why do most new businesses fail?
   2. What sources of capital are most readily available to entrepreneurs?
   3. What factors do venture capitalists look for before making an investment?

GETTING DOWN
TO BUSINESS

Creating Proforma Balance Sheets, Income Statements, and Cash Flow Statements

As we explained in this chapter, you will need to develop proforma financial statements for your new business. This exercise is designed to help you do that.

Step One: Develop 3-year proforma balance sheets for your new business, following the format shown here.

Your Company Name _____

	12/31/04	12/31/05	12/31/06
Cash			
Accounts Receivable			
Inventory			
Property and Equipment			
Less: Accumulated Depreciation			
Total Assets			
Accounts Payable			
Notes Payable			
Total Liabilities			
Stockholder Equity			
Total Liabilities and Equity			

Step Two: Develop 3-year proforma income statements for your new business, following the format shown here.

Your Company Name _____

	12/31/04	12/31/05	12/31/06
Sales			
Less: Cost of Goods Sold			
Gross Profit			
Less: Operating Expenses			
Less: Depreciation			
Net Profit (Loss)			

Step Three: Develop 3-year cash flow statements for your new business, following the format shown here.
1. Take your net profit on 12/31/04 and add back depreciation.
2. Subtract increases in accounts receivable or add decreases in accounts receivable.
3. Subtract increases in inventory or add decreases in inventory.
4. Add increases in accounts payable or subtract decreases in accounts payable.
5. Subtract decreases in notes/loans payable or add increases in notes/loans payable.
6. The resulting figure is your net cash flow for 2004.
7. Repeat for the other years.

Calculating Your Breakeven Level of Sales

In this chapter, we discussed the importance of conducting a breakeven analysis for your new venture. Breakeven analysis allows you to figure out how much sales volume you need to achieve to cover your costs. This exercise will help you to calculate the breakeven level of sales for your new venture so that you may include the information in a feasibility study. Follow these steps to do the calculation:

1. Determine the sales price (per unit) of your product or service. _____
2. Estimate the variable cost (per unit) of your product or service. _____

3. Subtract the variable cost per unit from the sales price to calculate your contribution margin (per unit). _____

4. Divide the contribution margin (per unit) by the sales price (per unit) to estimate your contribution margin percentage. _____

5. Estimate your business' fixed costs. _____

6. Divide the fixed costs by the contribution margin percentage to calculate the breakeven sales volume. _____

Evaluate your breakeven level of sales. Is it large or small? How does it compare to the average sales level of firms in your industry? How large a percentage of total sales in the market is your breakeven sales volume?

Cost of Capital

In this chapter, we discussed the venture capital method of calculating your venture's cost of capital. This exercise will help you to calculate your new venture's cost of capital so that you may include the information in a feasibility study. Please follow these steps to calculate your venture's cost of capital and report the proportion of equity that the investor would take to provide you with the capital that you need. Show all steps in the process of calculating this estimate.

1. Use your proforma income statements to estimate the venture's level of income in the year that you would expect the business to be acquired or go public.

2. Calculate the appropriate price-earnings ratio for acquisitions and public offerings in the same industry as the new venture.

3. Estimate the terminal value of the investment by multiplying the projected income by the price-earnings ratio.

4. Use the appropriate discount rate, based on the desired rate of return for the investment, to calculate the net present value of the terminal value.

5. Specify the portion of ownership that investors will take by dividing the investment amount by the net present value of the terminal value.

Enhanced Learning

You may select any combination of the case options below to enhance your understanding of the chapter material.

- **Appendix 1: Case Studies –** Thirteen cases provide opportunities to apply chapter concepts to realistic entrepreneurial situations. These brief cases call for careful analysis of real business problems and ask you to think about potential solutions.

- **Appendix 2: Video Case Library –** Nine cases are tied directly to video segments from the popular PBS television series *Small Business School*. These cases and video segments give you unparalleled access to today's entrepreneurs, with expert advice and insights on how to start, run, and grow a business.

- **Comprehensive Cases –** Visit the book support Web site at http://baron.swlearning.com for cases detailing real businesses whose successes and setbacks illustrate each stage of the entrepreneurial process. You will conduct in-depth analysis of entrepreneurial challenges through well-developed case studies.

Notes

1. Blanchflower, D., & Oswald, A. 1998. What makes an entrepreneur? *Journal of Labor Economics* 16(1): 26–60.

2. Casson, M. 1995. *Entrepreneurship and business culture.* London: Edward Elgar.

3. Shane, S., & Stuart, T. 2002. Organizational endowments and the performance of university start-ups. *Management Science* 48(1): 154–170.

4. Amit, R., Glosten, L., & Muller, E. 1990b. Entrepreneurial ability, venture investments, and risk sharing. *Management Science* 38(10): 1232–1245.

5. Arrow, K. 1974. Limited knowledge and economic analysis. *American Economic Review* 64(1): 1–10.

6. Bhide, A. 2000. *The origin and evolution of new businesses.* New York: Oxford University Press.

7. Wu, S. 1989. *Production, entrepreneurship and profits.* Cambridge, MA: Basil Blackwell.

8. Blanchflower, D., & Oswald, A. 1998. What makes an entrepreneur? *Journal of Labor Economics* 16(1): 26–60.

9. Barzel, Y. 1987. The entrepreneur's reward for self-policing. *Economic Inquiry* 25: 103–116.

10. Gompers, P. 1997. An examination of convertible securities in venture capital investments. *Working paper.* Harvard University.

11. Shane, S. (forthcoming). *A general theory of entrepreneurship: The individual opportunity nexus.* London: Edward Elgar.

12. Hoffman, H., & Blakely, J. 1987. You can negotiate with venture capitalists. *Harvard Business Review* (March–April): 6–24.

13. Barry, C. 1994. New directions in research on venture capital finance. *Financial Management* 23 (3): 3–15.

14. Sahlman, W. 1990. The structure and governance of venture capital organizations. *Journal of Financial Economics* 27: 473–521.

15. Sorenson, O., & Stuart, T. 2001. Syndication networks and the spatial distribution of venture capital investments. *American Journal of Sociology* 106(6): 1546–1588.

16. Ibid.

17. Lerner, J. 1994. The syndication of venture capital investments. *Financial Management* 23(3): 16–27.

18. Aldrich, H. 1999. *Organizations evolving.* London: Sage.

19. Bhide, A. 2000. *The origin and evolution of new businesses.* New York: Oxford University Press.

20. Debelak, D. 2003. Play your cards right. *Entrepreneur* (March): 106–110.

21. Baum, J. 1996. Organizational ecology. In S. Clegg, C. Hardy, & W. Nord (eds.). *Handbook of organization studies.* London: Sage, 77–114.

22. Aldrich, H. 1999. *Organizations evolving.* London: Sage.

23. Sap Story. http://www.entrepreneur.com/mag/article/0,1539,229518 - - - - 2-,00.html.

24. Shane, S. 2003. *A general theory of entrepreneurship: The individual-opportunity nexus.* London: Edward Elgar.

25. Ibid.

26. Bhide, A. 2000. *The origin and evolution of new businesses.* New York: Oxford University Press.

27. Giudici, G., & Paleari, S. 2000. The optimal staging of venture capital financing when entrepreneurs extract private benefits from their firms. *Enterprise and Innovation Management Studies* 1(2): 153–174.

28. Sorenson, O., & Stuart, T. 2001. Syndication networks and the spatial distribution of venture capital investments. *American Journal of Sociology* 106(6): 1546–1588.

29. Fuerst, O., & Geiger, U. 2003. *From concept to wall street: A complete guide to entrepreneurship and venture capital.* Upper Saddle River, NJ: Prentice Hall.

30. Shane, S., & Cable, D. 2002. Network ties, reputation, and the financing of new ventures. *Management Science* 48(3): 364–381.

31. Shane, S., & Stuart, T. 2002. Organizational endowments and the performance of university start-ups. *Management Science* 48(1): 154–170.

32. Uzzi, B. 1996. The sources and consequences of embeddedness for the economic performance of organizations: The network effect. *American Sociological Review* 61: 674–698.

33. Stuart, T., & Robinson, D. 2000. The emergence of interorganizational networks: Probation until reputation. *Working paper.* University of Chicago.

34. Burt, R. 1992. *Structural holes: The social structure of competition.* Boston: Harvard University Press.

35. Fernandez, M., & Weinberg, N. 1997. Sifting and sorting: Personal contacts and hiring in a retail bank. *American Sociological Review* 62: 883–902.

36. Shane, S. 2003. *A general theory of entrepreneurship: The individual-opportunity nexus.* London: Edward Elgar.

37. Dees, G., & Starr, J. 1992. Entrepreneurship through an ethical lens: Dilemmas and issues for research and practice. In D. Sexton & J. Kasarda (eds.). *The state of the art of entrepreneurship.* Boston: PWS–Kent, 89–116.

38. Bhide, A. 2000. *The origin and evolution of new businesses.* New York: Oxford University Press.

39. Roberts, E. 1991. *Entrepreneurs in high technology.* New York: Oxford University Press.

CHAPTER 7

WRITING AN EFFECTIVE BUSINESS PLAN: CRAFTING A ROAD MAP TO SUCCESS

LEARNING OBJECTIVES

After reading this chapter, you should be able to:

1 Define a business plan and explain why entrepreneurs should write one.

2 Explain how the process of persuasion plays a key role in business plans and in the success of new ventures.

3 Explain why the executive summary is a very important part of any business plan.

4 Describe the major sections of a business plan and the types of information they should include.

5 Describe the "seven deadly sins" of business plans—errors all entrepreneurs should avoid.

6 Explain why potential investors usually ask entrepreneurs to give verbal presentations describing their idea for new products or services and their company.

7 Describe steps entrepreneurs should take to make their verbal presentations to potential investors truly excellent.

Why Write a Business Plan? The Benefits of Clear-Cut Goals

Components of a Business Plan: Basic Requirements

The Executive Summary

Background, Product, and Purpose

Market Analysis

Development, Production, and Location

The Management Team

Financial Plans and Projections

Critical Risks: Describing What Might Go Wrong

Reaping the Rewards: Harvest and Exit

Scheduling and Milestones

Appendices

A Note on the Intangibles

Making an Effective Business Plan Presentation: The Ball Is Definitely in Your Court

Whether they realize it or not, most entrepreneurs accept these words as true. They are convinced that because *they* believe passionately in their ideas and their new ventures, others will, too, if given half a chance to do so. As a result, they are often dismayed when their initial efforts to obtain financial backing meet with lukewarm receptions (or worse!) from venture capitalists, business angels, and others who might readily provide the resources they need. "What's wrong with these people?" they wonder. "Can't they recognize a great thing when they see it?" The problem, of course, may not be a lack of discernment on the part of these persons. Rather, it may have much more to do with the kind of job the entrepreneur is doing in presenting her or his idea to others. Yes, the entrepreneur is enthusiastic and enthusiasm sells. But in order to induce other people—especially ones who have been taught by years of experience to view new ventures with a jaundiced eye—enthusiasm alone is rarely sufficient. In addition, entrepreneurs who want to succeed must realize that they face a very serious and very tough task, one centered around the process of **persuasion**—the task of inducing others to share our views and to see the world much as

we do. After all, why should total strangers entrust their hard-earned money to something as risky in nature as a new venture, especially if it is going to be run by someone who has had little if any experience in starting or running a business? Would you? Unless you are like the characters shown in Figure 7.1, and have fallen in love with an idea or industry, the answer is clear: No!

If enthusiasm alone is not enough, then what can entrepreneurs do to gain the resources they need? For many entrepreneurs, a large part of the answer involves preparing a truly first-rate business plan. This is a formal, written expression of the entrepreneur's vision for converting ideas into a profitable, going business, and in most cases, it is the entry card for serious consideration by venture capitalists, banks, and other sources of funding: Most won't even think about supporting a new venture until they have seen and carefully evaluated this document. This basic fact poses something of a dilemma for many entrepreneurs: They firmly believe in their ideas and their own ability to carry them through to success, but at the same time, they have had little practice in writing formal documents such as business plans. In fact, unless they have a background in business (which only some entrepreneurs possess), they may not even have a clear idea about what a business plan is or what it should contain. The result? Many do not prepare such plans; in fact, statistics show that more than 60 percent of small, new companies have no business plan—or no written plans of any kind, for that matter.[1]

Figure 7.1 Overeager Investors: A Very Rare Occurrence!

Sometimes, investors rush to offer funding to start-up companies in a "hot" industry, as happened during the late 1990s with respect to Internet companies. In most cases, however, they are much more careful about where they put their hard-earned money!

That brings us to the main purpose of this chapter: helping you understand what a business plan is and how to write one that will assist you in attaining the support you need, financial and otherwise. In order to reach this goal, we will proceed as follows. First, we will examine the question of why you should write a business plan, even if you are in the rare and truly glorious situation of not needing financial support to get started. As we will soon note, preparing this document can be helpful in several important ways. In fact, research findings indicate that entrepreneurs who prepare excellent business plans are more likely to attain success than those who do not—for reasons that will soon become clear. For instance, one recent and very carefully conducted study found that writing business plans significantly reduced the chances of venture failure and increased the rate of new business and new product development among a random sample of Swedish entrepreneurs.[2]

After explaining why it is usually helpful to write a thorough business plan, we will turn to the task of describing this document in detail—the key sections it should contain, how they should be put together, and so on. Throughout this discussion, we will do more than just describe the basic requirements: We will also provide you with tips and suggestions for making your plan excellent—an instrument for transmitting your own enthusiasm and vision to others. We think this is crucial information that will serve you well as you move toward starting your own venture.

After we have described the major sections of a formal business plan, we will return to a key theme we wish to emphasize throughout this chapter: Persuasion is, indeed, the name of the game where starting a new venture is concerned. For that reason, writing an excellent business plan, though certainly a crucial activity, is only the first step in a larger process. Persuading other people to support your new venture involves several other steps as well. For instance, if your plan is one that generates initial positive reactions on the part of venture capitalists and other investors to whom you send it (an outcome achieved by only a few percent of all plans), this will often lead to the next step: an invitation for you to visit and make a formal presentation. This presentation often plays an important role in decisions about whether and to what extent to support your venture, so it is a task you should definitely take very seriously. How can you "shine" in this context? Although we agree with John Ruskin (1749) who once wrote: "He who has truth at his heart need never fear the want of persuasion on his tongue," we also know that being persuasive involves much more than personal conviction. In a final section, therefore, we will provide suggestions for reaching these goals based on both careful research and our personal experiences as entrepreneurs.

WHY WRITE A BUSINESS PLAN? THE BENEFITS OF CLEAR-CUT GOALS

Make no mistake: Preparing a business plan requires a lot of hard work. In fact, it usually requires many hours of careful thought, followed by an equal or larger number of hours spent converting these thoughts into a written document. Although university professors may enjoy such activities (!), entrepreneurs generally do not. Often, they are eager to get started—to launch their business and make their vision happen. Many realize that once their business has been launched, it will rarely follow the steps and time line outlined in the business plan. So why should they stop and devote so much hard work to the task of preparing a first-rate business plan, even if, as we noted earlier, they are in the rare and enviable position of *not* needing outside resources to get started? Perhaps the simplest yet most important answer we can give is this: *It is truly difficult to arrive somewhere unless you know where you want to go.* In other words, a business plan is much more than a document designed to persuade skeptical people to invest in your new venture: *It is also a detailed road map for converting your ideas and vision into a real, functioning business.* Writing a business plan requires you, as an entrepreneur, to carefully and fully address a number of complex issues relating to the process of converting your idea and its accompanying vision into reality: how your product will be produced, the price at which it will sell, how and to whom it will be marketed, how it will compare with existing or potential competitors, what financial resources are needed and how these will be used, and so on.

In other words, the term "plan" in "business plan" is really appropriate: A carefully prepared and well-reasoned business plan will indeed help you with the process of planning; it really *will* provide the road map mentioned in the title of this chapter. More specifically, a well-prepared business plan will explain what the new venture is trying to accomplish and how it will go about attaining these goals. This is the kind of information venture capitalists and others who might support a new venture often seek, and in fact, the clearer the links between the goals sought and the means for accomplishing them, the more impressive (and persuasive) the business plan will be. But remember: Entrepreneurs do not write business plans solely to persuade others to invest in their new ventures. They also write them to provide themselves with a clearer understanding of the best ways of proceeding. That, we hope

LEARNING OBJECTIVE

1 Define a business plan and explain why entrepreneurs should write one.

you'll agree, is invaluable information that should be sought by all entrepreneurs early in the process.

Having made these points, we should now balance the scales, so to speak, by noting that a business plan is a *living document*—one that often changes—and changes often—as a new business develops. Because you can never know in advance just how your new business will develop, there is a limit to how much planning you can do. For this reason, successful entrepreneurs often avoid "analysis paralysis" in which they spend countless hours in the library developing long, formal business plans with lots of data and assumptions, fancy spreadsheets, and beautiful bindings. Instead, they do just enough planning to get their new companies started, and then use the information that they gather from actually running their new ventures to refine their plans in the light of reality. In essence, the successful entrepreneur's business planning model often looks like this: (1) Develop a simple, basic business plan, (2) start the business, (3) take the information that is gained from starting and running the new business and use it to refine the plan and obtain funding as this become necessary. For example, consider Alex D'Arbeloff, founder of Teradyne, a large public scientific instruments company. When D'Arbeloff founded his company, he wrote a short business plan only a few pages in length. He assumed that there was little benefit in developing a long, detailed business plan made up mostly of assumptions and analysis of data resting on largely unsupported assumptions. Rather, it was better to focus on the key pieces of information that he knew to be true and get the business started. Then, once the business was up and running, he revised his business plan many times, adding new information as it was acquired. D'Arbeloff's success as an entrepreneur made him quite wealthy, and he now works as a business angel who has backed such notable companies as Lotus. As a business angel, he maintains the same philosophy that he used when he started his own company: Look for entrepreneurs who have written simple, straightforward business plans that focus on key dimensions of business opportunities that are well understood, and then treat their business plans as "living documents" that change and develop with the new ventures.

The advantages of this approach are obvious: Entrepreneurs can spend their time getting their business started rather than on writing a formal business plan, and thus have something tangible to "sell" when they finally do seek large amounts of outside funding to expand their growing businesses. (See Figure 7.2 for a summary of the model of business planning we have just described.)

So overall, is it better to start with a long, detailed business plan or a shorter and simpler one? As you can guess, the answer is "It depends." In some situations, a long and detailed plan is necessary—for instance, when large amounts of funding are required to launch the new venture. In others, a shorter and less detailed plan will suffice—as long as it provides sufficient guidance to get the business started, and it is changed "on the fly" to reflect new information as it becomes available. The key rule, then, is to *always* engage in careful preparation and planning, but to be flexible and to match the form of the business plan you develop to the specific needs of your new venture.

Figure 7.2 A Model of Business Planning Used by Many Successful Entrerpneurs

Many successful entrepreneurs write relatively simple business plans that are based on information they actually know rather than on lots of untested assumptions. Then they start their businesses and use the information they gain from running them to both refine their business plans and to secure additional funding as needed. The cycle continues, thus making business plans true "living documents" that are open to change in response to new information.

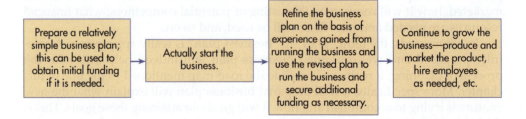

Prepare a relatively simple business plan; this can be used to obtain initial funding if it is needed.

Actually start the business.

Refine the business plan on the basis of experience gained from running the business and use the revised plan to run the business and secure additional funding as necessary.

Continue to grow the business—produce and market the product, hire employees as needed, etc.

- A business plan is a written document that explains the entrepreneur's vision and how it will be converted into a profitable, viable business.
- Venture capitalists and other potential sources of funding generally require a formal business plan as a first step for considering investments in new ventures.
- An additional step, and one that is often very important, involves a face-to-face presentation of the plan by the entrepreneur to venture capitalists or other interested parties.
- Preparing a formal business plan is useful for most entrepreneurs because doing so encourages them to formulate specific goals and concrete plans for reaching them, and these are invaluable both for converting ideas into viable companies and for raising needed capital.
- However, many successful entrepreneurs develop a fairly simple business plan, and then refine it in the light of information they gain from actually running the new venture.

COMPONENTS OF A BUSINESS PLAN: BASIC REQUIREMENTS

Business plans are as different in their specific contents as the persons who prepare them. Overall, though, there is general agreement that they must contain a number of basic sections that, together, address key questions anyone should ask before investing in a new venture:

- *What* is the basic idea for the new product of service?
- *Why* is this new product useful or appealing—and to whom?
- *How* will the idea for the new venture be realized—what is the overall plan for producing the product, for marketing it, for dealing with existing and future competition?
- *Who* are the entrepreneurs—do they have the required knowledge, experience, and skills to develop this idea and to run a new company?
- If the plan is designed to raise money, *how much* funding is needed, *what type of financing* is needed, *how* will it be used, and how will both the entrepreneurs and other persons realize a return on their investment?

As you can see, these are truly basic and important questions—the kind *you* would ask *yourself* before making an investment in a start-up company. A well-prepared business plan addresses all these questions and many others, too. Moreover, it does so in an *orderly, succinct,* and *persuasive* fashion. Pay careful attention to these terms, because they are truly crucial. As we noted earlier, the great majority of all business plans are rejected within a few minutes by experienced venture capitalists who see hundreds or even thousands of such documents each year. As a result of this experience, they employ a set of filters to determine which business plans are worthy of their time and which they can quickly discard. As an entrepreneur, you want to do everything in your power to assure that your business plan is one of the few that receive more than a cursory glance, and that requires careful attention to several basic principles:

- *The plan should be arranged and prepared in proper business form.* This means that it should start with a *cover page* showing the name and address of the company and the names and contact information (telephone, e-mail, etc.) for key contact people. This should be followed by a clear *table of contents* outlining the major sections. The table of contents should then be followed by an *executive summary*; this, in turn, should be followed by the major sections of the plan, each clearly headed and identified. Various appendices (e.g., detailed financial projections, complete resumes for the company's founders and key personnel) follow, often bound separately. Overall, the entire plan should adhere to the same basic rule: It should have the appearance of a serious business document, but should *not* seek to "wow" readers with showy illustrations or super-creative use of type fonts and styles. Remember: The first impression you make on venture capitalists, bankers, and other people important to your company's future will be made by your business plan, so make sure that it looks like what it is: A serious document prepared by serious people!

- *The plan should be succinct.* This is absolutely crucial; no one—not even your own family members—will plow through hundreds of pages of dense, convoluted prose (or complex financial figures). An effective business plan, therefore, should be as short and succinct as possible. Anything more than 40 to 50 pages is almost certainly overkill, and up to a point, the shorter the better. For instance, the business plan submitted by Teradyne was six pages in length, and that for Lotus Development was ten pages. The key goal is to address the major questions listed earlier (what, why, how, who, and how much?) in a clear and intelligent manner, without needless detail or redundancy. Always keep in mind that the people you want to read your plan are busy and highly experienced: They know how to cut rapidly to the heart of what your business is all about and to tell if you are smart enough to present it clearly.

- *The plan should be persuasive.* As we have tried to emphasize, you are facing a highly competitive situation in which you will have a small window of opportunity: Either you seize the attention of the people who read your plan early on and have additional chances to persuade them, or they conclude within minutes that reading further would be a waste of time. This is simply a fact of life: Experienced decision makers operate this way in many business contexts, not just with respect to evaluating business plans. For instance, research on job interviews indicates that many interviewers make their judgment about the suitability of each applicant within a minute or two.[3] Why? They simply don't have time to waste on applicants who are clearly not suitable, so they reach a decision about whether to continue the discussion very early in the process. If their decision is "this is not a suitable person," they conclude the interview very quickly. If, instead, they decide "this could be a good candidate," they keep it going in order to acquire more information. The same principle is at work with respect to business plans: Decisions are made very quickly by venture capitalists and other potential sources of funding and are rarely, if ever, reversed.[4] This means that you must begin strong, and continue strong, if you want to succeed. And the place where a business plan begins is the executive summary—the first major component of the business plan and, in some ways, the most important.

LEARNING OBJECTIVE

2   Explain how the process of persuasion plays a key role in business plans and in the success of new ventures.

One more point: We want to emphasize that, ultimately, it is the quality of the idea behind the new venture and the quality of the person or persons who have put it together that it are crucial. If the idea is not sound and has little economic potential, experienced investors will recognize this immediately, no matter how well-written or persuasive the plan appears to be. So before you decide to invest large amounts of time and effort into preparing a super-impressive business plan, you absolutely *must* get feedback on the idea behind your new venture. If this is not encouraging, stop right there, because proceeding is almost certain to be a waste of time.

The Executive Summary

LEARNING OBJECTIVE

3   Explain why the executive summary is a very important part of any business plan.

Have you ever heard the phrase "elevator pitch"? I (Robert Baron) first became familiar with it while working at a government agency (I was a program director at the National Science Foundation). I observed that many of my more experienced colleagues went to lunch at a specific time each day and that they jockeyed for position in front of the elevator. Why? Because they wanted to stand next to the division director—the person who made key decisions about how funds available to our part of the agency would be distributed—and they knew that she would be standing on the elevator when the door opened (because her office was on a higher floor). On the way down to the street, they made their "elevator pitches"—brief but impassioned statements about the wonderful things going on in their particular areas of science, and why funding of such work would be a great investment. The director usually made no concrete response, but in a few cases, I heard her remark, "That sounds interesting . . . make an appointment so we can discuss it." That signified great success because it meant that the one- or two-minute "pitch" delivered in the elevator had at least opened the door to further discussions—and the real possibility of additional funding.

The moral of such situations is clear: Often, we have just a brief opportunity to stimulate another person's interest—to get them interested enough to want to learn more. That, in essence, is the purpose of the executive summary. This part of the business plan—

which should be brief and to the point (many experienced investors suggest 2 to 3 pages at most)—should provide a short, clear, and persuasive overview of what the new venture is all about. In essence, it should provide brief answers to all the questions listed earlier: What is the idea for the new product or service? Why will it be appealing—and to whom? Who are the entrepreneurs? How much funding (and in what form) are they seeking?

Can all this be accomplished within a brief format? Absolutely. But it requires very careful and thoughtful writing—writing that delivers a lot of information per sentence (or even word), yet also transmits the entrepreneurs' excitement and enthusiasm. We wish we could provide you with a few simple rules for writing such a document, but in fact, we cannot: The precise contents will depend on the specific ideas being presented. But whatever these are, the executive summary should answer key questions briefly, but in enough detail so that a reader can form a clear picture of what this new venture is all about. Remember: This is an important part of the business plan, so it is worthy of special effort. It is your first and best chance (and often your only chance!) to generate interest in others, so by all means, make it your very best shot in all respects.

After the executive summary, major sections follow in an orderly arrangement. Many arrangements of these key sections are possible, but here is one that is used in many business plans and that seems quite logical. The specific order of the sections—as well as their content, however—should be dictated by the nature of the idea and what you are trying to communicate in the plan, not by any hard-and-fast preset rules.

LEARNING OBJECTIVE

4 Describe the major sections of a business plan and the types of information they should include.

- *Background and purpose.* A section describing your idea and the current state of your business.
- *Marketing:* A section describing the market for your product or service—who will want to use or buy it, and—most importantly—*why* they would want to do so.
- *Competition.* Information on existing competition and how it will be overcome, pricing, and related issues. (Sometimes this is a separate section, and sometimes it is included in the marketing section.)
- *Development, production, and location.* Where your product or service is right now in terms of development, how you will move toward actually producing or providing the product or service, and (if this is relevant to your company) information on where the new venture will be located. Information on operations, too, can be included in this section if this is an important factor in understanding what the business will do and why it has significant economic potential.
- *Management.* A section describing the experience, skills, and knowledge of the new venture's management team—what you have and what additional skills may be required in the months ahead. Information on current ownership should be included here.
- *Financial section.* This section provides information on the company's current financial state and offers projections for future needs, revenues, and other financial measures. It should also include information on the amount of funding being sought, when such funds are required, how they will be used, cash flow, and a break-even analysis.
- *Risk factors.* This section discusses various risks the new venture will face and the steps the management team is taking to protect against them.
- *Harvest or exit.* Investors are interested in understanding precisely how they will gain if the company is successful, so information on this important issue (e.g., when and how the company might go public) can often be very useful.
- *Scheduling and milestones.* Information on when each phase of the new venture will be completed should be included, so that potential investors will know just when key tasks (e.g., start of production, time to first sales, projected break-even point) will be completed. This can be a separate section, or it can be included in other sections, as appropriate.
- *Appendices.* Here is where detailed financial information and detailed resumes of the top management team should be presented.

To be complete, all business plans must cover these and closely related topics. However, depending on the specific nature of the new venture, the order can be altered, and the relative length adjusted. In other words, there are no hard-and-fast rules about how long or detailed each section should be; rather, this is a matter of good business judgment.

Now that we've provided an overview of the key sections included in a sound business plan, we'll describe each of these sections in more detail.

Background, Product, and Purpose

Among the first things potential investors in your new venture want to know are facts relating to the background of your product and your company and what, specifically, you hope to accomplish. As we noted in Chapters 2 and 3, ideas for new products or services do not arise in a vacuum; rather, such opportunities emerge out of changing economic, technological, and social conditions and are then recognized by specific persons who take action to develop them. A key question for potential investors, then, is "What is the nature of the idea driving your company and how did it arise?" This will often require discussing conditions in the industry in which your company is located, because it is these conditions, in part, that have suggested the idea you are now seeking to develop. For instance, suppose that an entrepreneur has developed a new material that gives the soles of shoes much better traction than any material now on the market. Potential investors will want to know why this is useful and who will want to use the new material (e.g., manufacturers of athletic shoes? manufacturers of medical devices for people who have been hurt in accidents or who have brittle bones?). In other words, this section should explain what the product has to offer—why it is unique and valuable, and therefore has potential for generating future profits. Unless these issues can be addressed clearly and successfully, investors are likely to conclude that the risks far outweigh any potential benefits.

Investors also usually want basic information about the existing company—its legal form, its current ownership, and its current financial condition. After all, no one wants to invest in a new venture in which thorny issues of ownership exist, or that has excessively high overhead.

This section should also address the company's goals: What does it hope to accomplish? Returning to the new material for shoes described earlier, this section should clarify whether it will be generally useful for all kinds of shoes or only for some (e.g., running shoes) and the benefits its use will confer. For instance, perhaps many thousands of persons are injured in falls each year, and perhaps many of these injuries could be prevented through use of the new material (see Figure 7.3). In that case, these potential benefits should be mentioned along with financial ones that will stem from the company's success. But again, the usefulness of such information depends very much on the idea behind the new venture, and it is more appropriate for some than others. It, like everything else in the plan, should only be included if it is relevant and will contribute to both planning by the entrepreneurs and to their ability to communicate the nature of the company to others.

In sum, after reading this initial section, potential investors will understand where and how the product was developed, the basic nature of the entrepreneur's company (its legal form, ownership, history), what it is that makes this product or service valuable or unique, and what the new venture will seek to accomplish—a brief statement of its mission. Together, this information provides a useful framework for understanding later sections of the business plan, so it is important that it be presented first.

Figure 7.3 Describing the New Venture's Goals or Mission

The first major section of a business plan should provide background information on the nature of the product and the start-up venture. It should also include information on the new venture's goals—a brief mission statement. For instance, a company that wants to develop a new material that gives shoes better traction might present data indicating that thousands of persons are injured each year in falls, and that the company's product would help reduce the frequency of such accidents.

© Wally McNamee/CORBIS

Market Analysis

Do you remember the gadgets described in Chapter 4—products that were brought to market but quickly vanished without a trace? If so, you may recall that one reason these products failed is that no one conducted careful market analysis before they were produced; in other words, no one bothered to find out if there was a market for them—whether anyone would really want to buy or use them. The result? Disaster for the entrepreneurs who invented them and for anyone who invested in the companies they started to produce and sell these items.

It is not surprising, then, that sophisticated investors want to see specific and detailed information concerning marketing as part of any strong business plan. Specifically, they want information on what entrepreneurs have done to identify the market for their product (e.g., have they conducted marketing surveys? detailed market analyses?). Moreover, they want to know how large these markets are, whether they are growing or shrinking, and how the new products or services will be promoted in these markets. This often requires detailed information about *competing products*—do they exist and, if so, how will the new product be demonstrably superior to them; *competing companies*—who are they, and how likely are they to respond to the entrepreneurs' new product; and *pricing*—how will the new product or service be priced relative to competing products or services, and why does this pricing strategy make sense.

For instance, consider Photowow.com, a company started by Robert Schiff in Los Angeles. Schiff's company makes large pieces of art—42″ x 42″ or even larger—for use in homes and businesses. This art is produced by large-format inkjet printers and can show almost anything—for instance, the buyer's children in pop montages resembling the style of a famous artist such as Andy Warhol. This is an entirely new product, so pricing it was a challenging task and required careful consideration of existing products (e.g., art posters). Marketing, too, raised complex questions: What would be the potential market for such art? Many possibilities existed: franchises, which would want to show a picture of their founders in every outlet; corporations, which might want to have a picture of the home office in every branch. Schiff explored all these, plus others, with the help of consultants and was then able to include this information in his business plan.

In essence, this section of a new venture's business plan should be designed to convince skeptical investors that the entrepreneurs have done their homework: They have examined potential markets for their product or service carefully and have evidence indicating that consumers or other businesses (depending on the product or service) will want to buy it when it becomes available. Further, investors want to know the specifics of how the new product or service will be promoted, and at what cost. Market projections are, of course, always uncertain; no one ever knows for certain how consumers will react to new products (see Figure 7.4). But at the very least, the entrepreneur should have engaged in state-of-the-art efforts to find out why people will want to buy or use their product, and to pinpoint an effective marketing strategy for it. If, instead, it is simply assumed that the product or service is so wonderful that people will line up to buy it, a loud alarm will sound for sophisticated investors, and they will quickly lose interest.

Figure 7.4 Market Analysis: Sometimes Uncertain, But Always Essential

Entrepreneurs should always devote careful attention to the following question: "What is the need for our product or service? Why, in other words, would anyone want to buy or use it?" Market research can often help to answer this question. The product on the left was introduced after market research indicated that consumers would want to buy it—and this is exactly what happened: It was a huge success. In contrast, the product on the right was introduced mainly because the company that produced it simply assumed that a market for it existed; in fact, consumers did not want it and the product largely failed.

© Roger Ressmeyer/CORBIS

AP/ Wide World Photos/Carlos Osorio

Development, Production, and Location

It is not possible to market a new product or service unless it is available, so another issue that must be carefully addressed in any effective business plan is product development and production. Potential investors want information about where the new venture's products and services are in this process: Are they still under development? Are they fully developed and ready to be manufactured? If so, what are the projected costs and timetable for making the product or for delivering the service? Related issues include steps to assure quality and safety for consumers or other users (e.g., has the company applied for Underwriters Laboratory approval, or similar certification?). As I learned while running my own company, such processes can require months—and considerable fees—so investors want to know that entrepreneurs are aware of these issues and have them well in hand.

The further along a start-up company is with respect to these issues, the more attractive it will be to potential investors—not simply because the company has developed beyond the initial launch phase, but also because this demonstrates that it is operating in a productive and rational manner. I (Robert Baron) recently invested in a new biotechnology company, mainly because I liked the basic idea (developing drugs for "orphan diseases"—ones that afflict too few people for major drug companies to bother with) and also because I know and respect the founders. Another important consideration for me, however, was where the company stood with respect to development of effective new drugs. My conclusion was that everything was in place to allow the new venture to move ahead quickly, but only time will tell whether I was correct in this judgment. In any case, I—like other potential investors—searched for information on this issue in the company's business plan and would certainly have been less enthusiastic about investing in it if such information were not included or was too general in scope to be informative.

The Management Team

Many venture capitalists note that they would rather invest in a first-rate team with a second-rate idea than a second-rate team with a first-rate idea. Although this is something of an exaggeration—venture capitalists and other investors actually focus on many different issues—there is actually a substantial grain of truth in such statements. What venture capitalists are saying, in essence, is that talented, experienced, and motivated people at the top of a new venture are very important for its success. It is for this reason that a key section of any business plan is the one dealing with the people who will run the new venture.

What, specifically, do potential investors want to know? Primarily that, taken together, these people have the experience, expertise, skills, and personal characteristics needed to run the new venture successfully. We say "taken together," because as we pointed out in Chapter 5, investors want to know that the management team has complementary skills, abilities, and experience: What one person is lacking, others provide, and vice versa. Further, they want to be reasonably certain that the members of the team have developed good working relationships: Each has clearly assigned roles and duties, and communication between them is good. Although investors may be willing to bend these requirements to a degree—for instance, they can't really require lots of experience from a very young group of entrepreneurs—they do demand at least some of them. If the management team of a new venture is lacking in experience, for instance, they may require that the entrepreneurs hire seasoned executives to assist in running the business—in other words, that they acquire needed experience from outside the new venture team itself. Similarly, if entrepreneurs are lacking in experience, investors may place greater weight on their training, their intelligence, and their interpersonal skills. Seasoned investors know from past experience that entrepreneurs who are good at getting along with others are more likely to succeed than ones who are "rough around the edges" and annoy or irritate the people with whom they deal. After all, why should anyone give their business to a stranger who rubs them the wrong way? Surely, it would take a vastly superior product or service to tip the balance this way. In fact, research findings indicate that entrepreneurs who are high in social skills are indeed more successful in running new ventures than ones who are not.[5]

In short, potential investors place a great deal of emphasis on the qualifications of entrepreneurs, and do everything they can to assure that the companies they fund are headed by people in whom they can have confidence. The source of such confidence is, ideally, past business experience, but if this is lacking, potential investors will seek to assure that this potential weakness is offset by other strengths brought to the table by the founding entrepreneurs: high intelligence (social and cognitive), a high level of technical skill, and yes—energy and enthusiasm!

Financial Plans and Projections

Every section of a business plan is important—of that there can be no doubt. But one that is absolutely certain to receive close and especially careful examination is the section dealing with financial matters. This section should include several major components, each of which must be carefully prepared. As we explained in Chapter 6, these elements provide a picture of the company's current financial state, how it will use funds it receives from investors, and how it will manage its financial resources to reach its major objectives.

The financial section should provide an assessment of what assets the venture will own, what debt it will have, and so on. As Chapter 6 explained, such information is summarized in a **proforma balance sheet**, showing projections of the company's financial condition at various times in the future; such information should be projected semiannually for the first three years. These projected balance sheets allow investors to determine if debt-to-equity ratios, working capital, inventory turnover, and other financial indices are within acceptable limits and justify initial and future funding of the company. In addition, as Chapter 6 explained, a **proforma income statement** should be prepared to illustrate projected operating results based on profit and loss. This statement records sales, costs of goods sold, expenses, and profit or loss, and should take careful account of sales forecasts, production costs, costs of advertising, distribution, storage, and administrative expenses. In short, it should provide a reasonable projection of operating results. Finally a **cash flow statement** showing the amount and timing of expected cash inflows and outflows should be prepared, again for a period of several years. By highlighting expected sales and capital expenditures over a specific period of time, this forecast will underscore the need for and timing of further financing and needs for working capital. These forms are summarized in Table 7.1

Another key part of the financial section—one also discussed in Chapter 6—should be a **break-even analysis**, a table showing the level of sales (and production) needed to cover all costs. This should include costs that vary with the level of production (manufacturing, labor, materials, sales) and costs that do not vary with production (interest charges, salaries, rent, and so on). The break-even analysis is a very important reality check for entrepreneurs who often have an overly-optimistic view of how quickly their new venture can become profitable, and it is often examined with considerable care by potential investors.

INCOME STATEMENT	CASH FLOW STATEMENT
Includes sales as they are generated.	Shows sales as "cash in" only when payment is received.
Includes depreciation.	Depreciations is added back in because it is not a cash expense.
Interest on loans is included.	Both interest and principle are included.
Beginning inventory and ending inventory are included in the calculation of cost of goods sold.	Inventory purchases are recorded as bills actually paid.

Table 7.1 Income Statements and Cash Flow Statements: Some Key Differences

Income statements and cash flow statements differ in several important respects.

Overall, the financial section of the business plan should provide potential investors with a clear picture of how the new venture will use the resources it already has, resources generated by continuing operations, and resources provided by investors to move toward its financial objectives. If there is any section in which entrepreneurs should strive to hold their enthusiasm and optimism in check, this is it: Many investors have learned to view entrepreneurs' financial projects with a healthy does of skepticism. They have seen too many overly-optimistic predictions to view the situation otherwise; in fact, many begin by discounting entrepreneurs' projections by a minimum of 50 percent!

Critical Risks: Describing What Might Go Wrong

You probably know this saying, known as "Murphy's Law": "If anything can go wrong, it will." Perhaps you have also heard the corollary: "Murphy was an optimist." Entrepreneurs, filled with enthusiasm for their new ventures, are not the most likely candidates on earth to think hard and long about what can go wrong with respect to their new ventures. On the contrary, they prefer to dwell on the upside and are often genuinely dismayed when things do *not* go according to plan. This is one reason why effective business plans should contain a section specifically focused on what might potentially go wrong—critical risks that can prevent the new venture from reaching its key objectives. Thinking about these risks is "good medicine" for entrepreneurs, and formulating ways of responding to these potential calamities before they occur can be constructive indeed!

What are the potential risks new ventures face? Here is a partial list:

- Price cutting by competitors, who refuse to "roll over and play dead" for the new venture
- Unforeseen industry trends that make the new venture's product or service less desirable—or less marketable
- Sales projections that are not achieved for a variety of reasons, thus reducing cash flow
- Design, manufacturing, or shipping costs that exceed estimates
- Product development or production schedules that are not met (people problems, such as low employee motivation, can play a role in each of the last three points; see Figure 7.5)

Figure 7.5 New Ventures Face Many Risks

New ventures confront many risks. Several of these (e.g., cost overruns in product design or manufacturing) involve employee motivation and morale.

"Do you ever catch yourself wondering what the hell's gone wrong with this corporation?"

- Problems stemming from top management's lack of experience (e.g., inability to negotiate contracts with suppliers or customers on favorable terms)
- Longer than expected lead times with respect to obtaining parts or raw materials
- Difficulties in raising additional, needed financing
- Unforeseen political, economic, social, or technological trends or developments (e.g., new government legislation or the sudden start of a major recession)

These are just a few of the many potential risks that can put new ventures badly off the track. To emphasize a point we made earlier, many are truly unexpected. For instance, consider Stephanie Anne, Inc., a Dallas-based company that produces ultra-high-quality children's furniture. The company ran into serious problems when many of its products were damaged during out-of-town shipments, despite the fact that they were shipped through a large moving company. The solution? Custom packaging that protected the products even through rough handling.

Truly, many of these problems are frightening to contemplate, so why should entrepreneurs describe them in detail in their business plans? Mainly because recognizing these dangers is the first step toward coming up with strategies to deal with them if they do in fact occur. Writing an appropriate risk-related section for their business plan obliges entrepreneurs to perform this task and take these potential risks into account.

Reaping the Rewards: Harvest and Exit

All good things must come to an end, and even the most enthusiastic of entrepreneurs realizes that at some point, they may want to leave the companies they start. This can be because they have reached a stage in life where they want to sit back a bit and enjoy the fruits of their labors or, alternatively, because it is the excitement of starting something new they crave, so they want to launch yet another new venture. Whatever the reason, every business plan should include a section that describes both *management succession*—how the founding entrepreneurs can, ultimately, be replaced—and *exit strategies for investors*—how they can ultimately reap the benefits of having funded the new venture. Initially, ownership of a new venture is not a liquid asset: Shares cannot readily be sold to other persons. Later, however, this can change radically if the company has an initial public offering (IPO) and its shares are subsequently traded on a national exchange. The business plan should address this and other potential exit strategies for investors, and for founders, too. In fact, this section is often very important to investors who fully understand the Arab proverb: "Think of the going out before your enter."

Scheduling and Milestones

A final section in the body of the business plan should address the question of when major activities will be performed and key milestones reached. Again, giving careful thought to the question of "when" various tasks will be performed or specific goals achieved is useful both for entrepreneurs and potential investors. Identifying target dates may help entrepreneurs overcome a powerful cognitive bias known as the *planning fallacy*, which we described in Chapter 3—the tendency to assume that we can accomplish more in a given period of time than is really possible.[6] In this way, it can serve as another important reality check. From the point of view of investors, it indicates that entrepreneurs are indeed paying careful attention to the operations of their company and have developed clear plans for its future progress. What are these milestones? Included among the most important are these:

- Formal incorporation of the new venture (if this has not already occurred)
- Completion of product or service design
- Completion of prototypes
- Hiring of initial personnel (sales or otherwise)
- Product display at trade shows
- Reaching agreements with distributors and suppliers
- Moving into actual production
- Receipt of initial orders

- First sales and deliveries
- Profitability

This list is just a small sample of the many milestones new ventures can include in their business plans; many others exist as well. The important point is to select milestones that make sense both from the point of view of the company's resources and the industry in which it is located.

Appendices

Because the main body of the plan should be relatively brief—as short as is adequate for presenting all essential information—several items are best included in separate appendices. Items typically included are detailed financial projections and full resumes of the founders and other members of the top management team. By including such items in appendices, entrepreneurs assure that this important information is present for persons who wish to examine it, but at the same time keep the length of the business plan itself within desirable limits.

A Note on the Intangibles

What we have described in the preceding section is an outline of the essentials—the sections that are generally viewed as necessary for any thorough business plan. What we haven't addressed, of course, is what might be termed the *intangibles*—the extra "something" that leads readers of a plan to drop their slightly jaded attitude and to conclude, perhaps with some excitement, that there is indeed something here worth a closer look. We have both done a large amount of writing, so we believe that such factors as organization, clarity, choice of words, and style do indeed matter. Unfortunately, no one has yet been able to draw a bead on how these factors operate or how you can turn them to your own advantage. Given the importance of the business plan in the future of your new venture, however, we do have a concrete suggestion: Before distributing it to potential investors, have a number of people who are known to be good writers read it. If they will do it as a favor, that's great; if not, pay them for their time. Then *listen carefully to their suggestions* and revise the plan accordingly. Honestly, we can't think of anything else you can do that is likely to yield as much benefit for you and for your new venture. (What about the downside—are there specific errors you should be careful to avoid because they can be the "kiss of death" to any business plan? Our answer is "Yes." And we have attempted to summarize the most important of these in the **"Danger! Pitfall Ahead!"** section.)

KEY POINTS

- All business plans should begin with an executive summary—a brief (2 to 3 pages) section that provides a brief, clear, and persuasive overview of what the new venture is all about.
- Subsequent sections should include:

  Background and purpose. A section describing your idea and the current state of the business.

  Marketing. A section describing the market for the new venture's product or service, why there is a need for the product and why anyone would want to buy one, plus information on existing competition and how it will be overcome, and pricing.

  Development, production, and location. Where the product or service is in terms of development, how it will be produced, and (if appropriate) information on where the business will be located.

  Management. A section describing the experience, skills, and knowledge of the new venture's management team.

  Financial section. A section that provides information on the company's current financial state, and offers projections for future needs, revenues, and other financial measures, as well as a break-even analysis.

  Risk factors. A section that discusses various risks the new venture will face, and the steps the management team is taking to protect against them.

  Harvest or exit. A section focused on how investors will gain if the company is successful.

  Scheduling and milestones. An overview of when each phase of the new venture will be completed, so that potential investors will know just when key tasks (e.g., start of production, time to first sales, projected break-even point) will be completed.

  Appendices. Detailed financial information and detailed resumes of the top management team.

DANGER! PITFALL AHEAD!

The Seven Deadly Sins for New Venture Business Plans

Let us say it again: less than five minutes. That's the amount of time your plan has in the hands of many potential investors before they decide to turn "thumbs up" or "thumbs down" on it. In other words, they evaluate a document that may have taken you weeks or even months to prepare in just a few moments. For this reason, it is absolutely imperative that you avoid errors that will doom your plan to the rejection pile no matter how good other sections of it may be. We term these the "Seven Deadly Sins of New Venture Business Plans." Here they are for you to recognize—and avoid:

Sin #1: The plan is poorly prepared and has an unprofessional look (e.g., no cover page, a cover page without contact information, glaring typos). This triggers the following investor reaction: "I'm dealing with a group of amateurs."

Sin #2: The plan is far too slick (e.g., it is bound like a book, is printed on shiny paper, uses flashy graphics). This leads investors to think: "What are they trying to hide behind all those fireworks?"

Sin #3: The executive summary is too long and rambling—it doesn't get right to the point. This leads investors to think: "If they can't describe their own idea and company succinctly, I don't want to waste my time with them."

Sin #4: It's not clear where the product is in terms of development—does it exist or not? Can it be readily manufactured? Investors conclude: "I can't tell whether this is real or just another pipe dream; I'll pass on this one."

Sin #5: No clear answer is provided to the question: "Why would anyone ever want to buy one?" Instead, many entrepreneurs seem to assume that their new product or service is so great that it will virtually sell itself. This leads investors to think: "How naïve can you get? Even a machine that grew hair on the heads of bald men would need a marketing plan. These are truly amateurs."

Sin #6: There is no clear statement of the qualifications of the management team. This leads investors to conclude: "They probably have no relevant experience—and may not even know what relevant experience would be!"

Sin #7: Financial projections are largely an exercise in wishful thinking. This leads potential investors to conclude: "They have no idea about what it is like to run a company, or (even worse) they think I am incredibly naïve or stupid. Pass!" (These "Seven Deadly Sins" are summarized in Figure 7.6.)

The moral is clear: Keep a sharp lookout for these seven deadly errors because if you commit even one, your chance of obtaining help from sophisticated investors will drop off the bottom of the scale.

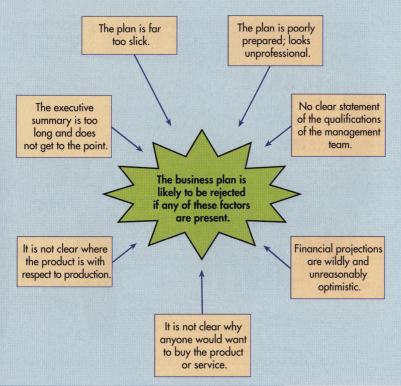

Figure 7.6 The Seven Deadly Sins for New Venture Business Plans

If one or more of these errors or problems are present in a business plan, it is likely to be rejected by potential investors, no matter how good other aspects of the plan may be.

The plan is far too slick.

The plan is poorly prepared; looks unprofessional.

The executive summary is too long and does not get to the point.

No clear statement of the qualifications of the management team.

The business plan is likely to be rejected if any of these factors are present.

It is not clear where the product is with respect to production.

Financial projections are wildly and unreasonably optimistic.

It is not clear why anyone would want to buy the product or service.

MAKING AN EFFECTIVE BUSINESS PLAN PRESENTATION: THE BALL IS DEFINITELY IN YOUR COURT

Researchers who study stress agree that the way in which people think about stressful situations is a powerful determinant of how they react to them. One possible reaction is to emphasize the downside—to imagine what will happen if you simply can't cope with the stressful situation. Many people feel this way about making formal presentations: They imagine forgetting what they planned to say or harsh rejection from the audience, and this causes them to experience high levels of anxiety that can, in turn, interfere with their actual performance. In contrast, another way to think about high-stress situations is to view them as a *challenge*—an opportunity to rise to the occasion and show the world what you've got. When people think about stressful situations in this way, they experience lower levels of anxiety, and their performance often matches their expectations: It *does* rise to new heights.[7]

This is how you should think about making a verbal presentation of your idea and company to venture capitalists or other potential investors or sources of funding. The fact that you have been invited to make the presentation indicates that you have successfully passed the first major hurdle: More than 90 percent of plans do not generate an invitation to make a presentation, so you are already in a select group. Because you have done such a good job in preparing your plan, why should you doubt your ability to make a dynamite presentation? Basically, you should not; on the contrary, confidence, not doubt, should be your guiding principle. But confidence does not automatically translate into a first-rate presentation. That, like writing an excellent business plan, requires a lot of preparation. Yes, as suggested by Figure 7.7, some people are better at making presentations—and at persuasion—than others. But almost everyone can improve their presentation skills if they try. So here are some concrete steps you can take (we really mean *should* take) to assure that your verbal presentation will match the high quality of your business plan—or even exceed it.

Figure 7.7 Some People Are Better at Making Presentations Than Others, But Everyone Can Improve

Some people start out with an advantage where making presentations is concerned: They are true "spellbinders." But research findings indicate that nearly everyone can improve substantially with respect to this activity if they exert the effort to do so.

"*Al, you've been chosen Businessman of the Year by the Junior Chamber of Commerce.*"

■ *Remember: This really is important.* Your carefully-prepared business plan has gotten you in the door. But venture capitalists, bankers, and business angels do not give funds to business plans—they give them to people. So how you handle this presentation has real and serious consequences for your company. It's important to keep this fact in mind because it will motivate you strongly to take the additional steps described below.

■ *Prepare, prepare, and then . . . prepare some more.* You are certainly the world's greatest expert on your idea and your company. But this doesn't mean that you will be able to describe them accurately, succinctly, and eloquently without careful preparation. So find out how much time you will have for your remarks (often this is 20 minutes or less, and it can be as short as 5 minutes in some settings) and then prepare your comments to fit this time.

■ *Choose the content carefully.* What, exactly, should you try to accomplish during this brief presentation? Several things, but first and foremost you want to demonstrate that there is indeed something unique and potentially valuable about your product and service, and that you understand precisely what this is. In this context, I'm reminded of the time I made the presentation that secured a manufacturing partner for my own company. The CEO of this large (more than $1 billion in annual sales) company turned to me and said, "OK, professor, tell us what you've got." His team of engineers had already tested our prototypes exhaustively, and his staff had read our business plan in detail, but he wanted to hear *me* summarize the nature and benefits of the product. Why? Partly, I'm sure, to find out whether I really understood them myself and also, as he later told me, to see how I performed under pressure. I had done my homework and was ready with a short presentation that got right to the point, so although many pointed questions followed later, I felt from the start that I was on the right track.

■ *Remember that you are trying to persuade, not overwhelm.* One potential trap for many entrepreneurs—especially ones from a technical background—is to lapse quickly into technical language that only other persons in their field would understand. This can be a serious tactical error, because although the people you are addressing are highly intelligent and have a wide range of business experience, they may not have the specific training needed to understand highly technical descriptions. In general, it is far better to focus on the big picture—what the product does and why it is superior to other, competing products, rather than to slip into technical language that is easy and comfortable for the entrepreneur, but which may be largely unfamiliar to at least some potential investors.

■ *Show enthusiasm—but temper it with reality checks.* Yes, you should definitely be enthusiastic; after all, this is *your* baby and *your* chance to shine. But temper your enthusiasm with hard facts and data. If you have completed marketing research, mention it briefly as you discuss marketing strategy. And be sure that any financial projections you mention keep at least one foot in contact with the ground; anyone can use a spreadsheet program to demonstrate sales that soon exceed the entire gross national product of the country. So, your audience will certainly *not* be dazzled—or influenced—by numbers that make little or no business sense.

■ *Rehearse!* There is no substitute for rehearsal where oral presentations are concerned. Some of these should be in front of friends and cofounders of your company so that you can get their feedback on how to improve. Others should be in front of people totally unfamiliar with your idea or company; that will help you find out whether your presentation makes sense to people learning about it for the first time. (Some of the people in the audience when you give your formal presentation will probably be in this situation, or—at most—they will have read your 2-page executive summary.) Some rehearsals don't even require an audience. It is often helpful to deliver portions of your presentations to the four walls of your own room or office, just to make sure that you have committed major points to memory.

■ *Don't overlook the basics.* It's amazing, but we have both personally attended many presentations that fell flat on their face because the people giving them had focused on the content, delivery, and level of their talks, but had forgotten about the basics. For instance, we have seen many talks in which the presenters spent precious time trying to figure out how to get their slides to appear on the screen, or in trying to explain charts or tables that were extremely complex or unreadable by the audience. In other cases, presenters failed to keep track of time and ran out of this precious commodity before they could make key points. *Don't overlook these basic issues.* If you do, all your hard work and careful presentation may go directly down the drain, and for very little reason.

■ *Adopt a cooperative, helpful approach to questions.* One thing that is sure to happen during and after your presentation is that members of the audience will ask you pointed, searching questions. This should come as no surprise. First, you are asking them to give you money—perhaps large amounts of money. Second, they are an experienced group who have seen lots of things go wrong with what seemed, at first, to be excellent start-up ventures. So they are cautious and will have no qualms about asking you to hold forth on virtually any point made in your business plan—and also on issues not considered in the plan. Your answers to these questions are important and must make good sense, but so, too, is your attitude. If you bristle with obvious annoyance when asked a pointed question, or when the person who asked it objects to your answer, this is a sign to potential investors that you may be lacking in the kind of emotional maturity they want to see in entrepreneurs, and you may *not* be a good bet. So your reaction to questions should be to take them seriously, try to answer them as best as possible, and to maintain a helpful, cooperative attitude no matter how intense the session becomes.

If you keep these points firmly in mind, we believe that you will have a good chance of making an excellent presentation—a much better chance than would be true if you ignore them or minimize their importance. But suppose that despite your best efforts, and despite the fact that you did an excellent job, you still receive a "no" from a group on which you pinned high hopes. Should you be discouraged? Not at all. Very few entrepreneurs obtain support from the first potential investors they approach. In fact, highly successful entrepreneurs often note that their companies were rejected by many investors initially. In view of this fact, you should view rejections as an opportunity to learn, and should try to obtain as much information as possible from them. Try to find out *why* your proposal was rejected, and whether there were aspects of the plan and your presentation that the potential investors found especially weak—or strong. Then, go back to the drawing boards and rework both your plan and your presentation. Along these lines, there are two key points you should keep firmly in mind: (1) There is almost always room for improvement, in virtually everything; and (2) success does *not* have to be immediate to be sweet. Good luck!

KEY POINTS

- Entrepreneurs should view invitations to give verbal presentations about their idea and their company as a challenge—a chance to shine—rather than as a high-stress situation in which they may be overwhelmed.
- Because such presentations are very important to the future of new ventures, entrepreneurs should take them very seriously and try to do an outstanding job.
- Steps that can help entrepreneurs accomplish this goal include selecting content carefully, avoiding technical jargon, showing enthusiasm tempered by reality, rehearsing carefully, paying careful attention to basic aspects of presentations (e.g., arriving early to set up audio-visual systems), and adopting a helpful cooperative attitude toward questions.
- Entrepreneurs should view rejections by potential investors as an opportunity to learn—to improve both their business plan and their verbal presentations.

Summary and Review of Key Points

- A business plan is a formal written document that explains the entrepreneur's vision and how it will be converted into a profitable, viable business.
- Venture capitalists and other potential sources of funding generally require a formal business plan as a first step for considering investments in new ventures.
- An additional step, and one that is often very important, involves a face-to-face presentation of the plan by the entrepreneur to venture capitalists or other interested parties.
- Preparing a formal business plan is useful for most entrepreneurs because doing so encourages them to formulate specific goals and concrete plans for reaching them, and these are invaluable both for converting ideas into viable companies and for raising needed capital.
- However, many successful entrepreneurs develop a fairly simple business plan, and then refine it in the light of information they gain from actually running the new venture.
- All business plans should begin with an executive summary—a brief (2 to 3 pages) section that provides a brief, clear, and persuasive overview of what the new venture is all about.
- Subsequent sections should include:
  Background and purpose. A section describing your idea and the current state of the business.
  Marketing. A section describing the market for the new venture's product or service, why there is a need for the product and why anyone would want to buy one, plus information on existing competition and how it will be overcome, and pricing.
  Development, production, and location. Where the product or service is in terms of development, how it will be produced, and (if appropriate) information on where the business will be located.
  Management. A section describing the experience, skills, and knowledge of the new venture's management team.
  Financial section. A section that provides information on the company's current financial state, and offers projections for future needs, revenues, and other financial measures, as well as a break-even analysis.
  Risk factors. A section that discusses various risks the new venture will face, and the steps the management team is taking to protect against them.
  Harvest or exit. A section focused on how investors will gain if the company is successful.
  Scheduling and milestones. An overview of when each phase of the new venture will be completed, so that potential investors will know just when key tasks (e.g., start of production, time to first sales, projected break-even point) will be completed.
  Appendices. Detailed financial information and detailed resumes of the top management team.
- Entrepreneurs should view invitations to give verbal presentations about their idea and their company as a challenge—a chance to shine—rather than as a high-stress situation in which they may be overwhelmed.
- Because such presentations are very important to the future of new ventures, entrepreneurs should take them very seriously and try to do an outstanding job.
- Steps that can help entrepreneurs accomplish this goal include selecting content carefully, avoiding technical jargon, showing enthusiasm tempered by reality, rehearsing carefully, paying careful attention to basic aspects of presentations (e.g., arriving early to set up audiovisual systems), and adopting a helpful cooperative attitude toward questions.
- Entrepreneurs should view rejections by potential investors as an opportunity to learn—to improve both their business plan and their verbal presentations.

Glossary

Break-Even Analysis: An analysis indicating the level of sales and production required to cover all costs.

Business Plan: A written expression of the entrepreneur's vision for converting ideas into a profitable, going business.

Cash Flow Statement: A form that forecasts cash flow over a specific period of time, given certain levels of projected sales and capital expenditures.

Persuasion: The task of inducing others to share our views and to see the world much as we do.

Proforma Balance Sheet: A form showing projections of the company's financial condition at various times in the future.

Proforma Income Statement: A form illustrating projected operating results based on profit and loss.

Discussion Questions

1. Although writing a business plan requires a lot of work, why should entrepreneurs do it? Why not just get the company started? Which approach would *you* prefer, and why?

2. Why is the executive summary at the start of a business plan so important? What should be its primary goal or goals?

3. Why it is important to explain where the new product or service is with respect to the production process (e.g., is an idea? a prototype? in production?)?

4. Why it is so important for a business plan to fully describe the experience and expertise of the new venture's management?

5. How much optimism should be built into financial projections? What is the potential "downside" of including too much optimism?

6. Why should business plans include a full disclosure and discussion of potential risk factors? Isn't this just calling attention to "negatives" that might prevent investors from providing financial support?

7. Some people are better than others at giving verbal presentations. Should entrepreneurs consider this factor when choosing potential cofounders?

InfoTrac Exercises

1. **The Ins and Outs of Turnons and Turnoffs.** (The Company Doctor)(developing sound business plans that will attract potential investors)(column)
Scott Clark
Long Island Business News, May 7, 1999 v46 i19 p35A(1)
Record: A54896541
Abstract: Many entrepreneurs develop, assemble, or present business plans that represent their life's dream so poorly that they fail to attract the interest of potential investors. All business plans ever written feature elements that will engage readers' interest, that may turn them on, or turn them off. Suggestions pertaining to business plan writing may help entrepreneurs to engage the immediate attention and, perhaps, the support of potential financiers.

   1. According to the article, what two purposes should a business plan achieve?
   2. What problems in a business plan are turnoffs to potential investors?
   3. What steps can you take to ensure your business plan turns on potential investors?

2. **Lights, Camera, Takeoff?** (business presentation by an entrepreneur before the Toronto Venture Group)
Joyce Lau
Canadian Business, December 26, 1997 v70 n18 p93(2)
Record: A20417604
Abstract: HIL-Tech International Ltd director Marc Hutchins had only five minutes to persuade investors at a monthly breakfast meeting of the Toronto Venture Group to provide $1 million in capital. He told the meeting that the additional capital would be used for distribution and marketing.

   1. According to the text, what key steps should you take to prepare for a business plan presentation?
   2. Evaluate Marc Hutchins' presentation. What steps might he have taken to improve his 5-minute presentation?
   3. Now you have five minutes to present your business plan. How would you prepare? What elements of the plan would you highlight?

GETTING DOWN
TO BUSINESS

Writing a Great Executive Summary

A first-rate executive summary is an important ingredient in any good business plan. Excellent summaries catch the attention and interest of potential investors who generally decide, on the basis of the executive summary, whether to continue reading—or to move on to the next business plan in the pile. For this reason, learning how to write an excellent executive summary is a very useful skill for entrepreneurs. Follow these steps to improve your skill with respect to this important task.

1. **Write an executive summary for your new venture.** Be sure that it is no more than 2 to 3 pages long.

2. **Now, ask several people you know to read it and comment on it.** In particular, ask them to rate the summary on the following dimensions. (Ratings should use a 5-point scale: 1 = very poor; 2 = poor; 3 = neutral; 4 = good; 5 = excellent.)
   a. It provides a clear description of the new product or service.
   b. It explains why the new product or service will be appealing in specific markets.
   c. It identifies these markets and explains how the product will be promoted in them.
   d. It explains where the product is with respect to production.
   e. It explains who the entrepreneurs are and describes their background and experience.
   f. It explains how much funding the entrepreneurs are seeking and the purposes for which it will be used.

3. **Obtain the average score on each dimension.** The features on which you scored low (3 or below) are the ones on which you should work. Prepare another, improved executive summary and have a different group of people rate it.

4. **Continue the process until the ratings on all dimensions are 4 or 5.**

Describing the New Venture's Management Team— And Putting It in a Favorable Light

Potential investors consider the quality of a new venture's management team to be a crucial factor—perhaps the most crucial—in their decision about whether to provide funding for it. This means that not only is it important to assemble an excellent team, but it is also essential to describe it fully and in terms that are as positive as possible. Unfortunately, some entrepreneurs don't seem to recognize the importance of this task. They fail to list past accomplishments or experience, and are just too modest overall. Carrying out the following steps can help you avoid these errors—and increase your chances of obtaining the funding you seek.

1. **List each member of the top management team of your new venture.**

2. **Describe their role in the new venture—what, specifically, will they do?**

3. **Next, ask each to provide information on the following items:**
   a. Where and when did they received their degrees, and in what fields.
   b. A description of *all* relevant experience—experience that is in any way related to the tasks they will perform. This can include work experience, offices held in social and professional organizations, experience in running previous businesses (even small, informal ones), writing experience—almost anything that is relevant to their role in the new venture.
   c. Honors, awards, and prizes they have received (academic, business, athletics, etc.).
   d. Personal references—the more experienced, well-known, and prestigious, the better.
   e. Anything else in their background or experience that is relevant to their role in the new venture and puts them in a favorable light (e.g., famous relatives? famous friends or associates? etc.).

4. **Match the information that you have about the members of the top management team to the roles that you defined.** Make sure to include all the information that supports their ability to fulfill these roles, but don't include information

that isn't relevant to the role. (For example, don't say that your head of marketing was the president of her high school chess club.)

5. **Finally, show the finished product to other members of the top management team and brainstorm with them about whether it presents your strengths in a way that will be obvious to potential investors.** If it does not, go back to the drawing board and start again!

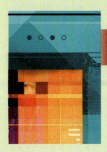

Enhanced Learning

You may select any combination of the case options below to enhance your understanding of the chapter material.

■ **Appendix 1: Case Studies** – Thirteen cases provide opportunities to apply chapter concepts to realistic entrepreneurial situations. These brief cases call for careful analysis of real business problems and ask you to think about potential solutions.

■ **Appendix 2: Video Case Library** – Nine cases are tied directly to video segments from the popular PBS television series *Small Business School.* These cases and video segments give you unparalleled access to today's entrepreneurs, with expert advice and insights on how to start, run, and grow a business.

■ **Comprehensive Cases** – Visit the book support Web site at http://baron.swlearning.com for cases detailing real businesses whose successes and setbacks illustrate each stage of the entrepreneurial process. You will conduct in-depth analysis of entrepreneurial challenges through well-developed case studies.

Notes

1 Mancuso, J.R. 1975. *How to write a winning business plan.* Englewood Cliffs, NJ: Prentice-Hall.

2 Delmar, F., & Shane, S. (forthcoming). Does business planning facilitate the development of new ventures? *Strategic Management Journal.*

3 Fletcher, C. 1979. Impression management in the selection interview. In R.A. Giacalone & P. Rosenfeld, P. (eds.). *Impression management in the selection interview* (pp. 269–272). Hillsdale, NJ: Erlbaum.

4 Zacharakis, A.L, & Shepherd, D.A. 2001. The nature of information and overconfidence on venture capialists' decision making. *Journal of Business Venturing* 16: 311–332.

5 Baron, R.A., & Markman, G.D. 2003. Beyond social capital: The role of entrepreneurs' social competence in their financial success. *Journal of Business Venturing* 18: 41–60.

6 Buehler, R., Griffin, D., & MacDonald, H. 1997. The role of motivated reasoning in optimistic time predictions. *Personality and Social Psychology Bulletin* 23: 237–247.

7 Greenberg, J., & Baron, R.A. 2003. *Behavior in organizations.* 7th ed. Upper Saddle River, NJ: Prentice-Hall.

PART 3

LAUNCHING THE NEW VENTURE

CHAPTER 8

The Legal Form of New Ventures—
And the Legal Environment in Which They Operate

CHAPTER 9

Marketing in a New Firm

CHAPTER 10

Strategy: Planning for Competitive Advantage

CHAPTER 11

Intellectual Property: Protecting Your Ideas

All new ventures must adopt a specific legal form, so choosing among these is a key step in actually launching a new venture. Once launched, new ventures need two key ingredients to succeed: specific marketing plans—ones that help them to actively sell their products or services—and an overall strategy for gaining and holding competitive advantage, and for overcoming the disadvantages faced by new companies that must compete with larger, well-established ones. Finally, new ventures need protection for their new products or services—protections that will assure that they, and not competitors, capture economic benefits from these products or services. Such protections can be legal (patents, copyrights) or nonlegal (first-mover advantage, possessing or quickly building complementary assets—assets required to provide a new product or service to customers, such as manufacturing equipment, and marketing and distribution facilities).

CHAPTER 8

THE LEGAL FORM OF NEW VENTURES— AND THE LEGAL ENVIRONMENT IN WHICH THEY OPERATE

LEARNING OBJECTIVES

After reading this chapter, you should be able to:

1 Describe the major forms of business ownership—sole proprietorship, partnerships, corporations—and explain the advantages and disadvantages of each.

2 Describe additional forms of business ownership—limited liability companies, joint ventures, and professional corporations—and the advantages and disadvantages of each.

3 Describe the basic components of business contracts, and explain what happens if these obligations are not met.

4 Define franchising and describe the two major types—tradename franchising and business format franchising.

5 Describe the advantages and disadvantages of becoming a franchisee.

6 Describe the legal requirements franchisors must meet in terms of disclosure to potential franchisees.

7 Describe current trends in franchising, such as smaller outlets in nontraditional locations, co-branding franchising, and international franchising.

The Legal Forms New Ventures Can Take
Sole Proprietorship: One Company, One Owner
Partnerships: Different Forms, Different Benefits
Corporations: Limited Liability, But at a Cost
The S Corporation
The Limited Liability Company (LLC)
The Joint Venture
The Professional Corporation

The Legal Environment of New Ventures: Some Basics
New Ventures and the Law
Business Contracts: Their Essential Components
Basic Elements of a Contract
Obligations Under Contracts

Franchising
Types of Franchising
The Benefits of Becoming a Franchisee
Drawbacks of Becoming a Franchisee
Legal Aspects of Franchising
The Future Shape of Franchising

All photos this page © PhotoDisc, Inc.

> "The business of the law is to make sense of the confusion of what we call human life—to reduce it to order but at the same time to give it possibility, scope, even dignity." (Archibald MacLeish, 1978)

When I started my first company in 1992, I (Robert Baron) didn't give much thought to the legal form it should take. I was certain from the word "Go!" that it should be a corporation. Why? Mainly for two reasons. First, I had been working for more than 25 years, so I had built up a reasonable amount of personal property (my house, stocks, real estate holdings). I realized that a corporation would protect these assets if, for some reason, the company did not succeed and ended up in debt. Second, I had experience with several other forms of ownership—joint ventures, various kinds of partnerships—and had found that they all suffered from serious drawbacks. For instance, I had been a limited partner in past investments where the controlling general partners had done pretty much as they pleased—including diverting the partnership's funds to their personal use. I wanted to avoid these problems, so I decided to make my new business a corporation. As I quickly discovered, though, this was more complicated—and expensive—than I had guessed. Many decisions had to be made: Would this be a regular (C) corporation, or an S corporation? How would shares be distributed? Would there be one kind of stock or several? No, forming a corporation was not easy; yet, it still seemed the right way to go. Ultimately, I discovered still additional problems; for instance, dissolving the corporation 9 years later turned out to be a nightmare of endless paperwork. Along the way, I found filing the required financial statements to be a difficult chore—especially in the early, hectic days when we were first getting started.

Looking back, and knowing what I know now, I realize that I actually had several choices aside from forming a corporation. In other words, my new venture could have taken one of several different legal forms. What are these forms and what advantages and disadvantages do they offer? These questions are the primary focus of the current chapter. The legal form taken by a new venture, however, is just one aspect of the total legal environment in which new companies operate. Taking account of this fact, we will also examine some basic legal issues of which all entrepreneurs should be aware—issues such as the basic elements of contracts and laws that directly affect all businesses (start-ups included). Although we agree with the quote and share MacLeish's conviction that laws do often bring order to the turmoil of daily life, we also realize that many entrepreneurs know very little about legal matters. The current chapter—plus related discussions at several other points in this book (see, e.g., Chapters 4, 11, and 13)—is designed to provide you, present or future entrepreneurs, with some basic insights into these legal issues. Finally, we will consider becoming a franchisee, yet another way in which individuals come to own a business. Examining it in the context of this chapter, which focuses on various forms of business ownership, is a logical place in which to do so. Please note that in this chapter we will focus on franchising from the perspective of the franchisee; in Chapter 10, we will examine franchising from the perspective of the franchisor.

THE LEGAL FORMS NEW VENTURES CAN TAKE

The next time you visit a dry-cleaning store, look at the moving belt that brings your clothing to the front counter. If it says "Railex," you are face-to-face with a product manufactured by a company started by my uncle Sid (see Figure 8.1 on page 188). In fact, several members of my family, including my grandfather and at least three uncles, started businesses and were—or are—entrepreneurs. Most of them chose to make their new ventures corporations, but my grandfather's business took a different form: It was a straightforward partnership, which he started with one other person. As I'll note later, this got him into serious difficulties and ultimately led to the demise of a profitable company. But that's getting ahead of the story. Let's turn now to an overview of the major legal forms new ventures can take, and the advantages and disadvantages offered by each.

Figure 8.1 Entrepreneurship in My Family

One of my uncles is a founder of the Railex Corporation. He and his brothers chose to make their company a corporation.

1 Describe the major forms of business ownership—sole proprietorship, partnerships, corporations—and explain the advantages and disadvantages of each.

Sole Proprietorship: One Company, One Owner

By far the simplest form of business ownership is the **sole proprietorship**—a situation in which a business is owned and managed by one individual. As shown in Figure 8.2, most businesses fall into this category—in fact, almost three-quarters are sole proprietorships. For reasons that will soon become clear, almost all of these are small companies. For instance, the person who mows my lawn owns his own company; similarly, the store in which I buy coffee, tea, and granola is owned and operated by one individual. The appeal of sole proprietorship is obvious. Such businesses are simple to create: All that's necessary is obtaining the required license or licenses from the state, county, or local governments; once these have been obtained, the owner can open for business. Indeed, some businesses don't require any license, so starting them is even simpler: The owner just opens for business. The costs involved in setting up a sole proprietorship are very low, so this, too, is a decided advantage. A third benefit of being the sole owner of a business is total control over its operations: The owner herself or himself makes all the decisions and, of course, gets to keep all the profits. If, one day, this person wants to the close the business, he or she just does so. Clearly, then, there are important "pluses" to being a sole proprietor: Entrepreneurs who choose this route are truly their own bosses, and as we noted in Chapter 1, that is one reason why many people choose to become entrepreneurs in the first place.

These benefits come at a considerable cost, however. The most important of these involves the fact that owners of sole proprietorships are subject to **unlimited personal liability**: They are personally liable for all debts incurred by the business. Not only can they lose their entire investment if the business goes "belly up," but they can also lose most of their personal assets too if the business is deeply in debt. Although most states permit owners to retain some equity in their homes or car, everything else is fair game for debtors, and the owner can be forced to sell them to pay off the debts the business has incurred.

A second disadvantage involves the fact that when individuals run a business by themselves, they represent the sum total of its management resources: If they lack the

Figure 8.2 Types of Business Ownership in the United States

Most businesses in the United States are sole proprietorships, with smaller percents being corporations or partnerships. A large proportion of the sole proprietorships are very small businesses, such as the lawn care company operated by one of my neighbors.

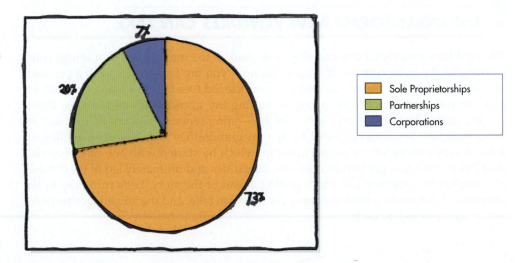

Sole Proprietorships
Partnerships
Corporations

knowledge or skill needed to run the business successfully, they must either hire someone who has what they lack, or the business may fail. Similarly, if the owner becomes ill or incapacitated, or if she or he chooses to retire, the business terminates unless there is a family member, close friend, or employee willing and able to operate it. Finally, sole proprietorships face a big disadvantage in obtaining capital: There are no shares in the business that can be sold to investors, and banks and other financial institutions may be reluctant to make loans because of the risks involved (e.g., the business will halt or terminate if something happens to the owner). In sum, although nearly everyone daydreams about owning their own business and being their own boss, sole proprietorship is generally not a suitable legal form for a new venture that its founder hopes to nurture into a large financial success.

Partnerships: Different Forms, Different Benefits

As I noted earlier, the business started by my grandfather was a **partnership**, which in the legal sense of this term is an association of two or more people who co-own a business for the purpose of making a profit. It is assumed that the co-owners (partners) will share the profits, assets, and liabilities of the business in accordance with agreed-upon terms. What are these terms? They can be anything the partners choose. For instance, partners could decide to divide the profits 50-50, 90-10, or according to any other formula they prefer. Whatever the terms, however, these should be stated as clearly as possible in a written **partnership agreement**, a document written with the assistance of an attorney and that states all of the terms under which the partnership will operate. The partnership agreement should spell out all the details—especially the ones about which bitter disagreements can emerge, such as how profits will be divided, what each partner will contribute, how decisions will be made, how disputes will be resolved, and how the partnership can be dissolved. Specifically, a standard partnership agreement will generally include the following kinds of information:

1. Name of the partnership
2. Purpose of the business
3. Location of the business
4. Names of the partners and their legal addresses
5. Duration of the partnership
6. Contributions of each partner to the business at the creation of the partnership and later
7. An agreement on how profits and losses will be distributed
8. An agreement on salaries or drawing rights against profits for each partner
9. Procedures for expanding or dissolving the business
10. Information on how the assets will be distributed if the partners choose to dissolve the partnership
11. How each partner can sell her or his interest in the business
12. What happens if one of the partners is disabled or absent
13. How alterations or modifications to the partnership agreement can be made

In other words, the partnership agreement covers all the major issues that are likely to arise as the partners seek to run their new venture. If partners do not prepare a written partnership agreement, regulations specified under the Uniform Partnership Act (UPA) will apply. This law specifies the rights and general obligations of partners and focuses on three key elements: ownership interest in the business, sharing of the business' profits and losses, and the right to participate in managing the operation of the partnership. Under the UPA, each partner has a right to:

1. Share in management and operations of the business
2. Share in any profits the business earns
3. Receive interest on additional advances made to the business

4. Receive compensation for expenses incurred on behalf of the partnership
5. Have access to the books and records of the partnership
6. Receive a formal accounting of the partnership's business affairs

In addition, the UPA specifies that each partner is obligated to:

1. Share in any losses
2. Work for the partnership without salary
3. Submit differences concerning the conduct of the business to a majority vote or arbitration
4. Give the other partner complete information about all activities of the business
5. Provide a formal accounting of the partnership's business activities

What are the advantages and disadvantages of a partnership? On the plus side of the ledger, partnerships are easy and inexpensive to establish: Owners must simply obtain required business licenses and complete a small number of forms. Similarly, partnerships provide a high level of flexibility: Partners can choose to divide profits and responsibilities in any way they choose. If the partners have complementary skills and knowledge, these can contribute to the successful operation of the business. Moreover, because each partner can contribute equity, the pool of financial resources available is expanded. Finally, partnerships are not subject to federal taxation; rather, net income or losses are *passed through* to the partners as individuals. This avoids the "double taxation" to which many corporations are exposed (taxation at the corporate level *and* at the individual level; we will return to this later in our discussion of corporations).

On the minus side, partners generally have unlimited liability, just as if each was a sole proprietor. (The exception is *limited partners* in a *limited partnership.*) Second, it is often difficult to continue a partnership if one of the partners becomes ill, becomes disabled, or dies. This is especially difficult when the partnership agreement puts restrictions on how each partner can dispose of his or her share of the business. Often, it is required that the partner wishing to sell must first offer it to the remaining partner or partners. If these people do not have the necessary funds, they may be forced to seek a new partner or to dissolve the partnership. This is what happened to my grandfather. During the Depression of the 1930s, his company (which manufactured clothing) remained profitable. However, his partner became seriously ill, and when my grandfather could not purchase his share, it became necessary to terminate the business. The same situation might have developed if my grandfather and his partner had experienced personal conflicts—a situation that often arises in partnerships when the partners disagree over important issues (see Figure 8.3). In short, partnerships definitely involve major risks, and any entrepreneur contemplating this form of ownership should consider these with care.

Limited Partnerships

Because partnerships cannot sell shares (as can corporations), they often experience difficulty in raising needed capital. One solution to this problem is to form a **limited partnership**, in which one or more partners are *general partners* who manage the business and others are *limited partners* who invest in the business but forego any right to manage the company. Such persons share in the profits in accordance with terms stated in the *limited partnership agreement* (which they sign when they become partners), but they have limited liability: They can only lose what they have invested. In contrast, the general partners have unlimited liability. In a sense, then, limited partnerships offer a combination of the benefits of partnerships and the benefits provided by corporations. One potential problem, however, is the danger that the general partners will run the business in a way that benefits them personally, while harming the interests of limited partners. Because the limited partners have no right to manage the company, unscrupulous general partners can strip a partnership of its valuable assets before limited partners are even aware that this is occurring.

*"Now that you've demonstrated your clout, let's
get on with the negotiations."*

Figure 8.3 Conflict Between
Partners: A Major Source of
Problems for Partnerships

*When partners disagree over
important issues and experience
conflict, the effects can be
devastating for their company.*

Other Forms of Partnerships: Limited Liability Partnerships (LLPs) and Master Limited Partnerships (MLPs)

An additional form of partnership is one that most states in the United States restrict to professionals such as physicians, attorneys, dentists, and accountants. Such partnerships are known as *limited liability partnerships (LLPs)*, and all partners in them are limited partners, with only limited liability for the debts of the partnership or for legal actions brought against other partners. An added benefit is that such partnerships pay no tax; rather, all profits and losses are passed through to the limited partners, who pay any taxes due as individuals.

A recent development is the *master limited partnership (MLP)*. Such partnerships issue shares that are traded like shares of common stock. MLPs offer limited liability to their partners while providing increased liquidity for their investments. However, such partnerships do pay taxes (the "double taxation" problem) unless they are involved in natural resources or real estate, which are specifically protected from such taxation.

KEY POINTS

- Sole proprietorships are the simplest form of business ownership: ownership by one person.
- Sole proprietorships are easy and inexpensive to establish, but the persons who own them are subject to unlimited liability for the businesses' debts, and in many cases, the business cannot continue if they become ill or incapacitated.
- Partnerships are an association of two or more persons who co-own a business. All partnerships should have a partnership agreement outlining the rights and obligations of all partners.
- In a partnership, at least one person must be designed as a general partner; this person has unlimited liability. In a limited partnership, one person is the general partner and all the others are limited partners.
- In a limited liability partnership, all persons are limited partners. Such partnerships are restricted to professionals practicing together (e.g., physicians, attorneys, accountants). In a master limited partnership, all partners have limited liability and shares of the partnership can be transferred to other persons; however, double taxation occurs.

Corporations: Limited Liability, But at a Cost

Ambrose Bierce (1881), the American author, once defined a corporation as follows: *"Corporation: An ingenious device for obtaining individual profit without individual responsibility."* To an extent he was right: A key advantage of corporations is that they are a form of business ownership that allows owners (persons holding shares in them) to receive profit while at the same time providing the significant advantage of limited liability: No matter how great the debts of the corporation, shareholders' liability is limited to the amount of their investment. In legal terms, **corporations** are separate legal entities apart from their owners, entities that may engage in business, make contracts, own property, pay taxes, and sue and be sued by others. The Supreme Court (1819) defined a corporation as: "an artificial being, invisible, intangible, and existing only in contemplation of the law."[1]

In the United States, corporations are created in specific states and are bound by the laws of those states; such laws vary somewhat from one state to another. A corporation doing business in the state in which it was created is a *domestic corporation*. A corporation doing business in another state is considered to be a *foreign corporation* in that state. Corporations formed in other countries are termed *alien corporations.*

Although entrepreneurs can form a corporation without the assistance of an attorney, the process is often complex, so the services of a good attorney are usually essential. (We will examine the question of how to select a good an attorney in a later section.) Registration of a corporation generally requires that the persons creating it provide the following information:

- The corporation's name
- A statement of purpose—what the corporation will do (e.g., "engage in sale of air filters")
- The length of time it will exist (this can be "for perpetuity" or for a specific duration)
- Names and addresses of the persons incorporating
- Place of business
- Capital stock authorization—how many shares of stock will be issued and whether there are different types of stock
- Restrictions on transferring shares, if these exist
- Names and addresses of the officers and directors of the corporation
- Bylaws—rules under which the corporation will operate

Once this information has been submitted and the required fees paid, the corporation receives approved *articles of incorporation*, which become its charter. The shareholders then must hold a meeting to formally elect directors. The directors, in turn, appoint the corporate officers.

Advantages of Corporations

We have already described a key advantage offered by corporations: limited liability for stockholders. In the past, these persons had no personal liability for debts or actions of the corporation. However, recent court decisions have made entrepreneurs—owners of small corporations—increasingly liable for legal claims against the corporation, especially with respect to environmental and pension-related matters. In other words, forming a corporation no longer offers shareholders total immunity to claims relating to these issues. So, for instance, if a start-up venture that has incorporated is creating an environmental hazard through its operations, the owners of the company as well as the corporation itself may be subject to prosecution for these violations. This is a sobering fact, and one that entrepreneurs should consider carefully.

Another key advantage of corporations is the ability to attract capital. Because they can sell shares, they can raise additional funds by doing so, as necessary. Similarly, corporations can continue indefinitely, long beyond the presence—or even lives—of their founders. Finally, shares are transferable; they can be sold to someone else. If the shares are traded publicly on a stock exchange, such liquidity can be very high. We will return to the issue of creating a public corporation in Chapter 14, in our discussion of exit strategies for entrepreneurs.

Disadvantages of Corporations

Like all forms of ownership, however, corporations also have a downside. First, it can be complex and expensive to start one; attorney's fees and government fees can exceed $2,500 in many cases. Even more important, because corporations are separate legal entities, any profits they earn can be subject to *double taxation*: The corporation itself must pay taxes on these profits, and then, if they are distributed to individual shareholders, these persons must pay tax on them again, as individuals.

Corporations, unlike partnerships or sole proprietorships, are subject to many legal and financial requirements. Corporate officers must record and report management decisions and actions, and must report financial data to both the federal and state governments. Corporations must hold annual meetings, and managers are required to consult with the board of directors about major decisions. If the shares of the company are traded publicly, it must file quarterly and annual reports with the Securities and Exchange Commissions (SEC). So, although corporations are a very useful form of business ownership, they have important drawbacks, too.

The S Corporation

What we have described so far is the standard (C) corporation. One way of avoiding the double taxation issue mentioned earlier is through formation of an **S corporation**. In such corporations, all profits and losses are passed through to shareholders, just as they are passed through to partners in a partnership. In addition, if assets that have appreciated in value are sold, there is no tax to the corporation; rather, individual shareholders pay taxes as individuals, based on the number of shares they hold.

In order to qualify as an S corporation, corporations must meet certain requirements:

- They must be a domestic (U.S.) corporation.
- They cannot have a nonresident alien as a shareholder.
- They can issue only one class of common stock.
- They must limit shareholders to individuals, estates, and certain trusts (recently, this has been extended to include employee stock ownership plans).
- They cannot have more than 75 shareholders.

If any of these conditions are violated, the corporation's S status is automatically ended.

Although the advantages offered by S corporations are important ones, they also suffer from disadvantages. First, benefits paid to shareholders who own 2 percent or more of stock cannot be deducted as business expenses; this means that reimbursements for meals, lodging, and travel are taxable income to the persons who receive them. In regular (C) corporations, in contrast, such expenses can be deducted as business expenses. Second, and more important, the marginal tax rate for individuals in the United States is currently higher (approximately 38 percent) than the rate for corporations (35 percent). This means that individuals actually pay at a higher rate than corporations, thus reducing some of the benefits provided by S corporations. Overall, it appears that this form of business ownership is especially advantageous when start-up ventures are showing large losses; these are passed through to individual shareholders, who can then use them to offset other sources of income.

The Limited Liability Company (LLC)

In recent years, a new form of business ownership known as the **limited liability company (LLC)** has appeared. This, too, is a cross between a corporation and partnership, and offers some of the benefits of both. As is true in S corporations, income flows through to owners (known as "members") who pay their own taxes as individuals.

LEARNING OBJECTIVE

2 Describe additional forms of business ownership—limited liability companies, joint ventures, and professional corporations—and the advantages and disadvantages of each.

Unlike S corporations, however, LLCs are not subject to so many government restrictions. They can have more than 75 shareholders, several classes of stock, and foreign shareholders. They *are* subject to some regulations, however. For instance, they can offer only *two* of the following characteristics of corporations: (1) limited liability, (2) continuity of life, (3) free transferability of interests in them, and (4) centralized management. Further, they must include the words "limited liability company" or "limited company" or the letters "LLC" in their names. Finally, in many states they are chartered for only 30 years; corporations can exist in perpetuity.

Because LLCs offer the advantages of a partnership and the legal protection of a corporation, they have become increasingly popular in recent years. However, because they are so new, there is as yet no uniform legislation governing them, and this introduces a degree of uncertainty into the equation. At present, though, they appear to offer a very promising form of business ownership.

The Joint Venture

Suppose that you located some very desirable land—acreage you were certain would increase in value. You could not afford to buy it alone and did not want to take a loan to do so. How could you purchase it? One possibility is by forming a **joint venture**—a form of business ownership that resembles a partnership, except that there are no general or limited partners and the purpose of the entity is very limited. You don't want to operate a business; you just want to buy, hold, and then sell a piece of land. In a joint venture, all participants can participate in the management of the venture and in decision making. The larger the number of shares they hold, they more votes they have; the number of shares, in turn, is determined by the size of their initial investment.

The income derived from a joint venture is taxed as if it arose from a partnership (it flows through to the participants), and the issue of liability is largely irrelevant, because the joint venture is formed for a limited, specific purpose. Generally, there is no reason for the joint venture to acquire debts, because capital contributions at the start are sufficient to launch the venture. Participants can elect specific persons to manage the day-to-day operations of the venture (e.g., pay bills as due), but all have an active role in key decisions, such as when to sell.

Table 8.1 Major Forms of Business Ownership

Major forms of business ownership and their key features are summarized here.

The Professional Corporation

Earlier, we described limited liability partnerships (LLPs)—a form of business ownership preferred by many professionals (physicians, attorneys, accountants). An alternative form of ownership is available to such individuals, and should be briefly mentioned—

	SOLE PROPRIETORSHIP	PARTNERSHIP	C CORPORATION	S CORPORATION	LIMITED LIABILITY COMPANY
Owner's liability	Unlimited	Unlimited for general partners, limited for limited partners	Limited	Limited	Limited
Number of owners	1	2 or more	Any number	Maximum of 75	2 or more
Tax liability	Proprietor pays at individual rate	Partners pay at individual rate	Double tax: corporation pays tax and shareholders pay tax on dividends	Owners pay at individual rate	Members pay at individual rate
Transferability of ownership	Fully transferable	May require consent of partners	Fully transferable	Transferable (but may affect S status)	Usually requires consent of all members
Continuity of business	Ends on death of proprietor or upon termination by proprietor	Dissolves upon death or retirement of general partner	Perpetual	Perpetual	Perpetual
Cost and ease of formation	Low; easy	Low, easy	High; more complex	High; more complex	High; relatively easy
Ability to raise capital	Limited	Moderate	Very high	Moderate to high	High
Maximum tax rate	38	38	35	38	38

the **professional corporation** (**PC**). In LLPs, the liability of the partners is limited by the fact that all are limited partners. In PCs, in contrast, this protection is afforded by the fact that the PC is a corporation. Thus, all shareholders in the PC are protected from malpractice lawsuits filed against the PC or against other shareholders, although they are still subject to legal actions filed against them as individuals.

In sum, many forms of business ownership are open to entrepreneurs. All offer a mixed pattern of advantages and disadvantages, so the task of choosing between them should be approached carefully—and with considerable caution. Also, it is important for entrepreneurs to note that they are not locked in forever to the form they select initially: Partnerships can become corporations, corporations can change from C to S forms (or vice versa), and so on. Some changes are easier to make than others (e.g., from sole proprietorship to partnership, from one form of partnership to another), but there is no reason to stick with an initial choice if conditions change and it becomes clear that it would be advantageous to change. We have covered a lot of ground in this section, so before proceeding, please examine Table 8.1 (on page 194) carefully; it provides an overview of all the types of business ownership we have discussed, and of the advantages and disadvantages they offer.

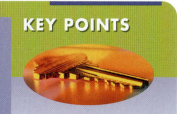

KEY POINTS

- Corporations are legal entities apart from their owners, entities that may engage in business, make contracts, own property, pay taxes, and sue and be sued by others.
- One key advantage of corporations is that they provide limited liability to their owners. Another key advantage of corporations is the ability to attract capital. However, corporations, unlike partnerships or sole proprietorships, are subject to many legal and financial requirements
- An S corporation is one in which all profits and losses are passed through to shareholders, just as they are passed through to partners in a partnership.
- Limited liability corporations resemble S corporations, but they are permitted by law to demonstrate only two of the following characteristics: (1) limited liability, (2) continuity of life, (3) free transferability of interests in them, and (4) centralized management.
- A joint venture is a form of business ownership that resembles a partnership, except that there are no general or limited partners, and the purpose of the entity is very limited.
- Professional corporations, a form of ownership often preferred by physicians, attorneys, and other professionals, provide limited liability to shareholders but are subject to double taxation.

THE LEGAL ENVIRONMENT OF NEW VENTURES: SOME BASICS

Choosing the legal form of a new venture is important, but it is far from the only thing entrepreneurs need to consider with respect to legal matters. Although most entrepreneurs are not interested in such topics, and may well share the negative views about attorneys that are so prevalent in the United States at the current time (see Figure 8.4 on page 196), it is important for them to know something about three additional issues: (1) laws that can affect their businesses, (2) laws concerning intellectual property, and (3) the nature of business contracts. We have already examined (1) in Chapter 4 and will consider (2) in detail in Chapter 11, so here we will focus on item (3). Specifically, we will seek to accomplish to two tasks. First, we will expand slightly our previous discussion of laws that can affect new ventures. Second, we will examine the nature of business contracts.

New Ventures and the Law

My first job, back in 1957, was as a counselor in a day camp; the children in my charge were four and five years old, and managing them was quite a chore. If I turned my back for a moment, one was sure to punch or kick another, so I spent much of my time breaking up fights. Also, unless I watched them constantly and kept them entertained, they would wander off in different directions and get totally

Figure 8.4 How Many People—Including Some Entrepreneurs—Currently View Attorneys

At the present time, many people hold negative views about attorneys and the legal system. However, entrepreneurs must put such views aside and acquire basic knowledge of legal matters that can strongly affect the success of their companies.

"Wait! First, his attorney."

lost. I did this job five days a week for ten weeks (my entire summer vacation) and was paid the princely sum of $100 plus tips (which amounted to another $140). Clearly, this was lower than minimum wage (which at the time was about 75¢ per hour), but I never thought about seeking a lawyer or filing any kind of claim; after all, I had accepted the job with my eyes open, and it was my decision to stay in it.

Today, as you probably know, things are very different. In recent decades, the federal government has enacted many laws designed to protect employees and to protect consumers. If you run a new venture, and if you hire employees, *it is imperative that you have at least basic knowledge of these laws.* If you don't, you run the real risk of finding out about them in a court of law, as you answer charges brought against you. We described three of the most important of these laws in Chapter 4: the Occupational Safety and Health Act, which requires all employers to take active measures to safeguard the health and safety of employees; Title VII of the Civil Rights Act of 1964, which prohibits employers from basing employment decisions on a person's race, color, religion, sex, or national origin; and the Americans with Disabilities Act, which prohibits discrimination against individuals with disabilities. Here, we simply want to remind you of the impact of these laws on new ventures, and to call your attention to one more: the **Immigration Reform and Control Act of 1986**.

This law was designed to accomplish two major goals: discourage illegal immigration into the United States and to strengthen the national origin provision of Title VII of the Civil Rights Act (1964). The law seeks to attain the first goal by requiring all employers to document the eligibility of persons they hire for jobs in the United States. Employers must complete a special form (Form I-9) for all new hires—a form that requires these employees to provide documentation proving their identity and their authorization to work in the United States. If an employer is found have hired people who are not eligible to work, it is subject to large fines and other punishments. The law seeks to accomplish the second goal by specifically forbidding discrimination against "foreign-sounding" or "foreign-looking" persons. Again, if an employer is found guilty of violating this provision, she or he can face stiff fines and be required to provide back pay for up to two years.

Additional laws exist as well, but rather than examine these, too, we will simply repeat the advice we offered in Chapter 4: New ventures are as subject to these laws as large, mature companies. So please do look before you leap: The business you save may be your own. (What can happen when entrepreneurs do not pay attention to these laws? For some examples, please see the **"Danger! Pitfall Ahead!"** section.)

DANGER! PITFALL AHEAD!

What Can Happen When Entrepreneurs Are Ignorant of the Law

Ignorance of the law, it is often said, is no excuse. Where regulations and laws governing the health and safety of employees are concerned, this is definitely true. An entrepreneur who violates these laws and later claims "I didn't know!" will receive little sympathy or consideration from the courts. Why? Because it is the responsibility of every person running a business to be familiar with these laws. When entrepreneurs ignore them, true horror stories can unfold. Here are a couple of examples:

- An entrepreneur who ran a small woman's clothing factory was approached by a sweet, elderly woman who asked for a job "at any wage, just to finish out my time." He hired her to clean desks. Less than two weeks later, she asked for a leave of absence "to take care of some family matters." The entrepreneur, being soft-hearted, agreed and told her to call him when she was ready to work once again. She never called, but her attorney did, informing the entrepreneur that she was suing him for $20,000 because working in his factory had caused her to experience double carpel tunnel syndrome, which would now prevent her from holding any job. After many months and mounting legal fees, the entrepreneur settled with her out of court, despite the fact that he had learned that the woman had lined up her lawyer even before asking him for a job!

- An employee in a small equipment-repair company in Philadelphia was often absent from work because of what he described as bursitis—an inflammation of the joints that would flare up at unpredictable times. The company was tolerant of these absences, but one day, the owner of the company was driving by the employee's home and saw him polishing his car with his "bad arm." The next day, he called the employee into his office for a talk. The employee entered, but when the entrepreneur closed the door, the employee made a U-turn and left without a word. The next day the local sheriff came to see the entrepreneur and served him with papers indicating that the employee had filed criminal charges against the entrepreneur. These charges included interference with the exercise of civil rights, assault and battery, stalking, and kidnapping. The employee claimed that he was held in a locked room against his will, threatened, and injured permanently when the entrepreneur pulled his arm. The entrepreneur spent many thousands of dollars defending himself against these claims; because they were criminal charges, his company's liability insurance did not cover them. We can only guess at how many times he told himself: "If only I had known that closing the door was risky . . . ."

We could go on to describe other, equally unsettling cases, but by now, you almost certainly get the point: Because of laws designed to protect the health and welfare of employees, the workplace is now a veritable minefield for employers who are unfamiliar with these laws and the rights they grant to employees. Wise entrepreneurs, therefore, will either become familiar with these laws themselves, or make sure that they have someone in their company who has this knowledge. Anything else amounts to gambling with the future of the business!

Business Contracts: Their Essential Components

Another aspect of the law with which entrepreneurs should be familiar is that governing **contracts**—promises that are enforceable by law. *Contract law* is a body of laws designed to assure that parties entering into contracts comply with the provisions in them; it also provides remedies to those parties harmed if a contract is broken.

A contract does not have to be written to be legal and enforceable. Indeed, many contracts are oral. In the United States, only contracts dealing with the following issues must be in writing: (1) the sale of real estate, (2) paying someone else's debt, (3) contracts that require longer than one year to perform, or (4) contracts that involve the sale of goods with a value of $500 or more.

> **LEARNING OBJECTIVE**
>
> **3** Describe the basic components of business contracts, and explain what happens if these obligations are not met.

Basic Elements of a Contract

A contract must meet four basic requirements in order to be binding on the parties involved:

- *Legality.* The contract must be intended to accomplish a legal purpose. For instance, you cannot write a contract to sell illegal drugs because doing so itself is not legal.

- *Agreement.* A legal contract must include a legitimate offer and a legitimate acceptance; this is known as *meeting of the minds* in legal terminology. If, for instance, an entrepreneur offers to sell some product to a customer for a specific price and the customer accepts, this is a contract. If there is no acceptance by the customer, then there is no contract.

- *Consideration.* Something of value must be exchanged between the parties involved for it to constitute a contract. If nothing of value is exchanged, then the agreement is about a gift and does not constitute a contract. For instance, suppose that a customer is so pleased with the product or service provided by an entrepreneur that she says, "I like your product so much that I'm going to give it free advertising." If she does not deliver on this promise, the entrepreneur cannot legally demand that she do so, because her offer did not involve the exchange of anything of value—it was a gift.

- *Capacity.* Not all persons have the capacity to legally enter into a contract. Minors or persons who are intoxicated or who have diminished mental ability cannot be bound by contracts. So if an entrepreneur makes a deal with a customer who is clearly intoxicated (several witnesses can testify to this fact), the entrepreneur cannot insist that the customer honor the agreement: The fact that he was intoxicated at the time means that the contract was not a valid one.

Obligations Under Contracts

If you have a contract with someone and they fail to hold up their end of the agreement, what can you do? Legally, this is known as a **breach of contract**, and several options are available. In most cases, the damaged party can sue for, and obtain, money or some specific action by the other party as compensation for the damages she or he has sustained. The goal is to restore the damaged party to the state he or she was in before the agreement was made. If money is awarded to the damaged party (the *plaintiff*), it is known as *compensatory damages*. This is an amount that, presumably, reflects the monetary extent of the damage.

If money alone is not enough to restore a person to her or his original state, a judge may order *specific performance* by the person who violated the contract. This requires the person who violated the contract to do exactly what she or he originally agreed to do. For instance, suppose that an entrepreneur sells her business to another person and signs a noncompete agreement indicating that she will not start or own a similar business in a specific geographic area for a certain period of time. Later, though, she changes her mind and starts such a business. This is a violation of the noncompete agreement (which is a contract), and under these circumstances, a judge may rule that money is not enough to compensate the purchaser for the harm done and may issue an injunction—a court order that prohibits the entrepreneur from operating the new business for the duration of the original agreement.

Contract law is very complex, and only a trained attorney can draw up a contract that is certain to meet the requirements outlined above. This, in turn, raises an intriguing question: How can entrepreneurs choose a good attorney? There is no simple answer, but there are some definite "do's" and "don'ts" well worth considering:

- Do *not* choose an attorney for your company simply because you know her or him; although this person may be a friend, she or he may lack the skills and experience you need in many business contexts.

- Do *not* choose an attorney for your company because she or he has handled other, unrelated matters for you (real estate transactions, estate planning, divorce); again, this person may be skilled in these areas, but may not necessarily be skilled with respect to business law

- Do seek an attorney by asking other people in business for referrals; they are likely to steer you to an attorney or law firm that has the skills you need.

- Do check credentials; law schools are not all alike, and attorneys who graduated from good ones are likely to be better trained than ones who graduated from lesser-known schools.

■ Do ask potential attorneys to describe their experience; if they are reluctant to do so, look elsewhere!

These are just general guidelines; choosing an attorney is a personal decision and should reflect your own preferences. But do be certain to obtain the services of an attorney who has worked with entrepreneurs and small businesses before; such a person will understand the many legal pitfalls that can threaten new ventures, and help you steer clear of them.

KEY POINTS

- In recent decades, many laws designed to protect the health and rights of employees have been enacted (e.g., OSHA, the Americans with Disabilities Act, the Immigration Reform and Control Act). Entrepreneurs need a working knowledge of these laws to avoid violating them.
- Another aspect of the law with which entrepreneurs should be familiar is that governing contracts—promises that are enforceable by law.
- Key elements of contracts are legality (the contract must be designed to accomplish a legal purpose), agreement (a legitimate offer and legitimate acceptance), consideration (something of value must be exchanged), and capacity (the persons involved must be capable of entering into a contract).
- If contracts are violated, the damaged party can seek redress in the form of compensatory damages or specific performance by the party that violated the contract.
- In choosing an attorney for a new venture, it is usually best to select one who has experience in business matters, and who has solid legal credentials.

FRANCHISING

If you drive down any major commercial street in virtually any town or city in the United States, you will probably see a scene like the one in Figure 8.5. If you recorded the names of all the businesses jostling each other for space—and your attention!—you would almost certainly find that a large percentage of them are ones you already know: McDonald's, Arby's, KFC, Subway, Domino's, Red Roof Inn, to mention just a few. Moreover, you would see the same names, and the same businesses, no matter where you happened to be. The reason for this is obvious: **Franchising** is a tremendously popular form of business ownership today, and all these companies are in franchises. What is franchising? In essence, it is a system of distribution in which legally independent business owners (*franchisees*) pay fees and royalties to a parent company (the *franchisor*) in return for the right to use its trademark, sell its products or services, and, in many cases, to use the business model and system it has developed. How popular is franchising? In the United States, there are more than 5,000 franchisors, which, together, operate more than 650,000 separate outlets (stores, restaurants, hotels, etc.).[2] Together, franchises account for more than 44 percent of all retail sales—sales totaling more than

Figure 8.5 Franchising: Definitely Big Business in the United States

As a drive down any busy commercial street or road suggests, franchising is very popular in the United States. In fact, there are more than 650,000 separate franchise outlets at the current time, and the number is growing rapidly.

$1 trillion per year; they employ more than 8 million people.[3] So franchising is indeed very big business.

Types of Franchising

Not all franchises are alike. Some, known as **trade-name franchising**, give franchisees the right to sell specific products under the franchisor's brand name and trademark. Good examples of such franchising are automobile dealers, who are granted the right to sell specific brands by the manufacturers (e.g., Audi, Honda, Chevrolet, Buick) and gasoline stations (Texaco, ExxonMobil). Again, the benefits to the franchisee involve association with brands and trademarks that are recognized, and trusted, by consumers.

The second type of franchising, known as **business format franchising**, involves providing the franchisee with a complete business system—a trademarked name, the products or services to be sold, the buildings in which the business will be operated, a marketing strategy, methods of actually operating the business, quality control, and assistance in actually running the business. This is the most rapidly growing type of franchising, and it is found in many different industries: business service firms, hotels, car rental agencies, beauty aid retailers, and, of course, fast-food restaurants (see Figure 8.6). Franchisees who enter into this kind of agreement with a franchisor virtually receive a "turnkey" operation: The franchisor sets up the business, trains the franchisee on how to run it, and then often helps the franchisee to operate it. In a sense, this is the farthest away from our definition of entrepreneurship, but as you can readily see, it offers important benefits for the franchisees—especially if they have little or no prior experience in running a business.

The Benefits of Becoming a Franchisee

We have already mentioned some of the benefits of franchising for the franchisee—they become associated with a well-known brand name or product and receive, to varying degrees, help in setting up and running a business. In essence, they benefit from the past experience of the franchisor who, if successful, has identified an effective and profitable business model and put it into operation hundreds or even thousands of times. But this is only part of the total picture; franchisees also gain additional benefits from their association with the franchisor. These are summarized in the following sections.

Figure 8.6 Franchises: Two Major Types

Two major kinds of franchises exist: (1) trade-name franchising (e.g., automobile dealers) and (2) business format franchising (e.g., Burger King, McDonald's, Dunkin' Donuts).

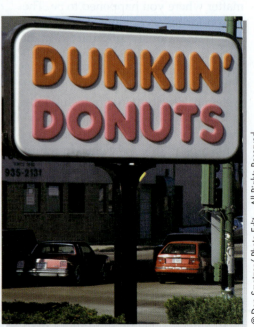

Training and Support

Have you ever heard of "Hamburger University"? It is the facility run by McDonald's corporation to train new franchisees. During a 14-day period, they receive instruction in everything from how to clean grills correctly to how to manage their businesses. Other major franchisors run similar operations—for instance, Dunkin' Donuts trains new franchisees for up to five weeks on tasks ranging from keeping financial records through making dough. Clearly, such training can be invaluable to new franchisees, and for many, the fees they pay for such training is money well spent. (As we will see, however, this is not always the case and can be a source of serious conflict between franchisees and franchisors.)

Standardized Products and Services

If you buy a hamburger in a Burger King outlet in Portland, Maine, it will be virtually identical to one you purchase at a Burger King outlet in Portland, Oregon. Why? Because major franchisors insist that products sold under their name meet strict standards. This is a big plus for franchisees, because it means that they do not have to work hard to convince potential customers that they are selling good products or services: The name on the door does this for them. In contrast, it may take years for independent business owners to build a solid reputation in their local communities—and then, of course, these reputations are only good within a limited geographic area.

National Advertising

Major franchisors launch equally major advertising campaigns—ones that consumers recognize and, on occasion, like. For instance, do you recall the ad campaign for Papa John's Pizza, in which the owner appeared in several franchise outlets and stressed the quality and freshness of the ingredients? Such campaigns are not free to franchisees: Usually, they pay a fee or a percent of their sales to support them. But given the fact that these campaigns appear on national television and are developed by top-notch advertising companies, this can be a bargain, and an important "plus" contributing to franchisees' success (see Figure 8.7).

Buying Power

Can you imagine how many pounds of potatoes are purchased by McDonald's Corp. each year? How about the number of pillows and towels purchased by major motel chains? The point of these statistics is simple: Major franchisors have huge "buying muscle." They can negotiate very favorable prices for the items they need, and which they then supply to their franchisees. Most pass along at least a portion of these savings to their franchisees—after all, they want these individuals to succeed. So although franchisees must purchase their supplies and equipment from the franchisors, this is often a very good deal for them, and it helps hold their costs below what they would be for independent businesses that do not benefit from this centralized buying power.

Financial Assistance

Although major franchisors do not generally loan money to potential franchisees, they do often help them in less direct ways. For instance, they assist them in establishing relationships with banks, investors, and other sources of funds. Moreover, they do sometimes offer highly qualified franchisees such benefits as in-house construction loans (e.g., in the hotel

Figure 8.7 National Advertising: An Important Benefit for Franchisees

Major franchisors often launch national advertising campaigns, which include television commercials, magazine ads, and billboards. These campaigns help increase business for their franchisees.

industry) and even short-term loans to cover franchising fees, which in some cases can be very large.

Site Selection and Territorial Protection

The location of any business can be crucial, and this is especially true for retail operations, which is what most new franchises are. Major franchisors often conduct careful site analyses to help pinpoint good locations for new outlets, and franchisees benefit from this expertise: Their businesses open in locations that draw on a large, potential market.

One problem for any new business is nearby competition. Major franchisors help to reduce this risk for franchisees by offering them *territorial protection*—they assure that no additional, competing outlets will be opened within a specified distance. This helps avoid dilution of sales and contributes to the success of new franchise outlets. But recent findings suggest many new franchisors won't offer this type of protection to franchisees because it hinders the franchisor's flexibility.[4]

A Business Model That Works

Perhaps most important of all, successful franchisors provide new franchisees with a proven business model. This means that franchisees do not have to learn by trial and error—the usual way in which new businesses grope their way to success. On the contrary, the business models of major franchisors have been honed and perfected through experiences gained in thousands of previously-opened outlets. The result is that the methods and systems supplied to new franchisees really do *work*. As long as the franchisees follow these methods and supply the required level of hard work and commitment, their chances of success are increased; at least, their chances are often higher than what is true for the owners of independent small businesses who must learn "on the fly" and often only manage to get it right after spending considerable time on the brink of failure.

Drawbacks of Becoming a Franchisee

Given the immense popularity of franchising, it is clear that growing numbers of people recognize the advantages. But becoming a franchisee is certainly not an unmixed blessing; there are also serious drawbacks to entering into this kind of business relationship. Here are some of the key ones.

Franchise Fees and Royalties

Recently, an Atlanta Bread Company outlet opened near where I live. (This is a rapidly-growing and relatively new franchisor.) When I visited it, I had a brief conversation with the new—and proud—owner. At one point, he mentioned the size of his investment, and I must admit that it staggered me: The figure was over $450,000. Even that pales by comparison with the amount required to open a new hotel in one of the leading franchise chains: more than $10 million! So start-up costs for franchisees are often quite high. On top of this, franchisees must pay royalties to the franchisor. This is usually based on a percent of gross sales and generally ranges between 3 and 7 percent. These fees must be paid even if the outlet is not profitable, so some franchisees find themselves facing a situation where the franchisors make money while they barely make ends meet—or worse. In such cases, it is as if they are simply an employee of the franchisor, working hard to make profits for this company rather than themselves. This is certainly not why they chose to open a business in the first place, so franchisees who face this situation can tell you—with lots of pain—about the potential downside of franchising.

Enforced Standardization

Many franchisees suffer from a basic misunderstanding: They believe that at first they will follow the strict guidelines established by the franchisor, but later, after they get the hang of running the business, they will be able to branch out and do things their way. In fact, this is not an option. Many franchise agreements require franchisees to run their businesses in a specific way, and violations of the rules can lead to serious consequences, including revocation of the franchise. I once knew of a McDonald's outlet that was frequently dirty—the floors, the tables, even the bathrooms. I was not surprised when one day, signs proclaiming "Under New Management" appeared. The previous owner's inability or unwillingness to adhere to the company's strict guidelines concerning cleanliness had ultimately cost him his franchise—and the large fees he had paid to open this outlet (more than $500,000).

Restricted Freedom over Purchasing and Product Lines

Franchisees also have little or no choice with respect to where they purchase their supplies: These must be obtained from the franchisor or sources specified by the franchisor, and they have little or no choice over the products they sell. If the franchisor decides to introduce a new product and it is one the franchisee thinks will not be popular locally, she or he can seek approval to refrain from offering it, but the final decision rests with the franchisor. So, for instance, if a large pizza franchisor decided to introduce kiwi fruit pizza, its franchisees would be required to add it to the menu and to stock the ingredients—even if they never sold a single kiwi pizza.

On the other side of the ledger, some highly successful franchisors invite input from franchisees—and really listen to it. In fact, at Subway—*Entrepreneur* magazine's top-rated franchisor[5]—franchisees serve on the advertising board and in the purchasing coop. They meet about every four months to discuss the direction of the company and have had a major hand in shaping its strategic plan. So, franchisees are not necessarily left out in the cold in terms of having input into how the parent company—and their own franchises—are run.

Poor Training Programs

McDonald's, Dunkin' Donuts, and many other major franchisors run excellent training programs for new franchisees. The quality of such programs varies greatly across the industry, however, and many franchisees complain that they have paid large fees for training and then received very little in return. Clearly, this can be discouraging for franchisees, so the general rule of "check before you invest" clearly applies here.

Market Saturation

Some experts feel that the "golden age" of franchising, at least in some industries, has already passed. Prime locations for fast-food restaurants, motels, auto service facilities, and many other kinds of franchises are already occupied, and new outlets are being placed in less desirable locations. Is that true? No one knows for sure, but I have often wondered about the location of some franchise outlets. For instance, a new Microtel motel was built about three years ago in a spot close to where I live. I wondered about this at the time because the location was far from the nearest highway and was in a neighborhood I would describe as basically residential in nature. The result? Whenever I passed this hotel, the parking lot was practically empty, and I assumed that soon, I would see a new name on the large sign outside the office; I did! (see Figure 8.8 on page 204).

Lower Ability to Coordinate Across Individual Units

We should briefly mention one further disadvantage faced by franchisees—especially those who own units in large franchise chains. Research findings indicate that such chains are less effective at coordinating their price and advertising as compared to corporations that own a large number of outlets (e.g., a restaurant chain that does not franchise its units).[6] Why? Because each individual owner gets "spillover" effects from efforts to improve sales through pricing or advertising. This reduces the incentive to coordinate with others and, overall, reduces effectiveness relative to corporate chains.

In sum, franchising, as a route to business ownership, offers a mixed assortment of potential benefits and potential drawbacks. Franchisees benefit from the brand name,

Photo courtesy of R.A. Baron.

Figure 8.8 Market Saturation: An Important Risk for Franchisees

The motel shown here was built in a location out of sight of any major highway, in a residential neighborhood. As a result, it seems empty most of the time. This may be the result of market saturation, which led the franchisor to choose a site that is far from ideal because all the good ones are already filled.

quality control, and national advertising provided by the franchisor, but must pay large fees, continuing royalties, and give up any dreams about operating a business the way they prefer. Moreover, one study indicates that franchisees actually make less money than independent entrepreneurs in the same industry.[7] Finally, we should note that despite all the advantages it can offer, rates of failure are quite high among franchisees; indeed, one recent study that obtained data from 800 franchise systems and 250,000 individual outlets over a 4-year period[8] found turnover rates in excess of 10 percent per year. (Turnover refers to instances in which a franchise unit is transferred from an existing owner to a new franchisee, cancellations of the franchise agreement or failure to renew it by the franchisor, and reacquisitions—the franchisor purchases the unit from the franchisee.) These failures stem from many factors, but central among them seems to be a basic misfit between the skills, abilities, and motives of the franchisee and the requirements of running a successful franchise unit.[9]

So, is becoming a franchisee for you? Or would you prefer to run your own business, make your own mistakes, and take the risks of learning as you go? Only you as an individual can answer this question, and to a large extent, it depends on the relative, subjective weights you place on receiving expert help, becoming part of a going concern, and personal freedom to run your business as you choose. Some people, like one couple described in a recent magazine article,[10] move back and forth between the two roles. This couple—call them Jack and Diane (not their real names)—tried running their own business (a golf apparel Web site) first. It failed because they were unwilling to quit their current jobs to become full-time entrepreneurs. They still wanted to run their own business, so they compromised this dream and purchased a franchise—an automobile quick-oil-change operation. They view this as a way to leverage their plan to run their own business by acquiring necessary capital from the franchise.

In short, the decision to become a franchisee is complex and should reflect not only economic realities, but personal dispositions and preferences as well. Remember: This choice, once made, is *not* set in stone; people can—and often do—switch from one role (franchisee) to the other (independent business owner) at different points in their lives.

Legal Aspects of Franchising

Whenever an industry booms, government regulations cannot be far behind, and franchising is no exception to this general rule. In the United States, the Federal Trade Commission has established rules (the Trade Regulation Rule) requiring all franchisors to disclose detailed information to potential franchisees at least ten days before a franchise contract is signed, and before any money is paid. The Trade Regulation Rule requires information on 23 points to be included in this written document; these are summarized in Table 8.2. As you can see, the Trade Regulation Rule requires franchisors to disclose important information useful to potential franchisees in making their decision about whether to proceed. Among the information that must be included is full disclosure of franchise fees and continuing payments (e.g., royalties, service fees, training fees, etc.), information on restrictions concerning the goods or services franchisees are permitted to sell, territorial protection, obligations of the franchisor, and a description of the conditions under which the franchisor can repurchase the franchise or refuse to renew it. Moreover, many states have additional rules that govern the relationship between franchisors and franchisees. If you are considering purchasing a franchise, you should examine whether the laws of your state offer you any additional protections as a franchisee.

1	Identify the franchisor and describe the franchisor's previous business experience
2	Describe the business experience of each of the franchisor's offices, directors, and management personnel
3	Information on lawsuits against the franchisor, its officers, directors, and managers
4	Information on any bankruptcies involving the franchisor
5	Information about initial franchise fee and other required payments
6	Information on continuing payments franchisees must make
7	Detail description of payments franchisee must make to meet initial investment requirement and how and to whom they are made
8	Information about quality restrictions on goods, services, equipment, supplies, inventory, and other items used in the franchise and where franchisees may purchase them
9	Statement of franchisee's obligations under the franchise contract (tabular form)
10	Description of any financial assistance available from the franchisor
11	Description of all obligations the franchisor must fulfill
12	Description of any territorial protection for franchisee
13	Information about franchisor's trademarks, service marks, trade names, logos, and commercial symbols
14	Similar information on any patents and copyrights owned by franchisor
15	Description of extent to which franchisees must participate personally in operating the franchise
16	Description of any restrictions on goods or services franchises are permitted to sell
17	Description of conditions under which the franchise may be repurchased or refused renewal by the franchisor
18	Description of involvement of celebrities and public figures in the franchise
19	Complete statement of the basis for any earnings claims made to the franchisee
20	Statistical information about the current number of franchises
21	Franchisor's financial statements
22	Copy of all franchise and other contracts the franchisee will be required to sign
23	Standardized, detachable "receipt" to prove that the prospective franchisee received a copy of the Uniform Franchise Offering Circular (required by federal law in the United States)

Table 8.2 Information Franchisors Must Disclose to Potential Franchisees

In the United States, federal law requires franchisors to disclose all of the information described here to potential franchisors. This must be supplied at least ten days before they sign a contract.

Anyone considering the possibility of purchasing a franchise should examine such information carefully, and then ask additional questions of the franchisor. It is also very useful, if possible, to talk with current franchisees. This latter group can give you important insights into how the franchisor treats franchisees, and to what extent it helps them achieve success. In any case, entering into an agreement with a franchisor is a very serious decision, and should only be made after careful consideration and only after doing one's homework (e.g., checking into the current financial state of the franchisor, its competition, and so on).

The Future Shape of Franchising

Any economic activity that is growing as rapidly as franchising is also very likely to be experiencing rapid change—and this is definitely true with respect to franchising. Here, briefly, are some of the trends that are currently emerging.

Smaller Outlets in Nontraditional Locations

Smart businesses go where the customers are, and major franchisors have begun to put this principle into operation. As a result, they are opening scaled-down outlets in places where a full-scale operation would not be appropriate. Franchise outlets are appearing in grocery stores on college campuses, in high school cafeterias, in hospitals, in zoos, and in theaters (see Figure 8.9 on page 206). These outlets put the products or services they sell directly in the path of potential customers, and so encourage them to buy. This trend is a new one, so it seems likely to continue for some time.

LEARNING OBJECTIVE

7 Describe current trends in franchising, such as smaller outlets in nontraditional locations, co-branding franchising, and international franchising.

© Getty Images

Figure 8.9 Franchise Outlets in Nontraditional Locations: A New Trend in Franchising

A recent trend in franchising is to place small outlets in places where they are convenient for potential customers (e.g., college campuses and theaters).

Co-Branding Franchising

Because many businesses have heavy volume at certain times of day or at certain times of the year but lower volume at other times, franchisors are *co-branding* many products to make more efficient use of costly retail space. For instance, rest areas along the New York Thruway generally contain three or more franchises, all selling different but compatible products. One combination I have seen in the rest areas is Roy Rogers (hamburgers, roast beef, fried chicken), Breyer's Ice Cream, and Dunkin' Donuts. The basic idea is that people eat more of each product at different times of the day and less at other times. For instance, they tend to eat donuts and drink coffee in the morning, but to consume hamburgers and fried chicken at lunch or dinner. And they tend to eat more ice cream in the afternoon and evening than in the morning. By taking advantage of these different patterns of consumption, the cost of renting expensive real estate can be spread across a greater volume of total sales.

International Franchising

In recent years, U.S. franchisors have moved into international markets. For instance, if you travel through Europe, you will see the familiar "Golden Arches" of the McDonald's Corp. not only in large cities, but increasingly in smaller towns, too. But as many franchisors have discovered, exporting their products or services is not always simple. In fact, products or services that sell very well in the United States sometimes seem strange or unpleasant to customers in other countries. Even brand names can be a source of difficulty. For instance, some years ago, Chevrolet was puzzled by the cool reception its Nova automobile received in Latin America—until someone pointed out that "No va" means "Doesn't go" in Spanish! So, franchisors who do not investigate local tastes and customs carefully can run into serious problems. The huge success of franchise outlets in Russia, China, and other international markets, however, suggests that this, too, is a trend that will continue in the years ahead.

A Huge Expansion in the Kinds of Business Being Franchised

At one time, most franchises were located in the food and retail trade industries—Baskin Robbins, Pizza Hut, Subway, Super 8 Motels, Days Inn, and other franchises spread from coast to coast and became household words. Recently, however, franchising has expanded into virtually every corner of the economy. For instance, franchises that provide a wide range of services for businesses—everything from advertising (e.g., Adventures in Adverstising) through management training (e.g., Leadership Management, Inc.) and staffing (Management Recruiters Worldwide)—are now growing rapidly. Similarly, franchises have entered the realm of education, and now provide many programs for children in such diverse areas as drama (e.g, Drama Kids International Inc.), fitness (e.g., Gymboree), and tutoring (e.g., Sylvan Learning Centers), to mention just a few. Other areas in which the number of franchises is growing rapidly include health services (e.g., Pearle Vision, Inc.), home improvements (e.g., Ubuild It), closet systems (e.g, Closets by Design), and recreation (e.g., Golf USA, Inc.). Overall, franchisors now offer potential franchisees a truly staggering array of businesses they can operate, and there is no sign that this expansion will end soon.

In sum, franchising is an immensely popular way for ambitious persons to own their own business without coming up with an idea for a new product or service and without developing their own, unique business model. For this reason, it seems likely to remain a large and growing activity for many years to come.

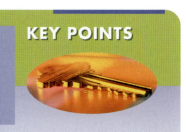

KEY POINTS

- Franchising is a system of distribution in which semi-independent business owners (franchisees) pay fees and royalties to a parent company (the franchisor) in return for the right to use its trademark, sell its products or services, and, in many cases, use the business model and system it has developed.
- Two basic types of franchising exist: trade-name franchising and business format franchising.
- Franchising offers important benefits to franchisees including training and support, standardized products, national advertising, site selection, and a proven business model that works.
- However, franchising also has a downside: Franchisees must pay substantial fees and royalties, they must deal with enforced standardization, and they have restricted freedom over purchasing and product lines.
- Franchising is regulated by the government, which requires that all prospective franchisees be given extensive information about the franchise agreement before signing it.
- Current trends in franchising include smaller outlets in nontraditional locations, co-branding franchising, international franchising, and a large expansion in the kinds of businesses being franchised.

Summary and Review of Key Points

- Sole proprietorships are the simplest form of business ownership: ownership by one person.
- Sole proprietorships are easy and inexpensive to establish, but the persons who own them are subject to unlimited liability for the businesses' debts, and in many cases, the business cannot continue if they become ill or incapacitated.
- Partnerships are an association of two or more persons who co-own a business. All partnerships should have a partnership agreement outlining the rights and obligations of all partners.
- In a partnership, at least one person must be designated as a general partner; this person has unlimited liability. In a limited partnership, one person is the general partner and all the others are limited partners.
- In a limited liability partnership, all persons are limited partners. Such partnerships are restricted to professionals practicing together (e.g., physicians, attorneys, accountants). In a master limited partnership, all partners have limited liability, and shares of the partnership can be transferred to other persons; however, double taxation occurs.
- Corporations are legal entities apart from their owners, entities that may engage in business, make contracts, own property, pay taxes, and sue and be sued by others.
- One key advantage of corporations is that they provide limited liability to their owners. Another key advantage of corporations is the ability to attract capital. However, corporations, unlike partnerships or sole proprietorships, are subject to many legal and financial requirements

- An S corporation is one in which all profits and losses are passed through to shareholders, just as they are passed through to partners in a partnership.
- Limited liability corporations resemble S corporations, but they are permitted by law to demonstrate only two of the following characteristics: (1) limited liability, (2) continuity of life, (3) free transferability of interests in them, and (4) centralized management.
- A joint venture is a form of business ownership that resembles a partnership, except that there are no general or limited partners and the purpose of the entity is very limited.
- Professional corporations, a form of ownership often preferred by physicians, attorneys, and other professionals, provide limited liability to shareholders but are subject to double taxation.
- In recent decades, many laws designed to protect the health and rights of employees have been enacted (e.g., OSHA, the Americans with Disabilities Act, the Immigration Reform and Control Act). Entrepreneurs need a working knowledge of these laws to avoid violating them.
- Another aspect of the law with which entrepreneurs should be familiar is that governing contracts—promises that are enforceable by law.
- Key elements of contracts are legality (the contract must be designed to accomplish a legal purpose), agreement (a legitimate offer and legitimate acceptance), consideration (something of value must be exchanged), and capacity (the persons involved must be capable of entering into a contract).

- If contracts are violated, the damaged party can seek redress in the form of compensatory damages or specific performance by the party that violated the contract.
- In choosing an attorney for a new venture, it is usually best to select one who has experience in business matters and who has solid legal credentials.
- Franchising is a system of distribution in which semi-independent business owners (franchisees) pay fees and royalties to a parent company (the franchisor) in return for the right to use its trademark, sell its products or services, and, in many cases, use the business model and system it has developed.
- Two basic types of franchising exist: trade-name franchising, and business format franchising.

- Franchising offers important benefits to franchisees including training and support, standardized products, national advertising, site selection, and a business model that works.
- However, franchising also has a downside: Franchisees must pay substantial fees and royalties, they must deal with enforced standardization, and they have restricted freedom over purchasing and product lines.
- Franchising is regulated by the government, which requires that all prospective franchisees be given extensive information about the franchise agreement before signing it.
- Current trends in franchising include smaller outlets in nontraditional locations, co-branding franchising, international franchising, and a large expansion in the kinds of businesses being franchised.

Glossary

Breach of Contract: A legal term referring to situations in which two parties have a legal contract and one fails to comply with the terms of the agreement.

Business Format Franchising: A type of franchising in which franchisees are provided with a complete business system by the franchisor—a trademarked name, the products or services to be sold, the buildings in which the business will be operated, a marketing strategy, methods of actually operating the business, quality control, and assistance in actually running the business.

Contracts: Promises that are enforceable by law.

Corporations: Legal entities separate from their owners that may engage in business, make contracts, own property, pay taxes, and sue and be sued by others.

Franchising: A system of distribution in which semi-independent business owners (franchisees) pay fees and royalties to a parent company (the franchisor) in return for the right to use its trademark, sell its products or services, and, in many cases, use the business model and system it has developed.

Immigration Reform and Control Act of 1986: A law designed to accomplish two major goals: discourage illegal immigration into the United States and strengthen the national origin provision of Title VII of the Civil Rights Act (1964).

Joint Venture: A form of business ownership that resembles a partnership, except that there are no general or limited partners, and the purpose of the entity is very limited.

Limited Liability Company (LLC): A cross between a corporation and partnership, offering some of the benefits of both. As is true in S corporations, income flows through to owners (known as "members") who pay their own taxes as individuals. Unlike S corporations, however, LLCs are not subject to so many government restrictions.

Limited Partnership: A partnership in which one or more partners are general partners who manage the business and others are limited partners who invest in the business but forego any right to manage the company.

Partnership: An association of two or more people who co-own a business for the purpose of making a profit.

Partnership Agreement: A document written with the assistance of an attorney, and that states all of the terms under which the partnership will operate.

Professional Corporation (PC): A form of business ownership in which owners have limited liability; generally restricted to professionals such as physicians, attorneys, and accountants.

S Corporation: Corporations in which all profits and losses are passed through to shareholders, just as they are passed through to partners in a partnership.

Sole Proprietorship: A type of business ownership in which a business is owned and managed by one individual.

Trade-Name Franchising: A type of franchising in which franchisors grant independent business owners the right to use the franchisor's name.

Unlimited Personal Liability: Occurs when business owners are personally liable for all of debts incurred by the business.

Discussion Questions

1. Recent court decisions have challenged the view that persons who own shares in corporations have limited liability for debts or actions of the corporation. What are the consequences of these court rulings for entrepreneurs?

2. In recent months, the U.S. Congress has begun to consider legislation that would eliminate double taxation on corporate dividends. If this legislation is enacted, do you think it will have positive or negative consequences for entrepreneurs?

3. Would you ever become a limited partner in a limited partnership? Why? Why not?

4. What are the advantages of a joint venture over a corporation? Of a corporation over a joint venture?

5. Why should entrepreneurs become familiar with laws designed to protect the safety and well-being of employees?

6. Suppose that one of your customers promises you an order but then does not place it. Can you sue this customer under contract law?

7. How can a franchisor considering the possibility of entering a foreign market find out, in advance, whether its products or services will be well-received in this new market?

InfoTrac Exercises

1. **Corporate Choice** (recent federal tax cuts effect on type of corporations)
   Ashlea Ebeling
   Forbes, July 7, 2003 v171 i14 p126
   Record: A104004189
   Full Text: COPYRIGHT 2003 *Forbes, Inc. C corp? S corp? LLC? The new tax law creates some new wrinkles.*

   1. Why have S corporations and other "passthrough" entities become more popular than traditional C corporations in recent years?

   2. How do tax cuts affect the type of corporation you might choose for your new business?

   3. Why, according to Peter Faber, is the LLC still the best choice for new businesses?

2. **Franchising Likely to Grow as Recently Jobless Seek to Mind Their Businesses** (opinion)
   Jerry Wilkerson
   Nation's Restaurant News, May 26, 2003 v37 i21 p27(2)
   Record: A102659658
   Full Text: COPYRIGHT 2003 Reproduced with permission of the copyright holder. Further reproduction or distribution is prohibited without permission.

   1. According to the text, what are the benefits of becoming a franchisee?

   2. According to the article, why do franchises grow in difficult economic conditions?

   3. What challenges do franchisees face in difficult economic conditions?

GETTING DOWN
TO BUSINESS

Choosing the Best Form for Your New Venture

Many entrepreneurs assume that the best form for their new venture is a regular corporation. In fact, though, this may not be true. Many other options exist (e.g., partnerships, limited liability companies, joint ventures, etc.) and choosing among them depends on the goals the entrepreneur wants to reach and which features of these many business forms are more important to the entrepreneur. Which of these business forms is best for *your* new venture? To gain practice in deciding, answer each of the following questions:

1. **How many owners will there be?**

2. **It is important for you to have limited liability?** (For instance, this may be relatively important to you if you have lots of personal wealth; if you do not, it may be less important.)

3. **Is transferability of ownership important or unimportant?**

4. **Do you anticipate that your new venture will pay any dividends?** If so, how important is to you that such dividends will be subject to double taxation?

5. **If you decide to leave the business, do you care whether it can continue to operate without you?**

6. **How important is keeping the costs of forming the business low?**

7. **How important is the ability to raise additional capital in the future as needed?**

Consider your answers in terms of the features of various business forms summarized in Table 8.1. On the basis of this information, rule out business forms that would definitely *not* meet your goals or requirements, and then choose among the remaining ones on the basis of how close a match they provide to these goals.

Is Franchising for You?

Franchising is a rapidly expanding activity. In fact, new franchises are being started every day, and the number is now in the thousands. Just because franchising is popular, though, doesn't necessarily mean that it is for you. To decide whether you should consider this option for owning your own business, answer the following questions:

1. How important is it to you to get help in starting your business—such things as training and support, standardized products, national advertising, site selection, and a proven business model that works? (These are the kinds of help often offered by successful franchisors.)

2. How important is it to you to really be your own boss—to be able to make decisions about running your business, the nature of your products or services, suppliers, advertising, and so on? (This will usually not be possible if you are a franchisee.)

3. How important is it to you to receive ongoing help in running your business—such things as assistance in hiring and training employees, continuous feedback on what you are doing right and what you are doing wrong, etc.?

4. What are your ultimate goals with respect to running your own business—to make money and have a secure life? Create something really new that changes people's lives? Obtain the personal freedom that can only come from being your own boss?

5. How important is it to you that the products or services you offer are well-known to potential customers—that they recognize the name over the door even if they have never visited your business before?

Consider your answers carefully in the light of the discussion in this chapter of the benefits and drawbacks to becoming a franchisee. Only you can decide whether franchises offer what you want out of running a business—and out of life. But answering these questions carefully and fully will at least help you make this decision in a rational manner. Whatever your choice—independent business or franchise—good luck!

Enhanced Learning

You may select any combination of the case options below to enhance your understanding of the chapter material.

- **Appendix 1: Case Studies –** Thirteen cases provide opportunities to apply chapter concepts to realistic entrepreneurial situations. These brief cases call for careful analysis of real business problems and ask you to think about potential solutions.

- **Appendix 2: Video Case Library –** Nine cases are tied directly to video segments from the popular PBS television series *Small Business School*. These cases and video segments give you unparalleled access to today's entrepreneurs, with expert advice and insights on how to start, run, and grow a business.

- **Comprehensive Cases –** Visit the book support Web site at http://baron.swlearning.com for cases detailing real businesses whose successes and setbacks illustrate each stage of the entrepreneurial process. You will conduct in-depth analysis of entrepreneurial challenges through well-developed case studies.

Notes

1. Chief Justice John Marshall, cited by Miller, R.L., & Jentz, G.A. 1994. *Business law today*. St. Paul, MN: West Publishing Co.
2. Buss, D.D. 1999. New dynamics for a new era. *Nation's Business* (June 1999): 45-48.
3. Tiffany, L. 1999. Breaking the mold. *Business start-ups* (April), 42–47.
4. Azoulay, P., & Shane, S. 2001. Entrepreneurs, contracts and the failure of young firms. *Management Science* 47(3): 337–358.
5. Torres, N.L. 2003. Do the math. Subway is the No. 1 franchise in Entrepreneurs' Franchise 500 . . . for the 11th time. *Entrepreneur* (January): 148, 150.
6. Michael, S.C. 2002. Can a franchise chain coordinate? *Journal of Business Venturing* 17: 325–341.
7. Bates, T. 1994. A comparison of franchise and independent small business survival rates. *Small Business Economics* 7: 1–12.
8. Holmberg, S.R., & Morgan, K.B. 2002. Franchise turnover and failure: New research and perspectives. *Journal of Business Venturing* 18: 403–418.
9. Stanworth, J., & Curran, J. 1999. Colas, burgers, shakes, and shirkers: Towards a sociological model of franchising in the market economy. *Journal of Business Venturing* 14: 323–344.
10. Maddocks, T.D. 2003. Driving forward. Jack and Diane look for new ways to get their small-business dreams moving. Will franchising be the right direction? *Entrepreneur* (March): 86, 88.

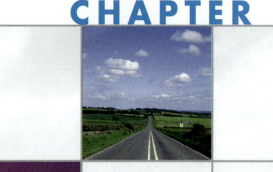
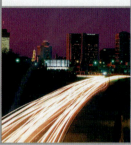

CHAPTER 9

MARKETING IN A NEW FIRM

LEARNING OBJECTIVES

After reading this chapter, you should be able to:

1 Identify a real customer need and explain why an entrepreneur should seek to develop a product or service that meets a real need.

2 Explain why entrepreneurs use different techniques to assess customer preferences in new and established markets, and identify those different techniques.

3 Explain conjoint analysis and indicate what information it provides for entrepreneurs.

4 Explain how large and growing markets help entrepreneurs.

5 Define the new product S-curve, and explain why it is important for entrepreneurs to understand the relationship between effort and product performance.

6 Describe the typical new product adoption pattern and explain how it influences entrepreneurial action.

7 Define "crossing the chasm" and explain why and how entrepreneurs "cross the chasm."

8 Explain how entrepreneurs should choose the customers to focus their initial efforts on.

9 Define a "dominant design" and a "technical standard" and explain how they influence the performance of new ventures.

10 Explain why personal selling is a very important part of entrepreneurs' marketing strategies.

11 Describe how entrepreneurs price new products.

Assessing The Market
Starting with a Real Need
Assessing Customer Preferences and the Market for New Products and Services
Conjoint Analysis: Determining Which Dimensions Are Most Important

Market Dynamics
Knowing Your Market: The Importance of Market Size and Market Growth
Timing the Market: The S-Curve Story

Achieving Market Acceptance
Adoption Patterns: Understanding Which Customers Adopt When
Moving from Early Adopters to the Early Majority
Focus: Choosing the Right Customers to Target First
Dominant Design: Product Convergence and Its Effect on New Ventures
Technical Standards: Getting Customers to Adopt Your Design as the Market Standard

The Marketing Process in a New Company
Personal Selling: The Central Component of Entrepreneurial Marketing
Pricing New Products: The Role of Cost Structure and Supply and Demand

"Try novelties for salesman's bait, for novelty wins everyone." (Goethe, *Faust: Part I*, 1808, Tr. Philip Wayne)

Recently, many publishers have been telling authors that electronic books will soon replace "real" books. This happened to me (Scott Shane) last year, when one large publisher suggested that I write an electronic textbook. The basic idea was simple: Students would purchase an access code that would allow them to view and download their textbook from a special Internet site. Students could then, at their discretion, highlight various sections, enter notes to help their studying, print individual chapters, or do anything else they wished to their electronic textbooks. I was a little skeptical; books are, after all, very convenient products. They can be carried through airport security without setting off alarms, can be read almost anywhere, even in places where no source of power is available, and they have additional uses, too—for instance, they, can be used to prop open doors and can even serve as makeshift fly-swatters!! All this led me to wonder: Would students really give up regular books for e-books in the next few years? The answer was quick in coming: No! Sales of the e-book versions of most texts are miniscule. Given a choice, students overwhelmingly choose books in their traditional form.

This outcome raises an intriguing question: Why did people invest millions of dollars in these ill-fated e-book projects? Didn't they do their homework first, to find out if anyone would want to buy this kind of product? The answer is complex and contains important lessons for entrepreneurs. In essence here is what happened: The companies involved *did* try to find out, in advance, whether students would buy these books—they conducted marketing research. But, as is frequently the case when entrepreneurs pursue new technology, it is very difficult to gauge the market for something that hasn't yet been introduced. Moreover, as the S-shaped curve in Figure 9.1 shows, when new products based on new technologies are introduced, they are often inferior in performance to existing alternatives and therefore are not adopted by mainstream customers. Only after further development has been undertaken to improve the new product's performance does it begin to perform better than the existing alternatives, and mainstream customers begin to adopt it in large numbers. The moral of this story is that talking to customers is only one part of the process of developing and marketing a new product. Gathering information in a way that gets useful answers, and understanding how new product performance develops, are also very important.

Figure 9.1 The Transition from Traditional Books to E-Books

When a new product based on a new technology is introduced, it often has inferior performance to the product it replaces. However, the new product makes up for this initial disadvantage as effort is put into improving it.

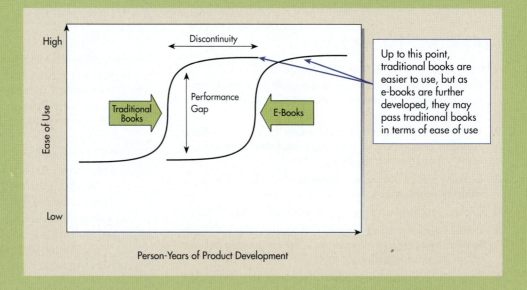

The remainder of this chapter will expand on marketing in a new firm. In the first section, we will discuss how entrepreneurs assess markets and customer needs. We will explain why it is important for entrepreneurs to develop new products or services to meet *real* customer needs—truly solving unsolved customer problems or offering products or services that are significantly better than existing alternatives. We will also explain how the appropriate techniques for entrepreneurs to use in order to assess markets and customer needs—focus groups, surveys, discussions with users, extrapolation of trends, discussions with experts, and so on—depend on whether the product or service would open up a new market or would be used in an existing market. The first section will also explain how entrepreneurs use **conjoint analysis** to determine the relative importance to customers of different product features.

In the second section, we will discuss market dynamics and explain what entrepreneurs need to know about them. We will explain why it is so important for entrepreneurs to estimate the size and growth rate of the market that they are entering when they begin their new ventures. In this section, we will also discuss how new products develop in the S-shaped pattern first described at the beginning of the chapter, and explain what this pattern of product development means for entrepreneurs, particularly for their timing of market entry.

In the third section, we will discuss how entrepreneurs achieve mainstream market acceptance for their new products and services. We will describe the typical adoption pattern for new products and services and explain why it is normally distributed, with few adoptions occurring early, many more later on, and then fewer later still. We will also discuss how entrepreneurs transition from the early adopters of new products and services to the early majority of adopters. This section will also explain why it is important for entrepreneurs to focus on a single product or service when their ventures begin and how they should choose which customers to target first. The third section will also discuss dominant designs for new products and how the tendency of products to converge on a single design over time influences the performance of new ventures. Finally, this section will also explain how technical standards influence new product adoption and how entrepreneurs can get customers to adopt their products as the **technical standard** in the market that they are targeting.

In the final section of the chapter, we will focus on the marketing process in new companies. We will discuss why entrepreneurs focus on personal selling as their main marketing tool, as opposed to relying heavily on advertising or brand name reputation to sell their products the way that many established companies do. This section will also discuss how entrepreneurs price their new products, focusing on the influence of the new venture's cost structure and supply and demand for products in the market.

ASSESSING THE MARKET

As we discussed in Chapter 4, successful entrepreneurs do not launch companies and begin to offer new products and services without first gathering information about the market and customer preferences. In particular, successful entrepreneurs make sure that there is a real need for their new product or service; assess customer preferences for the attributes of the new product or service that they are considering offering; and identify the key dimensions of customer needs that their product or service is meeting.

Starting with a Real Need

Successful entrepreneurs develop new products and services that are based on real customer needs. This sounds pretty obvious, right? Maybe, but surprisingly few entrepreneurs develop products that meet a real need; most end up failing to generate any sales. Why? Most entrepreneurs become enamored of the idea of starting a company and do not pay enough attention to whether they can provide a product or service that is better than existing alternatives. For example, when I (Scott Shane) was teaching at the Sloan School at MIT, one student proposed a business to provide Internet delivery of soap and shampoo. This being MIT, the other students in the class immediately assumed that he was going to come up with a complex electronic system for this product, and asked how he intended to put electronic sensors in the soap and shampoo dispensers so that the toiletries would automatically be ordered when they ran low. The student responded that he wasn't going to use electronic sensors; his business idea was just that people would go onto the Internet and order shampoo and soap when they ran low. When I asked why there was a need to order shampoo and soap over the Internet, as opposed to just going to the grocery store to

LEARNING OBJECTIVE

1 Identify a real customer need and explain why an entrepreneur should seek to develop a product or service that meets a real need.

get these items, the student answered that he could never remember to buy toiletries when he went to the grocery, and figured that this problem would be solved by Internet toiletry delivery. In reality, however, there is no need for this service. Unlike this student, most people can remember to stop at the drugstore or supermarket to buy toiletries. Even the most absent-minded people can run out to a 24-hour supermarket or drugstore to get these items at the last minute—especially when the alternative is to wait three days for UPS to deliver the online order of soap! So, although this entrepreneur thought he was serving customers, his business idea did not meet a *real* customer need (see Figure 9.2).

What does it mean for a *real* customer need to exist? It's a real need when customers have a problem that they want solved, but no existing products or services can do this. For example, a drug that cures lung cancer would meet a real need. Nothing today treats this disease very well, and people who have the disease would like a cure. A product or service also meets a real need when it is so much better at solving a problem that customers are motivated to switch to the new product or service from an existing alternative. Notice that we said "so much better at solving." Because people tend to prefer the status quo, a new product or service has to be much better than an old one to get people to switch to it. Just slightly better is rarely enough to motivate customers to change. For example, a microchip that triples computer-processing speed would meet a real need, but one that improved processing speed by 2 percent probably would not.

How do successful entrepreneurs determine whether there is a real customer need for a new product or service? In general, they follow a 4-step process. First, they look for customer problems. We will talk more about this a little later in the chapter, but basically, successful entrepreneurs search out problems that customers have that aren't being solved adequately. What gets customers frustrated? What makes them complain? Those things are usually the sign of a problem that represents a real customer need. For example, are people in the accounting departments of several companies complaining that the software they use is inadequate to manage both their payroll and inventory? If customers complain that they need to integrate records from different aspects of their business and existing accounting software can't do this, then customers might really need better, more integrated software.

Once the entrepreneur has figured out that customers have a real problem that is not being solved, the second step is to come up with a true solution to that problem.

Figure 9.2 To Succeed, a New Business Must Satisfy a Real Customer Need

Is there a need for this product? We doubt it. Because the product does not satisfy a real customer need, founding a company to exploit it would probably not make good business sense.

Otherwise, from an entrepreneur's perspective, it doesn't really matter that customers have an unsolved problem. In our accounting software example, it wouldn't matter that customers want software to integrate inventory and payroll records if the entrepreneur can't write software that would integrate the two any better than existing accounting software. If the entrepreneur's software were no better than existing alternatives, there would be no reason for him to start a new business to produce software.

But suppose that the customers have a real problem, and the entrepreneur has a true solution to that problem; the third step in the process is to figure out the economics of satisfying the customer's need. For example, it would only make sense for the entrepreneur to start a new business to offer a solution to the customer need for integrated accounting software if she could offer her product at a price that customers would pay and still make a profit. If the entrepreneur could develop the solution, but it would cost more than customers would be willing to pay for it, then starting a company to offer the new software wouldn't be worthwhile.

The final step in the process is to identify any alternatives to the entrepreneur's solution that exist or will come out in the very near future. This step is often the hardest for entrepreneurs to manage because people tend to convince themselves that the solutions that they come up with are better than those offered by anyone else. However, successful entrepreneurs know that they need to critically compare their solutions to solutions offered by others, keeping their egos from getting involved. To do this well, entrepreneurs often need to talk directly to potential customers or third parties to get a realistic opinion on the value of their solutions in comparison to other alternatives. For example, our accounting software entrepreneur might show her software and alternative software to accounting software experts and ask them what they think of them. Only if the entrepreneur's new product or service were actually better than the alternatives would there be a reason to start a new business.

Fixx Services, Inc., a retail management services company founded by Mark Bucher in Bethesda, Maryland, is a good example of a company established to exploit a real customer need. Bucher founded the company when he learned from restaurant and retail store owners that they needed a facility management service that would allow them to call one telephone number to get help with broken windows, plumbing problems, snow removal, and so on, rather than contracting with separate vendors for each of these services. Not only does Fixx Services take the headache out of finding all of these vendors—a real need for customers—but also customers can obtained discounted services from the vendors, who offer them reduced prices because of the referrals that Fixx Services provides.[1]

Assessing Customer Preferences and the Market for New Products and Services

As we explained in Chapter 4, entrepreneurs often need to gather information from potential customers when developing their new businesses. To do this, they use a variety of techniques, including focus groups, surveys, and conversations with existing customers and users of similar products. However, they also use other techniques, such as observation of customers, discussions with industry experts, and examination of trends.[2]

So how do entrepreneurs know what techniques to use to gather information from customers? The first step is to determine the kind of market that they're targeting. Is the target market already well-established, like the market for automobiles? Or is the target market new, like the market for Internet-based auction houses in the early 1990s? When the target market is already established, the process of assessing the market and customer preferences is much easier than when the target market is new, and generally involves using the focus groups and surveys that we discussed in detail in Chapter 4. The reason is that when the target market is established, customer preferences are not very uncertain because the basic characteristics of those preferences are known. For instance, anyone who wants to sell automobiles today pretty much knows what the market wants in a car. In addition, when the target market is established, customers find it much easier to communicate their preferences to entrepreneurs. This exchange

LEARNING OBJECTIVE

2 Explain why entrepreneurs use different techniques to assess customer preferences in new and established markets, and identify those different techniques.

of information makes it much easier to establish the good survey and focus group questions that we explained in Chapter 4 are essential to getting useful feedback from these techniques.

The second step is to figure out what kind of new product or service you are developing. Is your solution to customer needs already known and understood or is it a novel solution? For example, a faster processing computer chip made of silicon would be a well-known and understood solution because existing computer chips are made of silicon. In this example, the entrepreneur is producing a faster chip that works more or less the same way as previous chips. But there have been times when computer manufacturers offered novel solutions to the problem of making computers process information faster, as occurred when computer manufacturers shifted from using vacuum tubes to transistors and again from transistors to microchips. In the case of both of these transitions, the solution to the customer problem was based on new science and engineering and so was not well known or well understood by customers.

Similar to the case with a known target market, when knowledge of the solution is well known, the process of assessing the market and customer preferences is much easier. Entrepreneurs can again rely on the focus groups and survey techniques that we discussed in Chapter 4. Table 9.1 summarizes when different approaches to gathering information about customer preferences work the best. As the table shows, when the target market and solutions are well known, traditional market research techniques are quite effective. In contrast, when the target market and solutions are not well known, traditional market research techniques tend to do very poorly. Under these conditions, the people in the focus groups and surveys don't know enough to give you useful answers. For instance, when the laser and the photocopier first appeared, potential customers surveyed about these products said that there would be no use for them. In large part, this was because people could not envision the ways in which these products would ultimately be used.

So what should you do when the market or the solution you are offering is really novel? Under these circumstances, successful entrepreneurs have discussions with industry experts and extrapolate trends to figure out what features to include in new products and services. But be careful. These techniques appear to work best when the market or the solution is really new. When the market or the solution is well known, traditional market research techniques work better. You really have to know your target market and your product before deciding which techniques to use or you will get yourself into some serious trouble.

What about situations in which either the target market or the solution is known, but the other is not? Then the entrepreneur needs a blend of traditional market research techniques and futurist approaches. In these cases, anthropological expeditions, in which entrepreneurs put themselves in the shoes of the customer, or having in-depth conversations with early adopters and lead users of new products, or partnering with customers to develop the products often prove to be very effective strategies for learning about customer preferences.[3]

Although entrepreneurs can develop new products and services for existing markets using known solutions, they are far better off focusing on creating new products and services for new markets using new solutions. Why? The answer is that entrepreneurs are not the only people who develop new products and services. The managers of established companies do the same thing, often with more people and money behind the projects. To introduce a new product or service successfully, the

Table 9.1 Market Research Techniques Depend on the Type of Market

Entrepreneurs use different techniques to learn about customer needs in new and existing markets.

	EXISTING MARKET	NEW MARKET
Philosophy of market research	Deductive data analysis	Intuition
Techniques for gathering customer information	Focus groups, surveys, mall studies	Industry experts, trend extrapolation, future scenarios
Examples	New types of toothpaste, new car models	Internet auction houses, telephone

Source: Based on information contained in Barton, D. *Commercializing Technology: Imaginative Understanding of User Needs.* Harvard Business School Note 9-694-102.

entrepreneur not only has to satisfy a market need, but she also has to do so better than competitors. It really helps if the entrepreneur can introduce a new product or service that established companies aren't trying to develop, too.

When markets already exist, or new products are based on known solutions to customer problems, new firms are at a real disadvantage relative to established companies. Because established companies have already sold their products to customers, they have already gathered a large amount of information about customer preferences. Have you ever used a credit card at a retailer like JC Penney? That credit card allows the retailer to know exactly what you purchased, when you purchased it, how much you spent, whether it was on sale, whether you used a coupon, and so on. This information makes it pretty easy for JC Penney to figure out what your preferences are when they launch a new product, especially in comparison to an entrepreneur who is competing with JC Penney and is launching a new product for the first time.

When the market is new or the solution to customer needs is novel, however, entrepreneurs can offset the advantages that existing companies have in understanding customer preferences. Dorothy Leonard Barton, a professor at the Harvard Business School, has explained that existing companies have three major disadvantages when serving new markets with novel solutions to customer needs. The first, which she calls **core rigidities**, means that companies do well at things that they are accustomed to doing, not at doing things that are new. Existing companies aren't very good at coming up with new products to serve new markets or that are based on new solutions to customer needs because they have a hard time breaking away from old ways of doing things.

The second disadvantage of established firms, which professor Barton calls **tyranny of the current market**, means that established companies have a hard time coming up with new products for new markets because they listen to their customers. This might sound strange—after all, your marketing textbook probably told you how important it is to listen to your customers, and it is if you want to continue to serve your *existing* customers. However, listening to *existing* customers will make it difficult for a company to come up with new products for *new* markets. The reason? A firm's existing customers will always ask for improvements to current products, not for products for new markets. As a result, existing customers will keep established companies focused on making improvements to current products rather than on looking for ways to target new customers.

The third disadvantage of established firms is something professor Barton calls **user myopia**. This means that customers of existing firms can only see very narrow needs or solutions. Typically, they might see their own needs, but not the needs of other potential customers. This creates big problems when a new product is very useful for a different market. For example, when Halloid Corporation, the precursor to Xerox, introduced the first photocopy machine, its representatives went to the only people who reproduced documents at the time—offset printers—and asked them what they thought of the machines. The printers responded that they had no use for them; offset printing worked just fine. Fortunately, Halloid Corporation didn't listen to the printers because this was a classic case of user myopia. Sure, offset printing worked just fine for printers, who didn't need photocopiers. But, as you know, there was a huge need for photocopiers—in schools, offices, libraries, and so on. The printers didn't see this use because they couldn't see the needs and preferences of other segments of the market.[4]

The lesson here is counterintuitive. Although entrepreneurs often want to go after established markets with well-known solutions to customer needs because it is easier, that isn't the best approach. Entrepreneurs actually do better when they launch products based on novel solutions to customer needs in new markets. When established companies have sold products based on an older solution for a long time or when the market is so new and demand so unknown that it is very difficult to do much market research, entrepreneurs who launch businesses with novel products tend to do very well.

Conjoint Analysis: Determining Which Dimensions Are Most Important

Why do customers choose one product over another? Presumably, because the product they select offers an optimal combination of features—high rankings along the dimensions customers view as most important. But which of these dimensions weigh most heavily on customers' preferences and decisions? Price? Size? Weight? What about various combinations of these features? For instance, will customers accept larger size in return for a lower price?

Simply asking consumers "Which dimensions are most important to you?" will not solve this puzzle. Although people *believe* that they can explain why they behave as they do, a large body of evidence indicates that, in fact, they are not very good at this task: They don't really know the reasons they make various decisions.[5] For instance, recently, I visited a relative who had just purchased a huge SUV—one of the largest on the market. As he maneuvered this gigantic vehicle through dense city traffic, I asked him why he had decided to buy it. His answer? "I don't know . . . it just makes me feel good to drive it." I'm sure he had reasons for choosing this SUV, but he could certainly not describe them to me clearly.

A solution to this mystery is provided by **conjoint analysis**.[6] Conjoint analysis asks individuals to express their preferences for various products that are specially chosen to offer a *systematic array* of features. For instance, remember the lost object locator from Chapter 4? Perceptual mapping showed that people had different preferences about price, size, loudness of locater signal, weight, and battery life. To determine the relative importance of each of these dimensions for consumers, entrepreneurs present examples of locator devices (real, or perhaps just in photos or other images) to potential customers and ask them to indicate the likelihood that they would purchase each one. The products are specifically designed so that they are low or high on each of the key dimensions. For instance, one product would be high on the first dimension (price), but would be low on the others: size, loudness, weight, and battery life. A second would be low on price, as well as low on all the others, and so on. Because there are five different dimensions, this would generate a large number of products: 2 (low, high) × 2 (low, high) × 2 (low, high) × 2 (low, high) × 2 (low, high) = 32. Consumers might be shown pairs of items and asked to choose between them. Alternatively, they could be shown one at a time and asked to indicate the likelihood that they would purchase it (e.g., on a 7-point scale where 1 = very unlikely to buy it and 7 = very likely to buy it). As you can see, if the number of dimensions is large (e.g., 7 instead of 5) and if the products can be high, moderate, or low on each, the number of combinations would quickly get out of hand (e.g., 3 × 3 × 3 × 3 × 3 × 3 × 3 = 2,187). To reduce this problem, conjoint analysis often uses a *fractional factorial design*—only a fraction of all the combinations are presented to consumers. How is this fraction chosen? Largely on the basis of preliminary evidence from perceptual mapping. For instance, if perceptual mapping suggested that price, size, and loudness of signal are the most important dimensions, these would be fully represented in the array of products, while other dimensions might be represented only in combination with others. The data gathered by conjoint analysis (participants' ratings of each product or choices between them) are then analyzed statistically (e.g., by regression analysis). The results of such analyses indicate the relative importance of each variable (i.e., size, weight, loudness, etc.) in participant's decisions.

Although the statistical details of conjoint analysis are beyond the scope of this discussion, the overall strategy is straightforward: Instead of asking potential customers to tell us which dimensions are most important to them in choosing between various products, they actually make these choices, and their selections or stated preferences provide the information we seek.

Conjoint analysis can provide extremely valuable marketing information to entrepreneurs. Once they know what features are most important to consumers, entrepreneurs can build these into their new products, and so maximize the chances of success. In contrast, just going to market without gathering this information often leads to problematic results.

Given the importance to entrepreneurs of gathering and analyzing information from customers, most entrepreneurs try to gather customer information before they launch their new products. But some entrepreneurs do not gather adequate information before moving forward. Certainly, some of these entrepreneurs don't gather adequate information from customers before they start because they haven't taken entrepreneurship courses and read books like this one that explain why doing so is important. However, often entrepreneurs know that gathering information from customers is important, but fail to gather this information anyway because of the time and money pressures that they face. Sometimes, entrepreneurs don't gather information from customers because they don't have enough money to pay for focus groups, interviews, surveys, or other efforts to obtain customer information and still pay for the costs of developing the product itself. Other times, entrepreneurs don't gather information because they are worried that another entrepreneur will get to the market before them or because they are concerned that the opportunity will disappear before they can get their product out. For example, an entrepreneur in the fashion industry might want to survey customers about her new fall line of clothing, but realizes that, if she spends the time gathering information, she will be unable to get her clothing into retail stores until after Halloween, clearly too late to launch a fall line. The moral of this story is that gathering information from customers is important, but entrepreneurs often have to make difficult choices between spending their limited capital on assessing customer needs or spending it on other things, and between gathering information and meeting windows of opportunity in the market before they close (see Figure 9.3).

DILBERT reprinted by permission of United Feature Syndicate, Inc.

Figure 9.3 Entrepreneurs Need to Analyze Market Needs

Entrepreneurs often face a tension between meeting a market window and conducting the market research necessary to learn about the market.

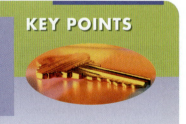

KEY POINTS

- Entrepreneurs are most successful when they start a company that meets a real need: a customer problem no products or services can solve or new product or service that is so much better at solving the problem that customers are motivated to switch.
- Entrepreneurs assess customer preferences differently when markets are new than when they are already established; entrepreneurs need to adopt the right assessment techniques for the type of market they are targeting.
- Entrepreneurs are better off targeting new markets than established markets because established firms face three obstacles in assessing new markets: core rigidities, the tyranny of the current market, and user myopia.
- Conjoint analysis is a useful technique for determining the relative importance, in the customer's preferences and decisions, of the dimensions that they consider important.
- Through the effective use of conjoint analysis, entrepreneurs can design products that will have high appeal to potential customers, and so maximize the chances of success of their new ventures.

MARKET DYNAMICS

Successful entrepreneurs realize that all markets are not equal. They understand that some markets, like the market for golf clubs, are larger than other markets, like the market for ping pong paddles. Successful entrepreneurs also realize that markets grow at different rates; for instance, the market for SUVs is currently growing much faster than the market for muscle cars. Last, they recognize that markets evolve as new products are born, mature, and grow old. Therefore, successful entrepreneurs understand the dynamics of the markets that they are thinking of entering before they begin their companies and launch their new products or services to make sure that they adopt the right marketing strategy for that market. In this section, we introduce you to some of the key market dynamics that successful entrepreneurs exploit to their advantage.

Knowing Your Market: The Importance of Market Size and Market Growth

One basic question that entrepreneurs need to ask when developing a marketing plan for their new venture is "How large is the market?" A large market is important because new businesses have a fixed cost to get started. The smaller the market, the lower will be the potential sales for the new venture and the higher share of the market the entrepreneur will need to obtain just to cover the cost of getting started. Moreover, a new venture can enter a large market without drawing a lot of attention from competitors, who notice what's going on in the market much more easily in small markets. Because the new venture often is not yet ready to compete—its products haven't been developed, its employees haven't been hired, and so on—going in "under the radar," as venture capitalists call it, is very important.

Entrepreneurs also need to determine how quickly the market is growing. A rapidly growing market is advantageous to entrepreneurs because it affects the sales process. In a stagnant market, the only way for a company to make sales is to take customers away from other companies. However, in a rapidly growing market, a company can grow quickly by serving customers who had not previously been customers in the market. It is much easier to capture new customers than customers served by other firms because in the latter case the other firms will compete with you to keep their customers. In addition, a rapidly growing market is beneficial to entrepreneurs because rapid growth means a larger volume of customers, providing the benefits of volume purchasing and scale economies that lower the entrepreneur's costs.

Timing the Market: The S-Curve Story

As we explained in the beginning of the chapter, products have life cycles that influence the ability of entrepreneurs to enter markets with new products. Researchers have shown that when products are first introduced, they are often inferior to alternative products on many of the dimensions that are important to customers, like quality, reliability, and performance.[7] For example, the first automobiles could not travel as far or go as fast as the typical horse and buggy that people used for transportation at the time. However, firms work their way up the learning curve as they figure out how to improve their products. They add new features, improve speed, enhance reliability, or otherwise make the new products better along the dimensions that customers care about.

Initially, this improvement is slow because learning new things is difficult. Many ideas about how to improve the product turn out to be dead ends. Moreover, as soon as people solve one problem, they often face another, precluding them from gaining rapid performance improvement. For example, when people built the first airplanes, each initial effort to improve the wings and the engines yielded only a few feet of additional flight. But after working through a variety of design problems, the early airplane entrepreneurs figured out the key solutions to wing and engine problems, and flight performance improved dramatically. This rapid improvement in performance continues for awhile, until it reaches a level of diminishing returns, where each amount of effort to improve yields very little benefit in terms of performance. For example, making an airplane capable of flying one additional mile takes much more of an investment than it took to get earlier airplanes to increase their range from one to two miles. As you probably figured out, this pattern of new product performance is shaped like an "S." Researchers call it the "**S-curve**."[8] In Figure 9.4, we show the S-curve for computer memory.

We have just described the S-curve for a successful new product. If things always worked the way we just described, then companies would produce new products all of the time, knowing that they would eventually perform better than the older products they already have. However, new products don't always end up performing better than old ones—or they do, but it takes so long that it isn't worthwhile developing the new product. For instance, in the 1970s, many people thought that nuclear power would replace fossil fuels like oil and coal in making electricity. Unfortunately for them, the entrepreneurs developing nuclear power plants ran into large obstacles in improving the safety of the plants. So nuclear power has never achieved superior performance to oil and coal in producing electricity on all the dimensions that customers care about. Although it might some day in the future, the fact that it hasn't for 30 years has meant that entrepreneurs who tried to launch companies to make electricity using nuclear power in the 1970s were unable to replace alternative products, like coal and oil, in a short enough time frame to survive.

The product development S-curve has important implications for entrepreneurs. First, introducing novel products is very difficult for entrepreneurs because new products start out with inferior performance on the dimensions that customers care about than existing product alternatives. To survive this early period, entrepreneurs need to find a source of capital that can sustain them until they can develop their new product's performance, or find a market segment that doesn't care that much about the performance of the new product and is willing to adopt it.

Second, entrepreneurs need to recognize that new product improvement is a function of effort, not time. Unless someone invests in the development of the new product, it will never become as good as existing product alternatives. Often, the entrepreneur can't just wait until the product is good enough to compete with existing products. If the entrepreneur doesn't produce the new product, it will never be as good as existing alternatives.

Third, identifying the point of acceleration in the S-curve is an important entrepreneurial skill. By knowing when a new product's performance is about to take off,

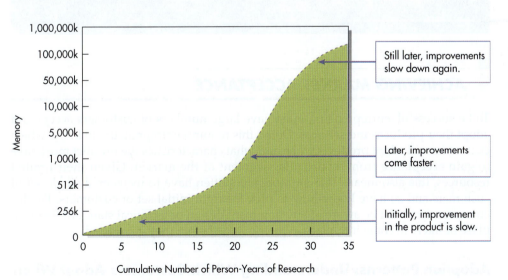

Figure 9.4 The S-Curve for Computer Memory

Entrepreneurs need to be aware that their new product introductions are often inferior to existing alternatives when they are first introduced; new products improve as people put more effort into their development.

Still later, improvements slow down again.

Later, improvements come faster.

Initially, improvement in the product is slow.

Cumulative Number of Person-Years of Research

Source: Based on information in Foster, R. 1986. *Innovation: The Attacker's Advantage.* New York: Summit Books.

the entrepreneur can better time hiring employees, expanding manufacturing, and raising capital. More importantly, entrepreneurs need to predict whether the S-curve will accelerate. If the new product's performance does not improve rapidly, it will never overtake existing products in terms of the performance that customers prefer. Like nuclear power, it will not replace existing products, like coal and oil, and so is not a very good product for entrepreneurs to develop.

Successful entrepreneurs also know that established firms will not compete with them to develop new products that lie at the early part of the S-curve. Because the new product begins with inferior performance to the products that established firms already have, the established firms have little incentive to change products. In fact, the inferiority of the new product often leads managers of established firms to believe that the new product will always have very limited appeal to customers and is something that they do not need to worry about. Worse come to worst, the managers of established firms figure that they can always improve their own products to compete with the new product. Established firms will almost always opt for improving their own product rather than adopting the new product because they have investments in the technology and human resources used to produce the older product. As a result, they will be unwilling to shift to the new product until after it has proved its superiority over the old one, at which point the entrepreneur has a big head start.[9]

KEY POINTS

- Entrepreneurs are more successful in large and growing markets because large markets amortize the fixed cost of getting started over a larger number of units, and because it is easier to sell in more rapidly growing markets.
- The performance of new products follows an S-shape. Initially, a large amount of effort is required to achieve small improvements in product performance. Then performance improvements accelerate, with a small amount of effort leading to large improvements in performance. Ultimately, a large amount of effort is again required to achieve small improvements in performance as the product confronts the law of diminishing returns.
- The product S-curve is important to entrepreneurs because new products begin with inferior performance to existing products, requiring entrepreneurs to obtain a source of capital to keep their ventures alive as they improve new product performance. The S-curve also shows that the improvement in new products is a function of effort, not time. Finally, it demonstrates the importance of timing organizing activities to the acceleration of the S-curve.
- Established companies rarely compete with entrepreneurs to develop new products on the early part of the S-curve because the new product generally begins with inferior performance to the established company's existing products, and because the managers of established firms often believe that they could always improve the performance of their existing products to compete with new products.

ACHIEVING MARKET ACCEPTANCE

To be successful, entrepreneurs must have large numbers of customers accept and adopt their products and services. Doing this requires entrepreneurs to know which customers will adopt products when and what characteristics the product must have to gain acceptance from a particular segment of the market. Given their limited resources, this also means that entrepreneurs often have to focus on a single set of customers and so have know-how to pick the right initial set of customers. Finally, entrepreneurs must be aware of any dominant design or technical standard that is in place or likely to come into place in their market before they get started.

Adoption Patterns: Understanding Which Customers Adopt When

Entrepreneurs are understandably thrilled when they are able to sell their first product or service. A first sale is quite an achievement—one that many entrepreneurs never accomplish. However, for entrepreneurs to really succeed with their new businesses, they need to do more than achieve a first sale. They need to achieve broad adoption of their new products or services.

How do entrepreneurs achieve broad acceptance of their products? The first step lies in understanding how customers adopt new products. In general, the adoption of new products and services follows a normal distribution, like the one shown in Figure 9.5. A small group of customers are innovators, who are the earliest customers of new products and services. Early adopters follow the innovators. The majority of customers adopt after that, followed by a smaller group that are laggards, and adopt new products pretty late in the process.[10] Although the adoption of products doesn't always work as precisely as is shown in our figure, largely because of differences in individual tastes and preferences, this pattern is a good starting point for entrepreneurs. On average, across the vast majority of products, adoption patterns follow the normal distribution shown in the figure.

In fact, you have probably seen this adoption pattern at work. Think about the adoption of DVD players. You probably know someone who was an innovator. They bought one of the very first DVD players to come out. You also probably have some friends who were early adopters. They bought their DVD players before most of the people you know bought them. Most of your friends probably bought their DVD players around the same time because most people are in the early or late majority of adopters. Last, we suspect that you know some people (your parents, perhaps?) who are laggards who still have not purchased a DVD player.

Why does this adoption pattern matter to entrepreneurs? Understanding adoption patterns helps to understand how to introduce new products and services. One thing that entrepreneurs need to know about Figure 9.5 is that different groups adopt products for different reasons.[11] Innovators often find that they "need" every new device and piece of technology on the market. They tend to be intrigued by new products and adopt them so that they can explore what is new. In many cases, they purchase new products before they are formally marketed, even offering to purchase prototypes and beta tests. These customers are very insensitive to price. They want to try what is new, and often there are no alternatives yet available at any price. Early adopters tend to appreciate the value of new products and adopt them without much marketing effort by sellers. Although these people do not "need" new products as quickly as the innovators, they do claim to have greater needs for new product features than the majority of ultimate adopters. They base their buying decisions on their intuition about the value of new products and do not require much information to make their purchasing decisions. The early majority appreciates the value of new products, but also is influenced by practicality. They often want to see references from satisfied customers or

Figure 9.5 The Typical Pattern of Adoption of New Products

Most new products face a normal distribution of adopters. Few customers adopt early or late in the adoption cycle; most customers adopt in the middle of the cycle.

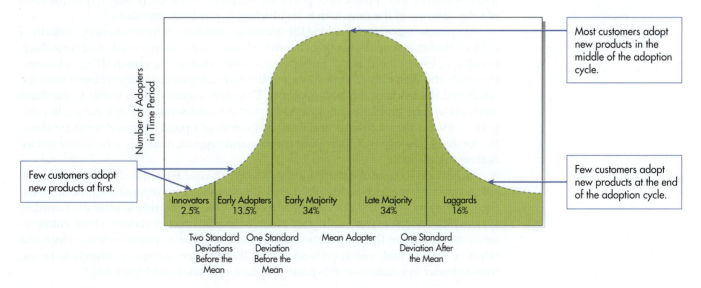

Few customers adopt new products at first.

Most customers adopt new products in the middle of the adoption cycle.

Few customers adopt new products at the end of the adoption cycle.

Number of Adopters in Time Period

| Innovators 2.5% | Early Adopters 13.5% | Early Majority 34% | Late Majority 34% | Laggards 16% |

Two Standard Deviations Before the Mean | One Standard Deviation Before the Mean | Mean Adopter | One Standard Deviation After the Mean

Source: Based on information contained in Rogers, E. 1983. *Diffusion of Innovations.* New York: Free Press.

endorsement by celebrities and other famous people before purchasing. The late majority tends not to be comfortable with new products and is driven to purchase by other considerations. They will wait for a product to become well established before purchasing it. Only when they are shown that the value of having the product clearly outweighs the cost do they adopt the product. The laggards avoid new products. In fact, they will do everything that they can to avoid adopting them. In many cases, laggards only adopt new products because the old products that they have been using are no longer available, as is the case with many very late adopters of computers who only adopted when typewriters became difficult to buy.[12]

Because different groups of customers adopt new products for different reasons, entrepreneurs need to know where the market is on the adoption curve when they start their new businesses and introduce their new products. If the early majority is not yet adopting the product, it might be too early for the entrepreneur to try large-scale promotion based on references from satisfied users or celebrity endorsements. In contrast, if the late majority is already adopting the product, the entrepreneur better have well-established support for the product if she hopes to get customer acceptance.[13]

In addition, entrepreneurs need to adjust their marketing message to fit the needs of the segment of customers who are adopting at the time. In general, this means offering more information and more support as part of marketing new products as the customer base shifts more toward late adopters who need this information and support to make their buying decisions.

Moving from Early Adopters to the Early Majority

LEARNING OBJECTIVE

7   Define "crossing the chasm" and explain why and how entrepreneurs "cross the chasm."

Transitioning from early adopters to the early majority is very important for entrepreneurs. In most markets, the innovators and the early adopters are too small a group to sustain new firms. Firms that sell only to them tend to die. But, because adopters of new products tend to follow a normal distribution, there is a very big increase in the number of customers when the entrepreneur moves from early adopters to early majority. Transitioning to the early majority allows new firms to get the volume of sales that they need to survive. Moreover, innovators and early adopters often demand customization of products. As a result, serving only these groups often becomes cost-ineffective for entrepreneurs who really need to develop products for larger volume markets to make a profit on them. Furthermore, profit margins are the highest at the middle of the adoption bell curve for many markets because the increase in volume of sales that occurs when firms transition to the early majority allow them to dramatically lower costs through higher volume of purchases and economies of scale. Last, the high cost of equity capital that many entrepreneurs incur to finance their business requires the transition to the early majority or the level of sales revenue of the new firm is insufficient to pay back investors.[14]

Despite its importance, making the transition from early adopters to early majority is difficult for entrepreneurs, leading Geoffrey Moore, a well-known marketing consultant, to call it "crossing the chasm." Entrepreneurs find crossing the chasm difficult because the needs and demands of innovators and the early adopters are very different from the needs and demands of the early majority. The early majority often wants to purchase solutions to their problems, not just novel products and services. For instance, in computer software, the innovators and early majority might purchase novel software alone, but the early majority will often want training and support, manuals, a customer service hotline, and so on.[15]

So how do successful entrepreneurs cross the chasm? First, they build the complete solution to customer needs described earlier, rather than offering just the product itself. Second, they focus on a single niche because they will not be able to offer the complete system that customers want if they try to serve too many niches at once. Third, entrepreneurs communicate the information about their solution to customers in a clear and effective way so that customers understand that the new company intends to be the market leader in solutions to this particular customer need (see Figure 9.6).[16]

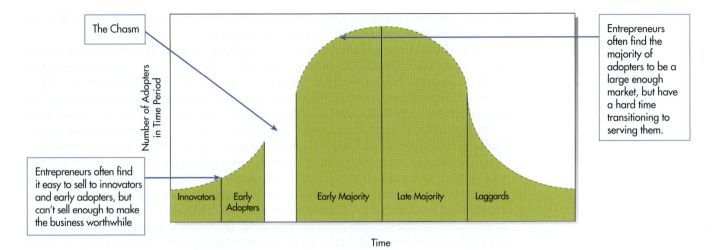

Source: Based on information contained in Moore, G. 1991. *Crossing the Chasm*. New York: Harper Collins.

Figure 9.6 Crossing the Chasm
Entrepreneurs often find it easy to sell their new products to innovators and early adopters, but find it difficult to transition to the early majority.

Focus: Choosing the Right Customers to Target First

To be successful, entrepreneurs need to focus. As we explained in the previous section, entrepreneurs need to focus to cross the chasm. Focusing is also essential in new businesses because entrepreneurs have limited resources. As we explained in Chapter 6, raising capital is difficult and costly; entrepreneurs rarely have enough capital for pursuing multiple market segments at the same time. Moreover, as we explained in Chapter 4, entrepreneurs have to gather a lot of information about markets and customers to develop new products and services and pursue their opportunities; entrepreneurs rarely have enough time to gather information about a number of market segments at the same time. Even the most determined entrepreneurs just can't work much more than 100 hours per week!

But focusing is only good if you focus on the right customers. How should an entrepreneur choose where to focus? By considering the customer. This involves figuring out which customers need to buy the product or service. Customers need to buy if the product or service gives them something that improves their productivity, reduces their costs, or gives them something that they could not have before.[17] For example, a package delivery company like UPS has a need to buy a global positioning system because it allows drivers to develop more precise routes and make their deliveries more efficient. Similarly, Hostess has a need to buy new product packaging that allows them to improve the storage life of Twinkies, because Hostess makes more money if its products can be kept longer on store shelves.[18]

Pigeon Control Professionals, a Redondo Beach, California, start-up founded by Robert Crespin, provides a good example of a new company that figured out which customers to focus on. Crespin's business uses a variety of devices, such as screens and bird repellent, to keep pigeons from doing their business on area businesses. How did Crespin know which customers to target first? A client of his maintenance business received repeated pigeon attacks on the same restaurant window, effectively destroying it. Crespin realized that the restaurant had a need for his service because the pigeon droppings were driving away the restaurant's customers and harming its business. He understood that getting rid of the pigeons would have clear value to the restaurant.[19]

Dominant Design: Product Convergence and Its Effect on New Ventures

Many markets have **dominant designs**. A dominant design is an arrangement that all companies producing a product will choose as the way of bringing together the different parts of a product or service.[20] A good example of a dominant design is the

LEARNING OBJECTIVE
8 Explain how entrepreneurs should choose the customers to focus their initial efforts on.

LEARNING OBJECTIVE
9 Define a "dominant design" and a "technical standard" and explain how they influence the performance of new ventures.

internal combustion engine. Once this design was introduced, all automobile makers adopted this design and it hasn't changed since then.

Why should entrepreneurs care about dominant designs? Because they influence an entrepreneur's likelihood of success. William Abernathy, a former professor at Harvard Business School, and Jim Utterback, a professor at the Sloan School at MIT, explain that products evolve through periods of incremental change, punctuated by radical breakthroughs. Radical breakthroughs are a new way of making something or a fundamentally new product design or architecture. Take computers as an example. Initially, computers used vacuum tubes. For many years, computer manufacturers made incremental improvements to vacuum tubes so that they would perform better and better. The computer manufacturers initially had different designs for vacuum tubes, but then converged on a single common design. Then the computer industry experienced a radical shift—to transistors. After that radical shift, computer manufacturers had different designs for their products. Then they converged on a dominant design for transistors, and again made incremental improvements, making the transistors better and better. Then there was another radical shift, this time to integrated circuits. For awhile, computer manufacturers had different integrated circuit designs, but ultimately converged on a dominant design. Again, after the dominant design, the computer makers made incremental improvements to the integrated circuit, reducing their size and increasing their processing speed.[21]

This pattern we just described is important because it very much affects the right time for an entrepreneur to start a new company. Every time there is a radical technological shift in an industry, new firms rush in and begin to compete because this is the point in the evolutionary cycle that is most favorable to new firms. Because there is no dominant design, new firms aren't handicapped by having to adopt a design that existing firms, who have more experience than they do, already use. Moreover, once firms converge on a dominant design, firms shift their basis of competition to efficiency and scale economies because the product design has become standardized. This shift favors established firms over new firms, which are not as efficient and often can't operate on the same scale as established firms.[22] How powerful are the effects of a dominant design? For a dramatic illustration of the far-reaching impact they command, please see the **"Danger! Pitfall Ahead!"** section.

Technical Standards: Getting Customers to Adopt Your Design as the Market Standard

In many industries, entrepreneurs must produce products or services that meet a **technical standard**. A technical standard is an agreed-upon basis on which a product or service operates. For example, the gauge of a railroad track is standard to make sure that all producers of railroad cars can operate on the same track.

The most important thing for entrepreneurs to know about technical standards is that getting the market to adopt your product design as the technical standard will make you super rich. One of the most famous technical standards is the Windows computer operating system. Bill Gates became the richest man in America largely because almost 80 percent of computers in the world operate the Windows operating system.

Those of you who are interested in becoming rich will be reassured to know that there are things that you can do to increase the likelihood that your market will adopt your product design as the technical standard. First, entrepreneurs can discount their prices when the new product is initially introduced, attracting more customers than if they charged a high price. Having this high volume is useful for getting suppliers because many suppliers would prefer to work with the largest producers who have the largest volume (for example, many software producers preferred Windows to the Macintosh operating system and would only write their software for Windows). Therefore, firms that generate the most customers quickly often stay ahead of competitors because suppliers prefer them to other alternatives. By being ahead of alternatives, the product becomes the technical standard in the industry.[23]

A second action that an entrepreneur can take to make her product the technical standard is to build relationships with producers of **complementary products**.

DANGER! PITFALL AHEAD!

Stymied by the Dominant Design: The Story of Electric Vehicles

Did you know that there were once more electric-powered vehicles in the United States than gasoline-powered ones? According to David Kirsch, a business historian and entrepreneurship professor at the University of Maryland, in 1900, vehicles using gasoline-powered internal combustion engines were actually the least common type. Steam-powered vehicles were the most common (have you ever seen a Stanley Steamer at an automobile museum?) and electric-powered vehicles were the second most common.[24] In 1900, very few people thought that the internal combustion engine would become the dominant design in automobiles. Electric- and steam-powered vehicles performed much better than gasoline-powered ones: They had greater range and could pull heavier loads. In fact, newspapers and magazines from that time period extolled the virtues of the electric vehicle and were often quite critical of the internal combustion engine. Many people predicted that the entrepreneurs who had founded electric- and steam-powered vehicle companies would become very wealthy, and those who formed gasoline-powered vehicle companies were destined to bankruptcy. But, as you probably know, the reverse occurred. The founders of the companies that made gasoline-powered vehicles went on to great wealth, and the entrepreneurs who lead the steam- and electric-powered vehicle companies ended up on the dustbin of history.

So what happened? Convergence on the dominant design that we have been talking about. Although electric and steam vehicles had better technical performance than gasoline-powered vehicles, they weren't as good as gasoline-powered vehicles for touring. In the early twentieth century, many Americans discovered the joy of driving for the fun of it. Electric vehicles weren't great for touring because they had batteries that had to be recharged. If a person went touring in the wrong direction, there was no place to recharge the car battery. Steam-powered vehicles tended to break down a lot on the terrible roads of the day. When people went touring, they preferred gasoline-powered cars, as long as they remembered to bring extra gasoline. As more people began to tour in gasoline-powered cars, other entrepreneurs began to serve them by building gasoline stations so that they could refuel their cars. Over time, as more and more people began to use gasoline-powered cars, the alternative product designs became less and less popular. The makers of those types of cars ran into financial trouble and went out of business, until ultimately the only design of car that anyone drove was a gasoline-powered car. The moral of this story for entrepreneurs is that industries often converge on a dominant design; those firms that produce the dominant design tend to survive and grow while other firms tend to fail, even if all the experts thought that the other product designs were better than the dominant design.

Complementary products are products that work together, like recorded movies and videotape recorders, or computer hardware and computer software. When VCRs first came out, Sony was locked in a major battle with Matsushita over whose VCR format would become the technical standard. Sony had the Betamax, and Matsushita had VHS. VHS became the technical standard, and Betamax disappeared largely because of a very wise decision by Matsushita. The executives at Matsushita pushed hard to get their standard adopted by the new video rental shops that were springing up around the country. In contrast, Sony didn't seem to care. Because recorded movies were an important complementary product to the VCR, once people started to rent movies and rental shops began to offer VHS tapes, most customers adopted the VHS standard and the Sony Betamax failed.[25]

A third action the entrepreneur can take to get her product adopted as the technical standard is to get to the market quickly rather than get to the market with the best version. Often this means starting with a simplified product that doesn't have all the best technology or features in it. It also means signing contracts with already existing manufacturers to produce the product for you rather than building new manufacturing plants from scratch. Finally, it involves simplifying the product so that mass production can occur.[26]

Getting to market quickly with less than perfect products is difficult for many entrepreneurs, who make the mistake of waiting to enter the market until they can make sure that their products are as close to perfect as they can get them. Sometimes this makes sense, but getting to market fast is a better approach when technical standards are up for grabs. As long as customers are more likely to switch to the new version of a company's products than to those produced by a competitor, the entrepreneur is better off entering the market quickly with an incomplete product than she is to wait until she has a completed product to offer. Waiting too long lets customers adopt another product design as the technical standard and makes it very hard for the entrepreneur to break into the market later.

KEY POINTS

- Customers tend to follow a normal distribution in the adoption of new products and services, and can be divided into five groups: innovators, early adopters, early majority, late majority and laggards, which adopt new products for different reasons.
- Entrepreneurs often find it difficult to transition from selling to the early adopters to selling to the early majority, a concept called "crossing the chasm," because the early majority have different needs and demands from innovators, most notably the desire for a whole solution to their problems.
- Successful entrepreneurs cross the chasm by building a complete solution to customer needs, by reducing the scope of their product offerings to focus on a single niche, and by communicating information about their solution to customers in a clear and effective way.
- Entrepreneurs consider the customer to choose the right segment to focus on initially, selecting those with the greatest need to buy as their initial target market.
- Many new products converge on a dominant design, or arrangement that all companies producing a product will choose as the way of bringing together the different parts of the product. New companies are most successful if they are founded before an industry converges on a dominant design, which leads to competition on the basis of efficiency and scale economies.
- In many industries, products must conform to a technical standard, or agreed-upon basis on which a product operates. Because having your product design be adopted as the technical standard is beneficial, entrepreneurs often try to get their design adopted as the standard through price discounting, building relationships with the producers of complementary products, and by getting to market quickly.

THE MARKETING PROCESS IN A NEW COMPANY

Perhaps the two most important aspects of the marketing process in a new company are selling and pricing. Much as people like to say, "a product sells itself," most new products don't. Entrepreneurs have to know how to sell to others. Entrepreneurs also have to figure out how to price their new products or services if they want to introduce them successfully. Although there are certainly other aspects of the marketing process in a new company, these two dimensions are central to that activity and probably account for most of the entrepreneur's marketing activity in the early days of the venture.

Personal Selling: The Central Component of Entrepreneurial Marketing

LEARNING OBJECTIVE

10 Explain why personal selling is a very important part of entrepreneurs' marketing strategies.

Personal selling is an effort by the entrepreneur to sell a product or service to customers through direct interaction with them. Although people often think of advertising, creating brand names, and building sales forces when they think of marketing, those aspects of marketing often occur relatively late in the life of a new venture. In the very beginning, most of the marketing effort by a new business consists of efforts by the entrepreneur to persuade customers to buy the new company's products or services (see Figure 9.7). For this reason, it is important for you to know what activities make people effective at selling.

Successful entrepreneurs understand that effective selling proceeds in the following way: First, the entrepreneur generates customer interest in the product or service.

This is usually done by letting the customer know that the entrepreneur has a product or service that will meet a need that they have. For example, suppose target customers are architects who want a better way to see what a building design will look like than constructing models out of mylar and foam. The entrepreneur can generate interest among target customers by letting them know that she has developed computer software that generates 3-dimensional images of buildings. By explaining that she has a solution to the customer's need, the entrepreneur can generate customer interest.[27]

Second, the entrepreneur identifies the customer's requirements for purchasing a new product. In the architectural example we just discussed, is the customer computer savvy or does she also want manuals and a customer support hotline along with the architectural design software? By determining customer requirements, the entrepreneur can figure out what aspects of the new product or service offering will "sell" the customer. This is a very important step in the sales process, and one that many people overlook. In their rush to persuade customers, entrepreneurs often forget to ask customers their requirements. As a result, they often tell customers about the wrong features of their products or services and hinder their ability to make sales.

The third step in the process is to overcome customer objections. Customers rarely purchase new products without challenging something that entrepreneurs tell them. To make the sale, entrepreneurs need to provide good answers to the objections and hesitations that customers have.[28] For example, architects might question whether the entrepreneur provides adequate customer support, whether the software can be linked to existing CAD/CAM software, or whether the product is easy to use. By providing explanations to these questions that customers feel are adequate and persuasive, the entrepreneur can make the customer feel comfortable enough to buy the new product or service.

The final step in the process is to close the sale. Many entrepreneurs often forget to close their sales, continuing to discuss the product until after the customer has expressed a conditional commitment to purchase.[29] As a result, they talk themselves out of a sale by making the customer feel that they are wasting their time. So how does the entrepreneur close a sale? When the customer has shown a conditional commitment to purchase, by indicating that they like the product or would like to have it, the entrepreneur should move to close the sale. Typically closing a sale involves asking closing questions, such as "Would you like to pay for that with a credit card or cash? Would you like to pick up the product or have us deliver it? Would you like one or two units?" These types of questions lead the discussion to its natural completion.

Figure 9.7 Personal Selling Is Central to Successful Marketing by Entrepreneurs

Direct personal selling is the entrepreneur's most important marketing tool—more important than advertising, building a brand name, or other marketing devices used by larger and more established companies.

Pricing New Products: The Role of Cost Structure and Supply and Demand

Entrepreneurs must set a price for their new products. Setting a price involves several important things. First, the entrepreneur must determine her costs and set a price that is greater than cost. Otherwise, the entrepreneur will not make a profit. Many an entrepreneur has failed to set prices relative to costs and has gone out of business while selling up a storm.

To understand his costs, the entrepreneur must make sure that he calculates both **fixed costs** and **variable costs**. Fixed costs are costs for things like facilities and equipment that do not change with the number of units that they produce. Variable costs are costs that are incurred on each unit that is produced, like a commission given to a salesperson or the cost of packaging for each shipped product. Although entrepreneurs are generally pretty good at estimating their variable costs, they often have trouble calculating the portion of their per unit costs that represent a share of the fixed cost. This is because the entrepreneur does not know how much volume she will produce. The more volume that the new venture produces, the lower the per unit portion of fixed costs. In fact, one of the reasons that many entrepreneurs fail is that they believe that

LEARNING OBJECTIVE

11 Describe how entrepreneurs price new products.

they will produce a much larger volume than they actually do. As a result, the per unit portion of their fixed costs becomes very high, leading costs to exceed revenue.

Second, the entrepreneur needs to pay attention to the market conditions. Most products sell within a limited range that creates a floor and ceiling on prices. The entrepreneur must make sure that she can sell her product within that range. If the entrepreneur's costs are too high to price within the existing range for products, she probably shouldn't launch a business providing that product or service because she will have a hard time attracting customers.

But what about the totally new products we talked about earlier in the chapter? Even for these products, the entrepreneur probably doesn't want to price the product above the range of existing products or services on the market. Why? One reason is that there is really no such thing as a product without alternatives, and a reasonable price is necessary to encourage customers to switch from those alternatives to the new product. For example, when the telephone was first developed, people still had the alternative of using the telegraph or mail to communicate. Similarly, when e-mail was first introduced, people could still use fax machines and telephones to communicate. If the entrepreneurs who first launched these products had priced them much higher than the alternative products on the market, then customers would not have been willing switch to the new product. A second reason is the same one we offered earlier in the chapter when we were talking about technical standards. Whenever an entrepreneur would benefit from widespread adoption of her product—like the case when the most popular product becomes the technical standard—it is a good idea to price the product at a reasonable level to encourage customers to buy it. By encouraging customer adoption, the low price generates the advantages that come from large sales volume. A third reason is, as we said earlier, that most truly new products perform much worse than existing alternatives when they are first introduced. If a new product performs worse than existing alternatives and is priced higher than those alternatives, then customers have no reason to try the new product.

Third, the entrepreneur must understand how customers trade off product attributes and price. Because no two products are exactly the same, customers are often willing to pay more for one product than for another. The price difference between the two products can be attributed to the different attributes that the two products have. This is relatively easy to do if two products are the same on all dimensions except one. But what if they have three different features—range, size, and brand name? Then assessing the price that each of these attributes represents is much more difficult. Entrepreneurs have a particularly difficult time accurately assessing the value of intangible attributes of competing products. For example, customers might be willing to pay more for an IBM computer because it is backed by the IBM brand name. Intangibles, such as customer service or brand name reputation, often account for differences in the price of otherwise similar products.

Last, the entrepreneur must factor in hidden costs or discounts in pricing. For example, if a competitor offers a 2 percent discount to customers paying immediately, rather than in 90 days, this discount affects the net price. Similarly, if competitors generally offer credit to customers, then the cost of raising the capital to provide this credit needs to be factored into the price (see Figure 9.8). In short, setting a price for a new product involves

Figure 9.8 Pricing Is an Important Part of Entrepreneurial Marketing

Entrepreneurs need to set an appropriate price for their new product or service; only the most foolish would try to sell a Kia sports car for the price of a Ferrari.

figuring out one's costs and not pricing below them; knowing what alternative products sell for and not pricing above them; figuring out the value to customers of different product attributes and using that information to accurately price the components that your product has; and factoring in any hidden costs or discounts that come from credit terms.

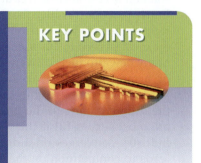

KEY POINTS

- Personal selling, or efforts to market a product or service to customers through direct interaction, is perhaps the most important marketing method available to entrepreneurs.
- Effective personal selling involves a process that begins with generating customer interest in the product or service, followed by identifying customer requirements, overcoming objections, and closing the sale.
- Entrepreneurs set the prices of their new products by considering several things: their cost structure, the supply and demand conditions in the market in which they operate, customer trade-offs between product attributes and price, and hidden costs and discounts.

Summary and Review of Key Points

- Entrepreneurs are most successful when they start a company that meets a real need: a customer problem no products or services can solve or new product or service that is so much better at solving the problem that customers are motivated to switch.
- Entrepreneurs assess customer preferences differently when markets are new than when they are already established; entrepreneurs need to adopt the right assessment techniques for the type of market they are targeting.
- Entrepreneurs are better off targeting new markets than established markets because established firms face three obstacles in assessing new markets: core rigidities, the tyranny of the current market, and user myopia.
- Conjoint analysis is a useful technique for determining the relative importance, in the customer's preferences and decisions, of the dimensions that they consider important.
- Through the effective use of conjoint analysis, entrepreneurs can design products that will have high appeal to potential customers, and so maximize the chances of success of their new ventures.
- Entrepreneurs are more successful in large and growing markets because large markets amortize the fixed cost of getting started over a larger number of units, and because it is easier to sell in more rapidly growing markets.
- The performance of new products follows an S-shape. Initially, a large amount of effort is required to achieve small improvements in performance. Then performance improvements accelerate, with a small amount of

effort leading to large improvements in performance. Ultimately, a large amount of effort is again required to achieve small improvements in performance as the product confronts the law of diminishing returns.
- The product S-curve is important to entrepreneurs because new products begin with inferior performance to existing products, requiring entrepreneurs to obtain a source of capital to keep their ventures alive as they improve new product performance. The S-curve also shows that the improvement in new products is a function of effort, not time. Finally, it demonstrates the importance of timing organizing activities to the acceleration of the S-curve.
- Established companies rarely compete with entrepreneurs to develop new products on the early part of the S-curve because the new product generally begins with inferior performance to the established company's existing products, and because the managers of established firms often believe that they could always improve the performance of their existing products to compete with new products.
- Customers tend to follow a normal distribution in the adoption of new products and services, and can be divided into five groups: innovators, early adopters, early majority, late majority and laggards, which adopt new products for different reasons.
- Entrepreneurs often find it difficult to transition from selling to the early adopters to selling to the early majority, a concept called "crossing the chasm," because the early majority have different needs and demands from innovators, most notably the desire for a whole solution to their problems.

- Successful entrepreneurs cross the chasm by building a complete solution to customer needs, by reducing the scope of their product offerings to focus on a single niche, and by communicating information about their solution to customers in a clear and effective way.
- Entrepreneurs consider the customer to choose the right segment to focus on initially, selecting those with the greatest need to buy as their initial target market.
- Many new products converge on a dominant design or arrangement that all companies producing a product will choose as the way of bringing together the different parts of the product. New companies are most successful if they are founded before an industry converges on a dominant design, which leads to competition on the basis of efficiency and scale economies.
- In many industries, products must conform to a technical standard, or agreed-upon basis on which a product operates. Because having your product design be adopted as the technical standard is beneficial, entrepreneurs often try to get their design adopted as the standard through price discounting, building relationships with the producers of complementary products, and by getting to market quickly.
- Effective personal selling involves a process that begins with generating customer interest in the product or service, followed by identifying customer requirements, overcoming objections, and closing the sale.
- Entrepreneurs set the prices of their new products by considering several things: their cost structure, the supply and demand conditions in the market in which they operate, customer trade-offs between product attributes and price, and hidden costs and discounts.

Glossary

Complementary Products: Complementary products are products that work together, like recorded movies and videotape recorders or computer hardware and computer software.

Conjoint Analysis: A technique for determining the relative importance of various dimensions in customers' evaluations of specific products.

Core Rigidities: The fact that companies tend to do well at things that they are accustomed to doing, not things that are new.

Dominant Design: An arrangement that all companies producing a product will chose as the way of bringing together the different parts of a product or service.

Fixed Costs: Costs of things like facilities and equipment that do not change with the number of units sold.

Personal Selling: An effort by an entrepreneur to sell a product or service through direct interaction with customers.

S-Curve: A graphical depiction of the typical pattern of performance improvement of new products or services as a function of the amount of effort put into them.

Technical Standard: An agreed-upon basis on which a product or service operates.

Tyranny of the Current Market: The fact that listening to customers will make it difficult for companies to come up with new products for new markets because a firm's current customers will always ask it for improvements to current products, not new products for new markets.

User Myopia: The fact that customers can only see very narrow needs or solutions, typically only their own needs, not those of other market segments.

Variable Costs: Costs incurred for each unit that is sold.

Discussion Questions

1. Think of some new products or services. Is there a real need for them? Why or why not? Try to rank order the new products or services that you came up with. For which ones is the need greater than the others? Why?

2. Assume that you have an idea for developing a business to create a new communication device to replace e-mail. How should you assess customer needs for the product? How would your assessment process differ from the one that you'd use if you were developing a business to create a new breakfast cereal?

3. Suppose you've developed a new product or service and the market size today is only $100,000. Should you pursue the new product or service? Why or why not?

4. Assume that you've just started a new company to sell spring break trips to Fort Lauderdale. What should you to do to market your product and make your first sales?

5. Suppose you've developed a new computer software package for inventory management. You've made some initial sales to innovators and early adopters. How are you going to make sales to the early majority of customers?

InfoTrac Exercises

1. **Early Adopters: Geeks or Pioneers?** (full disclosure) (how to buy cutting-edge technology products) (Column)
   Stephen Manes
   PC World, May 2003 v21 i5 p170(1)
   Record: A99910443
   Full Text: COPYRIGHT 2003 *PC World Communications, Inc.*

   1. According to the text, why do early adopters tend to adopt new products?
   2. According to the article, what distinguishes smart early adopters from "hapless geeks who overpay for new but inadequate products"?
   3. What price do early adopters sometimes have to pay for their product choices?

2. **The Internet and Personal Selling**
   Paul N. Romani
   American Salesman, March 2003 v48 i3 p3(8)
   Record: A98265212
   Full Text: COPYRIGHT 2003 National Research Bureau

   1. According to the text, what role does personal selling play in entrepreneurial marketing?
   2. Based on your reading of the article, do you think that the Internet can take the place of personal selling for an entrepreneur? Why or why not?
   3. Why did eToys fail as a new online venture?

GETTING DOWN
TO BUSINESS

Identifying a Real Need for a New Product or Service

In this chapter, we discussed the importance of identifying a product or service that meets a real customer need. This exercise will help you to develop a product or service that meets a customer need. Please follow these steps to complete the exercise.

Step One: In one paragraph, describe the new product or service that your business will create.

Step Two: List the features that your product or service will have (consider things like price, size, weight, and so on).

1.
2.
3.
4.
5.

Step Three: Specify how you will collect information from customers about their needs. Will you observe customers? Will you conduct focus groups? Will you conduct interviews? Will you distribute surveys?

Step Four: Collect information from customers about their needs, following the methodology you said that you would follow in step 2.

Step Five: Match customer needs to the features of your product or service. Does your product or service have attributes that meet the needs of the customer? If yes, explain why. If not, consider how you will modify the product or service to meet the needs of customers.

Step Six: Describe the optimal combination of features that customers want in your product or service. Use conjoint analysis, if you want. Otherwise, simply consider which features are particularly important to customers and make sure that those features are included in your product or service.

Developing a Marketing Plan

As this chapter explained, entrepreneurs need to develop plans to estimate market size and to convince potential customers to adopt their new products or services. To help you create a marketing plan for your new venture, we have designed this exercise. Please follow these steps:

Step One: Gather data on sales of similar products or services in your market over the past five years. Plot these data over time. Describe the shape of demand growth in your market over time. Use this information to project demand over the next five years. Estimate the size of your market over the next five years.

Step Two: Identify the market niche you will focus on. Explain how you will choose your customers. Make sure to explain why customers have a compelling reason to buy.

Step Three: Identify who will be the early adopters of your product or service. Explain why this segment of the market will adopt. Make sure to match the needs of early adopters to the characteristics of your product in explaining why the initial segment of the market will adopt your product or service. Also be sure to include any evidence from your customer feedback that explains why the features of your product or service will lead initial customers to adopt.

Step Four: Explain how your new venture will transition to mainstream customers. Explain what your venture will do to attract mainstream customers. How will you advertise and promote your product or service? What support will you provide along with your product or service? How will you achieve market leadership?

Step Five: Estimate the number of customers that your venture will attract over the next five years, and project your new venture's sales growth. Remember to consider the typical S-shaped curve of customer adoption. In addition, estimate the amount of resources that you will need to invest to attract customers over the next five years.

Step Six: Gather information on the share of the market held by the top three competitors, and use this information to calculate your projected market share over the next five years.

Learning to Sell

As we explained in this chapter, much of successful marketing in a new business involves personal selling. If you want to be a successful entrepreneur, you'll need to learn how to sell. This exercise will help you practice learning how to sell.

Step One: Find a partner in the class. The two of you will alternate being the customer and the salesperson.

Step Two: Identify a list of 10 things that you will try to sell (for example, a baseball cap, a car, tickets to spring break in Fort Lauderdale, and so on). Each of you will take five of these and try to sell them to the other.

Step Three: Try to sell your partner on the first object. Start by generating customer interest in the product or service. As we indicated earlier in the chapter, this is usually done by letting the customer know that you have a product or service that will meet a need that they have.

Then identify the customer's requirements for purchasing a new product. By determining customer requirements, you can figure out what aspects of the new product or service offering will "sell" your partner. Do not forget to ask your customer his requirements.

The third step in the process is to overcome your customer objections. Customers rarely purchase new products without challenging something that entrepreneurs tell them. To make the sale, you'll need to provide good answers to the objections and hesitations that your partner has.

The final step in the process is to close the sale. When your customer has shown a conditional commitment to purchase by indicating that they like the product or would like to have it, move to close the sale. Typically, closing a sale involves asking closing questions, such as "Would you like to pay for that with a credit card or cash? Would you like to pick up the product or have us deliver it? Would you like one or two units?"

Enhanced Learning

You may select any combination of the case options below to enhance your understanding of the chapter material.

- **Appendix 1: Case Studies –** Thirteen cases provide opportunities to apply chapter concepts to realistic entrepreneurial situations. These brief cases call for careful analysis of real business problems and ask you to think about potential solutions.

- **Appendix 2: Video Case Library –** Nine cases are tied directly to video segments from the popular PBS television series *Small Business School*. These cases and video segments give you unparalleled access to today's entrepreneurs, with expert advice and insights on how to start, run, and grow a business.

- **Comprehensive Cases –** Visit the book support Web site at http://baron.swlearning.com for cases detailing real businesses whose successes and setbacks illustrate each stage of the entrepreneurial process. You will conduct in-depth analysis of entrepreneurial challenges through well-developed case studies.

Notes

[1] Pedroza, G. 2003. Mr. Fix-it. *Entrepreneur* (March): 92.

[2] Barton, D. 1994. *Commercializing technology: Imaginative understanding of user needs.* Harvard Business School Note 9-694-102.

[3] Ibid.

[4] Ibid.

[5] Baumeister, R.F. (1998). The self. In D.T. Gilbert, S.T., Fiske, & G. Lindzey, (eds.). *Handbook of social psychology.* 4th ed., vol. 1, pp. 689–740.

[6] Green, P., & Rao, V. 1971. Conjoint measurement for quantifying judgmental data. *Journal of Marketing Research* 8: 355–363.

[7] Foster, R. 1986. *Innovation: The attacker's advantage.* New York: Summit Books.

[8] Ibid.

[9] Ibid.

[10] Rogers, E. 1983. *Diffusion of innovations.* New York: Free Press.

[11] Ibid.

[12] Moore, G. 1991. *Crossing the chasm.* New York: Harper Collins.

[13] Rogers, E. 1983. *Diffusion of innovations.* New York: Free Press.

[14] Moore, G. 1991. *Crossing the chasm.* New York: Harper Collins.

[15] Ibid.

[16] Ibid.

[17] Ibid.

[18] Ibid.

[19] Solving a problem. http://www.entrepreneur.comMagazines/MA_SegArticle/0,1539,230037----2,-00.

[20] Utterback, J. 1994. *Mastering the dynamics of innovation.* Cambridge: Harvard Business School Press.

21 Tushman, M., & Anderson, P. 1986. Technological discontinuities and organizational environments. *Administrative Science Quarterly* 31: 439–465.

22 Utterback, J. 1994. *Mastering the dynamics of innovation.* Cambridge: Harvard Business School Press.

23 Arthur, B. 1996. Increasing returns and the new world of business. *Harvard Business Review* (July–August): 100–109.

24 Kirsch, D. 2000. *Electric vehicles and the burden of history.* New Brunswick, NJ: Rutgers University Press.

25 Cusumano, M., Mylonadis, Y., & Rosenbloom, R, 1992. Strategic maneuvering and mass market dynamics: The triumph of VHS over beta. *Business History Review* 66: 51–94.

26 Arthur, B. 1996. Increasing returns and the new world of business. *Harvard Business Review* (July–August): 100–109.

27 Bhide, A. *Selling as a systematic process.* Harvard Business School Note 9-935-091.

28 Ibid.

29 Ibid.

CHAPTER 10

STRATEGY: PLANNING FOR COMPETITIVE ADVANTAGE

LEARNING OBJECTIVES

After reading this chapter, you should be able to:

1 Define a competitive advantage and explain why an entrepreneur needs to have one to be successful.

2 Describe a new firm strategy, and explain why entrepreneurs need one to protect their profits from opportunity exploitation.

3 Distinguish between efforts to keep others from learning about or understanding the business idea and barriers to imitation, and explain why both are important to entrepreneurs.

4 Define Arrow's paradox, and explain the problem of disclosure.

5 List several barriers to imitation that entrepreneurs use.

6 Identify different market mechanisms that entrepreneurs use to exploit opportunities, and explain why entrepreneurs use them.

7 Describe the strategic actions that entrepreneurs take to manage information asymmetry and uncertainty in the entrepreneurial process.

8 Explain why entrepreneurs often start their businesses on a small scale, and expand if they are successful.

9 Explain how alliances and partnerships with established firms help entrepreneurs to exploit their opportunities.

10 List actions that entrepreneurs undertake to make their new ventures appear more legitimate, and explain why they take these actions.

Competitive Advantage: An Essential Ingredient

Strategy: Protecting Profits from the Exploitation of Opportunity
  Secrecy: Keeping Others from Learning About or Understanding How to Exploit the Opportunity
  Establishing Barriers to Imitation

Franchising or Licensing? The Choice of Organizational Form
  Minimizing the Cost of Exploiting the Opportunity
  Accelerating the Pace to Market
  Making Use of the Best Capabilities
  Managing Information Problems in Organizing

Managing Information Asymmetry and Uncertainty in the Pursuit of Opportunity
  Growth from Small Scale
  Forming Alliances and Partnerships with Established Firms
  Legitimating the Opportunity and the New Venture

> "What sets us against one another is not our aims—they all come to the same thing—but our methods, which are the fruit of our varied reasoning." (Saint-Exupery, *Wind, Sand and Stars*, 1939)

In Chapter 9, we explained that entrepreneurs develop business ideas to sell something that meets a market need and introduce that product or service successfully into the mainstream market. However, just satisfying a market need does not mean that an entrepreneur will earn a profit. To make money, the entrepreneur also needs to develop a strategy that protects the business idea against competition. This chapter focuses on the entrepreneur's strategy.

What makes a strategy effective in protecting a business idea against competition? Existing evidence suggests that the answer involves two key types of action: (1) precluding others from gaining access to or understanding information about how to exploit the opportunity; and (2) creating barriers to the exploitation of the opportunity by others, even if they have access to information about the opportunity and understand how to exploit it.[1]

Robert Baron certainly used both of these types of strategic action when he developed the air filtration product that we discussed in Chapter 1. How did he preclude others from gaining access to or understanding information about the opportunity? He kept that information secret (see Figure 10.1). By not describing to other people where the information that triggered his recognition of the opportunity came from—the problem in his daughter's dorm room,

details of his research about how the physical environment affects human behavior, and his conversations with companies where he had worked as a Baron minimized the chance that others would gain access to the information that led him to learn of the opportunity. Furthermore, he kept others from understanding *how* to exploit the opportunity by making sure that he did not show other entrepreneurs or established companies, such as the manufacturers of existing air filters, how to design and manufacture a product that simultaneously filtered the air, reduced noise, and released fragrance.

How did Baron create barriers that would keep others from exploiting the opportunity in the same way that he did? By obtaining a patent on the PPS technology, Baron created a legal barrier that stopped others from imitating his approach to exploiting the opportunity. Even if air filter manufacturers had access to the same information that led Baron to recognize the opportunity, and even if they understood exactly how to design and manufacture the PPS product, the patent provided a legal barrier that kept the air filter manufacturers from acting. By adopting this two-part strategy, Baron protected the profits that his business idea generated against competition by others.

Figure 10.1 Entrepreneurs Must Keep Their Approaches to Exploiting Opportunities Secret

An entrepreneur will run into problems if he talks too much about his opportunity and plan to exploit it, even to his therapist!

"These dreams of yours wherein you find great tubs of money, Mr. Croy—can you describe the spot a little more exactly?"

The remainder of this chapter expands on the basic ideas behind entrepreneurial strategy. The first section discusses why new firms need a **competitive advantage** to exploit an entrepreneurial opportunity successfully. A competitive advantage is an attribute that allows a firm, and not its competitors, to capture the profits from exploiting an opportunity. Even though the typical new business has no competitive advantage, you want your new venture to have one. Why? The typical entrepreneurial effort lasts less than three years, never generates a profit, and is abandoned, or ends in bankruptcy.[2] So if you want to have a successful new business rather than a typical new business, you will need a competitive advantage.

The second section will return to the theme that we started to discuss at the beginning of the chapter. We will describe how the entrepreneur precludes others from gaining access to information about the opportunity and understanding how to exploit it, as well as how the entrepreneur creates barriers to the exploitation of the opportunity by others, even if they know about the opportunity and how to develop it.

The third section will discuss the organizational form that new ventures take. Although people normally think that entrepreneurs exploit opportunities by founding firms that own and operate all parts of the value chain, entrepreneurs often exploit opportunities by licensing their business ideas to others. Even when they found firms, entrepreneurs frequently rely on market-oriented modes of exploitation, such as franchising, or develop only part of the value chain, contracting with other firms to provide the rest. As you probably remember from Chapter 2, the value chain consists of the different stages in the process of creating and distributing a product or service to customers, including research and development, the supply of inputs and other raw materials, manufacturing, and distribution. We will explain when entrepreneurs should choose market-oriented modes of exploitation, like franchising and licensing, and when they are better off owning all parts of the value chain.

The last section of the chapter will discuss the strategies that entrepreneurs use to overcome the information asymmetry and uncertainty that are fundamental parts of the entrepreneurial process. As we explained in Chapter 2, people can never know for sure that their business idea will be successful until after they have exploited an opportunity, making the entrepreneur's pursuit of opportunity uncertain. In Chapter 3, we explained that entrepreneurs identify opportunities that others fail to recognize. To overcome the difficulties that uncertainty and information asymmetry generate in the pursuit of opportunity, entrepreneurs undertake several strategies that we discuss in the last section of the chapter.

LEARNING OBJECTIVE

1 Define a competitive advantage and explain why an entrepreneur needs to have one to be successful.

COMPETITIVE ADVANTAGE: AN ESSENTIAL INGREDIENT

In Chapter 1, we explained that the entrepreneurial process begins when the entrepreneur comes up with a business idea or way to exploit an opportunity. In Chapter 2, we pointed out that entrepreneurs typically devise these business ideas because they have access to better information about the opportunity or are better able to recognize the opportunity from the information that they have. In Chapter 9, we explained that, as a way to exploit their business ideas, entrepreneurs develop new products and services that customers value. This chapter focuses on ways to protect the value that the company derives from providing customers with valuable products and services.

At the very beginning of the process, no one else will have exactly the same business idea as the entrepreneur; the entrepreneur has a **monopoly** on it. A monopoly is a situation in which a firm is the only supplier of a product or service. For example, suppose that you have identified an opportunity to put a nightclub on the edge of campus because there is no place to listen to music or dance near school. At the beginning, your nightclub will be the only business satisfying the demand for a place in which to listen to music and dance.

What happens after you open your nightclub? Nothing—if you are wrong about the opportunity. If there is no demand to listen to music and dance, or if you can't make a profit because you can't get a liquor license or because the bands cost too much to book, then your nightclub will go under, and that will be the end of the story. But what if your nightclub is successful and you start making money? People will imitate your business idea. Your roommate, your boyfriend or girlfriend (assuming that they are not your roommate), and the owner of the local pizzeria will learn that the idea for a nightclub is profitable. Because they, too, would like to earn profits, they enter the market and set up nightclubs with the same design and the same music as your nightclub on, say, the three remaining corners of the street where your nightclub is located.

Left unchecked, these imitators will erode your profit from exploiting the opportunity. The imitators will try to acquire the resources needed to exploit the nightclub business idea, driving up the costs of those resources, and undermining profits. Now instead of booking a band cheaply because yours was the only gig in town, you have to outbid the other three nightclub owners for music talent. The imitators will also target your customers by cutting the cover, offering free drinks or free food, driving down your revenues and, consequently, your profits. This process of competition will continue until there are no profits left from the exploitation of the nightclub opportunity.

Not only can't you stop people from trying to imitate good business ideas, but also by starting a successful business you actually help them. The very act of pursuing a business idea provides other people—both individual entrepreneurs and existing companies—with the information that they need to develop a business idea that successfully exploits the same one that you have identified. In our nightclub example, for instance, you showed the others where to put their clubs and which bands to book by operating your nightclub.

To keep imitators from taking away the profits that you earned from coming up with a business idea that satisfies the needs of customers, you must develop a competitive advantage that deters imitation. If you can keep the information about the opportunity and how to exploit it from leaking out completely, then others will be unable to imitate your business idea completely. Similarly, if you can create some barrier that precludes others from taking action to exploit the opportunity in the same way that you did, you can also deter imitation.

In the nightclub example, suppose that you signed an exclusive contract with all of the really good local bands. Because those bands would only play in your club, and not in the three other clubs on the edge of campus, you would have a competitive advantage. As long as people want to hear specific bands, you would have a barrier to imitation of your business idea. If the imitators can't copy your business idea completely, and that idea generates a profit, then the profits from exploiting the opportunity will remain with you.

KEY POINTS

- The identification of a business opportunity that satisfies the needs of customers is not enough for an entrepreneur to earn profits; the entrepreneur also needs a competitive advantage.
- The exploitation of an opportunity will provide information to others about how to imitate the entrepreneur's business idea; imitation by others will erode the entrepreneur's profit from exploiting the opportunity.
- By developing a competitive advantage, the entrepreneur precludes others from imitating the business idea perfectly, and allows the entrepreneur to capture the profits from exploiting the opportunity.

STRATEGY: PROTECTING PROFITS FROM THE EXPLOITATION OF OPPORTUNITY

In general, entrepreneurs retain the profits from exploiting opportunities in two ways. First, they keep others from learning about their opportunities or understanding their business ideas for exploiting them. Entrepreneurs do this by keeping secret the information that allowed them to discover the opportunity, and by making it difficult for others to understand their methods of exploitation. Second, entrepreneurs use four types of barriers to block others from exploiting the opportunity in the same way that they do, even if the others have learned about the opportunity and understand how to exploit it: controlling resources, establishing legal barriers to imitation, building a reputation for satisfying customers, and by innovating to stay ahead of competitors.[3] This section will discuss these methods for protecting a business idea against competition.

Secrecy: Keeping Others from Learning About or Understanding How to Exploit the Opportunity

Stopping others from acquiring the information that allows an entrepreneur to identify an opportunity usually involves keeping that information secret. For example, suppose you learned that most college students wanted to go to Cancun instead of Fort Lauderdale on spring break. If you were planning to start a charter travel business that sold spring break package tours, you might not want to share this information about the preferences of your market with others. If other people didn't know that the hot destination for spring break was Cancun, and not Fort Lauderdale, then they wouldn't recognize that the key to the opportunity would lie in booking hotel rooms in Cancun, and wouldn't compete with you to gain access to the necessary resources (the beach-front rooms) to exploit the opportunity.

Because the goal of keeping information about the opportunity secret is to keep others from learning that the opportunity exists, this strategy works best when there are few ways of getting the information about the opportunity other than from talking to the entrepreneur. As you probably suspected, the spring break example is a tough one to protect just by keeping the information about the discovery of the opportunity secret. Too many people could obtain access to information about this opportunity from sources other than you. So even if you keep the information a secret, potential competitors could still get access to this information independently and exploit the opportunity in the same way that you do.

When are there few ways to get information about the opportunity other than from the first person to identify it? In general, when identification of the opportunity requires knowledge of a new and complex process that the entrepreneur retains as a **trade secret**, other people find it difficult to gain access to the information necessary to identify the opportunity on their own. A trade secret is a piece of intellectual property that is not patented, but is novel, nonobvious, and valuable, and provides a competitive advantage. We will talk more about trade secrets in the next chapter when we discuss intellectual property, but here is what you need to know for now: Sometimes people discover a new process for making something that other people haven't yet figured out. For example, suppose that you were working in the chemistry lab on campus and you figured out how to combine several chemicals into a formula that tripled the speed at which grass grew. You might want to start a fertilizer company to exploit your discovery. If you did, you would probably want to avoid telling other people that you had discovered this new formula for fertilizer. If other people didn't know that the new formula existed, then they wouldn't go looking for it. As a result, they wouldn't know that there was an opportunity to use the formula to produce fertilizer, and they wouldn't compete with your new fertilizer company.

The entrepreneur can also keep others from imitating the business idea if they can keep them from understanding how to exploit the opportunity, even if they have learned that the opportunity exists. Strategic management researchers call this concept **causal ambiguity** because other people do not understand the causal process that allows the entrepreneur to exploit the opportunity, only that the entrepreneur has recognized an opportunity and figured out how to exploit it.[4] For example, suppose that you and everyone else in your dorm know that the people in the town where your university is located really like fruit pie. The townies' preference for fruit pie creates demand conditions that make it possible for you to start a company to sell fruit pies (remember that in Chapter 2 we explained that demand conditions influence opportunities for new businesses). If the whole dorm knows that people in the town like pie, then the information about the opportunity is not a secret. You can't stop other people from imitating your business idea simply by keeping the information about the opportunity secret.

However, what if your grandmother gave you really great recipes for making pie—recipes so great that no other pie ever tastes as good as hers? Then you could exploit causal ambiguity to keep other people from learning how to exploit this business opportunity in the same way that you do. You could start a business making pie for the people in town, using your grandma's recipes. Even though the other people in your dorm know about the opportunity—the demand for pie in the town—they would not know how to exploit that opportunity—your grandmother's recipes. As a result, you could exploit the opportunity without losing out to competition from them.

An entrepreneur's ability to keep others from understanding an opportunity usually involves some type of **tacit knowledge**. Tacit knowledge is knowledge about how to do something that is not written down, or codified. Remember in Chapter 5 when we said that often people know what they do, but not why or how they do it? That's related to tacit knowledge. For instance, you probably know how to swim. If you do, we suspect that your knowledge is tacit. Unless you are really strange, you probably don't refer to written instructions on how to do the crawl each time you go swimming. In fact, if someone asked you to explain how to swim, you probably wouldn't even be able to explain the exact steps that you follow. Why? As we explained in Chapter 3, your knowledge about how to swim is tacit and is held in procedural memory (see Figure 10.2).

Many aspects of business are tacit. A good engineer might know how to operate a manufacturing plant, but not be able to give you step-by-step instructions on how to do it. A successful salesperson might know how to make a sale, but not be able to write a sales guide. Even the pie recipe example we just gave points out the value of tacit knowledge. Grandma's recipes are codified knowledge, or knowledge that is written down in documentary form. But when your grandmother makes pie, she might also exploit tacit knowledge, knowledge of things that she does that aren't actually written in the recipe. These things make her version of the pie taste better than when you follow the same recipe that she follows.

Tacit knowledge is better than codified knowledge for creating causal ambiguity about how to exploit an opportunity. When knowledge is codified in, say, a recipe for pie, anyone who wants to imitate the entrepreneur can do so by getting hold of the recipe. Although it may be more difficult to get hold of the recipe than to figure out that the opportunity exists, it is still not as easy as figuring out how your grandmother makes such great pie when the secret isn't written in the recipe.

When an entrepreneur has tacit knowledge about how to exploit an opportunity, other people have difficulty figuring out the causal relationships that drive the processes that the entrepreneur uses to produce, distribute, and organize.[5] Unless they can get inside the entrepreneur's head, they just can't figure out what those key production, distribution, and organizational processes are. If other people can't figure out the entrepreneur's processes, they can't imitate them, and this protects the entrepreneur's profits against imitation. For example, suppose that key to the successful exploitation of an opportunity to found a furniture store lies in an entrepreneur's tacit knowledge about how to sell. Even if other people started furniture businesses and located next door to the entrepreneur, selling exactly the same lines of furniture, the entrepreneur would still be able to retain the profits from the opportunity because the other people would not be able to imitate the entrepreneur's tacit knowledge about how to sell.

The use of causal ambiguity to keep other people from imitating a business idea is particularly effective when the tacit knowledge that the new venture is exploiting is

Figure 10.2 Tacit Knowledge Helps Entrepreneurs to Deter Imitation Even When Others Are Aware of the Opportunity

Much like swimming, exploiting opportunities involves tacit knowledge. Many entrepreneurs successfully keep others from imitating their business ideas by making use of tacit knowledge.

© Getty Images/ PhotoDisc

based on rare skills or experience.[6] If large numbers of people have the skills or experience to exploit the opportunity, then some of them will probably figure out how to exploit it, even if the entrepreneur keeps the tacit knowledge secret. However, if only a small number of people have the skills or experience to exploit a particular opportunity, an entrepreneur will be able to keep others from imitating just by keeping the tacit knowledge secret.

For example, Lynne Zucker, a sociologist at UCLA, and her husband Michael Darby, an economist at the UCLA business school, examined the performance of new biotechnology companies established in the United States. They discovered that the entrepreneurs who founded these companies were able to keep others from taking away their profits by exploiting their rare tacit knowledge about how to exploit certain biological research skills. Because very few people in the world (in each case about 10) could employ the same scientific techniques that they employed, these entrepreneurs were able to reap huge profits from using their tacit knowledge of particular scientific techniques to make new drugs, despite the widespread recognition that the drugs that they were developing were valuable.

The reasons that we just outlined are not the only ones for keeping ideas secret. There are many others, too. For a discussion of another potential problem that comes from not keeping knowledge of a business idea secret that can be especially dangerous for entrepreneurs, please see the **"Danger! Pitfall Ahead!"** section.

LEARNING OBJECTIVE

4 Define Arrow's paradox, and explain the problem of disclosure.

DANGER! PITFALL AHEAD!

Arrow's Paradox: The Problem of Disclosure

We just stressed the importance of keeping secret your opportunity and knowledge about how to exploit it. Although that may seem easy to do, it really isn't.

Suppose that you have come up with a great new design for a new windshield wiper, and have tested it out with several different people. They all love your new wipers, which work much better than other windshield wipers and only cost half as much to produce.

You know that you need to talk to potential customers about the wipers, so you send a letter to the major automakers telling them that you have developed a great new set of windshield wipers. One day you get a call back from the folks at one of the companies, who tell you that they'd like you to come in and talk to them. On the phone, the manager is really positive, telling you that your wiper design sounds like just the thing they have been looking for, and that they would like to buy it from you. They just need to learn a little more about the wipers. So you set up a meeting.

When you get to the meeting, a junior staffer ushers you into a huge oak-paneled conference room where seven or eight people are around the table waiting for you. Everyone is very excited to hear about your new windshield wipers.

The people at the company ask to see the prototype of your windshield wipers because they want to get a sense of what they look like. They ask you how you designed the windshield wipers because they want to make sure that the design is compatible with their vehicles. They ask you what materials you used, and how much time it took to produce the wipers

because they want to make sure that the process is as good as they imagine. All the while, they keep telling you that they love your windshield wipers, and that there is going to be a big check in the works for you. Because you want the sale, you answer all of their questions.

At the end of the meeting, they thank you and tell you that they will be in touch soon. But a few weeks pass and you hear nothing. You call to follow up, leaving voice mails, which elicit no response. You try to reach the people in the meeting, but you get shunted off to a secretary. Finally, you realize that they are never going to buy your windshield wiper design.

What happened? You have fallen victim to Arrow's paradox.[7] Kenneth Arrow, a Nobel prize–winning economist at Stanford University, explained that disclosing knowledge is a paradox. A buyer will never buy a piece of knowledge, like a design for a new windshield wiper, if its value is unknown. So to sell a piece of knowledge, its value has to be demonstrated. However, demonstration transfers the knowledge to someone else, and undermines the buyer's incentive to pay for it. So once demonstration has occurred, the buyer won't pay for the knowledge. Although there are a few solutions to this problem, such as patenting the technology that your business idea is based on, or getting people to sign a nondisclosure agreement—an agreement that those people you describe your idea to won't disclose it to anyone else—the problem cannot be eliminated. So we want you to pay attention to it. Many people will try to get you to disclose your business idea to them so that they can use it to exploit the opportunity that you have discovered. So please be careful. Keeping information about your opportunity and how to exploit it secret is harder than it looks.

Establishing Barriers to Imitation

Often, other people can imitate an entrepreneur's business idea once the entrepreneur has begun to exploit it because the entrepreneur cannot keep the information about the opportunity secret or cannot create causal ambiguity about the way it is exploited. If secrecy is not a viable strategy to prevent imitation, the entrepreneur can keep others from profiting from their opportunity by creating barriers to imitation of their method of exploiting it.[8] Creating barriers to imitation is also useful, even if the entrepreneur is trying to keep secret knowledge of the opportunity or how to exploit it. Even when people try to maintain secrecy, that secrecy is often breached; others can learn even tacit knowledge. Therefore, entrepreneurs establish four types of barriers to competition: obtaining control of the resources needed to exploit the opportunity, establishing legal obstacles to imitation, developing a reputation, and innovating to stay ahead of the competition.[9]

Obtaining Control of Resources

An entrepreneur can build a barrier to competition by gaining control over the key resources that are required to exploit the opportunity.[10] For example, suppose that you came up with a business idea to sell food at sporting events on your campus. Every university has a limited number of arenas and stadiums in which the sporting events take place. If you signed a contract to lease all of the food service space—the key resource for exploiting this opportunity—in all of the arenas and stadiums on campus, you would be able to stop other people from exploiting the same opportunity as you.

In addition to contracting with resource providers to obtain control over key resources, you could just purchase the source of supply of that resource. This would make the most sense if your opportunity depended on a key resource with a limited source of supply. Suppose, for example, that you were going to build a business selling diamond rings, like the South African company, De Beers. High-quality diamond gems can be found in only a few diamond mines in the world. By purchasing these mines, you would effectively preclude everyone else from gaining access to the gem-quality diamonds used in jewelry, just as DeBeers has done.

Obtaining a Legal Monopoly

A second barrier to competition that an entrepreneur could employ would be to obtain a legal monopoly on the process used to exploit the opportunity. **Patents** and **government permits** are two important types of legal monopolies on methods used to exploit opportunities. We will talk more about patents in the next chapter, but, basically, a patent is a right given by the government to be the only party that can use a particular invention for a specified period of time. The medical device industry provides a good example of the use of patents to deter competition. An entrepreneur who has invented a heart pacemaker could patent the design of the pacemaker to keep others from trying to exploit the market by producing the same pacemaker.

A permit is a right given by a government that makes you the only party allowed to do something in a particular geographical location. For example, many cities limit the number of liquor stores to one store in each geographic area. By obtaining a permit to establish a liquor store in a specific area, an entrepreneur can ensure that no one else can compete with them by establishing another liquor store in the same general area.[11]

Establishing a Reputation

Entrepreneurs also create a third barrier to competition, the establishment of a reputation for satisfying customers. By creating goodwill among customers, an entrepreneur can keep customers from shifting their allegiance to other firms, and thus keep the profit from exploiting the opportunity to themselves. For example, suppose that you developed a new type of mountain bike, and everyone agreed that your mountain bike was really excellent and wanted to buy it. The big problem for you would be that other people could imitate your mountain bike design and compete for a share of the mountain biking market and your profits. You might be able to keep customers from going to any of your competitors who imitated the design of your bike if you developed a reputation for excellent customer service. This reputation would be a competitive advantage that made your mountain bike company better than other ones, and allowed you to preserve profits against the efforts of competitors to take them away.

One tactic is particularly useful in developing a reputation as a barrier to competition. The entrepreneur can advertise heavily to promote the attributes of a new product or service to customers. This advertising creates customer expectations about the attributes of a product or service. If imitators can't or don't copy all of these attributes, the advertising makes customers reluctant to switch to the competitors' product or service, reducing competition from other firms.

Innovation

A fourth barrier to competition used by entrepreneurs is innovation. Innovation involves any effort to keep the entrepreneur's product or service ahead of the alternatives offered by competitors on any dimension desired by customers, including quality, features, speed, cost, and so on. For example, an entrepreneur who has developed a piece of financial planning software could add additional features to the base model, such as tax paying, bill paying, or estate planning capability. By innovating, the entrepreneur can take advantage of the learning curve that we discussed in Chapter 2. As long as the entrepreneur can make improvements to the initial product or service sooner than competitors, the entrepreneur can retain customers by always offering attributes of the product or service that the competitors' products and services don't have. (See Table 10.1 for some more examples of barriers to competition that entrepreneurs establish.) For the insights of one highly successful entrepreneur with respect to establishing competitive advantage, see **"The Voice of Experience"** section on page 248.

Daddy's Junk Music Stores Inc. provides a good example of a start-up company that used innovation to create a barrier to competition. Fred Bramante founded the company to sell music equipment through retail outlets in New England. An innovative start-up, the company received awards for its creative marketing and employee management programs. However, the establishment of eBay was a direct competitive challenge to Daddy's. Instead of going to the company's stores to trade their music equipment, people began to buy and sell them on eBay, eating into Daddy's sales. In response, Bramante closed Daddy's mail order business, improved its stores, expanded their network, enhanced employee compensation, and improved marketing by launching a TV program that included musical appearances and advertising by the company. As a result, Bramante was able to grow Daddy's despite competition from eBay and other firms.[12]

Table 10.1 Entrepreneurs Deter Imitation by Building Barriers to Competition
Entrepreneurs establish several different types of barriers to competition.

TYPE OF BARRIER	BUSINESS IDEA	EXAMPLE	REASONING BEHIND WHY THE BARRIER WORKS
Control of resources	Sell food at college basketball games	Signing a contract for the concession stands in the arena	Without access to concession stands, other entrepreneurs cannot sell food at the games.
Legal barriers to imitation	Sell DVD players	Obtaining a design patent on the DVD player	The patent precludes others from making a DVD player with the same design.
Reputation	Sell clothing	Develop a reputation for being the best clothing designer in Paris	The reputation keeps customers from defecting to your competition.
Innovation	Sell scooters	Develop scooters with better features every 6 months	By always making sure that your scooter has features that other scooters don't have, you can ensure that your scooter is more desirable to customers than the competition's scooters.

THE VOICE OF EXPERIENCE

Establishing Competitive Advantage: Recognize Your Strengths

Michael Herman is the past president and COO of the Kauffman Foundation, past president of the Kansas City Royals baseball team, and past president of Marion Labs. He is a cofounder of Dryden Co, a private investment banking firm in New York, and serves on the board of directors of many companies, including Janus Capital Corp., Cerner Corp., and Eloquent Inc. He is a trustee of the University of Chicago Graduate School of Business and Rensselaer Polytechnic Institute. He holds a degree in metallurgical engineering from Rensselaer and an MBA from the the University of Chicago. Herman is married to Karen Herman, and they have two children—Jolyan and Brooks. Herman enjoys golf, fishing, skiing, squash, bicycling, and music.

Every new venture needs a competitive advantage—something that allows it, and not its competitors, to capture the profits from exploiting an opportunity. In fact, new ventures that fail to establish—and maintain—competitive advantage usually have a short existence. In a recent conversation, Robert Baron asked Michael Herman, an entrepreneur with a wide range of experience in several different industries, to comment on how, in his view, entrepreneurs can seize, and hold, competitive advantage.

Baron: "It's a tough world out there, so even the combination of a great idea and supercompetent entrepreneur aren't enough, in and of themselves, to guarantee success. In other words, every new venture needs some kind of competitive advantage—something that allows it, and not its competitors, to capture the profits from an opportunity. What did you do to establish a competitive advantage in your own companies, and then to hold on to it?"

Herman: "You are right—having a competitive advantage is crucial. So you start out trying to develop it, but you never know just how that will turn out. The key thing is recognizing which competitive advantage you can get, and which is best for you. Let me give you an example. When I joined Marion Labs, which was founded by Ewing Kauffman, we didn't have the resources to do basic research—to develop new products. What we did have was outstanding sales and marketing capacity, plus a first-rate ability to deal with the FDA. Our value added was recognizing that there was technology all over the world that hadn't come into the United States yet (this was 1974). So we were able to go to Japan, Germany, and other countries, and get some great pharmaceutical products for the United States. That become our competitive advantage. We realized that we didn't have to do our own research; we could get new products from other countries and bring them into the United States."

Baron: "This sounds so obvious that I'm wondering why other companies didn't have the same idea."

Herman: "They didn't because they were stuck in groupthink. They convinced themselves that they had to do their own basic research. In Japan, for instance, we were the only people trying to license new products. The Japanese, and the Germans, too, weren't comfortable dealing with the FDA. So we came up with the concept that we would bring their products here and sell them. This gave us an incredible advantage. We didn't have the research, but we were willing to license foreign technology and import it into the U.S. market. Ten years later, in 1985 or 1986, everyone was there—but we were the first, and during the years that we had the advantage of being first, sales for Marion Labs went up more than one hundredfold. Again, the big companies were suffering from groupthink, and until they come around to recognizing the opportunities you have discovered, you have a big advantage over them."

Baron: "Can you give me another example of how new ventures can establish competitive advantage?"

Herman: "Sure. David Glass, the CEO of Wal-Mart, found competitive advantage in being the first to develop first-rate data systems. He invested heavily in them early on. The result was that people at Wal-Mart could meet on Saturday and have reports from all their stores through Friday; then they could make decisions about what merchandise to order on Saturday. Sears and other competitors didn't have data systems as good, so they couldn't get the reports until Monday, and couldn't interpret them fully until Wednesday. So Wal-Mart was a week ahead. That gave them a big competitive advantage. Someone else would hold the inventory until Wal-Mart needed it."

Baron: "Anything else to add?"

Herman: "Only this. It's important to remember that you will have a competitive advantage only for a period of time; then the marketplace will recognize it and catch up. At that point, you need another one. So it evolves continuously. The key thing is to remember that competitive advantages emerge, so you have to recognize them, seize them, and executive them when they do. Waiting can be a big mistake."

Commentary: Mr. Herman's views are closely related to several key points made in this chapter. First, having a competitive advantage is crucial; without it, entrepreneurs will not be able to reap the full benefits of the opportunities they identify. Second, there are many ways to attain competitive advantage, but among these, being innovative—creating a new product, developing a new distribution approach, entering a new market—is often one of the best. Third, competitive advantages, no matter how good they are, almost always have a limited life; after a time, competitors are able to move in and exploit the same opportunities. As a result, entrepreneurs can never afford to stand pat: On the contrary, they must continuously develop new competitive advantages to maintain their momentum. Over the long-term, nothing else really works.

FRANCHISING OR LICENSING? THE CHOICE OF ORGANIZATIONAL FORM

One popular misconception about entrepreneurship is that people always exploit opportunities by establishing a new organization that produces and distributes new products or services. Although it is true that entrepreneurs often found **vertically-integrated** companies—that is, firms that own successive stages of the value chain, including the purchase of inputs, manufacturing and production, and marketing and distribution outlets—entrepreneurs don't have to own all parts of the value chain. Instead, they can use what economists call market-based modes of opportunity exploitation.

> **LEARNING OBJECTIVE**
>
> 6 Identify different market mechanisms that entrepreneurs use to exploit opportunities, and explain why entrepreneurs use them.

Palm Computer provides a good example of a start-up that used a market-based mode of opportunity exploitation. Rather than build their computer organizer alone, the founders of Palm computing sought partnerships with other companies who produced the parts for their Palm Pilot according to Palm's specifications. For instance, The Windward Group, a California-based software developer, created the desktop computer applications for the Palm Pilot. By partnering with other companies that created the various parts of the Palm Pilot, the company's founders were able to increase their speed to market and reduce their costs—two important competitive advantages in the handheld computer market.[13]

The two most common market-based modes of opportunity exploitation are **licensing** and **franchising**. Licensing is a mode of business in which a person contracts with another to use the latter's business idea to make products and services for sale to end customers in return for a fee. Many entrepreneurs use licensing to exploit their business ideas. For example, Jerome Lemelson, a well-known inventor who established the Lemelson prize for America's greatest inventors, made a huge fortune by patenting his technological inventions and licensing them to established companies, rather than by founding new companies.

Franchising is a mode of business in which one party, the franchisor, develops a plan for the provision of a product or service to end customers. Another party, the franchisee, obtains the right to use the franchisor's plan in return for paying a fee and agreeing to oversight by the franchisor.[14] Many well-known companies like, McDonald's and Subway, were once new firms whose entrepreneurs chose to pursue their opportunities by franchising, rather than by owning all of their fast-food outlets.

With franchising, both the franchisor and the franchisee contribute to meeting customer needs. Because the franchisee is an entrepreneur who operates the outlets and directly serves customers, he is usually more motivated than a typical company manager. His willingness to work harder (and smarter) often enhances customer satisfaction and improves sales. The franchisor also provides a variety of assets that improve sales. First, the franchisor offers useful services on running a new business that have been honed from years of experience. These services include assistance in location selection, outlet setup and leasing, employee training, financing, and advertising. Second, the franchisor offers a brand name that helps to attract customers. Third, the franchisor offers the benefits of scale economies in purchasing of supplies and advertising.

Because one of the franchise system's main assets is its brand name, the franchisor maintains control over the marketing of the product or service that the franchise system provides. Close control of the brand name is necessary to ensure the value of the system's goodwill. Franchisors often maintain control by specifying quality standards that franchisees have to meet. For example, every McDonald's franchisee has to meet specific standards for cleaning the outlet's restrooms. These standards are very strict and even specify what cleaning supplies to use and how often to mop the floors. In many cases, franchisors require franchisees to adhere religiously to the terms of a thick manual of instructions on how to operate the outlet. These manuals often specify exactly what employee uniforms will look like, how storefronts should appear, how customers should be greeted, and so on.

Because you have a choice to use market-oriented modes of opportunity exploitation, like franchising and licensing, to exploit your business ideas, you should understand when each of these methods is most appropriate for a new venture. Researchers have identified four sets of factors that determine whether an entrepreneur should use a market-based mechanism to exploit an opportunity: cost, speed, capabilities, and information.[15]

Minimizing the Cost of Exploiting the Opportunity

Suppose that you don't have millions of dollars in savings, but you would like to exploit an opportunity to establish a chain of auto repair shops, each of which will require $500,000 in equipment. How will you exploit this opportunity? As we discussed in Chapter 6, you might go to an angel investor to try to get the capital that you need to set up the repair shops. But you have an alternative. You could franchise the repair shops to other people who would use your format for the stores to serve customers.

New businesses adopt **market-based modes** of exploiting opportunities when different parts of the business, such as manufacturing and marketing, are owned by different entities and are connected by a contractual relationship. New businesses adopt **hierarchical modes** of exploiting opportunities when one party owns all parts of the operation that produces and sells a product or service to end customers. A comparison between franchised and nonfranchised restaurants provides a good example of the difference between these modes of opportunity exploitation. A franchised restaurant uses a market-based mode of exploiting opportunities because one party, the franchisor, owns the restaurant's operating system—the recipes, design of the restaurant, hiring policies, and so on—and leases that system to another party, the franchisee, who owns and operates the restaurant itself. A nonfranchised restaurant uses a hierarchical mode of exploiting opportunities because one party owns both the operating system and the restaurant itself.

Entrepreneurs often use market-based modes of exploiting opportunities, such as franchising, because these modes take less capital than hierarchical modes, such as a chain of auto repair shops that owns all of the outlets. As we explained in Chapter 6, entrepreneurs have to raise capital from external sources to finance the exploitation of their opportunities because they lack cash flow from existing operations. External capital is more expensive than internally generated capital because investors demand a premium to compensate for risks that they bear from having less information about the opportunity and the business idea than the entrepreneur.[16]

To overcome the high cost of capital, entrepreneurs use franchising to tap franchisees as a source of capital to exploit their opportunities. In franchising, franchisees to pay franchisors up-front fees, in the tens, and sometimes hundreds, of thousands of dollars, to obtain the rights to use the franchisor's brand name and business format in an outlet that they, the franchisees, own.[17] Moreover, by franchising an outlet instead of owning it outright, the entrepreneur can transfer the cost of setting up the outlet to the franchisee (see Figure 10.3).

Similarly, technology entrepreneurs often license their technologies to established companies who use their manufacturing and distribution assets to produce products and services for end users. For example, many biotechnology entrepreneurs are unable to obtain the hundreds of millions of dollars that it takes to get a drug through all phases of FDA approval from venture capitalists or even from public markets. To finance drug development, they license their drugs to large pharmaceutical firms like Merck and Pfizer, who use the entrepreneur's technology to produce the actual drugs.

Accelerating the Pace to Market

Entrepreneurs also use market-based modes of opportunity exploitation to accelerate the pace of their efforts to exploit opportunities. Sometimes, an opportunity is too short-lived for an entrepreneur to assemble the entire value chain in time to exploit it. For instance, suppose that you discovered an opportunity for a board game based on a recent presidential election. By the time you set up an entire game company, the market window might have passed, and the opportunity would be lost. So you set up your new business by contracting with different people, who provide the different things that you need to produce the game. You contract with a game designer to develop the questions for the game; with a manufacturer to produce the pieces; with a packaging company to assemble and ship the games; and with an Internet site to sell it. By contracting instead of trying to build the whole value chain from scratch, you get the game out quickly and meet the opportunity window.

Using market-based modes of exploitation are also useful when the entrepreneur is in a race to be the first to enter a market. In certain businesses, being the **first mover**, or the first firm to serve customers in a market, provides a lot of advantages. For instance, if customers face a high cost to switching from one supplier to another, then being the first to serve the customer has lasting value. In addition, being quick to market matters a lot when a business faces **network externalities**. Network externalities exist when something has increasing value as more people use it. Take eBay as an example. The more people that use eBay, the more valuable eBay is. People prefer eBay to other auction sites because it is already the largest auction site and therefore is the easiest to use to sell goods. If a business has network externalities or first mover advantages, entrepreneurs often race to set up these businesses before their competitors. As a result, they often use contractual arrangements in exploiting their opportunities.

Making Use of the Best Capabilities

Sometimes the people who identify an opportunity are not the best at exploiting it. Other people or firms might have better access to capital, deeper knowledge of the relevant market, already established manufacturing and distribution facilities, or better experience selling new products or services to customers. Researchers have found that both the entrepreneur and the party that contracts for the use of the business idea gain from this mode of exploitation because performance goes up dramatically when people who have strong capabilities for exploiting opportunities do so in place of

Figure 10.3 To Minimize the Cost of Exploiting Opportunities, Entrepreneurs Often Franchise

Selling the rights to use a firm's business format and brand name to operate a retail outlet allows entrepreneurs to overcome financial constraints to exploiting their opportunities.

those who have weaker capabilities.[18] Therefore, entrepreneurs often use market-based modes of exploiting opportunities when they have inferior capabilities to others at the activities that are necessary to exploit the opportunity.

For example, many university professors of science and engineering who invent technologies choose to have their inventions licensed to established firms whose employees have strong marketing skills and business experience. Why? Because most science and engineering professors are lacking in the knowledge needed to start a new business. They will not necessarily know how to do most of the things necessary to establish a new firm—things that you have learned in this class—like evaluating the market, hiring people, raising capital, and evaluating the opportunity. Moreover, the established firm will have the advantages of existing cash flow and established marketing, distribution, and manufacturing facilities that make it easier and cheaper for that firm to exploit the opportunity than the university inventor could if he started his own company.

However, entrepreneurs need to take care in choosing their partners, especially if they license their technology to others. As we explained in Chapter 5, to make money, you need to find partners with the capabilities that you lack, but you also need to find partners that treat you fairly and that you trust. Figure 10.4 shows an inventor who found a partner with the better business capabilities that justify licensing, but not one who meets the criterion of perceived fairness that is crucial to making the licensing arrangement work.

Figure 10.4 Entrepreneurs Often License Their Technologies to Other People Who Have Better Capabilities at Exploiting Opportunities Than They Do

Inventors of technology often aren't the most capable entrepreneurs, but you should pick your partners more wisely than this inventor!

Managing Information Problems in Organizing

A final factor that influences entrepreneurs' use of market-based modes of exploitation lies in information. As we mentioned in the **"Danger! Pitfall Ahead!"** section on Arrow's paradox (on page 245), entrepreneurs often find it difficult to use market mechanisms to exploit opportunities because disclosure of their business ideas to potential buyers undermines the buyers' willingness to pay for these ideas. The use of patents mitigates this disclosure problem. If an entrepreneur patents the key technology underlying a business idea, she can disclose her idea to others without fear that the buyer will refuse to pay for it once it has been disclosed. Why? Unlike the situation we described in the **"Danger! Pitfall Ahead!"** section, when the entrepreneur discloses her business idea to a potential buyer to demonstrate its value, the buyer has to pay to use the entrepreneur's business idea. The patent blocks anyone but the entrepreneur from using the technology underlying the business idea unless the entrepreneur has given him or her the right to do so. Therefore, the use of market mechanisms, like licensing, to exploit opportunities is much more common if the entrepreneur's technology is patented because patents reduce disclosure problems.

Patents are not the only information-related factors that influence the use of market-based mechanisms for exploiting business ideas. Market-based mechanisms are also more common when a business idea can be codified, or written down, in a contract. When a business idea can be described in a contract, both sides can have confidence that the legal system will enforce the agreement that they have made. However, if the business idea is too uncertain or too vague to write down, contracts are difficult to use. Not only will negotiations between the buyer and the seller be likely to break down as the two parties have trouble agreeing on what they buying and selling,[19] but also the uncertainty of the idea makes any contract that they manage to write very difficult to enforce.

For example, suppose that you wanted to sell your business idea for levitating cars. The idea would have value to all of the commuters who get stuck in rush hour traffic. But, let's say that you don't know yet how you would make these levitating cars. You would have a hard time contracting with someone else to buy the business idea. What if it turned out that you could make the car, but the cost would be the same as the cost of producing the space shuttle, or that you would need the world's supply of titanium to make 14 of the vehicles. Under these circumstances, the buyer probably wouldn't want your business idea any more. To get the buyer to sign the contract in the first place, you'd have to be willing to let them out of the contract if the solution you came up with wasn't feasible for them. But once you do that, then the buyer will have a way out of any contract that they sign and the contract is no longer enforceable.

You shouldn't come away from this thinking that information-related factors always lead people to use hierarchical modes of opportunity exploitation. Although we have just described two information-related factors that lead to the use of hierarchies over market-based mechanisms—disclosure and tacitness—many times these factors make entrepreneurs better off using market-based mechanisms of exploitation.

Take, for example, a restaurant entrepreneur who is deciding whether to buy a franchise or create her own independent restaurant to serve barbecue pizza. Although there are a variety of factors that influence this decision—Does the would-be entrepreneur have a good pizza recipe? Does she need support in creating a new business or does she know how to do it?—the information-related problems of adverse selection and moral hazard also influence her decision. We first discussed these concepts when we talked about financing new ventures in Chapter 6. As you probably remember, adverse selection occurs when people with less desirable characteristics are more likely to put themselves in a particular situation, as would be the case if only those people with lousy business ideas sought venture capital and those with good ideas financed their ideas from their own savings. Moral hazard occurs when people take action that benefits them at the expense of others, as would be the case if people used venture capital to buy fancy sports cars instead of investing in the development of their new businesses.

Entrepreneurs often face the potential for adverse selection from employees whom they hire to work for them. Why? Remember in Chapter 5 when we said that people are adept at image management? That can cause a lot of problems when an entrepreneur is seeking to hire employees. Take our barbecue pizza restaurant example. Because restaurant managers are paid fixed wages, they often overstate their abilities in order to get hired. If they get the job, but aren't qualified to do it, they don't bear any cost of that error. To distinguish qualified managers from unqualified ones, the entrepreneur has to engage in expensive efforts to screen potential employees: having them fill out applications, checking references, and interviewing them. Even then, the entrepreneur could select the wrong person if the employee really wanted to misrepresent his abilities.

Franchising mitigates this problem. A franchisee has to pay the franchisor for the right to operate the restaurant, and is compensated from its profits. If a potential franchisee doesn't have the right skills to operate the outlet, she would not make any profits, and might even lose her investment by buying a franchised outlet. This means that only people with the right skills to operate the outlets are willing to buy franchises, making franchising an inexpensive way for entrepreneurs to separate high and low quality restaurant managers. The key lesson here is that when adverse selection is a major threat in hiring employees, entrepreneurs are better off using contractual modes of opportunity exploitation, like franchising, than owning and operating their own outlets.[20]

Entrepreneurs also face another potential problem, a type of moral hazard called **shirking**. Shirking is the failure to put forth all of the effort that a person is capable of putting forth. Employees often shirk if they will receive the same salary regardless of how hard they work. As we discussed in Chapter 5, the tendency to shirk is a major problem for entrepreneurs because perceived fairness is very important to most people.

Entrepreneurs can minimize shirking problems by using a contractual mode of opportunity exploitation, like franchising. Franchising replaces the employee's fixed wage with compensation based on the profits from their efforts, such as their efforts to manage a restaurant. If a restaurant franchisee does not put forth the full amount of effort necessary to manage their restaurant, his profits will fall, and he will earn less money. Therefore, when employee shirking is a major problem, entrepreneurs often use contractual modes of opportunity exploitation, like franchising.[21]

However, franchising doesn't solve all of the entrepreneur's problems. In fact, entrepreneurs face two kinds of information problems when they use franchising. The first is a type of moral hazard called *free riding*. This problem should be familiar to anyone who has ever done a group project in school. Think about what happens when the grades for a group project are assigned equally to all members of the group. Everyone in the group has an incentive to free ride and let someone else do the work. If one person does all of the work, and the group gets an "A," then the others are better off than if they did the work to get an "A" because they received the benefit of an "A" grade without having to go to the library.

The same problem exists in business—so those of you that know who the free riders are on class projects, make sure you set up the right business arrangement with this person later! For instance, take a sandwich shop that operates under the brand name, say, Scott's Super Subs. If there is only one outlet of Scott's Super Subs in a particular town, the owner of the sub shop has a strong incentive to advertise in the local paper. Suppose that the ad costs $50. If every ad that promotes the super cheese sub with 14 different types of cheese brings in 48 cheese-loving customers at a profit margin of $2.00 per super sub, it pays for the entrepreneur to advertise in the paper.

However, now suppose that there are four outlets of Scott's Super Subs in town. The $50 dollar ad will still bring in 48 cheese-loving customers, but they will be divided across the four outlets. Individually, each of the outlet owners would lose money if they placed the ad themselves because they would incur the $50 cost, but only earn the additional profit of $24 (12 of the 48 customers times $2.00 per sub). If all of the outlet owners got together and agreed to share the cost of the ad, they would all benefit. Unfortunately, each of the sub shop entrepreneurs has an incentive to free ride off the efforts of the others to advertise the Scott's Super Subs name. If the other three sub shop owners shared the $50 cost of the ad, the fourth shop owner could obtain the $24 profit without incurring a share of the cost. Why? Customers will respond to a newspaper ad and go to the nearest outlet to buy their hoagies, regardless of who paid for the ad. Sometimes, the owners can write contracts with each other to manage this problem, but at other times those contracts can be difficult to write and enforce. If the free-riding problem becomes severe, having a single person own all four of the outlets would be a better arrangement. Then, the party that paid for the ad would get the benefits from sales at all of the outlets, and there is no free riding. This is why company ownership, rather than franchising, is used when there is a threat of free riding.

An even more severe problem from franchising, called **hold-up**, also motivates entrepreneurs to use hierarchical arrangements to exploit opportunities. Hold-up is an attempt by one party to opportunistically renegotiate the terms of a contract after it has been made. For example, consider a franchisee that has established a car rental franchise at the airport. The agreement says that the franchisee will pay the franchisor 5 percent of its sales to use the franchisor's brand name, reservation system, and method of doing business. The franchisor can hold up the franchisee and demand better terms, say an 8 percent royalty rate on sales, by threatening to put a second rental car franchise at the airport.[22] Because the franchisee knows that her sales will drop if another person also is allowed to operate the same car rental franchise at the airport, she agrees to pay the higher royalty rate. Often, the intense fear that franchisors will engage in this type of action makes it very difficult for entrepreneurs to attract franchisees, and forces them to operate their own outlets. (See Table 10.2 for a description of several information problems and their effect on the mode of exploitation.) Although some state governments, like Iowa's, have established laws to protect franchisees from this problem by requiring franchisors to maintain at least 3 miles

TYPE OF PROBLEM	MODE OF EXPLOITATION	REASONING BEHIND THE CHOICE
Adverse selection of potential employees	Market-based	By making compensation directly dependent on performance, those of low ability will be unlikely to misrepresent their abilities.
Moral hazard—Shirking by employees	Market-based	The incentive to shirk is reduced by making compensation directly dependent on performance.
Moral hazard—Free riding by outlet operators	Hierarchical	The threat of free riding by independent operators makes it better to operate a single entity that makes all investments and reaps all rewards.
Hold-up of outlet operators	Hierarchical	The threat of opportunistic renegotiation of the contract makes it difficult to find buyers.
Disclosure of knowledge	Hierarchical	Arrow's paradox: Buyers will not purchase knowledge unless its value is demonstrated, but demonstration undermines their incentive to pay.
Tacit business idea	Hierarchical	It is difficult to negotiate and enforce a contract about a business idea that cannot be documented in writing.

Table 10.2 Information Problems Influence the Choice Between Market-Based and Hierarchical Modes of Exploiting Opportunities

Entrepreneurs choose between market-based and hierarchical modes of doing business for a variety of different reasons.

between franchisees, other states are less friendly toward franchisees, making this problem more severe. For instance, in states without any franchise regulation, franchisors can even put another outlet of their franchise next door to an existing outlet!

KEY POINTS

- Entrepreneurs can, and do, exploit opportunities through market-based modes of exploitation like franchising and licensing.
- Entrepreneurs often use these market-based modes of exploitation because they are less costly than efforts to own the entire value chain, which is important given the capital constraints that new ventures face.
- Entrepreneurs often use market mechanisms to exploit opportunities because these mechanisms accelerate the pace of exploitation, which is important when the opportunity is short-lived or entering a market first provides advantages to a new firm.
- Entrepreneurs often use market mechanisms to exploit opportunities when other parties have better capabilities than they do at opportunity exploitation.
- Entrepreneurs often use market mechanisms to exploit opportunities because these mechanisms minimize adverse selection and shirking by employees.
- However, information problems do not always lead to market-based modes of opportunity exploitation. When disclosure problems are severe, and business ideas cannot be codified easily, and when the threat of free riding and hold-up are present, hierarchical modes of opportunity exploitation are better.

MANAGING INFORMATION ASYMMETRY AND UNCERTAINTY IN THE PURSUIT OF OPPORTUNITY

As we explained in Chapter 6, the entrepreneurial process involves a great deal of uncertainty. When entrepreneurs found their firms, they face technical uncertainty because they do not know for sure that the product or service that they are developing is going to work, or if it works, that they will be able to produce it. Entrepreneurs also face market uncertainty because they never really know for sure that customers will want their new product until after introducing it, and, even if the customers like it, that they will demand a large enough volume, fast enough, and at a price at which the entrepreneur can make a profit. Last, entrepreneurs face competitive uncertainty because they do not know if they will be able to create a competitive advantage and capture the profits from exploiting an opportunity, or if other companies will take that profit away from them.[23]

LEARNING OBJECTIVE

7 Describe the strategic actions that entrepreneurs take to manage information asymmetry and uncertainty in the entrepreneurial process.

The entrepreneurial process also involves significant information asymmetry between the entrepreneur and her employees, investors, customers, and suppliers. As we explained in Chapter 3, entrepreneurs identify and exploit opportunities because they have access to better information or have greater ability to recognize opportunities from that information. Moreover, as we explained earlier in this chapter, entrepreneurs often keep secret their methods of exploiting opportunities to limit imitation. These two forces mean that entrepreneurs almost always have more information about their opportunities and their methods of exploiting them than their employees, investors, customers, and suppliers.[24]

Because uncertainty and information asymmetry are an important part of the entrepreneurial process, successful entrepreneurs must develop strategies for managing these dimensions of the entrepreneurial process. In this section, we discuss three important strategies that entrepreneurs use to do this: growth from small scale, forming alliances and partnerships with established firms, and creating legitimacy for the opportunity and the new venture.

Growth from Small Scale

LEARNING OBJECTIVE

8 Explain why entrepreneurs often start their businesses on a small scale, and expand if they are successful.

Earlier in this chapter, we talked about the benefits of economies of scale in advertising and production, and how they lower the cost structure of a new firm. Given the value to firms of operating on a large scale, why don't most entrepreneurs start their businesses on a large scale? The answer lies in the uncertainty and information asymmetry that new ventures face.

The uncertainty and information asymmetry that pervade the entrepreneurial process make it virtually impossible for entrepreneurs to establish their ventures on a large scale, and even if they could, uncertainty and information asymmetry make it very foolish to do so.[25] First, as we explained in Chapter 6, most entrepreneurs have to self-finance the development of their new ventures. Except for a few very wealthy individuals, most people do not have a large amount of savings. So even if they max out all of their credit cards (as many entrepreneurs do!), very few people could come up with all of the money that it would take to start a business on the same scale of their existing competitors (given the hundreds of million dollars that it would take to start a biotechnology company, the billion dollars it would take to start a semiconductor company, or the tens of billions of dollars it would take to start an auto company).

So what do typical entrepreneurs do? Instead of starting their companies with as broad product lines, as large manufacturing facilities, or as much advertising as established companies in their industries, entrepreneurs generally start with small companies focused on a single product line. Then, if they do a decent job with their initial efforts, the entrepreneurs attract external investors, who give them the money to grow their ventures to the size of the other firms in its industry.

Second, investors do not like to give entrepreneurs large sums of money all at once. For the reasons we discussed in Chapter 6, investors tend to make relatively small investments in new ventures over time, using real options reasoning. As a result, most entrepreneurs simply cannot raise the capital that it would take to start a company that is large from day one. There is just too much information asymmetry and uncertainty, not to mention too few investors with enough capital to finance a new aerospace company that is the size of Boeing, or a new pharmaceutical company that is the size of Merck.

Third, starting a company is risky. Most people, entrepreneurs included, would like to minimize risk. Risk in new ventures comes from making large, irreversible investments. A good example of a large, irreversible investment is a steel plant. Once you take cash and use it to build a steel plant, that is what you have. You aren't going to be able to change that steel plant into a biotechnology laboratory, no matter how hard you try, even if you find that your opportunity was really in biotechnology and not in steel.

So entrepreneurs keep their risks down by making investments in things that are not irreversible, such as using generic trucks instead of specialized, custom-made vehicles. That way, if their businesses fail, the entrepreneurs can always sell the trucks, making the investment reversible. This is also why entrepreneurs don't purchase most of the assets that they need, and lease or borrow instead.[26] A borrowed asset can be returned, and a lease canceled, much more easily than something can be sold.

It is also why many businesses begin as consulting or contract organizations and go into making products only if customers turn out to be interested.[27] For example, waiting to produce shrinkwrapped software until after an entrepreneur proves that customers are interested in the accounting program that she has written reduces the entrepreneur's risk of producing software that no one will buy. By working for the customer as a consultant and providing the accounting software for a fee first, the entrepreneur reduces this risk.

Unfortunately for the entrepreneur, some assets have to be made in irreversible form. There is just no way to get around it. For example, if you are going to make and sell a new electronic device, you don't really have much choice, but you have to take some of your money and use it to build a prototype of the device. This is where small-scale production comes into play in reducing your risk. If you start by building one prototype and, if it works, expanding to small-scale production, and, then, if that works, expanding to greater production, risk bearing is minimized. The most that you can lose if your business fails is the amount that you put into assets that have no liquidation value. The smaller that investment is, the less that you will have at risk if the venture fails.[28] In short, all of these factors lead entrepreneurs to start on a small scale and expand if the business idea proves to be successful (see Figure 10.5).

Moreover, uncertainty means that entrepreneurs need to be flexible and adaptive in their strategies. Remember that, at the very beginning, entrepreneurs do not know if they can produce a product, find a market for the product, or compete with other firms to earn profits from that product. If it turns out that they can't do these things, entrepreneurs have to change their plans. Moreover, events occur that require entrepreneurs to change their plans. For instance, you might have planned to launch a really high-end boutique hotel, but the economy tanks and you need to make the hotel appeal to families to get enough customers to survive. By starting small and not investing too much in any one direction until the technical, market, and competitive uncertainty is reduced, the new venture remains more flexible and adaptive, and the entrepreneur can change directions more easily.

Clay Christiansen, a professor at Harvard Business School, provides a good example of the way that entrepreneurs use a flexible, adaptive strategy to manage market uncertainty in the process of exploiting a new business idea. In a study of the hard disk drive industry in the United States from 1976 to 1989, Clay found that many new companies introduced new disk drives that were smaller than the disk drives made by established firms. Initially, the entrepreneurs thought that they would sell the disk drives to the customers of the established disk drive manufacturers. But, in

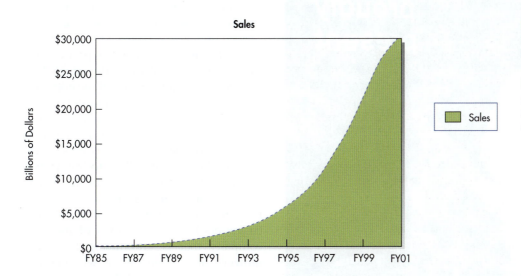

Figure 10.5 Most Entrepreneurs Start Their New Businesses at a Small Scale and Then Expand if the Initial Effort Proves Favorable

Even Microsoft, one of the world's largest companies, began as a tiny company and expanded from there.

Source: Based on data available at http://www.microsoft.com/msft.

all cases, when a new-sized disk drive was introduced, none of the existing customers wanted them. In every single case, the entrepreneurs had to search for new target markets, going for one after another until they found a segment with customers that were interested in their particular type of disk drive.[29]

Forming Alliances and Partnerships with Established Firms

Many new firms form alliances with established firms as part of their strategy to exploit their opportunities. For instance, many new biotechnology companies engage in research and development alliances with established pharmaceutical companies.

Researchers have explained that the formation of alliances and partnerships with established firms overcomes several major problems in the exploitation of entrepreneurial opportunities.[30] First, as we mentioned earlier, in our discussion of the use of market-based modes of opportunity exploitation, opportunities are often short-lived and entrepreneurs do not have enough time to obtain external financing to build needed assets, such as manufacturing plants or retail outlets. By forming alliances with established companies, the entrepreneur can gain access to already developed assets.[31] For example, when new biotechnology companies are in a race to be the first to develop a new drug, they often form alliances with pharmaceutical firms to gain access to research facilities and expertise because venture capitalists cannot provide them with the resources quickly enough to build these assets from scratch.

Second, as we mentioned in Chapter 6, entrepreneurs simply lack the capital that they need to purchase the resources that they need both because they must self-finance and because investors ration the capital that they provide to entrepreneurs. Alliances and partnerships with established firms provide a way to gain access to resources that they need—like plant and equipment, sales forces, and product development expertise—but don't have the money to purchase. Moreover, as we explained earlier in our discussion of starting on a small scale, allying with an established company that already has the equipment and facilities that the entrepreneur needs minimizes the potential downside loss that the entrepreneur would experience if the business idea turned out to be a failure.[32]

Third, an alliance or partnership with an established company helps the entrepreneur persuade others that her business idea is valuable. As we explained in Chapter 3, the identification of an entrepreneurial opportunity requires either the possession of information that other people do not have or a better ability to recognize the opportunity inherent in that information. Either way, the entrepreneurial process often involves the recognition of something that customers did not see. Human nature is such that people tend not to believe the value of things that they, themselves, don't see, making it hard to convince customers that a novel business idea is a good business idea.

Figure 10.6 Entrepreneurs Often Form Alliances and Partnerships with Established Firms

Partnering with Sears and other prominent retailers, George Foreman was able to achieve faster customer acceptance of his lean, mean, fat-grilling machine.

An entrepreneur can mitigate this problem by selling her new product or service under an established firm's brand name through an alliance or partnership (see Figure 10.6).[33] Because the established firm has a reputation to lose if the entrepreneur's product or service turns out not to be any good, potential customers see the established firm's support as evidence of the value of the new product or service, making them more willing to buy it. For example, think about a new business that wants to introduce an electric-powered lawn mower with a unique design. Potential customers have never heard of the new company that is introducing the lawn mower and are unsure of whether the design is really any good. This makes it dif-

ficult for the new company to sell its lawn mowers. The entrepreneur can get around this problem by forming an alliance with a big retailer like Sears. The alliance with Sears will lead people to associate the lawn mower with them. They will figure that the product must be okay or Sears wouldn't have partnered with the company. This, of course, makes it much easier for the start-up to sell the lawn mower than if it had to sell the lawn mower on its own.

Establishing alliances as part of an entrepreneur's strategy involves certain hazards. In particular, alliance partners may take advantage of the entrepreneur, exploiting their size and power in the relationship. Numerous examples have been found of entrepreneurs forming partnerships with large, established companies and then finding that the alliance partners had misrepresented the assets and capabilities that they could bring to the relationship, that the alliance partner waited for the new firm to make investments in the relationship and then exploiting the fact that those investments were sunk to extract a better deal from the entrepreneur, and that the alliance partner withheld promised resources and assets. Entrepreneurs need to factor in these hazards when evaluating the benefits of alliances and partnerships with other firms.

Legitimating the Opportunity and the New Venture

The uncertainty and information asymmetry inherent in the entrepreneurial process also means that entrepreneurs often have to generate **legitimacy** for their business ideas, particularly if those business ideas are novel. Legitimacy is a belief that an idea is correct and appropriate. For example, a new company called Lifegem has just introduced a new product that allows you to take the remains of your dead relatives, cremate them, and turn them into industrial diamonds that are then placed into jewelry. (We are not kidding. We saw a segment about this company on the *Today Show*). To succeed, this company will have to convince people that taking human remains and turning them into jewelry is a correct and appropriate action before they can worry about how to manufacture the jewelry or how to price it. Although you might think that this is impossible, it isn't. When life insurance was first introduced, people didn't think that it was appropriate or correct for the same reasons that people think that making jewelry from the cremated remains of relatives is incorrect and inappropriate.[34] Yet life insurance became an accepted product that many people buy.

LEARNING OBJECTIVE

10 List actions that entrepreneurs undertake to make their new ventures appear more legitimate, and explain why they take these actions.

Why do people have such a hard time accepting an entrepreneur's novel business idea as legitimate? First, the entrepreneur has information that others do not have, making it easier for the entrepreneur to visualize the value of the business idea than it is for other people to visualize that value. Second, new business ideas are inherently uncertain, and many of them will fail. Because people have a bias against uncertainty and failure, they tend to believe that the status quo is better than something new.

The tendency of people to resist viewing new business ideas as legitimate requires entrepreneurs to take action that demonstrates the legitimacy of their business ideas and opportunities to make them acceptable to customers, suppliers, investors, and employees. They do this in several ways. First, entrepreneurs show that their business ideas conform to existing rules and norms. For instance, the entrepreneur who came up with the first ethanol-powered car designed it to look like other cars, changing only the engine. Why? By keeping everything else in the car the same, potential customers would view the ethanol-powered vehicle as more legitimate and acceptable than if it didn't look like a standard car.

Another way that entrepreneurs demonstrate legitimacy is to imitate the routines and procedures of existing firms so that their ventures don't look like new companies. For example, many entrepreneurs "borrow" the offices of existing firms when trying to meet customers, instead of meeting their clients where they do business—in their homes or their garages. They do this because people tend not to trust or believe in businesses that don't look "real." By borrowing "real" offices, entrepreneurs "show" customers what looks like a regular business, not like some start-up in a garage.[35]

A third way that entrepreneurs demonstrate legitimacy for their new businesses is by engaging in collective actions. Entrepreneurs, particularly those in new industries,

© Bettmann/CORBIS

often join together in trade associations, or work together to set up common standards or designs. Common standards and designs make products and services less confusing to customers and reduce the level of effort to persuade customers that the opportunity is reliable and valid.[36] For example, entrepreneurs in the wireless telecommunications industry joined together to establish a trade association and standard-setting body in part to make sure that the government and general population understood the general value of wireless devices.

A fourth way that entrepreneurs demonstrate legitimacy for their business ideas is by obtaining certification by reputable authorities. People tend to believe in the reliability and validity of statements made by people in authority, in part because those people have greater expertise than the general population, and in part because people in authority have a lot to lose if they certify the value of something that turns out to have no

Figure 10.7 Entrepreneurs Often Have to Take Actions That Make Their Business Ideas Look Legitimate

The car shown here won contests sponsored by automotive magazines in the early twentieth century to test reliability and features, making it more appealing to customers than other car models.

value. Huggy Rao, a professor of organizational behavior at the Kellogg School at Northwestern University, showed the value of certification to new ventures in a study of automobile companies in the early twentieth century. Rao showed that new automobile companies that won contests sponsored by automotive magazines were more likely to survive than their competitors.[37] The victories in the magazines' contests led customers to perceive the automakers as better and more reliable than other auto companies. In short, to be successful, entrepreneurs need to establish legitimacy for their new businesses just as people need to establish legitimacy for anything new that they do (see Figure 10.7).

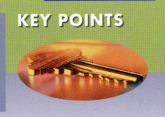

KEY POINTS

- Entrepreneurs engage in three strategies to manage the technical, market, and competitive uncertainty and information asymmetry that new ventures face: growth from a small scale, forming alliances and partnerships with established firms, and creating legitimacy for the opportunity and the new venture.
- Uncertainty and information asymmetry lead entrepreneurs to self-finance; lead investors to limit the size of their investments in new ventures; and require entrepreneurs to bear risk, all of which lead entrepreneurs to start at on a small scale and expand if they are successful.
- Entrepreneurs form alliances and partnerships with established firms to establish the value chain quickly; to overcome capital constraints to the assembly of necessary assets; and to use established brand names to demonstrate the value of their new products and services.
- Uncertainty and information asymmetry also make it difficult for people to believe that new business ideas are appropriate and correct, leading entrepreneurs to take actions to demonstrate the legitimacy of their opportunities and business ideas. Among the different ways that entrepreneurs demonstrate legitimacy are adhering to existing rules and norms; imitating the routines and procedures of existing firms; engaging in collective actions; and obtaining certification from reputable authorities.

Summary and Review of Key Points

- The identification of a business opportunity that satisfies the needs of customers is not enough for an entrepreneur to earn profits; the entrepreneur also needs a competitive advantage.

- The exploitation of an opportunity will provide information to others about how to imitate the entrepreneur's business idea; imitation by others will erode the entrepreneur's profit from exploiting the opportunity.

- By developing a competitive advantage, the entrepreneur precludes others from imitating the business idea perfectly, and allows the entrepreneur to capture the profits from exploiting the opportunity.

- Entrepreneurs protect their business ideas against competition in two ways: by keeping others from learning about the opportunity and understanding how they exploit it, and by blocking others from exploiting the opportunity in the same way that they do.

- Efforts to stop others from learning about an opportunity involve keeping secret the information that led to the discovery of the opportunity, which works best when the information about the opportunity requires knowledge of a new technical process.

- The entrepreneur can keep others from imitating the opportunity by taking advantage of causal ambiguity about how to exploit the opportunity, which works best when understanding how to exploit an opportunity involves tacit knowledge that is held by only a few people.

- Entrepreneurs deter competition by creating four barriers to imitation of their business ideas: obtaining control of the resources needed to exploit the opportunity; establishing legal obstacles to imitation, such as obtaining a patent or government permit; developing a reputation for satisfying the needs of customers; and innovating to keep their products or services ahead of those offered by the competition.

- Entrepreneurs can, and do, exploit opportunities through market-based modes of exploitation like franchising and licensing.

- Entrepreneurs often use these market-based modes of exploitation because they are less costly than efforts to own the entire value chain, which is important given the capital constraints that new ventures face.

- Entrepreneurs often use market mechanisms to exploit opportunities because these mechanisms accelerate the pace of exploitation, which is important when the opportunity is short-lived or entering a market first provides advantages to a new firm.

- Entrepreneurs often use market mechanisms to exploit opportunities when other parties have better capabilities than they do at opportunity exploitation.

- Entrepreneurs often use market mechanisms to exploit opportunities because these mechanisms minimize adverse selection and shirking by employees.

- However, information problems do not always lead to market-based modes of opportunity exploitation. When disclosure problems are severe, and business ideas cannot be codified easily, and when the threat of free riding and hold-up are present, hierarchical modes of opportunity exploitation are better.

- Entrepreneurs engage in three strategies to manage the technical, market, and competitive uncertainty and information asymmetry that new ventures face: growth from a small scale, forming alliances and partnerships with established firms, and creating legitimacy for the opportunity and the new venture.

- Uncertainty and information asymmetry lead entrepreneurs to self-finance; lead investors to limit the size of their investments in new ventures; and require entrepreneurs to bear risk, all of which lead entrepreneurs to start on a small scale and expand if they are successful.

- Entrepreneurs form alliances and partnerships with established firms to establish the value chain quickly; to overcome capital constraints to the assembly of necessary assets; and to use established brand names to demonstrate the value of their new products and services.

- Uncertainty and information asymmetry also make it difficult for people to believe that new business ideas are appropriate and correct, leading entrepreneurs to take actions to demonstrate the legitimacy of their opportunities and business ideas. Among the different ways that entrepreneurs demonstrate legitimacy are adhering to existing rules and norms; imitating the routines and procedures of existing firms; engaging in collective actions; and obtaining certification from reputable authorities.

Glossary

Causal Ambiguity: Indistinctness about the underlying process through which entrepreneurs exploit opportunities.

Competitive Advantage: A business attribute that allows a firm and not its competitors to capture the profits from exploiting an opportunity.

First Mover: The first firm to enter a particular market.

Franchising: A mode of business in which one party, the franchisor, develops a plan for the provision of a product or service to end customers, and another party, the franchisee, uses that plan in return for paying a fee and agreeing to oversight.

Government Permit: A right given by a government to be the only party allowed to do something in a particular geographical location.

Hierarchcial Modes: When one party owns all parts of the operation that produces and sells a product or service to end customers.

Hold-Up: An attempt by one party to a contract to opportunistically renegotiate the terms of an agreement after it has been made.

Legitimacy: A belief that something is correct and appropriate.

Licensing: A mode of business in which one party contracts with another to use the first party's ideas to make products and services for sale to end customers in return for a fee.

Market-Based Modes: When different parts of the business, such as manufacturing and marketing, are owned by different entities and are connected by a contractual relationship.

Monopoly: A situation in which a firm is the only supplier of a product or service.

Network Externalities: A situation in which something has increasing value as more people use it.

Patent: An exclusive right given by the government to preclude others from duplicating an invention for a specified period of time in return for disclosure of the invention.

Shirking: The failure to put forth all of the effort that a person is capable of providing.

Tacit Knowledge: A type of understanding that cannot be documented or even articulated. It is frequently contrasted with codified knowledge, which is a type of understanding that can be expressed in documentary form.

Trade Secret: A piece of knowledge that confers an advantage on firms and is protected by nondisclosure.

Vertically Integrated: A situation in which a firm owns successive stages of the value chain.

Discussion Questions

1. Suppose you started a company without a competitive advantage. What do you think would happen to your company? Why?

2. Think of five different new businesses. For each of these businesses, explain what you would do to increase your chances of keeping the profits from exploiting these business opportunities. Why would you choose the approach that you chose?

3. Assume that you've come up with an idea for a new restaurant specializing in chicken fingers. Should you pursue the opportunity through franchising or by establishing a chain of company-owned stores? Explain your choice.

4. When you start a new company, should you form a partnership or alliance with a large, established firm? Why or why not?

5. You've just started a new telecommunication company and other entrepreneurs in the industry invite you to join the telecom trade association. Should you join? Why or why not?

InfoTrac Exercises

1. **Competitive Advantage Through Specialty Franchising**
   John F. Preble; Richard C. Hoffman
   Journal of Consumer Marketing, Winter 1998 v15 n1 p64(14)

Record: A20514522

Abstract: A competitive advantage in terms of strategy and customer responsiveness can be developed through mobile franchising. Mobile franchises tend to be more focused in their strategies in terms of geography, product and market. They can establish their business where their clients are located or where the customer's "need" can be found. Semicustom work, fast cycle times, professional service, proximity to customer, and customer responsiveness are some of the significant elements of mobile franchises.

1. According to the text and the article, what are the benefits of franchising for entrepreneurs?

2. According to the article, how is competitive advantage developed through mobile franchising?

3. What market trends are fueling entrepreneurial opportunities in mobile franchising?

Let's Get Together (small-business alliance)(includes related article on how to tell if an alliance is right for one's small business)

Jack Sommars

Colorado Business Magazine, December 1996 v23 n12 p44(6)

Record: A19040320

Abstract: More and more businesses are entering partnerships as the number of small-business alliances grew by 25 percent since 1986. In Colorado, such alliances are particularly abundant in the telecommunications, biotechnology, and electronics industries. Small firms often opt to form an alliance with other companies for a more cost-effective way of reaching new customers and providing better services. Alliances succeed when partners work together and share equal commitment with one another.

1. What role do alliances with established firms play in the strategic development of a small business?

2. How have the companies mentioned in the article used alliances to build their businesses?

3. According to the article, when are alliances most likely to fail?

GETTING DOWN
TO BUSINESS

Developing a Strategy

This chapter discussed the importance of developing a strategy for your new venture. Without a strategy, you can still start a firm, but you're unlikely to be successful. For this reason, it's important to carefully think about your new venture strategy. Moreover, when you write a feasibility study on your venture opportunity or develop a business plan to exploit it, you'll need to specify your new venture's strategy. This exercise will help you to develop a strategy for your new venture. If you follow these steps, you'll find that you will be well on your way to defining a strategy for your new venture.

Step One: In no more than one paragraph, identify the opportunity that your new venture will exploit.

Step Two: Using the material you developed when you completed the exercises in Chapter 9, explain the customer need that your new venture's product or service will fill, and how your product or service will fill that need.

Step Three: Explain how your new venture will deter actions by other firms to meet this customer need with their products or services. Remember to consider the mechanisms discussed in this chapter: Will you develop a trade secret? Will you exploit causal ambiguity? Will you obtain control over resources through exclusive contracts, patents, government permits, or the purchase of the key source of supply? Will you build a reputation through advertising and the development of a brand name? Will you innovate and move ahead of competitors by providing superior product or service features?

Step Four: Choose your organizational form. Will you establish a vertically-integrated operation or will you franchise or license? Explain your choice. How do the factors that we discussed in the chapter—cost, speed, capabilities, and information—influence your decision?

Step Five: Explain how your new venture will overcome information asymmetry and uncertainty. How will your new venture grow? Will you create alliances and partnerships with established firms? If so, why and how? How will you create legitimacy for your new venture? Will you imitate the actions of large firms? Conform to norms? Engage in collective action? Seek certification from reputable authorities?

Write down your strategy for building your business. Explain how your business will grow from its initial size at the time it is formed to the size that it will be at the time of your exit strategy. In addition, explain how you will establish legitimacy for your new venture and explain how you will overcome problems of information asymmetry and uncertainty in developing the venture.

Identifying Your Competitors

This chapter has focused on the importance of establishing a competitive advantage in your new business. To establish a competitive advantage, entrepreneurs need to identify their competitors and specify how their new venture will provide better products or services than those offered by competitors. Unfortunately, most entrepreneurs have trouble identifying their competitors and evaluating their strengths and weaknesses. This exercise is designed to help you identify your competitors, evaluate their strengths and weaknesses, and pinpoint a strategy for offering better products and services than your competitors.

Step One: List all of the competitors that your new venture will face. Be careful to approach this question from the point of view of your customer. For example, if your new venture is a bakery, list all competing bakeries in your area. Also include all other companies that offer products that your customers might choose over your own, like donut shops and ice cream parlors. Remember to consider all firms (like your own) that might enter the market in the near future.

Step Two: Summarize the products and services that each of your competitors offers. Include information about the product features, price, quality, advertising and promotion strategy, distribution methods, after-sales service, and so on.

Step Three: For each of your competitors, list their strengths and weaknesses. Make sure to approach this analysis from your customers' perspective, and be fair to your competitors. If they have real strengths, acknowledge them. For each of your competitors' strengths, explain how you will overcome it. For each of their weaknesses, explain how you will exploit it.

Step Four: Identify the current strategies of each of your competitors. Are they adding new strengths? Do they have plans to overcome current weaknesses? Be prepared to explain how you will respond to the current strategies of each of your competitors.

Gathering Information on Competitors

Most entrepreneurs find it very difficult to gather information about their competitors. As a result, they write business plans based on inaccurate or outdated information about their competitors' strategies and strengths and weaknesses. To overcome this problem, you'll need to practice gathering information about your competition. For this reason, we've developed this exercise in gathering information on competitors. Please follow it to create a file on each of your new business's competitors.

1. **Conduct an Internet search on each of your competitors.** Take the information that you gather and divide it into categories such as strategy, products and services, problems, successes, and so on.

2. **Talk to your competitors and their customers.** Ask customers what they like and dislike about your competitors. Ask your competitors about their companies. You'll be surprised how much information people will give you. Add that information to the records that you created from your Internet search.

3. **Examine documentary sources.** Go to the library and conduct a database search on your competitors. What do articles in newspapers, magazines, and trade publications say about them? Have your competitors issued press releases that provide

useful information? Have their executives made presentations or speeches that provide information about their companies? Include the information from documentary sources in your records about competitors.

4. **Examine your competitors' advertising.** What do print, radio, television, Internet, billboard, and other advertising for your competitors show about them? What about displays at trade shows or other events? Do they provide useful information about your competition? The answer is probably yes. Again, add this information to your records.

Enhanced Learning

You may select any combination of the case options below to enhance your understanding of the chapter material.

■ **Appendix 1: Case Studies –** Thirteen cases provide opportunities to apply chapter concepts to realistic entrepreneurial situations. These brief cases call for careful analysis of real business problems and ask you to think about potential solutions.

■ **Appendix 2: Video Case Library –** Nine cases are tied directly to video segments from the popular PBS television series *Small Business School*. These cases and video segments give you unparalleled access to today's entrepreneurs, with expert advice and insights on how to start, run, and grow a business.

■ **Comprehensive Cases –** Visit the book support Web site at http://baron.swlearning.com for cases detailing real businesses whose successes and setbacks illustrate each stage of the entrepreneurial process. You will conduct in-depth analysis of entrepreneurial challenges through well-developed case studies.

Notes

1 Shane, S. (forthcoming). *A general theory of entrepreneurship: The individual-opportunity nexus.* London: Edward Elgar.
2 Schiller, B., & Crewson, P. 1997. Entrepreneurial origins: A longitudinal inquiry. *Economic Inquiry* 35: 523–531.
3 Shane, S. (forthcoming). *A general theory of entrepreneurship: The individual-opportunity nexus.* London: Edward Elgar.
4 Barney, J. 1991. Firm resources and sustained competitive advantage. *Journal of Management* 17(1): 99–120.
5 Nelson, R., & Winter, S. 1982. *An evolutionary theory of economic change.* Cambridge, MA: Belknap Press.
6 Amit, R., Glosten, L., & Muller, E. 1993. Challenges to theory development in entrepreneurship research. *Journal of Management Studies* 30: 815–834.
7 Arrow, K. 1962. Economic welfare and the allocation of resources for inventions. In R. Nelson (ed.). *The rate and direction of inventive activity.* Princeton, NJ: Princeton University Press.
8 Rumelt, R. 1987. Theory, strategy and entrepreneurship. In D. Teece (ed.). *The competitive challenge: Strategies for industrial innovation and renewal.* Cambridge, MA: Ballinger, 137–158.

9 Casson, M. 1982. *The entrepreneur.* Totowa, NJ: Barnes & Noble Books.
10 Shane, S. (forthcoming). *A general theory of entrepreneurship: The individual-opportunity nexus.* London: Edward Elgar.
11 Casson, M. 1982. *The entrepreneur.* Totowa, NJ: Barnes & Noble Books.
12 Practice makes perfect. http://www.entrepreneur.com/Magazines/Copy_of_MA_SegArticle/0,4453,302464----4,00.html.
13 Hendricks, M. 1998. The modular squad. *Entrepreneur* (March): 101.
14 Shane, S., & Foo, M. 1999. New firm survival: Institutional explanations for new franchisor mortality. *Management Science* 45(2): 142–159.
15 Venkataraman, S. 1997. The distinctive domain of entrepreneurship research: An editor's perspective. In J. Katz & R. Brockhaus (eds.). *Advances in Entrepreneurship, Firm Emergence, and Growth* 3: 119–138. Greenwich, CT: JAI Press.
16 Evans, D., & Leighton, L. 1989. Some empirical aspects of entrepreneurship. *American Economic Review* 79: 519–535.

17 Shane, S. 1998. Making new franchise systems work. *Strategic Management Journal* 19(7): 697–707.

18 Teece, D. 1986. Profiting from technological innovation: Implications for integration, collaboration, licensing, and public policy. *Research Policy* 15: 286–305.

19 Audretsch, D. 1997. Technological regimes, industrial demography and the evolution of industrial structures. *Industrial and Corporate Change* 49–82.

20 Shane, S. 1998. Making new franchise systems work. *Strategic Management Journal* 19(7): 697–707.

21 Ibid.

22 Azoulay, P., & Shane, S. 2001. Entrepreneurs, contracts and the failure of young firms. *Management Science* 47(3): 337–358.

23 Amit, R., Glosten, L., & Muller, E. 1990a. Does venture capital foster the most promising entrepreneurial firms? *California Management Review* (spring): 102–111.

24 Shane, S. (forthcoming). *A general theory of entrepreneurship: The individual-opportunity nexus.* London: Edward Elgar.

25 Bhide, A. 2000. *The origin and evolution of new businesses.* New York: Oxford University Press.

26 Starr, J., & MacMillan, I. 1990. Resource cooptation via social contracting: Resource acquisition strategies for new ventures. *Strategic Management Journal* 11: 79–92.

27 Roberts, E. 1991. *Entrepreneurs in high technology.* New York: Oxford University Press.

28 Caves, R. 1998. Industrial organization and new findings on the turnover and mobility of firms. *Journal of Economic Literature* 36: 1947–1982.

29 Christiansen, C. & Bower, J. 1996. Customer power, strategic investment, and the failure of leading firms. *Strategic Management Journal* 17: 197–218.

30 Stuart, T., Hoang, H., & Hybels, R. 1999. Interorganizational endorsements and the performance of entrepreneurial ventures. *Administrative Science Quarterly* 44: 315–349.

31 Katilla, R., & Mang, P. (forthcoming). Exploiting technological opportunities: The timing of collaborations. *Research Policy.*

32 Venkataraman, S. 1997. The distinctive domain of entrepreneurship research: An editor's perspective. In J. Katz & R. Brockhaus (eds.). *Advances in Entrepreneurship, Firm Emergence, and Growth* 3: 119–138. Greenwich, CT: JAI Press.

33 Eisenhardt, K., & Schoonhoven, K. 1990. Organizational growth: Linking founding team, strategy, environment, and growth among U.S. semiconductor ventures, 1978–1988. *Administrative Science Quarterly* 35: 504–529.

34 Aldrich, H. 1999. *Organizations evolving.* London: Sage.

35 Starr, J., & MacMillan, I. 1990. Resource cooptation via social contracting: Resource acquisition strategies for new ventures. *Strategic Management Journal* 11: 79–92.

36 Aldrich, H. 1999. *Organizations evolving.* London: Sage.

37 Rao, H. 1994. The social construction of reputation: Certification contests, legitimation and the survival of organizations in the American automobile industry: 1895–1912. *Strategic Management Journal* 13: 29–44.

CHAPTER 11

INTELLECTUAL PROPERTY: PROTECTING YOUR IDEAS

LEARNING OBJECTIVES

After reading this chapter, you should be able to:

1. Explain why product development in new firms is difficult, but why new firms tend to be better than established firms at product development in most industries.

2. Explain why established firms find it easy to imitate entrepreneurs' intellectual property quickly and at a low cost.

3. Define a patent, explain what conditions are necessary for an inventor to patent an invention, and outline the pros and cons of patenting.

4. Define a trade secret, explain what conditions are necessary for an invention to be a trade secret, and outline the pros and cons of trade secrets.

5. Define a trademark, describe why trademarks are useful to entrepreneurs, and explain how an entrepreneur can obtain a trademark.

6. Define a copyright, and describe how it protects an entrepreneur's intellectual property.

7. Describe a first-mover advantage and explain the conditions under which it provides a useful form of intellectual property protection.

8. Describe complementary assets, and explain when it is better for an entrepreneur to obtain control over complementary assets than to be innovative.

Capturing the Profits from New Products and Services
    The Product Development Process
    New Firm Advantages at Product Development
    Ease of Imitating Entrepreneurs' Intellectual Property

Legal Forms of Intellectual Property Protection
    Patents
    Trade Secrets
    Trademarks
    Copyrights

Nonlegal Forms of Intellectual Property Protection
    Learning Curves, Lead Time, and the First-Mover Advantage
    Complementary Assets

In the early 1990s, Bjorn Jakobson, a Swedish entrepreneur, invented a baby-carrying device. It was a very useful product because it allowed a person to carry a baby but still have his hands free to do other things (see Figure 11.1). As an experienced entrepreneur, Jakobson knew that other companies would soon try to imitate his product and that obtaining a patent would be a good way to protect the product against imitation.

However, the U.S. Patent and Trademark Office had already issued eight baby carrier patents. In 1951, Vera Maxwell received a patent on her infant carrier, followed by D.J. Hershman, who patented hers in 1966. In 1979, Sandra Hathaway patented a child carrier with an enveloping structure and suspension strap.[1] In 1983, Patricia Purtzer and William Lauer patented an infant carrier with a detachable pouch.[2] In 1990, Allison Poole and Jodi Badagliacca patented their infant carrier. In 1993, Junice Dotseh patented a baby carrier with head support,[3] and James Bicheler and Kenneth Morton patented another style of baby carrier. Finally, in 1996, Hakan Bergqvist patented still another baby carrier. Jakobson was concerned about these inventions. He knew that to obtain a patent, his baby carrier had to be something that hadn't already been invented by someone else.

At first glance, it might appear that Jakobson wouldn't be able to patent his new product because so many other people had already patented baby carriers. But, Jakobson knew that patents only protect what is stated in their *claims*. As we will explain in greater detail later in the chapter, a claim is the part of the patent that identifies the invention that is protected against imitation. As long as Jakobson didn't claim the same features as the other baby carriers, he could patent his baby carrier.

By carefully examining the claims of the previous baby carrier patents, Jakobson discovered that the prior inventions were different from his in several ways. As a result, he was able to claim the invention of "a baby carrier comprising two closed strap loops which are mutually connected at a point, the strap loops adapted to extend around respective shoulder regions of a user such that the point is located on a rear side of the user, a carrier piece which is connected to the strap loops both at an end part of the carrier piece and at laterally spaced sides of the carrier piece so as to form a baby supporting pouch, a pair of insert tongues secured to said strap loops, releasable fasteners providing connections between the strap loops and the laterally spaced sides of the carrier piece which, when released, enable the carrier piece to be dropped down fully around its end part, and a clasp secured to said end part of said carrier piece and including sleeves for respectively receiving said insert tongues so that said insert tongues are releasably interlocked with said clasp and a bar lock which a free length of the end part of the carrier piece is adjustable."[4]

As you probably noticed, Jakobson's patent claims are pretty narrow. This narrowness means that another person could patent another baby carrier even after Bjorn received his patent, as long as they did not violate the specific claims in his patent. In fact, just over 5 months after Jakobson's patent issued, Kevin Kohn of Atlanta, Georgia, filed a patent on another baby carrier.[5] The moral of this story for entrepreneurs is that a patent only protects what is stated in its claims. Even when other people have patented similar things before them, entrepreneurs can patent new products. But, remember that what goes around comes around. If an entrepreneur has to write narrow claims to avoid violating a previous patent, his patent will only protect the invention against a narrow range of imitators.

Figure 11.1 The Baby Bjorn: A Patented New Product

Many customers have found Bjorn Jakobson's baby carrier to be a very valuable new product, motivating the inventor to obtain a patent to protect it against imitation by others.

Photo courtesy of Lynne Schneider.

The remainder of this chapter will examine how entrepreneurs protect their intellectual property. In the first section, we will explain why protecting intellectual property is so important to entrepreneurs—because most of the time entrepreneurs' only advantages over established firms lie in product development. We will also explain how the product development process works, and why new firms tend to be better at it than established firms, at least in most industries. But this section will also discuss why it's very easy for people to imitate entrepreneurs' intellectual property.

In the second section, we will describe four legal forms of intellectual property protection—patents, trade secrets, trademarks, and copyrights. We'll explain how these tools work and the pros and cons of using each of them.

In the final section of the chapter, we will discuss forms of intellectual property protection that don't depend on legal barriers—first-mover advantages and complementary assets. We'll explain how these things work, and when entrepreneurs should use them to protect their intellectual property.

CAPTURING THE PROFITS FROM NEW PRODUCTS AND SERVICES

Protecting their intellectual property is very important for entrepreneurs because, most of the time (with the few exceptions described in Chapter 9 about serving new markets), the only advantages entrepreneurs have over established firms lie in product development. In general, established firms are much better than new firms at marketing and manufacturing.

But just being better than established firms at product development is not enough for entrepreneurs to be successful. If entrepreneurs can't protect their **intellectual property**, the core ideas about their new product or service, then it doesn't matter that they are better than established firms at product development. The established firms can wait for the entrepreneurs to complete their product development and then imitate the entrepreneurs' new products and services. In this section, we'll explain why it is very difficult for entrepreneurs to protect their intellectual property, and offer some suggestions for approaches that successful entrepreneurs have found to be effective. But first we need to explain how product development occurs and why new firms tend to be better at this activity than established firms.

The Product Development Process

Once an entrepreneur has identified an opportunity to pursue and has obtained at least the initial resources to begin pursuit of her opportunity, she must engage in **product development**. Product development is the process by which the entrepreneur creates the product or service that will be sold to customers.

Developing a new product or service is not easy. Even if the entrepreneur has recognized a clear need among potential customers, she still has to create a solution to that need, which can be produced and marketed for less than the customer would be willing to pay for it. That, of course, is easier said than done. For example, you probably know that cancer is a major medical problem and that people would clearly pay for a drug to treat it. Knowledge that this clear customer need exists doesn't mean that you can come up with a drug to treat cancer. Moreover, even if you could come up with the formula for a cancer-fighting drug, you might not be able to produce it in a cost-effective manner. For example, Taxol is a cancer drug made from the bark of the yew tree. Because yew trees are relatively rare and it takes a lot of the bark to make the drug, Taxol is very expensive. Taxol isn't a very good solution to many types of cancer, even if it were shown to be effective in treating these diseases. Medical insurers only cover the use of Taxol for very serious types of cancer that it works particularly well at treating. For other types of cancer, Taxol isn't a cost-effective solution.

The development of a new product or service is also difficult because it's very uncertain. Entrepreneurs don't know if the product development path will lead to a successful new product or service. In many cases, millions or even billions of dollars can be spent to develop a new product or service that doesn't work. For example, Motorola spent over a billion dollars on a satellite-based portable phone system and then scrapped the system because it didn't work well enough to attract the necessary volume of customers.

Other times, the product development path is successful, but at developing something different from what people set out to produce. For example, when Merck was seeking to develop a drug to treat prostate problems, they found that the drug that they developed, Propecia, had the side effect of stimulating hair growth. As a result, Merck ended up developing a drug to treat baldness rather than a drug to treat prostate problems.

What does the difficulty and uncertainty of product development mean for entrepreneurs? Basically, it means that entrepreneurs are most effective at product development if they quickly screen new product opportunities to identify the most promising ones. Rather than invest heavily in the evaluation of different product opportunities, entrepreneurs do well to actually integrate their analysis with action to develop the new product. For instance, suppose you have thought of making a device to download music from the Internet and play it, like an MP3 player. Instead of conducting extensive laboratory research to decide what features to put into the prototype—testing different features and comparing them to each other on a technical basis—before making the prototype and going into production, you'd be better off building the prototype without spending a lot of time on research. By showing your best guess to some customers, you could use their feedback to figure out what you need to change before production. This approach would integrate your analysis about product features with action to get customer feedback, and avoid wasting a lot of time and money in the laboratory testing alternatives that might never matter. In addition, to avoid getting stuck in a dead end, successful entrepreneurs don't make large, sunk investments in particular product development paths, but instead maintain flexibility by limiting their investments in any one course of action.

The difficulty and uncertainty of product development also means that luck is an important part of product development. In addition to the lucky break that Merck received in the discovery of the hair growth potential of their prostate drug, successful product development also involves other types of luck, such as lucky timing. For example, new companies that were in the process of completing the development of new computer-based voting machines just as the "hanging chad" controversy in the 2000 presidential election occurred had a significant advantage over companies that had completed their product development two years earlier and could not interest customers in their new products.

What is the lesson to be learned about the role of luck in product development? It isn't that we can teach you how to be lucky—if we could do that, we'd probably become professional gamblers instead of textbook authors. Rather, it is to point out that you can do everything right in product development and still fail if you are unlucky. In addition to making sure that you understand the costs and risks involved in developing a new business based on a new product or service, we want to emphasize the importance of approaching product development with a strategy of staying flexible and minimizing your investment of time and money. If there is any lesson that can be learned from the importance of luck, it's that having another chance is very valuable.

New Firm Advantages at Product Development

Product development is extremely important to entrepreneurs because it is one of the few parts of the process of producing and delivering a product to customers that established firms aren't better at doing. The advantage of new firms at product development is important because, in general, established firms are better than new firms at manufacturing products. They tend to have better access to capital, which allows them to buy better equipment. They also develop tacit knowledge about production processes from years of operation that new firms cannot replicate overnight. So new firms are often much less efficient and effective at manufacturing than established firms. Moreover, established firms also have advantages of economies of scale because they have built their manufacturing operations up over time. These scale advantages allow them to manufacture products at a lower cost than new firms.

Established firms also tend to be better at marketing than new firms (except, as we described in Chapter 9, for products in completely new markets). In already existing markets, established firms are better than new firms at marketing because they have access to previously developed knowledge of customer needs and preferences that help them sell their products more effectively. For example, they often know how to target customers using information on the customers' previous purchasing patterns. In addition, established firms gain reputations that enhance their ability to sell new products. Established firms also have developed social ties with customers, which make customers resistant to switching to new suppliers. Finally, they have marketing assets in place—things like an established sales force or retail outlets—that allow them to launch new products at a lower cost than new firms, which don't yet have these assets.

New firms make up for these marketing and manufacturing advantages of established firms with their superiority at product development. New firms tend to develop new products more easily and cheaply than more established firms because they don't have the bureaucratic structures and rules and procedures that established firms have developed over time—things like rules about how different parts of the organization should work together and communicate. Such rules often hinder new product development. As a result, new firms can transfer information back and forth between marketing and product design people more easily, facilitating the communication and coalition building that is important to success at any creative activity.[6]

Small and start-up firms also can offer better incentives to their employees to work hard to develop new products because they can more easily provide equity as an incentive. Not only does equity motivate people to work hard to get the new product or service developed quickly, but it also allows new firms to attract talented product development people, who want the chance to make a lot of money.[7] Large, established firms can rarely match the equity incentives of new, small firms. Giving adequate amounts of equity to motivate people is difficult in large established organizations because the equity in these firms is already allocated to investors, leaving little of it to give to product development people. In addition, the amount that the stock price of a new firm can rise in response to the successful efforts of product development people is much larger than the amount that the stock price of a large, established firm can rise in response to the efforts of these same people because the stock price of large firms is driven by the performance of the overall business. As a result, product development people simply can't earn the kind of capital gains on stock in established firms that they can on stock in new firms.[8]

Last, new and small organizations have a great deal of flexibility, which helps them to develop new products when unexpected things happen. Sometimes customers change their preferences in ways that people couldn't predict. Other times, people discover that something isn't really technically feasible. These changes require product developers to change course. Just as it is easier to shift course in a small speedboat than in an ocean liner, it is easier for new and small organizations to make these changes than it is for large, established ones to make them.

Having said all of this, we need to add a caveat. New, small firms aren't always better than large, established firms at developing new products. There are some industries in which large, established firms are better than new, small firms at product development (see Table 11.1 on page 272). To be an effective entrepreneur, you need to know about these important exceptions to the product development rules that we just presented.

So what makes large, established firms better than new, small firms at product development in some industries? First, large established firms tend to be much better at new product development in industries where production is concentrated in the hands of a few firms because these firms control access to the customer base. Second, large, established firms also tend to be better at product development in industries that are capital and advertising intensive. As we explained in Chapter 6, new and small firms have a much harder time raising capital than large, established firms, making them quite disadvantaged in industries that demand a lot of capital. Similarly, as we explained in Chapter 2, advertising depends heavily on economies of scale, making advertising-intensive industries much more favorable to large, established firms than to new, small firms. Third, new and small firms tend to be less effective at

Table 11.1 When Do Small
Firms Develop New Products?

*Large firms are better at innovation
in some industries, whereas small
firms are better at innovation in
others.*

INDUSTRY	RATIO OF LARGE FIRM TO SMALL FIRM INNOVATIONS
Aircraft	31.000
Pharmaceutical preparations	9.231
Photographic equipment	8.778
Office machinery	6.710
Surgical appliances and supplies	4.154
Industrial inorganic chemicals	4.000
Semiconductors	3.318
Toilet preparations	2.278
Environmental controls	2.200
Special industry machinery	2.048
Radio and TV equipment	1.153
Surgical and medical instruments	0.833
Electronic components	0.740
Fabricated metal products	0.706
Electronic computing	0.696
Industrial trucks and tractors	0.650
Valves and pipefitting	0.606
Instruments to measure electricity	0.596
Optical instruments and lenses	0.571
Scientific instruments	0.518
Plastics products	0.268
Measuring and controlling devices	0.067

> Small firms have an advantage in industries with a ratio below 1 and a disadvantage in industries with a ratio above 1.

Source: Based on information contained in Table 1 of Z. Acs and D. Audretsch. 1988. Innovation in large and small firms: An empirical analysis. *American Economic Review* 78(4): 678–690.

product development when industries are very research and development intensive, probably because they can not afford to maintain large research laboratories.[9]

The lesson here for entrepreneurs is quite straightforward. There isn't much of anything that entrepreneurs can do to compete with established firms in industries in which new firms are worse than established firms at product development because they are already worse than established firms at marketing and manufacturing. That's why we see so few new aircraft, pharmaceutical, and photographic equipment manufacturers, and we see even fewer successful ones. However, in industries in which entrepreneurs are better than established firms at developing new products—industries like medical devices, computers, and scientific instruments—entrepreneurs have a chance to compete with established firms by taking advantage of their superior ability to develop new products. That is, they can compete if they can protect their intellectual property, a point to which we will turn in a moment.

Ease of Imitating Entrepreneurs' Intellectual Property

As we just explained, in many industries, new firms are better than established firms at developing new products and services. So why do new firms rarely reap large profits from coming up with new products or services? Why do they often lose out to established firms that were worse than they are at product development? The answer is that, with a few exceptions, most entrepreneurs' new products and services, or the intellectual property underlying them, is very easy to imitate, and can generally be copied at a fairly low cost. In fact, research by Richard Levin, now president of Yale University, and his colleagues showed that the typical unpatented process innovation could be duplicated at less than 50 percent of the cost of developing the original innovation more than 40 percent of the time. For product innovations, the numbers were even stronger, with the typical unpatented product innovation being duplicated at less than 50 percent of the original development cost more than 52 percent of the time. In addition, most of the time a large number of firms can duplicate an entrepreneur's intellectual property. Levin and his colleagues found that almost half the time, the typical product or process innovation could be imitated by between six and ten competitors.[10]

One of the reasons why so many competitors can imitate an entrepreneur's intellectual property at such a low cost is that competitors have a wide variety of methods that they can use to imitate an entrepreneur's intellectual property. When the entrepreneur develops a new product, the competitors' engineers can purchase that product, take it apart, figure out how it works, and produce the same thing in a process called **reverse engineering**. Competitors can also hire away the entrepreneur's employees and suppliers or just have informal conversations with them as a way to gather information about an entrepreneur's new products and services. For example, Hewlett-Packard (HP) recently had its latest printer cartridge design copied before it had even launched the new product because one of its competitors obtained a copy of the product prototype from one of HP's suppliers. (The ease of getting information from suppliers and employees is one reason why it is so important for entrepreneurs to use nondisclosure and employment agreements, which are the subject of the **"Danger! Pitfall Ahead!"** section on page 274.) Moreover, competitors often can work on their own new product development and can imitate entrepreneurs' intellectual property simply by knowing that something new has been developed and putting their engineers and product development staff to work on copying the new product.[11]

Even patenting a technology, which we will discuss in more detail later in the chapter, does not stop imitation. In fact, because inventors are required to disclose how their inventions work in return for receiving a patent, patenting actually makes it easier for competitors to imitate the entrepreneur's intellectual property. As we will explain a little later in the chapter, the advantage of patents doesn't lie in making imitation difficult; it lies in making imitation illegal.

Our message to prospective entrepreneurs like you is pretty simple: You need to recognize that it takes only a short time for competitors to imitate your intellectual property. Figure 11.2 shows the number of months that competitors need to imitate a new product, at least according to one research study. So what should you do? The next two sections of the chapter discuss some ways that successful entrepreneurs keep other firms from copying their intellectual property. So please pay attention. The following sections will help you to develop a plan for managing your new venture's intellectual property.

Figure 11.2 Industries Differ Significantly in the Amount of Time It Takes Rivals to Understand How to Imitate a New Product

In most industries, it takes competitors less than 12 months to figure out how to imitate a new product.

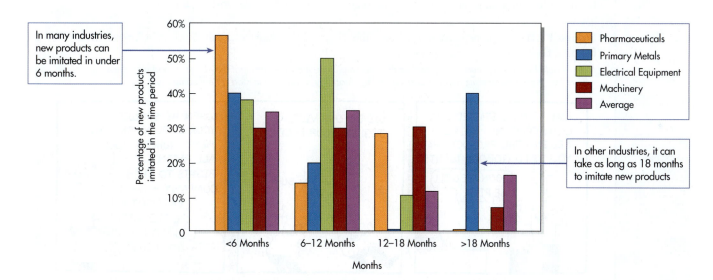

Source: Based on information contained in Table II of Mansfield, E. 1985. How rapidly does industrial technology leak out? *Journal of Industrial Economics* 34(2): 217–223.

DANGER! PITFALL AHEAD!

Nondisclosure and Noncompete Agreements

When I (Scott Shane) taught at the Sloan School at MIT, an MBA student came to my office one day asking for advice on starting a new company to produce a tissue grasper, a medical device that surgeons could use to hold back tissue during an operation. The student's invention had a unique design that made it much better than alternative tissue graspers. In fact, he had already talked to several surgeons about the product, and they were all wildly enthusiastic about it.

The student's story sounded very promising; he had a very good business opportunity for starting a company. As I began to describe MIT's 50K business plan competition to the student and suggest that he enter it as a way to get his new company started, he asked a question that began to raise a red flag. "How can I be sure that I won't have any trouble from my former employer if I start the company?" he asked. "Why are you concerned?" I replied. He explained to me that before going back to school for his MBA, he had worked for a large, medical device company. Although he had refined the tissue grasper in a product development class at MIT, he had designed the initial version of it while he was working at this company. The student explained that his former employer wasn't interested in pursuing the development of the tissue grasper and had no intention of patenting it. But, he explained, that as an employee, he had signed **nondisclosure** and **noncompete agreements**. The first agreement precludes a person from disclosing to others any information valuable to the employer that was developed while working at the company, typically for three to five years from the termination of employment. The second

agreement bars a person from working for a company that competes with the employer for a set period of time, often one to two years. I told the student that he should have a lawyer look over his nondisclosure and noncompete agreements before he did anything else with his new venture.

The lawyer's verdict was that the student might be able to get around those agreements because noncompete agreements cannot bar an employee from making a living in their profession. However, it would be something of a battle because the noncompete and nondisclosure agreements make it difficult to start a company based on knowledge developed in one's prior employment, particularly if the entrepreneur would compete against that employer. More importantly, he didn't recommend trying to start a company to make the tissue grasper. Not only would the legal fees take a lot of money the student didn't have, but also as long as the nondisclosure and noncompete agreements were unresolved issues with the former employer, it would be very difficult for the student to raise capital. Most venture capitalists and business angels simply avoid start-ups that are saddled with these kinds of legal obstacles at the start.

The moral of this story is that you need to be careful about making agreements with your current employer if you plan to start a company later. Noncompete and nondisclosure agreements can preclude you from using ideas that you developed during that employment to start a new company (see Figure 11.3). However, there is a bright side to all this. If you start a company and you hire employees, you can get them to sign noncompete and nondisclosure agreements, which will help you to keep them from quitting and starting their own companies to make use of the ideas that they develop while working for you.

Figure 11.3 Entrepreneurs Must Make Sure That They Have the Right to Use the Intellectual Property That Will Form the Basis of Their New Companies

Many would-be entrepreneurs do not realize that the employment agreements that they have signed with the companies where they work preclude them from using technology that they developed to start a new company.

LEGAL FORMS OF INTELLECTUAL PROPERTY PROTECTION

Entrepreneurs have several legal forms of intellectual property protection available to them. Although none of these completely deter competitors from imitating their intellectual property, all of them help to protect intellectual property in some way. Successful entrepreneurs understand the advantages and disadvantages of these tools—patents, trade secrets, trademarks, and copyrights. In this section, we will explain what these tools can do and what they can't do so that you can figure out the best way to use them to protect the intellectual property in your new venture.

Patents

A **patent** is a legal right granted by a national government that allows an inventor to preclude others from using the same invention for 20 years, in return for disclosing how the invention works. For an invention to be patented in the United States, certain conditions must be met: The invention must be novel; it must not be obvious to a person trained in the relevant field (e.g., a piece of computer software to a computer scientist); and it must be useful. In addition, to obtain a patent, the invention must be secret at the time that the patent application has been made. If the invention has been disclosed in print in any country, or has been offered for sale in the United States, the U.S. Patent and Trademark Office will not issue a patent on it.[12]

So what can you patent? A process, machine, manufacture, chemical formula, design, or piece of software.[13] You can't patent a business idea, like the idea of selling fast food through a drive-through window. Also, you can't patent something that doesn't work. Recently, the courts have allowed inventors to patent "business methods," such as Amazon.com's "One Click" system, which permits repeat purchasers to make purchases without reentering information about themselves.[14] Inventors can also obtain plant patents, which protect grafted or crossbred plants.[15] For example, Tropicana recently sued Florida orange growers who used experimental varieties of oranges that Tropicana had developed for Pure Premium orange juice. Because Tropicana had patented these varieties, it argued that the orange growers should be barred from using these varieties without license from Tropicana.

To obtain a patent, an inventor files an application with the U.S. Patent and Trademark Office, which then evaluates whether the invention is patentable. Because it takes an average of two years for a patent to issue, many inventors first file a **provisional patent application**. This document marks the start of the patent application process and does not require very much disclosure. However, it provides some initial protection of the invention and therefore helps the entrepreneur to obtain financing and to deter competition while the regular patent application is being processed.[16]

Because the inventor needs to demonstrate how the invention is different from existing patented inventions, the inventor or her patent attorney searches through existing patents to determine the **prior art**. Prior art is the set of previous patented inventions that are related to the new invention. If your invention builds on prior art, you have to cite it in your patent. For example, the patent for the Baby Bjorn described at the beginning of the chapter cited the patents on previous baby carriers because Bjorn Jakobson built upon their features when he invented his baby carrier. The phrase "built upon" is important. To obtain a patent, your invention has to improve upon prior art. If your invention does exactly what the prior art does, then your device isn't an invention and you won't be able to obtain a patent on it.

The most important aspect of this process is determining the set of **claims**, or statements about what was invented. Inventors and their patent attorneys write these claims very carefully and try to make them as broad as possible. Why? Because, as we explained at the beginning of the chapter, a patent precludes other people from duplicating only those things stated in the claims. This means that a claim for a device that heats metal, for example, will protect an inventor against a much wider range of imitators than a claim for a device that heats steel. In the first case, the patent would preclude other parties from using a device to heat any type of metal; in the second case, the patent would only preclude others from using only those devices that heat steel, and others would be free to develop devices that heat iron, copper, aluminum, and so on.

Because a U.S. patent is only issued to the first person (or team of people) who invents a technology, inventors need to keep records of their inventions, particularly the date when they first conceived of the idea. To do this, most inventors keep dated logs of their research and the development of their inventions in notebooks; they often have others witness those records.

Patents are very valuable tools for entrepreneurs, but they have some important disadvantages that you need to know. Table 11.2 summarizes the advantages and disadvantages of patents. Pay careful attention to the disadvantages: Many entrepreneurs get into trouble because they don't realize what they are. Among the important disadvantages of patents is the fact that they are costly to defend; are not always effective; require disclosure of the invention; and can be invented around.

The cost of patents is particularly important to entrepreneurs. A typical patent costs approximately $15,000 to obtain when all legal fees are considered. Moreover, to obtain patent protection in foreign countries, an entrepreneur has to file for patents in all of the countries where she seeks protection. Just obtaining patent protection in several countries—the United States, Japan, Canada, and the European Community—can run $40,000 to $50,000. Furthermore, in many cases, more than one patent is required to protect a product or service, greatly increasing this cost.

To enforce a patent, an entrepreneur needs to defend it against infringement by others by going to court. This process involves hiring lawyers who develop a court case to show that another party infringed the patent, or violated the monopoly right of the patent holder. Not only is the value of a patent dependent on how vigorously you defend it, but also failure to challenge people who violate your patent can undermine its effectiveness in other cases. Because defending a patent against infringement can be a very complex undertaking, especially if the case needs to go to

Table 11.2 The Advantages and Disadvantages of Patents

Although patents provide many advantages, entrepreneurs should not always patent their inventions. In many cases, the disadvantages of patents outweigh the advantages.

ADVANTAGES OF PATENTS	DISADVANTAGES OF PATENTS
Helps to raise capital by demonstrating the existence of a competitive advantage	Requires disclosure of the invention
Raises the cost of imitation by competitors	Provides only a temporary monopoly—20 years
Provides a monopoly right by blocking other people from doing the same thing	Can be circumvented, with competitors accomplishing the same goal, but avoiding the patent protection
Prevents a second party from using the invention as a trade secret	Requires stringent legal requirements to be valid and to show infringement, making it difficult and costly to defend a patent, especially against large companies
	Is less effective than other mechanisms at protecting intellectual property for most types of technology
	Can be irrelevant by the time the patent is granted if the technology is fast moving
	Requires patent application in all countries of the world, otherwise people can use the disclosure made in the United States to know how to exploit the invention in other places

court, obtaining and enforcing patents can become a very expensive proposition for entrepreneurs, with total costs rising easily into the hundreds of thousands and even millions of dollars.

Take, for example, Ron Chasteen's experience with his patented snowmobile fuel-injection system. Initially, he made a deal with Polaris Industries to provide them with his fuel-injection system. One year later, Polaris canceled the deal, saying that it was not going to use a fuel-injection system in its snowmobiles. When Polaris started selling a snowmobile with a very similar fuel-injection system to the one he had developed, Chasteen decided he had to sue. Because the litigation costs for his case were upwards of $2 million, he realized that he couldn't afford to cover the costs of a lawsuit himself. After working with five law firms, and spending a lot of his own money, Chasteen finally found a law firm that would take the case on contingency. Chasteen ultimately won a $70 million judgment against Polaris, but not until 11 years after he started his case.[17]

A second disadvantage of patents is that they aren't always effective. Some times there is so much prior art that an inventor can only obtain a patent on a small improvement to a technology. In addition, as we mentioned earlier, patents are only as strong as their claims, and sometimes patent examiners will only allow relatively weak claims to an invention. Topping all of this off is the fact that some technologies are advancing so fast that the new product or service is obsolete by the time that the patent issues, or so many different companies have claims to different aspects of a technology that every company is forced to license their inventions to other companies or no one can produce a product or service. Because the cost of patents stays pretty much the same regardless of how effective they are, sometimes patents are simply not effective enough to make them worthwhile.

A third disadvantage of patents is that they require disclosure of the invention. The 20-year monopoly that the government provides inventors is given in return for showing others how the invention works, thereby allowing others to make use of the inventor's discovery. To obtain a patent, the inventor has to describe the invention and how it works, providing any necessary drawings that help to demonstrate its operation. Doing this makes it much easier for someone else to duplicate the entrepreneur's invention, possibly undermining the entrepreneur's competitive advantage if the patent cannot be enforced.

A fourth disadvantage of patents is that they can often be invented around. To understand inventing around a patent, you first need to understand that the effectiveness of patents varies greatly across industries. In pharmaceuticals and biotechnology, for example, patents are very effective at preventing imitation, but in communications equipment, they don't work very well. Why? It has to do with how technology works. When a person invents a new drug, they can patent the drug's molecular structure. As those of you who have taken a lot of chemistry and biology know, the slightest change to molecular structure can dramatically change how a drug works. For example, if you take everything on the right-hand side of the molecular structure and put it on the left-hand side, you might go from an effective drug to something that kills people instantly. (Not a recommended medical treatment!) In contrast, you could easily take everything in a cellular telephone that was on the right-hand side of the device and put it on the left-hand side and have a perfectly effective cell phone. These differences in technology make it much harder for imitators to **invent around** biological and chemical patents than to invent around electrical patents. (Inventing around a patent means coming up with a solution that does not violate a patent but accomplishes the same goal).

The lesson here is that a good entrepreneur must balance the advantages and disadvantages to determine whether or not to patent. An entrepreneur should obtain a patent when a product or service meets the conditions of novelty, nonobviousness, and value, and the advantages of patenting outweigh the disadvantages. (To obtain more information about patents and to conduct a patent search, go to the United States Patent and Trademark Office Web site at http://www.uspto.gov.)

We need to discuss one other major issue about patents. There is no such thing as an international patent. Because patents are granted by national governments, an inventor needs to obtain a patent in every country where she wants to protect her invention. Please remember that patenting an invention in the United States does not protect the invention against imitation in France, Argentina, Japan, or anywhere else in the world.

Why does the need to patent in multiple countries to protect an invention matter for entrepreneurship? First, patenting is expensive, and the need to patent in multiple countries means that an entrepreneur has to make a very sizable investment in patent costs to protect his product or service against imitation.

Second, failure to patent in a particular country means that it is legal for someone else to imitate your invention in that country. As we explained earlier, to obtain a patent in the United States, an inventor has to disclose how the invention works. This means that anytime an entrepreneur patents his invention in the United States, but not everywhere else in the world, he is showing other people exactly how to develop the product or service. As a result, he is helping potential competitors to exploit the invention in the unprotected country!

Third, patent laws differ across countries. Although we cannot teach you all of the differences in patenting across countries—if you are really developing a new company based on a patented invention you should talk to a good intellectual property attorney about patenting your invention in different countries—we think that it is important for you to understand the wide range of differences in patent laws. One truly fundamental difference in patent laws is that between countries whose legal systems are based on English common law and those countries whose legal systems are based on Roman code law. Countries whose legal systems are based on English common law—the United States, Canada, the United Kingdom, and countries that were former British colonies in Africa and Asia—award patents to the first person to invent something, whether or not they were the first to file with the patent and trademark office. If an inventor can show, through such things as notarized notebooks detailing the work on the invention, that she invented something before anyone else, she will be awarded a patent in a common law country, even if someone else applied for a patent on the invention first. In contrast, countries whose legal systems are based on Roman code law—France, Spain and their former colonies in Asia, Africa, and Latin America—award patents to the first person to file for the patent, even if someone else invented the technology first. So you can see, there are very substantial differences across countries in patent laws, and an entrepreneur needs to understand how to navigate these differences when seeking to use patents to protect a new product or service.

Trade Secrets

A **trade secret** is a piece of knowledge that confers an advantage on a firm and is protected by nondisclosure. Examples of things that can be trade secrets are production processes, like the way a chemical company makes fertilizer; customer lists, such as the databases at a real estate agency; and food recipes, like Colonel Sanders' 11 herbs and spices.

Patents and trade secrets are mutually exclusive. An entrepreneur can't obtain a patent on something and then claim it as a trade secret. Because entrepreneurs must choose between patents and trade secrets, it is important for you to know the advantages and disadvantages of trade secrets.

The biggest advantage of trade secrets is that they provide a way for an entrepreneur to protect a competitive advantage without disclosing to others how a technology underlying a new product or service works. As you will remember from Chapter 10, maintaining secrecy about how to exploit an opportunity is a valuable method for preventing imitation, particularly when the entrepreneur's knowledge about the exploitation process is tacit.

However, trade secrets have several disadvantages as compared to patents. First, a trade secret must be kept hidden to remain valuable. In Chapter 10, we discussed how entrepreneurs often find it difficult to keep hidden their methods of exploiting opportunities, even if they have the best intentions to do so. With trade secrets, not only does the entrepreneur face the general difficulty of keeping secret their method of opportunity exploitation, but the entrepreneur must meet strict legal standards for demonstrating that they kept information secret. Their employees must sign nondisclosure forms. The entrepreneur must have procedures for keeping information secret, such as password protecting information on computers. She must demonstrate that certain information was kept secret by limiting access to the information and by keeping it from the view of visitors. For example, the chemical formula for Coca-Cola is a trade secret; only three executives in the company are allowed to see the actual formula, which is kept hidden in a vault in a bank in Atlanta (see Figure 11.4).

Second, unlike a patent, having a trade secret does not provide the inventor with a monopoly right. If other people independently discover the same invention (that is, they figure out the same thing without getting the information illegally), they are free to use it, too. On the other hand, if the trade secret were patented, then others would be barred from using it for 20 years from the date of the patent application. What does this mean in practical terms? Say you came up with the formula for Coca-Cola while experimenting in chemistry class. Because the formula isn't patented, as long as you obtained it without stealing information from Coca-Cola, you would be free to sell that beverage to anyone you wanted. Coca-Cola might sue you, claiming that you had somehow stolen their secret, but as long as you really figured out the formula on your own, you would win the lawsuit. U.S. intellectual property laws allow independent discovery and exploitation of trade secrets by multiple parties.

Third, to enforce a trade secret and claim damages in court, you must show a loss of a competitive advantage. This is a stricter standard than with a patent, which does not require you to have lost a competitive advantage. With a patent, all you need to do to obtain damages is show that someone copied your invention.

Drugstore.com is good example of a start-up that was sued by another company for violating its trade secrets. Wal-Mart Stores sued Drugstore.com and its venture capitalist, Kleiner Perkins, for stealing trade secrets about Wal-Mart's computer system. Wal-Mart charged that Drugstore.com stole its trade secrets by hiring former employees who helped to develop Wal-Mart's computer system, which was 15 years in the making. Because Drugstore.com competes with Wal-Mart through Internet retailing, Wal-Mart claims it has suffered a competitive loss.[18]

The lesson here is that a good entrepreneur must balance the advantages and disadvantages to determine whether or not to protect a new product or service through trade secrecy. An entrepreneur should use trade secrecy when a product or service confers an advantage on a firm and is protected by nondisclosure and the advantages of trade secrecy outweigh the disadvantages.

Trademarks

A **trademark** is a word, phrase, symbol, or design that distinguishes the goods and services of one company from those of another.[19] A good example of a trademark is McDonald's Golden Arches. Although trademarks don't offer the kind of intellectual property protection that patents or trade secrets offer, they are still useful because they can keep your competitors from making their products look just like yours. For example, by obtaining a trademark on its "swoosh" symbol, Nike can better develop its brand name. No other company can put that symbol on its sneakers, hats, shirts, and so on, making it easier for customers to recognize Nike products.

You can obtain a trademark in two ways: by actually using the mark or by filing an application with the U.S.

LEARNING OBJECTIVE

5 Define a trademark, describe why trademarks are useful to entrepreneurs, and explain how an entrepreneur can obtain a trademark.

Figure 11.4 Trade Secrecy Is an Important Type of Intellectual Property Protection for New Ventures

The founders of Coca-Cola chose to protect the formula for Coke by keeping it a trade secret, rather than by patenting it. This proved to be a wise decision, as the patent would have expired close to 100 years ago, but the formula for Coca-Cola still remains a secret.

Patent and Trademark Office.[20] The right to use a particular trademark—for example, the Nike "swoosh" or the Coca-Cola name—belongs to the first party to register or use the trademark, unless two companies have a conflict. If there is a conflict, the courts decide who has the rights to use the trademark. In general, the courts will not allow more than one company to use the same trademark if consumers would be likely to confuse one company's products with those of another (see Figure 11.5).[21]

The lesson here is that a good entrepreneur must often trademark a word, phrase, symbol, or design that distinguishes the goods and services of her company from those of another. An entrepreneur should use trademarks to protect these dimensions of her business, as well as to build up the new venture's brand name.

Copyrights

A **copyright** is a form of intellectual property protection provided to the authors of original works of authorship, including literary, dramatic, musical, artistic, and certain other intellectual work.[22] For example, when we wrote the first draft of this textbook, we obtained a copyright on the material contained in it. This copyright makes it illegal for anyone else to publish the material or use it in any way. That's why South-Western, our publisher, required us to sign a contract that assigned our copyright to them when they agreed to publish this book.

But books aren't the only things that are copyrighted. Also copyrighted are software, databases, music, study materials, plays, pantomimes, choreography, pictures, sculptures, graphics, motion pictures, recordings, and architectural designs.[23] The main requirement for something to be copyrighted is that it is tangible. You can copyright a written speech, but not an impromptu one. You also can't copyright titles, phrases, ideas, procedures, devices, or common property, such as standard calendars.[24]

A copyright gives the owner of the copyright and only those people she designates the right to reproduce, further derive, copy, or display the protected item. In the United States, copyright protection now extends from the time the work is created until 100 years after the death of the author. However, there is no way to obtain international copyright protection. Different countries have different copyright laws and you need to follow the laws of other countries if you want to obtain copyright protection outside the United States.

Perhaps more importantly, in works made for hire—that is when someone employs someone else to produce an original work of authorship—the employer receives the copyright. This is very valuable to entrepreneurs who need others to produce things that can be protected by copyright. For example, an entrepreneur who starts a company to sell accounting software can hold the copyright on the software even if he hires someone else to write the software program.

Figure 11.5 Trademarks Are an Important Source of Intellectual Property Protection for Entrepreneurs

Trademarks protect a word, phrase, symbol, or design that identifies a company's products or services.

You don't have to do anything to obtain a copyright. As soon as a document (or a CD, videotape, or anything else that can be copyrighted) is produced, it has copyright protection. You can apply for a copyright from the U.S. Patent and Trademark Office, but it's not necessary. In essence, you have copyright protection even before you apply. Showing the copyright symbol—©—on a document isn't necessary to get a copyright. It's only useful to stop someone from claiming "innocent infringement,"[25] which occurs when someone uses copyrighted material and claims that they did not know that it was copyrighted.

The lesson here is that a good entrepreneur must often use copyrights to protect aspects of her intellectual property that cannot be protected by patents or trade secrets—such things as software, databases, music, study materials, plays, pantomimes, choreography, pictures, sculptures, graphics, motion pictures, recordings, and architectural designs. When patents and trade secrets are not an option to protect intellectual property, copyrights become an important way that entrepreneurs can obtain legal protection for their intellectual property.

KEY POINTS

- Legal forms of intellectual property protection include patents, trade secrets, trademarks, and copyrights.
- A patent is a legal right granted by the government to preclude others from making use of the same invention in return for disclosing how the invention works.
- To obtain a patent, an inventor must show that the invention works, is novel, nonobvious to a person trained in the art, and useful. A process, machine, chemical formula, design, plant, piece of software or business method can be patented, but a business idea can't be patented.
- Patents provide several advantages, including a monopoly on use of the invention for 20 years; however, they also have several disadvantages, including the fact that they aren't always effective; require disclosure; and can be invented around.
- A trade secret is a piece of knowledge that confers an advantage and is kept hidden. Trade secrets have the advantage of providing a way to protect tacit knowledge without disclosure, but they also have the disadvantage of requiring the entrepreneur to keep the knowledge hidden; confer no monopoly rights; and demand evidence that they provide a competitive advantage.
- A trademark is an original word, phrase, design, or symbol that distinguishes the goods and services of one company from another. It belongs to the first company to register or use it.
- Copyrights are a form of intellectual property protection for original works of authorship in a wide variety of forms that last from creation of the work until 100 years after the death of the author.

NONLEGAL FORMS OF INTELLECTUAL PROPERTY PROTECTION

Although legal forms of intellectual property protection are used by many entrepreneurs, and are very useful in certain settings, patents and trade secrets are not appropriate forms of protection for certain types of intellectual property. For example, suppose an entrepreneur has come up with a new piece of computer software for Internet payment. The software might not meet the conditions required for patent or trade secret protection. However, entrepreneurs can use nonlegal forms of intellectual property protection, such as lead time, learning curves, first-mover advantages, and complementary assets to protect their new products or services against imitation. Moreover, researchers have shown that nonlegal forms of intellectual property protection actually are more effective than legal forms in preventing duplication of the entrepreneur's products or services. For example, a study conducted by Wes Cohen, a professor at Duke University, and his colleagues found that lead time/first-mover advantages, secrecy, and complementary assets were all more effective than patents in protecting both new products and new processes against imitation.[26]

Given the superiority of nonlegal forms of intellectual property protection, successful entrepreneurs develop and use these forms of protection more often than they use legal forms of intellectual property protection. Therefore, we want you to know what these forms of protection are and how to use them. That way, when you start your business, you can develop the best approach possible to protecting your intellectual property. Let's take a closer look at several kinds of nonlegal forms of protection.

Learning Curves, Lead Time, and the First-Mover Advantage

A firm's competitive advantage often involves speed and the timing of activities relative to those of competitors. Three different types of advantage come from speed and timing: first-mover advantages, lead-time advantages, and learning curve advantages. A **first-mover advantage** refers to any benefit that a firm receives from being the first to offer a product in a particular market. Sometimes a first mover advantage involves **lead time** or the benefits that are generated by doing something a few months or years before someone else. Other times, a first-mover advantage involves the learning curve. We first discussed learning curve advantages in Chapter 2. Because entrepreneurs often improve their new firms' activities as a result of their efforts to learn how to do things better, early efforts to learn often put firms at a relative advantage over their competitors. By doing something more times than others, an entrepreneur can improve her performance at that activity relative to the others, giving the entrepreneur an advantage at it. Successful entrepreneurs know that even when the intellectual property underlying their products or services can be completely imitated by other firms, being the first firm to serve a market provides an advantage that protects the products and services against competition.

Research has shown that being the first mover can protect an entrepreneur's product or service against imitation under certain conditions. First, when a business involves scarce assets, an entrepreneur can protect her intellectual property by obtaining control of the scarce assets before others can get to them.[27] For example, certain locations are better for drilling for oil than others. Early entrepreneurs in the oil industry were able to preclude complete imitation by later firms even though the later firms were able to perfectly imitate the initial entrepreneurs' oil drilling technology. How? By buying up the land where oil was close to the surface, the early movers were able to establish much lower production costs than subsequent followers.

Although buying up land where oil is close to the surface is a good way to gain a first-mover advantage in oil production, entrepreneurs don't have to obtain control over scarce physical assets, like land, to use this type of first-mover advantage. Entrepreneurs can also gain control over intangible assets. For instance, if there are a limited number of good suppliers of a product, an entrepreneur can exploit a first-mover advantage by signing contracts with the best suppliers, leaving the inferior suppliers to imitators.[28]

Second, being a first mover provides an entrepreneur with an advantage when products become more valuable as the number of people who use them increases (think eBay here). Remember in Chapter 10, when we explained that people rush to be the first mover when businesses have network externalities or increasing value as more people use them? Because these types of businesses have positive feedback, any early lead in getting customers works in favor of the entrepreneur and against any imitator further down the road.[29] People tend to use eBay as an online auction site because it is the most popular auction site. As a result, people naturally look at eBay first for online auctions, making it easier to attract attention on that site than on others. In short, when products become more valuable as more people use them, an entrepreneur gets a first-mover advantage because the entrepreneur performs better than the imitator as volume increases. Whoever is first to market tends to continue to perform better than anyone else (see Figure 11.6).

Third, anytime there are high costs to customers to switch from one product to another, first movers have an advantage. A good example is the English language typewriter keyboard. Take a look at the keyboard on your computer the next time you type a paper. The QWERTY format (named after the first six letters on the top row) is the original format and has never been replaced, even though studies have shown that other keyboard designs allow for faster and more accurate typing. Why has this product design remained dominant even though it isn't the best performer? Because the costs to people of switching to a new keyboard are very high—they would need to be trained to type on a new keyboard, make sure all the computers they use have that keyboard, make sure computer manufacturers who supply them produce the new keyboard, and so on. The costs of switching to the better keyboard just aren't worth it for any single firm, so we all still use the first—and not the best—keyboard design.[30]

Fourth, anytime people tend to be content with the status quo, being a first mover offers an advantage. As we explained in Chapter 9, people are frequently satisfied with the status quo and tend to adopt new products only if the new product is *significantly* better than the old one. If an entrepreneur is the first mover, any imitators need to come up with alternative products that are *much better* than the entrepreneur's initial product on some dimension that customers care about (quality, features, durability, and so on) to compete. Otherwise customers will not change to the new product. Being first forces any imitator to offer a better product to attract customers, and coming up with a significantly better alternative is often difficult to do.[31]

Fifth, being a first mover is an advantage whenever reputations are important. Do you remember the name of the second person to walk on the moon? No? That's because people tend to remember the first and not the second time something happened.[32] This is just as true for new products as it is for people who walk on the moon. The first product in a market tends to make a larger and more long-lasting impression on customers, providing an advantage to the company producing it.[33] As a result, later moving companies have to invest more heavily in advertising than the first mover to obtain the same amount of product recognition.[34] Moreover, the first product in a market often becomes the standard against which customers compare all other products, giving the first mover the advantage of being the default option.[35] For example, studies have shown that most customers treat Amazon.com as their default choice for online book purchases, only switching to other online booksellers when Amazon can't meet their needs.[36]

Sixth, entrepreneurs benefit from a first-mover advantage whenever the learning curve for producing a product or service is proprietary. Remember in Chapter 2 when we discussed the learning curve? We showed that the more times that someone does something, the better they become at doing it. This pattern means that a first mover can gain a significant advantage over any followers as long as what they learn can be kept from spreading to competitors. If the knowledge can be kept from spreading, then the first mover can develop significant cost advantages by learning how to do things better, such as produce or market products more efficiently (see Figure 11.7 on page 284).[37] Take Amazon.com as an example. Every day Amazon learns more about how to gather and store information about its customers so that it can provide better customer service. This effort to learn about customers allows Amazon to provide better customer service at a lower cost than other online retailers.[38]

Please be careful here. Being the first mover isn't always the best approach to protecting your intellectual property. When the six conditions just mentioned don't

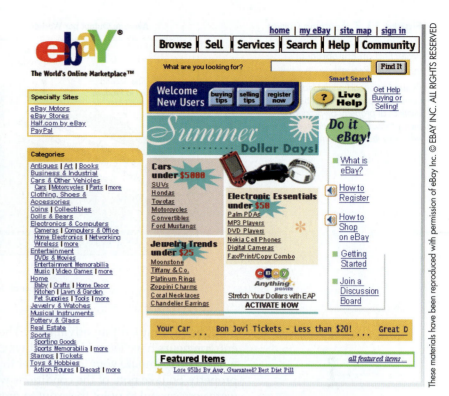

Figure 11.6 First-Mover Advantages Are Sometimes Very Helpful in Protecting an Entrepreneur's Intellectual Property

As eBay has shown, when a business demonstrates network externalities, entrepreneurs can benefit from being the first mover.

Figure 11.7 Learning Curves Provide an Important Method of Protecting an Entrepreneur's Intellectual Property

By moving ahead on the learning curve, entrepreneurs often protect their intellectual property by producing their products or services more efficiently than their competitors.

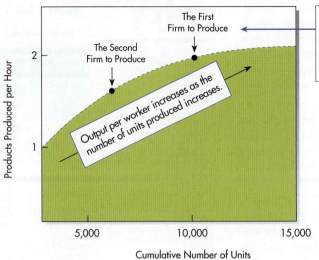

Average Output per Worker

The first firm has a learning curve advantage: Because it has produced the product for more time than the second firm, it can produce the product more efficiently.

hold, being first isn't an advantage. Then being first can be a problem. As many entrepreneurs have learned the hard way, being first sometimes shows other people what to do to imitate your ideas, rather than providing protection of your intellectual property. So take note of the conditions when being a first mover is a good idea. We were very careful to point these out to prevent you from making the mistake of being first when it isn't a good idea to do so.

Complementary Assets

As good as the first-mover story might sound, it isn't always good for an entrepreneur to focus on introducing new products or services. New companies that introduce new products or services don't always profit from their introduction. In many cases, established companies imitate the new products introduced by those pioneering entrepreneurs and they capture the profits from selling those products to customers.

Why don't new companies always profit from introducing new products or services? David Teece, a professor of business strategy at the Haas School of Business at the University of California at Berkeley, explains that the ability of new companies to profit from the introduction of new products depends on their ability to protect their intellectual property. According to Teece, three factors determine whether a new company will profit from introducing a new product: the ability to secure a strong patent; the presence or absence of a dominant design in the industry; and the presence of complementary assets in marketing and distribution.[39]

The decision about what to do about innovating is very simple if an entrepreneur can secure a strong patent on their intellectual property. If patent protection is strong, the entrepreneur will likely capture the profits from developing a new product. The strong patent precludes other companies from imitating the new firm's product.[40]

But what about situations in which the entrepreneur cannot obtain a strong patent, either because patents tend to be weak in the industry in which she operates or because the claims on her patent don't protect very much? Then it is important to know if the industry has converged on a dominant design. Remember in Chapter 9 when we explained that a dominant design is a common approach or standard to making a product on which firms in an industry have converged? In industries that have converged on a dominant design, then the firms that control the complementary assets are the ones that profit from the introduction of the new products.[41]

As we explained in Chapter 2, complementary assets are assets that must be used along with an innovation to provide a new product or service to customers, typically including manufacturing equipment, and marketing and distribution facilities. For example, in the auto industry, the internal combustion engine is a dominant design. The major automakers, companies like Ford, General Motors, and DaimlerChrysler, control the auto manufacturing plants and the dealerships where cars are sold. As a result, entrepreneurs who develop new designs for cars don't do very well. No matter how innovative the entrepreneurs are, the fact that patents are weak in the auto industry means that the major auto companies can imitate what the entrepreneurs do. Once they do this, they can use their manufacturing and marketing advantages to drive the entrepreneurs out of business.

The reason is that once there is a dominant design, new products have to follow a standard form that adheres to that design. (Remember that discussion in Chapter 9?) If established companies can imitate the entrepreneur's new product, and they control the marketing and manufacturing facilities in the industry, it is very easy for them to exploit the same product as the entrepreneur more cheaply by taking advantage of their complementary assets.

The only way that an entrepreneur can compete effectively under these circumstances is to build up her own complementary assets quickly. But in industries like automobile manufacturing where manufacturing plants cost hundreds of millions of dollars and thousands of dealerships are spread throughout the country, this is almost impossible to do.

What's the message here? Sometimes it is better to control complementary assets than to be the innovator of new products. Entrepreneurs need to know this because they tend not to do as well when controlling complementary assets is the key to success in an industry. Moreover, if they are going to try to compete in an industry in which controlling complementary assets is the key to success, then they need to know that they should focus on developing those assets. To help you figure these things out, Table 11.3 summarizes the conditions under which entrepreneurs will be more successful if they focus on gaining control over complementary assets and the conditions in which they will be more successful if they are innovative.

COMPLEMENTARY ASSETS ARE MORE IMPORTANT . . .	BEING INNOVATIVE IS MORE IMPORTANT . . .
When patents are not very effective	When patents are very effective
When a dominant design already exists in the industry	Before a dominant design exists in the industry
When learning curves are shallow or not proprietary	When learning curves are steep or proprietary
When knowledge is codified	When knowledge is tacit
When products are observable in use and so easy to imitate	When products are not observable in use and so difficult to imitate

Table 11.3 The Choice Between Controlling Complementary Assets and Being Innovative

Under certain conditions, entrepreneurs are better off investing their resources in being more innovative than in controlling complementary assets; under other conditions, the reverse is true.

KEY POINTS

- Nonlegal forms of intellectual property protection include first-mover advantages and complementary assets.
- A first-mover advantage is any type of benefit that a firm gets from being the first to offer a product or service in a market. First-mover advantages are particularly useful to entrepreneurs when key assets are scarce; when products become more valuable as more people use them; when customer switching costs are high; when imitators need to offer higher quality than initiators to attract adopters; when learning curves are proprietary; and when building a reputation is important to attracting customers.
- Complementary assets are assets, like marketing and manufacturing facilities, that are used along with an innovative new product or service. When patents are not very effective and an industry has converged on a dominant design, control of complementary assets is important to reap the rewards of innovation.

Summary and Review of Key Points

- New firms are better than established firms at product development because they do not have a bureaucratic structure; can offer better incentives to employees; and have greater flexibility.

- In industries in which established firms are better than new firms at product development, entrepreneurs have very little chance to succeed because established firms are better than new firms at marketing and manufacturing.

- New firms often fail to profit from developing new products and services because their intellectual property is easy, inexpensive, and not very time-consuming to imitate.

- Established firms can imitate entrepreneurs' intellectual property by reverse engineering entrepreneurs' products; by hiring their employees and suppliers; by having informal conversations with those people; and by conducting their own product development.

- Legal forms of intellectual property protection include patents, trade secrets, trademarks, and copyrights.

- A patent is a legal right granted by the government to preclude others from making use of the same invention in return for disclosing how the invention works.

- To obtain a patent, an inventor must show that the invention works, is novel, nonobvious to a person trained in the art, and useful. A process, machine, chemical formula, design, plant, piece of software, or business method can be patented, but a business idea can't be patented.

- Patents provide several advantages, including a monopoly on use of the invention for 20 years; however, they also have several disadvantages, including the fact that they aren't always effective; require disclosure; and can be invented around.

- A trade secret is a piece of knowledge that confers an advantage and is kept hidden. Trade secrets have the advantage of providing a way to protect tacit knowledge without disclosure, but they also have the disadvantage of requiring the entrepreneur to keep the knowledge hidden; confer no monopoly rights; and demand evidence that they provide a competitive advantage.

- A trademark is an original word, phrase, design, or symbol that distinguishes the goods and services of one company from another. It belongs to the first company to register or use it.

- Copyrights are a form of intellectual property protection for original works of authorship in a wide variety of forms that last from creation of the work until 100 years after the death of the author.

- Nonlegal forms of intellectual property protection include first-mover advantages and complementary assets.

- A first-mover advantage is any type of benefit that a firm gets from being the first to offer a product or service in a market. First-mover advantages are particularly useful to entrepreneurs when key assets are scarce; when products become more valuable as more people use them; when customer switching costs are high; when imitators need to offer higher quality than initiators to attract adopters; when learning curves are proprietary; and when building a reputation is important to attracting customers.

- Complementary assets are assets, like marketing and manufacturing facilities, that are used along with an innovative new product or service. When patents are not very effective and an industry has converged on a dominant design, control of complementary assets is important to reap the rewards of innovation.

Glossary

Claims: The part of a patent that states what was invented and what the patent precludes others from imitating.

Copyright: A form of intellectual property protection provided to the authors of original works of authorship, including literary, dramatic, musical, artistic, and certain other intellectual work.

First-Mover Advantage: Any benefit that a firm gets from being the first to offer a product in a particular market.

Intellectual Property: The core ideas about a new product or service that make the development of these products and services possible.

Invent Around: To come up with a solution that does not violate a patent but accomplishes the same goal as the patented approach.

Lead-Time Advantage: Any benefit that a firm receives by doing something before someone else.

Noncompete Agreement: A legal document in which a person agrees not to work for a company that will compete with her employer if she stops working for the employer.

Nondisclosure Agreement: A legal document in which a person agrees not to make private information public.

Patent: An exclusive right given by the government to preclude others from duplicating an invention for a specified period of time in return for disclosure of the invention.

Prior Art: Prior patents that a given patent cites as the building blocks of an invention.

Product Development: The process by which the entrepreneur creates the product or service that will be sold to customers.

Provisional Patent Application: A document, filed with the patent and trademark office, that states that a person intends to file a full patent application. It provides some protection against imitation of an invention during the patent application process.

Reverse Engineering: The process of taking apart a product to determine how it works.

Trademark: A word, phrase, symbol, design, or combination of these that identifies and distinguishes the goods and services of one company from those of another.

Trade Secret: A piece of knowledge that confers an advantage on firms and is protected by nondisclosure.

Discussion Questions

1. Suppose that you are founding a new company to produce a new form of surgical scalpel. Large companies, such as Johnson & Johnson, also have the same idea. Would your company or Johnson & Johnson be better at developing the new product? Explain why.

2. Assume that you have now developed your surgical scalpel. Will it be easy or difficult for Johnson & Johnson to imitate this new product? What could they do to imitate it? What can you do to stop them?

3. Think of five inventions that could be patented. Should you patent them? What are the advantages and disadvantages of patenting each of them?

4. Suppose that you are in charge of American Airlines' computer reservation system. A venture capital backed start-up that is creating an online airline reservation system wants to hire you as chief technology officer because of your expertise with American's reservation system. Under what conditions would you be allowed take the job?

5. Suppose that you are the first entrepreneur to develop an online dating service. Would being a first mover be an advantage in this business? Why or why not?

InfoTrac Exercises

1. **From Inventor to Entrepreneur: Safeguard Your Inventions and Your Profits** (includes a list of resource organizations)(tech issues)(brief article)
   Monique R. Brown
   Black Enterprise, February 1998 v28 n7 p54(2)
   Record: A20209030
   Full Text: COPYRIGHT 1998 *Earl G. Graves Publishing Co., Inc.*

   1. According to the American Bar Association, why do entrepreneurs generally receive little or no financial reward for their inventions?

   2. How can entrepreneurs increase the chances of successfully commercializing an invention?

   3. What are the benefits of licensing agreements?

2. **Locking Up Intellectual Property: Keep Your Secrets from Walking Out the Door** (small business advisor)
   F.S. Brewer
   Utah Business, March 2002 v16 i3 p52(2)
   Record: A84378378
   Full Text: COPYRIGHT 2002 *American Diversified Publishing Company, Inc.*

   1. What constitutes a trade secret?

   2. What is involved in a trade secret protection plan?

   3. What steps does Lee Saber recommend for protecting trade secrets?

GETTING DOWN
TO BUSINESS

Can You Obtain a Patent?

This chapter explained that patents are an important legal form of intellectual property protection that entrepreneurs use to keep their products and services from being imitated by competitors. Although many entrepreneurs *say* that they'll obtain a patent, getting a patent is far more difficult than saying you'll get one. This exercise is designed to help you determine if you can really obtain a patent to protect your new venture's product or service. Follow these steps to evaluate whether your new venture can obtain a patent.

Step One: Explain why your product or service is patentable. State explicitly why your product or service involves an invention that is novel, nonobvious, and valuable.

Step Two: Go to http://www.uspto.gov and conduct a search of existing patents. Search by the title of your product or service, and by what you are claiming as the invention. Has your product or service already been invented? If the answer is yes, stop here and explain why you cannot obtain a patent. If the answer is no, go on to step 3.

Step Three: Examine the claims of the existing patents. Are they broad or are they narrow? Based on the existing claims of previous patents, specify exactly what your invention will claim. Is this claim enough to protect your product or service against imitation? Why or why not?

Obtaining a Trademark

This chapter explained that entrepreneurs often obtain trademarks in their new businesses. This exercise is designed to help you to identify a trademark as a way to protect your new business's intellectual property. Follow these steps:

Step One: Identify a word, phrase, symbol, or design that you will seek to trademark.

Step Two: Go to http://www.uspto.gov and conduct a search of existing trademarks. Is the word, phrase, symbol, or design that you selected already trademarked? If so, please select another. If not, explain the steps that you'll take to obtain a trademark on it.

Step Three: Explain how your new venture will benefit from the trademark. What aspects of your intellectual property will the trademark protect? How will you make the trademark valuable?

Evaluating Nonlegal Forms of Intellectual Property Protection

This chapter pointed out that entrepreneurs can't always use legal forms of intellectual property protection to keep others from imitating their products and services. Instead, they use a variety of nonlegal forms of intellectual property protection. In this exercise, you will be asked to develop a plan to use nonlegal mechanisms to keep firms from imitating your new product or service. Follow these steps:

Step One: Identify any nonlegal forms of intellectual property protection that your new venture will use to keep other companies from imitating its intellectual property. Will your venture obtain a first-mover advantage? Will your venture have an advantage in lead time? Will your venture have a learning curve advantage? Will your venture control complementary assets in marketing and distribution?

Step Two: Explain why the nonlegal form of intellectual property protection that you plan to use will, in fact, protect your intellectual property. For instance, if your venture will have a first-mover advantage, explain why being a first mover is an advantage in your business. Is the business one of increasing returns? Is there limited supply? Are there high switching costs? Is reputation important? Is the learning curve proprietary? Are people biased toward the status quo? Remember to provide evidence in support of your argument.

Enhanced Learning

You may select any combination of the case options below to enhance your understanding of the chapter material.

■ **Appendix 1: Case Studies –** Thirteen cases provide opportunities to apply chapter concepts to realistic entrepreneurial situations. These brief cases call for careful analysis of real business problems and ask you to think about potential solutions.

■ **Appendix 2: Video Case Library –** Nine cases are tied directly to video segments from the popular PBS television series *Small Business School*. These cases and video segments give you unparalleled access to today's entrepreneurs, with expert advice and insights on how to start, run, and grow a business.

■ **Comprehensive Cases –** Visit the book support Web site at http://baron.swlearning.com for cases detailing real businesses whose successes and setbacks illustrate each stage of the entrepreneurial process. You will conduct in-depth analysis of entrepreneurial challenges through well-developed case studies.

Notes

1 U.S. Patent Number 4,139,131, http://www.uspto.gov.
2 U.S. Patent Number 4,402,440, http://www.uspto.gov.
3 U.S. Patent Number 5,246,152, http://www.uspto.gov.
4 U.S. Patent Number 5,732,861, http://www.uspto.gov.
5 U.S. Patent Number 6,009,839, http://www.uspto.gov.
6 Kanter, R, 1988. When a thousand flowers bloom: Structural, collective, and social conditions for innovations in organization. *Research in Organizational Behavior* 10: 169–211.
7 Holmstrom, B. 1989. Agency costs and innovation. *Journal of Economic Behavior and Organization* 12(3): 305–327.
8 Ibid.
9 Acs, Z., & Audrestch, D. 1988. Innovation in large and small firms: An empirical analysis. *American Economic Review* 78(4): 678–690.
10 Levin, R., Klevorick, A., Nelson, R., & Winter, S. 1987. Appropriating the returns from industrial research and development. *Brookings Papers on Economic Activity* 3: 783–832.
11 Ibid.
12 U.S. Department of Commerce. 1992. *General information concerning patents.* Washington, DC: U.S. Government Printing Office.
13 Ibid.

14 Fuerst, O., & Geiger, U. 2003. *From concept to Wall Street: A complete guide to entrepreneurship and venture capital.* New York: Prentice Hall.
15 U.S. Department of Commerce. 1992. *General information concerning patents.* Washington, DC: U.S. Government Printing Office.
16 Fuerst, O., & Geiger, U. 2003. *From concept to Wall Street: A complete guide to entrepreneurship and venture capital.* New York: Prentice Hall.
17 Paris, E. 1999. David v. Goliath. *Entrepreneur* (November).
18 Bahls, J. Been caught stealing? http://www.entrepreneur.com/Magazines/MA_SegArticle/0,1539,230037----8-,00.html.
19 U.S. Department of Commerce. 1992. *General information concerning trademarks.* Washington, DC: U.S. Government Printing Office.
20 Ibid.
21 Ibid.
22 U.S. Department of Commerce. 1992. *General information concerning copyrights.* Washington, DC: U.S. Government Printing Office.
23 Ibid.
24 Ibid.

25 Ibid.

26 Cohen, W., Nelson, R., & Walsh, J. 2000. Protecting their intellectual assets: Appropriability conditions and why U.S. manufacturing firms patent (or not). *NBER Working Paper No. 7552.*

27 Lieberman, M., & Montgomery, C. 1988. First mover advantages. *Strategic Management Journal* 9: 41–58.

28 Sandberg, K. 2001. Rethinking the first mover advantage. *Harvard Management Update* 6(5): 1–4.

29 Shapiro, C., & Varian, H. 1999. The art of standard wars. *California Management Review* (Winter): 8–32

30 David, P. 1985. Clio and the economics of QWERTY. *American Economic Review* 75: 332–337.

31 Shankar, V., Carpenter, G., & Krishnamurthi, L. 1998. Late mover advantages: How innovative late entrants outsell pioneers. *Journal of Marketing Research* 35: 54–70.

32 Sandberg, K. 2001. Rethinking the first mover advantage. *Harvard Management Update* 6(5): 1–4.

33 Boulding, W., & Christen, M. 2001. First mover disadvantage. *Harvard Business Review* (October): 20:21.

34 Kerin, R., Varadarajan, P., & Peterson, R. 1992. First mover advantage: A synthesis, conceptual framework, and research propositions. *Journal of Marketing* 56: 33–52.

35 Mellahi, M., & Johnson, M. 2000. Does it pay to be a first mover in e.commerce? *Management Decision* 38(7): 445–452.

36 Ibid.

37 Lieberman, M., & Montgomery, C. 1988. First mover advantages. *Strategic Management Journal* 9: 41–58.

38 Mellahi, M., & Johnson, M. 2000. Does it pay to be a first mover in e.commerce? *Management Decision* 38(7): 445–452.

39 Teece, D. Profiting from technological innovation: Implications for integration, collaboration, licensing and public policy. In D. Teeca (ed.), *The competitive challenge*. Cambridge, MA:Ballinger Publishing.

40 Ibid.

41 Ibid.

PART 4

RUNNING THE BUSINESS: BUILDING LASTING SUCCESS

CHAPTER 12

Essential Skills for Entrepreneurs: Enhancing Social Competence, Creating Trust, Managing Conflict, Exerting Influence, and Dealing with Stress

CHAPTER 13

Building the New Venture's Human Resources: Recruiting, Motivating, and Retaining High-Performing Employees

Once a new venture is launched, its founders face an emerging and complex set of issues. Instead of dealing mainly with ideas and plans, they must run a functioning company. This involves dealing with a wide range of people both inside and outside the new venture. Doing so requires entrepreneurs to possess—or quickly develop—several essential skills: social competence (the ability to get along well with others), the ability to enhance trust and cooperation and "defuse" conflicts, skill in exerting influence over others, and the ability to manage their own stress. In addition, because growing businesses require an ever-expanding labor force, entrepreneurs must be able to successfully recruit, motivate, and retain high-quality employees. In other words, entrepreneurs must learn to function like effective managers, at least to a degree, and as the chapters in this section point out, successfully accomplishing this task is crucial to the continued success of the new venture.

CHAPTER 12

ESSENTIAL SKILLS FOR ENTREPRENEURS: ENHANCING SOCIAL COMPETENCE, CREATING TRUST, MANAGING CONFLICT, EXERTING INFLUENCE, AND DEALING WITH STRESS

LEARNING OBJECTIVES

After reading this chapter, you should be able to:

1 Describe several social skills and explain how social competence (which is composed of these skills) can influence entrepreneurs' success.

2 Describe the difference between calculus-based trust and identification-based trust, and explain their role in the development of cooperative working relationships.

3 Define conflict and describe its major causes.

4 Explain how entrepreneurs can effectively manage conflict, especially affect-based conflict.

5 Describe the techniques that individuals use most frequently to influence others in work settings.

6 Describe various techniques that people use for gaining compliance—for getting others to agree to requests they have made—and the basic principles on which these rest.

7 Define stress and describe its major causes.

8 Describe the adverse effects of stress, and explain several techniques entrepreneurs can use to reduce the level of stress they experience.

Getting Along Well with Others: Building Social Competence
  The Nature of Social Skills
  The Impact of Social Competence on Entrepreneurs

Working Effectively with Others: Building Trust and Managing Conflict
  Building Cooperation: The Key Role of Trust
  Managing Conflict: Heading Off Trouble at the Pass

Influencing Others: From Persuasion to Vision
  Tactics of Influence: Which Ones Are Most Common?
  Other Tactics of Influence: From Ingratiation to the Foot-in-the-Door

Managing Stress: How Entrepreneurs Can Survive to Enjoy the Fruits of Their Labor
  Stress: Its Nature and Causes
  The Adverse Effects of Stress
  Personal Techniques for Managing Stress

All photos this page © PhotoDisc, Inc.

"Marvelous is the power which can be exercised, almost unconsciously, over a company, or an individual, or even upon a crowd by one person gifted with good temper, good digestion, good intellects, and good looks." (Anthony Trollope, 1863)

About ten years ago, I (Robert Baron)) obtained two patents for the new product described earlier in this book (Chapter 1)—a desktop unit that combined air filtration with additional features (e.g., noise control). Because I had only limited manufacturing experience, I decided that the best way to bring this invention to market was to license my patents to an established business. I contacted a number of companies that appeared to be appropriate as potential corporate partners, and was soon invited to visit several of them. As luck would have it, it was the third one I visited that ultimately licensed both patents. The events of that day are stamped indelibly on my memory.

When my partner Fred and I arrived, we waited for about 30 minutes, and were then brought to a room where the top people in the company were already seated: the president and CEO, the COO, the vice president for engineering, and the vice president for marketing. After brief introductions all around, the CEO turned to me and said:

"OK, professor, show us what you've got." I then made a presentation during which I described the benefits of my invention and demonstrated its major features. Was I enthusiastic? Absolutely! Did I wax poetic? I don't know, but I sure gave it a try! When I was done, the president rose and announced: "OK, thanks. Now, we're going to leave the room, but we'll be back in a few minutes." At that point, he and the other executives filed out, leaving my partner and me to wonder what was happening. We didn't wait long, because less than 10 minutes later they returned. When the president held out his hand and smiled, I knew that things had gone well. "OK, professor," he said, "we definitely want your product. I'll leave you to work out the details with Neville and Stan" (the V.P. for engineering and the COO).

In the months that followed, I got to know the president of the company quite well, and on one occasion I asked him how he made his decision so quickly. His answer was revealing: "Your prototype was good, and we had agreed before you came that you had something new that fit with our other products. But it was the way you handled yourself during the meeting that mattered most to me. I could tell right away that you knew the product and technology very well. More importantly, I could see that you are a high-energy person who gets things done. And I figured, 'OK, I can work with this guy; he's a man of his word.' You can bet that I'd *never* make a deal with someone I didn't trust or who couldn't get me excited about his product."

I learned many things from that experience, but perhaps the most important is this: Success often involves much more than technical knowledge, business acumen, and incredibly hard work; in many cases, it also requires *personal skills* that allow individuals to get along effectively with others. In a sense, that's what the opening quote suggests: Being able to get along with others is a highly valuable skill. In our view, it is truly essential for entrepreneurs. Think, for a moment, about what the founders of new ventures actually do. First, and foremost, they must get along well with each other—they must be able to work together cooperatively without experiencing the kind of angry, emotional conflicts that can destroy even the best of working relationships. In addition, they have to interact effectively with many other people—venture capitalists, potential customers, suppliers, and prospective employees, to name just a few. They must be able to persuade or influence these people (e.g., to get them to share their views or to say "yes" to various requests), to develop trust and cooperative working relationships with them, and to manage conflicts when they occur. If entrepreneurs cannot carry out these tasks effectively, the chances that their new venture will succeed may drop precipitously.

In short, in order to run a successful new venture, entrepreneurs need a wide variety of skills that, together, contribute to what has often been termed the **social capital** of their organizations—an important resource or asset that derives from close relationships among individuals in organizations or other social structures, relationships characterized by liking, mutual trust, and close identification with each other and the organization.[1] In this chapter, we will focus on several of the most important of the skills that contribute to the development of high levels of social capital in new ventures—and so provide them with sustainable competitive advantage.[2] These include all of the skills mentioned earlier: a general ability to get along well with others (often known as *social competence*[3]), the ability to develop cooperative working relationships with them (ones built on mutual trust) and to manage conflict, and the capacity to influence others—to persuade them or induce them to say "yes" to various requests. In addition, because entrepreneurs are truly *the* most valuable resource in their new ventures, we will also consider an additional topic—stress management.[4] Stress is often very high in new ventures, and unless it is managed effectively, it can place the health and well-being of the founding team at risk. So learning to deal with stress and reduce its potentially harmful effects is another valuable skill for entrepreneurs, one with beneficial effects not just for them, but for family, friends, and loved ones who care deeply about them and want them to realize their dreams.

GETTING ALONG WELL WITH OTHERS: BUILDING SOCIAL COMPETENCE

Look at the cartoon in Figure 12.1. Do you think the applicant will get the job? Almost certainly, he will not. Why? In part because he is presenting himself in a very unfavorable light—one that may well convince the interviewer that he is not a good bet as a new employee. So in essence, he is going to miss this potential opportunity because of poor social skills—an inability to get along well with others. As we will soon note, social skills have been found to influence the outcomes people experience in a wide range of business situations, so they are clearly important. Before describing these effects, though, let's first take a closer look at what these skills involve. After that, we will examine their impact on entrepreneurs' efforts to run successful new ventures.

The Nature of Social Skills

In essence, the term **social skills** refers to a set of competencies (discrete skills) that enable individuals to interact effectively with others.[5] Previous research on such skills indicates that many different ones exist, and that all are potentially useful to individuals in interacting with others. However, it is also clear that some of these skills are more directly relevant than others to the activities performed by entrepreneurs. (Some, in contrast, are more useful in purely social rather than business contexts.) Previous research has identified five social skills that may be especially helpful to entrepreneurs:[6]

- *Social perception.* Accuracy in perceiving others, including accurate perceptions of their motives, traits, and intentions. In other words, this refers to skill in "reading" others accurately.

- *Expressiveness.* Skill at expressing one's own reactions and emotions clearly so that they can be readily understood by others. This is very useful in generating enthusiasm in others.
- *Impression management.* Proficiency in the use of techniques for inducing positive reactions in others when we first meet them—for making a good first impression.
- *Persuasion and influence.* Skill at using various techniques for changing others' attitudes or behavior in desired directions
- *Social adaptability.* The ability to adapt to a wide range of social situations and to feel comfortable with individuals from a wide range of backgrounds

LEARNING OBJECTIVE

1 Describe several social skills and explain how social competence (which is composed of these skills) can influence entrepreneurs' success.

Figure 12.1 Social Skills: A Key Ingredient in Personal Success
Will this person get the job? Probably not! His lack of social skills will probably count heavily against him with the interviewer. Social skills also affect the outcomes people experience in many other business contexts, and can play an important role in entrepreneurs' success.

"Experienced! Are you kidding? I've had 12 jobs this year alone!"

Because these skills are often correlated (i.e., persons high in one are often high in others, too), they are often described by the summary term **social competence**. In other words, persons high on several social skills are described as being high in social competence, while those lower in several social skills are described as being relatively low in social competence. We will adopt that terminology in the current discussion.

The Impact of Social Competence on Entrepreneurs

Now that we have described several basic social skills, let's turn to their relevance to, and possible usefulness for, entrepreneurs.

Social Perception

Turning first to social perception, research findings suggest that this aspect of social competence is very helpful in many business contexts. For instance, interviewers high in social perception do a better job of choosing the best applicants than those who are low in this skill,[7] and managers who are adept at "reading" their subordinates are better able than those who are low in such skill to identify the causes of substandard performance (e.g., does it stem from lack of motivation, a lack of necessary resources, or other causes). Accurate identification of the causes of poor performance is a necessary first step in selecting effective corrective actions.[8]

Skill in social perception is also relevant to the activities entrepreneurs perform in attempting to build their new ventures. For example, consider the process of negotiation. Entrepreneurs engage in this activity frequently, especially during the early days of their new ventures' existence.[9] They must negotiate with partners, prospective employees, venture capitalists, suppliers, customers, and many others. As we noted in Chapter 5, research findings suggest that individuals who are skilled at social perception often find it easier to determine when their opponents are being honest and when, in contrast, these persons are bending the truth for their own advantage. Because knowledge of an opponent's actual break-even point plays an important role in successful negotiations,[10] it seems possible that proficiency in social perception may be an important plus for entrepreneurs, and can contribute significantly to their success.

Social perception is also relevant to another important task performed by entrepreneurs: choosing partners and key employees. As we noted in Chapter 5, individuals often attempt to conceal their true motives and intentions, and usually strive to place themselves in a favorable light. The ability to cut through such subterfuge—to perceive others accurately despite their efforts to conceal such information—can be invaluable to entrepreneurs when choosing partners and hiring key employees. In short, being adept at perceiving others accurately can be of considerable benefit to entrepreneurs in all these contexts, and provide them with an important competitive edge.

Expressiveness

Turning next to expressiveness, existing evidence suggests that persons high in the ability to express their emotions clearly often gain important advantages. For instance, physicians high in expressiveness are more popular with patients than ones who are less expressive,[11] and salespersons who are high in expressiveness are often much more successful than ones who are more "deadpan." For instance, in a study conducted with Toyota salespersons, those who were high in expressiveness sold many more cars than those low in expressiveness (see Figure 12.2 on page 296).[12] For entrepreneurs, being high in expressiveness may be an important means of generating enthusiasm in others—VCs, prospective customers, potential employees. In fact, venture capitalists often say that they invest in people who display passion when presenting their business plans. So again, expressiveness may be an important "plus" in terms of building a successful company.

Impression Management

A third social skill, impression management, has also been found to confer important advantages on those who can use it well. People employ many different techniques to

© CORBIS

create favorable impressions on others—everything from efforts to enhance one's own appearance and "image" through flattery and providing gifts to others during an initial meeting. Skill with respect to impression management has been found to enhance the outcomes experienced by job applicants (they are more likely to get the job)[13] and also to boost the ratings received by employees in annual performance reviews.[14] Skill at impression management may also be extremely helpful to entrepreneurs in their efforts to obtain needed capital. In describing how they go about making the decision to support or not support a particular project, venture capitalists often report that how entrepreneurs present themselves during face-to-face meetings and presentations is one of the factors they consider—one to which they give considerable weight.[15,16]

Figure 12.2 Expressiveness: A "Plus" in Many Business Contexts

Persons who are high in expressiveness gain an important advantage in many contexts. For instance, they tend to be more successful than persons lower in expressiveness as salespersons, and physicians high in expressiveness are more popular with patients than ones lower in expressiveness. Entrepreneurs, too, may benefit from being expressive, especially in contexts where it is important for them to generate enthusiasm in others.

Influencing Others

Skill in terms of influencing or persuading others has been found to be highly valuable in many business contexts. Persons who are high in persuasiveness generally attain higher success in many occupations—sales, law, and medicine—than persons lower in this skill.[17] Again, this is an aspect of social competence that may be useful to entrepreneurs in a wide range of contexts—everything from influencing their partners through convincing employees to expend even more effort on the job.

Social Adaptability

Have you ever known someone who was comfortable in almost any social situation? If so, he or she was probably high in social adaptability. Persons high in this aspect of social competence are able to talk to anyone about anything, introduce themselves to strangers with minimal discomfort, and adjust to a wide range of new social situations. For them the word "shy" is an unknown, unfamiliar concept, and they can fit comfortably into almost any social context. A large body of research findings suggests that persons high in such abilities attain greater success and more rapid promotions in many different contexts than persons low in such abilities;[18] indeed, it has even been found that professors high in social adaptability receive significantly higher ratings from their classes than professors low in social adaptability.[19]

Social adaptability can be helpful to entrepreneurs in many ways. For instance, entrepreneurs must often make many "cold calls" to strangers—potential customers and suppliers, to name just a few. These persons may be totally unfamiliar with the entrepreneur and his or her company, yet entrepreneurs must approach them and attempt to form business relationships with them. A high level of social adaptability can be very beneficial to entrepreneurs in this context.

In sum, being high in social competence can contribute to entrepreneurs' success in many different ways. The skills encompassed by social competence can help entrepreneurs to get along effectively with others and to successfully perform many activities required for building a successful company. We should note that this conclusion is far from mere speculation: Recent findings indicate that entrepreneurs who are rated by people who know them well as being high in social competence are actually more successful, in terms of the profitability of their new ventures, than entrepreneurs who are lower in such competence.[20]

Now, here's the most encouraging part: Social competence is definitely not set in stone. As is true for all the skills we will describe in this chapter, it is open to modification—and improvement. Almost anyone can enhance her or his social skills through a little practice. Special programs for building social skills have existed for decades—in fact, the famous Dale Carnegie programs focus, to a large degree, on building the social skills described here. In addition, many psychologists and other professionals specialize in helping people improve their social skills.

Although outside assistance of this kind is very useful, you can also improve your social skills yourself with a little help from friends or family who are willing to give you their honest reactions. One useful technique is to have someone videotape you while you interact with other people in a variety of contexts. Almost everyone is surprised by what they see on such tapes. For instance, many people are shocked to find that they cannot accurately "read" their own facial expressions. They believe that they are showing their feelings and emotions clearly but, in fact, they are not. Similarly, on viewing tapes of their own behavior, many persons are surprised to see how obvious their efforts at impression management or persuasion are. With a little practice, most people can substantially improve these and other aspects of their own social competence. Of course, the more help you receive, the better, but the key point is this: You *can* do better with respect to these key personal skills if you try. Given the benefits enhanced social competence can confer on entrepreneurs and their new ventures, this is effort very well spent indeed. For example, as we explained in Chapter 6, people typically obtain capital from others with whom they have some kind of social tie, and entrepreneurs who have better social competence are better at creating such links. (How important are social skills to entrepreneurs? For the thoughts of one highly successful entrepreneur on this issue, see **"The Voice of Experience"** section on page 298.)

KEY POINTS

- To run a successful new venture, entrepreneurs need a variety of personal skills that are helpful in building their company (e.g., social competence, the ability to develop trust and cooperative working relationships with others, to effectively manage conflicts).
- Social competence, the ability to get along well with others, encompasses a number of discrete social skills.
- Among these, the most relevant for entrepreneurs are social perception, expressiveness, impression management, skill at influencing others, and social adaptability.
- A large body of evidence indicates that persons high in these aspects of social competence experience more favorable outcomes in a wide range of business contexts. Further, entrepreneurs high in social competence tend to be more successful than those low in such competence.
- Social competence can be readily enhanced through appropriate training, so entrepreneurs should carefully consider devoting effort to this task—doing so may yield important benefits for both entrepreneurs and their new ventures.

WORKING EFFECTIVELY WITH OTHERS: BUILDING TRUST AND MANAGING CONFLICT

In Chapter 5, we noted that most new ventures are started not by a single entrepreneur, but by several cofounders. We also noted that, often, there is indeed strength in numbers: Teams of talented, highly motivated people working closely together can accomplish much more than they could by working alone. For these benefits to be realized, however, two important conditions must be met: (1) The people involved must work together cooperatively—they must pool their efforts and direct their activities toward the same goals—and (2) The inevitable conflicts that arise when bright, energetic people work together many hours each day must be handled effectively so that they do not interfere with teamwork and cooperation. These observations suggest that among the skills essential for entrepreneurs wishing to build their new ventures into successful organizations are ones relating to establishing close, cooperative working relations with others and skills relating to the effective management of conflict. Such skills help

THE VOICE OF EXPERIENCE

Why People Skills Really Matter

Nancy Mueller founded Nancy's Specialty Foods in 1977 and was president for 22 years until selling the company in July 1999. Nancy's is the largest processor and marketer of frozen quiche products in the world. The company's products are distributed throughout the United States and Canada through retail grocery stores, warehouse club stores, and food service channels.

Mueller received her bachelor's degree in chemistry from Russell Sage College in 1965. She was employed by Syntex Corporation as a research chemist for several years and was a community volunteer until she founded Nancy's. She currently serves on the board of directors of Rensselaer Polytechnic Institute, San Francisco Opera, and Palo Alto Medical Foundation, and is a member of the Committee of 200 and International Women's Forum. She has recently served on the advisory councils of the Stanford Graduate School of Business, Whitehead Institute, Castilleja School and Girl's Middle School, as well as having completed two terms on the Board of Avenidas—Serving Today's Seniors.

When Nancy Mueller started Nancy's Specialty Foods—a company she sold a few years ago for hundreds of millions of dollars—she was a housewife with two small children and a degree in chemistry. She had very little previous business experience, and

no clear idea about what it took to start a new venture. But she did have two important advantages: (1) an excellent product—people loved the miniature quiches she baked at home for parties—and (2) a high level of social competence—she was very good with people. I asked Ms. Mueller about the importance of these two factors in a recent interview, and here is what she said.

Baron: *"Many factors contribute to entrepreneurs' success—for instance, the quality of their idea for a new venture; the entrepreneurs' experience, background, and training; the availability of adequate financing; people skills. What factors do you think were most important in producing your success?"*

Mueller: *"First, you absolutely must make the best product so when people eat or use it, they are satisfied and want more. But there must be unvoiced need in the marketplace that naturally allows your product to be tried and accepted. Timing is important. In my case, women were joining the workforce and were thrilled to find tasty, low priced frozen appetizers ready to eat; a strong value proposition."*

Baron: *"But what about competitors—don't they try to make products as good or better than yours?"*

continued

Photo courtesy of Nancy Mueller.

entrepreneurs build the social capital of their new ventures, and recent findings indicate that organizations high in social capital (i.e., ones with high levels of trust, liking, and mutual identification among the persons working in them) are more effective and successful than ones low in social capital.[21] Both of these topics will be considered in this discussion.

Building Cooperation: The Key Role of Trust

If people can often accomplish more by working together than by working separately, why—you may be wondering—isn't cooperation "the name of the game"? Why, in other words, is it less common than purely utilitarian considerations would suggest? One answer involves a simple fact: Some goals cannot be shared. Two companies seeking orders from the same potential customer both want same result (the order!), but they cannot cooperate to attain it. On the contrary, they must compete vigorously against each other because this is clearly a "winner-takes-all" situation. Many other instances of this type exist and, in them, cooperation cannot occur.

In many other contexts, however, cooperation between individuals or organizations *is* possible. Whether it develops, however, depends on a number of different factors. For instance, some persons are simply more competitive than others, and will cooperate (i.e., work together as part of a team) only when there is no other choice. Similarly, within an organization, some reward structures encourage cooperation between individuals (reward structures in which raises and bonuses are distributed to teams) while others discourage such coordination (systems in which rewards are distributed on the basis of individual performance). Perhaps the most important factor in the development of cooperative working relationships, however, is **trust**—one person's degree of confidence in the words and actions of another.

Mueller: "Of course, so you have to keep improving your product all the time. The main point is always make sure the product is up to your standards. I can't tell you how much quiche I ate so that I could verify for myself that we were shipping the product consumers expected. Consumers are very sensitive, and they have a lot of choices, so you must make sure that you maintain quality."

Baron: "What else do you think contributed to your success?"

Mueller: "I'd have to say people skills—being able to get along with people, win them over, and gain their respect. When I started, I went to a lot of stores and sold my product directly. Later—and this was a big turning point—I took the product to Price Club (Costco today) two weeks before the holidays. They put it in their stores and it all sold in just two hours. At the time they had six stores in Northern California and that allowed me entry into this enormous distribution of club stores. Costco, Sam's, BJ's—that was what gave us the volume necessary to become a viable business. And we wouldn't have gotten the first order if the buyers at Price Club hadn't been excited to try our products and the customers didn't purchase and repurchase them."

Baron: "What about building your team and your company—were people skills important for those tasks, too?"

Mueller: "Absolutely. I didn't know anything about team building, and I had never managed people—although being the mother of two young children gave me some experience! But I was the person to communicate passion and vision—I led by example. I led by being sensitive to the issues of my people and helping them solve the issues they were dealing with. So when I hired people who had skills I didn't have—in marketing, sales, product, development, and man-ufacturing—I still remained the 'standard bearer.' My employees, especially in the production plant, liked it when I came in and gave a big 'good morning' to them; they wanted to see the leader behind them. That was my role—I was the leader, spokesperson, and the creative force. What was most important was making sure that you build a win-win situation for everyone—a situation where everyone feels they are getting out of the bargain what they want. Then everyone is happy and satisfied. My people skills also helped me create an environment where people felt valued. I also learned that if someone isn't cutting it, you have to make a change. People who don't share the vision pull the group back—they really hurt. You have to build a great team, not a bunch of 'yes' people, but smart people who are working toward the same goals; and that requires good people skills. You have to have passion and be able to make it rub off on others."

Commentary: What Ms. Mueller is saying, in essence, is that to launch a new venture, and run it successfully, you need a great product *and* the ability to get along well with other people—to influence them, motivate them, earn their trust, and stimulate their commitment and enthusiasm. Making sure the product is excellent is the first key task for entrepreneurs—one they cannot readily delegate to others, at least in the early days of their company. But building a successful business also involves managing the internal relationships as well as the external relationships with customers, suppliers, professional vendors, and so on. These tasks all require excellent people skills, and entrepreneurs who possess such skills gain an important advantage over those who do not. Having met Nancy Mueller on several occasions, I have no doubt that she scores very high on these skills and that this is one reason for her impressive success.

When we say that one person trusts another, this implies that the first person believes that the second will do what he or she says he or she will do, and will generally behave in predictable ways that are understandable in terms of the relationship between them. Moreover, the first person expects that the second will not act in ways that are harmful to her or his interests or well-being—as the characters in Figure 12.3 are doing!

Actually, there seem to be two distinct kinds of trust.[22] One—known as **calculus-based trust**—is based on deterrence. When we expect that another person will act in the ways they promise because they know they will be punished for doing otherwise, we are demonstrating calculus-based trust. For instance, if a customer of a new venture believes an entrepreneur's statement about when an initial order will be shipped, she may do so because of calculus-based trust. Both the customer and the entrepreneur know what will happen if the order is late: The customer may not order from the new venture again.

Figure 12.3 Trust: A Rare Commodity in the World of Business—And Many Other Spheres of Life

There are many situations when trust—confidence in the words and actions of others—is low. Low levels of trust, in turn, make it difficult to develop cooperative working relationships.

A second type of trust, in contrast, is the kind that develops in relationships when people work together over long periods of time and feel that they know and understand each other's motives and needs. This is known as **identification-based trust**, and when it exists, individuals expect others to behave as they promise to behave not because they will be punished for failing to do so, but because they believe that the person they trust has their well-being at heart. Clearly, this is the kind of trust that entrepreneurs want to exist between themselves and their cofounders, and between themselves and key employees (or perhaps all employees!) of their new ventures. The advantages of identification-based trust are obvious: When such trust exists, people can be depended upon to do the right thing—which in this case means they can be depended upon to act in ways that are beneficial to the company as a whole rather than to themselves. Figure 12.4 illustrates the difference between calculus-based and identification-based trust.

Needless to add, describing identification-based trust as a goal is one thing; attaining it is quite another. How can entrepreneurs build such trust into their working relationships? Several steps have been found to be useful. First, it is important to act as you promise. For example, if you promise to get something done by a specific time, you should try hard to do so. If you miss deadlines once in awhile, people will overlook it. But if you miss them regularly, their trust in you will be reduced. So, consistency between your words and your actions is one important trust-building step. For instance, if an entrepreneur repeatedly promises a customer that orders will be delivered at specific times but regularly fails to meet these targets, the customer's trust in the entrepreneur may be undermined.

Second, follow agreed-upon procedures. For people to trust you, it is not enough for you to do what you say you will do; in addition, you should do it in the way they expect, and the way you have outlined or suggested. For instance, suppose that an entrepreneur is trying to hire a marketing expert. She promises her cofounders that she will do this through a series of competitive interviews. (We will describe this process in Chapter 13.) In fact, though, she happens to meet someone at a party who is an expert in marketing and hires this person on the spot. Even if the new employee is highly competent, she may reduce her cofounders' trust in her; after all, she has *not* proceeded in the way they expected and on which they had previously agreed.

Third, trust can be built by engaging in what are known as **organizational citizenship behaviors**—employee behaviors that go beyond the role requirements of their jobs and that are not directly or explicitly recognized by formal reward systems.[23] Clearly, this is a kind of behavior many entrepreneurs demonstrate: They frequently engage in actions that demonstrate their deep and lasting commitment to the new venture—everything from working incredibly long hours and investing their entire personal fortunes in it, to forming very close and trusting relationships with initial employees—treating them more like family members or friends than employees. In a sense, then, they are models of organizational citizenship behavior to others in the new venture, and this can contribute strongly to high levels of trust. For instance, con-

Figure 12.4 Two Kinds of Trust

Calculus-based trust rests on deterrence: One person trusts another because if that person fails to behave as promised, she or he will be punished in some way. This implies that this person will behave as promised only when the threat of punishment is present. The other, identification-based trust, is based on one person's belief that another has her or his interests at heart, and will not do anything harmful to them. When this kind of trust exists, threat of punishment and surveillance are not necessary.

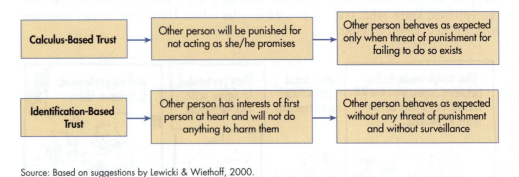

Source: Based on suggestions by Lewicki & Wiethoff, 2000.

sider Ron Schaich, founder of Panera Bread—a rapidly growing chain of bakery-cafes that sell high-quality bread and sandwiches. Schaich, who previously had founded another company with its roots firmly in bread—Au Bon Pain—is a model of commitment for his employees, many of whom are skilled bakers who share his passion for first-rate bread. As he puts it: "Nourishment for the soul . . . that's what we do. I believe if you give people something special, something worth going out of the way for, they'll buy it. This belief is rooted in tradition . . . in a fundamental commitment to handcrafter bread." Schaich's commitment to—and love for—high-quality bread is well-known to employees of Panera Bread, and he demonstrates it in personal visits to many of Panera's stores. His commitment and high standards help inspire employees, and have been a positive factor in Panera's success and rapid growth.

Finally, because identification-based trust requires that people understand and appreciate each others' motives and needs, it is important to discuss these with others as a basis for building trust. Where trust is concerned, in other words, ambiguity is not a good thing. To trust you, other people have to conclude that they know you, and how you are thinking. So a degree of openness is important from the point of view of establishing identification-based trust. For instance, if an entrepreneur discovers that his cofounder has entered into discussions for a cooperative arrangement with another company but hasn't discussed these tentative plans with him, his trust in this person may be weakened.

Managing Conflict: Heading Off Trouble at the Pass

There is an old saying to the effect that *"When emotions run high, reason flies out the window."* In other words, when people experience strong emotions, they stop thinking rationally—or predictably. A corollary to this saying might be, "And when they do, they stop recognizing their own self-interest." These thoughts are certainly true where certain kinds of conflict are concerned. **Conflict** is generally defined in management science as a process in which one party perceives that another party has taken or will soon take actions that are incompatible with its interests, and it takes two basic forms. In one, known as affective or emotional conflict, a strong element of anger or disliking is introduced into the situation. The two sides may or may not have opposing interests, but one thing is clear: They are upset with each other, do not trust each other, and experience strong, negative emotions (see Figure 12.5). A second kind of conflict, known as **cognitive conflict**, in contrast, is one in which individuals become aware of contrasting perspectives or interests, but focus on the issues and not on one another. For example, members of a board of advisers for a new venture may disagree with

each other about what advice to give the entrepreneurs with respect to marketing strategies without becoming upset or angry with one another: Their focus is on the issues, not on personalities. Research findings indicate that cognitive conflict can be constructive—it can induce both sides to consider each other's positions and possible solutions very carefully. The result may be a resolution acceptable to both sides. Affective conflict, in contrast, generally produces negative results.[24] In fact, when it is intense, such conflict can badly shatter working relationships and dissipate trust that has been painstakingly built up over months or even years.

Conflict is definitely relevant to entrepreneurs and their efforts to build strong, successful businesses. Indeed, recent findings suggest that when affective conflict is

LEARNING OBJECTIVE

3 Define conflict and describe its major causes.

Figure 12.5 Affect-Based Conflict

When conflict involves a strong emotional component, it may be especially difficult to resolve. Moreover, the persons involved may lose sight of their own self-interest as a result of the intense negative emotions they experience.

Photo courtesy of R.A. Baron.

high between cofounders of a new venture, the venture's performance may be significantly impaired.[25] Clearly, then this is an event entrepreneurs should strongly strive to avoid. In order to prevent such conflicts from erupting, it is useful to understand why they occur, so we will first consider the potential causes of such conflicts. We will then turn to ways of preventing them or managing them effectively if they do occur. Please note that in this discussion we will focus on **affective conflicts**—ones that involve a large emotional component rather than conflicts that emerge from incompatible interests or goals.

Causes of Affective Conflict

Because trust has a strong "upside," it is not surprising to learn that distrust has opposite effects. In fact, basic distrust between individuals or groups is a key cause of angry conflicts between them.[26] Another and closely related cause is preexisting grudges. Often, people import anger and resentment stemming from other situations into a current one, with the result that what might otherwise be minor conflicts erupt into intense and angry ones.

Additional causes of conflict involve what can be viewed as largely social factors—ones having more to do with relationships between people than with opposing interests or economic concerns. One such factor that plays a role in this respect is what have been termed faulty attributions—errors concerning the causes behind others' behavior.[27] When individuals find that their interests have been blocked (e.g., their recommendations were rejected and those of another person accepted), they generally try to determine why this occurred. Was it bad luck? A lack of planning on their part? A lack of needed resources? Or was it due to intentional interference by another person or group? If they conclude that the latter is true, then the seeds for an intense conflict may be planted—even if other persons actually had nothing to do with the negative outcomes they have experienced. In other words, erroneous attributions concerning the causes of such outcomes can, and often do, play an important role in conflicts, and sometimes cause them to occur when they could readily have been avoided.

Another social cause of conflict involves the tendency to perceive our own views as objective and resting firmly on reality, but those of others as biased or even irrational. As a result of this tendency, we tend to magnify differences between our views and those of others, and so also exaggerate conflicts of interest between us.

Finally, we should note that personal traits or characteristics, too, play a role in conflict. For example, Type-A individuals—ones who are highly competitive, always in a hurry, and quite irritable—tend to become involved in conflicts more often than calmer and less irritable Type-B persons.[28] This can be a particularly severe problem for entrepreneurs, who are more likely than others to be Type-A personalities.[29]

Overall, then, affective conflicts stem from several different sources. Fortunately, all of these can be diminished by the presence of a high degree of trust between cofounders or between entrepreneurs and their employees. When we have a high degree of identification-based trust in others, we tend to perceive their actions as stemming from positive rather than negative causes; at the least, we give them the benefit of the doubt. This can reduce the likelihood of emotion-laden conflict. Similarly, high levels of trust help to counter the tendency to perceive others' views as biased, self-centered, or worse. Basically, then, we are suggesting that there is a close link between trust within a new venture and the likelihood of affective conflict within it. The higher the trust, the less likely it is that such conflicts will develop. Once again, then, is seems clear that efforts to develop high levels of trust in a new venture between cofounders and between founders and employees are well worth the effort.

Techniques for Resolving Conflicts That Do Occur

Although trust can reduce the incidence of affective conflicts, it cannot reduce it to zero. This means that some conflicts, at least, will have to be resolved rather than avoided. Many techniques for resolving conflicts exist, but for entrepreneurs, the most relevant and useful involves **negotiation**—a process in which the opposing sides exchange offers, counteroffers, and concessions, either directly or though representatives.[30] If the process is successful, a solution acceptable to both sides is attained and the conflict is resolved. If, instead, bargaining is unsuccessful, costly deadlock may result and the conflict will intensify.

When the parties to a negotiation represent different companies, countries, or social groups (e.g., labor and management), the primary goal for each side may be to maximize its own outcomes, often at the cost of the opponent. Within a new venture, however, this makes little or no sense. Take, for example, an entrepreneur negotiating with her venture capitalist over a disagreement that they have concerning the new venture's strategy. Winning the argument with the VC might do the entrepreneur more harm than good, especially if the venture capitalist comes away from the discussions with the idea that the entrepreneur was difficult and not worthy of the same attention as other entrepreneurs in the VC's portfolio. Rather than win the debate, the two sides to any conflict should focus on obtaining what is known as a **win-win solution**—one that is acceptable to both sides and that meets the basic needs of both. Any other resolution will almost certainly be short-lived, and will, moreover, produce harmful consequences for the new venture. How can such solutions be obtained? Although there are no hard-and-fast rules, the following guidelines have been found to be useful:

- *Avoid tactics that reflect a win-lose approach* (one in which each side attempts to maximize its own outcomes). Among the tactics to be avoided are these: (1) beginning with an extreme initial offer—one that is very favorable to the side proposing it; this may put the recipient of the extreme offer at a disadvantage, but will also generate feelings of anger and resentment; (2) the "big-lie" technique—trying to convince the other side that one's break-even point is much higher than it is so that they offer more than would otherwise be the case; and (3) convincing the other side that you have an "out"—if they won't make a deal with you, you can go elsewhere and get even better terms. These and related strategies tend to throw kerosene on the flames and are counterproductive in terms of reducing the intensity of affective conflict.

- *Uncover the real issues.* As we noted earlier, many affective conflicts do not stem from opposing interests. Rather, they involve social and cognitive factors (grudges, faulty attributions concerning the cause of others' actions). A useful technique for reducing such conflicts, then, it to identify their true causes. This can require a lot of effort, but can ultimately save a lot of time—and frustration!

- *Broaden the scope of the issues considered.* Often, persons negotiating with each other have several issues on the table at once. This means that reciprocal concessions are possible: One side gives ground on one or more issues, while the other gives ground on others. For instance, if an entrepreneur is negotiating with a prospective employee, there may be several issues on the table: salary, stock options, fringe benefits, working hours, and so on. Perhaps the entrepreneur finds it easier to make concessions with respect to stock options and working hours than salary or fringe benefits. The potential employee might be willing to trade off immediate pay for these benefits; at the very least, it is worth considering such "logrolling," as it is sometimes termed.

In sum, it is best to avoid affective conflicts within a new venture: The potential costs are simply too high. When such conflicts do occur, however, savvy entrepreneurs can see them for what they are—dangerous traps for their working relationships with cofounders, employees, customers, VCs, and others—and then they can take steps such as the ones outlined here to defuse these conflicts, to resolve them, and so to prevent them from doing irreparable harm to the company they are working so hard to grow. (For a disturbing example of what can happen when people who work together do not attempt to avoid or resolve affective conflicts, see the **"Danger! Pitfall Ahead!"** section on page 304).

DANGER! PITFALL AHEAD!

How to Create an Affective Conflict When There Is None

Back in the mid-1990s, Delta Air Lines, like many other large carriers, was going through hard times, and for the first time in its history had to cut a number of jobs throughout the company. When asked by reporters to comment on the extent to which this had upset employees, Delta CEO Ronald W. Allen remarked, "So be it." This callous remark proved very costly. Delta's employees were furious, and let everyone—the media, passengers, and government officials—know about it. In fact, within a few days of Allen's remark, thousands of Delta employees donned "So Be It" buttons, and wore them proudly as a sign of their anger and contempt for Allen. Morale plunged, and the heat was truly on for Allen. In fact, the board of directors declined to renew his contract so that soon he, too, was out of a job.

What was going on here? A textbook illustration of affective conflict—a conflict that may have started with divergent interests, but which quickly escalated into a bitter dispute in which basic issues were quickly submerged in a tide of angry emotion. Consider the situation in the cold light of reason: Both Allen and Delta's employees wanted to save the company from a mounting sea of red ink. Yet, although some of their major interests coincided, Allen managed to drive a wedge between top management and Delta's employees—one that could only be healed by his departure.

There is an important message in these events for entrepreneurs: If affective conflict can prove so costly for a huge company like Delta Air Lines, imagine how devastating it can be when it occurs between members of the founding team or between this team and key employees. For this reason, being familiar with techniques for avoiding and defusing affective conflict is an important skill that entrepreneurs should definitely acquire—and practice!

In this context, do you recall the example of the tire recycling company described in Chapter 4? The founder of that company had an abrasive, irritating style and seemed to actually enjoy generating conflict. When he repeated this cycle with the head of a government office whose approval was needed before the company could install its new recycling process, however, the result was a total disaster: The government official refused to grant approval, and as a result, the new venture—which had a very high burn rate—ran out of cash and soon failed.

KEY POINTS

- Trust is an essential ingredient in building cooperative working relationships. Two kinds exist: calculus-based trust and identification-based trust.
- Calculus-based trust is based on the belief that if someone does not act as they say they will, they will be punished. In contrast, identification-based trust is based on the belief that the person in question has our best interests at heart.
- Calculus-based trust can be increased by acting as you promise to act, following agreed-upon procedures, and being open about your own motives and needs.
- Conflict is a process in which one party perceives that another party has taken or will take actions that are incompatible with its interests. It takes two basic forms: affective or emotional conflict, which involves a strong element of anger or disliking, and cognitive conflict, which focuses on issues rather than people.
- Affective conflicts stem from many causes, including distrust, long-standing grudges, social factors such as faulty attributions about the causes of others' behavior, and individual difference factors (e.g., the Type-A behavior pattern).
- The most useful means of resolving conflicts is negotiation—a process in which the opposing sides exchange offers, counteroffers, and concessions, either directly or though representatives.
- For negotiations to succeed, the participants should adopt a win-win perspective and avoid such tactics as extreme offers and "the big lie" technique. They should also seek to uncover the real issues and to broaden the scope of the issues discussed.

INFLUENCING OTHERS: FROM PERSUASION TO VISION

How many times each day does each of us attempt to influence others—to change their views or their behavior? How many times each day are we, in turn, exposed to influence attempts from other persons? Whatever the number is, it is very large. Every time you hear or see a commercial, or look at an ad in a newspaper or magazine, you are being exposed to an influence attempt (see Figure 12.6). Every time you ask someone for a favor or try to change a friend's mind about some issue, you are attempting to exert some type of influence (or, because it is directed toward other persons, *social influence*).

Organizations—including new ventures—are no exception to this general rule: They, too, are the scene of countless attempts by one or more persons to influence one or more others. Clearly, being successful at this task can yield important benefits; getting others to think the way you do or to agree to your requests can be very helpful in terms of reaching your goals. This is certainly true for entrepreneurs running new ventures. Virtually every day they come into contact with people they wish to influence—VCs, potential customers, suppliers, government officials, and many others. Further, in most cases, they have no direct power over these persons—they can't order them to do what they want. Rather, they must try to produce the results they want through their own skills with respect to influence. To the extent entrepreneurs can refine these skills, therefore, the more successful their companies are likely to be.

In this discussion, we will take a closer look at social influence and the many ways in which it is exerted. We believe that general knowledge of these techniques can prove useful in two key ways. First, this information can help you to choose among them more effectively, matching the appropriate technique to the specific situation. Second, such knowledge can help you recognize these tactics when they are used by other persons, and so can assist you in protecting yourself against them.

Tactics of Influence: Which Ones Are Most Common?

As you probably know from your own experience, people use many different strategies to influence others in works settings. Here is a brief description of the ones that appear to be most frequent in terms of use:[31]

LEARNING OBJECTIVE

5 Describe the techniques that individuals use most frequently to influence others in work settings.

Figure 12.6 Influence: A Fact of Modern Life

Each day, we are exposed to countless attempts to influence us—to change our attitudes or behavior. In return, we engage in many attempts to influence others, people with whom we live or work. Many of these influence attempts take place in work settings.

- *Rational persuasion*—Using logical arguments and facts to persuade another that a view is correct or accurate.
- *Inspirational appeal*—Arousing enthusiasm by appealing to the recipient's values and ideals.
- *Consultation*—Asking for participation in decision making or in planning a change.
- *Ingratiation*—Getting someone to do what you want by putting that person in a good mood or getting him or her to like you.
- *Exchange*—Promising some benefits in exchange for complying with a request.
- *Personal appeal*—Appealing to feelings of loyalty and friendship before making a request.
- *Coalition-building*—Persuading by seeking the assistance of others, or by noting the support of others.
- *Legitimating*—Pointing out one's authority to make a request, or verifying that the request is consistent with prevailing organizational policies and practices.
- *Pressure*—Seeking compliance by using demands, threats, or intimidation.

When are these various tactics used? Research findings suggest that different ones are preferred depending on whether influence attempts are directed at targets who are higher, lower, or equivalent to oneself in terms of status or position.[32] For example, in large organizations, people generally use rational persuasion, consultation, or personal appeals when dealing with others equal to or above them in rank, but are more likely to use pressure tactics or inspirational appeals when trying to influence subordinates.

What do entrepreneurs do? Some evidence[33] suggests that they frequently use inspirational appeals. Why? Because they often face the task of convincing others to share their beliefs about what the emerging organization can, and will, become. In other words, they must convince other people (VCs, prospective employees, potential customers) to accept their vision of what "might be," without much to back it up aside from their personal conviction or passion. In this context, inspirational appeals can be a very useful tactic. Indeed, recent findings indicate that the more clearly entrepreneurs can state their vision, the more successful are their new ventures.[34]

Other Tactics of Influence: From Ingratiation to the Foot-in-the-Door

Although the tactics described earlier are important, they are far from the entire picture where influence is concerned. Many other techniques are used for gaining compliance—for getting others to say "yes" to specific requests. Because this is often a goal for entrepreneurs (e.g., when they seek financial support, orders from customers, or attempt to hire new employees), it is worth taking a brief look at some of these tactics. Many of them exist, but all of them derive from a small number of basic principles:[35]

- *Friendship/liking.* The more other persons like us, the more willing they are to agree to our requests; several techniques for gaining compliance are based on this simple fact (e.g., flattery, ingratiation, efforts to enhance our own appearance). Recall that in Chapter 6 we pointed out that people are more likely to obtain capital from someone with whom they have a direct social relationship. That is one example of how friendship makes it easier to gain compliance—in this case, compliance with the entrepreneur's request for money.
- *Commitment/consistency.* Individuals wish to be consistent in their beliefs and actions. Thus, once they have adopted a position or committed themselves to a course of action, they experience strong pressure to comply with requests that are consistent with these initial commitments. In fact, they may find it virtually impossible to refuse such requests because doing so would force them to reject or disown actions or beliefs they previously adopted.
- *Scarcity.* As a general rule, opportunities, objects, or outcomes that are rare or hard to obtain are more highly valued that ones that are common or easy to get. Thus, requests that emphasize scarcity or the fact that some object, opportunity, or outcome is hard to obtain or will soon no longer be available are sometimes difficult to resist.

■ *Reciprocity.* Individuals generally experience powerful pressures to reciprocate benefits they have received from others. As a result, requests that activate this principle are more likely to be accepted than requests that do not.

These basic principles appear to underlie many tactics of influence. For example, ingratiation and impression management are closely related to the principle of liking/friendship. The basic idea here is simple: First get others to like you, and then once they do, ask them to do what you want.

The principle of commitment/consistency has been found to play an important role in several common, and often highly successful, tactics for gaining compliance. One of these is the *foot-in-the-door tactic*—starting with a small request, and once this is accepted, escalating to a larger one. For instance, an entrepreneur using this technique might at first ask a potential customer to accept a free sample of the new venture's product. Only later would she attempt to convert this into a sizeable order. Another tactic based on commitment/consistency is the *lowball*—attempting to change a deal or agreement by making it less attractive to the target person after it is negotiated. This latter tactic is often used by salespersons, and it goes something like this. An attractive deal is offered to a customer. Once the customer accepts, the salesperson indicates that the sales manager or someone else in the company has rejected the arrangement, and offers one less desirable to the customer. Rationally, people should walk away from such changes, but often, they don't: They feel committed to their initial decision, so they accept the less attractive deal.

Turning to the principle of scarcity, such tactics as *playing hard to get* and the *fast-approaching deadline technique* are widely used in the world of business. Job applicants who mention that they are under consideration for other positions or are very satisfied with their current position are using the hard-to-get tactic to manipulate important organizational outcomes in their favor. Similarly, large signs suggesting that "special sale prices" will only be in effect for a short period of time are often effective, and are based on the principle of scarcity (see Figure 12.7). Entrepreneurs sometimes use this tactic, too. For instance, they may tell a potential customer that they are offering a special price for a limited amount of time, thus putting pressure on this person to order now, before it is too late and the special deal has been withdrawn.

Finally, the principle of reciprocity is related to a tactic of influence known as the *door-in-the-face tactic*. In this strategy, individuals start with a request that is very large and certain to be rejected. Then they "scale down" their request to a more acceptable one, thus putting the target person under considerable pressure to reciprocate this concession. In fact, their concession is not a real one, but the tactic often works. Here's an example: A highly qualified prospective employee requests a 5 percent equity share in a new venture as part of his signing package. The entrepreneur refuses, offering only 1 percent. The prospective employee then backs down to 2 percent, which is the figure he wanted all along. Relieved, the entrepreneur accepts—and has, by doing so, fallen under the sway of the door-in-the-face technique.

As we noted earlier, knowing about these tactics is useful in two respects. By choosing them carefully to match specific situations, you may increase the likelihood of getting what you want—agreement to your requests by other persons. For instance, suppose that an

Figure 12.7 The "Fast-Appraoching Deadline" Technique

Several techniques for influencing others are based on the principle of scarcity: The suggestion that something people want is in short supply. Signs like the one shown here are using one procedure based on this principle: They suggest that if people don't act quickly, they will lose out on a special price or special deal.

entrepreneur is trying to persuade a customer to place an order in a market where all existing products, including the entrepreneur's, are highly similar. Here, tactics such as ingratiation (getting the customer to like him or her) might be useful. In contrast, when trying to get a repeat, and larger, order from a customer, the entrepreneur might remind this person that she placed a smaller order before, thus reminding this person of the initial commitment they made to the new venture's products. Of course, it is possible to use more than one tactic simultaneously, but the general rule remains the same: The better the match between the tactic chosen and the particular situation, the more likely it is to succeed.

In addition, knowing about these tactics can help entrepreneurs protect themselves against their use. For instance, if a supplier has made a favorable deal with an entrepreneur, but then seeks to change it in a way that is less favorable to the entrepreneur, this could be a sign that the low-ball tactic is being used; savvy entrepreneurs will walk away from such situations if they have any choice at all.

In sum, entrepreneurs often seek to exert influence over others—to change the way they think or act. For this reason, the more skilled they are with respect to persuasion and other tactics of influence, the more likely they are to attain success. And once again, we should note that almost anyone can, with a little careful practice, get better at this task. So this, too, can be a valuable skill entrepreneurs may wish to develop.

KEY POINTS

- Each day we attempt to influence the way others think or act, and are exposed, in turn, to many efforts to influence us.
- Many different tactics for exerting social influence exist, but among the most frequently used are rational persuasion and consultation. Various "pressure tactics" are used less often.
- Many other tactics for exerting social influence exist; most of these are based on several basic principles: friendship/liking, consistency, scarcity, and reciprocity.
- Familiarity with these techniques can help entrepreneurs use them effectively themselves, and also protect themselves against these tactics when used by others.

MANAGING STRESS: HOW ENTREPRENEURS CAN SURVIVE TO ENJOY THE FRUITS OF THEIR LABOR

Here is an intriguing puzzle: Most entrepreneurs make strenuous efforts to protect their new venture's resources, both intellectual and physical. As we saw in Chapter 6, they seek patents and trademarks, and they frequently purchase security systems to guard valuable equipment or raw materials. Yet, when it comes to their company's most precious resource—themselves—they often show a very different pattern. Rather than protecting this irreplaceable asset, they expose it to countless hazards: They work incredibly long hours, eat and sleep irregularly, and give up every enjoyable activity (from spending time with family and loved ones through hobbies) to work on their company. Certainly, we don't wish to seem critical of this steadfastness of purpose—far from it. But at the same time, we think it is important to note that by exposing themselves to incredibly high levels of stress for prolonged periods of time, entrepreneurs sometimes put their personal health at risk. It goes without saying that if their health is undermined so, too, is the future of their new ventures. For this reason, we believe it is crucial for entrepreneurs to know something about stress—its causes, effects, and most importantly, how to manage it—another important skill for entrepreneurs to acquire. Those are the topics we will consider next.

Stress: Its Nature and Causes

What precisely is **stress**? Definitions differ, but most experts agree that it refers to a pattern of emotional states and physiological reactions occurring in response to

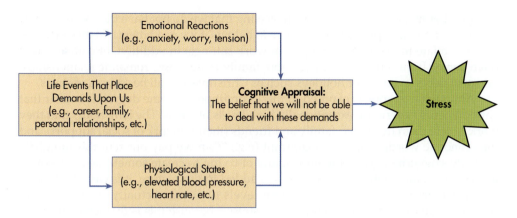

Figure 12.8 Stress: Its Basic Nature

Stress occurs when various events in our lives (known as stressors) induce a pattern of emotional states and physiological reactions that are accompanied by the growing belief that we will not be able to cope with the demands of these events. The result can be highly unpleasant—and downright dangerous to our personal health.

demands from many different events in our lives—our jobs, our families, our relationships, and so on. More specifically, these demands generate stress when the persons exposed to them engage in cognitive appraisal (i.e., they assess the situation) and conclude that they may soon be unable to deal with the demands upon them—when, in short, they feel in danger of being overwhelmed (see Figure 12.8). We're sure that this feeling is familiar to you, because everyone experiences it from time to time; we're also certain that you recognize it as a very unpleasant state—one you'd like to avoid or reduce as quickly as possible.

The specific conditions that generate stress are known as *stressors*, and many of these exist. One important source of stress is the demands of our jobs. As you can see from Table 12.1, occupations vary greatly in terms of their relative levels of stress. Interestingly, the role of entrepreneur is not included on this list, but we would guess, largely on the basis of case studies indicating that entrepreneurs' lives are highly stressful, that it is very near the top.

Other sources of stress will be all too familiar to you, such as the difficulties of juggling different roles we must play simultaneously (e.g., employee and parent; student and spouse). These roles often place incompatible demands on us—and so generate the feeling that we will soon be overwhelmed by them, which is the core of stress. This is an especially serious problem for entrepreneurs, who often find that the demands of running their new ventures, and the extremely long hours they work, make it impossible for them to devote the time and attention they would prefer to their families. Sadly, this is often a cause of great stress both for entrepreneurs and the people they love most—and can produce negative effects such as divorce or difficulties in dealing with children.

Responsibility for others is another key source of stress. For instance, several years ago, many newspapers ran a story about one entrepreneur who continued to pay his employees after a fire that destroyed his factory. Why? Because he felt deeply responsible for their well-being and experienced a great deal of stress over the economic hardships they faced. Sadly, this generosity ultimately caused him to go bankrupt, so we're not recommending such selfless practices; rather, we report this incident because it illustrates just how stressful responsibility for others can be.

HIGH-STRESS OCCUPATIONS (RANK)	STRESS SCORE	LOW-STRESS OCCUPATIONS (RANK)	STRESS SCORE
U.S. president	176.6	College professor	54.2
Firefighter	110.9	Economist	38.7
Senior executive	108.6	Mechanical engineer	38.3
Surgeon	99.5	Chiropractor	37.9
Air traffic controller	83.1	Accountant	31.1
Architect	66.9	Purchasing agent	28.9
Insurance agent	64.0	Actuary	20.2

Source: Based on data from *The Wall Street Journal*, 1997.

Table 12.1 Levels of Stress in Various Occupations

Some jobs are much more stressful than others. Although "entrepreneur" is not included on this list, case studies and other evidence suggest that it would be very close to the top.

Another major cause of stress is the feeling that we do not have the social support we need—that other people are not there to help us if we need them. All these sources of stress relate to events that happen in work settings; in addition, of course, stress often comes from our personal lives, too: family obligations, romantic relationships, personal debts, even major holidays such as Christmas can all be sources of stress.

Although everyone is exposed to these conditions to some degree, it is clear that entrepreneurs experience exceptionally high levels of stress. The long hours that they work isolate them from their family and friends (their network of social support), and the economic worries they must confront (e.g., "Can we pay our rent this month?") are truly staggering. When the uncertainty of trying to create something new—often in the face of unrelenting competition—is added to the picture, it is clear that many entrepreneurs are exposed to very high levels of stress. Actually, we should say "expose themselves to very high levels of stress," because this is the personal choice they have made; in contrast to persons who work for existing organizations, stress is not dropped on them from the outside—entrepreneurs choose it as a way of life—or at least, a temporary way of life.

The Adverse Effects of Stress

Common sense suggests that anything that feels as bad as stress and produces high levels of physiological arousal is probably harmful to our health. Indeed, a very large body of scientific evidence points to the conclusion that prolonged exposure to stress *is* harmful. In fact, medical authorities now believe that stress plays an important role in from 50 to 70 percent of all forms of physical illness.[36] The role of stress is particularly clear with respect to heart disease and strokes, but it is also involved in such varied illnesses as ulcers, diabetes, and even cancer. So clearly, stress is harmful to living things—including entrepreneurs!

In addition to its adverse effects on health, stress also interferes with performance on many different tasks. Although low levels of stress can sometimes enhance performance, especially on purely physical tasks requiring strength or speed, moderate or high levels of stress—especially if continued for long periods of time—reduce performance on a wide range of tasks.[37] Stress has also been implicated in what is sometimes described as *desk rage*—intense and often senseless lashing out at others in response to stressful conditions on the job.[38] This can be especially harmful to a new venture, where people work in close proximity many hours each day, and temper explosions by a stressed-out entrepreneur can have devastating effects on trust and morale. Finally, stress is a major cause of *burnout* (see Figure 12.9), a complex pattern of emotional, physical, and mental exhaustion that

LEARNING OBJECTIVE

8 Describe the adverse effects of stress, and explain several techniques entrepreneurs can use to reduce the level of stress they experience.

Figure 12.9 Burnout: A Key Adverse Effect of Stress

When individuals are exposed to very high levels of stress over prolonged periods of time, they may develop burnout—a pattern that may have devastating effects on the performance of a new venture.

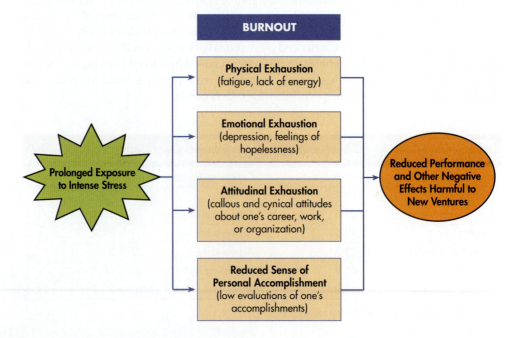

afflicts people who are exposed to stress for prolonged periods of time.[39] People suffering from burnout feel fatigued much of the time, and lose all enthusiasm for their work. In addition, they often feel hopeless and express cynical attitudes about their field and other people working in it. For instance, I once had a friend who was a physician, and who was clearly suffering from burnout. He frequently made comments such as: "Doctors know nothing and never help anyone; they are just a money-grubbing bunch of parasites." How serious is burnout? Suffice it to say that many studies suggest that if an organization acquires a substantial number of persons suffering from burnout, its effectiveness will soon drop off the charts.[40] This almost certainly applies to new ventures, too. Although entrepreneurs are known for their enthusiasm, high levels of stress can ultimately undermine passion; if the founders of a new venture suffer from burnout, it seems fair to say that the heart of the new venture itself has been consumed.

All in all, it is clear that stress produces many harmful effects. Entrepreneurs, who often accept incredibly high levels of stress as a normal part of their existence, are directly in the crosshairs where these adverse effects are concerned. True, they are probably on the high end of a dimension of "stress-tolerance" or "stress-resistance." But because they are certainly the most precious resource their new ventures possess, we think it is only prudent for them to take steps to protect themselves from the ravages of prolonged exposure to intense levels of stress. With that thought in mind, we will now describe some of the things entrepreneurs can do to protect their own health—and ensure that they will survive long enough to enjoy the fruits of their very hard labor.

Personal Techniques for Managing Stress

Stress-management techniques that you can build into your own life fall into two major categories: physical and behavioral. With respect to physical stress-management techniques, steps that strengthen personal health can be very helpful. Two of these involve ones we're sure you will find familiar: eating a healthy diet and getting into good physical shape. The fact that they are so familiar, though, shouldn't prevent you from recognizing their value. Research findings indicate that people who exercise regularly and eat a healthy diet are far less likely than persons who do not exercise regularly or eat a healthy diet to experience health problems when exposed to high levels of stress. For instance, in one impressive study, a large group of college students was tested for physical fitness.[41] In addition, the same students provided information on the level of stress they were experiencing in their lives. Finally, an objective measure of their personal health was obtained from records at the university health center. Results (see Figure 12.10) indicated that for students low in physical fitness, high levels of stress led to increased visits to the university health center for physical illnesses. Among those high in physical fitness, however, increased stress did not produce similar harmful effects on health. This and many others studies provide evidence for the following conclusion:

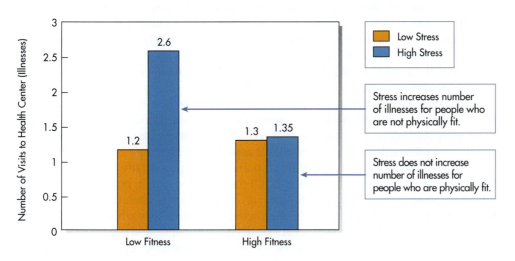

Figure 12.10 Being Phyiscally Fit: One Useful Technique for Managing Stress

Students who were physically fit showed little increase in frequency of illness when exposed to high levels of stress. In contrast, students who were not physically fit showed a much larger increase in illness.

Source: Based on data from Brown, 1991; see note 36.

Being in good physical condition can be an important means of warding off the adverse effects of stress. The message for entrepreneurs is clear: Taking the time to exercise regularly (as little as 20 to 30 minutes 3 to 4 times a week is often sufficient) is time well spent.

Turning to behavioral techniques (ones relating primarily to changes in our own thinking and behavior), several have been found to be very useful. The first has to do with efforts to curtail excessive worrying. Surveys indicate that almost 90 percent of all people feel that they worry too much. The key issue, though, is not the sheer volume of worry; rather, it is *what* people tend to worry about. In many cases, they report worrying about things that are either unimportant or not directly under their control. The result is that they add unnecessarily to their own levels of stress. To the extent this tendency is reduced, stress, too, can be lowered. Here's a concrete example of what we mean: Suppose an entrepreneur worries a lot about having enough cash flow to meet the payroll. Clearly, this is important and it is at least partly under the entrepreneurs' control (e.g., she can avoid buying new equipment for awhile if cash is truly short.) But now suppose that the same entrepreneur worries a lot about the possibility that a large competing company will come up with a better product. Certainly, this is important, but because there is not much she can do about it right now, there is little point in worrying about it. We're sure you get the main point: Worry only (or at least mainly) about important things that are at least partly under your control. Worrying about other combinations is mainly a waste of energy—and a cause of unnecessary stress. (The **"Getting Down to Business"** exercise (on page 316) will provide you with practice in this skill.)

Another useful behavioral technique involves what is known as the *incompatible reaction procedure*. When stress rises, so does physiological arousal, with the result that people's behavior tends to become increasingly intense: They speak faster and in a louder voice, and tend to tense their muscles. Consciously countering these natural inclinations can be very helpful. In other words, when faced with events that are very stressful, you should consciously try to speak more slowly and quietly, and consciously try to adopt a relaxed rather than tense posture. The result? The cycle of rising stress and rising tension can be broken, at least temporarily. It turns out that this is all we need: temporary "breaks" from stress. Research findings indicate that these are often sufficient to reduce the harmful effects that would otherwise occur.

Finally, managing stress often involves taking a step back from stressful situations and reminding oneself that even if things do not turn out as we wish—we do not get the financing we seek—this is *not* the end of the world. Human beings have a strong tendency to engage in what is sometimes termed *awfulizing*—they magnify the adverse effects of not being successful or perfect out of all proportion. The result? Even minor setbacks are interpreted as devastating calamities, and this greatly magnifies the intensity—and adverse impact—of stress. Entrepreneurs are passionate about their ideas and companies, so we are certainly not suggesting that they should reduce these commitments. But seeing current situations in perspective—against a broader backdrop—can help lessen the tendency to perceive any and all setbacks as catastrophes; that, in turn, can help lower stress to more tolerable levels. For instance, suppose an entrepreneur fails to secure an order from a customer after weeks of effort. Is this the end of the world? Probably not. There are other customers out there and other ways to market the new venture's products that may be more successful (see Chapter 9). So an adaptive response to this situation is for the entrepreneur to think: "Bad luck! But it's not the end of the world." A much less adaptive reaction would be to think: "This is a catastrophe! How can we ever recover from this giant setback?"

In sum, although stress is an inevitable aspect of starting a new venture, there are several steps entrepreneurs can take to manage this potentially harmful process. Though these differ greatly in form, they all rest, to some extent, on acceptance of the following basic principle: *No, we can't always change the world (make it the way we wish), but we can change our reactions to it.* In other words we can choose whether, and to what degree, to be upset or disturbed by various disappointments, and can choose either to manage the stress we inevitably experience or to let it dominate our thinking and our lives. The choice is always ours, and savvy entrepreneurs—those who want to remain in good health so that they can ultimately enjoy the rewards of their hard work—will definitely choose the former.

KEY POINTS

- Stress refers to a pattern of emotional states and physiological reactions occurring in response to demands from many different events in our lives.
- Stress exerts adverse effects on health, task performance, and psychological well-being. Entrepreneurs, who are exposed to high levels of stress for prolonged periods of time, are clearly at risk for such effects.
- A number of steps are helpful in managing stress. These include physical techniques, such as eating a healthy diet and getting into good physical shape, and behavioral techniques, such as avoiding excessive and unnecessary worry, taking short breaks away from stressful situations, and avoiding the tendency to magnify the adverse effects of setbacks or disappointment.
- Entrepreneurs can readily use these and many other techniques to manage stress, and so assure that they will survive in good health to enjoy the fruits of their labor.

Summary and Review of Key Points

- To run a successful new venture, entrepreneurs need a variety of personal skills that are helpful in building their company (e.g., social competence, the ability to develop trust and cooperative working relationships with others, to effectively manage conflicts).
- Social competence, the ability to get along well with others, encompasses a number of discrete social skills.
- Among these, the most relevant for entrepreneurs are social perception, expressiveness, impression management, skill at influencing others, and social adaptability.
- A large body of evidence indicates that persons high in these aspects of social competence experience more favorable outcomes in a wide range of business contexts. Further, entrepreneurs high in social competence tend to be more successful than those low in such competence.
- Social competence can be readily enhanced through appropriate training, so entrepreneurs should carefully consider devoting effort to this task; doing so may yield important benefits for both entrepreneurs and their new ventures.
- Trust is an essential ingredient in building cooperative working relationships. Two kinds exist: calculus-based trust and identification-based trust.
- Calculus-based trust is based on the belief that if someone does not act as they say they will, they will be punished. In contrast, identification-based trust is based on the belief that the person in question has our best interests at heart.

- Calculus-based trust can be increased by acting as you promise to act, following agreed-upon procedures, and being open about your own motives and needs.
- Conflict is a process in which one party perceives that another party has taken or will take actions that are incompatible with its interests. It takes two basic forms: affective or emotional conflict, which involves a strong element of anger or disliking, and cognitive conflict, which focuses on issues rather than people.
- Affective conflicts stem from many causes, including distrust, long-standing grudges, and social factors such as faulty attributions about the causes of others' behavior, and individual difference factors (e.g., the Type-A behavior pattern).
- The most useful means of resolving conflicts is negotiation—a process in which the opposing sides exchange offers, counteroffers, and concessions, either directly or though representatives.
- For negotiations to succeed, the participants should adopt a win-win perspective and avoid such tactics as extreme offers and "the big lie" technique. They should also seek to uncover the real issues and to broaden the scope of the issues discussed. Each day we attempt to influence the way others think or act, and are exposed, in turn, to many efforts to influence us.
- Many different tactic for exerting social influence exist, but among the most frequently used are rational persuasion and consultation. Various "pressure tactics" are used less often.

- Many other tactics for exerting social influence exist; most of these are based on several basic principles: friendship/liking, consistency, scarcity, and reciprocity.
- Familiarity with these techniques can help entrepreneurs use them effectively themselves, and also protect themselves against these tactics when used by others. Stress refers to a pattern of emotional states and physiological reactions occurring in response to demands from many different events in our lives.
- Stress exerts adverse effects on health, task performance, and psychological well-being. Entrepreneurs, who are exposed to high levels of stress for prolonged periods of time, are clearly at risk for such effects.

- A number of steps are helpful in managing stress. These include physical techniques such as eating a healthy diet and getting into good physical shape, and behavioral techniques such as avoiding excessive and unnecessary worry, taking short breaks away from stressful situations, and avoiding the tendency to magnify the adverse effects of setbacks or disappointment.
- Entrepreneurs can readily use these and many other techniques to manage stress, and so assure that they will survive in good health to enjoy the fruits of their labor.

Glossary

Affective Conflicts: Ones that involve a large emotional component rather than conflicts that emerge from incompatible interests or goals.

Calculus-Based Trust: Trust based on deterrence. When we expect that another person will act in the ways they promise because they know they will be punished in some way for doing otherwise, we are demonstrating calculus-based trust

Cognitive Conflict: Conflicts in which individuals become aware of contrasting perspectives or interests, but focus on the issues and not on one another.

Conflict: A process in which one party perceives that another party has taken or will take actions that are incompatible with its interests

Identification-Based Trust: Trust based on the belief that others will behave as they promise to behave not because they will be punished for failing to do so, but because they have the trusting person's well-being at heart.

Negotiation: A process in which the opposing sides exchange offers, counteroffers, and concessions, either directly or through representatives.

Organizational Citizenship Behaviors: Employee behaviors that go beyond the role requirements of their jobs and that are not directly or explicitly recognized by formal reward systems.

Social Capital: An important resource that derives from relationships among individuals in organizations or other social structures. Social capital involves close interpersonal relationships among individuals, characterized by mutual trust, liking, and identification.

Social Competence: A summary term for an individual's overall level of social skills.

Social Skills: A set of competencies (discrete skills) that enable individuals to interact effectively with others

Stress: A pattern of emotional states and physiological reactions occurring in response to demands from many different events in our lives.

Trust: One person's degree of confidence in the words and actions of another person—confidence that this person will generally behave in predictable ways that are understandable in terms of the relationship between them.

Win-Win Solution: One that is acceptable to both sides and that meets the basic needs of both.

Discussion Questions

1. If you had to choose between having excellent people skills and having a truly great product or service (versus a mediocre one), which would you prefer?

2. If people can readily acquire improved social skills, why don't they make the effort to do so? How can they enhance their own social skills?

3. Trust between cofounders of a new venture is often essential to its success. Suppose that for some reason, one of the cofounders loses her or his trust in another cofounder. Can such trust ever be restored? How?

4. Conflicts often start out as rational discussions over legitimate differences of opinion or perspective (cog-

nitive conflict), but then shift quickly into angry disputes (affective conflict). How can this costly change be avoided?

5. Beginning with an extreme initial offer in negotiations can often lead to better outcomes for the person using this strategy. Yet, we recommend against its use. What is the potential downside of using this tactic during negotiations?

6. After the CEO of Delta Airlines made his famous, insensitive remark about his reaction to laying off a large number of employees ("So be it."), he was faced with an immediate storm of anger from the company's employees. Was there anything he could have done to defuse this anger and save his own job?

7. What tactics of influence do you think are most useful to entrepreneurs when seeking financing for their companies? When attempting to build their customer base? Why?

8. Have you ever known any persons suffering from burnout? What were they like? Would you like to have them in your new venture?

InfoTrac Exercises

1. **Employee Conflicts Can't Be Ignored** (conflict resolution)

   HR Briefing, April 15, 2003 p7(1)

   Record: A99983489

   Full Text: COPYRIGHT 2003 Aspen Publishers, Inc.

   1. According to the text, what types of conflicts are easiest to resolve and why?

   2. According to the article, how can managers begin to hold employees accountable for their part in conflicts?

   3. What steps can managers take to begin to resolve conflicts?

2. **How to Sell an Idea**

   Ted Pollock

   Supervision, June 2003 v64 i6 p15(2)

   Record: A102677212

   Full Text: COPYRIGHT 2003

   1. Why do some people have a hard time selling their ideas?

   2. What steps can you take to show others that your idea has merits?

   3. What steps can you take to ensure you're communicating an idea most effectively?

GETTING DOWN
TO BUSINESS

Assessing Your Own Social Competence

Good social skills are a major "plus" for everyone, but they are especially important for entrepreneurs, who must interact with a large number of persons they did not know before starting their new venture. How do *you* rate with respect to social skills? To find out, ask at least five friends to rate you on each of the following dimensions. They should use the following scale for their ratings: 1 = very low, 2 = low, 3 = average, 4 = high, 5 = very high. They should place their ratings in the space before each dimension.

_____ **Social perception:** The ability to "read" other persons accurately.

_____ **Expressiveness:** The ability to express emotions clearly, so that other people can readily recognize them.

_____ **Skill at influencing others:** The ability to change others' views or behavior in desired directions.

_____ **Impression management:** The ability to make a good first impression on others.

_____ **Social adaptability:** The ability to adapt to, and feel comfortable in, any social situation.

Next, average the ratings your friends have provided. Dimensions on which you scored lower than 3 are ones where you have room for improvement. How can you enhance these skills? It is best to seek the help of a professional—for instance, a psychologist who specializes in improving social skills. But you can at least get started by viewing video-tapes of yourself as you interact with other people. These tapes will probably contain some major surprises, because most of us are not very good at recognizing how we come across to others. These surprises, in turn, may suggest specific things you can do to improve. For instance, if you are low in expressiveness, you can practice being more open in terms of expressing your feelings. Similarly, if you seem nervous on the tapes (e.g., you fidget a lot), you can work on changing these behaviors. Improving your own social skills is a challenging task, and one that takes time. But the potential benefits are so great that it is definitely worth the effort.

Don't Worry . . . Be Happy!

Here's a saying we like very much: "Worry is interest paid on problems in advance." Although this is not always true—there *are* things worth worrying about—research findings indicate that more than 80 percent of the topics or issues people worry about are ones they should probably *not* be worrying about. Excessive worry generates high levels of stress, which can be harmful to personal health.

To find out whether you are worrying too much, list all the things you worry about on a sheet of paper. Then, place each of these items in one of the following four quadrants.

	Things That Are Unimportant	**Things That Are Important**
Things I Can Control		
Things I Cannot Control		

What should you be worrying about? Rationally, only items that fit into the upper-right hand quadrant—ones that are both important *and* at least partly under your control. If you are worrying about items in the other three quadrants, it is time for a change; you are indeed worrying too much!

Enhanced Learning

You may select any combination of the case options below to enhance your understanding of the chapter material.

■ **Appendix 1: Case Studies –** Thirteen cases provide opportunities to apply chapter concepts to realistic entrepreneurial situations. These brief cases call for careful analysis of real business problems and ask you to think about potential solutions.

■ **Appendix 2: Video Case Library –** Nine cases are tied directly to video segments from the popular PBS television series *Small Business School*. These cases and video segments give you unparalleled access to today's entrepreneurs, with expert advice and insights on how to start, run, and grow a business.

■ **Comprehensive Cases –** Visit the book support Web site at http://baron.swlearning.com for cases detailing real businesses whose successes and setbacks illustrate each stage of the entrepreneurial process. You will conduct in-depth analysis of entrepreneurial challenges through well-developed case studies.

Notes

1 Nahapiet, J., & Ghoshal, S. 1998. Social capital, intellectual capital, and the organizational advantage. *Academy of Management Review* 23: 242–266.

2 Erikson, T. 2002. Entrepreneurial capital: The emerging venture's most important asset and competitive advantage. *Journal of Business Venturing* 17: 275–290.

3 Baron, R.A. 2000. Psychological perspectives on entrepreneurship: Cognitive and social factors In entrepreneurs' success. *Current Directions in Psychological Science* 9: 15–18.

4 Frese, M. 1985. Stress at work and psychosomatic complaints: A causal interpretation. *Journal of Applied Psychology* 70: 314–328.

5 Weber, A.L., & Harvey, J.H. (eds.). 1994. *Perspectives on close relationships*. Boston: Allyn & Bacon.

6 See note 1.

7 Eder, R.W., & Ferris, G.R. (eds). 1989. *The employment interview*. Newsbury Park, CA: Sage.

8 Heneman, R.L., Greenberg, D.B., & Anonyuo, C. 1989. Attributions and exchanges: The effects of interpersonal factors on the diagnosis of employee performance. *Academy of Management Journal* 32: 466–476.

9 Carter, N.M, Gartner, W.B., & Reynolds, P.D. 1996. Exploring start-up event sequences. *Journal of Business Venturing* 11: 151–166.

10 Thompson, L. 1998. *The mind and heart of the negotiator*. Upper Saddle River, NJ: Prentice-Hall.

11 Friedman, H.S., Riggio, R.E., & Casella, D.F. 1988. Nonverbal skills, personal charisma, and initial attraction. *Personality and Social Psychology Bulletin* 14: 203–211.

12 Friedman, H.S., Prince, L.M., Riggio, R.E., & DiMatteo, M.R. 1980. Understanding and assessing nonverbal expressiveness: The affective communications test. *Journal of Personality and Social Psychology* 39: 333–351.

13 Stevens, C.K., & Kristof, A.L. 1995. Making the right impression: A field study of applicant impression management during job interviews. *Journal of Applied Psychology* 80: 587–606.

14 Giacalone, R.A., & Rosenfeld, P. 1989. *Impression management in the organization*. Hillsdale, NJ: Lawrence Erlbaum Assoicates.

15 Hall, J., & Hofer, C.W. 1993. Venture capitalists' decision criteria in new venture evaluation. *Journal of Business Venturing* 8: 25–42.

16 Zacharakis, A.L., & Meyer, G.D. 1995. The venture capitalist decision: Understanding process versus outcome. In J. Hornaday, F. Tarpley, J. Timmons, & K. Vesper (eds.). *Frontiers of entrepreneurship research*. Wellsley, MA: Babson Center for Entrepreneurial Research, 115–123.

17 Wayne, S.J., & Ferris, G.R. 1990. Influence tactics and exchange quality in supervisor-subordinate interactions: A laboratory experiment and field study. *Journal of Applied Psychology* 75: 487–499.

18 Kilduff, M., & Day, D.V. 1994. Do chameleons get ahead? The effects of self-monitoring on managerial careers. *Academy of Management Journal* 37: 1047–1060.

19 Baron, R.A., & Byrne, D. 2002. *Social psychology*. 10th ed. Boston: Allyn & Bacon.

20 Baron, R.A., & Markman, G.D. 2003. Beyond social capital: The role of entrepreneurs' social competence in their financial success. *Journal of Business Venturing* 18: 41–60.

21 Leana, C.R., & Van Buren, H.J. 1999. Organizational social capital and employment practices. *Academy of Management Review* 24: 538–555.

22 Lewicki, R.J., & Wiethoff, C. 2000. Trust, trust development, and trust repair. In M. Deutsch & P. T. Coleman (eds.). *The handbook of conflict resolution*. San Francisco: Jossey-Bass, 86–107.

23 Podsakoff, P.M., MacKenzie, S.B., Paine, J.B., & Bachrach, D.G. 2000. Organizational citizenship behaviors: A critical review of the theoretical and empirical literature and suggestions for future research. *Journal of Management* 26: 513–563.

24 Amason, A.C., & Sapienza, H.J. 1997. The effects of top management team size and interaction norms on cognitive and affective conflict. *Journal of Management* 23: 495–516.

25 Ensley, M.D., Pearson, A.W., & Amason, A.C. 2002. Understanding the dynamics of new venture top management teams' cohesion, conflict, and new venture performance. *Journal of Business Venturing* 17: 365–386.

26 Thompson, L. 1998. *The mind and heart of the negotiator*. Upper Saddle River, NJ: Prentice-Hall.

27 Baron, R.A. 1988. Attributions and organizational conflict: The mediating role of apparent sincerity. *Organizational Behavior & Human Decision Processes* 41: 111–127.

28 Baron, R.A. 1989. Personality and organizational conflict; The type A behavior pattern and self-monitoring. *Organizational Behavior and Human Decision Processes* 44: 291–208.

29 Begley, T., & Boyd, D. 1987. A comparison of entrepreneurs and managers of small business firms. *Journal of Management* 13: 99–108

30 See note 21.

31 Yukl, G., & Tracey, J.B. 1992. Consequences of influence tactics used with subordinates, peers, and the boss. *Journal of Applied Psychology* 75: 246–257.

32 Yukl, G., Falbe, C.M., & Young, J.Y. 1993. Patterns of influence behavior for managers. *Group & Organization Management* 18: 5–28.

33 Gartner, W.B., Bird, B.J., & Starr, J.A. 1992. Acting as if: Differentiating entrepreneurial from organizational behavior. *Entrepreneurship Theory and Practice* 16: 13–32.

34 Baum, J.R., Locke, E.A., & Kirkpatrick, S. 2001. A longitudinal study of the relation of vision and vision communication to venture growth in entrepreneurial firms. *Journal of Applied Psychology* 83: 43–54.

35 Cialdini, R.B. 1994. Interpersonal influence. In S. Shavitt & T.C. Brock (eds.). *Persuasion*. Boston: Allyn & Bacon, 195–218.

36 Cohen, S., & Williamson, G.M. 1991. Stress and infectious disease in humans. *Psychological Bulletin* 109: 5–24.

37 Motowidlo, S.J., Packard, J.S., & Manning, M.R. 1986. Occupational stress: Its causes and consequences for job performance. *Journal of Applied Psychology* 71: 618–629.

38 Integra Reality Resources. 2000, *Business Week*, November 2, 2001.

39 Maslach, C. 1982. *Burnout: The cost of caring*. Englewood Cliffs, NJ: Prentice-Hall.

40 Gaines, J., & Jermier, J.M. 1983. Emotional exhaustion in high stress organizations. *Academy of Management Journal* 31: 567–586.

41 Brown, J.D. 1991. Staying fit and staying well: Physical fitness as a moderator of life stress. *Journal of Personality and Social Psychology* 60: 555–561.

BUILDING THE NEW VENTURE'S HUMAN RESOURCES: RECRUITING, MOTIVATING, AND RETAINING HIGH-PERFORMING EMPLOYEES

LEARNING OBJECTIVES

After reading this chapter, you should be able to:

1. Explain why information about recruiting, motivating, and retaining high-quality employees is useful to entrepreneurs.

2. Define "job analysis" and "job description" and explain why they are important initial steps in the search for new employees.

3. Define "reliability" and "validity" and explain why all techniques used for selection must be high on both. Describe structured interviews and explain why they are higher in validity than traditional employment interviews.

4. Describe the requirements for setting effective goals, and why it is so important to tie rewards to performance.

5. Describe the role of fairness in motivating employees.

6. Define "job enlargement" and "job enrichment" and why they are important in motivating employees.

7. Describe various means for relating pay and other rewards to performance.

8. Define "continuance commitment," "affective commitment," and "normative commitment" and explain their role in the retention of high-quality employees.

9. Define the "control barrier" and explain why it is so important for entrepreneurs to learn how to delegate authority to others.

Recruiting and Selecting High-Performing Employees
 The Search for High-Performing Employees: Knowing What You Need and Where to Look
 Selection: Techniques for Choosing the "Cream of the Crop"

Motivating Employees: Maximizing the Value of the New Venture's Human Resources
 Reaching for the Moon—Or at Least, the Next Level Up: The Key Role of Goals—And Vision
 Tying Rewards to Performance: The Role of Expectancies
 Fairness: An Essential Ingredient in Motivation
 Designing Jobs to Make Them Motivating

Retaining High-Performing Employees
 Reward Systems: Linking Pay and Performance
 Building Employee Commitment
 Overcoming the "Control Barrier": A Note on the Necessity of "Letting Go"

All photos this page © PhotoDisc, Inc.

> "Surround yourself with the best people you can find, delegate authority, and don't interfere."
> (Ronald Reagan, 1986)

It's a sad fact of life that, often, our actions produce exactly the opposite of what we want. This is certainly true for entrepreneurs—especially successful ones. If you ask them why they started their own ventures in the first place, many will make statements such as these: "I hated being a small cog in a big machine" or "I really wanted more personal freedom—to be able to do things the way *I* want to do them, not the way I'm told to do them." In new ventures, at least for awhile, this is precisely what entrepreneurs' hard work and dedication yield: They *do* get to make all the decisions and run the show. But then, if the new venture is successful, a strange paradox begins to develop: As their company grows in size, entrepreneurs find their freedom and sense of control increasingly restricted. They must spend more and more of their time overseeing a business that becomes—much to their dismay—increasingly like the large, complex organizations from which they fled! Talk about getting precisely what you *don't* want in life!

One way to deal with this situation is to limit further growth—to seek a safe market niche and continue to fill it—and some entrepreneurs do indeed choose this option. For those who want to see their new ventures become as large and successful as possible, however, there is another option—one we will describe in detail later in this chapter. In essence, this involves shifting from being a team leader—the person who inspires members of a small group of cofounders and initial employees—to becoming a leader of many teams, a very central person in the company, but one who, of necessity, delegates key tasks to other persons.[1] This is often a difficult transition for entrepreneurs, who have attained success in their lives by being proactive—by doing things themselves rather than by having others do them. As we will note repeatedly, this is an essential change if the new venture is to continue to grow. So the opening quote does indeed ring true: Ultimate and substantial success for new ventures derives *not* from a situation in which entrepreneurs are capable of doing everything, but rather from a smooth and orderly shift away from this early state to one in which the entrepreneur has assembled a first-rate team of employees to whom she or he then delegates many of the growing venture's key processes.

Although this shift involves many different changes, central to it are three basic tasks: attracting, motivating, and retaining high-quality employees. Initially, entrepreneurs seek to accomplish these tasks themselves—they want to choose everyone who joins their team and to play a central role in motivating and retaining these people. But at some point, they must entrust these tasks to others. If that's the case, then why should you, as current or future entrepreneurs, be interested in these tasks? After all, you will ultimately turn them over to others. We think the answer involves three major points. First, the process through which entrepreneurs delegate these "people" tasks to others is gradual rather than sudden. Thus, information on how to accomplish them skillfully is useful to entrepreneurs during the early phases of their new venture's growth, when they *will* be performing them. Second, most entrepreneurs want to place their personal "stamp" upon their companies, and one important way of doing this is to play an active role in establishing the systems through which first-rate employees are recruited, motivated, and retained. Third, when they delegate these tasks to others, entrepreneurs need to choose these persons well—to choose, as the opening quote suggests, "the best people." One way of assuring that this occurs is to understand just what these individuals will do. In sum, we think there are several reasons why it's important for you to understand the nature of these tasks (recruiting, motivating, and retaining excellent employees). In the remaining sections of this chapter, therefore, we will provide you with an overview of key factors relating to them. Our goal is certainly *not* to turn you into an expert on key aspects of human resource management; reaching that goal requires several years of specialized training. But we do want to arm you with basic information we believe you will find valuable as you seek to enhance the growth of your new venture, and so move toward achieving your personal dreams and goals.

RECRUITING AND SELECTING HIGH-PERFORMING EMPLOYEES

Earlier in this book (Chapter 5), we suggested that new ventures are at a serious disadvantage when they enter the labor market to attract high-quality employees. Because they are new, they are relatively unknown to potential employees and cannot offer the security or "brand familiarity" of established firms. Although there is currently little direct evidence on this issue, it seems reasonable to suggest that unless new ventures succeed in overcoming these obstacles, they may be doomed to failure—after all, they cannot grow if they fail to attract and retain essential and dedicated employees. How, then, should entrepreneurs approach this important task? To provide you with some useful guidelines, we will consider two basic questions: (1) Where should entrepreneurs search for high-quality employees? and (2) What specific techniques should they use to identify the best among them?

The Search for High-Performing Employees: Knowing What You Need and Where to Look

There is an old saying suggesting, "It's hard to get somewhere unless you know where you want to go." In other words, it's hard to reach a goal unless you have defined it clearly. That's certainly true with respect to hiring high-quality employees. Before beginning a search for such persons, it is crucial to first determine just what it is that your new venture is seeking. In the field of human resource management, this implies two preliminary tasks: a **job analysis**—determining just what the job involves and what it requires in terms of specific knowledge, skills, and abilities[2]—and formulation of a clear **job description**—an overview of what the job involves in terms of its duties, responsibilities, and working conditions. In large companies, job analyses can be very detailed and lead to highly specific job descriptions, but for entrepreneurs, especially in the very hectic early days of a new venture, when founders have to do virtually everything, it is usually sufficient for them to simply have a clear idea of what the person or persons they are seeking will actually do and a brief written description of the major duties and tasks they will perform.

Why are these initial steps so important? Because they provide a basis for choosing among potential employees—for selecting the ones most likely to succeed in a specific job. The best choice, all other factors being equal, is the person whose knowledge, skills, and abilities provide the closest match to the requirements of the job. If they have not conducted a job analysis and formulated a clear job description for a particular position, entrepreneurs (or the persons to whom they delegate this task) will still proceed to choose among potential employees—this is a task that *must* be accomplished. However, it will be more difficult for them to make these choices on the basis of job requirements. Instead, for instance, they may choose the persons they find most congenial or attractive, or applicants who somehow "stand out from the crowd" (see Figure 13.1 on page 322) rather than the person best qualified for the job. For this reason, it is best to formulate a clear idea of the specific requirements of any job before beginning the search-and-selection process.

Having said that, we should add that in some industries—ones that are on the cutting edge of technological advancement such as biotechnology, for instance—it may be very difficult to specify the requirements of various positions very precisely because conditions are changing so rapidly that the tasks people perform, too, will certainly change. But insofar as conditions will permit, it is a good idea to first determine, as precisely as possible, what is needed before beginning the search for new employees.

Once the task of specifying precisely what is needed—what skills and abilities new employees will provide to the growing venture—has been completed, the search for these persons can begin. In Chapter 5, we noted that new ventures often fill their initial needs for additional human resources largely through their founders' social

LEARNING OBJECTIVE

2 Define "job analysis" and "job description" and explain why they are important initial steps in the search for new employees.

Figure 13.1 Selecting Excellent Employees: It's Important to Know What You Need

Unless entrepreneurs know precisely what they are seeking in new employees—unless they begin with a careful job analysis—they may select employees on the basis of factors other than their qualifications for the job in question.

"*Well, you certainly seem to have a lot to offer this company, and, of course, the truffles are a hell of a plus.*"

networks. In other words, they tend to hire people they know either directly, from personal contact, or indirectly, through recommendations from people they do know and trust.[3] Here, we will expand on those comments just a bit by indicating that referrals from current or former employees are often especially helpful in this regard. If new ventures continue to grow, however, these sources may soon prove to be inadequate: They simply do not produce a sufficient number of potential employees or ones with the full array of knowledge and skills that the new venture needs.

At that point, entrepreneurs must expand their search. One way of doing so is through advertisements in carefully selected publications. For instance, ads may be placed in trade journals that reach specific, targeted audiences. Because new ventures usually lack the resources to screen large numbers of applicants, it is generally less useful for them to advertise in mass-circulation outlets such as large local newspapers (although, of course, there may be exceptions to this general rule). Other useful sources include visits to college and university employment centers; here, once again, it is possible to specify job requirements quite precisely and to be reasonably certain of interviewing only persons whose qualifications match these closely. In recent years, Internet sites (e.g., Career Mosaic, Headhunter, and Monster Board) have been developed to assist companies in finding employees, and potential employees in finding jobs. However, to date, these have turned out to be of only limited help to new ventures, so we can't recommend them strongly.

Entrepreneurs should not overlook current customers as a potential source of new employees. Customers know the new venture's products and are familiar with its operations, so they can often be a very helpful source of referrals. Finally, professional "headhunters" are often helpful. Venture capitalists often have working relationships with such firms to help the start-ups they fund obtain management talent. So this can be a very useful source for entrepreneurs who have obtained financial support from VCs. Together, the sources outlined here are often sufficient to provide growing new ventures with a pool of applicants from which they can choose. And that brings us to the next important step in the process: techniques for selecting the best people in this pool.

Selection: Techniques for Choosing the "Cream of the Crop"

Our experience tells us that, in many cases, new ventures do a reasonably good job of assembling a pool of potential employees: Their social networks, current customers, and other sources yield a number of persons who could, at first glance, be hired. Choosing among them, however, is another story. This is a difficult task under the best of conditions even in large organizations that have human resource departments with experts specifically trained to perform this task. (These are rarely found in companies that have fewer than several hundred employees.) Entrepreneurs, in contrast, often lack such specialized experience and, moreover, must try to fit the task of making these decisions into their extremely busy days. Further, serious mistakes—hiring an incompetent or unethical person—are even more costly for new ventures, with their limited resources, than for large, existing companies. So how can entrepreneurs accomplish this task effectively? The answer, basically, is through a combination of several techniques.

First, it is essential for us to insert a few words on the topics of reliability and validity, because these concepts are closely related to the question of selecting the best employees. **Reliability** refers to the extent to which measurements are consistent across time or between judges. For instance, if you step on your bathroom scale this morning and it reads "150 pounds" but then get back on it ten minutes later and it reads "140 pounds," you might question its reliability; your weight hasn't change in ten minutes, so the scale does not seem to be providing consistent measurements. (Perhaps it needs a new battery.) A good illustration of reliability across judges is the ratings given to champion figure skaters by a panel of judges. The more the judges agree, the more reliable (consistent) their ratings would be viewed to be.

In contrast, **validity** refers to the extent to which measurements actually reflect the underlying dimension to which they refer. For instance, consider the device shown in Figure 13.2. It purports to measure a person's "sexiness" when they hold the bulb on the bottom. Does it really measure this dimension? Of course not; it responds to the temperature of people's hands, and this may be more a reflection of what they have been holding lately (e.g., a cup of hot coffee) than their sex appeal. Such a device is low in validity: It does not measure what it purports to measure. (In fact, it is fair to say that it has no validity.)

Reliability and validity are closely related to the task of selecting the best persons for specific jobs for this reason: Only selection tools or techniques that are both reliable and valid are useful for this purpose—and legal under existing laws (e.g., EEOC, Americans with Disabilities Act). In fact, if the validity of any technique used for selection is doubtful, using that technique can result in costly lawsuits; keep this fact in mind if this is a type of trouble you would rather avoid!

So where do various selection tools stand with respect to reliability and validity? Many, it turns out, are quite low on both of these dimensions. Letters of recommendation, for instance, have been found to be almost totally unrelated to actual on-the-job performance, which means that they are very low in validity. Surprisingly, the same is true for standard employment interviews—the selection technique that is by far the most widely used. Traditional interviews, which are largely unstructured in nature and proceed in any way that the interviewer wishes, suffer from several major problems that tend to reduce their validity. For instance, interviewers often make their decisions very early, after only a few minutes—well before they have had a chance to gather pertinent information about an applicant.[4] Second, if interviewers ask different questions of each applicant, and allow the length of the interview to vary greatly, how can they later compare the various applicants in a systematic manner?[5] The answer is

LEARNING OBJECTIVE

3 Define "reliability" and "validity" and explain why all techniques used for selection must be high on both. Describe structured interviews and explain why they are higher in validity than traditional employment interviews.

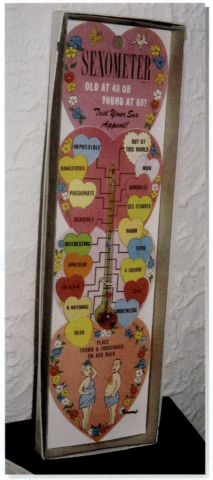

Figure 13.2 Low Validity: An Example

Validity refers to the extent to which any measuring device or instrument actually measures what it claims to measure. The device shown here, of course, is very low in validity: It really cannot measure what it claims to measure.

Photo courtesy of R.A. Baron.

that they can't, so validity suffers. Additional problems involve the fact that interviewers, like everyone else, are subject to subtle forms of bias in the way they perceive applicants. A large body of evidence indicates that attractive applicants, ones who are similar to the interviewer in various respects (age, background, ethnic identity), and ones who are good at impression management (see Chapter 5) tend to have a major edge over applicants who are less attractive, less similar to the interviewer, and less skilled at impression management.[6] Such factors are largely unrelated to the ability of various persons to perform the jobs for which they are being interviewed, so this means that the validity of such interviews is questionable, at best. Despite these drawbacks, and despite the bizarre results they often yield (see Table 13.1), most companies—including new ventures—continue to employ brief job interviews as the primary means through which they choose their employees. Why is this so? Probably because most persons, including entrepreneurs, suffer from the illusion that they are highly skilled at social perception (see Chapter 5). In other words, they believe that they can form an accurate impression of others' major traits, motives, and talents on the basis of a brief conversation with them.[7] In fact, however, systematic research suggests that we are unduly optimistic in this regard: The task of assessing others is far more difficult and subject to many more sources of error than most people realize. Because we discussed these in Chapter 4, we won't repeat that information here. Suffice it to say that we are generally less successful at this task than we believe and that this calls the validity of traditional job interviews into serious question.

Fortunately, the validity of interviews can be greatly improved by switching to what are known as **structured interviews**, in which all applicants are asked the same questions—ones chosen carefully to be truly job-related. Some of the questions (situational questions) ask the applicants how they would respond to particular work situations (e.g., "What would you do if you ran out of supplies?"). Others focus on job knowledge—do applicants have the necessary information. Additional questions focus on applicants' willingness to perform the job under current conditions (e.g., "What are your feelings about working overtime during very busy periods?"). Empirical evidence suggests that structured interviews are, perhaps, the most valid technique for selecting employees: Different interviewers come up with similar ratings for the same applicants, and these ratings do predict on-the-job performance. So although they are not perfect, structured interviews offer a useful technique—one that can help entrepreneurs make the correct decisions when choosing among several applicants.

Another technique for selecting employees and one that is reasonably high in validity involves **biodata**—information about their background, experiences, and preferences provided by employees on application forms. This information has been found to have moderate validity for predicting job performance—provided the questions asked are indeed relevant to the job in question. For instance, suppose that a job requires a lot of travel; a question on the application form might ask: "How willing are you to travel on the job?" or "How frequently did you travel in your previous job?" Clearly, applicants who are willing to travel are a better choice than ones who express

Table 13.1 Interviews: Sometimes They Yield Bizarre Results!

Traditional job interviews sometimes yield unexpected—and bizarre—results. The information shown here is based on actual interviews.

- Applicant entered and asked: "Why am I here?"
- When asked about his loyalty, applicant showed a tattoo of his girlfriend's name on his arm.
- Applicant said that if I hired him, "You will soon regret it!"
- The applicant arrived with a large snake around her neck and stated: "I take him everywhere."
- Applicant remarked: "If I am hired, I will teach you ballroom dancing for free." She then started demonstrating this skill.
- The applicant left a dry-cleaning tag on his jacket and remarked: "I wanted to show you how clean I am."
- The applicant took three cellular phone calls during the interview and said: "I have another business on the side."
- After a difficult question, the applicant said: "I need to leave the room to meditate before answering."

Source: Adapted from information presented by Gomez-Mejia, Balkin, & Cary, 2001.

reluctance to travel. But remember: Information collected in this manner is useful only to the extent that it is relevant to the job in question. In addition, as we noted in Chapter 4, certain kinds of questions cannot be asked, either in person or on application forms. Questions that inquire about an applicant's personal life, physical characteristics, personal health, prior arrest records, or personal habits can violate Equal Employment Opportunity laws and guidelines and land an entrepreneur in hot water. As long as questions are focused directly on knowledge, skills, preferences, and experience related to the job, these problems can be avoided, and structured interviews can be a valuable tool for choosing the best persons for specific jobs.

Although we have been emphasizing the use of interviews as a tool for selecting employees, it is important to note that many companies—new ventures included—often use such meetings with job applicants for another purpose: to build the image of the company. Up to a point, this can be a good strategy. But research findings indicate that it is often a big mistake to oversell a company, whether it is a new start-up or an established corporation. Painting too positive or rosy a picture of working conditions can set employees up for major disappointments once they are on the job, and this can undermine both their motivation and commitment. In general, it is much better to make sure that interviews reflect what are known as **realistic job previews**—efforts to present a balanced and accurate picture of the company to potential employees. In that way, unpleasant surprises are minimized, and new employees are more likely to remain on the job after they are hired.[8]

Why should you, as a current or future entrepreneur, want to know about these techniques and procedures? For two reasons we have already noted: (1) You will probably carry out the tasks of recruiting and selecting employees yourself, at least initially, and (2) later on, if you decide to delegate these tasks to others, you should still want to retain oversight, to assure that they are being handled correctly. Remember: Not only is recruitment of excellent employees crucial to the future of a new venture, but carrying out this task in an inappropriate manner can also put the company at risk for lawsuits stemming from violations of the laws we described in Chapter 4. Clearly, then, this is one more instance where the adage "Better safe than sorry" applies—and with a vengeance.

One final point: It is absolutely crucial to carefully check all references provided by job applicants and all claims they make concerning past experience and training. All people, unfortunately, are not completely honest, and applicants for jobs at new ventures are no exception to this general rule. To be on safe side, therefore, entrepreneurs should check at least major aspects of an applicant's resume before hiring this person. In all likelihood, the information is accurate, but in a few cases, there may be some big surprises lurking around the edges!

KEY POINTS

- Before beginning a search for new employees, it is very useful to carry out a job analysis and prepare a job description for each position to be filled. Only when these preliminary tasks are completed can clarity about what needs are to be met by new employees be obtained, and steps to choose the best persons for these positions be formulated.
- In their search for new employees, entrepreneurs focus primarily on their own social networks. However, as the new venture grows, it may be necessary to turn to other sources, such as advertisements in trade publications, the Internet, and referrals from customers.
- Reliability—the consistency of measurements over time or between judges—and validity—the extent to which measurements reflect the dimension to which they refer—are important considerations in selecting employees. Only techniques high in both reliability and validity are useful for this purpose and are legal under existing laws.
- Two employee selection techniques that are high in reliability and validity are structured interviews and biodata—information about applicants' background, experiences and preferences gathered by means of detailed application forms.
- It is best to provide potential employees with accurate information about working conditions in a company during an interview; such realistic job previews protect new hires from unpleasant surprises when they assume their jobs. This can improve motivation and retention.

MOTIVATING EMPLOYEES: MAXIMIZING THE VALUE OF THE NEW VENTURE'S HUMAN RESOURCES

Entrepreneurs are, by definition, highly motivated persons: In fact, as we noted in Chapter 12, their motivation for success is often so high that it exposes them to extreme levels of stress that can put their personal health in jeopardy. But entrepreneurs' high levels of motivation do not, in and of themselves, guarantee that everyone hired by their new ventures will share this perspective. True: Early hires may be acquaintances, former coworkers, or people referred to the entrepreneurs by close friends, so these individuals may well have high levels of motivation, too. But once a new venture begins to grow and to hire additional employees, the issue of motivation—of how to motivate these persons so that they will do their best work—arises, just as it does in every other organization. In fact, because every person on the payroll matters to a new venture, and it cannot afford to support "free riders" who coast along on the efforts of others, the question "How can employee motivation be maximized?" is a key one for entrepreneurs. In this section, we will offer some concrete suggestions for reaching this goal. Initially, most entrepreneurs use an inspiring vision of what their company can become to motivate new employees, and they are often highly skilled in this regard.[9] But this is just one technique that may be effective for building motivation, and we believe that it is very useful for entrepreneurs to at least be familiar with several others.

Before turning to these "motivation boosters," however, we should say few words about just what we mean by the term **motivation**. In the fields of human resource management and organizational behavior, the two branches of management that have focused most attention on this topic, motivation is usually defined as the processes that arouse, direct, and maintain human behavior toward attaining some goal. In other words, motivation refers to behavior that is energized by, and directed toward, reaching some desired target or objective. To fully understand motivation, all four components are necessary: Nothing happens without arousal (energy), and nothing is accomplished by random flailing around; to attain specific goals, behavior must be directed and generally continued over some period of time. Here's a simple example: Suppose that an entrepreneur wants to obtain financing for her new venture. She doesn't sit around daydreaming about this objective; rather, she takes active, energetic steps to reach it. And these steps are directed—they are not sheer random activity. For instance, she may use her network to identify possible "business angels" or to get her in contact with venture capitalists and other potential sources of funding. She doesn't, in contrast, go to a nearby intersection with a sign reading "Need money for a new venture" and try to solicit it from passing motorists. Further, her behavior persists over time: She doesn't quit after one or two setbacks. On the contrary, her desire to obtain financing is strong, so she continues to try over and over again. And her efforts are directed toward a specific goal—obtaining financing. Because all four components are present—energy, direction, persistence, and a clear objective or goal—her actions illustrate the basic nature of motivation. (See Figure 13.3 for a summary of these components.) Note, by the way, that this is an example of self-motivation: The entrepreneur is motivated to obtain financing by internal factors—her own goals and desires. Because a key task for entrepreneurs is that of motivating others, we will focus primarily on this issue in the current discussion.

Reaching for the Moon—Or at Least, the Next Level Up: The Key Role of Goals—And Vision

When you work on a task, do you set goals for yourself? For instance, when you began reading this chapter, did you set the goal of finishing all of it? Half? If you are like most ambitious, hard-working people the answer is probably *yes*. You probably already know that setting goals in this way can be highly motivating: They can help us maintain behavior for long periods of time. Why? Partly because knowing where we want to get

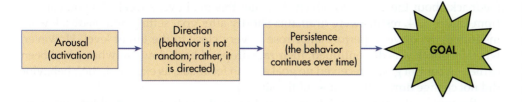

Figure 13.3 Motivation: Its Basic Components

Motivation involves three major components: arousal (activation), direction (toward some goal), maintenance of the behavior over time (persistence), and the goal toward which it is directed.

(our goal) helps us measure our progress: We can tell whether, and how quickly, we are getting where we want to be. That, it appears, helps us continue; in fact, research findings indicate that the closer we get to a specific goal, the stronger our motivation to reach it may become, and the greater the effort we expend trying to finally get there.[10]

So far, we have been talking about self-set goals—the goals people set for themselves. Clearly, entrepreneurs are masters at this task: In fact, the desire to set their own goals—to have personal control over their life and their own activities—is one reason why many people become entrepreneurs in the first place.[11] For instance, consider Jon Oringer, who recently started a software company (SurfSecret Software).[12] Oringer was a graduate student living comfortably in his parents' home, but he wanted the full independence that running his own business would provide. So, he gave up his secure life, moved into his own apartment, and started his company, which now employs four off-site programmers. In some ways, his life is certainly harder; but he now has the personal control he craved so, in his view, the trade-off was a very good one.

In contrast to entrepreneurs, many persons are not so self-directed: They do not seek total independence and do not always set goals for themselves. Or, if they do, they set goals that are so easy to reach that they are not very motivating. Echoing this basic fact, a vast number of research studies indicate that in many business contexts, setting goals for employees is an extremely useful way to increase their motivation—and their performance. In order to be maximally helpful, though, such goals must meet certain criteria:

- They must be *challenging*—the goals must be a "stretch" for the people involved, so that they have to work hard to expend effort to reach them. In contrast, goals that are not challenging do not increase motivation and performance.
- They must be *attainable*—setting impossible goals that people cannot reach does not increase their motivation or performance; on the contrary, it often encourages them to give up because they conclude that they cannot possibly reach the stated objective.
- They must be *specific*—just telling people to "do their best" or "increase your output" is practically useless. To motivate increased effort and performance, goals must be specific (e.g., "Increase your output by 15 percent within a month," "Reduce your error rate by 20 percent within two weeks.").
- They must be *accepted* by the persons involved—if people reject a goal because it is not consistent with their own wishes or objectives, it will have little if any impact on them; after all, it's not *their* goal so why should they try to attain it?
- *Feedback* concerning progress must be provided—the people involved must be kept informed about how they are doing. Are they moving toward the goal? At an acceptable pace? In the absence of such feedback, people have no idea about whether their efforts are paying off, and may soon become discouraged.

LEARNING OBJECTIVE

4 Describe the requirements for setting effective goals, and why it is so important to tie rewards to performance.

As we noted earlier, a large body of evidence suggests that setting goals that meet these criteria is a powerful technique for increasing motivation and performance.[13] Indeed, the results it produces are often nothing short of dramatic. For instance, in one recent study, operators of a pizza chain found that drivers who delivered its pizzas were not stopping fully at stop signs, thus putting themselves and the company at risk for accidents—and lawsuits. Goal setting coupled with concrete feedback was used to change this behavior: Drivers were given the specific goal of coming to a complete stop at least 75 percent of the time (versus the 45 percent rate they showed at the beginning of the study). Further, their driving was observed, and they were given feedback about the extent to which they met this goal every week. As you can see from Figure 13.4, results were dramatic: Shortly after goal setting and feedback were instituted, the drivers' performance rose to very close to the target level. However, when feedback was discontinued, their rate dropped back down to what it had been earlier. (A control group received no goal and no feedback; as expected, their behavior did not change during the course of the study.)

Because goal setting is relatively easy to use, it can be a powerful technique for entrepreneurs. To be effective, though, it must be applied in accordance with the guidelines described here. If these are ignored, results will probably be disappointing.

At this point, we wish to emphasize again a point we made earlier: Many entrepreneurs go beyond focusing on objectives relating to task performance. They focus, instead on *vision*—on what they want to achieve, and what their company can become. Communicating this clearly to employees and others, research findings suggest, can greatly enhance the growth of new ventures.[14]

One final comment: Throughout this discussion, we have mentioned motivation and performance together. It is important to note that they are definitely *not* the same thing. Motivation is a key ingredient in the performance of many tasks, but by itself, it is not a guarantee of improved performance. For instance, if employees lack required skills or knowledge to perform a job well, they will probably be unable to do so even if their motivation is very high—that's one reason why careful selection of job applicants is so important. Similarly, even highly motivated people may not be able to do a good job with poor or faulty equipment. So keep in mind that motivation is only one of the ingredients in good performance; it is often a crucial one, but it is by no means the entire story.

Tying Rewards to Performance: The Role of Expectancies

Do you recall our discussion of the optimistic bias in Chapter 3? We noted then that, in general, people are optimistic; they believe, more than is justified by the cold light of reason, that things will turn out well and that they will experience positive outcomes in many different situations.[15] This tendency is closely related to motivation: Because they are optimistic, people generally believe that the greater the effort they expend on a given task, the better they will perform it, and that good performance will generally yield larger rewards than poor performance. In many cases, these assumptions are reasonable ones; in others, though, they can be misleading. For instance, have you ever tried to perform a task with faulty tools or when you were lacking some necessary information? In such cases, working hard does not necessarily improve performance. I recall the first time I ever tried to build a bookcase; because I didn't know enough about how pieces of wood could be joined, it didn't matter how hard I worked: What I produced was still pretty shaky.

Figure 13.4 Goal Setting: A Highly Effective Technique for Motivating Employees

When a clear goal was established for the drivers of pizza delivery trucks and they were given feedback, their performance increased sharply. When feedback was removed, however, performance decreased to the level shown initially, before the goal was established.

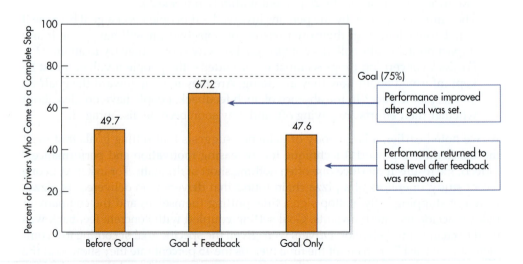

Source: Based on data from Ludwig & Geller, 1997; see note 12.

Similarly, you have probably experienced situations in your life where good performance was not recognized or rewarded; perhaps the situation was unfair, or your good work was just overlooked.

An important theory of motivation known as **expectancy theory**[16] suggests that both of these factors, plus one additional one, play a key role in motivation. Specifically, this theory—which has been verified by many different studies—suggests that people will be motivated to work hard on a task only when three conditions prevail: (1) they believe that expending effort will improve their performance (this is known as *expectancy*), (2) that good performance will be rewarded (this is known as *instrumentality*), and (3) the rewards offered are ones they really want or value (*valence*). When any of these factors is missing, motivation tends to drop to very low levels. This is eminently reasonable: Why, after all, should anyone exert effort on tasks when doing so won't help them perform better, or when there is no link between the quality of one's performance and the payoffs one receives? The answer is clear: Under these conditions, they will *not* expend the effort—they will not be motivated to work hard on this particular task.

Now here is where things get interesting: Because entrepreneurs are even more optimistic than other persons[17] and also higher in the belief that they can accomplish whatever they set out to accomplish (i.e., higher in self-efficacy), they tend to assume—implicitly, but strongly—that effort and performance are closely linked and that performance and rewards are also closely related to each other. So if working hard on a task doesn't succeed at first, they tend to redouble their efforts rather than give up. If at first the value of their hard work is not recognized, they tend to strive even harder to assure that, ultimately, it is. Other persons, however, may be more inclined to experience declines in motivation when confronted with these conditions. Thus, in running their new ventures, entrepreneurs should take careful note of this factor. It suggests several practical steps that they can implement to maintain the motivation of their employees at high levels:

- Make sure that effort does indeed lead to good performance—this means assuring that people have the training, equipment, and knowledge they need to perform their jobs well. If these are lacking, and effort does not produce improvements in performance, employees may get discouraged, with costly results for the new venture.

- Make sure that good performance is recognized and rewarded—that there is a close link between performance and rewards. This can be done through the reward system for pay, bonuses, and other positive outcomes established for the new venture. We will return to this in more detail in our discussion of steps useful in retaining first-rate employees. Here, we will merely note that when excellent performance is *not* recognized and rewarded, there is more at work than motivation—there is also a very real possibility that these people will decide to leave, and that can be devastating for a new venture.

- Make sure that the rewards provided for good performance are ones employees really want. This sounds obvious, but please remember: *Money is not the only thing people want from their jobs.* True, it is certainly important to them. But sometimes, people value other outcomes, such as specific kinds of fringe benefits, flexible working hours or vacation schedules, praise, and recognition. For instance, biotech start-ups often permit their scientists to publish research findings because being able to do so increases the motivation of these highly trained professionals. It is for this reason that organizations are currently offering employees a broad range of benefits, including all those shown in Table 13.2 on page 330. If you want to hold onto the best people in your company, this is a valuable principle to remember.

In sum, to the extent that the links between effort and performance or performance and reward are strong and clear for employees, their motivation will be high. Break or weaken these links, however, and the results may be a demoralized and demotivated workforce. Savvy entrepreneurs, therefore, will take careful note of these basic facts and do everything in their power to assure that conditions favoring high levels of motivation are the standard in their new ventures. Again, if they don't focus on

Table 13.2 Employee Benefits: Some New Forms

In order to keep employee motivation high, it is important to offer benefits that they find desirable. Here is a sample of the vast range of benefits offered to employees by actual companies. We're sure you will find some of these surprising.

BENEFITS (Description)	
Counseling (financial, legal, psychiatric/psychological)	Parking
Discounts on merchandise	Transportation to and from work
Tax preparation	Child adoption
Education subsidies	Clothing allowance
Child care	Subsidized food service
Housing allowance	Tool allowance
Elder care	Social and recreational opportunities
Emergency loans	Relocation expenses
Physical fitness programs	Credit union

Source: Based on information presented by Henderson, 1989; *Compensation management*, Prentice-Hall.

this task themselves, they should be certain that the people to whom they delegate it are using the techniques described here; if they are not, this may be reason for concern—and added oversight.

Fairness: An Essential Ingredient in Motivation

The summer between my freshman and sophomore years at college, I (Robert Baron) worked in the finance office of a large labor union. I was a summer fill-in, so the work was totally boring: I mainly filed forms and prepared new file folders by placing labels on them. My hours were long, and I had to punch a time clock when I arrived and when I left. I had only 45 minutes for lunch and one 15-minute break in the morning. I needed the money for college, so I would have gladly put up with all of this except for one thing: Another student also working there was treated much better. Tom, who was a year older than I was, arrived late every morning and often left early. He disappeared for long periods of time during the day, and often took 2-hour lunches. Worst of all, he was given the most interesting jobs to do. The final blow came when, by mistake, I received his paycheck. When I opened the envelope and discovered that it was 50 percent higher than mine, my head nearly exploded over the unfairness of it all. "Who the heck is this guy to get such special treatment?" I wondered. I soon found out: He was the nephew of the president of the union. End of mystery—but not of my feelings of being treated unfairly.

What do you think these feelings of unfairness did to my motivation? As you can readily guess, they caused it to drop to zero. "Why should I put out effort for an organization that treats me like this?" I remember thinking. In fact, this is one of the key effects of unfairness in business contexts: The people exposed to it experience a strong drop in motivation. Even worse, they often engage in instances of theft and sabotage, partly because of their anger toward the business that has treated them unfairly and partly because this is one way to "even the score," so to speak—to get what they feel they deserve, even if they have to take it themselves.[18]

This situation provides a clear illustration of one set of conditions that leads individuals to conclude that they are being treated unfairly—an imbalance between the contributions they make to the outcomes (rewards) they receive, relative to those of other persons. In general, we expect this ratio of contributions and rewards to be about the same for everyone in the group: The more each person contributes, the larger the rewards he or she receives. In other words, we seek **distributive justice** (or **equity**)—conditions under which available rewards are divided fairly among group members, according to what each has contributed to the group.[19] It was the absence of this kind of fairness that upset me in my summer job: My contributions were actually larger than those of the other student, yet his rewards were greater the mine (see Figure 13.5).

An imbalance between what they receive and what they contribute is not the only reason people feel unfairly treated, however. In addition, such feelings can arise when people feel that the procedures in dividing available rewards are not fair (*procedural justice*) or when they feel that the people who distribute these rewards have not explained

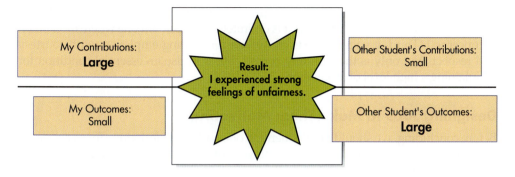

Figure 13.5 Distributive Justice: A Specific Example

In deciding whether we have been treated fairly, we often focus on distributive justice—the degree to which available rewards are divided in accordance with each person's contributions (the more each contributes, the larger the rewards they receive). In a summer job I once held, my contributions were larger but my outcomes were smaller than those of another student. The result: I experienced strong feelings of unfairness (inequity).

their decisions adequately or shown enough courtesy in their behavior (*interactional justice*).[20] Reactions to these kinds of injustice, too, are much the same: People become angry, feel resentment, and experience a drop in the desire to work hard. They may also demand larger rewards or more courteous treatment or—ultimately—take a walk and leave this exploitative workplace behind. (See the **"Danger! Pitfall Ahead!"** section for discussion of another, especially disturbing kind of reaction to unfairness on the part of employees.)

What does this mean for entrepreneurs? Several things. First, they should be very careful to be fair to people in their new ventures. This means that strong efforts must be made to link rewards to performance as closely as possible, so that the greater employees' contributions, the greater their rewards. Second, it means that it is important to establish fair procedures for evaluating performance and distributing

LEARNING OBJECTIVE

5 Describe the role of fairness in motivating employees.

DANGER! PITFALL AHEAD!

Employee Theft: Evening the Score with an Unfair Employer

- In the restaurant business—one in which many entrepreneurs operate—theft by employees costs between $15 billion and $25 billion each year in the United States alone.
- The average small store (many of which are operated by entrepreneurs) loses about $20,000 each year due to employee theft.
- In retail businesses around the world, more than 3 percent of employees admit that they steal every day and 8 percent admit that they steal at least once a week.
- Fraud costs businesses in the United States more than $400 million each year.

These numbers[21] suggest that employee theft is a major problem for many companies and that—more to the point—small businesses (including new ventures) are far from immune to this predicament. Why do employees steal? For many reasons, but research findings indicate that one of the most important is that they believe they are being treated unfairly.[22] In other words, they steal because they feel that they are entitled to do so—they are merely "evening the score," so to speak. Here's one disturbing example, from a small law office.

This office specialized in personal injury claims and employed a number of paralegals—people who do not hold a law degree but are trained in basic legal procedures. One of them, we'll call him Joe, was paid $7 per hour. Working conditions were terrible—to earn more money, the lawyers in the firm continually increased the number of cases they were handling, and although they earned huge fees, they did not share these with their hard-working employees. Most paralegals left after a few months, but Joe stuck it out. Why? Because he figured out a way to steal large amounts of money (more than $2,500 per month) from the company. Here's how: Because legal claims often drag on for years, clients would move away, give up, or simply forget about their cases after some period of time. So when checks arrived to settle these cases, there was often no client to receive her or his share. Joe simply forged the names of the people and cashed their checks. Rightfully, these leftover checks should have gone to his company, but as Joe put it, "They were underpaying me, so I figured they owed me." In this instance, it was a small law firm that suffered financial losses, but the same pattern can certainly develop in new ventures if employees feel that they are not being treated fairly. Because struggling start-up companies need all the revenue they can generate and can ill-afford losses stemming from employee theft, it is clear that building fairness into their culture is not only the ethical thing to do—it is the most practical, too!

available rewards—procedures that are understood by all employees. We will have more to say about this issue later, but it is definitely an important one where motivation is concerned. Third, it suggests a strong reason for treating employees with courtesy and respect. Not only is this ethically correct, but it is also an essential condition for maintaining a high level of motivation.

Designing Jobs to Make Them Motivating

Before concluding, we should briefly mention one additional technique for maintaining or increasing motivation among the employees of a new venture: designing the jobs they perform so that they are intrinsically motivating. Almost no one likes jobs that are totally routine and completely repetitive, and over which they have little or no control. People who find themselves in such jobs become "clock-watchers," impatiently waiting for the day to end so that they can get back to their real lives—the things they enjoy and that matter to them (see Figure 13.6). Certainly, their jobs are low on the list.

It is all too easy for entrepreneurs, who are excited about creating something new and are typically overstimulated every day, to overlook this fact. They forget that employees may not share in these feelings and may, in fact, be bored by the tasks they perform. This suggests that some attention to **job design**—to structuring jobs so that they increase people's interest in doing them (and hence their motivation)—is important. Fortunately, reaching this goal is not very difficult. Two basic steps can be very helpful in assuring that employees' jobs are not totally routine. One approach is known as *job enlargement*, and involves expanding jobs so that they include a wider variety of tasks and activities. For example, instead of having an employee pack products for shipment all day, this person can also be asked to help keep track of returns and perhaps play a role in ordering supplies needed in shipping.

The second basic technique of job design is *job enrichment*, which involves giving employees not simply more tasks, but ones requiring a higher level of skill and responsibility. For example, the boring summer job I described earlier could have been enriched by allowing me to answer requests from members for various forms or information booklets. Those tasks would involve a little more thought than filing endless forms, and would also be ones I could do at my own pace.

We have covered a lot of ground in this discussion, but in essence, the principles we have described are very straightforward and eminently reasonable. They can be summarized as follows:

- People will work harder when they are striving to reach challenging goals they accept than when they have no clear goals to attain.
  - People will work harder when they perceive clear links between their effort, their performance, and the rewards they receive, than if these links are weak or absent.
  - People will work harder when they feel that they are being treated fairly (in terms of rewards, procedures, and courtesy) than when they feel they are being treated unfairly.
  - People will work harder when their jobs are designed to be interesting to them.

All of these principles are ones that can be built into a new venture; indeed, new ventures have an advantage in this respect over large, existing companies in which complex and unreliable reward systems and organizational politics often get in the way. But these key ingredients in employee

Figure 13.6 Low Motivation: One Result of Failing to Design Jobs so That They Are Interesting to Employees

When their jobs are dull and tedious, employees generally have low motivation to perform them. This situation can be rectified through careful job design.

motivation will *not* take care of themselves. They will exist only to the extent that entrepreneurs or others to whom this task has been delegated take the time to assure their presence. Given the crucial role of employee motivation in the success of a new venture, this is a task entrepreneurs should definitely *not* neglect.

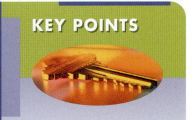

KEY POINTS

- Motivation is defined as the processes that arouse, direct, and maintain human behavior toward attaining some goal.
- Setting goals that are specific in nature, challenging but attainable, and accepted by the persons for whom they are established is a very effective technique for increasing motivation, provided that the persons in questions also receive feedback concerning progress toward these goals.
- Expectancy theory suggests that motivation will be high when there are clear links between effort and performance and between performance and rewards, and the rewards provided are ones people actually value.
- When employees feel that they are being treated unfairly in terms of outcomes, procedures, or courtesy they receive, motivation is sharply reduced. Thus, entrepreneurs should be careful to establish these kinds of fairness in their new ventures.
- Jobs can be designed to be interesting and motivating for the persons who perform them. This can be accomplished through job enlargement and job enrichment.

RETAINING HIGH-PERFORMING EMPLOYEES

Good people are always in demand, so new ventures face the same problems that all companies do: how to retain high-performing employees. Doing so is especially crucial for new ventures for two key reasons: Replacing good people requires time and other precious resources the new venture can ill afford, and if they leave, they may take important information with them—perhaps to competitors! (Recall that we discussed this problem in Chapter 11.) For these reasons, it is truly important for new ventures to retain their key employees. Many strategies can be useful in this regard, but two are most important: (1) developing excellent reward systems, and (2) building a high level of commitment and loyalty among employees. These two strategies are related, but because they involve somewhat different actions, we will discuss them separately, taking care to note links between them.

Reward Systems: Linking Pay and Performance

When bright, talented people come to work for a new venture, they are, in essence, taking a risk: Such persons can always find good jobs in large organizations—ones that offer higher levels of job security. So why do they choose to join relatively risky new ventures? Several factors probably play a role: the commitment and enthusiasm of the founders, who "tell a good story" about their company and its potential future; dissatisfaction with conditions in the large companies where they now work. Another factor that is crucial, and the one on which we will focus here, involves potential rewards: Good people come to work for new ventures because they perceive greater potential for rewards in this setting. If this is so, then it is also true that assuring that these beliefs are realized—or at least remain viable—is a crucial task for entrepreneurs. How can this goal be attained? Largely through the development of effective **reward systems**—systems in the new venture for recognizing and rewarding good performance.

In general terms, the kinds of systems most suitable for new ventures are described in the field of human resource management as **pay for performance systems** (or *incentive systems*). Such systems assume that employees differ in how much they contribute to the company's success, and that they should be rewarded in accordance with the scope of their contributions. In other words, such systems strive for the kind of distributive justice described earlier in this chapter. Several varieties of such plans exist. The most common type, *merit pay plans*, offers employees an increase in base pay, with the size of the increase being determined by their performance. The higher this is rated to be, the larger the raise. (Space limitations preclude our discussing the complexities involved in measuring and rating employees' performance, but it is crucial that these tasks be carried out in a systematic and accurate manner—far from an easy task. In fact, this matter is so complex that we recommend that entrepreneurs hire appropriate consultants to help them establish such systems of performance appraisal.)

Another type of individual pay for performance plan involves bonuses. In such plans, employees receive a bonus based, again, on their performance. A variant of these plans involves *awards*—tangible prizes such as paid vacations, electronic equipment, or other desirable items. In new ventures, entrepreneurs may also provide either actual stock in the company or stock options to employees. The latter give the employees the right to purchase shares of the company at a given price. Research findings indicate that new ventures that provide equity to employees grow faster and attain greater success than ones that do not, so this appears to be a technique well worth considering.[23]

All these pay for performance plans can be highly effective if designed and administered carefully. The advantages lie primarily in the fact that such plans translate the principles we described in our discussion of motivation into tangible actions important to employees. The link between performance and reward is strengthened, commitment to the company's goals is increased, and fairness (in terms of a balance between contributions and outcomes) is obtained. No wonder these plans often work!

Like every management procedure, however, pay for performance plans have a downside. Most important among these is the possibility that a "Do only what you get paid for" mentality may develop. In other words, employees may focus on whatever indicators of performance are part of the system, while neglecting everything else. For instance, in some school systems, teachers' pay has been linked to the scores their students attain on standardized tests. The result? The teachers focus on helping their students do well on these tests (e.g., by learning various test-taking tactics) rather than helping them understand the subject matter they are studying. Similarly, the number of "no-shows" (passengers who book tickets but don't show up) rose when airlines began compensating reservations agents on the number of reservations they booked.

Another problem with pay for performance plans is that they are hard to follow during tough economic times. When funds for raises and bonuses are severely limited—or even nonexistent—it may not be feasible to offer meaningful rewards to employees even for truly outstanding performance. Under these conditions, entrepreneurs need to be creative to hold onto their first-rate employees. People won't work hard forever without tangible rewards, so this, experts such as Marc Drizin of Walker Information Inc. suggest, is when effective communication with employees becomes essential. They should be fully informed about the current situation and about the entrepreneurs' plans to help things improve. In the meantime, entrepreneurs should do everything they can to demonstrate that they really do value excellent performance. For instance, they can offer nonmonetary support to hard-pressed employees such as adopting flexible hours and creating a pool of child-care resources. The main point is that ambitious, hard-working persons can put up with difficult situations—including a gap between their performance and their rewards—on a temporary basis. But to maintain their motivation, it is important to assure them that this state of affairs will not persist. If they conclude that it will not change, their motivation will drop, and they will head for the exit as soon as this is feasible.

In contrast to individual pay for performance plans, other reward systems offer incentives to teams of employees rather than to individuals. In such plans, all team members receive rewards based on the team's overall performance. This can lead to increased performance and a high level of cohesiveness among group members, but is unsatisfying to many people who prefer to "float or sink" on their own merits. It also encourages *free-riding* effects in which some team members do most of the work while others ride on their coattails.

Perhaps more useful to new ventures are *company-wide pay for performance plans*, in which all employees share in the company's profits. *Profit-sharing* plans distribute a portion of the company's earnings to employees; *employee stock ownership plans* reward employees with stock or options to purchase the company's stock at a specific (favorable) price. These plans make employees partners in the new venture, and this can work wonders for their motivation—and their desire to remain with the company. I am reminded of this every time I visit a Home Depot store. This large corporation has an unusually generous employee stock ownership plan, and it shows in the behavior of employees: Almost all are eager and happy to help, and when asked if they like working there, they reply "yes!" with enthusiasm (see Figure 13.7). Moreover, several have gone on to explain to me that they feel strong loyalty to Home Depot, mainly because they feel that own a share in it themselves.

Photo courtesy of R.A. Baron.

Figure 13.7 Making Employees Owners: An Effective Technique for Increasing Moviation

Every time I go into a Home Depot store, I find that employees are very eager to help me. Why? In part because Home Depot Corp. has a generous profiting-sharing plan— one that gives employees an equity stake in the company.

In sum, instituting an effective and fair reward system is one major technique through which new ventures can retain their best employees. Thus, this is an issue entrepreneurs should consider with care as their new ventures grow and they hire increasing numbers of employees.

Building Employee Commitment

Why do people decide to leave one job for another? The answer is definitely not as simple as "Because they can earn more money." On the contrary, the decision to leave appears to be a complex one, involving lots of thought and many factors.[24] How, then, can entrepreneurs tip this decision-making process in their favor, so that high-performing employees remain on board? A key factor involves **organizational commitment**—the extent to which an individual identifies and is involved with his or her organization and is, therefore, unwilling to leave it.[25] High levels of organizational commitment are often present in new ventures, where, at least initially, employees are recruited and hired by the founders. As new ventures grow and this task is delegated to others, however, there is the real risk that such commitment will decrease, so this is an important consideration entrepreneurs should not overlook.

Actually, three distinct kinds of organizational commitment exist. One, known as *continuance commitment*, refers mainly to the costs of leaving. If an individual would lose a lot by leaving (e.g., some portion of a pension plan, the opportunity to see close friends), this can weigh heavily in the balance and cause them to remain. For instance, stock contributions made by companies to retirement funds are nontaxable until employees redeem the stock. This can increase continuance commitment because employees want to remain with the company until the stock rises to high levels. Similarly, stock distributed as part of employee stock ownerships plans (ESOPs) may not become fully vested for employees until some period of time has elapsed. Again, this can increase continuance commitment. A second kind of commitment is known as *affective commitment*—it refers mainly to positive feelings toward the organization. If an individual shares the values of her or his company and holds it in high regard, this employee is less likely to leave than someone with the opposite feelings. Finally, individuals may remain with a company as a result of *normative commitment*—they stay because of a feeling of obligation to others who would be adversely affected by their departure. All three of these forms of commitment are important to new ventures, because each tends to help in the retention of employees. Employees of new ventures often identify with them because they believe in what the company is doing—that's why they came there in the first place! So to the extent such feelings can be strengthened, new ventures can retain their best employees. How can this be accomplished? Research findings offer several suggestions.

First, as job design suggests, making jobs interesting and giving employees some autonomy over running them is useful. Why would anyone become committed to an organization that assigns them to dull, routine tasks and gives them no say over their work? Second, affective commitment can be increased by aligning employees' interests with those of the company. Employee stock ownership plans are highly effective in this way because, as we noted earlier, they make employees "partners" in the new venture. To the extent they feel that they have a stake in the new venture, employees may be very reluctant to leave it. Finally, actively *listening* to employees—taking their input and suggestions seriously—can increase affective commitment. When entrepreneurs listen carefully to their employees, they send the message that the employees matter—that the company is committed to *them*. This, in turn, encourages feelings of commitment on the part of employees.

Is building a high level of organizational commitment worth the bother? Research findings indicate that it is. The higher employees' commitment, the less likely they are to leave for another job.[26] That, after all, is what entrepreneurs want—retention of persons they have worked hard to hire and who are essential to their company's continued growth. (For the thoughts of a highly successful entrepreneur on this and other issues relating to strengthening a new venture's human resources, see **"The Voice of Experience"** section.)

Overcoming the "Control Barrier": A Note on the Necessity of "Letting Go"

Before closing, we want to return to the quote with which we began this chapter—advice from a former President of the United States: "Surround yourself with the best people you can find, delegate authority, and don't interfere." (Ronald Reagan, 1986). Those words ring true, but they are sometimes hard for entrepreneurs to accept. Although they do want to surround themselves with the best people—to hire excellent employees—they often have a very hard time "letting to"—delegating authority to other people.[27] The reasons for this are understandable: Entrepreneurs have a passion for their companies and view them almost through the eyes of a doting parent. Just like loving parents, they find it difficult to surrender their authority and let other people control their new venture's fate by making important decisions or setting strategy. Yet—and here's the paradox—unless they can accomplish this task, they may put the future of their growing companies in jeopardy. To understand why, we need to take a brief look at how new ventures grow and move through successive stages of development.

Six Phases of Company Growth

Company growth is a continuous process, so dividing it into discrete phases is somewhat artificial. Still, many experts find it convenient to talk about six different phases through which many companies move:

- *Conception/existence phase.* This is the classic start-up phase, during which companies emerge and move toward the point at which they can deliver a product or service. During this phase, founders do essentially everything, so the issue of delegating does not arise.
- *Survival phase.* At this stage of development, the new venture has become a real company; it has customers and is earning revenues. During this phase, too, the issue of delegation is relatively unimportant; although there may be a small number of employees, the founders remain central in every aspects of its operation.
- *Profitability and stabilization.* During this phase, the company attains economic health: It is earning a profit and has a growing number of employees. Functional managers are hired, but because the company is still small, the founders continue to play a key role, and delegation is just beginning to become an important issue.

THE VOICE OF EXPERIENCE

The Four Pillars of New Venture Success

As one of the founders of Axiowave Networks, Mukesh Chatter brings with him more than 18 years' experience in the architecture, design, and development of state-of-the-art networking equipment and supercomputers and also holds several patents in these areas. Prior to founding Axiowave, he was the founder, president, and CEO of Nexabit Networks, Inc., a highly successful terabit switch/router company, which was acquired by Lucent Technologies in July 1999. A noted systems architect, Chatter invented the innovative scalable switching fabric technology that operates at multi-terabits per second. He subsequently served as vice president and general manager of IP products at Lucent. Chatter holds a master's degree in computer and systems engineering from Rensselaer Polytechnic Institute in New York and was its "Entrepreneur of the Year" in 2001.

What factors contribute to an entrepreneur's success? This is certainly a basic questions for the field of entrepreneurship and one that can only be answered fully through systematic research. But the insights of highly successful entrepreneurs, too, can be valuable in this respect. This is the topic I discussed with Mukesh Chatter in a recent interview.

Baron: "In your experience, what ingredients are necessary for an entrepreneur to succeed?"

Chatter: "I often think in terms of what I call the 'four pillars'—four things that you absolutely need to succeed. First, you must have a burning need—if you don't have this kind of passion, you really don't have an opportunity. Second, you must have a solution—something that is a lot better than what is out there—a solution that makes you top. Third, you must have money—you can't get anywhere without financial resources. Finally, you need a team that can execute—that can make it all happen. You need all four to really succeed."

Baron: "I'd like to hear more about the team—just what do you mean by 'a team that can execute'? How do you go about building one?"

Chatter: "You do it by building a corporate culture that values fairness and teamwork. Everyone is part of the team, including you. You are not the king—you a member of the team. You must

create a culture where every person matters and respect for people and their abilities is central. For instance, when we started, we bought used furniture and we all used it, me included; when we fly, we all fly coach—I would never dream of flying in front of the plane while the rest of the team travels in the back. There are no special privileges."

Baron: "But how do you assemble a great team—one that you can respect and on which you can rely?"

Chatter: "Communication is essential. Nobody teaches you this in college—no one tells you how to make a concise presentation or give a little pitch for your ideas. You need to practice this, because it is needed to attract good people. I think that every engineering student should take communication courses so that they can learn how to communicate. That is crucial for marketing, raising money, interacting with customers, talking on the street—and within your own organization. If you can communicate with your team effectively, you will be able to attract good people and keep them with you."

Baron: "What else, aside from the ability to communicate, is important?"

Chatter: "You have to show integrity, honesty, and social skills. Listening to others is important because we often learn from them, and this shows we respect them. You have to build your credibility because that makes for a strong team."

Commentary: We agree with Mr. Chatter: Building an outstanding team is crucial, because no matter how talented and motivated entrepreneurs are, they cannot do it alone—they need the help of other talented, motivated people, persons whose skills complement their own. Because first-rate people always have lots of choices, we also agree with Chatter's suggestion that creating a corporate culture that values people highly and reflects the entrepreneurs' integrity, honesty, and credibility is essential. In short, although the first three pillars Chatter mentions are certainly important—the entrepreneurs' passion, a product that is better than its competition, and sufficient financial resources—it is the fourth pillar, the new venture's team, that actually pulls these together and helps create a viable business.

- *Profitability and growth.* At this stage, the company moves toward real growth, and to reach this goal, its growing cash reserves are placed at risk (i.e., they are used to finance further growth). The founders are still central to all aspects of the company's business, but high-quality managers are needed to oversee its increasingly complex operations.
- *Take-off.* This is the pivotal phase of company growth from the point of view of delegation: The company is growing rapidly and becoming far too large for one founder or even a team of founders to oversee effectively. This necessitates the hiring of first-rate, professional managers—and these people will not come on

board, or remain, if they are not given sufficient authority and autonomy to do their jobs. This phase encompasses what some authors term the **control barrier**—the founders *must* surrender at least a significant amount of control over the company to others—people they have hired, bankers, or new shareholders who have provided needed capital. If they successfully pass through this barrier, the company can continue to grow; if they do not, its fortunes may begin to decline—a pattern that is far from rare.[28]

- *Maturity.* If founders successfully navigate their way through the control barrier, the company becomes truly mature: It has, in a sense "arrived" and is a significant player in its industry or market.

Here's a key point about these phases: In the early ones (phases 1 and 2), entrepreneurs' skills, abilities, and knowledge—their capacity to accomplish various tasks—are crucial to the success of the company. From the third phase on, however, their importance in determining the success of the company begins to decline. At the same time, though, the importance of another factor—the founders' ability to delegate—increases until, as shown in Figure 13.8, the two curves cross; this is the point at which the control barrier occurs. Beyond that point, success at delegating is crucial and, in fact, is closely tied with the company's ability to recruit, motivate, and retain high-quality employees and staff.

What all this suggests, in essence, is that entrepreneurs must change their style of leadership as their companies' grow. At first, as we suggested at the start of this chapter, they act as team leaders, persons who lead a small group of highly motivated people toward shared goals—primarily through the vision they describe and endorse. Later on, they must become leaders of teams—key decision makers who, nevertheless, delegate a large degree of authority and autonomy to other persons who lead various teams within the company—separate departments or, perhaps, integrated cross-functional teams. Whatever form the growing organization takes, founders *must* pay careful attention to President Reagan's advice and truly "let go." In other words, they must come to understand that control does not necessarily imply ownership of their company; on the contrary, it involves use of and access to assets.

To put it as clearly as we can, a 10 percent equity stake in a company worth $1,000,000,000 is clearly a lot more valuable to an entrepreneur than a 90 percent equity stake in a company worth $1 million! So letting go—delegating authority and trading equity for use of a much larger pool of assets—must, at some point, go hand in hand with the processes we have considered in this chapter: recruiting, motivating, and retaining first-rate people. Once they are on board, it is only reasonable for entrepreneurs to entrust them with key tasks; if this does not occur, why should these talented, energetic people stay around? The answer is simple: They won't. Letting go in an

Figure 13.8 Changing Roles for Entrepreneurs as Their Companies Grow

During early phases of growth, entrepreneurs' skills, abilities, and knowledge are crucial to the success of their new ventures. During later phases, however, the importance of these factors drops, while the importance of another factor—entrepreneurs' ability to delegate—grows in importance. The two curves cross at what is sometimes described as the control barrier.

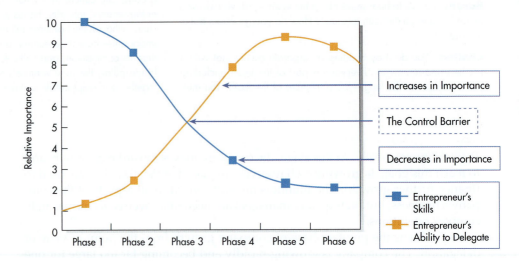

Source: Based on suggestions by Churchill, 2002; see note 27.

orderly manner and at the appropriate point in time is one of the best things founding entrepreneurs can do for their companies. And this is another reason why paying careful attention to recruiting, motivating, and retaining first-rate employees is crucial to the success of new ventures: When entrepreneurs do a good job at these tasks and are surrounded by truly excellent people, the pain of "letting go" may be significantly reduced: After all, they realize that they are placing the fortunes of their company in very good hands!

KEY POINTS

- In order to retain excellent employees, new ventures need pay systems that closely link rewards to performance.
- Pay for performance systems accomplish this goal by linking either individual or team performance to rewards such as pay, benefits, or equity in the company.
- Another important means for retaining excellent employees is strengthening their organizational commitment—their loyalty to the new venture. This can be accomplished in several ways.
- New ventures move through six relatively distinct phases of growth. During early phases, the entrepreneurs' skills, abilities, and knowledge play a key role in the new venture's success. In later phases, such success is closely linked to the entrepreneur's ability to cross the control barrier and delegate authority to others—the excellent employees the new ventures seeks to attract.
- Entrepreneurs who have done an excellent job with respect to recruiting, motivating, and retaining first-rate employees will often find this task easier to accomplish than entrepreneurs who have not.

Summary and Review of Key Points

- Before beginning a search for new employees, it is very useful to carry out a job analysis and prepare a job description for each position to be filled. Only when these preliminary tasks are completed can clarity about what needs are to be met by new employees be obtained, and steps to choose the best persons for these positions be formulated.
- In their search for new employees, entrepreneurs focus primarily on their own social networks. However, as the new venture grows, it may be necessary to turn to other sources, such as advertisements in trade publications, the Internet, and referrals from customers.
- Reliability—the consistency of measurements over time or between judges—and validity—the extent to which measurements reflect the dimension to which they refer—are important considerations in selecting employees. Only techniques high in both reliability and validity are useful for this purpose and are legal under existing laws.
- Two techniques for selecting employees that are high in reliability and validity are structured interviews and biodata—information about applicants' background, experiences, and preferences gathered by means of detailed application forms.

- It is best to provide potential employees with accurate information about working conditions in a company during an interview; such realistic job previews protect new hires from unpleasant surprises when they assume their jobs. This can improve retention.
- Motivation is defined as the processes that arouse, direct, and maintain human behavior toward attaining some goal.
- Setting goals that are specific in nature, challenging but attainable, and accepted by the persons for whom they are established is a very effective technique for increasing motivation, provided that the persons in question also receive feedback concerning progress toward these goals.
- Expectancy theory suggests that motivation will be high when there are clear links between effort and performance and between performance and rewards, and the rewards provided are ones people actually value.
- When employees feel that they are being treated unfairly in terms of outcomes, procedures, or courtesy they receive, motivation is sharply reduced. Thus, entrepreneurs should be careful to establish these kinds of fairness in their new ventures.

- Jobs can be designed to be interesting and motivating for the persons who perform them. This can be accomplished through job enlargement and job enrichment.
- In order to retain excellent employees, new ventures need reward systems that closely link rewards to performance.
- Pay for performance systems accomplish this goal by linking either individual or team performance to rewards such as pay, benefits, or equity in the company.
- Another important means for retaining excellent employees is strengthening their organizational commitment—their loyalty to the new venture. This can be accomplished in several ways.

- New ventures move through six relatively distinct phases of growth. During early phases, the entrepreneurs' skills, abilities, and knowledge play a key role in the new venture's success. In later phases, such success is closely linked to the entrepreneur's ability to cross the control barrier and delegate authority to others—the excellent employees the new ventures seeks to attract.
- Entrepreneurs who have done an excellent job with respect to recruiting, motivating, and retaining first-rate employees will often find this task easier to accomplish than entrepreneurs who have not.

Glossary

Biodata: Information about potential employees' background, experiences, and preferences provided by them on application forms.

Control Barrier: Refers to unwillingness of founders of new ventures to surrender control over the company to others.

Distributive Justice (Equity): Conditions under which available rewards are divided among group members according to what each has contributed to the group.

Expectancy Theory: A theory of motivation suggesting that in order for motivation be high, individuals must perceive clear links between their effort and their performance and their performance and their rewards, and that the rewards offered to them are ones they actually want.

Job Analysis: A careful analysis of a specific job to determine what it involves and what it requires in terms of specific knowledge, skills, and abilities.

Job Description: An overview of what the job involves in terms of its duties, responsibilities, and working conditions.

Job Design: Efforts to structure jobs so that they increase people's interest in doing them (and hence their motivation).

Motivation: The processes that arouse, direct, and maintain human behavior toward attaining some goal. In

other words, motivation refers to behavior that is energized by, and directed toward, reaching some desired target or objective.

Organizational Commitment: The extent to which an individual identifies and is involved with his or her organization and is, therefore, unwilling to leave it.

Pay for Performance Systems: Reward systems that assume that employees differ in how much they contribute to the company's success, and that they should be rewarded in accordance with the scope of their contributions.

Realistic Job Previews: Efforts to present a balanced and accurate picture of the company to potential employees, with the goal of improving future retention of these persons.

Reliability: The extent to which measurements are consistent across time or between judges.

Reward Systems: Systems in a new venture for recognizing and rewarding good performance.

Structured Interviews: Interview in which all applicants are asked the same questions—ones chosen carefully to be truly job-related.

Validity: The extent to which measurements actually reflect the underlying dimension to which they refer.

Discussion Questions

1. Why is it crucial that all techniques used to select employees be both reliable and valid?

2. Why are structured interviews superior, in choosing excellent employees, to regular job interviews?

3. From the point of view of goal setting, why is the strategy of telling employees to "Do your best!" generally ineffective?

4. Suppose that you want to give a bonus to high-performing employees for their excellent work. How should you go about doing this?

5. Why is it important to develop high levels of organizational commitment among employees in a new venture?

6. What is the control barrier and why is it crucial that entrepreneurs cross it successfully?

7. How can success in recruiting, motivating, and retaining first-rate employees make it easier for entrepreneurs to cross this barrier (i.e., the control barrier)?

InfoTrac Exercises

1. What's My Hiring Line? Here Are Some Valuable Pointers for How to Conduct a Successful Interview (hiring line)
Richard Ream
Information Today, May 2002 v19 i5 p18(2)
Record: A85410699
Full Text: COPYRIGHT 2002 Information Today, Inc.

1. How, as an interviewer, can you avoid a mismatch of culture?

2. How can you assess a job's context to value the traits and skills that will increase your opportunity to make a successful hire?

3. What steps can you take to ensure a successful interview?

2. Light Their Fires (motivating employees)
William Cottringer
Supervision, June 2003 v64 i6 p12(3)
Record: A102677211
Full Text: COPYRIGHT 2003 National Research Bureau

1. According to expectancy theory, what factors play a key role in motivation?

2. Do you agree with the following statement: "All employees have a drive to perform well"? Why or why not.

3. What tools can a supervisor use to motivate employees?

GETTING DOWN
TO BUSINESS

Setting Motivating Goals

Setting appropriate goals for ourselves is a very important task, not just because it strengthens and maintains motivation, but also because once goals are set, the strategies for reaching them are often clarified. You are already setting goals for yourself in many areas of life, but practice in this skill—choosing effective self-set goals—can be highly beneficial to entrepreneurs, or to anyone else. Follow these instructions to gain such practice.

1. **Consider goals you have set for yourself within the past few weeks.** For each, list the goal, and then describe it. (Some examples: "I set the goal of completing a term paper by a specific date." "I set the goal of writing a draft of my business plan by a specific date.")

   Goal 1:

   Goal 2:

   Goal 3:

   Goal 4:

   Goal 5:

2. **Now, for each goal you identified, rate the extent to which it met each of these criteria.** For each goal, place a number next to each criterion using the following

scale: 1 = very low in meeting this criterion; 2 = low in meeting this criterion; 3 = neither high nor low; 4 = high in meeting this criterion; 5 = very high in meeting this criterion.

- Specific: Was the goal specific? _____ (Place your rating here)
- Challenging: Was the goal challenging? _____
- Attainable: Was the goal attainable? _____
- Feedback: Could you readily assess your progress toward reaching this goal? _____

How high are your ratings? If they are not 4 or 5 on each goal, think carefully about how you could have redefined the goal so that it met these criteria. Remember: The more closely goals meet these criteria, the better they are for enhancing motivation and performance.

Perceived Fairness: The Self-Serving Bias Strikes Again

Fairness always rests in the eye of the beholder. In other words, each person decides for herself or himself whether the treatment they are receiving from other is fair. Remember our discussions of human perception and cognition in earlier chapters? These discussions emphasized the point that our thinking is not always 100 percent rational; on the contrary, it is often subject to important forms of error and bias. One of these is especially relevant to judgment of what is fair and what is not. This is the self-serving bias that we described in Chapter 5—the powerful tendency to attribute successful outcomes largely to internal causes (our own efforts, talents, or abilities) but unsuccessful ones largely to external cause (e.g., the failings or negligence of others).

This bias can often cloud our judgments where fairness is concerned. To demonstrate this fact for yourself—and to see why it is important to guard against this bias—try the following exercise.

1. **Think of a situation in the past when you worked closely with another person on a joint project, and the project was successful.** Now, divide 100 points between you and this other person according to how much you each contributed to the success of the project.

   _____ Points for me _____ Points for my partner

2. **Now, think of a situation in the past when you worked closely with another person on a joint project and the project was unsuccessful.** Again, divide 100 points between you and this other person indicating the extent to which you were each responsible.

   _____ Points for me _____ Points for my partner

Next, compare the pattern of your point assignments in the two instances. Did you give yourself more points in the first (success) case than in the second (failure)? Did you assign more points to your partner in the second (failure) instance than in the first (success)? If so, you may be demonstrating the self-serving bias. Alternatively, your perceptions might be accurate, so that you really *did* contribute more to the success than the failure; but watch out—the self-serving bias encourages us to reach such conclusions even when they are false.

Because it can distort perceptions of fairness, the self-serving bias can be an important cause of friction between cofounders of a new venture: Each tends to take credit for successes, but to blame the other for setbacks. The result? Their working relationship can be undermined. So beware of the self-serving bias and try to guard against it. One way of doing this is simply to remind yourself that this tendency exists and that in many cases, you should adjust your perceptions of your own contributions to successful outcomes downwards and your responsibility for reversals or setbacks upwards. The self-serving bias is powerful, but with sufficient effort, you can minimize its impact—and so secure better relations with your cofounders and other persons with whom you work.

Planning a Hiring Strategy: A Potential Plus for Your Business Plan

When you start your new venture—and especially if it grows as rapidly as you hope!—the chances are good that you will soon need to hire employees. Clearly, you want to do this well and attract the best people you can find. Although many entrepreneurs give little thought to this task, it is an important one; moreover, to the extent you can explain clearly in your business plan how you will accomplish it, this can be another "plus" in your column for venture capitalists and other investors. To start planning for your hiring strategy, complete the following steps.

1. **Job Descriptions and Analyses:** You can't hire the best people for a job until you know just what it is you want them to do. So begin by describing each position you think you will have to fill and by listing the skills, experience, and abilities required by each position.

   a. Position one:

   b. Position two:

   c. Position three:

   d. Position four:

   e. Position five:

   Continue as necessary.

2. **Attracting an Excellent Pool of Applicants:** For each position, you will want to attract a number of excellent candidates. How will you go about finding these people? In other words, what strategies will you follow to attract an excellent pool of applicants? Describe these here.

   a. Specific strategy:

   b. Specific strategy:

   c. Specific strategy:

3. **Selecting the Best Applicants:** Once you attract these candidates, how will you choose among them? In other words, what selection techniques and tools will you use (interviews, structured interviews, biodata?). Describe these and be sure to give careful consideration to whether these techniques are reliable and valid— and whether they are consistent with federal laws and regulations (e.g., EEOC guidelines).

   a. Selection technique #1:

   b. Selection technique #2:

   c. Selection technique #3:

Enhanced Learning

You may select any combination of the case options below to enhance your understanding of the chapter material.

- **Appendix 1: Case Studies –** Thirteen cases provide opportunities to apply chapter concepts to realistic entrepreneurial situations. These brief cases call for careful analysis of real business problems and ask you to think about potential solutions.

- **Appendix 2: Video Case Library –** Nine cases are tied directly to video segments from the popular PBS television series *Small Business School*. These cases and video segments give you unparalleled access to today's entrepreneurs, with expert advice and insights on how to start, run, and grow a business.

- **Comprehensive Cases –** Visit the book support Web site at http://baron.swlearning.com for cases detailing real businesses whose successes and setbacks illustrate each stage of the entrepreneurial process. You will conduct in-depth analysis of entrepreneurial challenges through well-developed case studies.

Notes

1 Levie, J., & Hay, M. 2000. Life beyond the "kitchen" culture. In S. Birley & D.F. Muzyka (eds.). *Mastering entrepreneurship.* Upper Saddle River, NJ: Prentice-Hall, 257–261.

2 Buckley, M.R., & Eder, R.W. 1988. B.M. Springbett and the notion of the "snap decision" in the interview. *Journal of Management* 14: 59–67.

3 Aldrich, H. 1999. *Organizations evolving.* London: Sage.

4 Judge, T.A., Higgins, C.A., & Cable, D.M. 2000. The employment interview: A review of recent research and recommendations for future research. *Human Resource Management Review* 10: 383–405.

5 Gomez-Mejia, L., Balkin, D.B., & Cardy, R.L. 2001. *Managing human resources.* 3rd ed. Upper Saddle River, NJ: Prentice-Hall.

6 Kacmar, K.M., Ratcliff, S.L., & Ferris, G.R. 1989. Employment interview rearech: Internal and external validity. In R.W. Eder & G.R. Ferris (eds.). *The employment interview: Theory, research, and practice.* Newbury Park, CA: Sage, 32–41.

7 Baron, R.A., & Byrne, D. 2002. *Social psychology.* 10th ed. Boston: Allyn & Bacon.

8 Wanous, H.P., & Coella, A. 1989. Organizational entry research: Current status and future directions. In G. Ferris & K. Rowlands (eds.). *Research in personnel and human resources management.* Greenwich, CT: JAI Press, 7: 59–120.

9 Baum, J.R., Locke, E.A., & Smith, K.G. 2001. A multidimensional model of venture groth. *Academy of Management Journal* 44: 292–303.

10 Locke, E.A., & Latham, G.P. 1990. *Goal setting.* Englewood Cliffs, NJ: Prentice-Hall.

11 Baron, R.A. (in press). The cognitive perspective: A valuable tool for answering entrepreneurship's basic "why?" questions. *Journal of Business Venturing.*

12 Pennington, A.Y. 2003. On a shoestring. *Entrepeneur.* (March): 96.

13 Ludwig, T.D., & Geller, E.S. 1997. Assigned versus participative goal setting and response generalization: Managing injury control among professional pizza deliverers. *Journal of Applied Psychology* 82: 253–261.

14 Baum, J.R., & Locke, E.A. (in press). The relationship of entrepreneurial traits, skill, and motivation to subsequent venture growth. *Journal of Applied Psychology.*

15 Shepperd, J.A., Ouellette, J.A., & Fernandez, J.K. 1996. Abandoning unrealistic optimistic performance estimates and the temporal proximity of self-relevant feedback. *Journal of Personality and Social Psychology* 70: 844–855.

16 Mitchell, T.R. 1983. Expectancy-value models in organizational psychology. In N. Feather (ed.). *Expectancy, incentive, and action.* Hillsdale, NJ: Lawrence Erlbaum Associates, 293–314.

17 Simon, M., Houghton, S.M., & Aquino, K. 2000. Cognitive biases, risk perception, and venture formation: How individuals decide to start companies. *Journal of Business Venturing* 15: 113–134.

18 Greenberg, J. 1998. The cognitive geometry of employee theft: Negotiating "the line" between taking and stealing. In R.W. Griffin, A. O'Leary-Kelly, & J.M. Collins (eds.). *Dysfunctional behavior in organizations: Non-violent dysfunctional behavior.* Stamford, CT: JAI Press, 147–194.

19 Brockner, J., & Wiesenfeld, B.M. 1996. An integrative framework for explaining reactions to decisions: The interactive effects of outcomes and procedures. *Psychological Bulletin* 120: 189–208.

20 Greenberg, J. 1997. *The quest for justice on the job.* Thousand Oaks, CA: Sage.

21 Kooker, N.R. 2000. Taking aim at crime—stealing the profits: Tighter controls, higher morale may safeguard bottom line. *Nation's Restaurant News* 34(21): 114–118.

22 Greenberg, J. 1998. The cognitive geometry of employee theft: Negotiating "the line" between taking and stealing. In R.W. Griffin, A. O'Leary-Kelly, & J.M. Collins (eds.). *Dysfunctional behavior in organizations: Non-violent dysfunctional behavior.* Stamford, CT: JAI Press, 147–194.

23 Cited in Levie & Hay; see note 1.

24 Mitchell, T.R., & Lee. T.W. 2001. The unfolding model of voluntary turnover and job embeddedness: Foundations for a comprehensive theory of attachment. In B.M. Staw & R.I. Sutton (eds.). *Research in organizational behavior.* Oxford, UK: Elsevier, vol 23, 189–246).

25 Meyer, J.P., & Allen, N.J. 1997. *Commitment in the workplace: Theory, research, and application.* Thousand Oaks, CA: Sage.

26 Lee, T.W., Ashford, S.J., Walsh, J.P., & Mowday, R.T. 1992. Commitment propensity, organizational commitment, and voluntary turnover: A longitudinal study of organizational entry processes. *Journal of Management* 18: 15–32.

27 Churchill, N.C., & Lewis, V.L. 1983. The five stages of small business growth. *Harvard Business Review* (May–June).

28 See note 1.

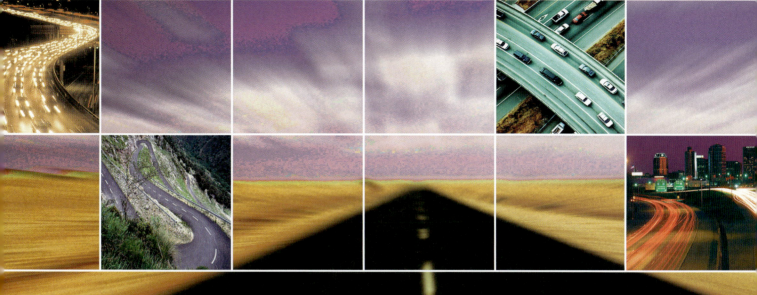

HARVESTING THE REWARDS

Exit Strategies for Entrepreneurs:
When—And How—To Harvest the Rewards

Even the best of things must come to an end, so at some point in time, entrepreneurs usually begin to consider various exit strategies—procedures through which they can transfer ownership of their businesses to other persons. Many of these exist, but all involve valuing the company so that negotiations with potential purchasers can proceed. Before initiating this final phase of the process, entrepreneurs should carefully consider what they want to do next, and this, in turn, can be closely linked to the phase of life they have reached. Exit strategies appropriate for young entrepreneurs in their 20s, 30s, or 40s may not be ideal for ones who have reached a later phase of life. So although exit strategies are primarily economic strategies, they must also take into account the preferences and current and future life styles of the specific entrepreneurs.

CHAPTER 14

EXIT STRATEGIES FOR ENTREPRENEURS: WHEN—AND HOW—TO HARVEST THE REWARDS

LEARNING OBJECTIVES

After reading this chapter, you should be able to:

1 Describe various strategies entrepreneurs can use to transfer ownership of their companies to family members.

2 Describe various strategies entrepreneurs can use to transfer ownership of their companies to other insiders (e.g., current management, employees).

3 Describe basic methods of valuing a business, including balance sheet methods, earnings-based methods, and market methods.

4 List the advantages and costs of an initial public offering.

5 Describe the basic nature of negotiation and explain the nature of several key bargaining tactics.

6 Explain why integrative agreements between negotiators are generally best, and explain the relationship of such agreements to the overall approach to negotiation (a "win-lose" versus a "win-win" approach).

7 Define "life transitions" and explain why entrepreneurs should consider their own age and phase of life before choosing an exit strategy.

Exit Strategies: The Major Forms
Sale or Transfer to Insiders: Succession, Leveraged Buyouts, and Employee Stock Ownership Plans
Sale to Outsiders: When Valuation Becomes Crucial
Determining the Value of a Business: A Little Art, a Little Science
Taking a Company Public: The Lure of IPOs

Negotiation: The Universal Process
Negotiation: Its Basic Nature
Tactics of Negotiation: Procedures for Reducing an Opponent's Aspirations

Exit Strategies and the Life Span: Different Needs—And Goals—At Different Times of Life

"All things change . . . There is nothing in the whole world which is permanent. Everything flows onward . . . the ages themselves glide by in constant movement." (Ovid, 10 B.C)

In the spring of 1987, I (Robert Baron) accepted a new position at Rensselaer Polytechnic Institute in New York. I was on the faculty of Purdue University at the time, and was living happily in a house I liked very much. It sat on a small hill surrounded by hundred-year-old oak trees, and I had redone it from top to bottom after buying it five years earlier—the kitchen, bathrooms, the works. But now, it was time to leave, so I put it up for sale. At first, I saw the sale purely as an economic transaction: I knew how much money I had invested in the house and wanted that plus a reasonable profit. As potential buyers appeared, though, I began to realize that more was going on than simple economics. One possible buyer told me: "I love the house, but the first thing I'm going to do if I buy it is cut down all those little trees over there." I shuddered because I had planted those trees myself—oaks, maples, and ashes—and I saw them as my gift to future generations. "Cut them down?" I mused. "What kind of person is he *anyway*?" When he made an offer, I rejected it, even though it was close to the price I was seeking.

Another potential buyer told me: "I like your house, but I don't know about that porch. It's too narrow. I'll probably have it torn down so I can build another." Again I found myself thinking, "Do I want this person to have my house?" I had built that porch myself, and was very proud of it. When this buyer made an offer, I found myself unwilling to agree to some of the terms she suggested. The real estate market was good at the time, so ultimately, I did get a buyer who seemed to appreciate the house just the way it was; he got it, and for a very attractive price.

By now you may be wondering, "What does all this have to do with entrepreneurship?" The answer is simple: It offers important insights into the final phase of the entrepreneurial process—the time when entrepreneurs harvest their well-deserved rewards through one of several exit strategies. Consider this: If "sweat equity" and other noneconomic factors sometimes play an important role with respect to the sale of houses (see Figure 14.1), imagine how powerful these factors can be when entrepreneurs consider selling the companies they have built from the ground up out of their own vision, energy, and spirit. Because entrepreneurs often feel a deep commitment to their companies ("their babies," as some describe them), they cannot readily view leaving them behind solely in economic terms.

We will take full account of this fact in the current chapter, which focuses on the various ways in which entrepreneurs can harvest their rewards and exit from the companies they have founded. Many different *exit strategies* exist, ranging from giving the business to family members to selling it to outsiders or taking it public; we will examine all the major ones carefully in an initial section. Although these strategies are basically economic arrangements, it is important to note that entrepreneurs' attitudes, values, and goals often play a crucial role in determining which of these exit strategies they choose and the specific terms they accept. For instance, all exit strategies involve the task of valuing a company—determining its economic worth. Is this based entirely on economic factors? Sometimes; but in many cases, additional factors enter into the equation, just as they do with respect to real estate transactions. As we have already noted, persons who put their houses up for sale often exaggerate the value of their property because of "sweat equity" or other psychological factors, and the same forces are at work for entrepreneurs. Often, they too overestimate the value of their companies because of the time and effort they have invested in building them. Indeed, given the magnitude of this investment, the impact of these forces is far stronger than in the case of merely selling a house. Even at this very basic level, then, factors other than economic ones play a role.

Figure 14.1 The Noneconomic Side of Economic Transactions

Many persons attach inflated values to their homes because of the effort they have invested in improving them ("sweat equity") and other psychological factors. For similar reasons, entrepreneurs sometimes find it difficult to view the sale of their businesses purely in economic terms.

© PhotoDisc, Inc.

After considering various exit strategies, we will turn to an aspect of the process that is crucial, but often receives very little attention from entrepreneurs: negotiation. This is the process through which entrepreneurs and potential purchasers of their company attempt to arrive at an agreement acceptable to both sides. Negotiation is complex, and it is important for entrepreneurs to understand several of its basic features if they are to be successful in arranging exit strategies that help them achieve their major goals. (We briefly considered negotiation in Chapter 12, as part of our discussion of resolving conflicts. Here, we will provide more detail on the nature of negotiation as a process and on the factors that affect it.)

We will conclude with a discussion of the interplay between some basic facts of human life (e.g., entrepreneurs' stage of life) and the exit strategies they choose. As human beings, we experience many changes as we move through the lifespan. Physical ones are the most obvious, but they are only a part of the total picture; as we age, we change cognitively and socially, too. The result is that our capabilities, goals, and social relationships change in subtle but important ways. For this reason, it is important for entrepreneurs to consider just where they are in this continuous process of development so that they can choose an exit strategy that makes sense personally as well as economically. In this final section, we will briefly review some of the factors entrepreneurs should consider as they contemplate their departure from the ventures they have founded—and that have shaped important portions of their lives.

EXIT STRATEGIES: THE MAJOR FORMS

Recently, I (Robert Baron) invested in a start-up biotechnology company. Why did I choose to risk my hard-earned capital on this new venture? Partly because I strongly liked the business model on which the company was based. The founders have chosen to focus their efforts on developing new drugs that will be helpful in treating what are known as "orphan diseases"—illnesses that afflict fewer than 200,000 people in the United States. Because the number of persons suffering from such illnesses is relatively small, large pharmaceutical companies have little interest in developing drugs to treat them. If the new company in which I invested is successful in identifying such drugs, however, it will become very attractive to these giant corporations, which may then seek to acquire it. If this happens, both the founders and early investors such as myself will reap very large rewards. In fact, this is precisely the scenario sought by the founding entrepreneurs: They realize that they cannot possibly hope to compete head-on with huge companies in the pharmaceutical industry. For instance, they certainly cannot match the size or experience of the sales staff or marketing departments of these companies. So instead of planning to compete with them, they hope to make enough progress to become an attractive candidate for a buyout—one that will be prove highly advantageous to the founders and early investors.

Acquisition by a larger company is just one of many different **exit strategies** open to entrepreneurs—procedures through which they transfer ownership of their businesses to other persons. In this chapter, we will examine all the major types. Before proceeding, though, it is important to note that there are many different reasons why entrepreneurs consider these strategies. In some cases, the entrepreneurs (like those who started the biotech company described above) want to harvest their rewards and move on to other activities—such as starting another venture. In other instances, the entrepreneurs realize that they need a large infusion of capital to continue growing the company, and that the best way of obtaining this is by selling a portion of their equity. The main point is that there are many good and legitimate reasons, both economic and personal, why new ventures do not continue forever in their original form, and why the entrepreneurs who founded them choose to share ownership with others. What are the specific strategies or options open to founding entrepreneurs who decide to do so? Many exist, but most are variations on three major themes: (1) sell or transfer ownership of the company to insiders—people already in the company, (2) sell or transfer ownership to outsiders, or (3) take the company public through an IPO (initial public offering). Let's take a closer look at each of these possibilities.

Sale or Transfer to Insiders: Succession, Leveraged Buyouts, and Employee Stock Ownership Plans

One very common way for entrepreneurs to exit from the companies they have founded is to turn over the reigns to a member of their own family. This makes very good sense for several reasons. First, these persons (spouses, children, brothers and sisters, parents, etc.) have often helped to build the company either through financial support or by assuming actual roles in it. Second, they often own large blocks of shares. Third, they have the trust and confidence of the entrepreneur and also know the company very well. Finally, one key goal for many entrepreneurs is that of building something of value for their children and other family members; given that goal, what better way to exit than by turning the company over to the people for whom it was built in the first place?

Succession in Family-Owned Businesses

Entrepreneurs wishing to follow this path can do so in many different ways: They can begin to share power with their chosen successors in a gradual manner. Alternatively, they can form a *limited partnership* in which they transfer a majority of the shares to the family members, but act as general partner, thus retaining control over the day-to-day operations of the business. Third, they can set up various kinds of *trusts*, agreements between the entrepreneur and trustees—generally bank officers or attorneys. The trustees receive legal title to the property (e.g., stock in the company) and hold this for the beneficiaries of the trust (e.g., the entrepreneurs' children). In this way, the entrepreneur retains control of the company for a limited period of time, after which, the beneficiaries receive title to the stock and assume control.

Which option is best? This depends on the goals of the entrepreneur, her or his relationships with family members, and various tax considerations: Entrepreneurs usually want to transfer ownership to family members in a way that will minimize estate and other taxes. Because the laws governing estates change constantly (they were substantially revised in the United States in 2000 and 2001), entrepreneurs must seek expert advice before proceeding. Whatever option is chosen, though, it is crucial that a clear *succession plan* be adopted—a plan that spells out in detail how and when the entrepreneur will transfer ownership in the company, and control of it, to designated successors. Further, it is important that these persons be chosen carefully, and with the consent of all interested parties. Successors must be individuals who want to play an active role in the business, and must be suited for this challenging task. If these factors are not taken carefully into account, serious difficulties can arise—including costly power struggles between family members who are unhappy with the entrepreneurs' choice of successor, their role in the company, or their share of the company's stock. As a general rule, the larger and more successful the company, the more bitter and costly these disputes, so entrepreneurs should do everything in their power to avoid them.

Why do founding entrepreneurs choose to transfer ownership of their businesses to other family members? For many reasons. As we will note in the final section of this chapter, they may simply have reached a point in their lives where they want more leisure time, or a simpler, less stressful life. Alternatively, they may feel that other family members have skills and expertise they lack, and that these are needed to cope with changing business conditions. Whatever the specific reasons, such transfers of equity should be done carefully and in accordance with carefully developed plans. Anything else runs the risk of severely damaging all the good work and effort entrepreneurs have invested in creating a successful business.

Leveraged Buyouts: When Managers Become Owners

Who knows and understands a company best? Presumably, its top management team—the people who run it on a day-to-day basis. They understand its products, its finances, its structure, and its prospects for the future. It's far from surprising, therefore, that when entrepreneurs decide to depart, these individuals often view that as an opportunity to purchase the company. They can do this in several ways. For instance, if they have enough cash, they can purchase it outright, or negotiate an agreement in which they pay a portion initially and the rest over a period of time (a cash plus note arrangement). Alternatively, they can arrange for a **leveraged buyout**. In this type of arrangement, the managers interested in purchasing the company borrow from a financial organization in order to pay the owner an agreed-upon price. The new owners pledge their stock as collateral for the loan or, depending on many factors, the lenders can accept an equity position in the company to cover part or all of the funds. Because the purchasers in leveraged buyouts are already running the company, disruption is minimized. This is one reason why leveraged buyouts are often a popular strategy for transfer of ownership of successful companies from their founders to the top management team these founders have assembled.

Leveraged buyouts are most useful for companies that have sufficient assets to serve as collateral for the loan required to purchase them. Companies purchased through leveraged buyouts generally have dependable cash flow from operations, a high ratio of fully depreciated fixed assets (equipment, plant, etc.), an established and successful product line, and low debt—both current and long term. If, in contrast, a company lacks these characteristics, its stock may not provide sufficient collateral for the required loan, and a leveraged buyout may not be either feasible or desirable.

Employee Stock Ownership Plans: Gradual Transfer to Employees

In Chapter 13, we discussed various techniques for motivating employees. At that time, we noted one of these involves **employee stock ownership plans (ESOPs)**—giving employees shares in the company as a bonus, with the size of these bonuses depending on the profitability of the company. Research findings indicate that this is indeed an excellent technique for building commitment and motivation among a company's employees: As part-owners, they have a stake in the future of the company and work hard to increase the value of their shares.[1]

ESOPs also provide a useful strategy that entrepreneurs can employ to gradually exit from their companies. Over a period of years, such plans allow entrepreneurs to transfer ownership of the business to its employees. Several variations on this basic approach exist. In the first, *ordinary ESOPs*, the entrepreneur sets up a trust (employee stock ownership trust; ESOT) and contributes up to 15 percent of the company's payroll annually in the form of cash or stock. If the contributions are in cash, the trust purchases shares of the company's stock at fair market value. If the contributions are in stock, the shares are simply held in the trust for employees. In this way, entrepreneurs (the current owners of the company) gradually transfer shares to employees. One advantage to the entrepreneurs is that the company's contributions to the ESOP are tax deductible, thus reducing tax liability for profitable companies.

A second type of ESOP is known as a *leveraged plan*. Here, the employee stock ownership trust borrows money from a financial institution and uses it to buy stock from the company. The company guarantees that in future years, it will contribute sufficient funds or stock to the ESOT to cover both the principal and interest on the loan, and it pledges stock in the company as collateral for the loan. The money paid by the company to the ESOT is fully deductible against current taxes—both interest and principal. Such plans are useful in speeding up the transfer of ownership of the company to its employees, because the ESOT can borrow sufficient funds to purchase large blocks of stock.

Finally, ESOPs can take the form of *transfer of ownership plans*. In these plans, the company makes cash contributions to the ESOT, which then uses these funds to purchase shares from existing stockholders—for instance, from the entrepreneur and members of her or his family—rather than on the open market. Figure 14.2 provides an overview of these three major forms of ESOPs.

ESOPs are a useful exit strategy when entrepreneurs wish to exit from the companies they have founded in a gradual manner rather than all at once, as often occurs in a sale to outsiders. In addition, ESOPs are useful when many employees in a company are highly committed to it and have been employed by it for long periods of time. In contrast, ESOPs are not as useful when turnover among employees is high

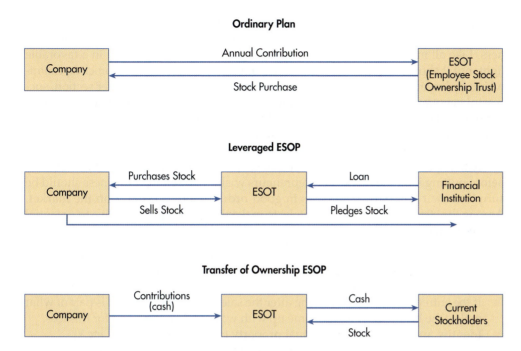

Figure 14.2 Different Types of ESOPs

Employee stock ownership plans can take several different forms.

and they have little or no interest in obtaining an equity position in the company that employees them.

In sum, entrepreneurs can exit from the companies they have founded by transferring ownership (and control) of the companies to insiders: family members, the top management team they have assembled, or other employees. In all of these cases, the agreements negotiated can involve continued active participation by the entrepreneur for a fixed period of time or, on the other hand, can involve an immediate exit—a severing of all ties between the entrepreneur and the company as soon as the strategy is executed. The specific form exit strategies take should depend on many factors—the preferences and wishes of the entrepreneurs, what is best for the company from an economic point of view, and tax and legal considerations to mention some of the more important ones (see Chapter 7).

Sale to Outsiders: When Valuation Becomes Crucial

Although many businesses founded by entrepreneurs are sold or transferred to insiders, many others are sold to outsiders—people not currently in the company who decide to acquire it. Several groups of potential buyers exist for any profitable business: *direct competitors*, who want to expand their market share; *nondirect competitors*—companies that do not compete directly with the entrepreneurs' company, but wish to enter to the markets it currently serves; and *noncompetitors*—buyers who simply see the company as a good opportunity—a good place to invest their surplus cash and their management skills.

Selling to outsiders is often a very good strategy. As we noted in Chapter 10, it is often very costly for a company to maintain its own manufacturing and distribution systems—especially when these already exist and are highly developed and efficient in other businesses. If a new venture becomes part of a larger company that already has such systems in place, these costs can be greatly reduced or even eliminated. Similarly, being part of a larger firm may offer economies of scale and scope that can be highly beneficial.

Although many potential buyers may exist for a sound business, finding them is not always a straightforward task. Sometimes, this involves hiring a *business broker*, a company that specializes in arranging for sales of existing businesses. Alternatively, if the business is already quite large, selling it may require the services of an investment banker who can arrange the large amount of financing needed for such a sale.

Whichever route is taken, sale of an existing business often involves preparation of a *selling memorandum*, a marketing document designed to attract interest in the business. Like all marketing documents, this one should put the company in a favorable light, but it should also be accurate and refrain from claims that will, on close examination by buyers, be found to be exaggerations. As we will note in a later section, successful negotiations rest, in part, on a foundation of mutual trust, and making false or exaggerated claims in a selling memorandum is one sure way to weaken such trust. It is also often useful to seek the help of professional advisers who may be aware of potential buyers not known to the entrepreneurs.

Just as people attempting to sell a house often make repairs and improvements before putting it on the market, entrepreneurs wishing to sell their business should be sure that their company's house is in good order before putting it on the market. Among the steps entrepreneurs can take to make their company attractive to potential buyers are the following:

- Sell at the right stage of development: In general, this is when the company is on the way up and is growing rapidly, not when it has already reached its peak.
- Sell when the business cycle is strong.
- If the entrepreneur will be leaving after the sale and her or his talent is part of what makes the business valuable, come up with ways of compensating for this loss.
- Identify and protect all intellectual property (patents, trademarks, etc.).
- Adopt transparent and conservative accounting policies appropriate to the business sector.
- Resolve any open questions that might make it difficult to estimate the value of the business—tax or other compliance issues, and legal issues.

Once potential buyers appear, two factors will play a key role in shaping the specific terms of the sale agreement: (1) valuation of the company, and (2) the negotiation process. We will consider negotiation, and the noneconomic factors that can affect it, in a later section. Here, therefore, we will turn to the issue of valuation—truly a crucial one for many exit strategies.

KEY POINTS

- Many different exit strategies exist, but most involve transfer of a business to family members, sale to insiders or outsiders, or an initial public offering.
- Transfer of the company to family members can occur through trusts or a limited partnership.
- Transfer to top management can occur through a leveraged buyout.
- Transfer to employees can be accomplished through employee stock ownership plans.
- Sales to outsiders offer important advantages over continuing to run an independent company and, in fact, a venture may have greater value as part of a larger organization than it does as an independent company.

Determining the Value of a Business: A Little Art, a Little Science

How much is a business worth? As we noted earlier, entrepreneurs and potential buyers may have sharply different perspectives on this issue. Entrepreneurs know the business intimately and are fully aware of the effort, stress, and sacrifice building it to its present level required. They also fully appreciate its **intangibles**—assets that are hard, if not impossible, to list on the balance sheet: the good will the company has acquired with customers and suppliers, its reputation in the industry, its success in attracting and motivating first-rate employees. As a result, entrepreneurs often have difficulty viewing the business in purely economic terms; it looms so large in their consciousness that it is hard for them to be totally objective. The result: They tend to perceive their business as having higher value, and greater future potential, than is actually the case, and this can impede its sale.

How can this important obstacle be overcome? In part by careful valuation of the company. As the heading of this section suggests, this is not a calculation that can be performed by a simple economic formula; in fact, experts in valuation can sometimes disagree considerably with respect to the numbers they generate. So, it is often best to value the company by using several different methods and then to negotiate a specific price on the basis of all this information. Putting such negotiations aside for the moment, let's look at three important ways of valuing a business—three ways of generating figures that can then serve as the starting point for discussions concerning a final selling price.

Balance Sheet Methods

One basis for valuing a company is in terms of its balance sheet. In the simplest approach, net worth is calculated according to this simple formula:

Net Worth = Assets – Liabilities

LEARNING OBJECTIVE

3 Describe basic methods of valuing a business, including balance sheet methods, earnings-based methods, and market methods.

The problem with this approach is that it fails to take account of the fact that the true market value of some assets may not be reflected in the balance sheet. For instance, many companies carry land and buildings on their books at prices considerably lower than their actual market value. Similarly, equipment and fixtures may be carried at higher or lower figures than fair market value—what it would cost to replace them. For this reason, valuation is usually computed by the *adjusted balance sheet technique*, in which the actual market value of assets is taken into account. This method estimates the value of such assets as inventories, supplies, and fixtures in terms of cost of last purchase and replacement value. Thus, it yields a more realistic valuation than a simple balance sheet approach.

Earnings Methods

When purchasers buy a business, they are buying not just current assets and liabilities. They are also buying future earnings—thus, another way of valuing a business is in terms of its future earnings. Three different methods of calculating the value of a business in terms of its future earnings are widely used.

Excess Earnings Method. Some businesses are more successful than others in their industry. To the extent this is the case, they have a higher value because they will generate greater future earnings. One method for calculating the value of a company, the **excess earnings method**, takes account of this fact. It estimates the extent to which a company will generate earnings in excess of the average for its industry and attributes these excess earnings to *goodwill*—an intangible asset of which entrepreneurs are highly aware, but which, as we noted earlier, is difficult to include in financial statements. The excess earnings method assumes that to the extent a company is outperforming its competitors, this is attributable to something that can be termed "goodwill." It makes no effort to determine how this factor arises or what it involves; to the extent a company is generating greater-than-average profits, it is assumed to possess this intangible asset.

Here are the basic steps in calculating the value of a business through this method:

1. *Adjusted tangible net worth* is calculated (for argument's sake, let's assume this is $500,000).

2. *Opportunity cost of investing in the business is calculated.* This represents the costs investors will incur by investing in this business rather than others, and it consists of (1) the rate or risk-free return (usually calculated in terms of U.S. treasury bonds or other similar financial instruments), (2) an adjustment for inflation, and (3) the risk allowance for investing in this particular business. The greater the risk, the higher the rate of return required by investors. A typical figure is 25 percent: Investors require a 25 percent return on their investment to justify the risks involved in purchasing an existing business. This can be higher or lower and, in fact, is open to negotiation between the entrepreneur and potential buyers.

Finally, because by purchasing the company the buyer will forego a salary that could be earned elsewhere, this figure is added to calculate total opportunity cost.

The opportunity cost, then, would be calculated as follows:

$500,000 (tangible net worth) × 25% = $125,000; adding the purchaser's "lost" salary (which we will assume is $50,000) to this = $125,000 + $50,000 = $175,000. This is total opportunity cost.

3. *Net earnings are projected.* Here, again, is where "art" enters the picture: The buyer must estimate the company's net earnings on the basis of past earnings, current trends, and any other factors she or he wishes to include. Let's assume that this figure is $200,000 for the upcoming year.

4. *Compute extra earning power.* Earnings over and above industry average are included here. This is the difference between net projected earnings ($200,000) and total opportunity costs ($175,000). As a result, extra earning power = $25,000.

5. *Estimate value of intangibles.* The extra earning power is then multiplied by a years-of-profit figure (usually 3 to 4) to compute the estimated value of goodwill over a period of several years. Let's assume that the buyer chooses a 3-year period: 3 × $25,000 = $75,000. This is extra earning power projected ahead—a measure of goodwill.

6. *Determine the value of the business.* Value of the business is then based on a simple calculation in which adjusted tangible net worth and value of the intangibles are summed. This would yield the following calculation: $500,000 (total tangible net worth) + $75,000 (estimated value of intangibles) = $575,000. This is the value of the business as computed by this method.

Capitalized Earnings Method. In this approach, expected net earnings are capitalized to determine value. This method is simpler and uses the following formula:

Capitalized net earnings = Net earnings (after deducting owner's salary)/Rate of return. In our example, this would be $200,000 – $50,000/.25 = $600,000. Notice that this figure is not very different from the $575,000 calculated using the excess earnings method.

Discounted Future Earnings Method. It is a basic fact of life that money received today is worth more than money that will be received in the future; after all, a bird in the hand is worth two (or at least 1.10!) in the bush. This principle is known as the *time value* of money. A third earnings-based method for valuing businesses takes account of this principle and is known as the **discounted future earnings method**. It calculates a company's value by discounting future earnings, which, after all, are far from certain. The basic steps are as follows:

1. *Future earnings are projected for five years.* Usually, in fact, three projections are made: pessimistic, most likely, and optimistic. Let's say that for our hypothetical company the most likely scenario is a total of $500,000 in earnings.

2. *These future earnings are discounted.* By how much? This again, is open to negotiation, but often a figure approaching 25 percent is used. Again, this reflects the risk that projections will not be achieved. Discounting future earnings by 25 percent for each future year (for five years) yields a projected discounted figure of $279,000.

3. *Income beyond the fifth year is calculated.* Often, this involves multiplying projected fifth-year income by 1/rate of return. Here, the figure is $120,000 (projected earnings)/25% = $480,000.

4. *Income beyond the fifth year is discounted by the present value factor.* This figure, and other figures for present value for years 1, 2, 3, 4, and 5, can be found in published tables that provide appropriate numbers for various discount rates (e.g., 20 percent, 25 percent, 30 percent, etc.). For our example, the figure is $480,000 × .26 = $124,800.

5. *Total value of the business is computed.* This involves adding the present value of the company's estimated earnings and the present values of its earnings from the sixth year. This figure is $500,000 + $124,800 = $624,800.

All three methods offer advantages and all involve disadvantages. But note that given the assumptions made here, the methods do not yield wildly different values (the range is $575,000 to $624,800). This is generally true: Regardless of which method is used, if reasonable assumptions about future earnings and opportunity costs are made, similar figures will be obtained through each method. The fact that differences remain, however, suggests that this is one point entrepreneurs and potential buyers must resolve: Which method will be used to value the company? If agreement on that point can't be reached, negotiations may well fail.

Market Method

A third major way of determining the value of a business involves comparing the price/earnings ratio of the business to that of other publicly traded companies in the same industry. This is known as the **market value** or *price-earnings* approach. Several companies comparable to the privately held company now up for sale are identified, and price/earnings ratios for those publicly traded companies obtained. This average figure is then multiplied by the estimated net earnings of the privately held company. For instance, in our example, let's assume that the average price-earnings ratio for companies similar to the business we are valuing is 3.10. Projected net earnings for the coming year are $200,000. Multiplying the two figures, we obtain $3.10 \times \$200,000 = \$630,000$. This is the value of the company.

One problem with this approach is the difficulty involved in identifying several publicly traded companies that are similar enough to the business up for sale to allow for meaningful comparisons. Similarly, this method compares publicly and privately held companies, and because privately held companies are basically illiquid (there is no market for their stock), assuming that the same price-earnings ratio applies is questionable; perhaps a much lower one would be appropriate. In fact, this is precisely what buyers will argue if this is the method of valuation preferred by the entrepreneur.

Taking a Company Public: The Lure of IPOs

Entrepreneurs have a multitude of goals and an abundance of visions of the future, but many do share one major dream: reaching the point at which they can take their company public through an **initial public offering (IPO)**. As recently as 1999, more than 300 companies went this route each year in the United Stated alone (although the number has now dropped considerably). Why is this particular exit strategy so appealing to many entrepreneurs? Perhaps the simplest answer is that going public often generates huge amounts of cash—more, in fact, than entrepreneurs ever thought possible. The entrepreneurs can use this infusion of capital (or at least, the portion they actually receive!) for major expansion of their companies. Further, as noted by Lelux,[2] publicly traded companies quickly acquire an aura of respectability in the eyes of various stakeholders, from investors to customers, and this can be a big "plus" from the point of view of gaining competitive advantage. Once a company has gone public, the market in which it is traded provides continuous, updated valuation of its worth; this can facilitate later rounds of financing and generally enhanced liquidity. A public company has other advantages as well: Public companies can use stock options for their employees more easily than privately held ones. Moreover, they can also more readily use their stock to acquire other companies.

There are important advantages to IPOs, but they come at a considerable cost—one entrepreneurs would be wise to consider carefully. First, going public is a tremendously expensive process; indeed, it can consume as much as 25 percent of the entire value of the offering! Not only are there direct costs of underwriting the issue and meeting strict legal and accounting standards of due diligence, but there are also the costs of having top management of the company literally tied up for months, as they participate in the "road show" that proceeds most initial public offerings, and is required by underwriters to assure that the new issue sells (see Figure 14.3 on page 358).

Another potential cost is the fact that most IPO's involve *lock-up agreements*, ones that prevent insiders—including entrepreneurs—from cashing in on the public offering.

LEARNING OBJECTIVE

4 List the advantages and costs of an initial public offering.

Figure 14.3 Participating in "Roadshows": One Cost of IPOs

Prior to an initial public offering (IPO), the top management of the company must engage in extensive promotion of the company and its future prospects, in cooperation with underwriters of the IPO. This takes them away from their regular jobs, and their absence often creates serious difficulties for the company. [Shown here is LeapFrog's president and CEO Mike Wood (center) at the New York Stock Exchange the day after its IPO.]

These agreements require that entrepreneurs retain their stock for months or even years after the initial public offering. Further, shares may be "underpriced" initially because underwriters want initial purchasers to experience an immediate rise in stock prices. These purchasers are often preferred customers of the underwriter and, in fact, they are often the group that benefits most initially.

Finally, entrepreneurs should recognize the fact that publicly traded companies are subject to very careful scrutiny—scrutiny that may limit the founding team's freedom to run the company as they prefer. For instance, markets tend to frown on risky business strategies so these will probably have to be avoided. Further, investors expect returns in the form of dividends or capital gains, so management's attention may be diverted to focusing on these issues and on short-term strategies designed to raise earning this year—or even this quarter—to make investors happy, rather than on longer-term goals. Before going public, entrepreneurs don't have to consider such matters, but after the IPO, they absolutely must consider them with care.

In general, an IPO involves four phases of activity. During Phase 1, efforts are made to prepare the company for "L-Day" (listing day). Lelux[3] has compared this to preparations for prom night in high schools—a process of getting the company to look its best so that it will shine on L-Day. Phase 2 involves working closely with the IPO work group (underwriters, investment bankers, attorneys) to prepare all IPO documentation (registration statement, prospectus, road show material). Phase 3 is the actual distribution exercise, which involves a 2- or 3-week road show by top management. Phase 4 should, ideally, continue the process by providing a constant flow of information to stock analysts and investors; this is needed to maintain public interest in the company and its shares. However, after the first three phases are complete, many companies are totally exhausted and find it extremely difficult to maintain this high level of activity. In addition, the need for the top management team to return to running the company may be acute, because they have been directing virtually all of their time and energies to the IPO process.

So, should entrepreneurs consider going public as a viable exit strategy? Many experts agree that the answer can be "yes" if the company truly needs large amounts of capital to grow and develop, and it is fortunate enough to possess an experienced management team that can handle the stress of the process and at the same time tell a great story to the public markets. Under these conditions, an IPO can provide entrepreneurs with the capital they need to fully realize their vision and, ultimately, with a very profitable exit route. On the other hand, many companies show excellent records of growth without an IPO (e.g., Cargill in the United States), so this is not a necessary ingredient in long-term success.

Beyond Exit Strategies: What Comes Next?

In sum, it is clear that many different exit strategies are available to entrepreneurs. Each offers a mixed bag of advantages and disadvantages, so the choice among them is neither simple nor easy. The selection of an exit strategy, moreover, is only the start of the process for entrepreneurs; once they have decided on whether they want to transfer ownership of their company to relatives, sell it to insiders or outsiders, or take it public, they must proceed to carry this strategy through to a satisfactory conclusion. This, in turn, often involves protracted discussions and negotiations with successors or potential buyers. Because the outcome of these discussions strongly shapes the future for both entrepreneurs and their companies, negotiation is a key process from the point of view of exit strategies, just as it is throughout the entrepreneurial process. For this reason, we will now take a closer look at this process and some of the key factors that affect it. (For the thoughts of one entrepreneur who has considered the choice among exit strategies very carefully, please see **"The Voice of Experience"** section on page 360.)

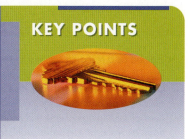

KEY POINTS

- Sale to outsiders involves valuation of the business. Several methods for accomplishing this task exist: balance sheet methods, earnings methods, and market methods.
- Entrepreneurs can also exit from their companies through initial public offerings. These offer important advantages (e.g., large infusions of cash) but come at a substantial cost (fees from underwriters are high, and the top management team must devote most of its energies to the IPO for several months). Thus, the decision to take a company public is a complex one that must be made with considerable care.

NEGOTIATION: THE UNIVERSAL PROCESS

Donald Trump (1987), a well-known businessman and entrepreneur, once remarked: "Deals are my art form. Other people paint beautifully on canvas or write wonderful poetry. I like making deals, preferably big deals. That's how I get my kicks." Trump himself would tell you that making deals involves **negotiation**—a process in which opposing sides exchange offers, counteroffers, and concessions either directly or through representatives. If the process is successful, an agreement acceptable to both sides is attained. If, instead, negotiations fail, the process ends, and each side seeks other parties with whom to make a deal. (We discussed negotiation briefly in Chapter 12 as a means of resolving conflicts; here we will expand on that discussion in the context of negotiations between entrepreneurs and other parties over the sale of their companies.)

As we noted in Chapter 12, entrepreneurs engage in negotiations with others throughout the entrepreneurial process. They negotiate agreements with venture capitalists or other sources of funding, negotiate with cofounders over roles and responsibilities, and with customers and suppliers over the terms of contracts. Finally, they negotiate with potential purchasers of their company, or with underwriters, in order to implement the exit strategy they have chosen. For these reasons, it is important that entrepreneurs understand some of the "basics" with respect to negotiation. Specifically, they need to understand the nature of this process and how to carry it out effectively. Fortunately, the importance of negotiation as a process has been widely recognized in several different fields (management, psychology, political science), so there is a wealth of knowledge on which to draw.[4] Here, we will summarize some of the key points that, we believe, will prove especially useful to entrepreneurs.

Negotiation: Its Basic Nature

We have already defined negotiation as a process in which opposing sides exchange offers, counteroffers, and concessions in an effort to obtain an agreement acceptable to both sides. Each side, of course, wishes to obtain an agreement favorable to its own interests, but each recognizes that the opponent is probably *not* going to lie down and surrender; rather, this person (or group of persons), too, will seek to maximize her or his outcomes. As a result, a key question becomes: "How can I persuade the other side to make concessions favorable to my interests?" Research findings indicate that the most basic answer involves the use of tactics that reduce the opposing side's aspirations—tactics that encourage opponents to conclude that they cannot get what they want and must, instead, settle for something much less favorable to them, but more

LEARNING OBJECTIVE

5 Describe the basic nature of negotiation and explain the nature of several key bargaining tactics.

THE VOICE OF EXPERIENCE

The Multiple Benefits of an Appropriate Exit Strategy

Trained as a research scientist in the field of biomedical engineering, Dr. Shreefal Mehta saw a gap in research development and commercial delivery of that research to patients. His curiosity about the process of technology commercialization led him to the field of technological entrepreneurship. He currently holds positions as research assistant professor of biotechnology management in the Lally School of Management and Technology at Rensselaer Polytechnic Institute in Troy, New York, and as CEO and cofounder of Myomatrix Therapeutics, a company devoted to the development of new drug treatments for cardiovascular diseases. His scientific experience (encompassing more than 12 years and more than 25 book chapters, presentations, and publications) has given him a broad background from which to approach and evaluate new emerging technologies.

Though not all entrepreneurs have a clear idea about how long they want to stay with the companies they found, many do—especially in certain industries where early exits are the rule rather than the exception. With this thought in mind, I recently interviewed Dr. Shreefal Mehta.

Baron: "Biotechnology is an exciting field, and I know that you have the perfect credentials for it. Can you describe those for me?"

Mehta: "I have a Ph.D. in bioengineering, and an MBA. Although I hold a Ph.D, my interest has always been in taking new technologies, developing them, and commercializing them. Or, as I like to put it, 'bringing science to fruition.'"

Baron: "That's certainly consistent with the mission of my university; when RPI was founded by Stephen Van Rensselaer back in 1824, he charged it with the mission of using science to enhance everyday life . . . and that's still the major focus of the university now."

Mehta: "I know, and that's why I came here for my MBA degree—that and the high proportion of outstanding scientists and engineers on the faculty."

Baron: "You are certainly putting your desire to 'bring science to fruition' to use in your new company, Myomatrix. Can you tell me what your goals are?"

Mehta: "We want to develop drugs for treating illnesses that are known as 'orphan diseases'—too few people have them for the large drug companies to bother with, with the result that the people suffering from them usually have very few treatment options."

Baron: "Suppose you are successful in developing such drugs, what comes next?"

Mehta: "We would prefer to sell Myomatrix to a large company. They would have the resources not only to develop the drugs we discover, but to bring them to market. The pharmaceutical industry is very competitive, so unless a company has a large marketing department and puts many salespersons in the field, it is very hard to get new drugs to doctors. If doctors don't know about new drugs and their benefits, they can't prescribe them for their patients, and these people go on suffering when in fact help for their condition is available. So for us, the best outcome would be an early sale—perhaps within the first three to five years of our existence."

Baron: "And that would fit with your key goal of bringing science to fruition."

Mehta: "Exactly—a large company can get the drugs to the people who need them much more quickly and effectively than we can."

Commentary: As you can see, Dr. Mehta has a clear exit strategy in mind for his company—one that is fully consistent with his vision of using science to benefit large numbers of persons. In our view, this strategy makes eminent good sense: As we noted in Chapter 9, small start-up companies generally can't compete with large established ones where marketing and sales are concerned. So Mehta's exit strategy is an excellent one in all respects—it will provide him and his partner (Dr. Lawrence Zisman) with financial rewards for their hard work and also fits well with his goals—and passion for helping people who, because of economic reasons, are not currently being helped by large pharmaceutical companies.

favorable to their opponent.[5] Let's take a look at some of these tactics and also at the question of whether it is ethical to use them.

Tactics of Negotiation: Procedures for Reducing an Opponent's Aspirations

The course and outcome of negotiations are influenced by many different factors. Among the most important of these, however, are specific *bargaining tactics* that are used to reduce an opponent's goals (see Figure 14.4). These include (1) beginning with an extreme initial offer—one that is very favorable to the side proposing it and is, in

Figure 14.4 Bargaining Tactics in Action

Bargaining tactics are procedures designed to reduce the aspirations (goals) of one's opponent. Mr. Dithers is using one of these in this cartoon.

fact, much more favorable than this side can realistically expect to get (e.g., an entrepreneur places a much higher value on her company than even she believes it merits); (2) the "big lie" technique—convincing the other side that one's break-even point is much higher than it is so that they offer more than would otherwise be the case (e.g., an entrepreneur seeks to convince a potential purchaser that he would rather continue to own the company than to sell for the price suggested by the would-be buyer); (3) convincing the other side that you have an "out"—another party with whom you can make a deal (e.g., an entrepreneur convinces a potential purchaser that he has another purchaser waiting in the wings—even if this is not true). Are these and related tactics ethical? Opinions differ, but research findings indicate that certain tactics are widely recognized as being unethical.[6] Here are the ones found to be most objectionable: (1) false promises—making false promises or commitments one has no intention of keeping; (2) misrepresentation—providing misleading or false information to an opponent; and (3) inappropriate information gathering—collecting information through theft, spying, etc. To the extent a negotiator engages in such actions, her or his behavior is generally viewed as unethical. According to these principles, then, an extreme initial offer is generally ethically acceptable (although risky, because if it is too extreme, it can anger or annoy an opponent), but both the "big lie" and fictitious claims about having an "out" are not—they involve false statements and misrepresentation. Please note: We're not saying that negotiators do not engage in such tactics; we are merely pointing out that most people consider doing so to be a violation of ethical standards. Thus, entrepreneurs who want to protect their reputation for making future deals or running additional companies should approach these tactics with caution: Using them can work in the short run, but it may prove very costly over longer periods of time.

Additional Techniques for Obtaining a Favorable Agreement

Although the tactics we have considered so far are among the most important, many others procedures for inducing one's opponent to make concessions during negotiations also exist. These do not focus on reducing opponent's aspirations; rather, they concentrate on inducing specific feelings and reactions in opponents—feelings or reactions that make it hard for them not to offer favorable terms to the person using such tactics. For instance, skilled negotiators often try to arrange their own concessions so that these produce pressures to reciprocate among opponents. More specifically, they make a series of small concessions on issues that they view as relatively unimportant. This puts subtle pressure on opponents to reciprocate—to make concessions of their own. If negotiators are truly skilled, they maneuver their opponents into the position where the concessions they make are precisely the ones the negotiators desire.[7]

A related tactic involves inducing *positive affect* (i.e., positive feelings or moods) among opponents. A large body of research findings indicate that when people experience positive affect, they are much more likely to agree to a request and to behave in cooperative ways.[8] How can positive affect be induced among opponents? By holding discussions in a very comfortable and pleasant settings, by providing lavish refreshments, and by treating them with respect and courtesy (see Figure 14.5 on page 362). Again, research findings indicate that such procedures often work: They make it easier, psychologically, for opponents to move toward the positions desired by the negotiators who use them.

© CORBIS

Figure 14.5 Positive Affect and the Course of Negotiations

Research findings indicate that putting one's opponent in a good mood is often a useful negotiating strategy. This is why important negotiations are often held in comfortable or even luxurious surroundings.

We could continue, but by now the main point should be clear: Many techniques for influencing the course of negotiations, and for obtaining positive outcomes from it, exist. For entrepreneurs, negotiation is almost a way of life—they engage in it throughout the entrepreneurial process, from discussions with potential investors through deliberations with potential purchasers when arranging exit strategies. For this reason, understanding its nature, and being able both to recognize various tactics and to use them effectively, is definitely well worth the effort. Please take note: Becoming a skilled negotiator requires years of practice, so our goal here is mainly that of acquainting you with the complexities of this process, not trying to turn you into experts. But being aware of the tactics we have discussed is a very good start, and will at least put you on the road toward improving what is certainly one of the most valuable skills you can develop.

Overall Orientation Toward Negotiation

Another aspect of negotiation has been found to be very important in determining the outcomes it produces. This is what is generally referred to as the **overall approach to negotiation** adopted by the persons participating in it. Research findings indicate that two basic approaches exist. One views negotiation as a "win-lose" situation in which gains by one side are necessarily linked with losses for the other. The other approach, in contrast, assumes that the interests of the two sides are not incompatible and that an agreement that maximizes the outcomes of both sides can be obtained; this is known as a "win-win" approach.

Not all situations offer the potential for win-win agreements, but many do provide such possibilities. If the parties to a negotiation are willing to explore all options carefully, they can sometimes attain what are known as **integrative agreements**—ones that maximize joint benefits—the gains experienced by both sides. Here's one well-known example: Two cooks are making different recipes, and both call for an orange; yet, the cooks have only one orange in their kitchen. What do they do? One possibility is to cut the orange in half; this works, but it leaves both chefs short of what they need. Another, and more creative (integrative) solution, is to notice that one cook needs all the juice while the other needs only the peel. So, one cook can take the peel and leave the juice for the other. This is a much better solution, because both get what they need; in other words, the joint outcomes are considerably better. Other strategies for reaching integrative solutions are summarized in Table 14.1.

One that is especially useful to entrepreneurs is *logrolling*, a technique in which each party makes concessions on issues that are relatively unimportant to it in exchange for concessions on other issues that it values more highly. Here's a concrete example: An entrepreneur wants a specific price for his company because he feels that he needs this amount in order to maintain his lifestyle in the years ahead. The potential purchaser is concerned with price, but an even more important issue for her is having the entrepreneur stay on with the company for a specified period of time, to smooth the transition. The entrepreneur would prefer to leave at once, but can handle staying on for a year—if that will help him get the price he wants. If the two sides are sharp enough to recognize this difference in the relative importance of these two issues, they can logroll: The purchaser raises her price and the entrepreneur agrees to stay on. Each side gets what is most important to it by making concessions

TECHNIQUE FOR REACHING INTEGRATIVE AGREEMENTS	DESCRIPTION AND EXAMPLES
Broadening the pie	Available resources are increased so that both sides can obtain their major goals (e.g., additional sources of funding for a purchase are obtained).
Nonspecific compensation	One side gets what it wants, and the other is compensated on an unrelated issue (e.g., entrepreneur gets the price she wants for her business, and the purchaser gets rights to patents held by the entrepreneur).
Logrolling	Each party makes concessions on low-priority issues in exchange for concessions on issues it values more highly (see text).
Cost-cutting	One party gets what it wants and the costs to the other party are reduced or eliminated (e.g., the entrepreneur gets the price he wants for the business, but the purchaser will pay this over a large number of years and in a way that makes the payments tax deductible).
Bridging	Neither party gets its initial demands, but a new option that satisfies the major interests of both sides is developed (e.g., the purchaser wants the entrepreneur to remain while the entrepreneur wants a straight sale; a new option in which the entrepreneur will train a replacement is worked out).

on issues it views as less important. Again, logrolling is not always possible, but when it is—or other integrative strategies are feasible—the outcome can be an agreement that meets the primary needs of both sides. That's an important point because research findings indicate that "winning" in a negotiation can prove costly: If one side manages to get most of what it wants (perhaps because it is bargaining from a position of real strength), the opponent may be forced to accept, but the seeds of future problems may be sown.[9] The losing side feels that it has not been treated fairly and may find various ways to "even the score," either overtly or covertly. This is a common occurrence in the realm of labor-management relations, where the ultimate outcome can be negative to both sides. For instance, during the 1950s and 1960s, unions representing employees in the newspaper industry staged repeated strikes, thus forcing costly concessions from the owners of many famous newspapers (e.g., the *Herald Tribune* in New York). Faced with this confrontational approach, many newspaper owners began to view the unions as totally unreasonable, and gradually concluded that it was impossible for them to earn reasonable rates of return in this industry. The result? They closed down many famous newspapers, thus costing well-paid union members their jobs and depriving the public of newspapers they had read for decades (see Figure 14.6).

Here's how this might operate with respect to entrepreneurs. Suppose that an entrepreneur is a skilled negotiator and manages to extract exceptionally favorable terms from a purchaser. When the purchaser reconsiders this deal at a later time, he concludes that he paid far too much. As a result, he feels justified in delaying payments to the entrepreneur or in saying negative things about this person, thus harming the entrepreneur's chances of obtaining funding to start another company. For this reason alone, integrative agreement and a "win-win" approach are strongly preferable to agreements in which one side sets out to defeat its opponent— and does so. (For an example of what can happen when negotiators focus on winning at all costs, please see the **"Danger! Pitfall Ahead!"** section on page 364).

What we have been saying throughout this section, in essence, is this: Negotiation is a complex process that is affected by more than purely economic factors. As we noted in Chapter 3, human beings are not entirely rational. On the contrary, they are

Table 14.1 Techniques for Reaching Integrative Agreements

Several techniques for reaching agreements that maximize joint outcomes (integrative agreements) exist, but they are not always easy to recognize. Negotiators who succeed in doing so can often attain highly satisfactory agreements.

Figure 14.6 The Potential Costs of a "Win-Lose" Approach to Negotiation

During the 1950s and 1960s, labor unions representing employees of large urban newspapers adopted a confrontational "win-lose" approach to negotiations with owners of these publications. As a result, many owners concluded that they were in a "no win" situation and closed the newspapers, including ones that were famous and highly regarded.

© Bettmann/CORBIS

DANGER! PITFALL AHEAD!

The Costs of Negotiating to Win: Watch Out for the "Ankle-Biters"!

Do you ever store food in plastic containers? If so, the chances are good that some of them, at least, say "Rubbermaid" on the lids. Until the mid-1990s, Rubbermaid had a virtual monopoly on small food-storage containers. But then something strange happened: Their products began to disappear from the shelves of supermarkets and large discount stores, where they had previously been prominently featured. I remember when this happened, and at the time, I wondered why. Now, I know. During the mid-1990s, the price of resin, the raw material for many of Rubermaid's products, soared, virtually doubling in only 18 months. Rubbermaid's reaction was to pass these price increases directly on to its customers, and when they protested, the company adopted a very tough negotiating stance. This was true even with respect to giant Wal-Mart, its largest single account. In other words, Rubbermaid "hung tough" and viewed negotiations with its customers as confrontations in which it set out to "defeat" these companies.

What happened next was classic. Stung by Rubbermaid's harsh treatment, and tempted by smaller companies who passed less of the price increase for resin on to customers, Wal-Mart and other large customers reduced the amount of shelf space they devoted to Rubbermaid's products. Consumers, in turn, were not as loyal to the Rubbermaid brand as the company expected and deserted its products for lower-priced ones that were not featured in the space previously occupied by Rubbermaid. Finally, Rubbermaid got the message and realized that the small companies they viewed as "ankle-biters" had used Rubbermaid's intransigence in negotiation with its customers to gain competitive advantage—and a larger share of this lucrative market.

Rubbermaid, of course, is a giant corporation. But the message for entrepreneurs—or anyone else entering into negotiations—is clear: If you choose to view your opponent as an enemy and seek to win the negotiation by defeating this person, get ready for some nasty surprises. It is rare in life that one side has all the power, and although you may triumph in the short run, the long-term costs may be more than you bargained for. This is a basic principle that is as true for giant corporations as it is for individual entrepreneurs negotiating with potential purchasers of their business. So, although integrative solutions that maximize joint outcomes are often hard to obtain, they are, often by far the best, and well worth the effort.

subject to many cognitive errors, and their thinking is often strongly influenced by their emotions.[10] For this reason, they sometimes lose sight of their basic self-interests during negotiations. These interests can be summarized in two major points: (1) obtain a favorable agreement with their opponent, and (2) avoid (insofar as possible) inducing feelings of anger, resentment, or outrage on the part of this person. This means that negotiators should seek fair and equitable agreements—not one-sided ones. The temptation to try to win by defeating one's opponent is often great but the likelihood that negotiations will succeed is much lower when this kind of win-lose strategy is adopted by one or both sides. Moreover, any agreement that is produced will tend to be unstable: The losing side will feel that it has been unfairly treated (perhaps tricked or exploited) and that, in turn, sets the stage for later, serious problems. Entrepreneurs who keep these basic points clearly in mind as they negotiate with potential purchasers over the sale of their company (or with anyone else over any other issue, for that matter), will ultimately obtain better and more lasting agreements than ones who revert to the standard approach of viewing their opponents as enemies against whom any and all tactics are acceptable. Obtaining integrative agreements requires more effort, thought, and greater creativity than the more obvious win-lose approach, but often, the outcome is well worth the additional cost.

- Negotiation is a process in which participants exchange offers and counteroffers until either an agreement is reached or negotiations deadlock. Skill in negotiating with others is very useful to entrepreneurs throughout the entrepreneurial process—from negotiating with potential investors to negotiating with potential buyers of the business.
- A key goal of negotiators is that of reducing the aspiration (goals) of their opponent. This can be accomplished through several specific bargaining tactics (e.g., extreme initial offers, the "big-lie" technique, claiming to have an "out").
- Other tactics involve efforts to generate pressures to reciprocate concessions on the part of opponents, and inducing them to experience positive affect.
- A key factor that affects the course and outcomes of negotiations is the negotiators' overall approach to this context: win-lose or win-win. A win-win approach offers much greater opportunity for reaching integrative agreements—ones that maximize joint outcomes.

EXIT STRATEGIES AND THE LIFE SPAN: DIFFERENT NEEDS—AND GOALS—AT DIFFERENT TIMES OF LIFE

Samuel Butler once wrote: "Life is like playing a violin solo in public and learning the instrument as one goes on." (1895). We agree; life does involve of a lot of ad-libbing, and we do indeed make it up as we go along. That's as true for entrepreneurs as anyone else; in fact, one could argue that they are the improvisers *par excellence*. After all, they are people who create something—viable new ventures—out of what, at first glance, appears to be nothing. Moreover, their energy, optimism, and belief in their own abilities (all characteristics confirmed by careful research)[11] equip them for long, productive working lives. Even entrepreneurs, however, must ultimately come face to face with the realities of the human life span. We do indeed change with the passing decades, and these changes take many different forms. Look at the photo in Figure 14.7, Part A. Do you recognize the person shown? (He is a famous entrepreneur.) Now turn to Figure 14.7, Part B, on page 366. Can you recognize him now? The kind of physical changes shown here are a normal part of growing older. Such change is slow at first, but speeds up for most people after they pass the age of 50. Energy, the acuteness of our senses, and stamina all decrease—although there are huge individual differences in this respect. For instance, research findings indicate that these processes are much slower for people who stay in good physical shape than for those who do not.[12] Thus, it is possible for a physically fit person age 60 to have more energy and stamina than a less fit person 20 or even 30 years younger. So the rate at which we decline physically, if not the decline itself, is somewhat under our control.

Physical changes, however, are only part of the total picture. As we move through the life span, we also change cognitively and socially, too. With respect to cognitive changes, it was once believed that memory, intelligence, and many other aspects of cognition decline with increasing age. Recent findings, however, suggest that such changes—if they occur—are much slower and smaller in

Figure 14.7, Part A
Who Is This?

Do you recognize the person shown here? Here's a hint: He is a very famous entrepreneur. To find out who he is, turn to page 366.

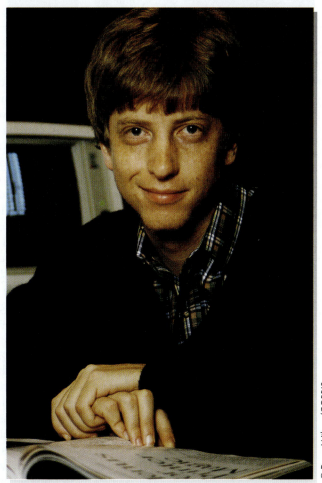

© Doug Wilson/CORBIS

© Reuters NewMedia Inc./CORBIS

Figure 14.7, Part B
Physical Change: A Basic Fact
of Life

*Now do you recognize the person
in the photo? Probably so; he is Bill
Gates. The differences in the two
photos (the one on this page, and
the one on page 365) indicate that
we all experience large physical
changes as we grow older.*

magnitude than was previously assumed.[13] For instance,
some aspects of memory do seem to decline with increasing age (e.g., our ability to transfer information from short-
term storage into long-term memory), but others remain
largely unchanged. For instance, semantic memory (general
knowledge) does not decline with age and may, in fact,
increase.[14] Similarly, procedural memory—the kind of memory involved in skilled motor activities—remains largely
unimpaired as we age. So if an entrepreneur happens to be
a skilled typist, he or she will probably retain that ability
over the decades.

Intelligence, too, changes only slowly, if at all, with
increasing age. In fact, recent studies suggest that the only
components of intelligence that decline with age are ones
directly related to speed—for instance, how quickly people
can retrieve information from memory or perform tasks
that require quick responses. In contrast, practical intelligence, a kind that is especially important to entrepreneurs,
may actually increase with age rather than decline.[15]

Additional research focused on creativity, too, points to
encouraging conclusions. Although most persons seem to
make their major contributions during their 30s and 40s,
this depends on the field in question. In highly quantitative
fields such as mathematics and theoretical physics, creativity peaks occur relatively early—when people are in their
20s and 30s. In other fields of science, however, the peak is
much later, occurring when scientists are in their 40s and
50s. Research findings indicate that many persons show a
second peak, late in life—in the 60s, 70s, or even 80s. For
instance, Picasso produced many of his famous paintings in
his 60s, 70s, or even 80s (see Figure 14.8), and Michelangelo
was painting until his death at 84. Composers, too, often show a second peak of productivity late in life. For instance, one of my favorite classical pieces is Rachimaninoff's
"Symphonic Dances," written just one year before his death, and decades after he composed his most famous works.

What this suggests for entrepreneurs, of course, is that they can continue working
productively for many decades—if they so choose—and if their families agree. That is an
important point, worth emphasizing: The demanding life of an entrepreneur can take a
heavy toll on family and personal relationships, and these people certainly should have
a voice in this decision. In other words, entrepreneurs have more to consider than simply
their own preferences. Just as the support of spouses, significant others, friends, and family members is essential at the start, so, too, is it important in deciding when and how to
exit. For instance, consider Bob Page, founder of Replacements Ltd., the world's largest
supplier of discontinued china, glassware, and flatware. As Page puts it, "My friends and
family discouraged me from quitting my job as an auditor . . . but I thought if I could
devote my time to doing what I love, I could make a living at it—even though it wouldn't
be as much as I would earn as a CPA." So he quit his job and started his company with
less than $5,000 in cash. The Small Business Administration turned down his request for
a loan, but by placing small ads in magazines, he built a customer base and grossed more
than $150,000 in sales during his first year. That soon convinced his family and friends
that he had made the right choice, and they responded by pitching in and supporting
him strongly. With their help, he built his business into a thriving success: Last year,
Replacements Ltd. grossed more than $60 million! When will it be time to quit? Page is
now 57, and will certainly take the wishes of his close family into account on choosing his
exit strategy. After all, as he and countless other entrepreneurs, recognize, you really *can't*
do it alone, and it is only fair that the people who helped you along the way should have
a voice in deciding when it is time to say "enough."

In any case, it is clear that at some point or other, all entrepreneurs face the following, key question: Do they wish to keep working and leading the same kind of hectic life, in which they devote 100 hours or more per week to their businesses? This is a question each person must answer for himself or herself, but research on human development across the life span suggests that most of us do reach a time when we want a simpler, less hectic life.

To summarize the main findings of this research,[16] it appears that we all pass through a series of distinct phases or eras in our lives, with each phase separated from the one before it by a turbulent transition period. One of these is the *age 30 transition*. At this time, individuals realize that they are nearing the point of no return: If they remain in their current job and life, they will have too much invested to change. Faced with this fact, they reexamine their initial choice and either make major changes or decide that they indeed chose the best course. This is one reason why many entrepreneurs decide to leave their jobs with large corporations soon after turning 30.[17]

The next life transition occurs when people are between 40 and 45 and is known as the *midlife transition*. It is a time when many individuals first begin to think about their own mortality. Up until this period, most view themselves as young, and life as a very long-term proposition, stretching off into a dimly visible future. After age 40, though, many persons come to see themselves as the older generation. This leads them to take stock of the success of their past choices and the likelihood of reaching their youthful dreams. The result can be a major change in a person's life—divorce, remarriage, a new career. Many individuals experience yet another period of transition between the ages of 50

© Hulton-Deutsch/CORBIS

Figure 14.8 Creativity: Does It Decline with Age?

Many famous persons—artists, scientists, composers, writers—make important contributions late in life. For instance, Pablo Picasso (shown here) produced many paintings when he was in his 70s and 80s. This suggests that creativity does not necessarily decrease with age.

and 55. This *late-adult transition* marks the close of the middle years of life, and the start of late adulthood. During this transition, individuals must come to terms with their impending retirement and the major changes this will bring. How long do they want to work? What do they want to do if they stop? These are questions most people never considered before, but begin to ponder with increasing frequency after age 50.

What does all this mean for entrepreneurs? Basically, that they should take such factors into account in deciding how and when to exit from their companies. As human beings, we definitely have different goals and needs at different stages of our lives, and these should be carefully considered by entrepreneurs when they think about leaving the companies they have created. Young entrepreneurs—those under 40—may well want to start another company, so they are likely to choose an exit strategy that yields significant cash on closing. Older entrepreneurs (e.g., those 50 or older) may be uncertain as to whether they want to start the whole process over again. Instead, they may consciously want to slow down and "smell the roses." For such persons, a gradual exit and payments over a period of time may make more sense. And still older entrepreneurs, who are already very secure financially, may want to focus on transferring ownership in their businesses to children or other family members.

The key point is this: No single exit strategy is best for all entrepreneurs. Rather, the choice among them, and the specific terms negotiated, should reflect not only economic realities (what is best for the company and its future), but personal ones, too. These should include what one researcher, Vernoka Kisfalvi, has recently described as central "life issues"—concerns that derive from the entrepreneurs' unique life experiences and are basic themes in everything they do, including the strategies they choose for running their new ventures (e.g., desire for autonomy, success, recognition, taking action, etc.).[18] These will vary from person to person, but we all have them in one form or another.

LEARNING OBJECTIVE

7 Define "life transitions" and explain why entrepreneurs should consider their own age and phase of life before choosing an exit strategy.

Similarly, the choice among exit strategies should reflect where the entrepreneur is in life's journey, and what he or she wants to do in the years ahead. The more entrepreneurs take these factors into account, the more likely they are to be able to echo the words of Javier Perez de Cuellar (1991), former Secretary-General of the United Nations, who, in speaking of his own retirement, remarked, "I am a free man. I feel as light as a feather." That is a fitting conclusion to a life of active achievement, and one to which, we believe, all entrepreneurs are entitled. Good luck! We wish you a smooth, interesting, and fulfilling journey through the decades that define our adult lives.

KEY POINTS

- As we age, we move through distinct phases or eras of life. These are separated by somewhat turbulent transition periods, during which many people examine their lives in the light of changing goals.
- The exit strategies entrepreneurs choose should reflect their phase of life. Young entrepreneurs (under age 40) may prefer a "clean exit" that yields a lot of cash because they want to start another company. Older ones, in contrast, may simply want to have enough future income to maintain their current lifestyle. Even older ones may simply want to transfer the company to family members or other persons.
- To the extent that entrepreneurs take careful account of these personal factors as well as economic ones, the exit strategies they choose and then negotiate will be ones that help them achieve the major goals they seek.

Summary and Review of Key Points

- Many different exit strategies exist, but most involve transfer of a business to family members, sale to insiders or outsiders, or an initial public offering.
- Transfer of the company to family members can occur through trusts or a limited partnership.
- Transfer to top management can occur through a leveraged buyout.
- Transfer to employees can be accomplished through employee stock ownership plans.
- Sales to outsiders offer important advantages over continuing to run an independent company, and in fact, a venture may have greater value as part of a larger organization than it does as an independent company.
- Sale to outsiders involves valuation of the business. Several methods for accomplishing this task exist: balance sheets methods, earnings methods, and market methods.
- Entrepreneurs can also exit from their companies through initial public offerings. These offer important advantages (e.g., large infusions of cash) but come at a substantial cost (fees from underwriters are high, and the top management team must devote most of its energies to the IPO for several months). Thus, the decision to take a company public is a complex one that must be made the considerable care.

- Negotiation is a process in which participants exchange offers and counteroffers until either an agreement is reached or negotiations deadlock.
- A key goal of negotiators is that of reducing the aspiration (goals) of their opponent. This can be accomplished through several specific bargaining tactics (e.g., extreme initial offers, the "big-lie" technique, claiming to have an "out").
- Other tactics involve efforts to generate pressures to reciprocate concessions on the part of opponents, and inducing them to experience positive affect.
- A key factor that affects the course and outcomes of negotiations is the negotiator's overall approach to this context: "win-lose" or "win-win." A win-win approach offers much greater opportunity for reaching integrative agreements—ones that maximize joint outcomes.
- Skill in negotiating with others is very useful to entrepreneurs throughout the entrepreneurial process—from negotiating with potential investors to negotiating with potential buyers of the business.
- As we age, we move through distinct phases or eras of life. These are separated by somewhat turbulent transition periods, during which many people examine their lives in the light of changing goals.

- The exit strategies entrepreneurs choose should reflect their phase of life. Young entrepreneurs (under age 40) may prefer a "clean exit" that yields a lot of cash because they want to start another company. Older ones, in contrast, may simply want to have enough future income to maintain their current lifestyle. Even older ones may simply want to transfer the company to family members or other persons.
- To the extent that entrepreneurs take careful account of these personal factors as well as economic ones, the exit strategies they choose and then negotiate will be ones that help them achieve the major goals they seek.

Glossary

Balance Sheet Methods (of valuation): Methods for valuing businesses based on their balance sheets.

Capitalized Earnings Method: A method for valuing businesses based on capitalized net earnings.

Discounted Future Earnings Method: A method of valuing businesses based on discounted future earnings.

Earnings Methods: Methods of valuing businesses based on their future earnings.

Employee Stock Ownership Plans (ESOPs): Methods of transferring ownership of a company to its employees in which current owners contribute to an employee stock ownership trust. Contributions are often based on the profitability of the company.

Excess Earnings Method: A method of valuing businesses based on the extent to which a company will generate earnings in excess of the average for its industry.

Exit Strategies: Procedures through which entrepreneurs transfer ownership of their businesses to other persons.

Initial Public Offering (IPO): Initial sale of stock in a company to the public.

Intangibles: Assets that are hard, if not impossible, to list on the balance sheet: the goodwill the company has acquired with customers and suppliers, its reputation in the industry, its success in attracting and motivating first-rate employees.

Integrative Agreements: Ones that maximize joint benefits—the gains experienced by both sides.

Leveraged Buyout: Procedures for transferring ownership of a company to its current managers. These persons borrow from a financial organization in order to pay the owner an agreed-upon price.

Market Value (price-earnings approach): Procedures for valuing businesses based on the price-earnings ratios for comparable publicly owned companies.

Negotiation: A process in which opposing sides exchange offers, counteroffers, and concessions either directly or through representatives.

Overall Approach to Negotiation: The overall approach to negotiation adopted by the persons participating in it. Two basic patterns are a "win-lose" approach and a "win-win" approach.

Discussion Questions

1. How important do you think emotional and other "nonrational" factors are in shaping entrepreneurs' exit strategies? Can you think of ways in which the impact of these factors can be reduced?

2. How can entrepreneurs decide which of several family members is the best person to be their successor in running the company? Should they seek outside help in making this choice?

3. What are the advantages of selling a company to insiders (e.g., its current executives)? What are the advantages of selling a company to outsiders? On balance, do you think one of these strategies is superior to the other?

4. Sometimes, all methods for valuing a company—balance sheet, earnings, and market approaches—yield similar results. On other occasions, however, they do not. Why?

5. Many entrepreneurs work toward the goal of an initial public offering (IPO). Although this can yield large amounts of cash, such offerings have a downside, too. What is this and why should entrepreneurs consider it carefully before seeking an IPO?

6. Why does holding negotiations in a very pleasant environment sometimes help participants to reach an agreement?

7. What do the effects of aging have to do with entrepreneurs' choice of an exit strategy?

InfoTrac Exercises

1. **Identify All Possible Exits; Too Many Businesses Are Launched Without a Thought for the Day When the Founder Will Move On. Big Mistake, Says This Veteran Entrepreneur** (entrepreneur's byline)(advice for entrepreneurs on exit strategies)
   William J. Link.

   Business Week Online, December 6, 2002 pNA

   Record: A94978856

   Full Text: COPYRIGHT 2002 The McGraw-Hill Companies, Inc. Byline: William J. Link

   1. According to the article, what types of entrepreneurs should consider an exit strategy at start-up?

   2. What four steps are necessary to build a business for a smooth exit?

   3. Why is developing an exit strategy first important in the success of a new business?

2. **Negotiate from Strength** (the art of negotiation in business)
   Scott Smith

   Success, July 2000 v47 i3 p74

   Record: A63091354

   Full Text: COPYRIGHT 2000 Success Holdings Company, LLC

   1. According to the article, when do negotiations begin?

   2. Explain this quote from Chester L. Karrass, chairman of Karrass, the world's largest negotiating training company: "Fact-finding is the mother's milk of negotiation."

   3. What questions should you answer to prepare for a negotiation situation?

GETTING DOWN
TO BUSINESS

Valuing Your Company

As we saw in an earlier section, there are many ways of valuing your company. Because every entrepreneur who runs a successful business will, ultimately, exit from it, we think it is important for you to gain practice in the basics of this process—although, almost certainly, you will have the help and guidance of a financial expert when the time comes to prepare an actual valuation. Follow these steps to gain familiarity with the major valuation methods.

1. **Balance sheet method.** Using the adjusted balance sheet method, compute the net worth of your company. (Net worth = Assets – Liabilities)

2. **Earnings methods.** Choose one of the three basic earnings methods of valuation (excess earnings method, capitalized earnings, discounted future earnings method) and, following steps outlined in the text, use it to value your company.

3. **Market method.** Use the market method to value your company.

Now, compare the three figures you obtained. Do they differ? If so, why? What assumptions did you make as a basis for these calculations? Would you feel comfortable explaining these to potential purchasers of your company? Remember, valuation is just a starting point for complex negotiations with potential purchasers of your company, so our comments about negotiation certainly apply: Excessive valuations that are based on unconvincing assumptions will usually *not* help you to obtain a higher price; they may, instead, get negotiations off to a bad start. So think carefully about the assumptions you make in any method of valuation; if they are unrealistically inflated, the probably won't contribute in a positive way to reaching a satisfactory agreement.

Improving Your Negotiating Skills

Negotiation truly is the universal process; whether we realize it or not, we engage in it several times each day. For instance, do you ever divide chores between yourself and roommates or significant others? If so, you almost certainly negotiated with them about this issue. Have you ever arranged the division of tasks between yourself and coworkers, or arranged for a coworker to cover for you while you took needed time off? Again, negotiation was almost certainly involved.

To gain insights into how often you are negotiating, and how well you are handling this process, follow these steps.

1. For one week, keep a record of all the occasions on which you engage in negotiation with others. Write down
   a. The issue over which you negotiated
   b. The person with whom you negotiated
   c. The tactics you used during the negotiations
   d. The outcome
   e. The satisfaction of both you and the other person with the arrangement you made

2. Next, consider negotiations carefully in terms of the following questions:
   a. Are you satisfied with the tactics you used, or do you think you could have chosen better ones?
   b. What about the stability of the arrangements you negotiated—are they ones that are fully acceptable to both you and the other person? (If not, these arrangements probably won't last.)
   c. Did you use different tactics depending on your relationship with the other person? (e.g., one set of tactics with people you must deal with regularly, but another set with people you may never see again?)

3. Finally, ask yourself this question—and answer honestly: When you approached each of these situations, did you adopt a "win-win" approach in which you genuinely sought an agreement that would be fully satisfactory to both you and the other person? Or did you adopt a "win-lose" approach, in which you concentrated mainly on getting what you wanted? Remember: Agreements obtained through a confrontational, "win-lose" approach may be attractive in the short run, but they can come back to haunt you—with interest—later on.

Enhanced Learning

You may select any combination of the case options below to enhance your understanding of the chapter material.

- **Appendix 1: Case Studies –** Thirteen cases provide opportunities to apply chapter concepts to realistic entrepreneurial situations. These brief cases call for careful analysis of real business problems and ask you to think about potential solutions.

- **Appendix 2: Video Case Library –** Nine cases are tied directly to video segments from the popular PBS television series *Small Business School*. These cases and video segments give you unparalleled access to today's entrepreneurs, with expert advice and insights on how to start, run, and grow a business.

■ **Comprehensive Cases –** Visit the book support Web site at http://baron.swlearning.com for cases detailing real businesses whose successes and setbacks illustrate each stage of the entrepreneurial process. You will conduct in-depth analysis of entrepreneurial challenges through well-developed case studies.

Notes

1. Gomez-Mejia, L., Balkin, D.B., & Cardy, R.L. 2001. *Managing human resources.* 3rd ed. Upper Saddle River, NJ: Prentice-Hall.

2. Lelux, B. 2000. Riding the wave of IPOs. In S. Birley & D.F. Muzyka (eds.). *Mastering entrepreneurship.* London: Prentice-Hall.

3. See note 2.

4. Thompson, L. 1998. *The mind and heart of the negotiator.* Upper Saddle River, NJ: Prentice-Hall.

5. Pruitt, D.G., & Carnevale, P.J. 1993. *Negotiation in social conflict.* Pacific Grove, CA: Brooks/Cole.

6. See note 4.

7. Baron, R.A., & Byrne, D. 2002. *Social psychology.* 10th ed. Boston: Allyn & Bacon.

8. Isen, A.M. 1984. Toward understanding the role of affect in cognition. In R.S. Wyer & T.K. Srull (eds.), *Handbook of social cognition.* Hillsdale, NJ: Erlbaum, vol. 3, 179–236.

9. See note 5.

10. Forgas, J.P. 1995. Mood and judgment: The affect infusion model (AIM). *Psychological Bulletin* 117: 39–66.

11. Shane, S. (in press). *The individual-opportunity nexus approach to entrepreneurship.* Amsterdam: Kluwer.

12. Arking, R. 1991. *Biology of aging: Observations and principles.* Englewood Cliffs, NJ: Prentic-Hall.

13. Park, D.C., Smith, A.D., Lautenschlager, G., Earles, J.L., Frieseke, D., Zwahr, M., & Gaines, C.L. 1996. Mediators of long-term memory performance across the lifespan. *Psychology and Aging* 11: 621–637.

14. Shimamura, A.P., & Jurica, P.J. 1994. Memory interference effects and aging: Findings from a test of frontal lobe function. *Neuropsychology* 8: 408–412.

15. Sternberg, R.J., Wagner, R.K., Williams, W.M., & Horvath, J.A. 1995. Testing common sense. *American Psychologist* 50: 912–927.

16. Levinson, D.J. 1986. A conception of adult development. *American Psychologist* 41: 3–13.

17. Zimmerer, T.W., & Scarborough, N.M. (1996). *Entrepreneurship and new venture formation.* Upper Saddle River, NJ: Prentice-Hall.

18. Kisfalvi, V. 2002. The entrepreneurs' character, life issues, and strategy making: A field study. *Journal of Business Venturing* 17: 489–518.

Appendix 1: Case Studies

CHAPTER TWO

EXAMINING THE INDUSTRY

John Hargan and Rita Maylor decided to launch a new business to produce and distribute noncarbonated, high-quality soft drinks. They decided on a location in Colorado partly because they believed access to high-quality, pure water would provide them with a competitive edge. A business consultant recommended they construct a comprehensive business plan that would include a clear and thorough assessment of the beverage industry. This exercise should help them understand their challenges and help position this new product. The two partners have spent two months of their spare time (since they both work for another employer full-time) trying to gather research to validate their idea. Because their current employer is not in the beverage industry, they are struggling to find sources of information. John and Rita realize that before any type of viable business plan can be developed, the beverage industry needs to be assessed. The specific elements of this type of assessment are unclear to both of them, however.

Questions

1. What elements of the industry should John and Rita examine?
2. Is the beverage industry a good industry for launching a start-up? Why or why not?
3. Is there a source of opportunity for a new business here? If so, what is it? If not, why not?
4. Is this an opportunity that favors new firms? Why or why not?

Source: From Entrepreneurship: Theory, Process, Practice with InfoTrac College Edition 6th Edition by Kuratko/Hodgetts. Copyright 2004. Reprinted with permission of South-Western, a division of Thomson Learning: http://www.thomsonrights.com. Fax 800-730-2215.

CHAPTER THREE

PROFESSIONAL SPORTS AUTHENTICATOR GROWING AN INTERNET SERVICE BUSINESS®

David Hall is no Mark McGwire. He wasn't even much of a Little League slugger. Yet Hall, 51, does have a pretty good eye.

He and his crack team at eight-year-old Professional Sports Authenticator (PSA), based in Newport Beach, Calif., can spot a phony 1991 Topps Sammy Sosa card. They can pick out a doctored 1953 Topps Mickey Mantle #82 by holding a magnifying glass to the card's edges. And they've shown a knack for turning that skill—the grading of collectible sports cards—into a fast-growing enterprise.

Hall chalks up some of PSA's success to the recent wave of sports-card trading on the Internet, which has made the company's card-authentication service all the more popular, because on-line buyers purchase cards sight unseen. Not content with the niche, however, Hall is swinging for more distant fences. PSA and its corporate parent, Collectors Universe, are trying to leverage the PSA brand in bold ventures linked to Internet auctions and, strange as it seems, DNA marking. Previously, they had scored a marketing coup: tying PSA's name to Mark McGwire and Sammy Sosa, the stars of the 1998 home-run derby.

The company can afford to think big. Owing to the hoopla surrounding McGwire and Sosa, PSA's card-grading business has been booming. Calls to its 800 number tripled during the home-run mania season, soaring from 600 to 1,800 in a four-week stretch. Two receptionists quit because they couldn't hack the volume. By year's end, claims Hall, the number of cards the company was grading—it evaluates a card's condition on a scale from one to 10—had increased almost fivefold, to roughly 80,000 cards a month.

"It just kind of exploded," says Hall, who's also chairman of Collectors Universe. Besides PSA, which has 35 employees, Collectors Universe runs a coin grading service, an Internet company featuring a wide assortment of collectibles-related Web sites, and a music collectibles business. Hall declines to provide PSA's revenues for past years but projects a total of $30 million in sales this year for all Collectors Universe businesses. However, given that PSA charged an average of $15 for each of the 370,000 cards the company says it graded last year, it's easy to do the math for that portion of the business. The card-grading business (covering football, basketball, hockey, and baseball cards) has apparently been very good to PSA.

Indeed, veteran sports-card dealers say the company has almost single-handedly created widespread demand for neutral third-party grading in the $700-million-a-year trade in collectible sports cards. Now few collectors would think of spending big money on a card that PSA hadn't inspected. "People who call our number or fax us, or E-mail us, are asking for one thing," says Levi Bleam, the owner of 707 Sports Cards, in Plumsteadville, Pa. "They're asking for PSA-graded cards."

Winning the kind of brand recognition PSA now commands hasn't come easy. A native Californian and a rare-coin nut from an early age, Hall founded Professional Coin Grading Service, one of PSA's sister companies, in 1986, before turning to sports cards. Hall was convinced that just as coin collectors relied on grading experts, sports-card hobbyists needed a way to be sure that the vintage cards they were buying were real and hadn't been recut or reglossed to hide decades of wear and tear. But convincing dealers was a different matter.

PSA president Stephen Rocchi remembers spending many a fruitless weekend at sports-card conventions trying to sell dealers on the need for third-party grading. The vast majority, he says, had zero interest in letting an outsider like PSA inspect—and potentially diminish the selling price of—their wares.

For its first three years, PSA lost an average of $10,000 a month and stayed afloat only through regular capital infusions from Hall's successful coin-grading business. Gradually, though, dealers began submitting their cards for PSA grading as more card buyers demanded it. By 1996 thousands of PSA-graded cards were circulating at sports-card shows, says Rocchi, and PSA was grading almost 10,000 cards a month.

Now, thanks in part to the wave of trading on the Internet, the demand for the company's services has snowballed even more. A sports-card buff jittery about on-line buying may be far less likely to balk if the 1915 "Shoeless" Joe Jackson he wants carries PSA's seal of approval. Consequently, dealers eager to sell on the Internet have first been shipping cards to PSA to grade, in ever-increasing numbers.

PSA, according to Web-commerce experts, is one of a handful of companies performing a vital new function: giving peace of mind to people making on-line, sight-unseen purchases. [Another] such business, Schiffman Grow & Co., an accounting firm based in Columbus, Ohio, inspects commercial Web sites, awarding some Internet entrepreneurs its seal of approval. Still another company, i-Escrow, based in San Mateo, Calif., offers a third-party escrow service. It holds on-line shoppers' payments in a bank account until the goods or services have been received. "In a lot of regards, the Internet is still the wild, wild West," says Michael Brader-Arje, founder and CEO of OpenSite Technologies, based in Research Triangle Park, N.C. Companies like PSA, he adds, are helping to make the new frontier far safer.

Questions

1. How did David Hall go about recognizing the opportunity he is exploiting in his company, PSA?

2. What conditions or factors generated this opportunity? Did they exist ten years ago? Ten years ago?

3. Do you think that his application of techniques used for grading rare coins to grading sports cards shows creativity? If so, why? If not, why?

Source: From "Ticket to the Show." INC: The Magazine for Growing Companies by Susan Hansen. Copyright 1999 by Bus Innovator Group Resources/INC. Reproduced with permission of Bus Innovator Group Resources/INC in the format Textbook via Copyright Clearance Center.

CHAPTER FOUR

TIX4U.COM

Growing up in the Southeast, Randy Lee had two passions—music and sports. Some of his best memories were traveling with his dad to a large city in a neighboring state to watch major league baseball and football games. Inevitably, Randy and his dad would arrive at the stadium in plenty of time to negotiate with others to trade tickets for better seats. They would always have a couple of extra tickets to sell in case they needed more money to pay for their upgraded seats.

When Randy attended college in the same city, he found himself again negotiating ticket sales and trades for music concerts. He became so well-known that many students, and even some professors, approached him for tickets to sold-out shows and sporting events. Randy majored in computer science, and after graduation, he moved back home to work in a small IT department with a manufacturing company.

Although working full time, Randy never lost his passion for sporting events and concerts. After a couple of months, Randy developed a Web site, TIX4U.com, for customers who wanted to trade concert tickets over the Internet. His business strategy was fairly simple. He developed a message board for users who were interested in buying, selling, or trading tickets to contact each other. For this service, he would charge a yearly membership fee.

What started out as a part-time endeavor quickly grew. Randy resigned from his IT position after only six months to devote his energy to running the business full time. Customers from several surrounding states had bought memberships, and he eventually began hiring employees to help with the growing workload.

Seven years after he started TIX4U.com, his hometown had turned into a city. Corporate sponsors lobbied for, and were awarded, expansion franchises in two major league sports. This was on top of two minor league teams that were already there. The minor league teams generated a lot of excitement and fan support, and he had already expanded his company's services to provide a bulletin board for these sports fans. Now, with the major league teams on their way, Randy was both excited and overwhelmed.

TIX4.com's staff had grown from one to 17 full-time employees over the last seven years. Randy estimated that his company's size would need to double, if not triple, to handle the increased demand for tickets with year-round sports games and concerts. While exciting, these changes created a unique set of challenges for Randy. He realized that he needed a comprehensive plan that would provide strategic guidance for him and his growing number of employees. The company had started out small, but dramatic changes in the environment meant that he would need to make significant investments in computer hardware and personnel to meet this growing demand. These challenges and opportunities now surpassed Randy's ability to effectively manage them alone. If he was going to remain successful and capitalize on the growing market, he would need a business strategy to provide operational plans for both the short and long term. Randy was overwhelmed and not sure where to begin. How could he develop a strategic plan that would give TIX4U.com a competitive advantage and better ensure its future viability?

Questions

1. What government policies and regulation will Randy Lee have to consider as the number of employees in his company rises? Which are most important?

2. How has the changing business environment created problems for TIX4U.com? What opportunities have been created these changing condition?

3. When Randy begins developing a comprehensive business strategy, he will almost certainly do so in consultation with some of his top employees. What kind of errors in decision making should he be aware of, and guard against?

Source: From Management: Challenges for Tomorrow's Lenders with Xtra! CD-ROM and InfoTrac College Edition 4th Edition by Lewis/Goodman/Fandt. Copyright 2004. Reprinted with permission of South-Western, a division of Thomson Learning: http://www.thomsonrights.com. Fax 800-730-2215.

CHAPTER FIVE

TRILOGY SOFTWARE, INC.

As a student at Stanford University, Joe Liemandt did part-time consulting jobs for various Palo Alto computer companies. On these consulting jobs, he noticed that computer companies were very inefficient in selling and delivering their products. "He was surprised at how primitive the process was. Much of it was handwritten, using cumbersome inventory manuals and often requiring lengthy consultation between the company's salespeople and its engineers." Intrigued by this order-processing (or sales configuration) problem, Liemandt began to work on a software idea that would become the foundation of his software development company.

Liemandt saw opportunity stamped all over the sales configuration problem. His research on the problem revealed that other companies like IBM and Hewlett-Packard were working on it as well. With this kind of competition he worried that his window of opportunity was closing. So a few months before graduation in 1990, 21-year-old Joe Liemandt dropped out of Stanford to start Trilogy Software. He convinced four classmates to join him, three of whom juggled classes and work until they graduated.

Liemandt says, "Starting Trilogy was the easy part. Keeping it going in the early years wasn't." Venture capitalists were not interested in investing in Trilogy. To keep the firm financially afloat, Liemandt took consulting jobs and leveraged one credit card against another, having 22 credit cards outstanding at one point. After moving the company to Austin, Texas, in 1991, Hewlett-Packard signed a $3.5 million contract with Trilogy for sales configuration software and support services. Hewlett-Packard in effect abandoned its own effort to develop sales configuration software.

Soon other big customers purchased Trilogy's software. Called *Selling Chain*, the software enabled companies to "use computers to configure orders for a range of products from airplanes to shoes to telephone switches, and to perform other complex tasks." Boeing, for instance, used *Selling Chain* to cut the cost of processing aircraft orders. A Boeing 747 contains more than six million parts, and customers can select from hundred of options. Without Trilogy's software, the sales configuration process required a salesperson to make numerous customer visits. The salesperson also had to spend considerable time working with Boeing engineers "to make sure all the chosen pieces fit together, renegotiating the price at every step." However, use of the *Selling Chain* software enabled the salesperson to make a single visit to a customer and, using a laptop computer, to configure the 747 complete with a price quote. This was possible because *Selling Chain* knew "which parts go together and how much they cost."

Trilogy's business grew rapidly. For more than 10 years now, the company has provided sales configuration technology and tools to the largest companies in the computer equipment manufacturing industry, including enterprise server and storage manufacturers such as Hewlett-Packard, NCR, Motorola and SGI. Trilogy also provides guided selling applications to the computer industry. These applications help manufacturers "market and sell products and services online and across all sales channels, with solution discovery and customization, customer-specific pricing, order management, and more."

Trilogy has become one of the largest privately owned enterprise software companies. It specializes in developing e-business solutions for other companies in the computer, automotive, communications, and financial services industries. Trilogy provides industry-specific solutions that "help large enterprises increase the effectiveness, efficiency, and profitability of customer-facing activities like sales, marketing, and service."

What is the secret to Trilogy's astounding growth and success? Liemandt credits Trilogy's success to the types of people the company hires and how they are treated. Most of Trilogy's new employees come from computer science departments at top-flight schools such as MIT, Harvard, Carnegie-Mellon, Rice, Stanford, and Berkeley. Trilogy attracts top talent by giving employees a lot of responsibility right away. One 22 year old, in describing the attraction of working for Trilogy, says the company gives people more responsibility than they think they can possibly handle and then lets them go do the job. According to Liemandt, "What matters is the ability to learn, adapt, and figure out what the answer is. You've got to be willing to get in over your head and struggle to make things happen." Trilogy expects "everyone in the company to demonstrate leadership capability, regardless of their role."

Liemandt also looks for risk takers. He says, "You've got to be willing to jump off a cliff for your idea." Indeed, a significant element of Trilogy's training for new recruits focuses on developing their risk-taking propensity. Liemandt asserts that "he learned the hard way that taking risks and suffering the consequences are a crucial part of business. And he wants new hires to understand the experience firsthand."

Liemandt puts Trilogy's college recruits through a rigorous three-month-long corporate boot camp known as Trilogy University. During the first month, training sessions last from 8:00 a.m. until midnight. In the second week, new hires are divided into teams and given three weeks to complete difficult projects. Teams that do well win a two-day trip to Las Vegas, where Liemandt also encourages the recruits to take risks. The objective of Trilogy University is "to develop creative people who work well in teams, adapt to swift changes in customer demands—and take chances." Liemandt maintains that nothing "brings a group of people together like risk."

"By hiring great people and giving them mission-critical responsibilities from the first day on the job," Trilogy is better able to respond to competitive challenges and achieve its goals.

Questions

1. Joe Liemandt appears to be hiring only people similar to himself for his company. So far, this has worked well, but do you perceive any potential problems in continuing this policy?

2. Do you think that the policy of "giving people more responsibility than they think they can possibly handle" is a good one? Why? Could it possibly generate problems for the company? What kind?

3. If everyone in the company is expected to demonstrate leadership, can this lead to confusion over specific roles—who is supposed to do what?

Source: From Organizational Behavior: Foundations, Realities, and Challenges 4th Edition by Nelson/Quick. Copyright 2003. Reprinted with permission of South-Western, a division of Thomson Learning: http://www.thomsonrights.com. Fax 800-730-2215. This case was written by Michael K. McCuddy, The Louis S. and Mary L. Morgal Professor of Christian Business Ethics and Professor of Management, College of Business Administration, Valparaiso University. This case was developed from material contained on Trilogy's Web site at http://www.trilogy.com and in the following articles: J. Maloney & E. Brown, "So You Want to Be a Software Superstar," *Fortune* (June 10, 1996): 104–111; J. McHugh, "Holy Cow, No One's Done This!" *Forbes* (June 3, 1996): 122–128; E. Ramstad, "High Rollers: How Trilogy Software Trains Its Recruits to Be Risk Takers," *The Wall Street Journal* (September 21, 1998): A1 & A10.

CHAPTER SIX

STEGMART
Projecting Financial Requirements®

Angela Martin is a sophomore English major attending Central State University, a small liberal arts college in Missouri. She is president of the journalism club, which is where she first met her dorm roommate and good friend Ashlie Stegemoller. Stegemoller is a junior computer science major. Martin and Stegemoller have been discussing the possibility of a new business venture. After months of brainstorming, they have agreed to start a venture that would offer students and local businesses help in preparing term papers and reports. Both young entrepreneurs recently attended a local seminar entitled "How to Start a New Business." From this experience, they realized the need for preparing pro forma financial statements to obtain necessary financing and also to help them better visualize the merits of the venture.

Research Findings

Research indicates an unfulfilled demand for quality report-preparation services on campus. Market projections estimate a potential volume of 19,200 reports a year from Central State's students. Additionally, there are over 100 small businesses within two miles of the university that have indicated an interest in the service.

The majority of the students at Central State University are enrolled in classes that require two or three reports each semester, ranging from 5 to 50 pages in length. The venture's secondary target market consists of businesses in the nearby city of Emmett, Missouri, which has an SMA (Standard Metropolitan Area) population of approximately 150,000. There are two office building complexes within two miles of the university, each containing over 50 small businesses.

Statement of Financial Assumptions

Drawing on their findings, Martin and Stegemoller have made the following observations:

1. Sales projections related to the preparation of student reports and term papers are based on the following assumptions:
   a. Eighty percent of the 12,000 students at the university, or 9,600 students, prepare at least two reports each 12-month period. This gives a projection of 19,200 reports ($9,600 \times 2 = 19,200$).
   b. The firm will get 3 percent of the student market in the first year, which will increase to 5 percent and 7 percent in the following two years, respectively.
   c. Student reports will average 16 pages in length, for which the firm will receive $20 per report.

2. Revenue forecasts associated with the businesses needing the firm's services are based on the following assumptions:
   a. Sixty percent of the 100 local businesses will need at least 10 reports each 12-month period.
   b. The firm will obtain 6 percent of the business market in the first year, which will increase to 10 percent and 12 percent in the following two years, respectively.
   c. Business reports will average 30 pages in length, for which the firm will receive $40 per report.

3. On average, students will want one copy of their report in addition to the original; businesses will want five copies. The firm will charge $0.06 a page for copies.

4. Practically all copies of reports will be bound, for a charge of $1 per copy.

5. The effective income tax rate will be 20 percent.

6. The firm will extend credit to its business customers. Accounts receivable should be about 15 percent of annual business sales, and inventories should run about 12 percent of annual total sales. However, suppliers are expected to provide credit to the firm, which is estimated at 6 percent of annual sales.

7. The average cost of producing each report is estimated to be $12 in labor and $0.50 in materials.

Martin and Stegemoller have an option for a rent-free office in the university's student activities building. This arrangement was negotiated based on an understanding that they will provide the university with a special pricing schedule after 12 months of operation.

The initial operation will include two personal computers with word-processing, spreadsheet, and database software. One laser printer and two photocopying machines will also be needed. The total equipment costs will be as follows:

Computers	$12,000
Printers and copiers	$ 5,000
Total equipment costs	$17,000

The equipment will be depreciated on a straight-line basis over a five-year life expectancy.

Financing is expected to come from the following sources:

■ As the founders, Martin and Stegemoller will each invest $2,000 in the business.

■ Additional equity will be raised in the amount of $4,000 from an outside investor: $3,000 will be invested at startup and the remaining $1,000 at the conclusion of the first year of operations.

■ The National Bank of Emmett has agreed to loan the firm $3,000, to be repaid within one year, but with the option to renew each year, provided the business is doing well. The interest rate is expected to be 9 percent.

■ The $17,000 in equipment will be purchased with a down payment of $7,000; the remaining balance will be paid off at $2,000 in principal per year, plus interest due on the remaining balance at an interest rate of 10 percent.

Question

Given the above information, help Martin and Stegemoller prepare pro forma income statements, balance sheets, and cash flow statements for the first three years of their operation.

Source: From Small Business Management: An Entrepreneurial Emphasis with CD-ROM 12th Edition by Longenecker/Moore/Petty. Copyright 2003. Reprinted with permission of South-Western, a division of Thomson Learning: http://www.thomsonrights.com. Fax 800-730-2215.

CHAPTER SEVEN

ROBINSON ASSOCIATES, INC.

Business Plan for a New Venture®

This case presents a business plan for a proposed management consulting firm. This plan was prepared by a graduate student in business who set up the firm to support himself both during and after his period of graduate study. A few details, such as name and location, have been changed, but the situation is real.

Business Plan for David R. Robinson Minneapolis, Minnesota

Scope of the Business

Personal. I plan to start a business consulting service in conjunction with USA Consultants (a nationwide business consulting firm).

History of USA Consultants. USA is over 30 years old. It originated in Boston and Atlanta. It started out as P. Miller Management Consultants. The name changed to USA in 1972. Paul Miller III is the current president of USA, which has over 160 consultants in more than 50 cities.

Specific Areas of Focus

Company (Brochure Available on Request)

1. Analysis Phase
2. Implementation Phase (selected examples)
   a. Marketing programs
   b. Organization planning
   c. Personnel training programs
   d. Cost reduction programs
   e. Loan package preparation
   f. Inventory control systems
   g. Financial control and reporting
   h. Mergers and acquisitions
   i. Strategic business planning
   j. Business evaluation

Personal. With my accounting background (CPA–inactive) and current experience consulting with small businesses, I would concentrate on:

1. Analysis phase
2. Implementation phase—especially on:
   a. Organization planning
   b. Loan package preparation
   c. Strategic business planning
   d. Financi al control and reporting systems
3. USA continuing education programs in various areas in which I could update my skills.

Goals

Personal

1. I plan to begin the business July 1 and operate it part-time for three months. I will limit my hours to 32 per week. I will still be eligible for full-time benefits including health insurance and tuition remission. I will go into the business full-time starting October 1.

2. I plan to continue pursuing a Ph.D. in business administration. This is entirely compatible with the consulting business. (See attached projected cash flow statements [Table C8-1].)

Financial. I plan to reach the following cumulative gross billing goals [Table C8-2]:

Six months	$ 22,500
Twelve months	$ 86,500
Eighteen months	$137,000
Twenty-four months	$191,000

Management Capability

See attached résumé [Figure C8-1].

Strong Points

1. Four years of consulting experience with Small Business Development Centers.

2. Admitted to Ph.D. program at the university in business administration. Major: Management; minor: International Business, with current G.P.A. of 4.0, out of possible 4.0.

3. Accepted by USA. USA advertised in The *Wall Street Journal, Inc.*, and *USA Today*. To date, they have received over 3,000 applications but approved only 158.

4. Education will be continued through schooling and USA's continuing education program.

Marketing

Competition

External:

1. Review of the Minneapolis–St. Paul *Webb's Directory* on management consultants shows no direct competition.

2. Typically, consultants specialize in one to three areas. No firm can offer the wide range of services that USA can.

Internal: There are two other USA consultants in the Minneapolis–St. Paul area. One started his business in December of last year, and the second is just starting. Both are on the Minneapolis side of the river. There appears to be plenty of room in the market for a third USA consultant.

Customer Analysis. USA billing rates are $125/hour to $300/hour. These rates will preclude very small businesses from using my services in most cases. The firms that appear to be best suited for using a USA consultant would be firms with 30 to 400 employees. These firms can be identified through the use of *Webb's Directory* and various other publications.

Reaching the Customer. There are three primary methods to reach customers:

1. *Salesperson.* USA will assist the consultant in hiring and training.

2. *MAS services to small accounting firms.* USA works with accounting firms that do not have an MAS department to provide them with consulting services.

3. *Personal contacts.* Extensive contacts have been developed on both sides of the river and will be used to assist in identifying potential customers.

Market Trends. Many businesses today are downsizing. Typically, the person that businesses are outplacing is in middle management. Businesses will still have the same problems as before. Businesses will then turn to a consultant to assist in solving these problems.

Financial

Amount Needed:

$ 7,500	Initial deposit*
$ 1,000	Supplies**
$ 4,000	Working capital***
$12,500	Bank financing
$ 9,500	Personal collateral (certificate of deposit)
$22,000	Total

*To be refunded when $50,000 in gross billings have been achieved.
**Supplies include Webb's Directory, file cabinet, office supplies, shelving, business subscriptions, and business phone.
***See attached cash flow statement for details.

Questions

1. Does this business plan include all the major components discussed in this chapter? If not, what's missing?

2. What part of the plan would impress a potential investor most favorably? What part seems weakest?

3. What additional information should be added to strengthen the plan?

4. What would be main points the founder of Robinson Associates Inc. would want to make to potential investors in a face-to-face presentation? In other words, what points would be most impressive to potential investors?

Source: This case was prepared by Philip R. Carpenter. From Small Business Management: An Entrepreneurial Emphasis with CD-ROM 12th Edition by Longenecker/Moore/Petty. Copyright 2003. Reprinted with permission of South-Western, a division of Thomson Learning: http://www.thomson-rights.com. Fax 800-730-2215.

CHAPTER EIGHT

A QUESTION OF INCORPORATION

The Harlow family opened its first motel in 1982. Initially, business was slow. It took almost 11 months to break even and three years for the Harlows to feel that the operation was going to be a success. They stuck with it, and by 1987 they were able to increase the size of the motel from 28 to 50 rooms. They expanded again in 1989, this time to 100 rooms. In each case, the motel's occupancy rate was so high that the Harlows had to turn people away during the months of April to September, and the occupancy rate was 85 percent during the other months. By industry standards, their business was one of the most successful motels in the country.

As they entered the 1990s, Harold and Becky Harlow decided that, rather than expanding, they would be better off buying another motel, perhaps in a nearby locale. They chose to hire someone to run their current operation and spend most of their time at the new location until they had it running properly. In 1992, they made their purchase. Like their first motel, the second location was an overwhelming success within a few years. From then on, the Harlows bought a number of new motels. By 1999, they had seven motels with an average of 100 rooms per unit.

During all of this time, Becky and Harold kept their own financial records, bringing in a certified public accountant only once a year to close the books and prepare their income tax returns. Last week the new accountant asked them how long they intended to keep running seven motels. The Harlows told him that they enjoyed the operation and hoped to keep at it for another ten years, when they planned to sell out and retire.

Harold admitted that trying to keep all of the motels going at the same time was difficult but noted that he had some excellent managers working for him. The accountant asked him whether he would consider incorporating. "If you incorporate," he said, "you could sell stock and use the money to buy more motels. Additionally, you could keep some of the stock for yourself so you could maintain control of the operation, sell some for expansion purposes, and sell the rest to raise some money you can put aside in a savings account or some conservative investment. That way, if things go bad, you still will have a nest egg built up." The accountant also explained to Harold and Becky that, as a partnership, they are currently responsible for all business debts. With a corporation, they would have limited liability; that is, if the corporation failed, the creditors could not sue them for their personal assets. In this way, their assets would be protected, so the money Harold would get for selling the stock would be safely tucked away.

The Harlows admitted that they had never really considered another form of organization. They always assumed that a partnership was the best form for them. Now they are willing to examine the benefits of a corporation, and they will go ahead and incorporate their business if this approach promises them greater advantages.

Questions

1. What are the advantages and disadvantages of a partnership?

2. Contrast the advantages and disadvantages of a partnership with those of a corporation.

3. Should the Harlows incorporate? Why? Why not? If they do incorporate, should the company be a regular C-corporation of an S-Corporation? Why?

4. Would the LLC option be useful for them?

5. Should they possibly consider franchising their operation, since it seems to be so successful?

Source: From Entrepreneurship: Theory, Process, Practice with InfoTrac College Edition 6th Edition by Kuratko/Hodgetts. Copyright 2004. Reprinted with permission of South-Western, a division of Thomson Learning: http://www.thomsonrights.com. Fax 800-730-2215.

CHAPTER NINE

SCRUBADUB AUTO WASH

Waxing Philosophical®

Imagine charging more than competitors for a number of your services, yet maintaining a higher market share and profit margin. ScrubaDub Auto Wash, based in Natick, Massachusetts, does just that. With eight locations and sales of more than $5 million, ScrubaDub is the largest auto-wash chain in the Boston area. And the company has continued its growth—posting annual sales increases of 10 percent in recent years—despite a long-lasting and punishing recession in its home state.

"Nineteen ninety-two was an absolutely disastrous year for the economy in Massachusetts, but it was one of the best years we ever had," recounts Marshall Paisner, who owns and operates the chain with his wife, Elaine, and their sons, Dan and Bob.

Their secret? ScrubaDub combines an expertise in the science of cleaning cars with a flair for the art of marketing. The company has turned an otherwise mundane chore—getting the car washed—into a pleasant service interlude. Employees sweat the details that define the experience for customers, and the company tracks [customers'] buying habits to improve customer service and boost sales. ScrubaDub then backs up its work with guarantees, ensuring that customers are satisfied with the results.

In short, ScrubaDub's managers and employees think from the customer's point of view, says Paul M. Cole, vice president of marketing services at the Lexington, Massachusetts, office of Mercer Management Consulting Inc. The ScrubaDub staff looks beyond the moment to anticipate how customers will feel about the company's services and its long-term role in the community . . . from the performance guarantees to Halloween charity events. "They're looking for every opportunity to demonstrate concern for customers," Cole says.

Details and Data

Better yet, ScrubaDub didn't need the resources of an industry giant to create its marketing and service programs. Instead, the 100-plus employee company has focused on cutting overhead—by automating functions such as cash management—to free up funds to invest in labor, computer operations and customer service.

Here are seven lessons from the car-wash chain that might apply to your business as well:

Pay attention to the details. Just as the hospitality industry wants travelers to feel pampered, the Paisners want customers to view the car-wash service as a pleasant experience. The first clues to this service philosophy: flower beds decorate the entrance to the wash, neatly groomed employees greet customers courteously, and car owners receive little treats such as peanuts as they enter the cleaning tunnel.

Inside, the cars are cleaned by an equipment system the Paisners configured for the most effective treatment possible (as opposed to the standard systems used by some competitors) and scrubbed with a soap that's exclusive to the chain. Meanwhile, any kids on board may be delighted to see cartoon characters like Garfield or Bart Simpson mounted on poles inside the tunnel. These familiar characters help calm children who are frightened when the washing machine descends on their family car—and thus allow their parents to relax. (Of course, kids like to be scared around Halloween, so then the chain decorates its tunnels like haunted houses.)

Once drivers emerge from the wash, they can go to a waiting room and get free coffee if they want the insides of their cars cleaned. Some customers—depending on the make of their car and the level of service they've chosen—have their wheels cleaned with a toothbrush. Others can go to the "satisfaction center," a final service checkpoint, for any extra attention they feel the car needs. The goal is to make sure customers feel well taken care of when they drive out of the lot.

Know the customer. ScrubaDub's marketing and service programs rely heavily on the tracking of customers' buying habits. For example, the company develops vehicle histories of its "club members," who spend $5.95 for a membership pass that entitles them to certain specials, such as a free wash after 10 paid cleanings. ScrubaDub uses a computer database to track the frequency of these customers' visits and the services purchased. Each time a member visits, an employee scans a bar-code sticker that's placed on the vehicle's window and logs information into the database.

Behind the scenes, the company analyzes the vehicle histories, along with other sales and profit data, to track buying habits and identify sales opportunities. To punch up its relatively slow business in the evening hours, for example, ScrubaDub introduced a "night wash" special with a $1 savings and doubled its volume. And if a review of the data shows that certain club members haven't been to the store for a while, the company sends out a "We miss you letter" to invite them back.

More recently, ScrubaDub has moved its vehicle histories out of the back office and onto the car-wash lot to improve its customer service. Now, when club members enter the car wash, sales advisors can call up their histories on a computer terminal. That way, they can address customers by name and remind them of services they've purchased before, such as an undercarriage wash, a special wax treatment, or a wheel cleaning.

What's more, employees can now use the histories to suggest service upgrades. If a customer usually gets a regular wash, for example, a sales advisor might recommend an undercarriage wash if the car has been coated by heavily salted roads. ScrubaDub counts on these special options to generate income above the base price of $5.95 (the average purchase above that level is $1.60), but it also wants employees to suggest only those services appropriate to the vehicle and the customer. The point-of-sale histories help guide the sales advisor to the customer's buying preferences.

Mine new prospects. ScrubaDub is always on the lookout for new prospects, using both mass-market means (such as radio jingles) and more targeted approaches to draw them in. New car buyers are obvious prospects, so the company works with local car dealers to distribute 30-day passes for free washes to their customers. To reach new home buyers, another target group, ScrubaDub uses an outside service to generate names from property-transfer records, then sends [those buyers] coupons for its services.

Last year, the company also launched a direct-mail campaign to reach people with $75,000 or more in income and homes close to one of its locations. The $30,000 mailing invited [those people] to become club members, who tend to be steady customers and purchase more add-on services. The mailing yielded more than 1,000 new members and generated a $45,000 return in its first year.

Fix the problems. If a customer believes the car wash has damaged his or her car in any way, the manager can spend up to $150 in labor or merchandise to fix the problem, no questions asked. Even if ScrubaDub is not at fault, the Paisners don't want customers driving away with a sour memory. When one customer's tire began to leak, for example, an employee spotted it, helped the customer change the tire and got the leaky one repaired. After a problem is fixed, says Elaine Paisner, ScrubaDub sends the customer "a little warm fuzzy" of flowers, cookies, or candy.

It also backs up its work with guarantees. Customers who purchase the basic wash can get a rewash if they're not satisfied, while club members are entitled to some added protection. In exchange for these customers' loyalty and investment, ScrubaDub offers them a free replacement wash if it rains or snows within 24 hours after they've left the lot. With some of the more expensive treatments, customers are guaranteed a clean car for three days. If the driver goes through a puddle or parks under a flock of pigeons, the company will wash the car again for free.

The benefit of such guarantees? They help a company stay competitive by acknowledging that a bad service experience eats away at a customer's good will, says Christopher W. L. Hart, president of TQM Group, a Boston consulting firm. Of course, this forces a company to determine what services it can afford to guarantee and to improve operations so that mistakes are the exception. But the cost of fulfilling guarantees should be viewed as a marketing investment and a second chance to make a good impression, not as a loss. "View it as something to celebrate," says Hart.

Monitor customer satisfaction. The Paisners use a variety of feedback mechanisms to evaluate the quality of their service at the eight locations. These include comment cards available to all customers and special reports which the managers personally ask some drivers to fill out each month. In addition, ScrubaDub recently added a new service questionnaire for customers getting the insides of their cars cleaned. This feedback mechanism, which a ScrubaDub manager adopted from a noncompeting operator, allows the company to make sure its inside-cleaning service is as detailed as customers expect.

Together, these forms give ScrubaDub enough feedback to rate overall customer satisfaction and calculate it on an index ranging to 100. To supplement its own research, the company also employs an outside firm to send people through the car wash and generate professional "shoppers' reports" on their experiences.

Use training and incentives to ensure good service. If you want high-quality service, says Paisner, then get the message across with your hiring, training, and pay practices. His company tries to set itself apart from competitors by hiring well-groomed employees, for example, and Paisner believes you get what you ask for in the recruiting process. "If you expect clean-cut kids who are willing to wear shirts and ties, you're going to get them," he says.

Once hired, employees go through various training modules in a classroom setting—an unusual practice in the car-wash business—to make sure service will be consistent from location to location. New employees also must meet the approval of their coworkers, since the staff at each location is viewed as a team with its own sales and expense goals to meet.

Indeed, up to half of employees' pay is tied to such goals; the incentive-pay proportion for each individual varies according to the sales and management content of his or her job. (Managers' incentive pay is more heavily weighted toward incentives than that of employees who vacuum the cars.) The teams also compete for contest awards, based on specific sales goals and their satisfaction ratings from customer feedback mechanisms.

Finally, several employees from each location join an improvement team that meets regularly to discuss new ways to enhance customer service. Employees recently designed a new "QuickShine" program, aimed at 4 percent of customers, comprised of a wax treatment that's applied in 25 minutes and provides 90 days of protection.

Demonstrate respect for the community. One of the subtler ways ScrubaDub impresses customers is by being a good neighbor. In these days of environmental awareness, ScrubaDub reclaims some of the water used and treats the dirt that's eliminated for recycling as fill. And the company links its decorated Halloween tunnels—always a neighborhood attraction—to the problem of child poverty and homelessness. ScrubaDub donates a portion of its sales over a three-day period to nearby homeless shelters that use the cash to buy winter clothes for their young clients.

Continuous Improvements

There's a final lesson to be drawn from ScrubaDub's operations, says Cole of Mercer Management. As inventive as the company has been, the managers didn't always start from scratch in devising ways to improve their marketing and customer service. Instead, they adapted ideas from other industries for their own use. Doctors and dentists, for instance, use cartoon characters to make kids happier. And many industries, including airlines and long-distance telephone companies, use sophisticated databases to track customers' buying habits and create new marketing programs.

The important point is to foster curiosity and a constant desire to improve among employees—an objective that's well within reach of small companies. "Small business can be at the cutting edge. It doesn't require monolithic companies with huge resources and lines of MBAs," says Cole.

Paisner, for his part, believes that the companies best poised for long-term growth are those committed to keeping new ideas in the pipeline. "There's no such thing as staying the same anymore. You have to be prepared to improve all the time," he says.

Questions

1. Which type of marketing philosophy has ScrubaDub adopted? Do you think this is the best choice? Why or why not?

2. What methods of marketing research were used by ScrubaDub? What additional research could it do to better understand its customers?

3. Do you think the promotional activities of ScrubaDub could be improved and/or extended? Explain.

4. What kind of forecasting method do you believe would be most appropriate to estimate ScrubaDub's market potential?

Source: From Small Business Management: An Entrepreneurial Emphasis with CD-ROM 12th Edition by Longenecker/Moore/Petty. Copyright 2003. Reprinted with permission of South-Western, a division of Thomson Learning: http://www.thomsonrights.com. Fax 800-730-2215.

CHAPTER TEN

THE FANTASTIC CATALOGUE COMPANY
Gaining a Competitive Advantage in the Mail Order Market®

It would be quite a wedding; the nuptials would take place in the stone chapel at the school from which the bride and groom had graduated. A reception for 400 guests would follow at the seaside home of the bride's parents. And from start to finish, the festivities would be imbued with Gatsby-esque elegance and style. Kathleen Mahoney, the bride herself, would see to that.

"I researched every aspect of it to the nth degree," she says, recalling the year of preparation. "I went haywire. I looked at 20 guest books, 20 bridesmaids' gifts, 20 different goblets, and so on. I wanted everything to be perfect."

Only the finest items would do, and finding them was frustrating. "There's a decentralized flow of information and goods in the wedding industry," Mahoney says. "There was no source for the upscale bride to find all the high-quality, tasteful wedding accessories she'd need." Her search took her to some 50 stores from Boston to San Francisco—gift shops, bridal boutiques, stationery stores.

All of which got her thinking. And by the time Mahoney and Ozzie Ayscue were married in June 1990, she had a new business on her hands. One-stop shopping for brides—the idea seemed irresistible. "It made intuitive sense to me, from my own experience," says Mahoney, 31. "I did some research with friends, and it made sense to everyone."

With 2.5 million weddings a year in the United States, a huge and lucrative market beckoned. The most promising targets, Mahoney reasoned, were career women, brides age 26 and up. They'd have the discretionary income to purchase topflight wedding goods but not the time to hunt for them.

How best to capitalize on the opportunity? She had dismissed a retail store as too limiting—hers was a national concept. A catalog, though, could put the products right at brides' fingertips. Mahoney was a catalog nut—she loved them. She didn't know the first thing about publishing one, she admits, but she figured she could learn.

The timing was fortunate. Mahoney was at American Express in Manhattan, in the direct-mail travel business. Ayscue was working for a travel-industry startup in San Francisco, where the couple had decided to settle. In late 1989, Mahoney left American Express and moved west, itching to take a crack at the catalog game.

It's no cakewalk to start a consumer catalog from scratch. Typically, retailers branch into mail order to augment established store-based operations. Other merchants tiptoe into the field by first advertising a few items in magazines. That's a cost-effective way of learning what sells while building a buyer file. Gradually, their product lines expand to fill full-blown catalogs. That's how Lands' End got started, for example.

One impediment to launching cold is capital. Catalogs inhale money. One might open a retail store for, say, $50,000, but that won't even get you off the ground in the catalog trade. It can easily cost $150,000 or more to get that first book in the mail, and follow-on editions are needed to build a buyer file. First come production costs for photography, copywriting, layout, and design—the "creative" end of the business. Then come costs for list rental, photographic color separation, printing, fulfillment, data processing, and postage. And even before that first order comes in, a startup needs to stock most of the featured items.

Mind you, all that happens before you know if the phone will ever ring. What if all the recipients throw your catalog in the trash? By definition, a startup has zero name recognition. And with an estimated 9,000 consumer catalogs in the country, mailing hundreds of millions of copies, it's easy to get lost in the clutter. Given that saturation, catalogs are creeping into ever smaller niches, staking out tiny franchises in hopes of survival.

Even so, most of them don't last long. Industry lore is replete with tales of first-timers who sank $1 million or more into a black hole before calling it quits. The market is ruthless in weeding out the glut. According to Leslie Mackenzie, publisher of *The Directory of Mail Order Catalogs*, between 1,000 and 1,500 of them fail or cease operations every year.

It is a business, analysts stress, in which you must get everything right. For instance, you might have terrific merchandise, a superb shipping operation, and a good mailing list. But you drop the ball on the creative—the product photos and the copy don't quite click. In that case, says consultant Bill Nicolai, "you are toast. It's a very tricky business, but it's one where sharp entrepreneurs can find their way in."

As Mahoney mapped her plans, however, she felt confident. A private investor had promised her $1 million, for 30 percent of the company, plus a $500,000 loan. That would sustain business for two years or more. The wedding niche, moreover, seemed solid. "I knew in my heart it was a good idea, so I didn't do much formal market research other than some demographics," she says.

She presented her concept to Jeff Haggin, chairman of the MoreNow Corp., a catalog-production firm in Sausalito, Calif. Over the years, MoreNow had handled the creative work for many prominent catalogers—Smith & Hawken, Sierra Club, and dozens more. Haggin knew the industry cold, and he thought Mahoney's idea had real merit.

That's all she needed to hear. And thus was born, in February 1990, The Wedding Fantastic, Inc.

With that start date, the earliest Mahoney could mail her first catalog would be July. That wasn't optimal. The big wedding season is spring and summer, and she would miss most of it. But impatient to get something into the market, she plunged in, headquartered in her San Francisco apartment.

Ayscue pitched in and joined the company in July as copresident. Two years as an analyst with Morgan Stanley had given him strong number-crunching skills. He'd handle strategic planning, statistical analysis, and financial management, while Mahoney concentrated on merchandising and marketing. Working with list brokers, she identified between 3.5 million and 10 million rentable names that met her demographic profile. Industry wisdom has it that you must mail at least 100,000 books to get a reasonable response. To reach her target market, she rented 100,000 names from Bloomingdale's, Williams Sonoma, Victoria's Secret, Neiman-Marcus, and 16 other upscale catalogers. She also rented from bridal-magazine subscriber lists. "I wanted to reach not just brides but brides' mothers, aunts, and shower throwers," she says.

From each list she rented a "cell" of 5,000 names. As a rule, names rent for about a dime each for onetime use, with rates rising to 15¢ depending on the number of "selects." That is, a renter can request names based on such factors as the timing, frequency, and monetary value of the customers' catalog purchases. Mahoney shot for people who had ordered through the mail in the previous six months, a common select.

The use of competing cells is key. It allows a cataloger to see which lists work best, so that when more names are needed, one can mine deeper into good ones. Essentially, a cataloger cold calls people in their mailboxes, and on average only 1.66 percent of the prospects respond. In other words, for every 100 catalogs mailed to rented names, better than 98 yield no sales. And those who do respond place smaller orders than established buyers.

To succeed, a mail-order operator must build a buyer file so that repeat customers represent a substantial percentage of total circulation. That can take several years. In Mahoney's model, the critical mass would be reached in 1994, when, she calculated, 12 percent of the 7 million people receiving her catalog would be buyers. That's the point at which her business would turn profitable. Her plan projected net sales that year of $12.5 million, with purchases averaging $95. That translates to more than 131,500 orders, enough that the company could amortize its costs over a far larger business base. General operating expenses, for example, would shrink from 41 percent of net sales in 1991 to 8 percent in 1994. Publicity expenses—creative work, color separation, printing, list rental—would drop from 89.5 percent of sales to 30 percent. And net income would rise from a 1991 loss of $837,000 to a positive $484,000.

Economies of scale work their magic all over the place once catalogs grow large, but reaching the magic number of 236,000 was, and remains, an ambitious goal. By comparison, Gump's, an old-line San Francisco gift cataloger, has a buyer file of about 100,000 names.

Pressing on, Mahoney contracted with MoreNow for production and arranged to have the book printed by Alden Press, a catalog specialty house in Elk Grove Village, Illinois. Fulfillment—everything from inventory storage to order taking to product packing—was farmed out to a small San Francisco company. United Parcel Service would handle deliveries.

Time was short. To get the catalog out in July, all the merchandise had to be selected and turned over to MoreNow by April 1, to start photography. It was a crash project, but Mahoney made it. Just three weeks after she and Ayscue exchanged vows, 100,000 copies of the inaugural edition of The Wedding Fantastic hit the mail.

It was very classy, a glossy, beautifully designed 32-pager featuring pretty much everything an upscale bride would need except a gown and a groom. Most items were the fruits of Mahoney's research for her own nuptials. There was a personalized Limoges porcelain ring box ($125), an heirloom-quality moiré hatbox ($298), a lace picture frame ($85), and even a sterling-silver service for the wedding cake (knife and server, $95 each).

The other half of the equation called for putting wedding gifts right in the catalog, to make it a complete wedding resource. They included some of Mahoney's personal favorites, among them a sterling ice-cream scoop ($95), a Zen rock garden ($48), and a birdhouse shaped like a Victorian manor ($145)—"mainstream products," she says, "but with a twist." In all, the catalog had 120 handpicked items.

Established catalogers know from experience how much inventory to carry. Startups don't know which items will be best-sellers and which will be dogs, and guessing wrong either way can be costly. "That's one of the hardest things we do," says Ayscue. "If you overstock, you are stuck with products. If you understock, you have to back-order and you might not make the sale." Going conservative, Mahoney went with a bare-bones inventory.

Competing not on price but on quality and uniqueness, she marked the products up 60 percent on average. On shipping and handling charges she aimed for break-even. The order form listed an 800 number and a fax number and allowed payment by check, money order, or credit card. On page three, a chatty "Dear brides" letter from Mahoney touted her commitment to top-quality goods and superb customer service, plus a full refund-exchange policy.

Getting that first book out was pricey. MoreNow's bill for the creative was $74,000—over $2,300 per page. Color separation added another $30,000. Alden charged $0.22 each for the 112,000 copies printed (there were some extras), and postage totaled $24,640. The combined in-the-mail cost came to $153,000, excluding list rental.

So handsome was the book that it won second prize that year in a new-catalog competition. "Even the most cynical of readers cannot help but be charmed by the catalog's sentimental approach to weddings," gushed trade journal *Catalog Age*.

The problem, however, was meager response, well below the 1.66 percent industry average for prospects. Response fell further when Mahoney "dropped" the second batch, 88,000, in September 1990, and further still when 127,000 went out in November. On the up side, however, the average order was $90, against an industry average of $61.

The new, updated spring edition hit the mail in three volleys, in February, March, and May of 1991. With 40 pages, it featured new items as well as top sellers from the first book. A total of 501,000 copies went out, half of them in May. With timing on the edition's side, the response rates climbed across the board. The new mailings generated sales of $917 per 1,000 catalogs, versus $547 for the first edition. Still, the response rate remained discouragingly below the industry standard, and the average order dipped to $81. "The wedding books were very narrowly targeted," Mahoney says now, "but we were taking a shotgun approach."

Needing something with broader appeal, she and Ayscue brought forth in September 1991 a brand-new catalog—The Christmas Fantastic. Weddings were seasonal, so why not launch a sister publication for the hottest shopping time of the year?

Working again with MoreNow, they developed a 32-page version known in the trade as a "slim jim." By virtue of its dimensions, 6 inches by 11 inches, it was cheaper to print and mail. To give the new catalog a better product mix, Mahoney and her employee sidekick, Georgina Sanger, scoured gift shows all over the country and developed several exclusives with California artists.

As with the wedding catalog, the products in The Christmas Fantastic were eclectic and fairly expensive. The new book featured about 150 items, everything from personalized tree ornaments and stockings to a hand-painted "kitty privy" and a $795 "Grand Mr. President" desk set. There were books and CDs, festive party invitations, even a beer-brewing kit. Some old favorites encored—the silver ice-cream scoop, the Victorian birdhouse, and the Zen rock garden.

The company sent out a test quantity of 112,000 catalogs in three mailings (early returns provide a "product read" that removes some inventory guesswork), and this time it hit pay dirt. The response rate topped the national norm, orders averaged $97, and sales per 1,000 catalogs mailed hit $1,584, beating the industry standard by $566.

So compelling were the overall economics that Mahoney and Ayscue retooled, shifting entirely away from the bridal market and into the gift business. There will be no new The Wedding Fantastic this spring, although some of its products are featured in full-page ads in bridal magazines, and a leftover 10,000 copies are available for $3 each. Instead, they launched another new catalog—The Celebration Fantastic—and changed their name to the Fantastic Catalogue Company.

The newest book, a 32-page slim jim, is billed as a way to "celebrate life's special occasions with romance, whimsy and imagination!" While some core items remain—the birdhouse, for one—the new catalog is heavy on unusual gifts for Easter, Mother's Day, Father's Day, graduations, anniversaries, and new babies. Its 120 items include everything from a complete gourmet picnic hamper for six ($525) to donkey and elephant earrings for election years ($34). Like Mahoney's other books, it strikes an upscale and upbeat tone.

"We think now we are sending the right message to the right people," she says. "Our targeting is getting more refined."

If The Celebration Fantastic yields results comparable with the Christmas edition's, as Mahoney expects, she will have a strengthening, nonseasonal business and a more secure foothold in the $2-billion mail-order consumer gift market.

But as they say, that's a big if. Having virtually abandoned the wedding niche, she is stepping into a gift sector already sated with some 630 catalog companies, many of them large and resource rich. The Fantastic Catalogue Company has to establish itself fast. "We need to become the household name, the completely trusted brand name for this whole celebration segment," Mahoney says.

To do that she feels she has to expand quickly. She'd like to circulate a million copies of The Christmas Fantastic this fall to aggressively build her buyer file from its current 15,000 names. But with the initial financing of $1.5 million fast depleting, that hinges on raising $1.25 million or so by summer. And another $1 million will be needed in 1993 to move The Celebration Fantastic beyond the test phase.

As the company expands and Mahoney increasingly understands exactly who her customer is, she has begun to focus on servicing that customer better. Toward that end, she brought the company's fulfillment operations in-house early this year, a move that will require more employees and might produce as-yet-unseen complications.

Questions

1. Do you think Mahoney has correctly assessed the basic nature of the competition she faces? Why or why not?

2. What is the competitive advantage Mahoney is trying to create? Do you agree with this appeal? Why?

3. What market segmentation strategy is The Fantastic Catalogue Company following?

4. How can this firm use customer service to gain a competitive advantage?

5. Do you think Mahoney leaped before looking? What should she have done differently?

CHAPTER ELEVEN

A PATENT MATTER

Technological breakthroughs in the machine industry are commonplace. Thus, whenever one company announces a new development, some of the first customers are that company's competitors. The latter will purchase the machine, strip it down, examine the new technology, and then look for ways to improve it. The original breakthroughs always are patented by the firm that discovers them, even though the technology is soon surpassed.

A few weeks ago Tom Farrington completed the development of a specialized lathe machine that is 25 percent faster and 9 percent more efficient than anything currently on the market. This technological breakthrough was a result of careful analysis of competitive products. "Until I saw some of the latest developments in the field," Tom told his wife, "I didn't realize how easy it would be to increase the speed and efficiency of the machine. But once I saw the competition's products, I knew immediately how to proceed."

Tom has shown his machine to five major firms in the industry, and all have placed orders with him. Tom has little doubt he will make a great deal of money from his invention. Before beginning production, however, Tom intends to get a patent on his invention. He believes his machine is so much more sophisticated and complex than any other machine on the market that it will take his competitors at least four years to develop a better product. "By that time I hope to have improved on my invention and continue to remain ahead of them," he noted.

Tom has talked to an attorney about filing for a patent. The attorney believes Tom should answer two questions before proceeding: (1) How long will it take the competition to improve on your patent? (2) How far are you willing to go in defending your patent right? Part of the attorney's comments were as follows: "It will take us about three years to get a patent. If, during this time, the competition is able to come out with something that is better than what you have, we will have wasted a lot of time and effort. The patent will have little value since no one will be interested in using it. Since some of your first sales will be to the competition, this is something to which you have to give serious thought. Second, even if it takes four years for the competition to catch up, would you be interested in fighting those who copy your invention after, say, two years? Simply put, we can get you a patent, but I'm not sure it will provide you as much protection as you think."

Questions

1. Given the nature of the industry, how valuable will a patent be to Tom? Explain.

2. If Tom does get a patent, can he bring action against infringers? Will it be worth the time and expense? Why or why not?

3. What do you think Tom should do? Why?

Source: From Entrepreneurship: Theory, Process, Practice with InfoTrac College Edition 6th Edition by Kuratko/Hodgetts. Copyright 2004. Reprinted with permission of South-Western, a division of Thomson Learning: http://www.thomsonrights.com. Fax 800-730-2215.

CHAPTER TWELVE

WHEN EVERYTHING ISN'T HALF ENOUGH

"You have 18 new messages." Norman Spencer looked at his watch, shook his head, and let out a sharp sigh. Was it possible that he had received 18 voice mail messages in the time he had spent at lunch and the gym? He'd only been gone for two hours.

He dropped into his desk chair and unhappily poked at the number 1 key to let the messages play.

The first was from Tim Carson, chief trader at Arrowhead Capital Management, the San Francisco investment firm that Norman had founded and where he was owner, president, and CEO. After 22 years in business, Arrowhead had about $25 billion in assets under management and was well known on Wall Street as a top-notch boutique firm, specializing in the quantitative analysis of small and midcap technology stocks. Over the years, Norman had put together one of the best teams of "quant jocks" in the business. But that wasn't the only reason Arrowhead had soared, and he knew it. The new economy was the rising tide that lifted all ships.

"Hi, Norm, it's me," Tim said, "just giving you the noon update. We're off to a great start today—up a point and a half against the market. Another fantastic week for us. That ought to cheer you up—and hey, I'll check in again at the close."

Norman hit the delete key and leaned back. Like everything else lately, Tim's news had left him feeling numb. He gazed out over San Francisco Bay from his 34th-floor office and wondered why anyone really cared how his firm performed on any given day. The market went up and the market went down. Same story, year in and year out.

Second message. "Hello, Norm. Frank Keller here. I wanted to remind you that there's a Permanent Endowment Committee meeting next Monday night at 7:30. We're really going to need you there this time, Norm—your leadership, that is. It makes such a difference. . . ." Norm punched the delete button to cut Keller off. He was sick and tired of the Permanent Endowment Committee; he was sick and tired of being a trustee at his daughter's private high school—period. Serving on the board had once been a real kick for him. They'd turned around the school, doubled the endowment, built a science building, and raised teachers' salaries enough to make a difference. Now all Norm wanted to do was find a gracious way to quit.

"Third message, sent at 12:08 pm." At first there was silence. Then someone on the other end was breathing unevenly. Finally: "Uh, Dad, this is Danny. It's after 12. You were supposed to meet me and Mom at Dr. Blanton's at 11:30. We'll keep waiting." More silence, then Dan again, this time whispering: "Dad, I think you might have forgotten. You've been forgetting a lot lately. I'm worried about you. . . ."

Again, Norm hit the delete key. The last thing he needed was a 13-year-old kid worrying about him. And what the heck were he and his mother doing at this Dr. Blanton's office in the middle of the day? They'd never mentioned any appointment to him. Or had they?

Norm cut off voice mail and reluctantly dialed home. First he'd have to deal with Dan's fretting, then Nancy's screeching. As it turned out, he got them both at once—on separate lines. The noise coming at him reminded Norman of everything he'd been going through for the past few months—half the world buzzing around him, wringing their hands and urging him to "get help" for his crankiness and insomnia; the other half marching back and forth, shouting at him to buck up and count his four million blessings.

Norman silently dropped the phone back into its cradle. He didn't have to listen. The truth was, he didn't have to do anything anymore. By every measure, Arrowhead was an unmitigated success. Yes, it had been tough at the beginning. Every start-up has its moments of difficulty, even its moments of staring straight into the headlights of failure. But these days, Arrowhead could boast 15 straight years of solid growth. The firm was making so much money now it felt illegal. No wonder so many breathless buyers were courting him, and dozens of potential institutional clients—some of them very major—were lined up at the door, clamoring to be let in.

As for his family, Norman didn't have to do anything else for them either. There was nothing left to buy. They had everything: the mansion in Pacific Heights, the yacht, and just for the heck of it, the new "cottage" in Nantucket. His 17-year-old daughter drove a BMW, his son was taking flying lessons in his own small plane, and recently his wife had found a new way to spend money: a personal feng shui adviser to help her redecorate the house—again.

And it wasn't as if Norman himself had been left out of the spoils. Over the past decade, he had accumulated every material possession a man could want. His whole life, he had wanted a 1965 Corvette. He owned several now. He'd wanted a pool. He had two—one inside the house and one outside. He'd wanted to dress well. His closet was now filled with suits made on Saville Row, most of which he never wore. These days, he didn't even know why he'd bought the stupid suits at $3,000 a pop. What a waste.

Norman gazed out his window again and felt a strange mix of defiance and sadness. I'm 48 years old, he told himself, and I've finally earned the right to say what I'm really thinking and to act the way I'm really feeling. I've finally earned the right not to answer every voice mail message, show up at every meeting, or remember every little detail about everyone's little life. I don't have to prove myself anymore. In fact, I don't even have to come into the office anymore. But I don't know what else to do. I just keep doing the same things I've always done—only now I do them without giving a damn. I wish the world would just go away.

Norman leaned back in his chair, covered his face in his hands, and, for the first time since he was a child, felt tears rise.

Questions

1. Do you think that Norman Spencer has good, satisfying relations with the other people in his life—people in his business, his family, friends? If he does not, why is this the case?

2. Do you think that Norman Spencer is suffering from *burnout*? If so, why, and what can he do about it?

3. Do you think that the person in this case manages conflict with others well or poorly? And what about his ability to influence others? Do you think he is high or low with respect to this skill?

4. Overall, what do you predict will happen to him—will he get his life straightened out, or experience more and more distress and unhappiness?

Source: Reprinted by permission of Harvard Business Review. From "When Everything Isn't Half Enough," by Suzy Wetlaufer, March/April 2000. Copyright 2000 by the Harvard Business School Publishing Corporation; all rights reserved.

CHAPTER THIRTEEN

WATERWAY INDUSTRIES

Waterway Industries was founded in the late 1960s as a small manufacturer of high-quality canoes. Based in Lake Placid, New York, the company quickly gained a solid reputation throughout the Northeast and began building a small customer base in the Pacific Northwest as well. By the late 1980s, Waterway was comfortably ensconced in the canoe market. Although earnings growth was fairly steady, CEO Cyrus Maher was persuaded by a friend to venture into kayaks. After Waterway began selling its own line of compact, inexpensive kayaks in 1998, Maher quickly learned that the decision was a good one. Most of Waterway's existing canoe customers placed sizable kayak orders, and a number of private-label companies also began contacting Maher about making kayaks for their companies. When Lee Carter was hired to establish a formal marketing department at Waterway, things really took off. Carter began bringing in so many large orders that the company had to contract with other manufacturers to keep up.

Managers began to envision the day when Waterway would be a major player in water sports equipment. They developed a long-range strategic plan that called for aggressive growth, new product designs, and nationwide marketing and distribution by 2003. Maher believes most employees are adjusting well to the faster pace at the company. Many of the shop-floor employees are outdoor enthusiasts who like making quality products that they and their friends use. Waterway has always had a relaxed, informal working atmosphere, where employees get along well, enjoy their jobs, and get their work completed on time. However, the greater work load means people have less time for horsing around, and they can no longer leave by 3 PM to enjoy canoeing or kayaking when the weather is good.

Maher thinks workers have been given adequate raises to compensate for the faster work pace, but he has recently been hearing complaints from the shop floor about inadequate pay. He recently turned down a request from the plant supervisor for additional hourly wage increases for top performers, insisting that wages were in line with what other local manufacturers were paying. Unfortunately, a new auto-motive parts plant offering a slightly higher wage recently lured away three of his best workers.

Several managers have also approached Maher about salary adjustments. Waterway's two designers suggested that they would be interested in equity (part ownership) in the company, whereby they would receive a share of the profits if their designs did well. Maher's response was to give the senior designer a modest pay raise and extra vacation and to increase the bonuses for both designers. Both seemed satisfied with the new arrangement. Waterway's CFO, on the other hand, recently left the company to take a position with a power boat manufacturer after Maher twice refused his request for a redesigned compensation package to include equity. Now, on a trip to the cafeteria to get a cup of coffee, Maher has just over-heard Lee Carter discussing a possible job opportunity with another company. He is well aware of the lucrative packages being offered to sales and marketing managers in the sporting goods industry, and he doesn't want to lose Carter. He would like to find a way to recognize her hard work and keep her at Waterway for at least a few more years.

Maher has asked you, the company's sole human resource manager, for advice about changing the company's compensation system. In the past, he has handled things informally, giving employees annual salary increases and bonuses, and dealing with employees one-on-one (as he did with the designers) when they have concerns about their current compensation. Now, Maher is wondering if his company has grown to the point where he needs to establish some kind of formal compensation system that can recognize employees who make outstanding contributions to the company's success.

Questions

1. Do you think that Waterway Industries is doing a good job of recruiting production employees? What steps could it take to find and attract people interested in the products it makes?

2. What's wrong with Waterway's current compensation policies for (a) shop-floor employees, and (b) managers? How could these weaknesses be corrected?

3. Should CEO Cyrus Maher re-consider his policy of refusing to give equity to key employees? Why? Why do you think he is reluctant to include equity in compensation packages for these people?

4. What else, aside from increase in compensation, can the company offer to employees to increase their motivation and their commitment—their desire to stay? (Hint: Changes in working hours or conditions might be useful

Source: Based on Robert D. Nicoson, "Growing Pains," *Harvard Business Review* (July-August 1996), 20–36.

CHAPTER FOURTEEN

THE BONNEAU COMPANY

An Entrepreneur's Experience in Exiting His Firm

Ed Bonneau was the founder of The Bonneau Company and had been the owner for some 30 years. He described his decision to sell his company and his experiences during the harvesting process:

I thought about selling the firm five years before I did. At that time, a friend of mine in a similar business had cashed out. His decision caused me to reflect on selling my firm also. The same people who bought his firm talked to us about combining the two companies; it would have been a good deal. However, I was a year late in starting. As we progressed in those conversations, two things happened. First, our company hit a dip with a major account, so it decreased our profits a bit. They then came back with a much lower offering price. Second, their company also experienced a downturn for whatever reason. Thus, if I had started the year before, it would have been perfect—it was our most profitable year ever.

What really prompted me to sell was the terrible time we were having in the business. We were not having a good year to begin with—probably a break-even or loss year. Then an account went down, costing us $5 million. That loss was the wakeup call that prompted me to try to figure out a way to get out of the business. I really became serious about selling the company and harvesting my investment.

When we encountered the loss, I didn't think that the company was in the right position to sell at that time. I thought we had to hunker down and operate for a while to get out of a bad situation. We could then start thinking about a sale. However, Benson Eyecare contacted me about a possible sale. I said I was interested if they were willing to look at the company and consider the bad year an aberration—to look at the firm's value without the loss. They said they would do so.

Bonneau was asked if he considered other options for exiting besides selling.

I really didn't know what other options I had. An IPO was suggested to me a number of times over the years. However, nobody ever explained to me the up-side of going public. I had some investment bankers come and look at our company to talk about going public; they said "Yeah, you can go public." They then asked me why I wanted to go public. I said "For one thing, I want some money out of the company. I have every dime I've got stuck in here." They responded that I couldn't do that. I asked what they meant. They said getting money out was not the purpose of going public. So I just quit thinking about it if I couldn't get something out of the firm. They said I could take a little, say $1 million. I wasn't interested in answering to other people about running the company if in fact I couldn't get any money out. Also, one of the disadvantages to me of going public would have been my competitors' gaining information about my company. When you have a very entrepreneurial company, that would really be distracting. They could know who your major accounts were and the volume you did; they could know some stuff they wouldn't otherwise know about your firm.

Bonneau offered the following description of how he determined the value of his company.

I don't know. They were the ones doing the valuation. I was just looking at the offer and negotiating with them in terms of what I thought the value of the company should be, but I didn't actually use a method to value the business. Neither did I have a value in mind in the beginning. When they approached us, I handled the negotiation through somebody else, and I didn't talk to them. They worked through the numbers, and only when they came back with their first offer did I start thinking in terms of what it should be; I started negotiating after the first offer. I thought the first offer was good, but we increased it a couple million dollars. But only when you sift through and read the fine print are you able to determine how good the offer is. It can be a big number, but you also have to consider the terms. The terms determine the eventual payout, and the likelihood of your receiving the value.

I was pleased with the value received. However, the value was bittersweet to me. I thought I was fortunate to get that amount of money for the company at the time. I knew that there was a previous point in time when the company was worth considerably more, but I was past that point—thus, the bittersweet. In looking at what had happened to the company, I thought we were fortunate to get what we did.

When asked to describe the harvesting process, Bonneau made the following comments.

I had gone through purchasing three companies, but they weren't anything like this. The complications of doing this deal were unbelievable to me, as well as the effort required to do it. All of my key people had to work on the sale, but they also had full-time regular jobs. We had to run the company during this time, and this was so demanding, while at the same time gathering all the needed information for the sale. Also, legal costs were way beyond what I had anticipated they would be, along with the madness of the communication in legal terms. My sitting on the sideline hearing things being discussed by attorneys for both sides was difficult because I didn't understand the points they were discussing or what the effects of those points were.

I ended up getting the value the company was worth. Also, I got free from the business. I didn't want a situation where I was still dependent on the firm's performance, because I didn't know whom I was selling to and that's always full of surprises. Also, there was certainly an emotional toll that took place during this process. Managing the business while at the same time trying to sell the company created a lot of stress. You then feel even more stress because you have a company that's been a close, family company and all that anxiety with all of the people in the company. You have the anxiety about what the future is going to be for personnel, and particularly your key personnel. You are having to keep business on an even keel when you don't even know yourself what the future's going to be after someone else buys the firm. Also, we had family involvement, which caused strain, because it meant something to members of our family who worked at the company, as well as to my wife and myself.

From my own perspective, I achieved my goals. I was satisfied that the time was right for me. I needed to get out and do something else. Our business had become very difficult and wasn't nearly as much fun as when we started. The subsequent events confirmed that the time was right.

Questions

1. Consider the steps entrepreneurs can take to make their company attractive to outsider purchasers. Which of these did Ed Bonneau take? In view of these steps, do you think he sold at the right time?

2. What method was used to value the company? Who did the valuing? Do you think the way this crucial part of the process was handled adversely affected the results achieved by Bonneau?

3. Do you think that Mr. Bonneau would have done better is he had negotiated with the buyer directly instead of through an agent?

4. Why do you think Bonneau did not consider other options aside from an outright sale of the company? What options would *you* have considered if you were in his place?

5. Do you think Bonneau's age played a role in his decision to sell, and in the way he acted on this decision? (He had been the owner for more than thirty years at the time of the sale, so clearly, he was not a young person.)

Source: Adapted from J. William Petty, John D. Martin, and John Kensinger, *Harvesting the Value of a Privately Held Company* (Morristown, NJ: Financial and Executive Research Foundation, 1999).

Appendix 2: Video Case Library

 **SmallBusinessSchool** ◘
the Series on PBS stations and the Web

Hattie Bryant, producer, *Small Business School*, the series on PBS stations and the Web site
http://smallbusinessschool.org

 CHAPTER TWO

WAHOO'S FISH TACOS

In this episode of *Small Business School,* we go to the U.S. International Surfing Competition; in addition to seeing the best surfers in the world, you'll meet surfers who are building a chain of surfer food joints, Wahoo's Fish Taco.

There's something truly special happening here. The founders are three brothers, immigrants from Brazil, whose parents are from China. Then to add to the diversity, they adopted a fourth partner, an immigrant from Greece. New Americans continue to introduce new insights and fresh ideas. A beacon to creative people around the world, this country is a place to actualize dreams; in this television show, you meet four new Americans who are changing the look of restaurants around the country.

In Southern California, we find some of the most beautiful scenery in the world, but inside Wahoo's, it's different. It's noisy. It's friendly. It's chaos. But the food is delicious. And, it's healthy. Though each place feels like a one of a kind, there are a lot of similarities within all of them. Here it feels like the people in charge are just doing this for the fun of it, and the customers and staff blend in some sort of free form dance. This is the new America. More like the Wild West. More intimate. More tribal . . . it is where people really know your name. These people do not want the pristine and predictable; they want a little Baja and the romance of an endless summer.

In this show, you will be introduced to the boarding tribe, people bonded by common experiences based on surfboards, snowboards, skateboards, and boards of any kind. The founders opened the first Wahoo's in 1988 because there was no place for surfers to meet and eat like the places they loved in Baja.

Wahoo's is a restaurant. But it is also a joint. A dive. And, it is one of the places that helps to make the restaurant industry the nation's largest private-sector employer, providing jobs for 11.3 million individuals. About 78% of us get our first job and learn a little about the nature of work in a restaurant. But Wahoo's is no Burger King. Here you'll see lines out the door and smiling faces of surfers just up from the beach.

Customers come back twice a day, several days a week. One surfer said, "I eat this food every day." Another comments, "It's embarrassing how much I come here." So we must warn you now, this place is contagious, and it is not business as usual.

Key Ideas

1. **Identify your market and identify *with* your market.**
    There is nothing like a well-defined market. But this is more than that. This show opens with scenes from the Phillips U.S. Open of Surfing in Huntington Beach, where some of the best surfers of the world compete. This is the biggest event in California and even the legends of surfing gather to watch the competition. Matt George, editor

of *Surfing Magazine* says, "The U.S. has given the world two icons—the cowboy and the surfer. They're one in the same. There's a total dedication to adventure." Surfing is a global sport but the iconic roots are found in Southern California. And part of that legacy is "where there are surfers, there are plenty of girls."

Chuck Allen, former surfing coach at Huntington Beach High School and founder of the national Scholastic Surfing Association and the USA Snowboard Association, comments, "You have to be a heck of an athlete to surf; it is very difficult." When you see a surfer doing the surfer handshake with Chuck Allen, he says, "I love you, Brother" Now that is tribal bonding.

Topic for discussion: What does it mean to have a tribe? How does it go beyond just "defining your market"?

2. **Do something where you have expertise.**
   We define business as . . . *creating enough of something of value that it can be sold or exchanged for something else of value.* Creating something of value is also a good "first principle" to live a meaningful life. But the two always comingle within small businesses.

   Wing Lam, Ed Lee, Mingo Lee, and Steve Karafidis appear to be enjoying life. Though the brothers started Wahoo's Fish Tacos as a final attempt before getting "real jobs," they had a deep-seated sense of the business. Mingo says, "As little kids we stood on coke crates to peel shrimp."

Topic for discussion: Why was it easy for the founders to spot the opportunity they are now engaged in?

3. **If you don't like systems, hire someone who does.**
   Steve Karfaridis to the rescue. As the business grew bigger than they expected, the brothers felt it had outgrown their ability to lead. Steve is Greek and as Wing said, "Every restaurant needs a Greek chef."

Topic for discussion: What did Steve bring to the party?

Answer: Big kitchen, white table cloth, and 5-star hotel experience. Remember that the brothers only know about very small business. Their parents have just one restaurant. Steve understood immediately that rigid systems must be put in place to guarantee consistency and quality, and to motivate employees, too. Employees don't want to work in the shadow of owners who pop in and change things on a whim. Steve is now the interface with all the leadership at each location. In fact, Wing is not allowed to go into a Wahoo's and make a change of any kind. He must express himself to Steve, who then figures out how to implement the idea if it has merit.

Topic for discussion: What is one of Steve's rules?

4. **Serve clean food, piled high and priced low if you're feeding young men.**

Topic for discussion: What is clean food?

5. **Do not discount your product; give it away.**
   Wing says, "We do not discount. If you do, you cheapen the image of the product." Their policy is, "It's either full-price or it is free. There is nothing in-between." When they give something, they give it with no strings attached. Wing says, "You don't do it because you want something; you do it because you can make a difference."

Topic for discussion: What do you think happens when Wing gives away food?

6. **The dishwasher and the CEO are treated the same.**
   At Wahoo's, the people strategy is magical. They want to have every person discover their best gifts and capitalize on them. Even the oldest brother and spiritual

founder, Wing, was pushed to define himself further. Everybody gets it. The baby brother is the CEO, Wing is only in charge of marketing, and Ed is in charge of real estate. Steve, the fourth partner, is in charge of operations.

Topic for discussion: How can such a management policy work?

7. Follow the process and the sales will happen.

Topic for discussion: Why does Steve tell employees never to worry about sales?

  Source: Hattie Bryant, producer, *Small Business School*, the series on PBS stations and the Web site http://smallbusinessschool.org.

CHAPTER THREE

ZIBA DESIGN WITH SOHRAB VOSSOUGHI

In this episode of *Small Business School,* we go to the City of Roses where we visit Ziba Designs and its founder, Sohrab Vossoughi. Not just any industrial design firm, this is a business filled with creative perfectionists from across the globe. Drawn to Portland by the opportunity to work with its revered founder, this diverse group of professionals is as driven to work in an environment based upon Ziba's design philosophy: Strive for simplicity, innovation, human-centered interaction, visual interest, and efficiency.

Design is a continuum. It never ends, and it can always be done better. The results of that philosophy are impressive. In fact, in 2001, Ziba became the first firm in the world to ever win four Gold Awards in the annual Industrial Design Excellence Awards Competition run by the Industrial Designers Society of America. With clients in the Who's Who of big business like Procter & Gamble, McDonald's, FedEx, Nike, and Ford, it's no accident that these firms have entrusted their brands to Ziba's unrelenting pursuit of perfection.

How do you account for that success?

It all began with the Cleret Squeegee, the firm's now legendary creation to solve a universal, yet simple problem: wet shower doors. Its beautiful, yet functional design has earned it a place in the permanent collection of the Smithsonian, and earned Ziba a reputation that warrants offices in Tokyo, Taipei, Boston, and San Jose, staffed by 80 people from 17 countries.

Sohrab immigrated from Iran in 1970 at the age of 14. He became a U.S. citizen a year later, finished college, got some business experience, and set out to solve "some of the world's big problems" through innovative design. He had a total of $400 in savings, but he aggressively went about minimizing all his fixed costs.

Today, the opportunity to study with and learn from the master attracts students from the world over. What they gain once they "arrive," however, is more than design principles. With so many people from so many backgrounds working so closely together, different attitudes and values inevitably work their way into the discussion. The team learns a lot about the world just working within the four walls. Culture is not just nationality, but also a way of seeing things from a different perspective and the source of Ziba's international acclaim.

At one of the best industrial design firms in the world, we find a hotbed of creativity—a wonderful mélange of personalities and nationalities. With other offices in Tokyo, Taipei, Boston, and San Jose, a total of 80 people representing 17 countries, Ziba generates $12 million in annual sales by working with a long, list of big business clients.

Key Ideas

1. Creativity is an environment and a way of thinking.

Sohrab Vossoughi says, "Design is a continuum. It never ends; you know once you do something, you know it can be done better. We are a brand consultancy with our expertise in product development . . . developing brands in the dimension of spaces."

Topic for discussion: Sohrab says, "You know it can be done better." Everything? What makes better "better"? We grow up learning the basic comparative analysis—good, better, best—but what is the best? Can anything ever be perfect?

Topic for discussion: Do you think it is true that those among us who are no longer striving for a higher perfection have simply lost their vision and hope for the future? Do you think that striving is at the heart of creativity?

2. **Submit yourself to the scrutiny of peers.**
   In 2001, Ziba became the first firm in the world to ever win four Gold Awards in the annual Industrial Design Excellence Awards Competition run by the Industrial Designers Society of America. Topic for discussion: Why would the Museum of Modern Art in New York City make a plastic squeegee part of its permanent exhibit?

3. **In every discipline there is a balance between form and function.**
   You see many products that Ziba has designed, including the Microsoft keyboard and the Coleman smoke detector.

Topic for discussion: Why are some products such an outrageous success?

4. **Create a cross-discipline, team-oriented experience.**
   "The world is diverse and a global village," yet we so often fail to be inclusive. It is too easy to think local. So when Steve McCallion says, "Culture is not just nationality, but culture is also all the different backgrounds people bring here . . . " it becomes a very important and compelling piece of this story.

Topic for discussion: With so many varying backgrounds assembled in work areas with no walls, what is the common language? How does Sohrab orchestrate the achievement of goals?

5. **Word-of-mouth marketing is key to growth and stability.**
   Sohrab said this himself, although winning awards and investing in print and Web materials to extend the word-of-mouth is important. He has paid his dues in the industry and is now at a point where he can say "no" to work that doesn't interest him, and he can say "no" to work that will not generate enough revenue to support his expanding overhead.

Topic for discussion: Why is word-of-mouth so efficient?

6. **Customers can become excellent mentors.**
   Here is the ultimate reality check from a customer, friend, and mentor. Bob Marchant says, " . . . the Ziba folks understand that it is not enough for the form to be interesting or exciting—or for the form to generate market acceptance. It's important for the form to be profitable, for somebody to be able to make it and for it to work reliably." Bob Marchant completely enjoys doing business with Ziba and, over the years, he has become a mentor to Sohrab.

Topic for discussion: Why are mentors important?

7. **An ESOP can propel a business to the next level.**
   Sohrab says, "One of my golden rules is that what is good for the goose is good for the gander. Whatever is good for me should be good for the next person. If you want them to feel like this is their own company, give them what you have."

Topic for discussion: What is an employee stock ownership plan?

Topic for discussion: How did an employee stock ownership plan help Sohrab?

Source: Hattie Bryant, producer, *Small Business School*, the series on PBS stations and the Web site http://smallbusinessschool.org.

CHAPTER FIVE

SUNDANCE CATALOG WITH HARRY ROSENTHAL

"We always try to deliver such high quality that when it shows up at the customer's door, it's always at least a little better than they even thought it was going to be."
Harry Rosenthal

In this episode of *Small Business School*, the series on PBS stations, you will meet Harry Rosenthal. When Robert Redford made the decision to create a catalog company to sell the products carried in his resort gift shop located not far from Provo, Utah, he knew he didn't know where to begin. Research led him to Harry, an attorney-turned-entrepreneur who had launched and run a profitable catalog called *Right Start*. Harry sold out of *Right Start*, which (by the way) is thriving today, to take on the challenge of another startup.

Robert Redford brought to the table the Sundance Resort and Sundance Film Festival brand that he had been building since the late 1960s, and he was smart to hire and allow a person with experience to deploy the catalog. Customers drove the entire idea, which is why I think the business succeeds today. Guests at the resort would buy in the gift shop and then get home and want to purchase items and have them sent to friends. The inbound calls to the gift shop motivated the enterprise and, besides, the Sundance operation needed cash to preserve its land and do its charity work.

I was fascinated by the product selection meeting you will see and the attention to detail taken to keep technology powerful enough to support a growing business. I was surprised to hear Harry speak candidly that having a celebrity spokesperson is not all a bed of roses. He warns to be careful using this technique because of what happened with Hertz and the O.J. Simpson association. This episode will give you terrific insight into a well-conceived and well-run small business.

Key Ideas

1. **You can build a business faster with an existing brand than without one.**

   Most of us who start a business from scratch don't have brand recognition. Harry certainly did not have brand awareness when he started his children's products catalog. When he started the Sundance catalog, the lodge already existed and soon the film festival also bore the name "Sundance." As a result, the festival helps the catalog, the catalog helps the lodge, and the lodge helps the festival. With 12 million catalogs being mailed per year, the catalog is building brand awareness for all of Mr. Redford's enterprises.

   In another program coming up this season, you'll meet a Web site creator who has the cyberspace rights to the animated character "Gumby." Having this known brand will bring traffic to the Web site. You can either find a way to attach yourself to an existing brand or invest in building your own name. Big businesses spend millions in advertising to build their brands because they know you can build a business faster with a brand than without one.

   Topic for discussion: What is the difference between a brand and a product?

   Topic for discussion: What is the Sundance brand known for?

   Topic for discussion: Can or should a very small business worry about brand?

2. **Use a spokesperson with caution.**

   Topic for discussion: Why does using Robert Redford as a spokesperson work for Sundance catalog?

3. **Somebody has to live, eat, sleep the business.**

   Topic for discussion: Why did Harry say this to Robert Redford?

   Topic for discussion: What does a small business owner need to do to attract talent?

4. **Admit what you don't know.**

Topic for discussion: What experience taught Harry this lesson?

5. **Sometimes it many look like you are flying by the seat of your pants.**

Topic for discussion: Did Harry fly by the seat of his pants when he practiced law?

 Source: Hattie Bryant, producer, *Small Business School*, the series on PBS stations and the Web site http://smallbusinessschool.org.

CHAPTER SIX

BRIDGECREEK DEVELOPMENT WITH FRANK JAO

This show is about a man who came to the United States in 1975 on a C-130 through Camp Pendleton. His name is Frank Jao. He was the middle child of a large, poor family with a Vietnamese mother and Chinese father. He left home at the age of 11 and got a job delivering newspapers to support himself. By the age of 13, he and his six "employees" were the delivery system for a local Da Nang newspaper. By the time he turned 18, he was working for the U.S. Marines as a translator.

Within a day of arriving in California, he got a job as a vacuum cleaner salesman; within a year, he had taken the courses and qualified to become a realtor; within four years, he became the founder of Bridgecreek Development, and he broke ground on his first building of 50,000 square feet in 1979.

This was the beginning of Little Saigon. He now has over nearly 2 million square feet of commercial space and he has inspired the development of even more. This place has become his home and the home of over 400,000 Vietnamese and their *de facto* capital outside of Vietnam. Frank Jao has been recognized by the president of the United States, and today Frank is the president of the Pan Asian American Chamber of Commerce and helping U.S. companies do business in Asia.

Bridgecreek has 15 employees who handle 1,100 tenants occupying commercial space in 10 buildings. Frank inspired others to build, and his Asian Garden is at the heart of a 4.5 square mile area. Just 4.5 square miles of our planet. A relatively small space. But it is at an exit of the interstate highway, and Kathy Buchoz, the former mayor of Westminster, says, " . . . never could anyone imagine that it was going to become the metropolis that it is." Over 400,000 Vietnamese-Americans say this is their cultural and commercial capital. Frank Jao has changed our world. He has made it a better place.

Frank and Cathie came to the United States from their offices in Vietnam; they did not even have time to return home to gather their belongings. But by witnessing their tenacity, hard work and bold decisions, you will learn about how to create something out of nothing (*creatio ex nihilo*).

Key Ideas

1. **Change the world by setting your sights high.**
   When Frank finally found what he loved doing in America, he continued searching for the right spot in this industry. He started selling real estate and noticed that the men in his office selling commercial property had more prestige than did the women who sold residential property. He might have also been impressed by larger commissions from larger sales on in the commercial arena, but told me that he liked the way the men were treated. Frank wanted to be treated with respect, and he would do what he had to do to make this happen.

Topic for discussion: How did Frank see himself even when he was living in a tiny apartment?

2. **One person's trash can be another's treasure.**

Frank was and still is striving for answers to questions. He is driven to learn and to do. Where street people search trash bins for food and recyclables that can be redeemed for money for food, Frank's search was for insight.

Topic for discussion: How did Frank prepare to ask a bank for a $3 million dollar loan?

3. **There are no secret formulas in business or in life.**

Frank says, "There is nothing to me that is a secret, including business formulas. That is the principal that I have always operated on." What a pearl of insight!

Topic for discussion: If each of us lived our life confident that we can find an answer to any question, where would we be?

Topic for discussion: When have you said "I don't know" or "That's a mystery" and did not attempt to find the answer? What would have happened to Frank if he had not sought the answer to the banker's question, "Where is your loan package?"

4. **Starting a business is easier than maintaining and building it.**

Frank gives us Management 101. He says, " . . . buying an automobile is not as difficult as keeping it in the top shape over a long time." His formula is to create space that includes culture, education, entertainment, and art in a location where the property can be acquired at a reasonable price and developed with the encouragement of the local government. Then, he focuses on having foot traffic see this place as a destination to buy things. But he turns the management over to people who like managing and he spends his time troubleshooting.

Topic for discussion: Why do most entrepreneurs have a twinkle in their eye when they tell you about their startup and then they get very sober when talking about the growth?

5. **Groom your replacement.**

Frank has proven he can develop successful projects without being present himself. Ryan Hubris, the young president of Bridgecreek, has been selected and trained so that Frank can go on to more expansive goals.

Topic for discussion: Why do most small business owners fail at replacing themselves?

 Source: Hattie Bryant, producer, *Small Business School*, the series on PBS stations and the Web site http://smallbusinessschool.org.

CHAPTER NINE

RODGERS CHEVROLET WITH PAMELA RODGERS

In this episode of *Small Business School*, we get up close and personal with one woman's involvement in a very American love affair. For Pamela Rodgers, Americans' love of their cars is as real and palpable as any romance going, and at her Chevrolet dealership, located in the quiet Detroit suburb of Woodhaven, helping customers to act upon that passion is her business.

An ardent student of what's under the hood as well as inside the company financials, she is equally adept at the psychology of her customers and making sure they keep coming back for more.

The key to her repeat business success is service. From her originally designed, colorful waiting area featuring a speedway theme to a team of highly skilled service advisors, Rodgers Chevrolet is a company that never misfires when it comes to building long-term relationships with customers. This is a team that's as well trained in the mechanics of human dynamics as they are the electronics of today's automobile engine. Keeping that relationship running smoothly is a matter of individualized communications where customer satisfaction is not an optional service.

Pamela's story is all the more unique in that she is one of the few women in the world to own a dealership in her own right. It wasn't passed on to her by her father or a husband, and she took a failing location and turned it around. Today, with a team of 85 employees, Rodgers Chevrolet generates $73 million in revenue annually by selling nearly 200 and servicing as many as 1,200 cars per month.

In an industry defined by steel, rubber, and oil, Pamela Rodgers is a woman in a man's world, where it's more common to see grease under the fingernails than a French manicure. Yet, her philosophy has always been that the two are compatible, and that strong, smart leadership—regardless of gender—is what matters. As a product of an influential mentor herself, Pamela is intensely focused on the softer side of what it takes to sell cars, and she invests heavily in the raw materials—the people—in her business. From training to development to advancement, Pamela understands that business is all about providing good service to your customers—and employees.

Her dealership is a fine-tuned organization with capable women in critical jobs: business manager, parts manager, controller, and of course, sales. And, their placement is anything but gratuitous. Statistics show that women own or purchase 50 percent of all automobiles sold and influence the purchase decision on 85 percent to 90 percent of all autos purchased. But, it's the quality of their experience at Rodgers Chevrolet that determines if and when they'll return. Judging from Pamela's track record, that happens more often than not—and in the car business that is where the rubber meets the road.

Meet Pamela Rodgers, owner of Pamela Rodgers Chevrolet, one of the few automobile dealerships owned by an African-American woman in the United States.

Key Ideas

1. ### Service should be the backbone and not the back end.
   The old-fashioned, hard-driving car salesman is now passé. While we all may occasionally run into a throwback to the 1970s, Pamela Rodgers is an example of the new way car dealership owners think and plan. Pamela is not interested in a quick buck—she is interested in building a strong, long-lived company. By studying the history of car dealerships and by determining that she wants to be running this business years from now, she clearly defined for everyone in her organization that the path to real prosperity is service.

Topic for discussion: Are there still companies out there who succeed with the old sales-driven model?

2. ### Know who has the buying power in your market.
   Pamela knows who her customers are. She knows, for example that many single women buy cars. She also knows that married women influence their husbands so the net affect is that women make more car-buying decisions than men.

Topic for discussion: How does this fact give Pamela an advantage over her competitors?

Topic for discussion: What do you see in this episode that makes the dealership female-friendly?

3. ### Counseling is better than selling.
   The people who work at Rodgers Chevrolet see themselves as counselors rather than salespeople. You saw Brenda, the business manager, and she spoke about helping the customer understand the implications of taking on a monthly loan payment. Rodgers does not want to make a loan to a person who might not be thinking clearly about the total picture of their personal finances.

In the short run, this strategy might mean that fewer people buy cars. However, this is the responsible tack to take, knowing that service is the backbone, not the back end, at Rodgers. Brenda is delivering a service when she helps a customer understand what level of debt is prudent for them

4. Create some magic for customers.

Life is hard, so when any of us have a chance to make people smile and feel good, we should take it. To make her customers smile, Pamela hired a theater set designer to create a fun environment for the service department. Rather than the clean, crisp walls we see in the rest of the dealership, the customer section of the service department is so remarkable that it has become what Pamela considers to be one of her best business decisions.

Topic for discussion: Ms. Rodger's Neighborhood is metaphor, and the artwork is a daily, visible reminder about the fun side of automobiles. In your mind's eye, paint over the walls and eliminate the awnings and windows, and you have a typical car dealer's entry area to the service and collision centers. What does this artwork do? Why are aesthetics important?

Topic for discussion: What can you do in your business to tap the power of art?

5. Provide communication skills training for everyone.

There was a quick shot in the program of a training session going on. The person leading the session is an outside specialist because Pamela believes fresh ideas need to be infused in the company on an ongoing basis.

Topic for discussion: Why aren't more employees in more training sessions?

6. Know your basic numbers and your key critical ratios.

If you are not making money you are a charity. How do you know if you're making money? What are the numbers you keep your eye on daily? Do you read your financials? Do you know what questions to ask? Do you have a key critical ratio that you always analyze?

Topic for discussion: Why does Pamela's CFO enjoy working for her?

7. When you're stuck, find a mentor.

Pamela credits her mentor with creating breakthrough opportunities. She earned the right to take action on his ideas, but it took an established mentor in the industry to help open the door for a young black woman.

Topic for discussion: Successful business owners know that without the insight, advice, and direction from people who took time to guide them, they would not be where they are today. I don't know any business owners who are operating strong companies who are not quick to acknowledge the help they have received. Why doesn't everyone have a mentor?

8. "Buy low, sell high" is a multidimensional truism.

Be it stocks, property, or a business, the truism works. Most things cannot be bought low. The truism is asking that we see the beauty in the ugly ducklings. Every business, every family, and every community has an ugly duckling.

Topic for discussion: So, what happens when we look for the beauty in the ugly duckling?

Topic for discussion: Did Pamela have a choice when she bought the ugly duckling?

9. Target your marketing dollars.

Everything at Rodgers Chevrolet is done by the numbers. Pamela has an MBA in finance, and she wants to measure everything, including every dollar they spend on marketing. They know that their current and future customers are people who live within a 15-mile radius of the dealership. With this knowledge, they hone in on that market.

Topic for discussion: Why is target marketing hard for many very small business owners?

Topic for discussion: What does Joe include in every direct mail piece he designs?

10. **Laughter is good for morale.**
    When was the last time there was a good laugh around your office? Recently? Well, when was the last time there was laughter and it was not at the expense of another? That is a very different story. Let's look at laughter.

Topic for discussion: What example of humor did you see in the program?

Topic for discussion: What can you do to have more fun and get more people to smile and laugh more often?

11. **Being nice can translate to the bottom line.**

Topic for discussion: Pamela Rodgers is very nice. She would fit right into Mr. Fred Rodger's Neighborhood. Some may think that being nice is being soft, so we leave our nice-side at the door when we walk into our place of business. Why can being nice increase your profits?

12. **Don't get comfortable.**
    Thank you, Pamela. The third point of our mission statement says, "If you are not living on the edge, you're taking up too much space." The actual quote begins, "Continue the climb and do not fear the falls . . . "

Topic for discussion: Why do you think Pamela says she never wants to be comfortable?

  Source: Hattie Bryant, producer, *Small Business School,* the series on PBS stations and the Web site http://smallbusinessschool.org.

CHAPTER ELEVEN

NOUVIR WITH RUTH ELLEN MILLER

In this excerpt of *Small Business School*, the series on PBS stations, you will meet Ruth Ellen and Jack Miller, founders of NoUVIR Research. The name stands for, "no ultra violet no infra red" and the company builds fiber optic lighting systems that today illuminate many of the world's most valuable objects.

In 2000, Ruth Ellen was named Small Business Person of Year from the small state of Delaware because she is making a huge impact on the way we see art. With nine employees, she and her father are shipping their products to places like the Baseball Hall of Fame and the Smithsonian. Their invention, the cold nose projector, is used to light the original copy of the Constitution and the Declaration of Independence because fiber optic lighting contains no damage-causing rays.

To win new customers, they conduct full-day seminars at museums that are good prospects for their systems. In addition, they mail catalogs and flyers to a targeted list. The Web site has proven to be a time saver as it clearly explains, in a fun way, why NoUVIR's products should be considered.

Their strategy from day one was to invent a way to allow museum-goers to see art in optimum light and at the same time not destroy the precious objects. NoUVIR targets the museum market because most large manufacturers don't take time to develop for what they would consider a limited marketplace. Once again, small business owners find their niche and proceed to get rich.

With over 100 patents between them, Ruth Ellen and Jack are respected scientists who spent three years in the development of their first projector, and now their company is growing faster than they imagined. I loved watching the two of them "ping pong" ideas, which is how they describe their creative process.

Key Ideas

1. **Make a quantum leap.**
   Starting a business by launching a new product is nearly impossible. You have to love the idea and enjoy the pain of doing something no one has ever done. You can look for paths to follow or mentors to guide you, but so often you will find yourself very alone.

   Topic for discussion: What did Jack and Ruth Ellen have to do to achieve their breakthrough?

2. **Position for profitability.**
   In the case of Jack and Ruth Ellen, their years in California taught them that it is not a friendly place for a company that wants to manufacture a product.

   Topic for discussion: Why make a drastic change in lifestyle by moving from California to Delaware even before you have a product perfected?

3. **Prepare for a long-term ramp up.**
   There are thousands of inventors but very few new projects that actually make it to the marketplace.

   Topic for discussion: Why do so few products succeed?

4. **Two patents are better than one.**
   In the case of the cold-nosed projector, Jack and Ruth Ellen have 16 patents in this one product.

   Topic for discussion: Why bother doing so much paperwork?

5. **There's a difference between patents, trademarks and copyrights.**
   Ruth Ellen said, "Patents protect your product. They keep competitors from copying you and from making exactly what you're making. The copyright protects your literature. This includes your catalogs, instruction manuals, ads, and photographs. Your trademark is your name. It is the thing that identifies you.

   Topic for discussion: What is important about a trademark?

6. **Protecting ideas creates prosperity for all.**
   Before patent, trademark, and copyright laws were put in place, the primary source of wealth was land. More than 5 million patents have been issued in the United Sates since the first patent law of 1790. The system is working.

   Topic for discussion: How is wealth created by a protected idea?

7. **Date before you marry.**
   Very few people get married without going through a dating phase. It sounds weird to most of us when we hear about mail-order brides and arranged marriages. But, in businesses everyday, people are hired without any trial period.

   Topic for discussion: What is the hiring process at NoUVIR?

   Topic for discussion: How could you/should you fine-tune your hiring process to improve the productivity of your team?

8. **Inventors must become teachers.**
   A new product usually doesn't sell itself. A new product needs to be sold by educating the prospects.

Topic for discussion: How does NoUVIR win new customers?

9.   **A problem should make you smile.**
     Jack's background in research and teaching trained him to see a problem as an opportunity to learn something new. He knows: If there's a problem, what is being done now isn't working, so someone has to come up with a solution, which implies a new product or service needs to be invented.

Topic for discussion: Since life really is about decision making and problem solving, why do so many run from the difficult problems?

  Source: Hattie Bryant, producer, *Small Business School*, the series on PBS stations and the Web site http://smallbusinessschool.org.

CHAPTER TWELVE

GADABOUT SALON AND SPAS WITH PAM MCNAIR

In this excerpt of *Small Business School*, the series on PBS stations, you will meet Pam McNair, the founder of Gadabout Salon and Spas. Though most spa customers check in for a week to be pampered, to eat low-fat foods, and to participate in endless exercise classes, day spas are different. Here you'll find only the pampering part. Although the day-spa segment of the industry is enjoying rapid growth, I discovered that Gadabout is a leader. Pam and her team are working to bring the salon business into the mainstream. In Tucson, Arizona, with five locations and 225 employees, Pam is making an impact.

Forty percent of small businesses are in the service sector, and Pam learned early that to attract and keep great service providers, she needed to meet their needs holistically. At Gadabout, employees told us over and over, "Pam saved my life." "Pam changed my life." "If I hadn't met Pam, I don't know what shape my life would be in today." And, these people are not talking about a beauty makeover. Can the owner of a company have the same effect on people as a minister, or a priest, or a surgeon, or a therapist? These employees have been profoundly impacted by Pam and I conclude that the answer is "yes." We've learned in business that "The customer is king." But, if you grow past the point where you as the owner are no longer delivering all of the customer service, how do you guarantee that every employee learns that the customer is king?

Just as Herb Kellerer of SouthWest Airlines teaches, I watched Pam treating the employees like kings and queens. The leadership theory is: Employees will treat customers the way employees are treated by the owner. Rather than pouring energy into customer service to grow, pour energy into employee service. The owner is rewarded with loyalty because people don't leave where they're loved.

Key Ideas

1.   **People are more important than cash.**
     Some would say that Pam was lucky to open her doors for business with a trained, happy, and loyal team of employees. I would say, Pam was lucky to learn early that business is about people.

Topic for discussion: What was Pam's startup dilemma?

2.   **The way you make people feel will determine your success at growing a business.**
     The only way to grow a business is to grow a team of some sort. We have studied companies that outsource most tasks, but the leadership still has to work with the people to whom the outsourcing has been done. There is no way to get around it.

People are the raw materials you must commit to working with, day in and day out, if you want to grow a company.

Businesses that lead with service must fully understand this concept because delivering service requires psychological heavy lifting. Every service provider needs psychological muscle and lots of it. Psychological muscle gives the employees strength to cope with mean, demanding people and even turn them into nice people. The strong employee can bounce back quickly from a situation that made them feel bad. They are mature and can admit being wrong and can look a person in the eye and say "thank you" and "I'm sorry," when necessary.

Topic for discussion: Why does the owner have to deal with a person's feelings?

3. **Think deeply about what people need.**
Pam thinks about what she needs and what her employees need all the time. This seems to be what occupies her most. She points out that in the salon and spa business there are many people who suffer from low-self esteem. I would say, there are many people who suffer from low-self esteem in every business. Pam is simply speaking from her own experience and knows, as the leader of people, that she must help each person feel good about who they are now and who they can become.

Topic for discussion: What are the results of thinking about needs rather than just wants?

Topic for discussion: What do the people who work for you need to be doing that they are not now doing? What can you do to move them in the right direction?

4. **Do it differently.**
Pam's business model is innovative compared to what others do in her industry. Although most shop owners lease a space for hairdressers to do their own thing, Pam has everyone on her payroll. Also, new-hires spends 18 months as interns before they are allowed to handle customers alone.

Topic for discussion: What type of person does Gadabout attract?

5. **Teach communication skills constantly.**
Great communicators can have what they want and do what they want in life. We see this proven in every field, and although Pam is not a public speaker, she is a powerful communicator. She understands that communication is the oil in the service machine. Gadabout sells plenty of products, but it leads with service, and in all service-based businesses, communication becomes the product.

Topic for discussion: What kind of communications training had all the employees just completed when we taped this story?

6. **Establish high expectations.**
There are no losers at Gadabout. The reason is that winners want to work in a place that is demanding. A loser wants to be where they can hide and ride on the coat tails of others.

Topic for discussion: How does Pam inspire people to rise to her expectations?

7. **Put controls in places where they didn't exist before.**
Business is about rules and numbers. It is regulated on many levels. Owners are asked to tell the truth, file reports, pay taxes, and keep records. By being one of the few salons in the country that treats its employees as professionals, Pam took on the paperwork burden.

Topic for discussion: Why bother to do the hard things when nobody else is doing them?

8. **Do for employees what you do for customers.**
   Pam believes in salon and spa products and services enough to sell them to customers, so she finds ways to give them to her employees.

Topic for discussion: How do the employees of Gadabout afford the services they provide to clients?

9. **As the owner, you are minister, social worker and therapist.**
   Employees at Gadabout told me that Pam has had a tremendous impact on their lives. Some had difficulty explaining why they feel so close to her, but one said, "I'm among a large number of people who've had the opportunity to completely transform their lives working here."

Topic for discussion: What benefit does Pam receive because she is willing to be a minister, social worker, and therapist?

10. **Delegate with design.**
    Spoken like a true artist. Pam is a hairdresser-turned-businesswoman. Her formal training was all about making her client look her best. How does a great hairdresser do that? She studies the client. She thinks about the type of hair the client has, the shape of her face, her lifestyle, and personality. Only then does the artist begin to cut and color a person's hair.

Topic for discussion: What do you think Pam means when she says, "delegate with design?"

  Source: Hattie Bryant, producer, *Small Business School*, the series on PBS stations and the Web site http://smallbusinessschool.org.

CHAPTER THIRTEEN

ON TARGET SUPPLIES AND LOGO WITH ALBERT BLACK.

This episode of *Small Business School* is the story of Albert Black. With no money and no mentors early on, Albert launched On Target Supplies and Logistics because he wanted to create jobs in the poor neighborhood of his childhood.

He worked a second job for 10 years before he was able to put himself on the payroll. On weekends, he went to school to get an MBA. Within 10 years, he had over 40 employees and major companies as clients. Within 20 years, he had over 100 employees and is a major supplier and a corporate leader in the Dallas–Fort Worth community. Albert is constantly retooling his business; the focus is on being a logistics company. Through continuous improvement, On Target's just-in-time deliveries to specific supply rooms within large corporations help to minimize inventories.

Key Ideas

1. **You don't have to have your own money to start a business.**

Topic for discussion: How did Albert get started in business?

2. **Make some of the biggest companies in town your customers.**
   The biggest and most prestigious company in Dallas is a customer of On Target's.

Topic for discussion: With fierce competition in the supply business, how does On Target hold on to these customers?

3. **Community service is a marketing strategy.**

   Albert's passion is community service, and by accident he found this to be his best marketing strategy.

Topic for discussion: Why is volunteering to work with a nonprofit organization good for the soul and also such a good marketing technique?

4. **Establish a board of advisors.**

   Albert is not going it alone. He has a board of advisors and a board of directors. The board of advisors is made up of customers; the board of directors is a group Albert expects to be tough on him.

   When Albert met John Castle, Albert called him and asked if they could go to lunch. After the two had developed a friendship, John suggested to Albert that On Target needed a board of directors. Albert agreed and asked John to chair the board. Two or three times a year, Albert meets with his board of directors. He, as the Japanese would say, opens the kimono. Albert shares the financials and every detail of his business with the board. He listens as people he trusts gives him their best thinking.

Topic for discussion: Where would you be in your life and in your business if you had several mentors guiding you through the rough waters?

5. **Provide a learning environment.**

   At On Target, learning is a priority and it isn't just learning how to do a specific job for which a person has been hired. It is about all employees improving their lives. Albert is the role model. Even after his company was enjoying great success, he got his MBA through Southern Methodist University's weekend program. It took three years of attending class most weekends while working spending at least 60 hours a week at On Target.

Topic for Discussion: Can a small business afford to fund employee education?

6. **Work is better than welfare.**

   We believe that working works. Work structures time. Work is a conduit for us to contribute to the lives of others. Work creates extended families and teaches us enduring lessons. All work is good if it serves another, and all businesses are in business to serve. We small business owners should accept the challenge in front of us and that is to help every American earn a living wage.

Topic for discussion: Why is On Target a great place for people who are trying to improve their lives by getting off of welfare?

Answer: The teaching starts where the person is. There are no pretensions. If a person wants to learn, they are given a chance and plenty of time to grow.

7. **Grow your own team.**

   Albert has developed his own team. In the beginning, he didn't have money to hire people with loads of experience. So, Albert hired people who he believed he could turn into leaders.

Topic for discussion: What is Albert's people philosophy?

8. **Use tough love.**

   Everybody needs to learn the basic lessons of cause and effect.

Topic for discussion: Does Albert feel so sorry for new hires from welfare that he is soft on them?

Topic for discussion: Is a person easily fired from On Target?

Topic for discussion: Should a company lower its standard to accommodate an employee learning curve?

9. **Get yourself a big goal.**

   Albert's mission is to create jobs and make the American dream possible for his employees. The American dream he talks about is ownership. He wants employees to own stock in the company, to become what he calls a 20 percent saver, to go to college and build happy, productive lives. Having this very big goal is motivating. Albert is fired up to help people, not to get rich himself.

Topic for discussion: How is Albert helping his employees achieve their goals?

 Source: Hattie Bryant, producer, *Small Business School*, the series on PBS stations and the Web site http://smallbusinessschool.org.

CHAPTER FOURTEEN

SELLING TO A PUBLIC COMPANY WITH BOB ORENSTEIN AND TRACY MYERS

The business press continually reports the stories of big businesses acquiring small businesses as part of a growth strategy. If you are running a good business and have market share in your industry segment, you should consider preparing for that call or knock on the door from a publicly traded company.

In a typical episode of this show, we explore how and why the founder of a business gets started and how they get over the hurdles. This episode is about two founders who received large checks for the fruits of their labor. They sold to big companies for millions and millions of dollars.

Bob Orenstein started International Wine Accessories in the spare room of his condominium, and Tracy Myers rented 1,100 square feet with a partner to open the Advertising Arts College.

Tracy's story is for all of us who are not even thinking about selling. Then there comes a knock on the door. Bob's story is for the rest of us who know that we have created a substantial asset. Bob, however, knew that his "time" was coming. Bob was strategic and spent several years getting ready for the day; then, it took over 4 years to consummate a deal.

To say the least, every one of us should have an exit strategy. The question for all of us, even if you are in the first step of starting, is "How is this all going to end?" Over 70 percent of all businesses fail to transfer to the next generation. But that does not disclose an even more dismal statistic: 70 percent of all small business startups fail within their first year.

There has to be a better way! Working together, learning from the best among us, we can stem the growth of negative numbers and open ways to increase the positive. Let's see if we can help build a better business infrastructure that causes more businesses to reach sustainability. Just think about how our quality of life would improve if more small businesses made it—really made it to sustainability—and could more readily and abundantly support their communities and families.

Key Ideas

1. **Think about selling one day.**

   When do responsible parents start saving for their children's education? Sometimes, before they are born!

Topic for discussion: Your business is your baby. How do you nurture it through its life cycle?

Topic for discussion: Like all of us, businesses have a life cycle. They are embryonic (remember when you first had that great idea?), are born, grow to maturity (oh, the challenge of those early years!), live the adult life, age, and finally, pass on. If you create a business with a longer life cycle than your planned working period, you'll have something of value to hand over to someone else! As you build your business, you are creating an annuity. How do you capitalize on that?

2. **Take charge of your day-to-day existence as you took charge of your launch.**
   We know this is difficult. It's particularly difficult to think long range when you are wondering how you are going to make payroll this week, whether or not you really need a check this month. But never lose sight of the fact that you are creating something, something of real value. Prepare yourself now to demonstrate that value in the future.

Topic for discussion: As you build value in your company, how do you prepare to someday liquidate that value for your personal benefit?

Topic for discussion: Each of us comes to our business with certain expertise and with an inadequate skill set in some of the other areas necessary to operate a successful business. We "fill the gaps" with employees, consultants, and by learning, expanding our own skill set. Most likely, you'll need all three when the time comes to exit.

Take the time now to educate yourself about succession planning. Learn the difference between price, cost, and value. Read books, attend lectures, visit with business brokers at Chamber luncheons, etc. Be confident that someday you'll need this knowledge.

3. **Hire the right experts for you.**
   When you are ready to sell, you'll need a business broker if you don't have your own buyer, an attorney for the legal documents, a CPA, and, potentially, a banker.

Topic for discussion: How do you identify the right experts?

Topic for discussion: Beyond the broker, should you use the same experts that have worked with your company over the years?

Topic for discussion: Is the CPA who has done your tax planning and tax returns over the years able to help you with the valuation of your business?

4. **Calculate your EBITDA.**
   This is a little technical but understanding this concept and why it matters is critical to your ultimate exit strategy. EBITDA stands for "earnings before interest, taxes, depreciation, and amortization."

   Calculating your EBITDA is easy. Take the bottom line of your income statement and add back all those items (interest, taxes, depreciation, and amortization). Simple, right? But understanding EBITDA and why it's important is what matters to you.

Topic for discussion: Why the focus on EBITDA?

Topic for discussion: The more profitable the business, the higher the price the buyer will pay because the business will provide an economic return justifying a larger investment.
EBITDA isn't the only thing the buyer will evaluate.

If your business operates with a significant investment in equipment, the buyer will have the equipment appraised. What kind of capital investment will be required beyond the purchase price? If your equipment is aging and needs to be replaced, this could have a big impact on the purchase price. The buyer considers necessary capital improvements separately; that's why depreciation and amortization are not included in EBITDA.

Topic for discussion: Why add back taxes to calculate EBITDA? Isn't that a cost paid from cash flow? Won't the buyer have to pay the same taxes you did?

5. **Build goodwill to collect even more cash.**
   Goodwill is what accountants call an "intangible asset." Goodwill is just as real an asset as cash or inventory, but you can't touch it. Another favorite definition of accountants for goodwill is "earnings capacity."

Topic for discussion: How do I know how much goodwill my company has?

Topic for discussion: Where is the goodwill in your business?

Topic for discussion: If goodwill is an asset, why doesn't my CPA put it on my books?

6. **Play hardball because the buyer will.**
   As hard as it may be to accept the idea, buying or selling a business is a lot like buying or selling a classic car: As long as you keep it up, it can actually appreciate with age. It all boils down to the age-old rule: Value is defined based on the willing buyer/willing seller maxim. Lots of assets, such as cash and accounts receivable, and liabilities are readily valued at cost. Long-term assets such as buildings, land, and equipment often require a professional appraisal.
   There's a little "wiggle room" here, but not too much. Frequently, both the buyer and the seller obtain appraisals, and the resultant amounts are averaged to arrive at the purchase price component.
   The challenge is always in valuing that goodwill. Don't underestimate that value, and be prepared for the buyer, and his or her team, to underestimate it as much as they think they can.

Topic for discussion: How do I get the highest price possible for my business without scaring the buyer away?

Topic for discussion: What are the advantages to the buyer of buying a business that dovetails seamlessly into his or her current operations?

7. **Strategic Buyers Want Continuity.**
   You recognized long before you thought about selling your business that your most important asset was the team you had put together. Every successful business owes its success to some extent or another to the people of the organization. You are the most critical employee of all. Don't be surprised if the buyer wants an employment contract as part of "the deal." What this means is that you may have to exit 1–3 years before you really want to exit!

Topic for discussion: When should you tell your employees that you are selling the company?

Topic for discussion: What will be the effect on your rank-and-file if you tell them you are selling the company and then the deal falls through?

8. **Marketing spin can get you attention, but numbers are the way the "big boys" keep score.**
   You'll want to have 5 years of audited financial statements when the time comes to sell your business. This doesn't mean that you have to have annual audits beginning with your first year of business. It doesn't even mean that you have to have annual audits done when you think you might be within 5 years of selling, it does mean that your books need to be "auditable" for that period.

Topic for discussion: When I do decide to sell my business, how do I make sure that I have the necessary books and records to satisfy the buyer?

Source: Hattie Bryant, producer, *Small Business School*, the series on PBS stations and the Web site http://smallbusinessschool.org.

GLOSSARY

A

Adverse Selection: The choice of someone or something without a desired quality because of the inability to distinguish between those who have a desired quality and those who don't.

Affective Conflicts: Ones that involve a large emotional component rather than conflicts that emerge from incompatible interests or goals.

Americans with Disabilities Act (ADA): This law prohibits discrimination against persons with disabilities who, despite these disabilities, are able to perform the essential functions of the job. The law also requires employers to provide reasonable accommodation for such persons—actions that accommodate the known disabilities of job applicants or employees.

Amortized: A method of distributing the cost of an investment over the number of units produced or sold.

Antidilution Provisions: Contract provisions that require entrepreneurs to provide investors with additional shares in a new venture so that the investor's percentage of ownership is not reduced in later rounds of financing.

Asset-Based Financing: A type of loan in which the assets being purchased are used as collateral for the loan.

B

Balance Sheet Methods (of valuation): Methods for valuing businesses based on their balance sheets.

Big Five Dimensions of Personality: Basic dimensions of personality that have been found to strongly affect behavior in a wide range of situations.

Biodata: Information about potential employees' background, experiences, and preferences provided by them on application forms.

Breach of Contract: A legal term referring to situations in which two parties have a legal contract and one fails to comply with the terms of the agreement.

Break-Even Analysis: An analysis indicating the level of sales and production required to cover all costs.

Burn Rate: The pace at which a new venture uses capital provided by investors.

Business Angel: A person who invests in new ventures as a private individual.

Business Format Franchising: A type of franchising in which franchisees are provided with a complete business system by the franchisor—a trademarked name, the products or services to be sold, the buildings in which the business will be operated, a marketing strategy, methods of actually operating the business, quality control, and assistance in actually running the business.

Business Plan: A written expression of the entrepreneur's vision for converting ideas into a profitable, going business.

C

Calculus-Based Trust: Trust based on deterrence. When we expect that another person will act in the ways they promise because they know they will be punished in some way for doing otherwise, we are demonstrating calculus-based trust

Cannibalize: An effort to produce and sell a product or service that replaces a product or service that one already produces and sells.

Capital Intensive: The degree to which the production process in a firm or industry relies on capital rather than on labor.

Capitalized Earnings Method: A method for valuing businesses based on capitalized net earnings.

Case Method: A research method in which large amounts of data about one organization or specific persons are gathered and then used to reach conclusions about what factors have influenced important outcomes such as economic success.

Cash Flow: The internally generated funds available to a firm after costs and depreciation are subtracted from revenues.

Cash Flow Statement: A form that forecasts cash flow over a specific period of time, given certain levels of projected sales and capital expenditures.

Causal Ambiguity: Indistinctness about the underlying process through which entrepreneurs exploit opportunities.

Claims: The part of a patent that states what was invented and what the patent precludes others from imitating.

Cognitive Conflict: Conflicts in which individuals become aware of contrasting perspectives or interests, but focus on the issues and not on one another.

Collateral: Something of value that an entrepreneur pledges to sell to reimburse investors in the event that there are insufficient proceeds from a venture to return the investors' principal.

Commercial Loan: A form of bank financing in which the borrower pays interest on the money borrowed.

Competence-Destroying: A form of change that undermines the skills and capabilities of people who are already doing something. It is contrasted with competence-enhancing change, which enhances the skills and capabilities of people who are already doing something.

Competitive Advantage: A business attribute that allows a firm and not its competitors to capture the profits from exploiting an opportunity.

Complementary Assets: Assets that must be used along with an innovation to provide a new product or service to customers, typically including manufacturing equipment, and marketing and distribution facilities.

Complementary Products: Complementary products are products that work together, like recorded movies and videotape recorders or computer hardware and computer software.

415

Concentration: The proportion of market share that lies in the hands of the largest firms in an industry. This concept is commonly measured by the four-firm concentration ratio, a government measure of the market share that lies in the hands of the four largest firms in an industry.

Concepts: Categories for objects or events that are somehow similar to each other in certain respects.

Confirmation Candidates: Alternatives that are not really considered seriously; rather, they are raised mainly for the purpose of helping groups convince themselves that initial favorite is indeed correct.

Confluence Approach: A view suggesting that creativity emerges out of the confluence (i.e., convergence) of several basic resources.

Conflict: A process in which one party perceives that another party has taken or will take actions that are incompatible with its interests

Conjoint Analysis: A technique for determining the relative importance of various dimensions in customers' evaluations of specific products.

Contracts: Promises that are enforceable by law.

Control Barrier: Refers to unwillingness of founders of new ventures to surrender control over the company to others.

Control Rights: The right to decide what to do with a venture's assets.

Convertible Securities: Financial instruments that allow investors to convert preferred stock, which gets preferential treatment in the event of a liquidation, into common stock at the investor's option.

Copyright: A form of intellectual property protection provided to the authors of original works of authorship, including literary, dramatic, musical, artistic, and certain other intellectual work.

Core Rigidities: The fact that companies tend to do well at things that they are accustomed to doing, not things that are new.

Corporations: Legal entities separate from their owners that may engage in business, make contracts, own property, pay taxes, and sue and be sued by others.

Covenants: Restrictions on the behavior of entrepreneurs contractually agreed upon by investors and entrepreneurs.

Creativity: The generation of ideas that are both novel (original, unexpected) and appropriate or useful; they meet relevant constraints.

D

Debt: A financial obligation to return money provided plus a scheduled amount of interest.

Deception: Efforts to mislead others by withholding information or presenting false information.

Devil's Advocate Technique: A procedure for improving group decision making in which one group member is assigned the task of disagreeing with and criticizing whatever plan or decision is the initial favorite.

Discount Rate: The annual percentage rate that an investor reduces the value of an investment to calculate its present value.

Discounted Future Earnings Method: A method of valuing businesses based on discounted future earnings.

Discrete: A characteristic of a new product or service that makes it independent of a system of other assets necessary to use the product or service.

Distributive Justice: A principle of perceived fairness suggesting that all parties to a relationship should receive a share of the available rewards commensurate with the scope of their contributions.

Dominant Design: An arrangement that all companies producing a product will chose as the way of bringing together the different parts of a product or service.

Due Diligence: The review of a new venture's management, business opportunity, technology, legal status, and finances prior to investment.

E

Earnings Methods: Methods of valuing businesses based on their future earnings.

Economies of Scale: A reduction in the cost of each unit produced as the volume of production increases.

Employee Stock Ownership Plans (ESOPs): Methods of transferring ownership of a company to its employees in which current owners contribute to an employee stock ownership trust. Contributions are often based on the profitability of the company.

Equity: The ownership of a company, which takes the form of stock. It also equals assets minus liabilities or net worth.

Excess Earnings Method: A method of valuing businesses based on the extent to which a company will generate earnings in excess of the average for its industry.

Exit Strategies: Procedures through which entrepreneurs transfer ownership of their businesses to other persons.

Expectancy Theory: A theory of motivation suggesting that in order for motivation be high, individuals must perceive clear links between their effort and their performance and their performance and their rewards, and that the rewards offered to them are ones they actually want.

Experimentation: A research method in which one variable is systematically changed in order to determine whether such changes affect one or more other variables.

F

Factor: Specialized organizations that purchase the accounts receivable of businesses at a discount.

First Mover: The first firm to enter a particular market.

First-Mover Advantage: Any benefit that a firm gets from being the first to offer a product in a particular market.

Fixed Costs: Costs of things like facilities and equipment that do not change with the number of units sold.

Focus Groups: Groups of from 8 to 12 people who are similar to potential customers and who meet for one to two hours to describe their perceptions of and reactions to relevant products.

Forfeiture Provisions: Contract terms that require an entrepreneur to lose ownership of her venture if she fails to meet agreed-upon milestones.

Franchising: A mode of business in which one party, the franchisor, develops a plan for the provision of a product or service to end customers, and another party, the franchisee, uses that plan in return for paying a fee and agreeing to oversight.

Franchising: A system of distribution in which semi-independent business owners (franchisees) pay fees and royalties to a parent company (the franchisor) in return for the right to use its trademark, sell its products or services, and, in many cases, use the business model and system it has developed.

G

Government Permit: A right given by a government to be the only party allowed to do something in a particular geographical location.

Group Polarization: The tendency for members of decision-making groups to shift toward views more extreme than the ones with which they began.

Groupthink: A strong tendency for decision-making groups to close ranks, cognitively, around a decision, assuming that the group can't be wrong, that all members must support the decision strongly, and that any information contrary to the decision should be rejected.

H

Heuristics: Simple rules for making complex decisions or drawing inferences in a rapid and seemingly effortless manner.

Hierarchcial Modes: When one party owns all parts of the operation that produces and sells a product or service to end customers.

Hold-Up: An attempt by one party to a contract to opportunistically renegotiate the terms of an agreement after it has been made.

Human Capital: Investment or value in human resources rather than physical assets.

Human Cognition: The mental processes through which we acquire information, enter it into storage, transform it, and use it to accomplish a wide range of tasks.

Hypothesis: An as yet untested prediction or explanation for a set of facts.

I

Idea Generation: The production of ideas for something new; very close in meaning to *creativity*.

Identification-Based Trust: Trust based on the belief that others will behave as they promise to behave not because they will be punished for failing to do so, but because they have the trusting person's well-being at heart.

Illiquidity Premium: Additional return demanded by investors to compensate them for the fact that an investment cannot be sold easily.

Immigration Reform and Control Act of 1986: A law designed to accomplish two major goals: discourage illegal immigration into the United States and strengthen the national origin provision of Title VII of the Civil Rights Act (1964).

Implicit Favorite: The decisions initially favored by a majority of members of a decision-making group. Often, this is the decision made by the group.

Impression Management: Tactics used by individuals to make a good first impression on others.

Information Asymmetry: The imbalance in knowledge about something between two parties.

Initial Public Offering (IPO): Initial sale of stock in a company to the public.

Intangibles: Assets that are hard, if not impossible, to list on the balance sheet: the goodwill the company has acquired with customers and suppliers, its reputation in the industry, its success in attracting and motivating first-rate employees.

Integrative Agreements: Ones that maximize joint benefits—the gains experienced by both sides.

Intellectual Property: The core ideas about a new product or service that make the development of these products and services possible.

Intelligence: Individuals' abilities to understand complex ideas, to adapt effectively to the world around them, to learn from experience, to engage in various forms of reasoning, and to overcome a wide range of obstacles.

Invent Around: To come up with a solution that does not violate a patent but accomplishes the same goal as the patented approach.

Intrapreneurs: Persons who create something new, but inside an existing company rather than through founding a new venture.

J

Job Analysis: A careful analysis of a specific job to determine what it involves and what it requires in terms of specific knowledge, skills, and abilities.

Job Description: An overview of what the job involves in terms of its duties, responsibilities, and working conditions.

Job Design: Efforts to structure jobs so that they increase people's interest in doing them (and hence their motivation).

Joint Venture: A form of business ownership that resembles a partnership, except that there are no general or limited partners, and the purpose of the entity is very limited.

K

Knowledge Spillovers: The accidental transfer of information about how to create new products, production processes, ways of marketing, or ways of organizing, from one firm to another.

L

Lead-Time Advantage: Any benefit that a firm receives by doing something before someone else.

Learning Curve: A relationship that measures the per-unit performance at production as a function of the cumulative number of units produced.

Legitimacy: A belief that something is correct and appropriate.

Leveraged Buyout: Procedures for transferring ownership of a company to its current managers. These persons borrow from a financial organization in order to pay the owner an agreed-upon price.

Licensing: A mode of business in which one party contracts with another to use the first party's ideas to make products and services for sale to end customers in return for a fee.

Limited Liability Company (LLC): A cross between a corporation and partnership, offering some of the benefits of both. As is true in S corporations, income flows through to owners (known as "members") who pay their own taxes as individuals. Unlike S corporations, however, LLCs are not subject to so many government restrictions.

Limited Partnership: A partnership in which one or more partners are general partners who manage the business and others are limited partners who invest in the business but forego any right to manage the company.

Line of Credit: An agreement to allow entrepreneurs to draw up to a set amount of money at a particular interest rate whenever they need it.

Locus of Innovation: The location, both within the value chain and between the public and private sector, in which efforts to apply new knowledge to the creation of new products, production processes, and ways of organizing occurs.

M

Macro (Perspective): A "top-down" perspective that seeks to understand the entrepreneurial process by focusing largely on environmental factors (i.e., economic, financial, political factors) that are largely beyond the direct control of an individual.

Mandatory Redemption Rights: Contract terms that require an entrepreneur to give investors their investment back at any time.

Market-Based Modes: When different parts of the business, such as manufacturing and marketing, are owned by different entities and are connected by a contractual relationship.

Market Value (price-earnings approach): Procedures for valuing businesses based on the price-earnings ratios for comparable publicly owned companies.

Memory: Our cognitive systems for storing and retrieving information.

Micro (Perspective): A "bottom-up" perspective that seeks to understand the entrepreneurial process by focusing on the behavior and thought of individuals or groups of individuals (e.g., founding partners).

Milestone: A jointly agreed-upon goal between entrepreneurs and investors that the entrepreneur needs to meet to receive another stage of financing.

Monopoly: A situation in which a firm is the only supplier of a product or service.

Motivation: The processes that arouse, direct, and maintain human behavior toward attaining some goal. In other words, motivation refers to behavior that is energized by, and directed toward, reaching some desired target or objective.

N

Negotiation: A process in which the opposing sides exchange offers, counteroffers, and concessions, either directly or through representatives.

Network Externalities: A situation in which something has increasing value as more people use it.

Noncompete Agreement: A legal document in which a person agrees not to work for a company that will compete with her employer if she stops working for the employer.

Nondisclosure Agreement: A legal document in which a person agrees not to make private information public.

Nonverbal Cues: Cues relating to facial expressions, eye contact, body posture or movements, or nonverbal aspects of speech. These cues can be very helpful in the detection of deception.

O

Occupational Safety and Health Act of 1970 (OSHA): An act designed to protect the health and safety of employees in the United States. The act requires employers to (1) provide a safe and healthy work environment—a workplace free from recognized hazards likely to cause harm to employees; (2) comply with specific occupational safety and health standards—rules dealing with various occupa-

tions and industries; (3) keep records of occupational injuries and illnesses.

Opportunity: The potential to create something new (new products or services, new markets, new production processes, new raw materials, new ways of organizing existing technologies, etc.) that has emerged from a complex pattern of changing conditions—changes in knowledge, technology, or economic, political, social, and demographic conditions.

Opportunity Recognition: The process through which individuals conclude that they have identified the potential to create something new that has the capacity to generate economic value (i.e., potential future profits).

Option: A right, but not an obligation, to make a future investment.

Organizational Citizenship Behaviors: Employee behaviors that go beyond the role requirements of their jobs and that are not directly or explicitly recognized by formal reward systems.

Organizational Commitment: The extent to which an individual identifies and is involved with his or her organization and is, therefore, unwilling to leave it.

Overall Approach to Negotiation: The overall approach to negotiation adopted by the persons participating in it. Two basic patterns are a "win-lose" approach and a "win-win" approach.

P

Partnership: An association of two or more people who co-own a business for the purpose of making a profit.

Partnership Agreement: A document written with the assistance of an attorney, and that states all of the terms under which the partnership will operate.

Patent: An exclusive right given by the government to preclude others from duplicating an invention for a specified period of time in return for disclosure of the invention.

Pay for Performance Systems: Reward systems that assume that employees differ in how much they contribute to the company's success, and that they should be rewarded in accordance with the scope of their contributions.

Perceptual Mapping: A technique for identifying the key dimensions along which potential customers evaluate products.

Personal Selling: An effort by an entrepreneur to sell a product or service through direct interaction with customers.

Persuasion: The task of inducing others to share our views and to see the world much as we do.

Practical Intelligence: Being intelligent in a practical sense; persons high in such intelligence are adept at solving the problems of everyday life and have "street smarts."

Prior Art: Prior patents that a given patent cites as the building blocks of an invention.

Product Development: The process by which the entrepreneur creates the product or service that will be sold to customers.

Professional Corporation (PC): A form of business ownership in which owners have limited liability; generally restricted to professionals such as physicians, attorneys, and accountants.

Proforma Balance Sheet: A form showing projections of the company's financial condition at various times in the future.

Proforma Income Statement: A form illustrating projected operating results based on profit and loss.

Protected Class: A group that suffered discrimination in the past.

Prototypes: Mental representations of categories of events or objects.

Provisional Patent Application: A document, filed with the patent and trademark office, that states that a person intends to file a full patent application. It provides some protection against imitation of an invention during the patent application process.

R

R&D Intensity: The proportion of a firm's sales that are devoted to creating new scientific knowledge and applying that knowledge to the creation of new products and production processes.

Realistic Job Previews: Efforts to present a balanced and accurate picture of the company to potential employees, with the goal of improving future retention of these persons.

Regulatory Focus Theory: A theory that suggests that in regulating their own behavior to achieve desired ends, individuals adopt one of two contrasting perspectives: a promotion focus (main goal is accomplishment) or a prevention focus (main goal is prevention of losses).

Reliability: The extent to which measurements are consistent across time or between judges.

Reverse Engineering: The process of taking apart a product to determine how it works.

Reward Systems: Systems in a new venture for recognizing and rewarding good performance.

Roles: The set of behaviors that individuals occupying specific positions within a group are expected to perform.

S

S Corporation: Corporations in which all profits and losses are passed through to shareholders, just as they are passed through to partners in a partnership.

S-Curve: A graphical depiction of the typical pattern of performance improvement of new products or services as a function of the amount of effort put into them.

Schemas: Cognitive frameworks representing our knowledge and assumptions about specific aspects of the world.

Self-Assessment: An inventory of the knowledge, experience, training, motives, and characteristics they themselves possess and can contribute to the new venture.

Self-Serving Bias: The tendency to attribute successful outcomes largely to internal causes (our own efforts, talents, or abilities) but unsuccessful ones largely to external cause (e.g., the failings or negligence of others).

Shirking: The failure to put forth all of the effort that a person is capable of providing.

Signal Detection Theory: A theory suggesting that in situations where individuals attempt to determine whether a stimulus is present or absent, four possibilities exist: The stimulus exists and the perceiver concludes that it is present; the stimulus exists but the perceiver fails to recognize it; the stimulus does not exist and the perceiver concludes, erroneously, that it is present; the stimulus does not exist and the perceiver correctly concludes that it is not present.

Small Business Innovation Research (SBIR): A government program designed to encourage innovation in the United States by requiring participating federal agencies to set aside 2 percent of their budgets for funding contracts, grants, or cooperative agreements through the SBIR.

Social Capital: An important resource that derives from relationships among individuals in organizations or other social structures. Social capital involves close interpersonal relationships among individuals, characterized by mutual trust, liking, and identification.

Social Competence: A summary term for an individual's overall level of social skills.

Social Perception: The process through which we come to know and understand other persons.

Social Skills: A set of competencies (discrete skills) that enable individuals to interact effectively with others

Sole Proprietorship: A type of business ownership in which a business is owned and managed by one individual.

Staging: The provision of capital in pieces conditional on the achievement of specified milestones.

Stress: A pattern of emotional states and physiological reactions occurring in response to demands from many different events in our lives.

Structured Interviews: Interview in which all applicants are asked the same questions—ones chosen carefully to be truly job-related.

Successful Intelligence: A balanced blend of analytic, creative, and practical intelligence. Successful intelligence is the kind of intelligence needed by entrepreneurs.

Sunk Costs or Escalation of Commitment: The tendency to become trapped in bad decisions and stick to them even though they yield increasingly negative results.

Syndicate: The sharing of an investment across a group of investors.

Systematic Observation: A research method in which certain aspects of the world are observed systematically, keeping careful records of what is detected. This information is then used as a basis for reaching conclusions about the topics under investigation.

T

Tacit Knowledge: A type of understanding that cannot be documented or even articulated. It is frequently contrasted with codified knowledge, which is a type of understanding that can be expressed in documentary form.

Technical Standard: An agreed-upon basis on which a product or service operates.

Terminal Value: The estimated value of a new venture at the time that the investment is liquidated in an initial public offering or an acquisition.

Theory: Refers to effort to go beyond merely describing various phenomena and, instead, to explain them.

Title VII of the Civil Rights Act of 1964: A law designed to prevent discrimination in workplaces. The law prohibits employers from basing employment decisions on a person's race, color, religion, sex, or national origin.

Trade Secret: A piece of knowledge that confers an advantage on firms and is protected by nondisclosure.

Trade-Name Franchising: A type of franchising in which franchisors grant independent business owners the right to use the franchisor's name.

Trademark: A word, phrase, symbol, design, or combination of these that identifies and distinguishes the goods and services of one company from those of another.

Trust: One person's degree of confidence in the words and actions of another person—confidence that this person will generally behave in predictable ways that are understandable in terms of the relationship between them.

Tyranny of the Current Market: The fact that listening to customers will make it difficult for companies to come up with new products for new markets because a firm's current customers will always ask it for improvements to current products, not new products for new markets.

U

Uncertainty: A condition in which the future is unknown.

Unlimited Personal Liability: Occurs when business owners are personally liable for all of debts incurred by the business.

User Myopia: The fact that customers can only see very narrow needs or solutions, typically only their own needs, not those of other market segments.

V

Validity: The extent to which measurements actually reflect the underlying dimension to which they refer.

Variable Costs: Costs incurred for each unit that is sold.

Variables: Aspects of the world that can take different values.

Venture Capital Method: How venture capitalists calculate the amount of equity that they will take in a new venture in return for their investment of capital.

Venture Capitalist: A person who works for an organization that raises money from institutional investors and invests those funds in new firms.

Vertically Integrated: A situation in which a firm owns successive stages of the value chain.

Vesting Periods: A period of time when entrepreneurs cannot cash out of their investments.

W

Win-Win Solution: One that is acceptable to both sides and that meets the basic needs of both.

NAME INDEX

A

Abernathy, W., 228
Abetti, P.A., 17, 26
ACM Enterprises, 140–141
Acs, Z., 26, 51, 79, 289
Advertures in Advertising, 206
Albany Molecular Research, 73
Alba-Ramirez, A., 26
Aldrich, H., 80, 132, 162, 266, 344
Allen, N.J., 345
Allen, R.W., 304
Amason, A.C., 106, 132, 318
Amazon.com, 33, 275
Americans with Disabilities Act (ADA) of 1990, 95–96, 103, 323
Amit, R., 162, 265, 266
Anderson, P., 51, 238
Anderson, P., 134
Anonyou, C., 317
Aquino, K., 79, 344
Arby's, 199
Ardichvili, Al, 26, 50
Arking, R., 372
Arrow, K., 51, 162, 245, 265
Arthur, B., 238
Ashford, S.J., 345
Ash, M.K., 7
Atkinson, B., 268
Atlanta Bread Company, 202
Au Bon Pain, 301
Audrestsch, D.B., 26, 51, 79, 266, 289
Azoulay, P., 211, 266

B

Bachrach, D.G., 318
Badagliacca, J., 268
Bahls, J., 289
Baj, Pam, 77
Baldwin, J., 134
Balkin, D.B., 26, 344, 372
Bamford, C., 51
Barnett, W., 51
Barney, J.B., 79, 265
Baron, R.A., 3, 6, 13, 26, 58, 79, 80, 83, 91, 96, 117, 131, 132, 168, 184, 187, 240, 293, 317, 318, 330, 344, 349, 350, 372
Barrick, M.R., 131
Barry, C., 162
Barton, D.L., 219, 237
Barzel, Y., 162
Baskin Robbins, 206
Bates, T., 211
Baumeister, R.F., 237
Baum, J.R., 51, 162, 318, 344
Bay Networks, Inc., 101
Bedeian, A.G., 26
Begley, T., 318
Bell, A.G., 10
Bergqvist, H., 268
Bezos, J., 33
Bhat, S., 77
Bhide, A., 30, 51, 140, 162, 238, 266
Bicheler, J., 268
Bird, B.J., 318

Birley, S., 26, 80, 344, 372
Blakely, J., 162
Blanchflower, D., 80, 162
Bollinger, M., 26
Borstein, D.J., 84
Boulding, W., 290
Bower, J., 51, 266
Boyd, D., 318
Bramante, F., 247
Brandstatter, M., 106
Bresson, R., 64
Brewer, F.S., 287
Breyer's Ice Cream, 206
Brockhaus, R., 265, 266
Brockner, J., 80, 344
Brock, T.C., 318
Brown, J.D., 132, 318
Brown, K.S., 106
Brown, M.R., 287
Brown, R., 51
Bucher, M., 217
Buchholtz, A.K., 131
Buchholz, R.A., 132
Buckley, M.R., 344
Buehler, R., 184
Burger King, 201
Burnstein, E., 106
Burt, R., 162
Busenitz, L.W., 79
Buss, D.D., 211
Butler, S., 108
Bygrave, W., 80, 132
Byrne, D., 132, 317, 344, 372

C

Cable, D.M., 344
Cafe Ladro, 56
Camacho, C.J., 80
Cameron, M., 150
CAPLine Program of the U.S. Small Business Administration, 150
Cardozo, R., 26, 50
Cardy, R.L., 132, 344, 372
Career Mosaic, 322
Carland, J.C., 26
Carland, J.W., 26
Carnegie, A., 7
Carnegie, D., 297
Carnevale, P.J., 372
Carpenter, G., 290
Carter, N., 132
Carter, N.M., 317
Carter, S., 80
Casella, D.F., 317
Casson, M., 162, 265
Caves, R., 266
Cerner Corp., 248
Chasteen, R., 277
Chatter, M., 13, 337
Chen, C.C., 26
Chen, J.J., 106
Chocolate Gecko, The, 54
Christen, M., 290
Christiansen, C., 51, 257–258, 266
Churchill, N.C., 80, 345

Cialdini, R.B., 318
Ciavarella, M.A., 131
Civil Rights Act of 1964, 95, 103, 196
Clark, M.S., 132
Clark, S., 182
Clegg, S., 162
Closets by Design, 206
Coca-Cola, 279, 280
Coella, A., 344
Coeurderoy, R., 80
Cohen, W., 281, 290
Coleman, P.T., 318
Collins, C.J., 11, 26
Collins, J.M., 344, 345
Connell, J.B., 106
Cooper, A., 131, 132
Corbett, A.C., 80
Corning Glass Works, 120
Cottringer, W., 341
Coutriaux, J., 80
Cramer, J., 80
Crespin, R., 227
Crewson, P., 265
Crick, A., 26
Cropanzano, R.D., 132
Curran, J., 211
Cusumano, M., 238
Cycletech Inc., 96

D

Daddy's Junk Music Stores, Inc., 247
Daimler Chrysler, 285
D'Ambra, T., 73
Dana Farber Cancer Institute, 101
D'Aquanni, L., 54
D'Arbeloff, A., 166
Darby, M., 245
David, P., 290
Davidsson, P., 131, 132
DaVinci, L., 61
Davis, J.H., 106
Day, D.V., 132, 317
Days Inn, 206
Dean, T., 51
De Beers, 246
Debelak, D., 162
de Cuellar, J.P., 368
Dees, G., 162
DeFigueiredo, J.N., 106
De Goncourt, E., 83
Dell, M., 7
Delmar, F., 184
Delta Air Lines, 304
de Mestral, G., 63–64
Design Toscano, Inc., 32
DeTienne, D.R., 79
Deutsch, M., 318
Diderot, 14
DiMatteo, M.R., 317
Dobbin, F., 51
Dollinger, M.J., 80
Domino's, 199
Donovan, J.J., 131
Dotseh, Junice, 268
Dowd, T., 51

Doyle, A.C., 88
Drama Kids International, Inc., 206
Drizin, M., 334
Drucker, P., 23
Drugstore.com, 279
Dryden Co., 248
Dunkelberg, W., 131
Dunkin' Donuts, 203, 206
Dunley, P., 115
Durand, R., 80
Dweck, C.S., 80

E

Earles, J.L., 372
ebay, 282
Ebeling, A., 209
Eckhardt, J., 28, 50, 51
Eder, R.W., 317, 344
Edison, T., 61, 64
8(a) Business Development Program, 92
8 minute Dating, 122
Einstein, A., 61, 64
Eisenhardt, K., 51, 132, 266
Ellis, J., 159
Eloquent Inc., 248
Enron, 13
Ensley, M.D., 106, 132, 318
Erikson, T., 131, 317
Evans, D., 26, 265
Expedia.com, 8

F

Falbe, C.M., 318
Federal Express, 138
Feldman, M., 31, 51
Fernandez, J.K., 344
Fernandez, M., 162
Ferris, G.R., 26, 131, 132, 317, 344
Fiet, J.O., 80
Finke, R.A., 80
Fiske, S.T., 237
Fixx Services, Inc., 217
Fletcher, C., 184
Flynn, B., 159
Folta, T., 132
Foo, M., 265
Ford, 36, 285
Forgas, J.P., 372
Foster-Fishman, P.G., 106
Foster, R., 237
Franz, T.M., 106
Frese, M., 317
Freud, S., 61
Friedman, H.S., 317
Frieseke, D., 372
Fuerst, O., 162, 289

G

Gadda, C., 134
Gaglio,C., 68, 80
Gaines, C.L., 372
Gaines, J., 318
Galkin, D.B., 132
Gartner, W.B., 26, 132, 317, 318
Gates, B., 7, 228, 366
Gatewood, E., 80
Gatewood, R.D., 131
Geiger, U., 162, 289
Geller, E.S., 344
General Electric (GE), 6, 98–99
General Motors, 36, 285
Genghis Grills, 58
Gentry, W., 106
George, J.M., 131
Gerpott, T.J., 132
Ghoshal, S., 317

Giacalone, R.A., 317
Gibson, D., 120
Gigone, D., 106
Gilbert, D.T., 237
Gimeno, J., 132
Giudici, G., 162
Glass, D., 248
Glosten, L., 162, 265, 266
Gnuschke, J.E., 23
Goldfarb, B., 106
Golf USA, Inc., 206
Gomez-Mejia, L.R., 132, 344, 372
Gompers, P., 162
Grady, C.L., 79
Graf, I.K., 132
Greenberg, D.B., 317
Greenberg, J., 26, 131, 184, 344, 345
Green, P., 237
Green, P.G., 26
Griffin, D., 184
Griffin, R.W., 344, 345
Grigorenko, E.L., 80
Grote, N.K., 132
Gupta, M., 80
Gymboree, 206

H

Hafer, C.L., 132
Hallam, M., 26
Hall, J., 317
Halloid Corporation, 219
Hall, Seth, 33–34
Hamburger University, 201
Hampson, E., 13, 26
Hardin, C.D., 79
Hardy, C., 162
Harris, C., 134
Harrison, J.S., 129
Harvey, J.H., 317
Hastie, R., 106
Hathaway, S., 268
Haxby, J.V., 79
Hay, M., 344, 345
Headhunter, 322
Heckhausen, J., 80
Heilman, M.E., 106
Hendeles, Y., 80
Hendricks, M., 265
Heneman, R.L., 317
Henrekson, M., 106
Herman, M., 248
Herron, L., 79
Hershman, D.J., 268
Higgins, C.A., 344
Higgins, E.T., 80
Hirt, E.R., 106
Hitt, M.A., 129
Hmieleski, K.M., 80
Hoang, H., 266
Hockhwarter, W.Q., 132
Hofer, C.W., 317
Hoffman, H., 162
Hoffman, R.C., 262
Holmberg, S.R., 211
Holmes, S., 88
Holmes, T., 51
Holmstrom, B., 289
Honig, B., 131
Hornaday, J., 317
Horvath, J.A., 372
Horwitz, B., 79
Hoskisson, R.E., 129
Houghton, S.M., 79, 344
Hoy, F., 80
Hubbard, R., 106
HubZone Empowerment Contracting
    Program, 93

Humphrey, H., 3
Hurtz, G.M., 131
Hybels, R., 266
Hyrsky, K., 80

I

Idson, L.C., 80
IEP, Inc., 3
Immigration Reform and Control Act of
    1986, 196, 208
Inca, 63
Interlan, Inc., 101
Ireland, R.D., 129
Isen, A.M., 372

J

Jafee, T., 122
Jakobson, B., 268, 276
Janis, I.L., 106
Janus Capital Corp., 248
Jentz, G.A., 211
Jermier, J.M., 318
Johansson, E., 80
John Paul Getty Foundation, 21
Johnson, M., 290
Jones, Coy A., 23
Judge, T.A., 344
Jurica, P.J., 372

K

Kacmar, K.M., 26, 344
Kalakanis, L., 26
Kangasharju, A., 80
Kansas City Royals, 248
Kanter, R., 289
Kasarda, J., 162
Katilla, R., 266
Katz, J., 68, 80, 265, 266
Kauffman, E., 248
Kauffman Foundation, 248
Keller, R.T., 132
Kelley, T., 104
Kelly, J., 56
Kennedy, J.F., 54, 72
Kerin, R., 290
KFC, 199
Kilduff, M., 132, 317
Kirkpatrick, S., 318
Kirsch, D., 229, 238
Kirzner, I., 29, 50
Kisfalvi, V., 367, 372
Kleiner Perkins, 279
Klepper, S., 80
Klevorick, A., 289
Knott, A.M., 106
Kodithuwakku, S.S., 26
Koen, P.A., 26
Kohn, Kevin, 268
Kooker, N.R., 345
Krantz, J.H., 132
Krishnamurthi, L., 290
Kristof, A.L., 317
Krueger, N.F., Jr., 26, 79
Kunda, Z., 79, 106
Kurlantzick, J., 104

L

Laats, A., 134
Langdon, N., 132
Langlois, J.H., 26
La Rouchefoucauld, 28
Larson, A., 26
Larson, J.R., Jr., 106
Latham, G.P., 344
Lauer, W., 268

Lau, J., 182
Lautenschlager, G., 372
Lave, L., 80
Laverack, B., 134
Leadership Management, Inc., 206
Leana, C.R., 318
Lee, T.W., 345
Leighton, L., 26, 265
Lelux, B., 358, 372
Lemelson, J., 249
Lerner, J., 162
Lerner, M., 80
Levie, J., 344, 345
Levin, R., 272–273, 289
Levinson, D.J., 372
Lewicki, R.J., 318
Lewin, K., 26
Lewis, V.L., 345
Liberman, N., 80
Liden, R.C., 132
Lieberman, M., 290
Lindzey, G., 237
Link, W.J., 370
Loan Guarantee Program of the U.S.
    Small business Administration, 150
Locke, E.A., 11, 26, 318, 344
Lotus Development, 168
Low, M.B., 80
Lubart, T., 80
Lucent Technologies, 13, 337
Ludwig, T.D., 344

M

MacDonald, H., 184
MacKenzie, S.B., 318
MacLeish, A., 187
MacMillan, I., 266
Maddocks, T.D., 211
Mahmood, T., 51
Maisog, J.M., 79
Management Recruiters Worldwide, 206
Mancuso, J.R., 184
Manes, S., 235
Mang, P., 266
Manigart, C., 80
Manning, M.R., 318
Mansfield, E., 51
Marion Labs, 248
Markman, G.D., 26, 80, 132, 184, 317
Markman, K.D., 106
Marshall, John, 211
Maslach, C., 318
Mason, C., 80, 132
Massachusetts Technology Development
    Corp. (MTDC), 101
Mata, J., 51
Matlin, M.W., 79
Matusik, S., 132
Maxwell, V., 268
McCline, R.L., 77
McDonald's, 199, 201, 203, 206, 249, 279
McDougall, P., 132
MCK Communications, 101
McKinsey & Company, 120
Media 100, 101
Mehta, S., 360
Mellahi, M., 290
Merck, 270
Meyer, G., 80
Meyer, G.D., 317
Meyer, J.P., 345
Michael, S.C., 211
Micom Systems, 101
Miller, R.L., 211
Mitchell, T.R., 344, 345
Monster Board, 322
Montagu, M., 21

Montgomery, C., 290
Moore, G., 237
Morgan, K.B., 211
Morganthaler Ventures, 134
Morton, D., 76
Morton, K., 268
Motorola, 269
Motowidlo, S.J., 318
Mount, M.K., 131
Mowday, R.T., 345
Mueller, N., 5, 10, 298–299
Muller, E., 162, 265, 266
Murray, L., 106
Muzyka, D.F., 344, 372
Mylonadis, Y., 238
Myomatrix Therapeutics, 360

N

Nahapiet, J., 317
Nancy's Specialty Foods, 5, 10, 298–299
NASDAQ, 101
NBX Corporation, 134
Nelson, R., 265, 289, 290
Nemeth, C., 106
Neubert, M.J., 131
Newton, 64
Nexabit Networks, Inc., 337
Nike, 279–280
Nord, W., 162
Nortel Networks, 101

O

Occupational Safety and Health Act of
    1970 (OSHA), 196
Ohly, Bob, 56
O'Leary-Kelly, A., 344, 345
Oliver, C., 51
Olson, J.M., 132
Opalka, C., 73
O'Reilly, B., 26
Oringer, J., 327
Orradio Industries, Inc., 76
Orr, J.H., 76
Oswald, A., 80, 162
Ouellette, J.A., 344
Ovid, 349

P

Packard, J.S., 318
Pagac, S., 141
Page, B., 366
Paine, J.B., 318
Paleari, S., 162
Palm Computer, 249
Palm Pilot, 249
Panera Bread, 301
Papa John's Pizza, 201
Paris, E., 289
Park, D.C., 372
Peale, N.V., 164
Pearle Vision, 206
Pearson, A.W., 106, 132, 318
Pedroza, C., 237
Pennington, A.Y., 344
Personal Privacy System (PPS), 3
Peterson, R., 290
Photowow.com, 171
Pietrini, P., 79
Pigeon Control Professionals, 227
Pizza Hut, 206
Plous, S., 26
Podsakoff, P.M., 318
Pollock, T., 315
Poole, A., 268
Portugal, P., 51
Preble, J.F., 262

Prince, L.M., 317
Propecia, 270
Pruitt, D.G., 372
Purtzer, P., 268

R

Railex, 187
Rao, H., 260, 266
Rao, V., 237
Ratcliff, S.L., 344
Ray, S., 26, 50
Reagan, R., 320, 336
Ream, R., 341
Red Roof Inn, 199
Replacements Ltd., 366
Resource Alliance Group, 13
Reynolds, P., 80, 132
Reynolds, P.D., 317
Ricchiuto, J., 26
Riggio, R.E., 317
Riordan, C.M., 131
Roberts, E., 162, 266
Robinson, D., 162
Robson, M., 106
Rockefeller, J.D., 7
Rogers, E., 237
Rogers, J.D., 106
Rogers, R.J., 132
Rosa, P., 26
Rosenbloom, R., 238
Rosenfeld, P., 317
Ross, J., 79
Rothman, A.J., 79
Roth, P.L., 26
Rotner, Phil, 134
Rowland, K.M., 131, 344
Roy Rogers, 206
Rubbermaid, 362–363
Rubenstein, A.J., 26
Ruef, M., 51
Rumelt, R., 265
Rutherford, E., 63

S

Sahlman, W., 162
Salgado, J.F., 131
Sandberg, K., 290
Sapienza, H.J., 79, 318
Sarasvathy, D., 80
Scarborough, N.M., 372
Schaich, R., 301
Schefcyzk, M., 132
Schiff, R., 171
Schiller, B., 265
Schmitz, J., 51
Schoonhoven, K., 51, 132, 266
Schumpeter, J.A., 50, 51
Schumpeter, J., 29–30
Sears, 259
Securities and Exchange Commission
    (SEC), 193
Segal, A., 122
Severino, P., 101–102
Sexton, D., 162
Shane, S.A., 4, 5, 11, 26, 28, 31, 51, 79, 80,
    145–146, 162, 184, 211, 213, 265, 266,
    274, 372
Shankar, V., 290
Shapiro, C., 290
Shaver, K., 80
Shavitt, S., 318
Shepherd, D.A., 79, 184
Shepperd, J.A., 344
Shimamura, A.P., 372
Shutjens, V., 132
Silberman, I., 80
Silly Putty, 89

Simon, H., 80
Simon, M., 79, 344
SkyMall, 141
Sleeper, S., 80
Small Business Innovation Research
    (SBIR), 92, 103, 150
Smith, A.D., 372
Smith, F., 138
Smith, K.G., 344
Smith, P., 51
Smith, S., 370
Smith, S.M., 80
Smoot, M., 26
Sommars, J., 263
Sonus Networks, 101
SONY Corporation, 63
Sorenson, O., 162
Source One Spares Inc., 33–34
Srull, T.K., 372
Stanworth, J., 211
Starr, J.A., 162, 266, 318
Staw, B.M., 79, 345
Stephanie Anne, Inc., 175
Steria, 17
Sternberg, R.J., 80, 372
Sternberg, R., 65
Stevens, C.K., 317
Stewart, G.L., 131
Stewart, W.H., Jr., 26
Stocker-Kriechgauer, G., 106
Stokes, G.S., 131
Stopka, M., 32
Stuart, T., 162, 266
Subway, 199, 203, 206, 249
Super 8 Motels, 206
SurfSecret Software, 327
Sutton, R.I., 345
Swets, J.A., 80
Sylvan Learning Centers, 206

T

Tarpley, F., 317
Tax and Accounting Software Corp., 91
Taxol, 269
Taylor, L., 132
Teece, D., 265, 284, 290

Tele-Publishing International (TPI), 122
Teradyne, 166, 168
Terry, R.L., 132
Thompson, L., 132, 317, 318, 372
Thornhill, S., 13, 26
Tiffany, L., 211
Timmons, J., 317
Tiscione, A., 140–141
Tiscione, J., 140–141
Title VII of the Civil Rights Act of 1964,
    95, 103, 196
Tjosvold, D., 132
Torres, N.L., 211
Toyota, 295
Tracey, J.B., 318
Trollope, A., 293
Tropicana, 275
Trump, D., 359
Tushman, M., 51, 238

U

Ubuild It, 206
Ungerleider, L.G., 79
Uniform Partnership Act (UPA), 189
U.S. Patent and Trademark Office, 275,
    279–280, 281
Utterback, J., 33, 51, 237, 228, 238
Uzzi, B., 162

V

Van Buren, H.J., 318
Vanderbilt, C., 7
Van Praag, C., 80
Varadarajan, P., 290
Varian, H., 290
Venkataraman, S., 4, 5, 26, 265, 266
Vesper, K., 317
Vonk, R., 132

W

Wagner, R.K., 372
Walker Information Inc., 334
Wal-Mart, 248, 279, 364
Walsh, J., 290
Walsh, J.P., 345

Wanous, H.P., 344
Ward, T.B., 80
Warren, C., 106
Warren, S., 106
Watson, Dr., 88
Watson, W.E., 26
Wayne, P., 214
Wayne, S.J., 132, 317
Weber, A.L., 317
Weinberg, N., 162
Wellfleet Communications, Inc., 101
Wesson, T., 106
Wetzel, W., 80
Wever, E., 132
White, R.E., 13, 26
White, S., 132
Whitney, J.H., 134
Wiesenfeld, B.M., 344
Wiethoff, C., 318
Wilkerson, J., 209
Williams, W.M., 372
Winders, B., 58
Windward Group, 249
Winter, S., 51, 265, 289
Witt, L.A., 132
Woo, C., 131, 132
Wu, S., 162
Wyer, R.S., 372

X

Xerox, 219
X-Ray Optical Systems, Inc., 120

Y

Young, J.Y., 318
Yukl, G., 318

Z

Zacharakis, A.L., 79, 184, 317
Zhou, J., 131
Zimmerer, T.W., 372
Zucker, L., 245
Zurada, J., 80
Zwahr, M., 372

SUBJECT INDEX

A

Acceptance, in a new market
  See Marketing, in new firms
Acquisition, as exit strategy, 350
ADA
  See Americans with Disabilities Act
Adaptability, 257–258
Adjusted balance sheet technique, 355
Adoption patterns, 224–226
Adverse impact, 95
Adverse selection, 136, 158, 253
Advertising-intensive industries, 39
Affect infusion, 60
Affective commitment, 335
Affective conflict
  causes of, 302, 304
  defined, 301–302, 314
African-Americans
  as entrepreneurs, government support
    of, 92
  as a protected class, 95
Age 30 transition, 367
Agreeableness, as a point in self-assessment, 111
Agreement (contracts), 198
Alien corporation, 192
Alliances, 258–259
Americans with Disabilities Act (ADA)
  of 1990, 95–96 103, 323
Amortized, 36, 47
Analogy, 63
Analytic intelligence, 64
Anchoring-and-adjustment heuristic, 60
Angel network, 73
Angels (business), 147, 158, 250
Ankle-biters, 364
Antidilution provisions, 138, 158
Appendices (business plan), 169, 176
Arrow's paradox, 245
Articles of incorporation, 192
Asian-Pacific American entrepreneurs,
  government support of, 92
Asset-based financing, 146, 158
  lenders, 149
Assets, complementary, 41–42, 47
Availability heuristic, 59, 60
Awards, 334
Awfulizing, 312

B

Background (business plan), 169, 170
Balance sheet method of valuing a company, 355, 369
Banks, as source of capital, 149
Bargaining tactics, 360–361
Barriers to imitation
  control of resources, 246
  innovation, 247
  legal monopoly, 246
  reputation, 246–247
Behaviors, that encourage investors,
  155–156
Bias
  confirmation, 59, 60, 85

optimistic, 59, 60
  self-serving, 121, 128, 342
"Big Five Dimensions" of personality,
  111–112, 128
  ratings for self, 129–130
Big-lie technique, 303, 361
Biodata, 324–325, 340
Bottom-up approach to management, 9
Breach of contract, 198, 208
Breakeven analysis, 144–145, 158,
  160–161, 173–174, 181
Burnout, 310–311
Burn rate, 146, 158
Business angels, 147, 158, 250
Business broker, 353
Business contracts
  See Contracts
Business format franchising, 199, 208
Business plan, 11, 22, 181
  components, 167
    appendices, 169, 176
    background and purpose, 169, 170
    development, production, and location, 169, 172
    executive summary, 168–169,
      182–183
    financial plans, 169, 173–174
    harvest or exit, 169, 175
    intangibles, 176
    management team, 169, 172–173,
      183–184
    market analysis, 169, 171
    product, 170
    risk factors, 169, 174–175
    scheduling and milestones, 169,
      175–176
  goals, benefits of, 165–166
  key questions, 167
  model (figure), 166
  persuasion and, 164
  presentation of, 178–180
  principles, 167–168
  seven deadly sins, 177

C

Calculus-based trust, 299, 314
Cannibalize, 42–43, 47
Capacity (contracts), 198
Capital
  See Financing
Capital intensive, 47
Capital intensive industries, 38–39
Capitalized earnings method of valuing
  a company, 356, 369
CAPLine Program of the U.S. Small
  Business Administration, 150
Case method, 17–18, 22
Cash flow, 41, 47
Cash flow statements, 142–144, 158,
  159–160, 173–174, 181
Causal ambiguity, 243, 244–245, 262
C corporation
  See Corporations
Change

competence-destroying, 42, 47
  external, 29–30
  political and regulatory, 31
  social and demographic, 31–32
  technological, 30–31
Civil Rights Act of 1964, 95, 103, 196
Claims, 268, 276, 286
Co-branding franchising, 206
Codified knowledge, 244
Cofounders, of a new venture
  See Human resources
Cognitive conflict, 301
Cognitive processes
  capacity to process information, 58–60
  heuristics, 59
  memory, 56–57
  prototypes, 58
  schemas, 57–58
Collateral, 137, 158
Collective entrapment, 61
Commercial loans, 149, 158
Commitment, as a point in self-assessment,
  111
Commitment/consistency (influence),
  306, 307
Commitment, employee, 335–336
Communication, 337
  among cofounders, 122–124
Company growth, six phases of, 336–339
Company-wide pay for performance
  plans, 335
Compensatory damages, 198
Competence-destroying change, 42, 47
Competition
  defending against, 33, 240
  direct competitors, nondirect competitors, noncompetitors, 356
  discussed in a business plan, 169, 171
  opportunity and, 33
  See also Strategy
Competitive advantage, 248, 262
  trade secrets and, 279
  See also Strategy
Competitive edge, 101–102
Complementarity, with cofounders, 108,
  109–110, 112
Complementary assets, 41–42, 47
  intellectual property and, 284–285
Complementary products, 228–229, 234
Concentration, 39, 47
Conception/existence phase of company
  growth, 336, 338
Concepts, 62, 75
  stretching or expanding, 63–64
Confirmation bias, 59, 60, 85
Confirmation candidates, 97, 103
Conflict, 297
  affective
    causes of, 302, 304
    defined, 301–302
  cognitive, 301, 314
  defined, 301
  managing, 301–302
  resolving, techniques for, 302–303
  role, among cofounders, 119

Confluence approach (to creativity), 65–67, 75
Conjoint analysis, 220–221, 234
Conscientiousness, as a point in self-assessment, 111
Consideration (contracts), 198
Constructive criticism, 123–124
Continuance commitment, 335
Contract law, 197
Contract provisions, 138–139
Contracts, 208, 252
  basic elements, 197–198
  breach of, 198, 208
  choosing an attorney for, 198–199
  obligations under, 198–199
Control barrier, 336–339, 340
Control rights, 138–139, 158
Convergence of factors (opportunity), 10
Convertible securities, 138, 158
Copyrights, 286
  defined, 280
  obtaining, 281
  protections, 280
  what can be copyrighted, 280
Core rigidities, 219, 234
Corporations, 194, 208
  advantages, 192–193
  alien, 192
  defined, 192
  disadvantages, 193
  domestic, 192
  foreign, 192
  professional corporation (PC), 194–195
  S corporation, 193
  as source of capital, 149
Correct identification, 70–71
Correct rejection, 70–71, 72
Costs
  of exploiting opportunity, 250–251
  fixed, 231, 234
  hidden, 232
  variable, 231, 234
Covenants, 138, 158
Cover page (business plan), 167
Creative intelligence, 64–65
Creativity, 75
  concepts, 62–64
  confluence approach, 65–67
  defined, 54, 61–62
  encouraging, 65–67
  generating, 61–62
  how it occurs, 63
  human age and, 366
  human intelligence and, 64–65
  importance of, 62
  major implications for (positive and negative), 62–63
  prototypes, 58
  schemas, 57–58
  See also Human cognition
Credit
  lines of, 149, 158
  supplier, 146
Crisis, "danger" and "opportunity," 72
Criticism, 123–124
Customers
  perceptions of, 86
  surveys of, 86
  why they buy, 227
  See also Marketing, in new firms
Customer surveys, 86

D

Debt, 146, 158
Debt financing, 146
Deception, 115–117, 128

Decision-making groups
  improving, 105–106
  potential pitfalls for
    countering, 100
    group polarization, 98
    groupthink, 98–99
    implicit favorite, 97–98
    shared information, ignoring, 99
Delegating authority, 336–339
Demand conditions, 36–37
Demographic change, 31–32
Depreciation, 91
Deregulation, 31
Desk rage, 310
Destructive criticism, 123–124
Development (business plan), 169, 172
Devil's advocate technique, 100, 103, 105–106
Direct competitors, 353
Disclosing knowledge, dangers of, 245
Discounted future earnings of valuing a company, 356–357, 369
Discount rate, 154, 158
Discounts, in pricing, 232–233
Discovery test, 91
Discrete products and services, 43, 47
Discrete skills, 294
Discrimination
  entrepreneurial awareness of laws against, 196–197
  laws against, 94–96
  See also Equal employment opportunities laws; Minority entrepreneurs
Disparate treatment, 95
Distributive justice, 121, 128, 330–331, 340
Domestic corporation, 192
Dominant design, 38, 47, 227–228, 229, 234, 285
Door-in-the-face tactic, 307
Double taxation, 190, 191, 193
Downsizing, 7
Due diligence, 114, 151–152, 158

E

Early adopters, 225
Early majority, 225–226
Earnings methods of valuing a company, 355–357
Economies of scale, 256
  as asset of established firms, 41
  defined, 47
  in established firms, 39
  franchisors and, 250
Elevator pitch, 168
Emotional stability, as point in self-assessment, 112
Employees
  number needed, 125
  social networks as source of, 124–125
  temporary or permanent?, 126
  theft by, 331
  See also Motivating employees; Recruiting and selecting employees; Retaining employees
Employee stock ownership plans (ESOPs), 335, 352–353, 369
Employment contract, 7
Employment interviews, 323–325
Entrepreneurial opportunities
  See Opportunity
Entrepreneurs
  deception by, 116–117
  examples, 5
  good done by, 21
  impact of, on economies, 7
  key characteristics of, 24

kinds of intelligence needed, 64–65
life transitions, 367
moral for, 83
numbers of, 6
overcoming control barrier, 336–339
required resources for, 11
test of potential, 24
See also Minority entrepreneurs
Entrepreneurship
  as an activity, 4–5
  defined, 5, 7
  as a field of business, 4
  intrapreneurship and, 6
  knowledge and, sources of, 14
    experimentation, 16–17
    reflection, 17–18
    systematic observation, 15–16
    theory, 18–20
  nature and roots, 4–9
  older disciplines and, 7–9
  procedural memory and, 57
  process, 3, 7
    (figure), 12
    key phases in, 9–11
    ongoing, 12
    opportunities and individuals, intersection of, 13–14
    variables, 12–13
  requirements for, 5–6
  resources required for, 11
  static view of, avoiding, 11–12
  See also Knowledge, routes to; Theory
Environment, creativity and, 66–67
Equal Employment Opportunity Commission, 95
Equal employment opportunity laws, 94
  Americans with Disabilities Act (ADA) of 1990, 95–96, 103, 323
  Title VII of the Civil Rights Act of 1964, 95, 103, 196
Equity, 146, 158, 330, 340
Equity financing, 146
  process, 151–152
  See also Financing
Escalation of commitment (sunk costs), 60, 61, 76
Established firms
  disadvantages when serving new markets, 219
  existing customers, satisfying, 43
  forming alliances and partnerships with, 258–259
  opportunities favoring, 40–42
  product development and, 271–272
  social ties and, 271
E-tailers, fraud as problem for, 116–117
Event reaction questionnaire, 78–79
Exaggerated agreement, 115
Excess earnings method of valuing a company, 355–356, 369
Executive summary (business plan), 167–169, 182–183
Exit strategies, 349, 369
  acquisition by larger companies, 350
  in a business plan, 169
  determining the value of a business, 370
    balance sheet methods, 355
    capitalized earnings method, 356
    discounted future earnings method, 356–357
    excess earnings method, 355–356
    intangibles, 354–355
    market method, 357
  human life span and, 365–368
  for investors, 175
  negotiation

basic nature of, 359–360
danger of ankle-biters, 364
improving your skills, 371
overall approach to, 362–364
tactics, 360–362
sale or transfer to insiders
employee stock ownership plans
(ESOPs), 352–353
leveraged buyouts by managers,
351–352
succession in family-owned businesses, 351
sale to outsiders, 353–354
taking a company public (IPO-initial
public offering), 357–358
Expectancy theory, 329, 340
Experience
importance of, 73
openness to, 112
Experimentation, 14, 16–17, 22
Exploitation of opportunity
See Strategy
Expressiveness, 294, 295
Extraversion-introversion, as a point in
self-assessment, 111
Eye contact, 116

F

Facial expressions, exaggerated, 116
Factors, 149, 158
Factual information, 57
Fairness
as employee motivator, 330–332
perceived
among founders, 119–122
exercise about, 342
shirking and, 253–254
False alarm, 70–71, 72, 73, 74
Family, as source of capital, 147
Fast-approaching deadline, 307
Faulty attributions, 302
Financial plans (business plan), 169,
173–174
Financial resources, as required resource
for entrepreneurs, 11
Financing
asset-based, 146
behaviors that encourage investors,
155–156
capital, sources of
asset-based lenders, 149
banks, 149
business angels, 147
corporations, 149
factors, 149
friends and family, 147
government programs, 150
savings, 147
venture capitalists, 147–149
debt financing capital, 146
debt guaranteed by entrepreneur's personal assets or earning power, 146
difficulty of
information asymmetry problems,
135–136
uncertainty problems, 137
equity financing capital, 146
problems of, solutions to
contract provisions, 138–139
geographically localized investing, 139
self-financing, 137–138
specialization, 139
syndication, 139
social ties
example, 134
raising money through, 155–156

start-up capital
amount needed, 140–141
breakeven analysis, 144–145, 160–161
cash flow statements, 142–144,
159–160
income statements, 159–160
list of costs and use of proceeds,
141–142
proforma financial statements, 142,
143, 159–160
structure of
cost of capital, 152–154, 161
equity financing process, 151–152
staging of investment, 152, 153
supplier credit, 146
venture capital, 134
Firms
See Established firms; New firms
First mover, 251, 262, 286
advantage, in intellectual property,
282–283
Fixed costs, 231, 234
Flattery, 115, 296
Flexibility, 257–258, 270
of established firms, 271
Float or sink, 334
Focus groups, 86–87, 103, 217–218
Focus, on a market, 227
Foot-in-the-door tactics, 307
Foreign corporation, 192
Forfeiture provisions, 138, 158
Founding of a new venture
See Human resources (cofounders)
Fractional factorial design, 220
Franchisees, 199
Franchise fees, 202
Franchising, 199, 208, 262
benefits of, 200–202
brand name, as main asset, 250
business format, 200
co-branding, 206
competitive advantage, 249
determining when to use (four factors),
250–255
drawbacks of, 202–204
expansion of (kinds), 206
free riding problem, 254
future shape of, 205–206
hold-up problem, 254–255
international, 206
is it for you?, 210
legal aspects, 204–205
operation of, described, 249–250
smaller outlets in nontraditional locations, 205
trade-name, 200
Franchisor, 199
Fraud, e-tailing problem, 116–117
Free riding, 254, 334
Friends, as source of capital, 147
Friendship/liking (influence), 306, 307

G

General partners, 148, 190
Geographically localized investing, 139
Goals
in a business plan, 165–166
role of, in motivating employees,
326–328, 341–342
Government permits, 246, 262
Government programs, as source of capital, 150
Government regulations, 89
anti-discrimination laws, 94–96
entrepreneur's experience (example),
101–102

innovation, support of, 92
minority entrepreneurs, support of,
92–93
OSHA, 94
taxes
incentives, 91
legal forms of new ventures and tax
rates, 90
overall rate, 90
Granger Causality, 17
Group-level variables of the entrepreneurship process, 12–13
Group polarization, 98, 103
Groups
See Decision making groups
Groupthink, 98–99, 103, 248
resisting, 105

H

Harvest, discussed in the business plan,
169, 175
See also Exit strategy
Headhunters, 322
Heuristics, 59–60, 75
Hidden costs, 232
Hierarchical modes of exploiting oppor-
tunities, 262
versus market-based modes, 250–255
Hispanic Americans entrepreneurs
government support of, 92
as a protected class, 95
Hit, 70, 74
Hold-up, 254–255, 262
HubZone Empowerment Contracting
Program, 93
Human capital, 43–44, 47
Human cognition, 75
defined, 54–55
errors in, 59–60
limited capacity to process information,
58–60
Human intelligence
See Intelligence
Human resources
"Big Five Dimensions" of personality,
111–112
ratings for self, 129–130
cofounders of a new venture, 108
choosing, 113–118
communication, 122–124
perceived fairness, 119–122
role conflict, 119
roles, 118–119
self-assessment, 110–112
similarity versus complementarity,
109–112
See also Deception; Impression management
employees
number needed, 125
social networks as source of, 124–125
temporary or permanent?, 126
as required resource for entrepreneurs,
11
See also Motivating employees;
Recruiting and selecting employees;
Retaining employees
Hypothesis, 15, 22

I

Idea generation, 75
sources of, 55
See also Creativity; Opportunity recognition
Identification-based trust, 300, 301, 302,
314

Illiquidity premium, 153, 158
Illusion of control, 59
Imitation, intellectual property and, 272–273
Imitators, 242
See also Barriers to imitation
Immigration Reform and Control Act of 1986, 196, 208
Implicit favorite, 97, 103
Impression management, 128, 294, 295–296
due diligence in checking, 114
flattery, exaggerated agreement, 115
intimidation, 114
other-enhancement, 113, 114
self-enhancement, 113, 114
slime effect, 114
social skills, 114
Incentive systems, 333–335
Income statements, 159–160
Incompatible reaction procedure, 312
Individual-level variables of the entrepreneurship process, 12–13
Industries
See Opportunity
Industry life cycles, 37–38
Industry structure
See New firms
Influence, 294, 296
principles
commitment/consistency, 306, 307
friendship/liking, 306, 307
reciprocity, 307
scarcity, 306, 307
strategies of, 305–306
Information
access to, increasing, 74
customer preferences and markets for new products and services, 217–219
experience and, 56
factual, 57
inappropriate gathering of, 361
interpreting, potential pitfalls and countering pitfalls, 100
group polarization, 98
groupthink, 98–99
implicit favorite, 97–98
shared information, ignoring, 99
lack of, venture failure because of (example), 96
limited capacity to process, 58–60
opportunity recognition and, 68–69, 70
problems in organizing, managing, 252–255
as required resource for entrepreneurs, 11
as source of opportunity, 29
unshared, 99, 105
using and transforming
prototypes, 58
schemas, 57–58
See also Marketing information
Information asymmetry and uncertainty in the pursuit of opportunity, 255
alliances and partnerships with established firms, 258–259
growth from small-scale, 256–258
legitimacy, generating, 259–260
problems, 135–136, 137, 158
Initial public offering (IPO), 357–358, 369
Innocent infringement, 281
Innovation, 35–36, 272–273
as a barrier to imitation, 247
government support of, 92
Innovators, 225
Instrumentality, 329
Intangibles, 369

in a business plan, 176
in determining the value of a business, 354–355
Integrative agreements, 362–363, 369
Intellectual property, 243, 286
legal forms of protection
copyrights, 280–281
patents, 275–278, 288
trademarks, 279–280, 288
trade secrets, 278–279
nondisclosures and noncompete agreements, 274
nonlegal forms of protection, 281
complementary assets, 284–285
evaluating, 288–289
learning curves, lead time, and first-mover advantage, 282–284
profits from new products and services
imitation, 272–273
new firm advantages, 270–272
product development, 269–270
Intellectual abilities, 65
Intelligence, 75
analytic, 64
creative, 64
defined, 64
human age and, 366
practical, 64, 74, 76
social, 64
successful, 65, 76
Interactional justice, 331
Interchannel discrepancies, 115
International franchising, 206
Interpersonal-level variables of the entrepreneurship process, 12–13
Interviews
See Employment interviews
Intimidation, 114
Intrapreneurs, 6, 22
Intrapreneurship, 6
Introversion-extraversion, as point in self-assessment, 111
Invent around, 277, 286
Investors
See Financing
IPO
See Initial public offering

J

Job analysis, 321, 340
Job description, 321, 340
Job design, 332–333, 340
Job enlargement, 332–333
Job enrichment, 332–333
Joint venture, 194, 208
Justice
distributive, 121, 128, 330–331, 340
interactional, 331
procedural, 330–331

K

Knowledge
base of, broad and rich, 65–66, 72, 73
as basis for ideas, 55
codified, 244
connections among kinds of, 74
disclosing, dangers of, 245
organization of, 73
as point in self-assessment, 111
tacit, 244, 262
Knowledge conditions, 35–36
Knowledge, routes to, 14
experimentation, 16–17
reflection, 17–18
systematic observation, 15–16

theory
defined, 18
example, 19–20
interest of entrepreneurship in, 20
process of, 18–19
role of, in entrepreneurship research (figure), 19
Knowledge spillovers, 35–36, 47

L

Laggards, 225–226
Late-adult transition, 367
Late majority, 225–226
Lead time, 286
in intellectual property, 282–283
Learning curve, 41, 47
in intellectual property, 282–284
Legal form of new ventures, 187
contracts
elements, 197–198
obligations under, 198–199
corporations
advantages, 192–193
disadvantages, 193
S corporation, 193
franchising, 199
benefits of, 200–202
co-branding, 206
drawbacks of, 202–204
expansion of (kinds), 206
future shape of, 205–206
international, 206
legal aspects, 204–205
self-questions about, 210
types of, 200
joint venture, 194
laws, 195–196
legal environment, 195–199
limited liability company (LLC), 193–194
partnerships, 189–190
limited, 190
limited liability (LLPs), 191
master limited (MLP), 191
professional corporation (PC), 194–195
sole proprietorship, 188–189
Legal forms of intellectual property
See Intellectual property
Legitimacy, 259–260, 262
Leveraged buyouts, 351–352, 369
Leveraged plan (ESOP), 352
Liability, unlimited personal, 188, 190
Licensing, 262
competitive advantage, 249
determining when to use (four factors), 250–255
Life span (human) and exit strategies
See Exit strategies
Limited liability company (LLC), 193–194, 208
Limited liability partnerships (LLPs), 191, 194
Limited partners, 148, 190
Limited partnership, 190, 208, 351
Limited partnership agreement, 190
Lines of credit, 149, 158
Loan Guarantee Program of the U.S. Small Business Administration, 150
Loans, commercial, 149
Location (business plan), 169, 172
Lock-up agreements, 357–358
Locus of innovation, 35–36, 47
Logrolling, 362–363
Long-term memory, 56–57
Lowball, 307

M

Macro perspective, 9, 12–13, 22
Management team (business plan), 169, 172–173, 183–184
Mandatory redemption rights, 138, 158
Manufacturing learning curve, 41
Market, new
    See Opportunity
Market analysis, discussed in a business plan, 169, 171
Market-based modes of opportunity exploitation, 249, 262
    capabilities considerations, 251–252
    cost considerations, 250–251
    information problems in organizing, 252–255
    speed considerations, 251
    when to use franchising or licensing, 250–255
Market conditions, 232
Market dynamics
    See Marketing, in new firms
Market growth, 36–37, 222
Marketing information, 84
    gathering, direct techniques for, 85
        customer surveys, 86
        focus groups, 86–87
        perceptual mapping, 86, 87
    gathering, indirect techniques for, 104–105
        observation, 88
        secondary data, 88
    knowing, before start-up, 101–102
    no guarantee of success, 88–89
Marketing, in new firms, 214
    acceptance, achieving
        adoption patterns, 224–226
        dominant design, 227–228
        early adopters become early majority adopters, 226–227
        initial target market, 227
        technical standards, 228–230
    assessing the market
        conjoint analysis, 220–221
        customer preferences, 217–219
        needs, 235
        real needs, 215–217
    market dynamics
        market size and growth, 222
        S-curve, 222–224
        timing, 222–224
    marketing plan, 236
    process of
        personal selling, 230–231, 236–237
        pricing, 231–233
Marketing plan, developing, 236
Market saturation, 203
Market segmentation, 36–37
Market size, 36–37, 222
Market value method of valuing a company, 357, 369
Master limited partnerships (MLPs), 191
Maturity stage of company growth, 338
Meeting of the minds (contracts), 198
Memory, 75
    long-term, 56–57, 62
    procedural, 57
    working, 56, 58
Mental ruts, 63
Mental shortcuts, 58
    heuristics, 59
    See also Human cognition (errors in)
Merit pay plans, 334
Microexpressions, 115
Micro perspective, 9, 12–13, 22
Midlife transition, 367

Milestone, 152, 158, 175–176
    discussed in a business plan, 169
Minority entrepreneurs, government support of, 92–93
Miss, 70–71, 72
Monopoly
    defined, 241, 262
    legal, 246
    patents, trade secrets, and, 279
Moral hazard, 253–254
Motivating employees
    decline in motivation, 329
    expectancy theory in, 329
    fairness, 330–332
    goals, 326–328, 341–342
    job design, 332–333
    maintaining, 329–330
    tying rewards to performance, 328–330
Motivation, 340
    creativity and, 66
    defined, 326
    regulatory focus theory and, 71–72
Motives, as a point in self-assessment, 111

N

Native American entrepreneurs
    government support of, 92
    as a protected class, 95
Needs
    See Marketing, in new firms
Negotiation, 303, 314, 369
    See also Exit strategies
Network externalities, 251, 262
New firms
    demand conditions favorable to, 36–37
    government policy favorable to, 91–93
    hindered by economies of scale, 41
    industry life cycles favorable to, 37–38
    industry structure impact on
        advertising-intensive, 39
        capital intensive, 38–39
        concentrated industries, 39
        economies of scale, 39
        size, 39
    knowledge conditions favorable to
        innovation process, 36
        knowledge spillovers, 35–36
        locus of innovation, 35–36
        R&D intensity, 35
    opportunities favoring, 42–44, 45
    product development and, 271–272
    young industries better than old, 37–38
    See also Government regulations; Marketing, in new firms; Product development; Human resources (cofounders)
Noncompete agreements, 273, 274, 287
Noncompetitors, 353
Nondirect competitors, 353
Nondisclosure agreements, 273, 274, 278–279, 287
Nonverbal aspects of speech, 116
Nonverbal cues, 115–116, 128
Normative commitment, 335

O

Observation, 14
    of customers, 217–219
    as information-gathering technique, 88
    systematic observation, 15–16, 23
Occupational Safety and Health Act of 1970 (OSHA), 94, 103, 196
Opportunity, 22
    competition and, 33
    defined, 9

favorable industries (table), 28
favoring established firms, 40–42
favoring new firms, 42–44, 45
forms of, 33–34
generation of, 13–14
industries favorable to new firms, 34
    demand conditions, 36–37
    industry life cycles, 37–38
    industry structure, 38–39
    knowledge conditions, 35–36
new market, 4–5, 9, 33–34
new method of production, 4–5, 9, 33–34
new product or service, 3, 4–5, 9, 33–34
new raw material, 4–5, 33–34
new way of organizing, 4–5, 9, 33–34
protecting, from imitators or competitors
    See Strategy
recognition of, 9–11, 14
sources of
    external change, 29–30
    information, 29
    political and regulatory change, 31
    social and demographic change, 31–32
    technological change, 30–31
    value differences, 28
    See also Opportunity recognition
Opportunity recognition, 67, 76
    cognitive science insights, 69
        regulatory focus theory, 71–72
        signal detection theory, 70–71
    defined, 54
    information, access to and use of, 68–69, 70
    information, central role of (figure), 70
    personal prototype, finding, 77
    prototypes, 58
    schema of entrepreneurial alertness, 69
    schemas, 57–58
    techniques for increasing, 72–74
    See also Human cognition
Optimistic bias, 59, 60, 328
Option, 152, 158
Ordinary ESOPs, 352
Organizational citizenship behaviors, 300–301, 314
Organizational commitment, 335, 340
Organizing, new way of
    See Opportunity
OSHA
    See Occupational Safety and Health Act of 1970
Other-enhancement, 113, 114
Overall approach to negotiation, 362–364, 369

P

Partners
    general, 148, 190
    limited, 148, 190
Partnership agreement, 189, 208
Partnerships, 189, 194, 208
    with established firms, 258–259
    limited liability partnerships (LLPs), 191
    limited partnerships, 190
    master limited partnerships (MLPs), 191
Patents, 246, 252, 262, 287
    advantages (table), 276
    claims, 276
    cost of, 276
    defined, 275
    disadvantages, 276–277
    enforcing, 276
    no international patents, 277–278
    obtaining, 275–276, 288

of technology, 273
trade secrets and, mutually exclusive, 278
what can be patented, 275
Pay for performance systems, 333–335, 340
Perceived fairness, 253–254, 342
among cofounders, 119–122
Perceptual mapping, 86, 87, 103, 220
Permits, 246
Personal attributes, as a point in self-assessment, 111
Personality attributes, creativity and, 66
Personal selling, 230–231, 234
learning, 236–237
Personal skills
See Conflict; Influence; Persuasion; Social competence; Stress; Trust
Persuasion, 181
in a business plan, 164
See also Influence
Plaintiff, 198
Planning fallacy, 59, 60, 175
Playing hard to get, 307
Political change, 31
Positive affect, inducing, 361
Practical intelligence, 64–65, 76
building, 74
Prevention focus, 71–72
personal, testing for, 77–79
Price-earnings method of valuing a company, 357, 369
Pricing, of new products, 231–233
Prior art, 275–276, 277, 287
Pro-cartel policies, 31
Procedural justice, 330–331
Procedural memory, 57
Product (business plan), 170
Product development, 287
defined, 269
difficulty of, 269–270
imitation, ease of, 272–273
new firm advantages, 270–272
nondisclosures and noncompete agreements, 274
Production (business plan), 169, 172
Production, new method of
See Opportunity
Product or service, new
See Marketing, in new firms; Opportunity
Professional corporation (PC), 194–195, 208
Profitability and growth stage of company growth, 337
Profitability and stabilization phase of company growth, 336
Profit-sharing plans, 335
Proforma balance sheet, 173–174, 181
Proforma financial statements, 142, 143, 159–160
Proforma income statement, 173–174, 181
Promotion focus, 71–72
personal, testing for, 77–79
Protected class, 95, 103
Prototypes, 58, 76, 270
of opportunity, finding one's personal, 77
Provisional patent application, 275, 287
Purpose (business plan), 169, 170

R

Radical breakthroughs, 228
Rate of return, high, demanded by investors, 152–154
Raw material, new, 4–5, 33–34

for creativity and opportunity recognition
capacity to process information, 58–60
memory, 56–57
prototypes, 58
schemas, 57–58
knowledge as, 55
See also Opportunity
R&D intensity, 35, 47
Realistic job previews, 325, 340
Reciprocity (influence), 307
Recruiting and selecting employees
know what you need and where to look, 321–322
planning for, 343
techniques for, 322–325
Reflection, 14, 17–18
Regulatory change, 31
Regulatory focus theory, 71–72, 76
personal, testing for, 77–79
Reliability (of employee-selection measures), 323, 340
Repertory grid, 87
Representative heuristic, 60
Reputation, 41
as a barrier to imitation, 246–247
first-mover advantage, 283
Retaining employees
control barrier, overcoming, 336–339
employee commitment, building, 335–336
pay and performance, linking (reward system), 333–335
Reverse engineering, 273, 287
Rewards, harvesting, 11
See also Exit strategies
Rewards (for employees), 340
tying to performance, 328–330
See also Retaining employees
Right-sizing, 7
Risk, 256–257
discussed in a business plan, 169, 174–175
Role conflict, among cofounders, 123–124
Roles, 128
among cofounders, 118–119
Royalties (franchises), 202

S

Savings, as source of capital, 147
SBIR
See Small Business Innovation Research
Scarcity (influence), 306, 307
Scheduling (business plan), 169, 175–176
Schemas, 57–58, 76
of entrepreneurial alertness, 69
S corporation, 90, 193, 194, 208
See also Corporation
Scripts, 58
S-curve, 222–224, 234
Secondary data, 88
Secrecy, about opportunity, 243–246
Self-assessment, 108, 110–112, 128
Self-enhancement, 113, 114
Self-financing, 137–138, 256
Self-serving bias, 121, 128, 342
Self-set goals, 327
Selling, personal, 230–231, 234, 236–237
Selling memorandum, 354
Shirking, 121, 253–254, 262
Signal detection theory, 70–71, 76
Similarity, with cofounders, 108, 109–110, 112
Size, as challenge of new firms, 39
Skills

as point in self-assessment, 111
social, 114
See also Conflict; Influence; Social competence; Stress; Trust; Persuasion
Slime effect, 114
Small Business Innovation Research grants (SBIR), 92, 103, 150
Small business investment companies (SBICs), 150
Small Disadvantaged Businesses, 92
Social adaptability, 294, 296–297
Social capital, 293, 314
Social change, 31–32
Social competence, 293, 298, 314
assessing your own, 315–316
social skills, impact of, on entrepreneurs, 294–295
expressiveness, 294, 295
impression management, 294, 295–296
influencing others, 294, 296
persuasion, 294, 296
social adaptability, 294, 296–297
social perception, 294, 295
Social influence
See Influence
Social networks, as source of employees, 124–125
Social perception, 113, 128, 294, 295
Social skills, 337
defined, 314
as predictor of job performance ratings, 114
See also Social competence
Social ties
of established firms, 271
importance of, 134
raising money through, 155
Societal-level variables of the entrepreneurship process, 12–13
Sole proprietorship, 188–189, 194, 208
Specialization, 139
Specific performance, 198
Speech, nonverbal aspects of, 116
Staging, of investment, 152, 153, 158
Start-up capital
See Financing
Strategy
competitive advantage, 241–242, 248
competitors
gathering information on, 264–265
identifying, 264
developing, 263–264
imitators, stopping, 242
information asymmetry and uncertainty challenges, 255
alliances and partnerships with established firms, 258–259
growth from small-scale, 256–258
legitimacy, generating, 259–260
organizational form: choosing franchising or licensing, 249
capabilities considerations, 251–252
cost considerations, 250–251
information management and organizing considerations, 252–255
speed considerations, 251
protecting profits from exploitation of opportunity, 242
barriers to imitation, 246–247
secrecy, 243–245
protection against competition, 240
See also Competitive advantage
Street smarts, 64
Stress, 314
adverse effects of, 310–311
defined, 308–309
generators of (stressors), 309–310

techniques for managing, 311–313
Stressors, 309
Stress resistance, 311
Stress-tolerance, 311
Structured interviews, 324, 340
Subcontinent-Asian Americans, as entre-
    preneurs, government support of, 92
Success
    building, 11
    four pillars of, 337
Successful intelligence, 65, 76
Succession, 351
Sunk costs, 60, 61, 76
Supplier credit, 146
Surveys, 217–218
    customer, 86
Survival phase of company growth, 336,
    338
Syndication, 139, 158
Systematic observation, 15–16, 23

T
Table of contents (business plan), 167
Tacit knowledge, 244, 262
Take-off stage of company growth,
    337–338
Target markets, 217–219, 227
Tax credit, 91
Taxes
    double taxation, 190, 191, 193
    legal forms of new ventures and tax
        rates, 90
    marginal tax rate, 90
    overall rate, 90
Tax incentives, 91
Technical standards, 228–230, 234
Technological change

as source of opportunity, 30–31
    speed with which new firms can
        make, 43
Technology, patenting, 273
Terminal value of an investment, 154, 158
Territorial protection (franchises), 202
Theory, 23
    defined, 18
    example, 19–20
    interest of entrepreneurship in, 20
    process of, 18–19
    role of, in entrepreneurship research
        (figure), 19
Thinking, creativity and, 66
Timing, in the market, 222–224
Title VII of the Civil Rights Act of 1964,
    95, 103, 196
Top-down approach to management, 9
Trademarks, 287
    defined, 279
    obtaining, 279–280, 288
Trade-name franchising, 199, 208
Trade secret, 243, 262, 287
    advantages, 278
    defined, 278
    disadvantages, 278–279
    patents and, mutually exclusive, 278
Transfer of ownership plan (ESOP), 352
Trust, 297, 314
    calculus-based, 299, 314
    cooperation and, building, 298–301
    defined, 298
    identification-based, 300, 301, 302, 314
    option of exit strategy, 351
    organizational citizenship behaviors,
        300–301
    in selling a business, 354
Tyranny of the current market, 219, 234

U
Uncertainty problems, 137, 158
    See also Information asymmetry
Unlimited personal liability, 188, 190, 208
User myopia, 219, 234

V
Valence, 329
Validity (of employee-selection measures),
    323, 340
Values, of entrepreneurs, 7
Variable costs, 231, 234
Variables, 23
    of the entrepreneurship process, 12–13
Venture capital, advantages to (table), 134
    See also Financing
Venture capitalists, 147–149, 158
    what they want (table), 148
Venture capital method, 153–154, 158
Ventures, launching, 11
Vertically-integrated companies, 249, 262
Vesting periods, 139, 158
Vision, 328

W
Win-lose approach, 303
Win-win solution, 303, 314, 361–362
Women entrepreneurs
    government support of, 92
    as a protected class, 95
Working memory, 56, 58
Worry, assessing your own, 316
    See also Stress